D0382302

EERL With
Surplus/Dup

Guide TO TECHNICAL SERVICES RESOURCES

PEGGY JOHNSON
EDITOR

With Chapters by

Sheila S. Intner

Karen A. Schmidt

Janet Swan Hill

Nancy J. Williamson

Stephen S. Hearn

Sarah E. Thomas and Anne Blankenbaker

Marcia L. Tuttle

Peggy Johnson

Wesley L. Boomgaarden

Erich J. Kesse

Christina Perkins Meyer

Farideh Tehrani

Z
731.
G9
1994

American Library Association
Chicago and London 1994

RASMUSON LIBRARY
UNIVERSITY OF ALASKA-FAIRBANKS

Project Publisher: Arthur Plotnik

Production Editor: Joan A. Grygel

Copy Editor: Carla Babrick

Indexer: Carol Kelm

Cover designed by: Richmond Jones

Text designed by: Dianne M. Rooney

Composed by Alexander Graphics
  in Palatino/Bodoni on Datalogics

Printed on 50-pound Glatfelter, a pH-neutral stock, and
  bound in Holliston Roxite A by Braun-Brumfield

The paper used in this publication meets the minimum
requirements of American National Standard for Information Sciences—Permanence of Paper for Printed Library
Materials, ANSI Z39.48-1984.∞

Library of Congress Cataloging-in-Publication Data

Guide to technical services resources / Peggy Johnson,
    editor ; with chapters by Sheila S. Intner . . . [et al.].
      p. cm.
    Includes bibliographical references and index.
    ISBN 0-8389-0624-9 (alk. paper)
    1. Processing (Libraries)—United States—
Bibliography. 2. Processing (Libraries)—Canada—
    Bibliography. I. Johnson, Peggy, 1948– . II.
    Intner, Sheila S.
Z731.G9 1993
016.02502—dc20   93-1966

Copyright © 1994 by the American Library Association.
All rights reserved except those which may be granted by
Sections 107 and 108 of the Copyright Revision Act of
1976.

Printed in the United States of America.

98 97 96 95 94   5 4 3 2 1

CONTENTS

A

Technical Services:

An Overview | 5

B

Acquisitions | 27

C

Descriptive Cataloging | 45

D

Subject Analysis Systems | 68

E
Authority Control | 86

F
Filing and Indexing | 104

G
Serials Management | 120

H
Collection Management | 136

I
Preservation | 166

J

Reproduction of Library
Materials | 196

K
Database Management | 214

L
Access Services | 237

ACRONYMS

AACR	*Anglo-American Cataloging Rules*	CAP	Collection Analysis Project
AACR2	*Anglo-American Cataloguing Rules, 2nd edition*	CC:DA	Committee on Cataloging: Description and Access
AACR2R	*Anglo-American Cataloguing Rules, 2nd edition revised*	CCF	Common Communication Format
		CCS	Cataloging and Classification Section
ACRL	Association of College and Research Libraries		
		CD-ROM	Compact-disc read-only memory
A&I	abstracting and indexing	CIC	Committee on Institutional Cooperation
AI	artificial intelligence		
AIC	American Institute for Conservation of Historic and Artistic Works	CLR	Council on Library Resources
		CMDS	Collection Management and Development Section
AIIM	Association for Information and Image Management		
		CNI	Coalition for Networked Information
ALA	American Library Association		
ALCTS	Association of Library Collections and Technical Services	CODES	Collection Development and Evaluation Section
		CONSER	Cooperative Online Serials
ALISE	Association for Library and Information Science Education	CRL	Center for Research Libraries
AMC	Archival and Manuscripts Control		
ANSI	American National Standards Institute	DDC	Dewey Decimal Classification
ARL	Association of Research Libraries	EDI	Electronic Data Interchange
ASI	American Society of Indexers	EIM	electronic imaging management
ASIS	American Society for Information Science	EMIERT	Ethnic Materials and Information Exchange Roundtable
		ERIC	Education Resources Information Center
BGN	Board on Geographic Names		
BISAC	Book Industry Systems Advisory Committee	ESS	Editorial Support System
BLDSC	British Library Document Supply Centre	FID	International Federation for Information and Documentation

FID/CR	FID Committee on Classification Research	LIRN	Library and Information Resources for the Northwest
FTP	file transfer protocol	LIS	library information science
		LISA	Library and Information Science Abstracts
GARE	Guidelines for Authority and Reference Entries	LITA	Library Information and Technology Association
GPO	U.S. Government Printing Office		
GRC	General Research Corporation	LSP	Linked Systems Project
ICA	International Council on Archives	MARBI	Committee on Machine-Readable Bibliographic Information
ICCROM	International Centre for the Study of the Preservation and Restoration of Cultural Property	MARC	MAchine-Readable Cataloging
		MeSH	Medical Subject Headings
IFLA	International Federation of Library Associations and Institutions	METRO	New York Metropolitan Reference and Research Library Agency
ILL	interlibrary loan	MOUG	Music OCLC Users Group
INFOTERM	International Information Centre for Terminology	NACO	Name Authority Cooperative; also, National Coordinated Cataloging Operations
I&R	information and referral systems		
IRS	Internal Revenue Service	NAG	National Acquisitions Group
ISADN	International Standard Authority Data Number	NASIG	North American Serials Interest Group
ISBD	International Standards for Bibliographic Description	NCCP	National Coordinated Cataloging Program
ISBN	International Standard Book Number	NCIP	North American Collections Inventory Project
ISO	International Organization for Standardization	NEDCC	Northeast Document Conservation Center
IS&T	Society for Imaging Science and Technology	NFAIS	National Federation of Abstracting and Information Services
ISSN	International Standard Serial Number	NFPA	National Fire Protection Association
		NISO	National Information Standards Organization
ITAL	Information Technology and Libraries	NIST	National Institute for Standards and Technology
JSC	Joint Steering Committee for the Revision of *AACR2*	NLM	National Library of Medicine
		NMP	NACO Music Project
		NUC	National Union Catalog
LAMA	Library Administration and Management Association		
LAN	local area network	OLAC	On-Line Audiovisual Catalogers
LBI	Library Binding Institute	OPAC	online public access catalog
LC	U.S. Library of Congress	OSI	Open Systems Interconnection
LCC	Library of Congress Classification	PAC	IFLA Core Programme on Preservation and Conservation
LCRI	Library of Congress Rule Interpretations		
		PRECIS	Preserved Context Indexing System
LCSH	Library of Congress subject headings	PRIMA	Program for Information Management

RAMP	Records and Archives Management Programme (of UNESCO)	SNI	Standard Network Interconnection
RASD	Reference and Adult Services Division	SPIE	Society of Photo-optical Instrumentation Engineers
REMUS	Retrospective Music Project	SSP	Society for Scholarly Publishing
RFP	request for proposal	TAPPI	Technical Association of the Pulp and Paper Industry
RI	rule interpretation		
RLG	Research Libraries Group	TCP/IP	Transmission Control Protocol/ Internet Protocol
RLIN	Research Libraries Information Network	TESLA	LITA Technical Standards Committee
RTSD	Resources and Technical Services Division		
		UBCIM	Universal Bibliographic Control and International MARC Programme
SAA	Society of American Archivists	UDC	Universal Decimal Classification
SAC	Subject Analysis Committee	UNISIST	United Nations Intergovernmental Programme for Co-Operation in the Field of Scientific and Technical Information
SGML	Standard Generalized Mark-Up Language		
SIG/CR	Special Interest Group on Classification Research		
SISAC	Serials Industry Systems Advisory Committee	WAIS	wide area information server
		WESS	Western European Subject Specialists
SMPTE	Society of Motion Picture and Television Engineers		
SNA	systems network architecture		

CHAPTER EDITORS

A | Technical Services: An Overview

Sheila S. Intner, Professor, Graduate School of Library and Information Science, Simmons College, Boston, Massachusetts, with the assistance of Samson C. Soong, Interim Head of Technical and Automated Systems, Rutgers University Libraries, and Judy Jeng, Head, Technical Services and Media, Newark Campus Libraries, Rutgers University.

B | Acquisitions

Karen A. Schmidt, Acquisitions Librarian, University Libraries, University of Illinois at Urbana-Champaign.

C | Descriptive Cataloging

Janet Swan Hill, Associate Director, Technical Services, University Libraries, University of Colorado at Boulder Libraries, Boulder, Colorado.

D | Subject Analysis Systems

Nancy J. Williamson, Professor, Faculty of Library and Information Science, University of Toronto, Toronto, Ontario, Canada.

E | Authority Work

Stephen S. Hearn, Authority Control Coordinator, University Libraries, University of Minnesota, Minneapolis, Minnesota.

F | Filing and Indexing

Sarah E. Thomas, Director for Cataloging, Library of Congress, Washington, D.C., and Anne Blanken-

baker, Library of Congress Intern, 1992–94 Intern Program.

G | Serials

Marcia L. Tuttle, Head, Serials Department, University of North Carolina Libraries, Chapel Hill, North Carolina.

H | Collection Management

Peggy Johnson, Assistant Director, St. Paul Campus Libraries, University of Minnesota, St. Paul, Minnesota.

I | Preservation

Wesley L. Boomgaarden, Preservation Officer, The Ohio State University Libraries, Columbus, Ohio.

J | Reproduction of Library Materials

Erich J. Kesse, Preservation Officer, Smathers Libraries, University of Florida, Gainesville, Florida.

K | Database Management

Christina Perkins Meyer, Head, Database Management, University Libraries, University of Minnesota, Minneapolis, Minnesota.

L | Access Services

Farideh Tehrani, Head of Access Services, Alexander Library, Rutgers University, State University of New Jersey, New Brunswick, New Jersey.

ADVISORS

Barry B. Baker, Assistant Director for Technical Services, University of Georgia Libraries, Athens

Doris H. Clack, Professor, School of Library and Information Studies, Florida State University, Tallahassee

Frances Corcoran, Coordinator, Instructional Materials, Des Plaines (Illinois) Public Schools, District 62

Karen M. Drabenstott, Associate Professor, School of Library and Information Studies, University of Michigan, Ann Arbor

Doina Farkas, Head, Technical Services, University of North Texas, Denton

Joe A. Hewitt, University Librarian, University of North Carolina, Chapel Hill

Denise Kaplan Hildreth, Head, Information Systems, King County Library System, Seattle, Washington

Dodie Ownes, Client Services, CARL Systems, Inc., Denver, Colorado

Vivian M. Pisano, Supervising Librarian for Technical Services, Oakland Public Library, Oakland, California

Laura Stalker, Assistant Director for Technical Services, Huntington Library, San Marino, California

William E. Studwell, Head Cataloger, Professor, University Libraries, Northern Illinois University, De Kalb

Penelope Swanson, Technical Services Librarian, Douglas College, New Westminster, British Columbia, Canada

Ex officio, as chair, ALA Association for Library Collections and Technical Services Publishing Committee: Bill Robnett, Director, Central and Sciences, Libraries, Vanderbilt University, Nashville, Tennessee

Introduction

The *Guide to Technical Services Resources* is a first attempt at a comprehensive and practical guide to the principal information resources for technical services practitioners, educators, and students.

The nature of library technical services is changing rapidly, and the information describing these changes is dispersed through a variety of media from monographs and periodicals to electronic bulletin boards. No single source has previously gathered and organized the most important recent information resources in the full range of technical services. This *Guide* will serve that function, providing annotated and evaluative references to the primary tools for those who work, study, research, and teach in the areas of library technical services.

The idea of an ALA guide for technical services staff was inspired in part by ALA's *Guide to Reference Books*, a standard work that has been refined through ten editions with a history dating back to 1902. Although the two guides vary fundamentally in content, purpose, and audience, it seemed that the organizing principles of the reference guide could be applied to a large body of sources for technical services work. Thus, while we make no pretense to the scholarly depth that characterizes the *Guide to Reference Books*, users will see a similarity in format between the two guides. Indeed, the *Guide to Technical Services Resources* has been physically de-signed to sit proudly by the reference guide in professional collections, symbolizing the equal importance of technical services and reference information in forging the responsive, client-oriented library of today.

Without the benefit of a ninety-year history, however, the present *Guide* appears in its first rude incarnation, with several unresolved challenges in the selection, description, and organization of thousands of resources in the protean areas of technical services. To withhold this *Guide* until such challenges were resolved would have been to delay the publication while its content aged. We preferred to provide the information but share with users our several practical decisions and caveats, below, along with our hope that criticisms will come forth abundantly and constructively to help improve the value of future supplements and editions.

Scope

Since even a guide of comprehensive range cannot be all-inclusive, works in each section have been selected according to several criteria: Currency is a primary consideration. The *Guide to Technical Services Resources* contains few works published before 1985; it is not a literature review. Works are included if they serve as a basic tool or resource, contribute in a significant way to the theory of the field, or identify and address a unique problem. Where appropriate, standards and resources about their application are included. A few older resources are included when they are important for understanding current practice or for solving problems with older formats, policies, and procedures. For additional titles, readers may consult the manuals, guides, and bibliographies listed along with the major bibliographic sources for the field—*ERIC Abstracts*, *Information Science Abstracts*, *Library and Information Science Abstracts* (LISA), and *Library Literature*.

Chapter authors have sought to be evaluative, selecting the best and most useful tools and identifying any shortcomings. Each chapter author also has applied his or her own criteria, affected by the nature of the topic covered, in selecting materials to include. Some fields—those with a lengthy history or those now generating intense interest—have an extensive literature of texts, manuals, research articles, and more, from which the author has chosen selectively. Other fields are newer or less clearly defined and have fewer and different types of tools for practitioners. As a result, chapters vary considerably in length.

The *Guide to Technical Services Resources* is intended primarily as a tool for technical services as practiced in North American libraries and contains a preponderance of English-language, North American publications. However, some selected resources are included that are outside this general body of publications.

To be timely and practical the *Guide* includes several types of information resources. Chapter authors sought to describe the tools that they would like at their fingertips and that they would use on a regular basis in an ideal library. Each chapter is comprehensive without being exhaustive. Journal titles, including electronic journals, are cited if the journal is read and consulted regularly by practitioners. We also suggest in each chapter additional avenues for professional support and expertise. These include relevant professional associations, conferences and institutes, vendor support groups, and electronic discussion groups. Since such technical-services leadership has largely come from two American Library Association divisions, we refer frequently to products and activities of the Association for Library Collections and Technical Services (ALCTS) and Library Information and Technology Association (LITA). Contact them in care of the American Library Association, 50 E. Huron St., Chicago, IL 60611.

Currency

Because we have sought to be as current as possible, we have included some information that may become outdated rapidly. This applies particularly to standards, codes, and information about library automation. The continuing accuracy of access instructions for the electronic resources is a particular problem. Nevertheless, this material serves as an alert to the important sources for up-to-date information and the chance to participate in lively discussions. Readers, therefore, are advised to verify that the tool they are consulting is the most recent edition or version and to check one of the several directories of electronic journals, newsletters, and discussion groups if instructions provided here for gaining access to these sources fail. We plan to update the *Guide* regularly with periodic supplements and cumulate editions. To that end, we solicit and encourage readers to inform the editor of errors, omissions, and new, valuable tools.

Style and Structure

Because the *Guide to Technical Services Resources* lists many types of resources, we have selected a citation style that is used in most bibliographies. We felt that certain types of references (for example, journal articles) would become exceedingly cumbersome if we applied the *Anglo-American Cataloguing Rules*, second edition, 1988 revision. No consensus has yet been achieved on how to cite electronic resources; we tried to handle these consistently throughout the *Guide* and to provide sufficient information for the reader to locate them.

The *Guide to Technical Services Resources* is divided into twelve chapters that parallel the organization and divisions found in many technical services operations. These twelve topics do not represent the only or the ideal organizational structure, but they serve as a convenient way to organize resources along functional lines. Nearly all the chapter authors have reported that their particular area of responsibility is in transition and that the effects of automation are pervasive. This, plus the interrelated nature of technical services work, means that many resources could be listed appropriately in several sections. Cross-references are provided to works described in detail elsewhere in the *Guide*. Readers may consult the index for topical resources located throughout the book.

While types of resources will vary in the different chapters and not all types are available for all subjects, the same categories recur in many of the sections and subsections, i.e., textbooks, guides, manuals, directories, and bibliographies.

Topical Introductions

Each section begins with an overview of the subject area it covers. These are not intended as comprehensive histories but serve to define and frame issues of current concern. For example, the chapter on database management briefly traces the history of MARC (MAchine-Readable Communication) formats in addition to listing resources for using MARC. The chapter on collection management presents a concise survey of the expanse and variety of collections responsibilities before listing tools for each. Many subsections within chapters also provide introductions to the topics that follow.

In effect, the *Guide to Technical Services Resources* serves a textbooklike function of revealing the nature of technical services today as well as describing the principal sources.

Acknowledgments

I wish to acknowledge my sincere appreciation and gratitude to the chapter authors. Each of them has worked diligently on a project that grew far beyond their initial expectations about the work involved in identifying, locating, reading, reviewing, and evaluating hundreds of resources in order to select and annotate those included in each chapter.

The advisors are owed a debt of gratitude for their willingness to read and review drafts in progress,

their helpful comments on organization and content, and their suggestions for additional entries—all within a very demanding time frame.

The substance of these chapters bears testament to the expertise and sound advice of all who have worked on it. Criticism of such errors and shortcomings as may have escaped attention would be rightly directed to this editor.

I cannot conclude these acknowledgments without personal expression of gratitude to Thomas Shaughnessy, University Librarian, and Richard Rohrer, Director of St. Paul Campus Libraries, at the University of Minnesota Libraries, who supported my work on this project, and to Art Plotnik, ALA Publishing, an ideal editor. Finally, I wish to thank my family for their continuing encouragement and help, and the cheer and reassurance they provided even during the most hectic times.

The *Guide to Technical Services Resources* answers a compelling need of the library profession. In the past, we have devoted our energies to preparing indexes and bibliographies that served the information needs of our patrons. This *Guide*, by bringing together in one reference tool a comprehensive guide to the major resources about library technical services, meets our own information needs.

Peggy Johnson, Editor

A

Technical Services: An Overview

Sheila S. Intner, with the assistance of Samson C. Soong and Judy Jeng

Technical services usually are defined as that set of activities performed without direct contact with the public. Technical services librarians, then, would be those librarians whose work does not bring them in contact with the public. Used this way, "technical" is the opposite of "public." But this definition also covers library housekeeping staff and grounds-keepers, a good many members of the administrative staff, and even some reference assistants who work behind the scenes in the reference office. What makes the technical services distinctively technical must be more than lack of public contact. I submit the salient feature is the fact that these activities and operations, being based on compilations of bibliographic data, require special, "technical" bibliographic knowledge in order to perform or manage them.

As they grow larger, bibliographic compilations become increasingly complicated and difficult to manipulate. Large bibliographic databases require special kinds of expertise on the part of technical service librarians who serve as system designers and managers. Such expertise may be acquired in schools of library and information science, in courses that deal with identification, definition, creation, arrangement, and uses of bibliographic data. The courses may be called "technical services" or they may have other titles, from the most generic—

"information science," the systematic study of information—to more specific ones, such as "information storage and retrieval systems," or "information organization." Still more specific courses may deal with individual elements in the structuring of bibliographic information and may be called, accordingly, by the name of the element on which they focus: "cataloging," "classification," "indexing," "bibliography," etc. It is the content that counts. After graduation, important experience is acquired on the job, where the specialist uses the principles learned in coursework and adds knowledge of practice to the theoretical foundations learned.

Functional definitions of technical services are not universal. Historically, the two functions of acquisition and cataloging of library materials have been central to technical services. In some libraries, acquisition operations have been divided into two separate units, one handling monographic materials and another dealing with continuing or serial publications, thus adding another function—serials control—to the technical services department. Some libraries include other collection-related responsibilities—planning, budgeting, selecting, and evaluating collections—adding collection management to the array of technical services as well. Cataloging and classification of newly acquired materials often are paired with processing them for use by marking spines with call numbers and inserting identification in the materials. Processing operations link logically with other activities that maintain the physical well-being of materials, so binding, repair, and other preservation functions also may come under the technical services umbrella, and the same staff members who prepare new books also may be trained to repair older ones when necessary. One other function that may be included with technical services is inventory control. It is a logical extension of the responsibility for shelf listing and the shelf arrangement. Thus, circulation control and shelf maintenance frequently come under the authority of the technical services department, even though circulation-desk work includes interacting with the public.

Forty years ago, Maurice Tauber and associates said, in a seminal work, *Technical Services in Libraries: Acquisitions, Cataloging, Classification, Binding, Reproduction and Circulation Operations (New York: Columbia University Press, 1954):*

> In most modern libraries . . . many of the library personnel are not known to the clientele. These are the order or acquisition librarians, the catalogers and classifiers, the binding librarians, the photographic assistants, and certain members of the circulation staff. These are not all the personnel who work behind the scenes, away from the service desks, but, primarily, they are the ones who perform the technical work of acquiring, recording, preserving, and circulating materials for the use of patrons.

Today, some administrators, educators, and writers include all these functions in defining technical services (*see* Fox, AB2; Godden, AA4; Intner and Fang, AA7; and Gorman, AA5). Others take a more conservative view, subsuming only some of them under this department and parceling the others out to public service departments or elsewhere on the library's organizational chart. *See,* for example, the discussion in Sheila S. Intner, "Education for Technical Services: Challenges for the Twenty-First Century," in *Technical Services in Libraries: Systems and Applications,* edited by Thomas W. Leonhardt (AA8), 2–7.

There are many styles of organization, each with its group of followers. At the Library of Congress, Collections Services include both the traditional functions of acquisitions and cataloging as well as collection development and preservation. This nomenclature is useful, since technical services focuses primarily on collections or materials, leaving the services that concentrate on people (or, as you choose, patrons, clients, readers, users) to public services. At the same time, it should not be taken as absolute, because organizational lines blur significantly in the integrated online environment, where bibliographic records and responsibilities may be distributed differently.

The advent of computerized bibliographic networks in the late 1960s and early 1970s and a concomitant decline of the volume of original cataloging in large numbers of libraries caused some observers to predict the demise of technical services departments in all but a few libraries. But just as changing the tools of bibliographic services did not mean the services themselves would disappear, so, also, broadening the role of technical services specialists did not mean the specialty itself would disappear. Instead, it has broadened to include database design, construction, and management, and responsibility for helping both the library staff and the public use computerized bibliographic systems.

The notion that knowledge of bibliographic systems is central to the core of all library service is one that seems to make sense intellectually and also is consistent with recent organizational trends to combine professional, technical, and reference functions into a single job description. Today's compleat librarian is expected to accomplish more than two librarians—one a technical specialist and one a reference specialist—might have done in an earlier time, albeit with the assistance of well-trained paraprofessional and clerical personnel and automated systems. Technical knowledge of the library's local systems also may be an added responsibility. Thus, it should come as no surprise that some recently published citations in this bibliography appeared in *The Reference Librarian* or that their titles contain the words "reference," "public," or "readers" services.

Chapter Content and Organization

This chapter is necessarily briefer than some that follow, since I adhered rather strictly to the principle that entries in the "overview" must cover multiple functions of technical services, and, preferably, cover all of them. For example, authors sometimes use the term "technical services librarian" when what they mean is "cataloger"; I have left to subsequent chapters these and similar resources that have a narrower focus. Also, if a resource containing individual chapters with relevant material is listed as a whole, the individual chapters are not listed, although a few exceptions were made to this rule. Journals devoted to a single technical services area, such as *The Serials Librarian* (GAD10), are not included, although a more general article appearing in such a journal may be listed.

The literature was searched from 1987 forward, and, for the most part, the citations go back only to that date. However, items published earlier and cited often by authors writing between 1987 and the present are included, also, on the grounds that the fact they were often cited meant they were particularly useful or provocative and should not be overlooked.

I thank Samson Soong and Judy Jeng, librarians at Rutgers University Libraries, who contributed sections on costs and on expert systems, respectively. Their help was invaluable and their work excellent. I am eternally grateful to Linda Watkins and Christine Turner, librarians at Simmons College's Graduate School of Library and Information Science Library, who patiently helped me to locate and supplied me with countless candidates to be examined for the listing. I hasten to add that all the material that follows is my responsibility alone, and any and all errors herein are mine, whether they occur in the citations or in misinterpretation of their contents and summary in the annotations. For any such entirely unintentional mistakes both the authors of the material and the readers of this chapter have my sincere apologies.

Technical services is a dynamic area in a field—library and information science—that is undergoing profound changes. To the reader of this chapter I suggest that all factual information represented here be understood to be accurate (to the best of each author's efforts to ascertain) solely as of its writing and publication, but not for all time.

AA
General Works

AA1. Bishoff, Lizbeth, ed. "Technical Services in the Small Library." *Library Resources & Technical Services* 29 (Apr./June 1985): 118–71.

A theme issue devoted to technical services topics from the perspective of librarians working in small academic and public libraries. Articles address automation, bibliographic control, serials control, collection development, and preservation. It is somewhat dated but is one of only a few examples aimed particularly at small libraries.

AA2. Corbin, John. "Technical Services for the Electronic Library." *Library Administration & Management* 6 (Spring 1992): 86–90.

This article discusses potential functions of technical services in an electronic library of the future. It examines the acquisition of electronic materials; their bibliographic control; systems planning, evaluation, and support; and staffing.

AA3. Crawford, Walt. *Technical Standards: An Introduction for Librarians.* 2nd ed. Boston: G. K. Hall, 1991.

Aims to improve understanding of individual standards and the standard-making process. The first section of the book covers standards and standardization in general. The second part addresses standards for libraries, publishing, and information science. Useful for all technical services librarians, who increasingly must rely on and use standards.

AA4. Godden, Irene P., ed. *Library Technical Services: Operations and Management.* 2nd ed. San Diego: Academic Press, 1991.

This all-purpose text explains the processing and preparation of materials for the use and management of those operations. Attention is focused primarily on books, although computer databases and other new technologies are addressed in some chapters. An update of the 1984 first edition, it emphasizes automation and drops separate chapters on acquisition by gifts and exchanges and circulation control included in the first edition. Six chapters remain in the current edition: introduction, by editor Godden; administration, by Leslie Manning; automation, by Karen Horny; acquisitions, by Sara Heitshu (the author was Marion Reid in the first edition); bibliographic control, by Betty Bengtson; and preservation by Dean Larsen and Randy Silverman (authored by Larsen alone in the first edition). Chapters contain lengthy bibliographies of references and other information sources. Provides a good overview of technical services functions, although the treatments of individual topics are uneven—not unexpected with a multiauthored work.

AA5. Gorman, Michael, and Associates. *Technical Services Today and Tomorrow.* Englewood, Colo.: Libraries Unlimited, 1990.

A text that describes the state of the art of acquisitions, bibliographic control, preservation, and circulation in large university research libraries. The associates—as Tauber called his coauthors in his 1954 classic text on technical services—include well-known practitioners Karen Schmidt, Betsy Kruger, Jennifer Cargill, Arnold Wajenberg, William Gray Potter, Jennifer Younger, D. Kaye Gapen, and others, as well as library educators Lois Mai Chan and Theodora Hodges.

The logic of the topical arrangement in the book's five main sections is not entirely clear. Acquisitions and bibliographic control make up the first two sections, each containing multiple chapters on subtopics such as ordering, book gathering plans, gifts and exchanges, serials, etc., and descriptive cataloging, subject cataloging and classification, authority work, copy cataloging, etc. Preservation is found in the third section, "Special Topics," along with a chapter on Slavic technical services, and circulation is in the next section, "Automation and Technical Services," paired with a chapter about online catalogs. The fifth section, "Administration of Technical Services," covers departmental organization and budgeting. The book closes with a "Postscriptum," a brief philosophical essay in which Gorman assures readers that technical services will not wither away, but change. Nonprint media figure importantly in his future scenario, although this book gives them little notice. Topics are carefully and thoroughly covered in this book, and it provides a clear, though conservative, profile of technical services activities in one segment of the library community.

AA6. Hagler, Ronald. *The Bibliographic Record & Information Technology.* 2nd ed. Chicago: American Library Association, 1991.

Here is a clear and complete explanation of the central source of data for all technical services activities—the bibliographic record—in the context of the current environment of computer technology. It discusses the integrated management of bibliographic data within and outside of individual libraries, and provides a valuable foundation for all technical services librarians.

AA7. Intner, Sheila S., and Josephine Riss Fang. *Technical Services in the Medium-Sized Library.* Hamden, Conn.: Shoe String Press, 1991.

Based on responses to a questionnaire sent to more than one hundred institutions, this all-purpose text describes technical services operations currently performed in medium-sized academic and public libraries. It begins by defining technical services, introducing the setting, and discussing the impact of computing. Then it covers acquisitions and collection management; preservation management; cataloging, classification, and indexing; document delivery; and coordinated collection development. The book closes with a forecast by Pamela McKirdy of what lies beyond the 1990s in the electronic library. In each of the central chapters, profiles of corresponding units in the surveyed libraries are summarized and respondents' comments added. A production error dropped the survey form from the appendixes, which include a list of participants, a glossary, and an annotated bibliography augmenting the notes and suggested reading lists in individual chapters. This text offers a different perspective than Godden (AA4) or Gorman (AA5), focusing on smaller, nonresearch libraries with a different mix of staff, budget, and environmental resources. The survey profiles relate theory and practice, giving a balanced picture especially useful for readers unfamiliar with technical services.

AA8. Leonhardt, Thomas W., ed. *Technical Services in Libraries: Systems and Applications.* Greenwich, Conn.: JAI Press, 1992.

The emphasis in this volume is on practical management of technical services, although it opens with a chapter about education for the specialty. Twelve subsequent chapters cover organization design of the department, general management, managing the catalog department, copy cataloging, online catalog, acquisitions (two chapters), serials, emerging technologies, staffing, and vendors (two chapters). Preservation and circulation are not addressed. Authors include editor Leonhardt, who also edits *Information Technology and Libraries* (AF10), Marion T. Reid, William Gray Potter, Tamara Frost Trujillo, Dana and Frank D'Andraia, Sheila S. Intner, and others. Topics are treated unevenly, with some authors providing thorough, scholarly descriptions with copious notes and others giving first-person opinion pieces with no references to other work on the subject. However, the latter can be useful in practice; e.g., Potter offers twenty valuable lessons about online catalogs he has learned from experience. There is no introduction or bibliography. The brief index does little to amplify the table of contents.

AA9. Libbey, Maurice C., ed. "Education for Technical Services." *Illinois Libraries* 67 (May 1985): 431–96.

Twenty articles have been compiled into a special issue of *Illinois Libraries* in which practitioners, library educators, and people trained as librarians but working outside the field offer opinions, describe experiences, and report research on education for technical services. The articles are organized into eight sections covering history, acquisitions, cataloging, serials, media, automation, management, and the world outside the library.

AB
Textbooks, Guides, and Manuals

AB1. Bloomberg, Marty, and G. Edward Evans. *Introduction to Technical Services for Library Technicians.* 5th ed. Littleton, Colo.: Libraries Unlimited, 1985.

This is a heavily illustrated standard textbook for paraprofessional staff, who play an increasingly important role in the execution of technical services operations in libraries of all types and sizes. It describes technical services functions and the role of technicians, automation, and networking; it then explains each aspect of the work of acquisitions (eleven chapters) and cataloging (twelve chapters). It features review questions at the end of each chapter, a glossary of terms, and a lengthy, albeit dated, bibliography.

AB2. Fox, Beth Wheeler. *Behind the Scenes at the Dynamic Library: Simplifying Essential Operations.* Chicago: American Library Association, 1990.

How to conduct a library's technical operations is explained with flowcharts, sample forms, and many illustrations, as well as brief discussions giving time-saving hints: e.g., on vendor services vs. in-house cataloging or processing. It covers the functions of acquisitions, cataloging and classification, catalog and collection maintenance, processing, circulation, communication, finances, and computers. It is geared toward small libraries that use Dewey Decimal Classification and collect children's and popular adult materials. Brief, eclectic bibliography.

AB3. Hahn, Harvey. *Technical Services in the Small Library.* Chicago: American Library Association, 1987.

A very brief introduction to acquisitions, cataloging and classification, materials processing, repair and maintenance, and withdrawals. Intended for staff members working in small libraries, it emphasizes simplification over the kinds of processes appropriate to larger libraries. Just twelve pages long, the work is not designed to provide discussion of alternatives and examples of procedures, which could be helpful for inexperienced staff.

AB4. Karpisek, Marian. *Policymaking for School Library Media Programs.* Chicago: American Library Association, 1989.

After a section devoted to steps in policy making, chapters discuss policies for the functions of circulation, selection, weeding, ordering materials, and serials control, among other policies, all in the elementary and secondary school settings.

AB5. Saffady, William. *Introduction to Automation for Librarians.* 2nd ed. Chicago: American Library Association, 1989.

A primer for librarians on the subject of automation, this revision of Saffady's basic textbook covers hardware, software, data processing concepts, and standard office systems in its first part and library applications in the second. Among the functions for which applications are discussed are acquisitions, serials control, cataloging, and circulation.

AC
Directories

AC1. Bailey, Charles W., Jr. *Library-Oriented Lists and Electronic Serials.* [database online] Houston: Public-Access Computer Systems News, 1992– . (Available on BITNET and INTERNET)

This electronically accessed directory, available through INTERNET, enumerates more than 100 computer conferences, known as "lists," devoted to topics in library and information science, and other electronic serial publications. Some lists are clearly focused on particular technical services areas, e.g., AUTOCAT (Library Cataloging and Authorities Discussion Group), *see* CAF3; CIRCPLUS (Circulation and Access Services), *see* LAC10; COLLDV-L (Library Collection Development List), *see* HAE10; and Conservation DistList (Conservation of Archive, Library, and Museum Materials), *see* IAJ1. Others are more general, although they also might be expected to discuss technical services issues on a regular basis, e.g., COSNDISC@BITNIC (Consortium for School

Networking) and LAW-LIB (Law Librarians). The lists are organized by the type of software used to access the list. Instructions for subscribing are provided. For further information, the author's electronic user ids are **LIB3@UHUPVM1** (BITNET) or **LIB3@UHUPVM1** (INTERNET).

AC2. Corbin, John B., and Joseph R. Matthews. *Directory of Automated Library Systems.* 2nd ed. New York: Neal-Schuman Publishers, 1989.

This book provides information on automated library systems from twenty-three vendors. It is organized into three sections: (1) eight tables summarizing vendor offerings and system capabilities; (2) directory of vendors and their installations, with names and telephone numbers of contact people at customer libraries; (3) indexes. It describes the individual functions of acquisitions, cataloging, circulation, online public access catalogs, and serials control. It also includes more general information or discussion about how to acquire and implement an automated library system, system costs, and reasons libraries change systems. Although the factual details in this type of book become dated quickly, the background is invaluable for anyone entering the market. Librarians unfamiliar with particular automated systems can use the contacts listed here for input on automation planning.

AC3. Dewey, Patrick. *101 Software Packages to Use in Your Library: Descriptions, Evaluations, Practical Advice.* Chicago: American Library Association, 1987.

Although dated by computing standards, this is a first-rate selection tool for microcomputer software intended for technical service activities (*see also* AC4). Arranged by type of application, it includes acquisitions, bibliography production, cataloging, circulation, communications and gateway programs for online databases, database management, integrated software, interlibrary loan, serials control, spreadsheets and statistics, training programs, utilities, and more. Reviews are based on the author's hands-on experience. They give vendor, price, hardware requirements, evaluation of the documentation, related programs, uses, etc., and are written in readable style.

AC4. _____. *202(+) Software Packages to Use in Your Library: Descriptions, Evaluations, and Practical Advice.* Chicago: American Library Association, 1992.

This update to the previous work (AC3) is bigger and better, covering more than 250 microcomputer software packages recommended by the author.

AC5. Strangelove, Michael. *Directory of Electronic Serials.* [database online] Ottawa, Ont., n.d.

This is an electronically accessed directory of electronic serials. To retrieve the directory, send the following email message to **LISTSERV@UOTTAWA** or **LISTSERV@ ACADVM1.UOTTAWA.CA: GET EJOURNL1 DIRECTRY F=MAIL** or **GET EJOURNL2 DIRECTRY F=MAIL.**

AD
Bibliographies

AD1. Anderson, Terry. *Occasional Bibliography #10: Technical Services and the Small Library.* Clarion, Pa.: Center for the Study of Rural Librarianship, School of Library Science, Clarion State College, 1980.

A brief alphabetic listing of approximately 125 books and articles published primarily between 1970 and 1978, although some were brought out in 1979. Focuses on a variety of subtopics in technical services. Included are selection and acquisition of materials; cataloging, indexing, and classification; filing; circulation; and interlibrary loan. Except for the title of this item, entries do not, for the most part, indicate that the works selected for inclusion are geared particularly to small and/or rural libraries, although there are a few exceptions, e.g., "Book Reviews: A Highly Selective List, Carefully Chosen Especially for Small Libraries to Towns under 10,000 Population." This is a no-frills work typographically, with no introduction, compiler's commentary, or annotations.

AD2. Christensen, John O. *Management of Technical Services in Libraries in the 1980's: A Selective Bibliography.* Monticello, Ill.: Vance Bibliographies, 1989. Public Administration Series, P-2759.

This is one of the briefest bibliographies (10 pages) in the Vance series, several of which were compiled by this author. Considering the large number of publications devoted to the topic that appeared in the decade, this can only include a minute fraction of the universe of available publications.

AD3. Hudson, Judith, and Geraldene Walker. "The Year's Work in Technical Services Research 1986." *Library Resources & Technical Services* 31 (Oct./Dec. 1987): 275–86.

See also annotation under AD9. The authors discuss the methodologies of thirty-eight research studies investigating aspects of technical services activities. The discussion is organized by function: cataloging, subject access, user interface, acquisitions, and administration. The authors conclude that the majority of studies reviewed either were purely descriptive, relying heavily on survey questionnaires or interviews, or were case studies. The studies focused on what was known or how something was done, but not why. A few studies employed experimental designs. Generally, levels of statistical analysis were rudimentary. The authors note that few of the findings appear to have been implemented in practice, and question when practitioners will begin to acknowledge research and use it in their work.

AD4. Kaplan, Denise P. "The Year's Work in Technical Services Automation, 1989." *Library Resources & Technical Services* 34 (1990): 299–312.

This bibliographic essay reviews the year's literature on the subject of technical services automation, with a listing of 113 relevant items published during 1989. It documents the changing nature of technical services departments within library organizations. Increasing evidence of the mergers of technical service with public service departments emerges as the year's key issue.

AD5. Magrill, Rose Mary, and Constance Rinehart, comps. "Technical Services Organization." In *Library Technical Services: A Selected, Annotated Bibliography.* Westport, Conn.: Greenwood Press, 1977, 1–43.

No comprehensive annotated bibliography on technical services has been published since this dated one. Chapter 1, "Technical Services Organization," cited here, contains 269 works divided into bibliographies, reviews, general works, works by library type, time and cost studies, personnel, automation, networks, and the Resources and Technical Services Division (RTSD) of the American Library Association, known since a 1990 name change as the Association for Library Collections and Technical Services (ALCTS). Includes books and journal articles published between 1960 and 1975, with a few notable exceptions, such as Maurice Tauber's 1954 monograph *Technical Services in Libraries.* Chronologically arranged annotations are purely descriptive and highlight bibliographic resources. This work will be useful for retrospective material, but some care must be taken in using it. Entries range from one- or two-page news items to full-length books, and some have a sufficiently narrow focus to warrant placement in subsequent chapters on individual technical service functions, e.g., "A Case Study of Catalogers in Three University Libraries . . ." (#81) and "Acquisitions Section Report" (#261).

AD6. Simpson, Charles W. "Technical Services Research, 1988–1991." *Library Resources & Technical Services* 36 (Oct. 1992): 383–408.

This bibliographic essay continues the journal's "Year's Work" literature reviews after a four-year hiatus (*see* AD3 and AD9). It begins with a philosophical discussion of what constitutes technical services and its body of research, given the changing nature of the specialty, followed by analysis of the major issues in acquisitions, authority control, automation, cataloging, classification, preservation, serials, subject access, and technical services costs and organization. Approximately 100 studies are listed and reviewed. The author provides a valuable source of bibliographic information as well as readable commentaries on the state of technical services in libraries.

AD7. St. Clair, Gloriana, Jane Treadwell, and Vicki Baker. "Notable Literature of the 1980s for Technical Services." *Journal of Library Administration* 9 (1988): 137–54.

Annotations of selected articles addressing the management of technical services and published between 1980 and 1987, when the issue went to press. Entries are organized by topic, including automation, education, managing external constituents, management techniques, personnel, and the role of technical services in the library. Extensive annotations are descriptive; selection for inclusion is evidence of an item's quality and/or usefulness.

AD8. Stenstrom, Patricia F. "Current Management Literature for Technical Services." *Illinois Libraries* 69 (1987): 96–103.

This compilation includes journal articles, books, and reports published since 1980, taken from the professional library literature. It begins with a bibliographic essay, stating immediately that most of the research in this area emanates from college and university libraries, and urging public librarians to write and publicize their in-house research. Topics include budget and finance, personnel (i.e., "people"), automation (i.e., "machines"), space, and time. The essay is followed by an alphabetic author listing of approximately seventy-five items. There are no individual annotations.

AD9. Walker, Geraldene, and Judith P. Hudson. "Research Methodology in Technical Services: The Case of 1987." *Library Resources & Technical Services* 32 (Oct. 1988): 352-65.

See also annotation under AD3. The authors list thirty-eight citations for research studies, divided into the following technical services functions: cataloging, subject analysis, authority control, use of the online catalog, acquisitions, preservation, and overview. They discuss the methodologies employed by each study. The authors conclude, once again, that little use was being made of innovative research designs and few of the findings were being utilized in practice.

AE
Handbooks

AE1. Eberhart, George M., comp. *The Whole Library Handbook: Current Data, Professional Advice, and Curiosa about Libraries and Library Services.* Chicago: American Library Association, 1991.

This is an eclectic compendium in the style of its non-library predecessors (e.g., *The Whole Earth Catalog*). Includes material relevant to technical services and automation, along with statistics, policies, career information, and other useful or entertaining material. The book furnishes a lot of reading for the price.

AE2. Futas, Elizabeth. *The Library Forms Illustrated Handbook.* New York: Neal-Schuman Publishers, 1984.

A large, loose-leaf compilation of forms used in library operations, divided by function, with brief discussions of the purposes and basic structures taken from both pre-printed commercial forms and independently developed forms from organizations, associations, or individual institutions.

AE3. Kershner, Lois M. *Forms for Automated Library Systems: An Illustrated Guide for Selection, Design and Use.* New York: Neal-Schuman Publishers, 1988.

This is an update—or, perhaps, it is more accurate to say an emulation—of the previous work (AE2), focusing on offline manual forms used for computerized systems rather than manually performed tasks. Its loose-leaf format is practical for librarians who wish to remove and copy a particular form for use. The material is divided into nine categories, nearly all related to various technical services, although public services functions are represented also. Examples come from a broad cross-section of public and academic libraries.

AF
Periodicals

AF1. *Advanced Technology/Libraries.* New York: G. K. Hall. v. 1– , 1972– . Monthly. ISSN 0044-636X.

A newsletter announcing products, describing operations, and offering summary news about conferences, people, and activities relating to library technology. It occasionally includes annotations for published articles and reports. Write-ups are brief but informative, and give vendor addresses and telephone numbers so readers can obtain additional information. Descriptions do not distinguish between applications in technical or public services, but cover both. The publication has a distinguished editorial board, but it is unclear how the editors and/or writers select material to include, whether any effort is made to survey the field comprehensively, or whether any areas are routinely excluded.

AF2. *Advances in Library Administration and Organization: A Research Annual.* Edited by Gerard B. McCabe and Bernard Kreissman. Greenwich, Conn.: JAI Press. v. 1– , 1982– . Annual. ISSN 0732-0671.

An annual compendium of papers reporting research on diverse topics relating to the administration of technical service functions. The term "organization" in the title may appear misleading to readers who expect papers solely on administrative organization, not bibliographic organization, but it will be clear enough to technical services managers and librarians.

AF3. *Advances in Library Automation and Networking: A Research Annual*. Edited by Joe A. Hewitt. Greenwich, Conn.: JAI Press. v. 1– , 1987– . Annual. ISSN 1048-4752.

This annual compendium of papers is similar to the previous entry (AF2), reporting research on topics in networking in online environments aimed at the educated nonspecialist. Material is well focused and well edited.

AF4. *ALCTS Network News*. [serial online] Chicago: Association for Library Collections and Technical Services. v. 1– , May 13, 1990– . ISSN 1056-6694. Irregular.

Also called *AN2*, this electronic newsletter contains notices of ALCTS activities and other timely information of interest to ALCTS members. To subscribe, send a message to **LISTSERV@UIUCVM** (BITNET) or **LISTSERV@UICVM.UIC.EDU** (INTERNET) with the command: **SUB ALCTS [YOUR NAME].**

The editor can be reached at **U34261@UICVM**. For information about backfiles and other ALCTS documents, send a message to **LISTSERV@UICVM** with the command: **SEND ACLTS FILELIST.**

AF5. *ALCTS Newsletter*. Chicago: Association for Library Collections and Technical Services. v. 1– , 1990– . Frequency varies. ISSN 1047-949X. Continues *RTSD Newsletter* (AF20).

This ALA divisional newsletter reports news about ALCTS activities from division administrators and officers, chairs of sections, committees, etc., and includes a column or brief article or two on topics of general interest, such as journal pricing and management practices. It has a book review column that mainly gives citations with a descriptive sentence or two for some items, and covers Education Resources Information Center (ERIC) documents and occasional serial and audiovisual titles in addition to books.

AF6. *Bulletin of the American Society for Information Science*. Silver Spring, Md.: American Society for Information Science. v. 1– , June/July 1974– . Bimonthly. ISSN 0095-4403.

In the words of the masthead, this is a "news magazine concentrating on issues affecting the information field; management reports; opinion, and news of people and events in ASIS and the information community." It also includes articles, some of which relate to technical services interests.

AF7. *CMC News*. Cannon Falls, Minn.: CMC News. v. 1– , 1979– . Three times a year. ISSN 0738-8845.

Subtitled "Computers and the Media Center," this desktop publication aimed at school library media specialists carries news of new computer systems, software, meetings, etc., much of which is relevant to technical services.

AF8. *IFLA Journal*. Munich: K. G. Saur. v. 1– , 1975– . Quarterly. ISSN 0340-0352.

This is the official journal of the International Federation of Library Associations and Institutions (IFLA). Each issue averages between four and eight scholarly articles on a broad range of topics, many of which relate to technical services, including cataloging, collection development, preservation, serials control, automation, management, education, standards, and so on, with an international flavor—e.g., cataloging in Country *X*, or preservation in Country *Y*. It also includes details of IFLA activities and reports from officers and committees, working groups, etc., many of which are devoted to tasks affecting one or more of the technical services.

AF9. *Information Retrieval & Library Automation*. Mt. Airy, Md.: Lomond Publications. v. 9, nos. 2– , July 1973– . Monthly. ISSN 0020-0220. Continues *Information Retrieval & Library Automation Letter*.

This brief newsletter provides short descriptions of new techniques, new equipment, events, meetings, case studies, federal policy, international developments, networks, communications, media, publications, and other topics of interest to automation librarians. Much of this material is of interest to technical services librarians. Recent issues included information about the use of census data and related software, optical disk technologies, the 15th edition of *Library of Congress Subject Headings*, Dialog's document delivery service SourceOne, and five meetings and six publications in addition to LCSH15, including Discovering RLIN. Current editor is Susan W. Johnson.

AF10. *Information Technology and Libraries*. Chicago: Library and Information Technology Association. v. 1– , Mar. 1982– . Quarterly. ISSN 0730-9295. Continues *Journal of Library Automation*.

The scholarly journal of the American Library Association division devoted to information technology. It contains lengthy, refereed articles on a variety of topics involving technology, primarily about computing, video, and telecommunications or their combinations, as well as library applications of information technologies such as the MARC formats, online catalogs, electronic publishing, and interactive media. Most items are relevant to technical services or one of its subtopics. Some of the issues also include shorter "Communications," and groups of long, signed book and media reviews. It is currently edited by Thomas W. Leonhardt.

AF11. *Journal of the American Society for Information Science*. New York: John Wiley & Sons for the Society. v. 21– , Jan./Feb. 1970– . Ten times a year. ISSN 0002-8231. Continues *American Documentation*.

The official journal of ASIS features scholarly articles, reports of research, opinion pieces, and book reviews, often of interest to technical services librarians. A recent theme issue contained nine articles about standards and the standards-making process as well as articles about name-matching algorithms, the problem of aging books, and knowledge acquisition for expert systems—all pertinent to issues in the technical services. Donald H. Kraft is the current editor.

AF12. *Library Hi Tech*. Ann Arbor, Mich.: Pierian Press. v. 1– , Summer 1983– . Monthly, plus special issues. ISSN 0737-8831.

This is an attractive, sophisticated, commercially sponsored professional magazine. Each issue contains between six and ten articles, often illustrated, on topics in library automation, including online catalogs, database design, networking, hardware and software, integrated systems, training, etc. There also are occasional theme issues, e.g., two recent issues focus on the Open Systems Interconnection. Well-edited and topical, *LHT* is oriented to computer-literate readers. Contributors are recognized authors who also publish in more scholarly library and information science journals.

AF13. *Library Resources & Technical Services*. Chicago: Association for Library Collections and Technical Services. v. 1– , Winter 1957– . Quarterly. ISSN 0024-2527.

This is the scholarly journal of the American Library Association division devoted to technical services. It addresses technical services topics in general as well as the special-interest areas of the group's six sections: Acquisitions, Cataloging and Classification, Collection Development, Preservation, Reproduction of Library Materials, and Serials. Each issue contains between four and eight full-length, refereed articles, some shorter pieces describing innovations in operations or studies in progress, and a varying number of thorough, evaluative, signed book reviews. Periodic literature reviews in its interest areas are a valuable source of information. The broad area covered by this journal results in a small proportion of truly general items compared with those on more specific topics. Generalists must peruse tables of contents carefully to determine the relevancy of individual items to their needs. A preponderance of articles fall into the areas of cataloging/classification and collection development/acquisitions.

AF14. *Library Software Review: SR*. Westport, Conn.: Meckler. v. 3– , Mar. 1984– . Bimonthly. ISSN 0742-5759. Continues *Software Review*.

Ostensibly devoted to reviewing software packages, *LSR* also includes articles of a more general nature dealing with library automation, networking, and specific systems, much of which is of interest to technical services librarians. Some issues contain executive summaries of papers delivered at the Computers in Libraries Conferences, sponsored by the publisher.

AF15. *Library Systems Newsletter*. Chicago: Library Technology Reports, American Library Association. v. 1– , July 1981– . Monthly. ISSN 0277-0288.

A newsletter containing up-to-date information on library-related computer products, hardware and software upgrades and new releases, and other news of interest to technical services managers. Well-edited for a number of years by Richard W. Boss and Judy McQueen, *Library Systems Newsletter* is easy to read and takes a practical, down-to-earth approach.

AF16. *Library Technology Reports*. Chicago: American Library Association. v. 12– , 1976– . Bimonthly. ISSN 0024-2586.

Lengthy issues give in-depth reviews of products and services for libraries, ranging from copiers and microform readers to bibliographic utilities and CD-ROM–based catalogs. Reviewers usually provide a comprehensive description of generally desirable characteristics and capabilities of the type of item(s) under review, followed by objective descriptions and evaluations of all or most of the offerings currently available. They usually include extensive bibliographies for further reference. This is an invaluable "consumer" guide for library purchasers.

AF17. *LITA Newsletter*. Chicago: Library and Information Technology Association. no. 1– , Winter 1980– . Frequency varies; occasional supplements. ISSN 0196-1799.

The membership newsletter of the Library and Information Technology Association, a division of the American Library Association. In addition to news of division activities, it also carries features and articles of interest to technical services librarians, e.g., "Standard Fare," a regular column on standards. It is a valuable source of news, internal politics, and topical information. Innovative editor Walt Crawford brought out a supplement to volume 13 titled *LITA Yearbook 1992*, featuring twenty-seven summaries of papers and programs from the 1992 ALA Annual Conference.

AF18. *The One-Person Library: A Newsletter for Librarians and Management*. New York: OPL Resources. v. 1– , May 1984– . Monthly. ISSN 0748-8831.

Possibly the only periodical devoted exclusively to persons working alone as the sole staff of an information agency. Within its eight pages, it features information-sharing columns (e.g., "What Would You Do?", "Feedback"), news of meetings and workshops, summaries of programs, and reviews of useful materials.

AF19. *Resource Sharing and Information Networks*. Binghamton, N.Y.: Haworth Press. v. 1– , Fall/Winter 1983– . Biannually. ISSN 0737-7797.

This is one of Haworth Press's many titles devoted to specialties in librarianship. Each issue contains between eight and ten articles on topics in library networking, broadly interpreted, that may include online catalogs, new automated systems, document supply, collection development, etc., as well as telecommunications and information networks. Some theme issues narrow the focus; for example, in volume 6, number 2, four authors wrote about cooperatives in music, fine arts, special collections, and performing arts. Editor since 1990, Robert P. Holley has contributed useful annotated bibliographies of relevant papers from IFLA conferences.

AF20. *RTSD Newsletter*. Chicago: Resources and Technical Services Division, American Library Association. v. 1–14, no. 6, 1976–1989. Frequency varied. ISSN 0360-5906. Continued by *ALCTS Newsletter* (AF5).

The membership newsletter of ALA's RTSD, which became ALCTS (*see* AF5). It emphasized reports of ongoing division, section, committee, and discussion group activities, plus a sprinkling of short articles of a topical nature. Columns that ran in several issues covered research, technical services management, automation, and other issues of interest. During the period covered by this title, division and section annual reports, annual awards, and the Dewey Decimal Editorial Board annual report were not found here, but were published instead in *Library Resources & Technical Services* (AF13).

AF21. *The School Librarian's Workshop*. Berkeley Heights, N.J.: Library Learning Resources. v. 1– , Sept. 1980– . Monthly, except July and August. ISSN 0271-3667.

Aimed at school librarians, this practical newsletter includes occasional articles on library automation, circulation, catalogs and cataloging systems, bar codes, etc., relating to technical services.

AF22. *Technical Services Quarterly*. Binghamton, N.Y.: Haworth Press. v. 1– , Fall/Winter 1983– . Quarterly. ISSN 0731-7131.

Another of Haworth Press's many titles devoted to library specialties, this one on technical services. Each issue contains between eight and ten articles on topics in technical services, broadly defined, that may include aspects of automation, networking, type-of-library, and management issues as well as issues in individual technical services. Each issue also contains several lengthy, signed reviews of recent publications, including an occasional nonprint item and, sometimes, a news section summarizing recent conferences or noteworthy announcements. Well-edited and useful, although coverage overlaps with other Haworth titles such as *Cataloging & Classification Quarterly* (CAE3), *The Acquisitions Librarian* (BAD2), *The Reference Librarian*, *The Serials Librarian* (GAD10), etc.

AF23. *Technicalities*. Lincoln, Nebr.: Media Periodicals, a division of Westport Publishers. v. 1– , Dec. 1980– . Monthly. ISSN 0272-0884.

Edited by Brian Alley since its inception, current issues include a front-page editorial, news, reviews of new products and publications, bimonthly columns on general issues of interest by Sheila Intner ("Interfaces"), collection development by Peggy Johnson ("Dollars and Sense"), online databases by Pat Ensor ("Database Commentary"), and Library of Congress subject headings indexing by William Studwell ("Cataloging Forum"), plus articles on topics of interest by well-known practitioners and theorists such as David Tyckoson, Pauline Cochrane, David Genaway, and James Dwyer, plus interviews with notables from the worlds of automation, multimedia, and emerging technologies. Early volumes contain a now-renowned cataloging series by Sanford Berman of Hennepin County Library. Aimed at all library types, its features and articles are topical and provocative—a good source of ideas and practical information.

AG
Sources of Expertise

AGA
Professional Associations

AGA1. American Society for Information Science (ASIS). Headquarters: 8720 Georgia Avenue, Suite 501, Silver Spring, MD 20910-3602. Executive Director: Richard B. Hill.

As its name suggests, ASIS is devoted to serving scholars and professionals in the field of information science, which includes areas relevant to several technical services areas, especially classification and indexing, and automated bibliographic systems. Members can participate in special-interest groups devoted to these and other topics within the information science field.

AGA2. Association for Library and Information Science Education (ALISE). Headquarters: 4101 Lake Boone Trail, Suite 201, Raleigh, NC 27607-4916. Executive Director: Sally Nicholson.

Primarily organized in support of library and information science educators, ALISE has a Special Interest Group on Technical Services Education that conducts programs and/or discussions on relevant topics at the association's annual meeting.

AGA3. ALA Association for Library Collections and Technical Services (ALCTS). Executive Director: Karen Muller.

This is the division of the American Library Association aimed at librarians working with collections and/or in the technical services. In 1990, the group changed its name from "Resources and Technical Services Division" to the current title. The division is organized into six sections: Acquisitions, Cataloging and Classification, Collection Management and Development, Preservation, Reproduction of Library Materials, and Serials. Each section has numerous committees and discussion groups devoted to particular aspects of work in the specialty as well as research, education, etc.

Division periodicals are listed above (*see* AF4, AF5, AF13, and AF20), but individual units also issue occasional papers, bibliographies, guides, and other helpful literature. ALCTS participates in interdivisional activities with other divisions and organizations and sends representatives and liaisons to them, e.g., the Committee on Machine-Readable Bibliographic Information, the Hugh Atkinson Memorial Award, the Joint Steering Committee for the Revision of Anglo-American Cataloguing Rules, the Joint Advisory Committee on Nonbook Materials.

Division-wide committees of general interest include the following: Audiovisual, Catalog Form and Function, Commercial Technical Services, Duplicates Exchange Union, Education, International Relations, Legislation, Library Materials Price Index, *Library Resources & Technical Services* Editorial Board, Preservation Microfilming, Publisher/Vendor-Library Relations, Research and Statistics, Scholarly Communications, and Technical Services Measurements.

AGA4. International Federation of Library Associations and Institutions (IFLA). Headquarters: c/o The Royal Library POB 95312, 2509CH, The Hague, The Netherlands. Secretary General: Paul Nauta.

IFLA is an international organization for library and information professionals, with a broad range of activities, programs, committees, discussion groups, etc., on the entire range of library and information topics. IFLA standards include the family of International Standard Bibliographic Descriptions and international applications of the MARC Format, and its publications program includes monographs, proceedings of its conferences, and periodicals (*see* AF8). Appointments to committees, working parties, etc., are made with attention to a broad distribution among nations. Many U.S. libraries maintain membership in IFLA, as do the American Library Association, the Association of Research Libraries, and other U.S. professional organizations.

AGA5. Library and Information Technology Association of the ALA (LITA). Executive Director: Linda J. Knutson.

This is the division of the American Library Association aimed at librarians working with computers and information technology. The division is organized into committees and interest groups. Division periodicals are listed above (*see* AF10 and AF17), but LITA also issues proceedings of its conferences and other monographic materials in book and nonbook formats. LITA participates in interdivisional activities with other divisions and organizations and sends representatives and liaisons to them; e.g., the Committee on Machine-Readable Bibliographic Information (MARBI) and the Hugh Atkinson Memorial Award.

Division-wide committees of general interest include the following: Education, International Relations, *Information Technology and Libraries* Editorial Board, Legislation and Regulation, Technical Standards for Library Automation, and Technology and Access. Interest groups of general interest include the following: Adaptive Technologies, Artificial Intelligence/Expert Systems, Customized Applications for Library Microcomputers, Desktop Publishing, Distributed Systems, Electronic Mail/Electronic Bulletin Boards, Emerging Technologies, Human/Machine Interface, Hypertext/Hypermedia, Imagineering, Library Consortia/Automated Systems, Microcomputer Users, Optical Information Systems, Programmer/Analyst, Small Integrated Library Systems, Telecommunications, and Vendor/User.

AGA6. National Information Standards Organization (NISO). Headquarters: P.O. Box 1956, Bethesda, MD 20827. Executive Director: Patricia Harris.

Previously known as the Z-39 group of the American National Standards Institute (ANSI), NISO is a professional membership organization that develops, publishes, monitors, and promotes the use of standards relating to information systems, operations, and entities. Many NISO standards are directly employed in technical services work, e.g., standard address numbers (used in ordering library materials), bibliographic record formats, thesaurus construction, computer system protocols. NISO publishes a quarterly journal edited by Patricia Ensor titled *Information Standards Quarterly* and holds an annual meeting in the fall. NISO activities are the focus of the LITA Technical Standards Committee (TESLA) and are reported by Lois N. Upham in her column "The Standards Connection" in *Journal of Education for Library and Information Science*.

AGA7. [State/Region] Technical Services Librarians (e.g., New York Technical Services Librarians, New England Technical Services Librarians).

Statewide or regional groups for technical services librarians usually are affiliated with state or regional library associations, although they also may be independent organizations. They may offer any or all of a variety of local activities, including collegial gatherings, newsletters and other materials of interest and use to practitioners, and educational programs, workshops, and institutes in convenient locations.

AGB
Conferences

AGB1. American Library Association Conferences. Twice a year; January (midwinter) and June/July (annual).

The annual conference is the largest gathering of librarians and information specialists (approximately 15,000–20,000 attendees) with programs and meetings, exhibits, tours, institutes, preconferences, and other related educational and social activities. Midwinter meetings, more business-related, draw some 8,000 to 12,000.

AGB2. American Society for Information Science Conferences. Twice a year; April (midyear) and October (annual).

ASIS conference schedules include programs and meetings, panel discussions, plenary sessions, exhibits, tours, institutes, preconferences, and other related educational and social activities. Papers read at the conference are refereed and published in its proceedings.

AGB3. Association for Library and Information Science Education Annual Conference. Once a year; January.

ALISE conference schedules include programs and meetings, plenary sessions, exhibits, tours, institutes, and other related educational and social activities. Perhaps because of the overlap in membership and general interests, the ALISE annual conference is held in the same city and with an overlapping schedule with the American Library Association Midwinter Conference each year.

AGB4. International Federation of Library Associations and Institutions Conference. Once a year; August.

IFLA conference schedules include programs, panels, meetings, and a broad range of educational and social activities, many of which are of interest to technical services librarians. Scholarly papers, etc., read during the conference appear in an annual proceedings, *The IFLA Annual*, published by K. G. Saur.

AGB5. ALA Library and Information Technology Association National Conference. Every second year; October.

LITA national conference schedules include programs and meetings, panel discussions, product demonstrations, exhibits, tours, institutes, preconferences, and related educational and social activities. Papers read at the conference are refereed and may be published in its proceedings.

AH
Administration

AH1. Adan, A. "Organizational Change in Law Libraries: The Impact of Automation on Traditional Library Structure." *Law Library Journal* 81 (Winter 1989): 97–102.

The author examines reorganizations taking place in academic libraries and suggests alternatives appropriate for smaller libraries, concluding that the traditional division between technical and public services is counterproductive.

AH2. Anderson, A. J. "How Do You Manage?" [column in] *Library Journal*. New York: Bowker. ISSN 0363-0277.

Anderson provides artful sketches of problems and incidents typically encountered in academic or public libraries, many of which relate to technical services activities. Two respondents selected by the publisher—usually practitioners, but sometimes library educators—analyze the problem and provide solutions. These columns furnish interested readers with a group of case studies illustrating a broad variety of issues.

AH3. Bonhomme, Mary, ed. "Technical Services: The 1990s." *Illinois Libraries* 72 (Sept. 1990): 471–519.

Here is an issue of *Illinois Libraries* devoted to an exploration of current and future trends in technical services administration, systems, and operations. Staffing and

automation are among the topics discussed, along with long-range planning and emerging technologies.

AH4. Boss, Richard W. *Library Manager's Guide to Automation.* 3rd ed. Boston: G. K. Hall, 1990.

The author examines the manager's role in automating libraries, as well as the current state of the art and future trends in local systems, emphasizing multiuser systems. Chapters cover hardware, software, communications, standards, implementation, and costs. This book contains a good mix of general principles and practical advice for the real world.

AH5. Busch, B. J., comp. *Automation and Reorganization of Technical and Public Services.* SPEC Kit, no. 112. Washington, D.C.: Association of Research Libraries, Office of Management Services, 1985.

This brief compilation reports the results of a 1984 survey of eighty-two ARL libraries conducted to determine to what extent research libraries have integrated technical and public services staff and the role played by automation in planning organizational change. Those with some degree of integrated staffing numbered fewer than half the respondents. None had integrated completely. The introduction of integrated automated systems ranked first among the forces motivating these changes. Staff integration (described as consisting of multiple- and dual-role job descriptions, i.e., one individual performing two major roles or dividing his or her responsibilities between cataloging and reference) took place in thirty-eight of the libraries. In addition to survey data, a variety of documents (memoranda, reports, letters, organization charts, etc.) from thirteen universities on the topic of organizational integration are included.

AH6. Busch, Joe. "Coming Out of the Back Room: Management Issues for Technical Services in the Eighties." *Technical Services Quarterly* 2 (Spring–Summer 1985): 115–41.

Busch introduces three papers presented at a 1983 New England Technical Services Librarians meeting by Dorothy Ladd (a just-retired associate director at Boston University Libraries), Fay Zipkowitz (then Rhode Island state librarian), and Michael Simonds (technical services librarian at Norwalk Public Library in Connecticut) on a number of vexing problems, including volunteer public service duties for catalogers, cataloging backlogs, retrospective conversion, work rules for inputters, and other issues relating to automation. Following the papers is a bibliographic essay/annotated bibliography by Busch on the subject of health-related effects of working on video display terminals. Partly dated, partly useful, the bibliography describes or annotates about fifteen items, mostly articles, but also a few monographs.

AH7. Cargill, Jennifer S., ed. "Library Management and Technical Services: The Changing Role of Technical Services in Library Organizations." *Journal of Library Administration* 9 (1988): 1–154.

This special issue offered timely contributions on managerial issues. Technical services librarians, department heads, vendor representatives, and administrators were asked to focus on change—in particular, the changes occurring in various aspects of the technical services. Eleven contributions plus an annotated bibliography (*see* AD7) cover topics such as leadership, staffing, impact of automation, relationship with public services, etc. Among the authors are Diane J. Cimbala, James R. Dwyer, Karin E. Ford, Constance L. Foster, Donald E. Riggs, Janet Swan Hill, Brian Alley, Gisela M. Webb, Dana C. Rooks, and Linda L. Thompson. Some articles have extensive bibliographies (e.g., Dwyer, Ford, Foster, Hill).

AH8. Corbin, John B. *Implementing the Library Automated System.* Phoenix: Oryx Press, 1988.

In this update to *Managing the Library Automation Project* (AH9), the author broadens the scope of systems to include acquisition, serials control, online catalogs, and integrated systems as well as circulation control systems. The book maintains a similar step-by-step approach to the processes of determining needs, designing a request for proposal, and implementing a stand-alone mini- or microcomputer-based system from among those available in the marketplace.

AH9. _____. *Managing the Library Automation Project.* Phoenix: Oryx Press, 1985.

See also annotation under AH8. One of the early books devoted to walking the library manager through the steps of choosing, acquiring, and implementing a stand-alone computer system. Examples focus primarily on circulation control systems. Each chapter includes helpful summaries, checklists, and forms. Appendixes provide complete versions of automation projects.

AH10. Cotta-Schonberg, Michael von. "Automation and the Academic Library Structure." *Libri* 39 (Mar. 1989): 47–63.

After exploring the functional structure for technical services, the author proposes a service-oriented organization for the library in which departments have both internal and external functions. Also suggested is the adoption of "permeable" departmental boundaries defined in such a way that all staff members can participate in direct service functions.

AH11. De Klerk, Ann, and Joanne R. Euster. "Technology and Organizational Metamorphoses." *Library Trends* 37 (1989): 457–68.

Reports on an informal survey of library directors about their perceptions and expectations for changes in organizational structure, initiated by the seeming disparity between expectations that automation would elicit widespread change and the results of the 1985 ARL survey indicating it had not occurred (*see* AH4). The authors describe the blurring of lines between public and technical services departments and shifts of roles among librarians, paraprofessionals, and clerical personnel. They call for redefinition of both organizational structures and staffing patterns.

AH12. Dumont, Paul E. "Creativity, Innovation, and Entrepreneurship in Technical Services." *Journal of Library Administration* 10, no. 2 (1989): 57–68.

The author sees technical services librarians as the change agents who implemented automation, and who benefited by developing flexibility and adaptability. He suggests they continue to facilitate change through an emphasis on entrepreneurship, innovation, risk taking, and creativity.

AH13. Fayen, Emily Gallup. "Beyond Technology: Rethinking 'Librarian.'" *American Libraries* 17 (Apr. 1986): 240–42.

The author speculates on how libraries and librarians might take the opportunity afforded by the introduction of automation to redefine their goals and service objectives. She asks that librarians stop ducking responsibility for finding and giving information to patrons by expecting patrons to do their own searching, which devalues library services and librarians' worth in the process. It is a strongly argued position in a well-written opinion piece.

AH14. Gleason, Maureen L., and Robert C. Miller. "Technical Services: Direction or Coordination?" *Technical Services Quarterly* 4, no. 3 (1987): 13–19.

The authors claim librarians have lost confidence in traditional bureaucratic administrative structures, but, in reality, have not made extensive changes to them. They suggest assistant directors be replaced by coordinators who do not manage departmental activities but monitor the flow of work and ensure that redundancy is eliminated and staff and systems are used effectively. Departmental management then moves downward to department heads, who should have the expertise and authority to plan, budget, staff, and make decisions. The authors argue persuasively that coordination can infuse library administration with needed flexibility as well as save money.

AH15. Graham, Peter S. "Electronic Information and Research Library Technical Services." *College & Research Libraries* 51, no. 3 (1990): 241–50.

Technical services, states the author, has changed from a traditional definition that includes acquisitions and cataloging to a new one based on different perceptions about technology and bibliographic data. He contends that technical services in the research library setting should not wait for decisions to be made elsewhere but should be a driving agent as well. Among the new tasks the author suggests technical services should undertake is linking access systems. He says technical services librarians must move to preserve and provide access to electronic data, without waiting for library administrators to decide it should be done.

AH16. Harrington, Sue Ann. "The Changing Environment in Technical Services." *Technical Services Quarterly* 4 (Winter 1986): 7–19.

The author claims that technical services staffs are feeling the greatest impact of the changes resulting from the introduction of electronic technologies in libraries. Their work environment is changing drastically. She urges technical services librarians to take control of these changes—which include a declining need for professional staff in technical services and merger of public and technical services departments—and be willing to adapt to new environments.

AH17. Hershey, Johanna. "The Impact of the Implementation of NOTIS on the Technical Services Workflow at the Milton S. Eisenhower Library, Johns Hopkins University." *Cataloging & Classification Quarterly* 9, no. 1 (1988): 19–26.

The author describes the changes made in workflow at Eisenhower Library after the implementation of NOTIS, an integrated automated system for technical services. The primary objective of the reorganization was to use the same bibliographic record for ordering and cataloging, with the result that the work of the acquisitions and cataloging departments now is interdependent.

AH18. Horny, Karen L. "Quality Work, Quality Control in Technical Services." *The Journal of Academic Librarianship* 11, no. 4 (1985): 206–10.

An examination of the effects of automation on the perennial tradeoff between quantity and quality. The author says key elements to be considered when discussing quality control include standards, user needs, access, and individual human capabilities and needs. Important skills for technical services managers and staff members are discussed, as are the ways computing can contribute both to higher productivity and higher quality work. The author provides both the scholarly context and practical evidence to aid readers in understanding a complex issue.

AH19. Intner, Sheila S. "For Technical Services: The Future is Now. The Future is Us." *Catholic Library World* 62 (May–June 1991): 420–27.

The author examines current trends such as changes in technical services job descriptions, integration of library functions, and shift of responsibility for generating new bibliographic data from the Library of Congress to local libraries. She urges that technical services librarians prepare to shoulder new responsibilities emphasizing management skills, research capabilities, and technological expertise, then use them to accomplish goals and objectives.

AH20. _____. "Interfaces." [column in] *Technicalities* 7– (Feb. 1987–).

This is a bimonthly column devoted to issues important to both technical and public services librarians and that act as "interfaces" between them, e.g., collection development, access services, preservation, catalog instruction, although some columns are of interest primarily to technical services librarians.

AH21. _____. "Interfaces: The Technical Services Mystique." *Technicalities* 7 (Jan. 1987): 8–11.

The author speculates on the negative psychological impact of names given to library departments performing technical services work, including "support" services, "processing" services, and the most popular term used,

"technical" services. She suggests the use of "bibliographic" services in place of these, in order to emphasize the similarities of this department's work to that of other library units, to strengthen the department's links with other library units, and because it more accurately describes the department's focus.

AH22. Jacob, M. E. L., ed. *Planning in OCLC Member Libraries.* Dublin, Ohio: OCLC, Inc., 1988.

This report analyzes and reports more than 2,000 responses to a 1987 survey about the planning process in academic research libraries, public libraries, state libraries, and special libraries. It covers data gathering and statistics as well as applications in library planning.

AH23. Johnson, Peggy. *Automation and Organizational Change in Libraries.* Boston: G. K. Hall, 1991.

The author reports responses of fifty-four Association of Research Libraries members to a survey documenting changes caused by the introduction of automation. She suggests methods of implementing changes in libraries, and relates what is happening in the library world to what is occurring in society at large. She concludes that support staff are performing more complex tasks and that lower level workers are decreasing in number. The author claims that libraries having long experience with automation show fewer organizational levels and exhibit changes in the distribution of responsibility and authority. The book provides a thorough analysis of the issues, furnishing hard data to support its conclusions. Clear and readable.

AH24. _____. "Matrix Management: An Organizational Alternative for Libraries." *The Journal of Academic Librarianship* 16 (Sept. 1990): 222–29.

The author offers a new model for library organization—the matrix structure—to address deficiencies of the traditional hierarchical structure for coordinating and integrating functions in the complex, high-tech library of today. She credits matrix management with providing more flexibility, greater independence on the part of professional librarians, and more balanced decision making.

AH25. Leonhardt, Thomas W. "Technical Services Management." *RTSD Newsletter* 9, nos. 1–7. (1984).

The author instituted a series of columns discussing current issues in technical services management. The first one was coauthored with Frederick C. Lynden. The intent was to provide practical analyses of common problems from the administrator's perspective. Begun by Leonhardt before he became editor of the newsletter, this column is continued by Marion Reid (*see* AH35).

AH26. Leonhardt, Thomas W., and Maureen Sullivan. "Self-Management in Technical Services: The Yale Experience." *Library Administration & Management* 4 (1989): 20–23.

The principles of self-management outlined in publications such as Tom Peters' *Thriving on Chaos: Handbook for the Management Revolution* and J. Richard Hackman's *Improving Life at Work* as applied to libraries, which now find themselves in need of flexibility and responsiveness to rapid change. It details recent experiences at Yale University Library's technical services departments, in which the authors played leadership roles.

AH27. Lowry, Charles B. "Technology in Libraries: Six Rules for Management." *Library Hi Tech* 3, no. 11 (1985): 27–29.

The author suggests the following six rules for managing change following the introduction of technology: (1) become informed, (2) discriminate, (3) understand finances, (4) select knowledgeable personnel, (5) know one's organization, and (6) manage people wisely. Far from applying solely to changes motivated by computerizing the library, these six suggestions can be productively applied by library managers to any library at any time.

AH28. Lynch, Beverly P., ed. *The Academic Library in Transition: Planning for the 1990s.* New York: Neal-Schuman Publishers, 1989.

The author documents the forty-year development of the University of Illinois at Chicago Library from a small undergraduate college library to a major research university library. Overall, the book illustrates trends in acquisitions, cataloging, networking, and other functions. Individual papers are written by current and former UIC librarians. The book provides a comprehensive and instructive case study, but does not furnish a planning guide as readers might expect from the title.

AH29. Marchant, Maurice P., and Mark M. England. "Changing Management Techniques as Libraries Automate." *Library Trends* 37, no. 4 (1989): 469–83.

In a carefully researched scholarly paper, the authors state that problems of adjustment to automation in libraries are similar to those occurring throughout society, and that deeper and more radical changes are yet to come. They argue for a change in library organization from pyramid to flat models and in style from authoritarian to participatory management. Libraries need to recognize that their greatest assets are human resources and information, and must aim to maximize librarians' potential for flexibility and innovation—essential in the rapidly changing technological environment.

AH30. Martin, Susan K. "Library Management and Emerging Technology: The Immovable Force and the Irresistible Object." *Library Trends* 37 (Winter 1989): 374–82.

The author discusses the window of opportunity afforded by emerging technologies for a complete restructuring of the library workplace and offers reasons why library technology hasn't moved faster (costs, lack of standards, copyright, etc.). She advises caution in introducing technology to ensure that the library doesn't pull too far ahead of its parental culture, is fair to the staff, and is consistent with the character of the management team. She sees the following problem areas: managing traditional and new formats simultaneously; keeping the library building active and interesting while also supporting remote sites more fully; accepting the likelihood that libraries and computer centers will not merge; deriving

changes from management's desire to change, not because technology requires it; and recognizing that failure to change may still require new communication links between people in different parts of the library. This is an exceptionally thoughtful analysis that makes worthwhile reading.

AH31. McCombs, Gillian M., ed. *Access Services: The Convergence of Reference and Technical Services.* New York: Haworth Press, 1991. Also published as *The Reference Librarian* 34 (1991).

Here are thirteen papers that, together, examine the changed nature of access services in light of current (i.e., in 1990–1991) interactions between public and technical services. The papers are divided into four parts: public services perspective, technical services perspective, the new access services, and national library-wide concerns. The editor urges that "public and technical services redefine both their own roles and their relationship in order to provide the services needed by patrons through the year 2000."

AH32. _____. "Technical Services in the 1990s: A Process of Convergent Evolution." *Library Resources & Technical Services* 36 (Apr. 1992): 135–48.

The author uses the theory of biological convergent evolution to illustrate heightened levels of integration achieved by technical services, public services, and collection development in academic research libraries, resulting from automation. She provides a theoretical rationale for explaining the changes in workflow that have occurred and are likely to continue to develop. This item is useful both for its review of fifteen years of change in library technical services and for its speculations on future developments.

AH33. Niles, Judith. "Technical Services Reorganization for an Online Integrated Environment." *Cataloging & Classification Quarterly* 9, no. 1 (1988): 11–17.

The author reports the experiences of the University of Louisville (Kentucky) Libraries in making decisions to reorganize technical services work flow upon the implementation of a NOTIS automated system. Among the more important results: the acquisitions department became responsible for bibliographic record selection along with searching and verification.

AH34. Racine, Drew, ed. *Managing Technical Services in the 90s.* Binghamton, N.Y.: Haworth Press, 1991. Also published as *Journal of Library Administration* 15, nos. 1/2.

This monograph consists of eight papers by William A. Gosling, Delmus E. Williams, Arnold Hirshon, Sharon L. Walbridge, Wayne R. Perryman, Olivia M. A. Madison, Kenneth John Bierman, and Jennifer A. Younger, and an introduction by the editor, which originally appeared as the *Journal of Library Administration*, volume 15, numbers 1/2. It provides an overview of a selection of current issues and problems in technical services activities primarily relating to the academic library setting, including high-tech products, personnel, the information world, relationships with other library units, information access, bibliographic access, and the role of librarians. Bierman's chapter examines the public library setting. It presents a potpourri of different styles, approaches, and perspectives.

AH35. Reid, Marion T. "Technical Services Management." *RTSD Newsletter* 10, no. 3 (1985) through 14, no. 5 (1989). Continued in *ALCTS Newsletter* 1, no. 2 (1990): 11–12.

This author continues Leonhardt's column (AH25) on various issues in technical services management. Currently Director of Libraries of California State University at San Marcos, Reid previously headed technical services at Louisiana State University. Some columns are written by guest authors. Columns attempt to analyze current problems and set out alternative solutions in an objective manner.

AH36. Stevenson, Gordon, and Sally Stevenson. "Reference Services and Technical Services: Interactions in Library Practice." *The Reference Librarian* 9 (Fall/Winter 1983): 1–163.

Here are thirteen papers that, together, constitute one of the earliest examinations of the overlapping roles of public and technical services workers, and the contributions of technical services workers to end-user services. Following Gordon Stevenson's introductory essay "The Nature of the Problem, If It Is a Problem," the issue is divided into five main sections: historical background, overview, organizational arrangements, document description, and subject organization and access. It is instructive to review the list of current issues, other than administrative organization, outlined by the editor in his overview article: national standards, complexity, online catalog, Library of Congress Subject Headings, and classification. Among the authors are Wayne Wiegand, Pauline Cochrane, Michael Gorman, Larry Earl Bone, Carol Ishimoto, Norman Stevens, Francis Miksa, and Sanford Berman.

AH37. Timko, Georgene. "Technical Services Behind Closed Doors." In *Energies for Transitions: Proceedings of the Fourth National Conference of the Association for College and Research Libraries*, edited by Danuta Nitecki, 112–14. Chicago: ACRL, 1986.

The author calls for a publicity campaign by technical services in order to raise public consciousness about the work, which frequently is conducted out of sight of both the public and other librarians. Here is an idea whose time has not merely come but is long overdue.

AH38. Weintraub, D. Kathryn, ed. "Shall We Throw Out the Technical Services—and Then What?" *Library Resources & Technical Services* 33 (July 1989): 284–96; 34 (Jan. 1990): 95–99; 34 (Apr. 1990): 251–55; 34 (July 1990): 401–405.

This series of four articles by D. Kaye Gapen, Liz Bishoff, Lois Kershner, and Joan Rapp provides descriptive detail about changing directions in technical services and ways to implement desired changes. The papers were originally presented at the 1987 annual meeting of the California Library Association Technical Services Chapter.

AHA
Decision Making

AHA1. Burkholder, Sue A., ed. *Statistical Applications in Library Technical Services: An Annotated Bibliography.* Prepared by LAMA, Statistics Section, Task Force: Statistical Applications in Technical Services, Linda S. Vertrees, Chairperson. Chicago: Library Administration and Management Association, American Library Association, 1987.

This work cites reports of statistical research in technical services published between 1975 and 1985 in a listing intended to aid practitioners and researchers as well as to encourage additional work in this area. The compilers cover acquisitions, serials, cataloging, catalog structure and use, collection development, analysis and management, and preservation and conservation, and emphasize practical studies over theoretical ones. Forty-eight journals from major English-speaking nations were surveyed comprehensively and 727 citations compiled and abstracted, although the compilers do not claim to be comprehensive for the subject. The arrangement is topical and, within categories, in reverse chronological order. The abstracts are short and purely descriptive. Items may appear more than once. The compilation contains author and subject/keyword indexes. This is a good place to begin when planning any technical services study.

AHA2. Hernon, Peter, ed. *Statistics for Library Decision Making: A Handbook.* Norwood, N.J.: Ablex, 1989.

This is not a statistics textbook, but a complementary work that places a selection of statistical techniques in context for library research and decision making. It has chapters on the t-test, Mann-Whitney test, correlation, and analysis of variance and regression, among other techniques. It provides numerous references and summaries of research studies reported in the literature.

AHA3. Hernon, Peter, and Charles M. McClure. *Evaluation and Library Decision Making.* Norwood, N.J.: Ablex, 1990.

Here is a basic text on library evaluation, containing many illustrative examples. It includes discussions of study design, sampling, data collection techniques, reporting, etc. It has study questions at the end of chapters, and an excellent bibliography of source materials.

AHA4. Lantz, Brian. "Evaluation of Technical Services Functions: Towards a Management Information System." *Journal of Librarianship* 18, no. 4 (1986): 257–77.

This article describes Birmingham Polytechnic Library's current combination of micro- and minicomputer-based technical services statistical reporting, and explores ways in which automation does not merely overcome existing problems but provides the basis for a full management information system for technical services evaluation and decision making. The author's thesis—that technical services managers must identify what information they need and press vendors of automated systems to incorporate them into system designs—is as valid today as it was when this article was written.

AHA5. McClure, Charles R., and others. *Planning and Role Setting for Public Libraries: A Manual of Options and Procedures.* Chicago: American Library Association, 1987.

See also annotation under AHA7. Although not specifically geared to planning technical services activities, this useful tool provides public librarians with easily followed procedures for managing change in their institutions and directing those changes toward desired and desirable ends.

AHA6. Phillips, Linda L., and William Lyons. "Analyzing Library Survey Data Using Factor Analysis." *College & Research Libraries* 51 (Sept. 1990): 483–89.

The authors describe how factor analysis, a statistical technique that attempts to group variables, can be applied to large data sets such as those resulting from library surveys. They illustrate use of the technique, originally developed to deal with psychology data, in analyzing survey data at the University of Tennessee, Knoxville.

AHA7. Van House, Nancy A., and others. *Output Measures for Public Libraries: A Manual of Standardized Procedures.* 2nd ed. Chicago: American Library Association, 1987.

This work describes twelve output measures in detail, with step-by-step instructions for their execution as well as explanations of how to use the results to evaluate services and aid in decision making. It is an appropriate companion volume to *Planning and Role Setting for Public Libraries* (AHA5).

AHA8. Van House, Nancy A., B. T. Weil, and Charles R. McClure. *Measuring Academic Library Performance: A Practical Approach.* Chicago: American Library Association, 1990.

Like the previous entry (AHA7), this is a practical manual furnishing step-by-step instructions in the measurement of outputs such as overall user success, availability of materials, etc., to be used in planning and decision making; but this book is aimed at academic libraries. It includes sample forms for data collection and helpful examples.

AHB
Costs

Compiled and annotated
by Samson C. Soong

AHB1. Bedford, Denise A. D. "Technical Services Costs in Large Academic Research Libraries: A Preliminary Report on the Findings of the Samuel Lazerow Fellowship Project." *Technical Services Quarterly* 6, nos. 3/4 (1989): 29–48.

The author reports preliminary findings of a project whose objective was to survey technical processing costs in large academic research libraries. The project defined seven functional categories that encompassed all technical services tasks: materials acquisitions, searching and verification, cataloging, catalog record production and maintenance, collection resources maintenance, serials control, and physical processing. The survey methodology used is adaptable to different technical services cost studies and projects.

AHB2. Breeding, Marshall. "Multipurpose Technical Services Workstations: Access to NOTIS/OCLC/GTO with a Single Microcomputer." *Library Hi Tech* 9 (1991): 69.

Multipurpose technical services workstations and the procedures outlined in this brief article can reduce equipment costs, save desktop space, and facilitate access to OCLC while reducing telecommunication costs. The general approach described here can serve as a model and be applied to other library systems and bibliographic utilities.

AHB3. Cochrane, Lynn Scott, and Carolyn Warmann. "Cost Analysis of Library Services at Virginia Polytechnic Institute and State University." In *Building on the First Century: Proceedings of the Fifth National Conference of the Association of College and Research Libraries, Cincinnati, Ohio, April 5–8, 1989,* edited by Janice C. Fennell, 55–62. Chicago: ACRL, 1989.

The authors analyze the costs of purchasing, cataloging, binding, and shelving monographs and serials at Virginia Polytechnic Institute. They interviewed departmental managers to obtain basic cost data, then added university overhead costs to arrive at average figures of more than $100 for monographs and $180 for periodicals and other serials.

AHB4. Dougherty, Richard M., and L. E. Leonard. *Management and Costs of Technical Processes: A Bibliographic Review 1876–1969.* Metuchen, N.J.: Scarecrow Press, 1970.

Although it now is dated, this review provides its reader with the material needed to gain a historical appreciation of the background and context in which today's cost studies can be understood.

AHB5. Getz, Malcolm, and Doug Phelps. "Labor Costs in the Technical Operation of Three Research Libraries." *The Journal of Academic Librarianship* 10 (Sept. 1984): 209–19.

The authors report the results of an analysis of the technical services activities of three middle-sized research libraries. The investigation focused on the costs of labor and the effects on these costs of library automation. This is good reading for all technical services managers.

AHB6. Hoermann, Heidi L., comp. *Technical Services Cost Studies in ARL Libraries.* SPEC Kit, no. 125. Washington, D.C.: Association of Research Libraries–Office of Management Studies, Systems and Procedures Exchange Center, 1986.

A brief work that includes the results of a 1986 survey of ARL libraries, a statistical questionnaire with definitions used by several Canadian libraries to obtain comparative data, an outline of a management information system for total library analysis with a specific section on technical services activities, a breakdown of all technical services activities into a menu of processing modules used for cost recovery, and two studies analyzing costs of specific products—the card catalog and retrospective conversion. It includes a brief bibliography of recent sources. This SPEC kit will be useful to librarians seeking to determine costs.

AHB7. Juergens, Bonnie. "Costs and New Technologies: The View from the Network/Broker." *Technical Services Quarterly* 8, no. 1 (1990): 17–28.

The author discusses the economics of obtaining technology-based products and services through membership in regional networks such as Amigos Bibliographic Council. The article is useful in an examination of cost-to-benefit issues at the individual library level in a network-specific context.

AHB8. Leonhardt, Thomas W. "Technical Services Management: Hidden Costs." *RTSD Newsletter* 9, no. 5 (1984): 49–50.

The author uses gifts, exchange agreements, service contracts, supplies, increases in the library material budget, and set processing for large microform sets as examples to illustrate activities with hidden costs. He points out the multiplicity of factors to be considered in making a decision and a commitment.

AHB9. Mandel, Carol A. "Trade-Offs: Quantifying Quality in Library Technical Services." *The Journal of Academic Librarianship* 14 (Sept. 1988): 214–20.

The author offers a practical, step-by-step guide to methods of translating perceptions of quality into concrete terms that can be represented in dollars and cents. She uses examples to demonstrate how librarians can determine the cost of implementing various cataloging alternatives and, thus, arrive at a considered decision to take a particular course of action.

AHB10. Martin, Murray S. "Automation in Technical Services: Its Effects and Costs." *Technical Services Quarterly* 8, no. 3 (1991): 3–18.

The author states that automation has changed both procedures and cost distribution in technical services. Introduction of automation increases nonpersonnel costs. New and substitute expenditures will differ library by library, but will fall broadly into three categories: staff costs, contract costs, and ongoing miscellaneous costs. Managers concerned about the budgetary effects of automation on technical services should find this article useful.

AHB11. Michalko, James. "Costly Boundaries: Costs, New Technologies, and Bibliographic Utilities." *Technical Services Quarterly* 8, no. 1 (1990): 29–36.

An article that offers the author's observations on the changing nature of library and utility costs and argues that the boundaries between library, network, and data resource costs have shifted even as the total costs have grown. He suggests costs and new technologies are creating centrifugal forces that could compromise the viability and usefulness of central data resources such as the Research Libraries Information Network (RLIN) and OCLC. He believes this may be helpful in decision making about the use of central data resources or other mechanisms to support library technical processing activities.

AHB12. Pitkin, Gary M., ed. *Cost-Effective Technical Services: How to Track, Manage, and Justify Internal Operations.* New York: Neal-Schuman Publishers, 1989.

This book contains papers from an ALA Technical Services Costs Preconference and reaction pieces solicited from attendees after the session. Cost studies described in the papers vary in scope and coverage. One section looks at issues involved in standardizing operational costs for the purposes of uniform study and application, and a ninety-six-page bibliography annotates selected sources published between 1970 and 1988. This work meets a basic need for managers seeking to identify and analyze costs and/or justify operational practices.

AHB13. Rosenberg, Philip. *Cost Finding for Public Libraries: A Manager's Handbook.* Chicago: American Library Association, 1985.

This book introduces methodologies used in cost finding and provides an overview of cost concepts. Steps for cost finding include (1) identifying the cost center, (2) determining activities and tasks within a cost center, (3) selecting units of measure, (4) capturing unit cost information, and (5) analyzing the data. A glossary of terms, guidelines for costing, and blank worksheet forms are given. Technical services managers in public libraries will find this a useful and practical approach.

AHB14. Smith, G. Stevenson. "Managerial Accounting and Changing Models of Administrative Behavior: New Methods for New Models." *Library Trends* 38, no. 2 (1989): 189–203.

The author explains that accounting information can be prepared for cost control, performance evaluation, or decision making for the future. In this paper, the focus is on the use of new managerial accounting techniques used to evaluate upper-level administrators, who, according to current theories of administrative behavior, may be contravening institutional goals by shirking their responsibilities and/or putting their personal interests ahead of the interests of the institution. It describes how performance audits, recording deferred items, and value-lost determinations (i.e., examining actions *not* taken) can be used to reveal problem behaviors. Were they to be applied to library administrators by their parent bodies, performance accounting techniques could be a sobering experience and might reveal the costs of poor management—clearly a disturbing idea.

AHB15. Spyers-Duran, Peter. "Cost of Library Technologies: The Bottomless Pit of the 1990s?" *Technical Services Quarterly* 8, no. 1 (1990): 3–16.

The author discusses the pressure on libraries that installed automated systems during the 1970s and early 1980s to upgrade these systems to meet the higher expectations of users in the current environment. The author recommends the cooperative approach to library automation to share the cost of establishing and maintaining automated systems. This paper provides a useful overview of many aspects of local library networking.

AHB16. Walton, Robert. "Shared Automated Library Systems: Is There a Fair Way to Divide the Costs?" *Library Journal* 115, no. 7 (1990): 68–69.

The author analyzes issues involved when budget administration requires that costs of integrated systems be allocated among different lines and categories. He highlights the need to reorganize budget administration to keep pace with changes in the way systems and services are organized and administered in libraries.

AHC
Expert Systems

Compiled and annotated
by Judy Jeng

AHC1. Aluri, Rao, and Donald E. Riggs. "Application of Expert Systems to Libraries." *Advances in Library Automation and Networking* 2 (1988): 1–43.

A good introduction to expert systems, covering definitions, history, architecture, design methodology, basic components, commonly used programming languages and shells, the user interface, knowledge representation, and evaluation. It addresses the psychological impact on staff of introduction of expert systems, i.e., fear of being replaced by a machine. It illustrates applications of expert systems in reference, government documents, indexing, and cataloging.

AHC2. Anderson, P. F. "Expert Systems, Expertise, and the Library and Information Professions." *Library & Information Science Research* 10 (Oct./Dec. 1988): 367–88.

In this article, the author reports an investigation of the application of expert systems technologies to various library functions, many of which fall into the area of technical services work, e.g., cataloging, indexing, the user interface, searching, and information retrieval.

AHC3. Bailey, Charles W., Jr., comp. *Expert Systems in ARL Libraries.* SPEC Kit, no. 174. Washington, D.C.: Association of Research Libraries, Systems and Procedures Exchange Center, 1991.

This compilation summarizes a 1990 survey assessing perceptions of research librarians about expert systems and determining the level of development activity in progress in ARL libraries. It includes documents describing expert systems at the University of Houston, University of Illinois, Louisiana State University, Northwestern University, the National Agricultural Library, and Stanford University.

AHC4. _____. "Intelligent Library Systems: Artificial Intelligence Technology and Library Automation Systems." *Advances in Library Automation and Networking* 4 (1991): 1–23.

This paper examines certain key aspects of artificial intelligence that determine its potential utility as a tool for building library systems. It discusses the barriers that inhibit the development of intelligent library systems and suggests possible strategies for making progress in this important area.

AHC5. Cavanagh, Joseph M. A. "Library Applications of Knowledge-Based Systems." *The Reference Librarian* 23 (1989): 1–19.

The author identifies a broad range of library applications for expert systems, including descriptions for approval plans, descriptive cataloging, classification, subject indexing, journal selection for indexing, and selective dissemination of information. The author predicts the development of expert systems for interlibrary loan and interactive reader advisory service.

AHC6. Chang, Ray. "The Expert Systems Are Coming." *Technicalities* 6 (July 1986): 9–11.

The author defines expert systems and outlines their capabilities and limitations. He describes the history and background of their development and gives examples of four successful expert systems: MYCIN, PROSPECTOR, XCON, and TAXADVISOR. He discusses artificial intelligence programming, basic components of an expert system, and potential application areas for libraries, including management, cataloging, and collection analysis. Good introductory reading for the uninitiated, the article is brief, clear, and light on jargon.

AHC7. Dabrowski, Christopher E., and Elizabeth N. Fong. *Guide to Expert System Building Tools for Microcomputers.* NIST Special Publication 500-188. Gaithersburg, Md.: Computer Systems Laboratory, National Institute of Standards and Technology, U.S. Department of Commerce, 1991.

This highly readable monograph provides an overview of expert systems concepts and technology. It discusses criteria for selecting a domain for expert systems application and analyzes expert systems building tools in microcomputer-based environments.

AHC8. Fenly, Charles, and Howard Harris. *Expert Systems: Concepts and Applications.* Advances in Library Information Technology, no. 1. Washington, D.C.: Cataloging Distribution Service, Library of Congress, 1988.

The author reports on investigations into the use of expert systems at the Library of Congress. The brief report is divided into two sections: the first is a general definition and description of expert systems technologies; the second includes descriptions of the author's research methodology, characteristics of suitable expert systems domains in Library of Congress collections and processing operations, and conclusions about the feasibility of applications for various operations in cataloging, acquisitions work, and serials management.

AHC9. Fox, Mark S. "AI and Expert System Myths, Legends, and Facts." *IEEE Expert* 5, no. 1 (1990): 8–20.

The author seeks the reasons for ineffective artificial intelligence (AI) applications. Common perceptions and misperceptions are identified and grouped into three categories: myths—perceptions not based on any fact; legends—perceptions once based on fact that have been distorted; and facts—perceptions with a real basis in fact. Examples of successful AI applications now in use worldwide outside of libraries also are discussed.

AHC10. Holthoff, Tim. "Expert Librarian Applications of Expert Systems to Library Technical Services." *Technical Services Quarterly* 7, no. 1 (1989): 1–16.

This paper begins with an introduction to artificial intelligence generally and the basics of expert systems. Specific expert systems relating to technical services functions are discussed. Finally, the author speculates on the effects of expert systems research on technical services librarianship.

AHC11. Keyes, Jessica. "Why Expert Systems Fail." *AI Expert* 4, no. 11 (1989): 50–53.

The author analyzes the reason for success and failure of expert systems development. An excellent list of DOs and DON'Ts is provided, which should be of great help to beginning systems developers.

AHC12. McDonald, Craig, and John Weckert, eds. *Libraries and Expert Systems: Proceedings of a Conference and Workshop Held at Charles Sturt University–Riverina, Australia, July 1990.* New York: T. Graham, 1991.

See also annotation under AHC14. The conference brought together librarians, information managers, and developers of expert systems from throughout the world. Individual papers explore the technology, applications in information management, implications for librarians, and managerial/social issues.

AHC13. Vickery, Alina, and Helen Brooks. "Expert Systems and Their Applications in LIS." *Online Review* 11, no. 3 (1987): 149–65.

This article discusses briefly what expert systems are and why they might be of interest to the developers of library information systems (LIS). It outlines interesting work being done using expert systems techniques in libraries, then goes on to detail an expert system for retrieval named PLEXUS, developed by a team at the University of London. Although PLEXUS is not perfect, it engages in intelligent problem solving with the user. It has the capacity to exclude concepts from the user's query and makes intelligent use of equivalent terms and synonyms to broaden a search.

AHC14. Weckert, John, and Craig McDonald, eds. "A Special Issue on Artificial Intelligence, Knowledge Sys-

tems, and the Future Library." *Library Hi Tech* 10, nos. 1–2 (1992).

See also annotation under AHC12. This special issue contains twelve articles by a group of Australian and British authors plus a brief introduction by the editors in an issue devoted to expert systems and their applications in library and information science. Following these articles, but presumably not part of them, is an entertaining quiz by Walt Crawford for readers of his column on personal computing.

AHD
Staffing and Training

AHD1. Altmann, Anna E. "The Academic Library of Tomorrow: Who Will Do What?" *Canadian Library Journal* 45 (1988): 147–52.

In a provocative article, the author challenges the traditional division of public and technical services in academic libraries and suggests a new collegial arrangement in which subject concentrations will replace library functions as the principle by which libraries are organized.

AHD2. Association of Research Libraries, Office of Management Studies. *Training of Technical Services Staff in the Automated Environment.* SPEC Kit, no. 171. Washington, D.C.: Association of Research Libraries-Office of Management Studies, Systems and Procedures Exchange Center, 1991.

This compilation reports the results of a survey of 119 ARL libraries to which sixty-six libraries responded, identifying the numbers of technical services staff in the library, types of automated systems used in technical services, and kinds of training procedures in use in sixty-one libraries (the others had no online catalog). It also includes planning documents, training schedules, evaluation forms, training documents, outlines of training procedures and guidelines, and a brief bibliography. Managers will find the planning documents particularly helpful as well as several rather complete sample training documents. Schedules alert them to the time training takes to maximize staff effectiveness.

AHD3. Bishoff, Liz. "Technical Services/Public Services Cooperation: What's Next?" *Technical Services Quarterly* 6, nos. 3 and 4 (1989): 23–27.

The author suggests that a decade of technical and public services librarians working together on the design and implementation of online catalogs is extending beyond that one area into the area of information and referral systems (I&R). Traditionally an area assigned solely to public services librarians, the author believes cooperative experiences with catalogers are encouraging the application of cataloging skills to problems of I&R systems design.

AHD4. Cargill, Jennifer S. "Integrating Public and Technical Services Staffs to Implement the New Mission of

Libraries." *Journal of Library Administration* 10, no. 4 (1988): 21–31.

The author takes the position that the introduction of technology into libraries and resulting improvements in access to information are changing the mission of libraries. As a result, librarians' activities are changing and will continue to change from acquiring, processing, servicing, and warehousing information to teaching access and search skills to patrons and, in doing so, competing with other information providers. The author believes a different perspective on library organization is needed that is consistent with a new and different array of tasks librarians will be called upon to perform. It provides an astute analysis, offering justifications for integration based on task analysis.

AHD5. Daily, Jay Edward. *Staff Personality Problems in the Library Automation Process.* Littleton, Colo.: Libraries Unlimited, 1985.

The author uses case studies to illustrate how libraries can implement automation projects despite the resistance of some employees. He describes stereotypical library personalities, and recommends methods of dealing with them. Readers need to be reasonably cautious in applying these stereotypes to real people.

AHD6. DeLoach, Marva L. "Human Resource Management in Technical Services." *Illinois Libraries* 69 (Feb. 1987): 112–16.

This overview shows how the concepts of personnel management can be applied successfully to library technical services personnel resources. It explores different schools of thought and weighs each carefully before suggesting strategies for libraries. It gives the manager's perspective, and is followed in the same issue by an article giving the employee's perspective (*see* AHD17).

AHD7. Glogoff, Stuart, and James P. Flynn. "Developing a Systematic In-House Training Program for Integrated Library Systems." *College & Research Libraries* 48 (Nov. 1987): 528–36.

This article discusses the link between applied learning theory and development of a university library training program. It offers a solid rationale for revising staff training programs to ensure they serve organizational goals, designing the training program according to principles of learning theory and selecting trainers because they are competent trainers rather than because they happen to be available. The authors use the experience at the University of Delaware to demonstrate application of the principles and methods.

AHD8. High, Walter M. "The Role of the Professional in Technical Services." *RTSD Newsletter* 11 (1986): 58–60.

The author discusses tasks and responsibilities characteristic of professional, contrasted with paraprofessional or clerical, job descriptions. This article was written at a time when the advent of copy cataloging and other computer-based technical services operations were recognized as having resulted in profound changes in the procedures, workflow, and staffing of departments.

AHD9. Ho, James. "Basic Strategy in Personnel Planning for Library Technical Services." *Library Administration & Management* 2, no. 4 (1988): 196–99.

The author suggests a methodology for applying management by objectives to technical services staffing. It takes into consideration such variables as the volume of materials, total materials budget, number of staff members, total working hours, specific tasks, and productivity, and demonstrates how mathematical formulas can describe their relationships. Valuable as one of the few analyses that considers the total job to be done as well as the parameters of individual productivity.

AHD10. Horny, Karen L. "Fifteen Years of Automation: Evolution of Technical Services Staffing." *Library Resources & Technical Services* 31 (Jan./Mar. 1987): 69–76.

The author discusses how automation affects the processing operation's staffing and costs in the context of Northwestern University's long-term experience with computerization. Staff reallocations and reductions are described along with positive impacts on services and savings in salaries.

AHD11. Lawson, V. Lonnie, and Charles E. Slattery. "Involvement in Bibliographic Instruction among Technical Services Librarians in Missouri Academic Libraries." *Library Resources & Technical Services* 34 (July 1990): 245–48.

This article reports a survey of participation in bibliographic instruction by technical services librarians in the State of Missouri. It documents the small role played by technical services librarians in a minority of libraries and questions whether such librarians might not have more to contribute.

AHD12. Morris, Anne, and Stephen Barnacle. "The Human Side of Library Automation." *Electronic Library* 7 (Apr. 1989): 84–92.

The work environment of an automated technical services department is described, with emphasis on ergonomic matters such as health, safety, and design as well as organizational issues. It examines the problems of staff members whose work requires that they sit for long periods of time at computer terminals and draws attention to their plight.

AHD13. Presley, Roger L., and Carolyn L. Robison. "Changing Roles of Support Staff in an Online Environment." *Technical Services Quarterly* 4 (Fall 1986): 25–39.

The authors discuss the implementation of local serials control systems at Georgia State University's Pullen Library Acquisitions Department, and how it served as a catalyst in effecting new organizational structure. The article highlights how staff participated in the process, changing both their expectations and their roles in the new work environment. Good analysis of the situation and suggestions for maintaining morale during times of change.

AHD14. Rubin, Richard, ed. "Critical Issues in Library Personnel Management." *Library Trends* 38 (Summer 1989): 1–148.

Here is an examination of current issues by eleven authors including Kathleen M. Heim (now McCook), James G. Neal, Sharon L. Baker, Anne Grodzins Lipow, Charles A. Bunge, and others. Some of the issues are of particular importance in technical services departments, e.g., stress management, salary-benefit determinations, training, resistance to change, and turnover.

AHD15. Rushing, Darla H. "Caught in the Middle: Systems, Staff and Maintenance in the Medium-Sized Academic Library." *Journal of Library Administration* 13, nos. 1–2 (1990): 157–73.

The author reports a survey of seven libraries in universities with book holdings between 250,000 and 600,000 volumes to determine how automation has affected technical services staffing and operations. The participants were Creighton, DePaul (Chicago), Loyola (New Orleans), Pepperdine, Stetson, and Trinity (San Antonio) universities and the University of Richmond. The findings include that staffs were not greatly reduced; integrated systems were absent for the most part; and problems of coordination and territoriality arose as integrated systems began to be introduced, which required creative solutions in order to facilitate the use of newer systems.

AHD16. Webb, Gisela M. "Strategies for Recruiting Technical Services Personnel." *Technicalities* 8 (Nov. 1988): 13–15.

This author suggests that libraries having difficulty recruiting librarians for technical services positions might take the opportunity to review personnel needs. Reviews should begin with an institutional profile and include budgets, presence of backlogs, state of automation, and definition of professional responsibilities. She then offers strategies for recruiting entry-level staff and departmental managers. This is practical advice, especially useful for the personnel officer who lacks familiarity with technical services work.

AHD17. Wendler, Ann V. J. "Management: An Employee Perspective." *Illinois Libraries* 69 (Feb. 1987): 116–20.

This companion to DeLoach's article (AHD6) gives a professional librarian's reaction to working under different managerial styles and techniques. It covers a selection of styles and techniques with which the author has had experience or that are of current interest, including participative management, quality circles, and management by objectives, and collegial systems in academic libraries. It also explores different methods of evaluating staff.

B

Acquisitions

Karen A. Schmidt

Overview

Acquisitions as defined today includes the ordering, claiming, and receiving of materials in a library. Acquisitions usually, but not necessarily, includes bibliographic searching, and it embraces both monographic and serial publications, whether or not the library pays for them. Acquisitions is also the link between the for-profit and the not-for-profit worlds of publishing and bookselling on the one hand and library collection and use on the other. After selection, it is in most libraries the point at which the entire library process begins. Acquisitions also can be, unfortunately, the area that is least understood by librarians and staff.

The literature of acquisitions is particularly wide ranging. Persons concerned with acquisitions must be familiar with many of the more common resources of librarianship, such as *Books in Print* (BAB2) and *Ulrich's International Periodicals Directory* (GAB12), and refer regularly to commercial readings in the fields of publishing, scholarly communication, and bookselling, such as *Publishers Weekly* (BAD9). Acquisitions also holds close connections with collection development issues, serial and monograph pricing discussions, library management concerns, interlibrary lending and borrowing, and new technology procurement. For these reasons, publications in acquisitions often include diverse topics that are procedural rather than theoretical in nature.

Acquisitions has not always enjoyed a prominent role in technical services librarianship, although it has remained one of a handful of areas—such as reference and cataloging—essential to the management of a library. Although it was part of the original curriculum of library science, after a few decades training for acquisitions (or "order work," as it was commonly known) became sporadic among the library schools in the United States. In contemporary times, consistent training in acquisitions has become more difficult to find in library schools. The paucity of textbooks on the topic reflects this uneven approach to the subject over the last century, just as the more recent publishing activity in this field reflects the renewed interest that acquisitions has generated.

Chapter Content and Organization

A scan of the sections of this chapter on acquisitions demonstrates the range of topics that acquisitions covers, and points out the relatively new nature of present-day acquisitions work. Of the nine specialized topics on the list, four—approval plans, automation, administration, and vendor selection and evaluation—are subjects that have two decades or fewer of history in the acquisitions literature.

Although acquisitions as a generic term can and often does encompass serials, the focus of this chapter is on monographic acquisitions, with serials acquisitions discussed more thoroughly in Chapter G. A discussion of the sections covered here follows.

The general works section includes the few textbooks that are available in acquisitions, covering a span of library history from 1930 to the present. The American Library Association began publishing textbooks early in its history and, fortunately, has continued to carry this responsibility to the present day with the publication of the basic texts in this area. There are no current directories of vendors or acquisitions librarians that are common reference tools in this area of the profession, although the listing of librarians subscribing to *ACQNET* (BAD1), the electronic newsletter, comes quite close to being a directory of acquisitions professionals. It is the publishing industry that has provided us with the directories we have available to obtain materials. The few articles listed in this section demonstrate the interest being taken in the field to describe and enhance the work of the acquisitions librarian.

Approval plans are credited to Richard Abel, who developed the idea in the 1970s through his work in a bookstore in Portland, Oregon. From a seemingly trivial start, these plans have become a significant part of library acquisitions and bookselling, and the subject of some of the best statistical studies in technical services work. Most academic libraries, and many other types of libraries, use approval plans for some proportion of their acquisitions, as a way of providing a steady flow of important publications at a reasonable discount. A good understanding of approval plans requires some working knowledge of bookselling and contract negotiation, vendor evaluation, and publishing. The publications listed in this subsection show the growth of approval plans over the past twenty years.

Acquisitions is one of the last areas of librarianship to become automated. Perhaps because of the duality of acquisitions, where both business and library practices have had to be melded into one automated system, work in acquisitions automation came well after the advent of cataloging and circulation systems. While the bibliographic and accounting portions of this work are now available from various automated systems, and many libraries are communicating electronically with booksellers, the final link between publishers and vendors/libraries has yet to be firmly established. Electronic codes for monographs and serials, called BISAC and SISAC (Book Industry Systems Advisory Committee and Serials Industry Systems Advisory Committee, respectively), similar in concept to MARC (MAchine-Readable Cataloging) tags for cataloging, as well as the transmission protocol for data exchange called

X12 have been developed but not agreed upon uniformly. By 2001 these standards, or some close cousin to them, likely will be successfully in place.

Gifts and exchanges have always been an important part of acquisitions procedures, especially in larger libraries. Indeed, many of the largest and best foreign collections in the United States are the result of exchanges with libraries in foreign countries. Gifts of books to libraries may range from the more mundane, such as textbooks, to the truly unique collections of first editions and authors' manuscripts. All of these items serve to enhance the collection of a library in significant ways, and a library that nurtures acquisitions through these means is able to develop its collection in inestimable ways. Recent new tax laws in the United States have made information about gift procedures especially important to good acquisitions management.

Acquisitions often relies on large numbers of staff at all levels, from students to clerical staff to technical assistants to librarians. The literature of acquisitions management addresses the concerns of dealing with personnel issues in a labor-intensive environment. In recent years, readings in this area show a concern for hiring the appropriate level of staff and for the optimum organization of acquisitions work. Another continuing component in this portion of the literature is the ongoing discussion of whether serials departments and acquisitions departments should be merged or kept separate. The debate began in earnest in the 1970s and has not yet been answered satisfactorily for many. Also included here are discussions of the nuts and bolts of acquisitions: purchasing processes, requests for proposal, and other general topics. Citations in this area show a somewhat sparse literature that is beginning to gain some momentum as automation, acquisitions conferences, and electronic discussions about management issues become more prevalent.

The common thread of librarianship is publishing, which is the inherent domain of acquisitions and collection development. The literature of publishing is large, and much of it is peripheral to the library community. However, there is a constant need for librarians, particularly acquisitions librarians, to understand the basic nature of the publishing industry and to keep abreast of current trends in the field. The resources covering publishing that are included in this chapter give a good overview of the industry and marketplace and pinpoint areas of common concern to librarians and publishers alike.

Out-of-print (o.p.) and antiquarian markets are another important source of acquisitions for many libraries. Out-of-print works can encompass recent publications that have had small print runs and older works that are beyond copyright and will likely never be reprinted. A subset of o.p. acquisitions is antiquarian books, which can include rare editions, fine bindings, and unique collections. Specialists in o.p. acquisitions are familiar with this corner of the acquisitions market and generally know dealers in specific categories of materials. The literature of the o.p. market includes writings from publishing and librarianship and guides to finding dealers and descriptions of new services on the market.

A good portion of the literature of acquisitions in the past two decades has been devoted to the selection and evaluation of vendors of library materials. The area is fraught with controversy over whether one should identify vendors that are being studied and how statistically correct samples can be drawn so that studies are fair. The question of statistical validity has been answered fairly clearly, especially with the introduction of automated acquisitions systems to produce data, but the ethical issue continues to draw discussion. Knowledgeable vendor selection and evaluation can save a library significant amounts of money and ensure quick and accurate delivery of desired material.

Ethics is a relatively new area of acquisitions discussion that has garnered a lot of interest in the past decade. It can include the concerns about revealing vendors in an evaluation study, as noted above, about accepting meals from vendors, about discussion negotiations with other librarians and vendors, and other uncharted areas. The emergence of an ethics committee in the acquisitions section of ALCTS demonstrates the recent interest in this topic, as does the recent publication of essays.

Acquisitions is a fundamental part of technical services. A firm understanding of its principles and procedures ensures that all librarians, not just acquisitions librarians, work effectively to develop and use library collections. This chapter serves to introduce the student and novice librarian to the area of acquisitions and to give in-depth help to the more seasoned acquisitions librarian.

BA
General Works

The titles described here all have general significance for the acquisitions librarian, although many are equally useful for other areas of librarianship. General aspects of acquisitions include the obvious elements of the work—ordering, claiming, and receiving—as well as the tangential areas of publishing and vending that support acquisitions work. As noted in the introduction, acquisitions librarians need to keep abreast of movements in many different areas as they strive to bridge the for-profit and not-for-profit worlds. The sources listed below serve as a good introduction to this mission.

BA1. Atkinson, Ross. "The Acquisitions Librarian as Change Agent in the Transition to the Electronic Library." *Library Resources & Technical Services* 36 (Jan. 1992): 7–20.

This essay investigates the role of the acquisitions librarian in handling new technology and proposes new functions and relationships for acquisitions within the library. It is an important contribution to acquisitions literature because of the attention it focuses on acquisitions as an aspect of librarianship.

BA2. Barker, Joseph W. "Acquisitions and Collection Development: 2001." *Library Acquisitions: Practice and Theory* 12 (1988): 243–48.

A future-oriented discussion of acquisitions and collection development that sets out the challenges acquisitions librarians will face by the turn of the century. Included is an analysis of the changing nature of acquisitions work. It is one of the few predictive essays in acquisitions.

BA3. Hewitt, Joe A. "On the Nature of Acquisitions." *Library Resources & Technical Services* 33 (Apr. 1989): 105–22.

Hewitt won the Best of *LRTS* Award for this essay, which explores the content of acquisitions librarianship and gives voice to an area that has seemed neglected in recent decades. He describes the work of acquisitions and the role of the professional in this area. Considered by most of the acquisitions community as a "must read."

BA4. Ogburn, Joyce. "Theory in Acquisitions: Defining the Principles Behind the Practice." *Library Acquisitions: Practice and Theory* 17 (Spring 1993): 33–39.

This article came from a presentation at the Feather River acquisitions conference, May 1992, held in Blairsden, California. Ogburn discusses the potential theoretical underpinnings of acquisitions work, basing much of her discussion on paradigms found in other disciplines. There is very little written on this issue for any aspect of librarianship, and this is a particularly interesting contribution.

BAA
Textbooks, Guides, and Manuals

BAA1. Chapman, Liz. *Buying Books for Libraries.* London: Clive Bingley, 1989.

Chapman's text provides a British point of view to acquisitions work, which is not all that different from the U.S. approach. Included is some information that may be helpful to support staff in acquisitions, such as preorder searching and bibliographic work. Information on the Net Book agreement is useful.

BAA2. Dessauer, John P. *Book Industry Trends*. New York: Prepared for the Book Industry Study Group, 1977– . Annual. ISSN 0160-970X.

The unique information contained in these annual compilations is valuable for study of the publishing industry, both past and future. Statistics provide five-year overviews, and allow in a general way for acquisitions librarians to make predictions about the coming years and to compare acquisitions levels of previous years.

BAA3. Drury, F. K. W. *Order Work for Libraries*. Chicago: American Library Association, 1930.

Drury is the grandfather textbook of acquisitions, fondly remembered by the older librarians as "Dreary Drury." It encapsulates aspects of acquisitions training found in early ALA acquisitions textbooks. Much of what is included about procedures is still valid and valuable.

BAA4. Eaglen, Audrey. *Buying Books: A How-to-Do-It Manual for Librarians*. New York: Neal-Schuman Publishers, 1989.

This text provides librarians with the public librarian's perspective on acquisitions, and is useful for its insights into the publishing industry, marketing, pricing, and selling. The list of book wholesalers, glossary, and bibliography are helpful.

BAA5. Ford, Stephen. *The Acquisition of Library Materials*. Rev. ed. Chicago: American Library Association, 1978.

Ford's text stood for a number of years as the most modern of acquisitions textbooks available. It focuses on procedural issues, as did the earlier work by Drury, and continues to be a useful reference for deciding how to deal with some current acquisitions questions about organization, forms, etc.

BAA6. Kohl, David F. *Acquisitions, Collection Development, and Collection Use: A Handbook of Library Management*. Santa Barbara, Calif.: ABC Clio Information Services, 1985.

This draws together information on management issues in acquisitions and collection development published between 1960 and 1985, which in some cases can cut down on literature searches. For example, if information on approval plan success rates is desired, the *Handbook* gives salient statistical citations, covering 1960 through 1985. For beginning literature searches—and recognizing the limitations of the 1985 publication date—it is a good place to start.

BAA7. Magrill, Rose Mary, and John Corbin. *Acquisitions Management and Collection Development in Libraries*. 2nd ed. Chicago: American Library Association, 1989.

This is a basic work that weaves together the work of acquisitions and collection development in a meaningful way. Twelve essays on the two topics discuss the role of each in a general library setting and provide an excellent introduction to the area. The bibliographies at the end of each chapter are especially helpful.

BAA8. Melcher, David. *Melcher on Acquisitions*. Chicago: American Library Association, 1971.

Melcher provides an often-overlooked series of essays and observations written from the perspective of an experienced publisher. This is a factual overview, both educational and entertaining, focusing mainly on academic libraries and giving a "Dutch uncle" approach to library acquisitions.

BAA9. Schmidt, Karen A., ed. *Understanding the Business of Library Acquisitions*. Chicago: American Library Association, 1990.

Chapters covering book publishing to payment are included here. The focus is not procedural so much as theoretical: why books are priced as they are, how approval plans can enhance efficiency, what factors should be included in vendor selection decisions, etc.

BAB
Directories

BAB1. *American Book Trade Directory*. New York: R. R. Bowker, 1925– . Annual. ISSN 0065-759X.

This annual provides a listing of wholesalers and retailers (arranged by city with specialty information) and general book trade information on auctioneers, appraisers, associations, export-import dealers, and related areas. It is indexed and can be useful in tracking down purchasing information.

BAB2. *Books in Print: Publishers*. New Providence, N.J.: R. R. Bowker, 1948– . Annual. ISSN 0068-0214.

This is a representative entry of the *BIP* volume that lists publishers' addresses and other miscellaneous information of use to the acquisitions librarian. This is one of the fundamental reference tools whose latest editions should be available in an acquisitions unit. *Books in Print* is available in machine-readable versions—tapes that can be loaded on mainframe computers and CD-ROM and updated at least quarterly. The CD-ROM, *Books In Print Plus*, has more than 750,000 citations included in the print versions of *Books in Print*, *Subject Guide to Books in Print*, *Supplement to Books in Print*, *Forthcoming Books in Print*, and *Children's Books in Print*.

BAB3. *Directory of Specialized American Bookdealers*. New York: Arco Press, 1981– . Annual. ISSN 0739-778X.

This specialty directory can be useful for finding out-of-print dealers or tracking unusual subject specialties. The subject arrangement is fairly well detailed.

BAB4. *International Literary Market Place*. New York: R. R. Bowker, 1971/72– . Annual. ISSN 0074-6827.

With listings by country, *ILMP* is a good place to start looking for information about publishers and book dealers overseas. It also includes listing of libraries, prizes, etc., that may occasionally be useful in acquisitions work.

BAB5. *Literary Market Place*. New York: R. R. Bowker, 1989– . Annual. ISSN 0000-1155.

The most useful section of *LMP* is the listing of publishers with addresses and telephone and fax numbers. It also includes book clubs, agents, publishing services, and other support agencies associated with the publishing industry. Continues the earlier *Literary Market Place, with Names & Numbers*.

BAB6. Perryman, Wayne R., and Lenore Wilkas. *International Subscription Agents: An Annotated Directory*. 5th ed. Chicago: American Library Association, 1986.

Directories of vendors of any kind of materials are difficult to find: the information can go out of date quickly, and it is difficult to be comprehensive. This directory is a useful guide to the international periodicals markets, listing the scope of vendors' work and details about their purchase requirements. Current information about the international vending market can be obtained from WESS, the Western European Subject Specialists group within ALA.

BAB7. *Publishers Directory 1993*. 13th ed. Detroit: Gale Research, 1993.

This is subtitled "A Guide to New and Established, Commercial and Nonprofit, Private and Alternative, Corporate and Association, Government and Institution Publishing Programs and Their Distributors; Includes Producers of Books, Classroom Materials, Prints, Reports, and Databases." This sums up the scope of this ambitious directory quite well. In its thirteenth edition (edited by Wendy S. Van de Sande), the directory contains several thousand entries of both well-known and obscure presses.

BAB8. Robinson, Ruth, and Dayush Farudi. *Buy Books Where—Sell Books Where*. Morgantown, W. Va.: R. E. Robinson Books, 1978– . Annual. ISSN 0732-6599.

Out-of-print searching is made much easier with this directory. The subject access and entries are detailed, and the accuracy of the entries is quite good.

BAC
Dictionaries

BAC1. Brownstone, David M., and Irene M. Franck. *The Dictionary of Publishing*. New York: Van Nostrand Reinhold, 1982.

Although this does not include many of the new words associated with electronic/computer publishing, this is a standard reference for interpreting the language of the publishing industry. The definitions are clear to librarian and layman alike.

BAC2. Glaister, Geoffrey Ashall. *Glaister's Glossary of the Book: Terms Used in Papermaking, Printing, Bookbinding and*

Publishing with Notes on Illuminated Manuscripts and Private Presses. 2nd ed. Berkeley, Calif.: University of California Press, 1979.

Glaister provides a historical and scholarly approach to publishing terms that can be useful when dealing with the antiquarian market. Current terminology used in electronic publishing is not included.

BAD
Periodicals

BAD1. *ACQNET*. [serial online] Ithaca, N.Y.: Cornell University Library, Christian Boissonnas. no. 1– , 1990– . Irregular. ISSN 1057-5308.

Also called *The Acquisitions Librarian's Electronic Network*, this electronic newsletter devoted to acquisitions is available through INTERNET and BITNET to any interested party. Edited by Christian Boissonnas, it provides a forum for discussion of current acquisitions topics, ranging from procedural to professional association issues, and is mandatory reading for acquisitions administrators. To subscribe, send a request to Christian Boissonnas at: **CRI@CORNELLC** (BITNET).

BAD2. *The Acquisitions Librarian*. New York: Haworth Press. no. 1– , 1989– . Irregular. ISSN 0896-3576.

Each issue of this irregular periodical is devoted to a separate topic. Issues draw together experts in various areas of acquisitions to contribute essays on topics ranging from approval plans to cost accounting to organization. Issues are also published as separate monographs. Edited by Bill Katz.

BAD3. *Against the Grain*. Charleston, S.C.: Katina Strauch. v. 1– , 1989– . Five times a year. ISSN 1043-2094.

ATG is an independent forum for discussion of any issue pertaining to acquisitions and collection development. The editor, Katina Strauch, strives to generate discussion and controversy on topics such as pricing, ethics, and vendor-librarian interactions. News from related fields is also published.

BAD4. *AB Bookman's Weekly*. New York: AB Bookman Publications. v. 1– , Jan. 3, 1948– . Weekly. ISSN 0001-0340.

This is the periodical for the out-of-print and antiquarian market. Contributions are addressed to the book dealer for the most part. Libraries publish their desiderata lists for dealers to scan, and issues are filled with ads for available titles. Librarians handling o.p. and antiquarian acquisitions should be familiar with it.

BAD5. *Collection Management*. New York: Haworth Press. v. 1– , 1976– . Quarterly. ISSN 0146-2679.

Collection Management is a refereed journal accepting articles covering acquisitions and collection development topics. Acquisitions studies are found here frequently enough to make this journal useful to scan on a regular basis.

BAD6. *Library Acquisitions: Practice and Theory*. New York: Pergamon Press. v. 1– , 1977– . Quarterly. ISSN 0364-6408.

This is the first journal devoted exclusively to acquisitions work. It is refereed and includes topics on procedures as well as principles in acquisitions. It also provides summaries of the major acquisitions conferences throughout the year and often includes the best papers from these meetings.

BAD7. *The Library Bookseller: Books Wanted by College and University Libraries*. Berkeley, Calif.: Scott Saifer. v. 1– , 1949– . Biweekly. ISSN 0024-2217.

Originally called *TAAB: The American Antiquarian Bookman*, and still often referred to as TAAB, this periodical lists the desiderata of academic libraries throughout the country. The process of "TAABing" a book is still used widely in acquisitions departments.

BAD8. *Library Resources & Technical Services*. Chicago: Association of Library Collections and Technical Services. v. 1– , 1957– . Quarterly. ISSN 0024-2527.

See also annotation under AF13. ALA's divisional publication (from ALCTS) covers all of technical services, including—especially in later years—acquisitions. It is refereed, and acquisitions articles tend to be theoretical or statistically based.

BAD9. *Publishers Weekly*. New Providence, N.J.: R. R. Bowker. v. 1– , Jan. 18, 1872– . Weekly. ISSN 0000-0019.

Focused on the publishing industry, *PW* includes news and articles of interest to agents, marketing departments, and the many other aspects of publishing. Acquisitions librarians will find it useful for information on new publications, publishing formats, marketing for libraries, and current events throughout the international publishing arena.

BAD10. *Scholarly Publishing*. Toronto: University of Toronto Press. v. 1– , Oct. 1969– . Quarterly. ISSN 0036-634X.

Many of the articles found here discuss the developments in the university and scholarly publishing communities. Topics include copyright issues and discussions of where the scholarly publishing market is headed.

BAD11. *Taking Stock: Libraries and the Book Trade*. Leeds, England: National Acquisitions Group. v. 1– , May 1992– . Biannual. ISSN 0966-6745.

British acquisitions librarians work through a professional association named the National Acquisitions Group (NAG). NAG has published a newsletter for a number of years; this journal is an expansion of that effort. *Taking Stock* covers items of immediate interest to acquisitions librarians, collection development specialists, publishers, and booksellers. Includes articles on the publishing, vending, and acquisitions work handled, most generally, in academic libraries.

BAE
Sources of Expertise

Acquisitions has been a growing part of the profession of librarianship, as the spurt of new groups in the American Library Association devoted to acquisitions will attest. Recently, ALA's Association for Library Collections and Technical Services (ALCTS) Resources Section separated into two sections: the Acquisitions Section and the Collection Management and Development Section. This move will likely spur more discussion groups devoted to the many specializations found in this chapter. Acquisitions committees and discussion groups are now found within the Acquisitions Section of ALCTS (AGA3).

In addition, a number of interesting conferences on acquisitions have shown a vitality not often found in general conferences. These conferences, for the most part, have had a small number of participants, which has added to the interplay of ideas and is reminiscent of some of the early ALA conferences held 100 years ago. When acquisitions librarians cannot attend these meetings, they should look for the proceedings, entries from which are included throughout the sections of this chapter.

PROFESSIONAL ASSOCIATIONS

BAE1. ALA Association for Library Collections and Technical Services. Acquisitions Section.

The following committees and discussion groups focus on particular topics of interest to acquisitions librarians:

Committees
  Education Committee
  Publications Committee
  Technology for Acquisitions Committee
  Acquisitions Administrators Discussion Group
  Acquisitions Librarians/Vendors of Library Materials
Discussion Groups
  Acquisitions Topics for Public Libraries Discussion
   Group
  Gifts and Exchanges Discussion Group

BAE2. ALA Association for Library Collections and Technical Services. Serials Section.

This section has an Acquisitions Committee.

BAE3. ALA Association of American Publishers–ALCTS Committee.

This is a joint committee of the Association of American Publishers and ALCTS.

BAE4. ALA ALCTS Publisher/Vendor–Library Relations Committee.

This association-level committee serves as a review and advisory committee on all matters of vendors of library materials–library relationships. It is charged with investigating these relationships, preparing recommendations, and developing guidelines of acceptable performance for libraries and vendors for ordering and supplying library materials.

CONFERENCES

BAE5. Acquisitions, Budgets and Material Costs: Issues and Approaches. Once a year; spring.

This conference is held at the University of Oklahoma Libraries. Each conference addresses a different aspect of acquisitions and collection management issues, with speakers invited from throughout the acquisitions and collection development communities. Sul Lee, Dean of Libraries at the University of Oklahoma, directs this conference.

BAE6. The College of Charleston Conference: Issues in Book and Serial Acquisitions. Once a year; November.

Held at the College of Charleston, South Carolina, this conference has gained the reputation of being one of the best sources of new ideas and open discussion among acquisitions librarians, vendors, and publishers. For information, contact the conference convener, Katina Strauch, College of Charleston Library, Charleston, SC 29424.

BAE7. The Feather River Institute on Acquisitions and Collection Development. Once a year; May.

This conference has been called the west coast version of the College of Charleston conference. It is held at the Feather River resort in Blairsden, California. Information on this conference may be obtained by contacting Thomas Leonhardt, University of Oklahoma Libraries, Norman, OK 73019.

BB
Approval Plans

Approval plans have been in full flower in many libraries for close to twenty years, and the literature that encompasses this area is equally prolific. The resources included here represent a sampling of the many titles that are available in library literature, with essays on procedural and philosophical issues as well as detailed statistical analyses that monitor the success or failure of various programs. Approval plans are international in scope as well, as can be seen from some of the articles listed. There is a great deal of foreign literature that reflects the international aspects of approval plans that is not covered

here but that can be followed up through *Library Literature* (Bronx, N.Y.: H. W. Wilson Co. 1933/35– . Bimonthly. ISSN 0024-2373) and *Library and Information Science Abstracts* (London: Library Association. v. 1– , 1969– . Monthly. ISSN 0024-2179).

BB1. Alessi, Dana, and Kathleen Goforth. "Standing Orders and Approval Plans: Are They Compatible?" *The Serials Librarian* 13 (Oct./Nov. 1987): 21–41.

Alessi and Goforth, representatives of two booksellers, discuss the problems of the interface between approval plans and standing orders. Duplication between these two areas is highly likely when series are involved. Practical advice is found here.

BB2. Barker, Joseph W. "Vendor Studies Redux: Evaluating the Approval Plan Option from Within." *Library Acquisitions: Practice and Theory* 13 (1989): 133–41.

This study compares the efficiency and effectiveness of approval plan acquisition versus firm ordering acquisition. It also looks at European and U.S. approval plans, and at the types of services that vendors might provide.

BB3. Biblarz, Dora. "Richard Abel—Part 1: The Origin and Development of the Approval Plan." *Against the Grain* 4, no. 3 (June 1992): 24–27; "Richard Abel—Part 2: The Approval Plan Is Born." *Against the Grain* 4, no. 4 (Sept. 1992): 20–24; "Richard Abel—Part 3: The Company Goes International, Turnkey Libraries, and Conclusion." *Against the Grain* 4, no. 5 (Nov. 1992): 35–39.

This three-part interview with Richard Abel follows the development of the modern approval plan in libraries through the eyes of its inventor, Richard Abel. Abel revolutionized the acquisitions process with his approach to approval plans. The history is unique and so is the man.

BB4. Bostic, Mary J. "Approval Acquisitions and Vendor Relations: An Overview." In *Vendors and Library Acquisitions*, edited by Bill Katz, 129–44. New York: Haworth Press, 1991.

This serves as a good literature review of approval plans and demonstrates the importance of this type of acquisitions to the average library. It is useful as a general overview.

BB5. Calhoun, John C., James K. Bracken, and Kenneth L. Firestein. "Modeling an Academic Approval Program." *Library Resources & Technical Services* 34 (July 1990): 367–79.

Using the 80/20 rule as a model, the authors provide a strategy for selecting approval plan books. The suggestion is made that a core selection of books can be purchased most efficiently using a domestic, publisher-based plan.

BB6. Cargill, Jennifer S., and Brian Alley. *Practical Approval Plan Management.* Phoenix: Oryx Press, 1979.

This is a practical, operational guide to setting up and managing approval plans on a daily basis. Included are chapters on bidding, public relations, profiling, financial management, and problem solving.

BB7. Ferguson, Anthony W. "British Approval Plan Books: American or British Vendor?" *Collection Building* 8, no. 4 (1987): 18–22.

The topic of purchasing British approval plan books is a recurring one in acquisitions, made more difficult by the close connection between British and U.S. publishers. Ferguson uses a case study approach to examine the many issues attendant with choosing a British approval plan vendor.

BB8. Grant, Joan. "Approval Plans: The Vendor as Preselector." In *Understanding the Business of Library Acquisitions*, edited by Karen A. Schmidt, 153–64. Chicago: American Library Association, 1990.

Here is a beginning discussion of approval plans: making the decision to have them, setting them up correctly, and managing them in tandem with other acquisitions operations. This is a good place to start to learn about this topic.

BB9. Howard, Clinton, comp. *Approval Plans in ARL Libraries.* SPEC Kit, no. 141. Washington, D.C.: Association of Research Libraries, Office of Management Studies, 1988.

Approval plans are important enough in large academic libraries to have SPEC kits on them updated fairly regularly. This SPEC kit provides a good overview of how large libraries are handling approval plans and investigates the satisfaction level. It also gives one an opportunity to identify libraries that have instituted specific types of approval plans. Updates SPEC Kit no. 83 (1982).

BB10. Kaatrude, Peter B. "Approval Plan versus Conventional Selection: Determining the Overlap." *Collection Management* 11, nos. 1/2 (1989): 145–50.

This statistical case study of the efficacy of an approval plan looks at the functioning of a plan and whether duplication of effort in selection and collection management was occurring. A good example of the use of statistics from an online system for evaluating an approval plan.

BB11. Lockman, Edward J., Edna Laughrey, and Kevin Coyle. "A Perspective on Library Book Gathering Plans." In *Technical Services Today and Tomorrow*, edited by Michael Gorman, 15–22. Englewood, Colo.: Libraries Unlimited, 1990.

The three authors offer a thorough overview of the benefits of approval plans, from the perspective of both the vendor and the librarian. The chapter also offers a unique perspective on these types of plans that would change the type of service given to libraries. This is an interesting thought-piece as well as a good first article on the topic.

BB12. McCullough, Kathleen, Edwin D. Posey, and Doyle C. Pickett. *Approval Plans in Academic Libraries.* Phoenix: Oryx Press, 1977.

Three views of approval plans are offered, from the vendor's, subject specialist's, and acquisitions librarian's perspectives. Information is based on a survey conducted in the mid-1970s, when approval plans were becoming an increasingly common part of acquisitions. Much of the findings reported here are still valid.

BB13. Magrill, Rose Mary, and John Corbin. "Vendor-Controlled Order Plans." In their *Acquisitions Management and Collection Development in Libraries*, 120–37. 2nd ed. Chicago: American Library Association, 1989.

Magrill and Corbin distinguish among the various types of vendor-supplied acquisitions: approval plans, standing orders, blanket orders, gathering plans, etc. This is the textbook discussion of approval plans and how they fit into the whole scheme of acquiring books.

BB14. Pasterczyk, Catherine E. "A Quantitative Methodology for Evaluating Approval Plan Performance." *Collection Management* 10, nos. 1/2 (1988): 25–38.

This is an excellent example of the statistical work that can be done with approval plan data. The author looks at approval plan returns to determine if the subject codes assigned by vendors are detailed enough to work well for all areas of a library.

BB15. Reidelbach, John H., and Gary M. Shirk. "Selecting an Approval Plan Vendor: A Step by Step Process." *Library Acquisitions: Practice and Theory* 7 (1983): 115–22; "Selecting an Approval Plan Vendor II: Comparative Vendor Data." *Library Acquisitions: Practice and Theory* 8 (1984): 157–202; "Selecting an Approval Plan Vendor III: Academic Librarians' Evaluation of Eight United States Approval Plan Vendors." *Library Acquisitions: Practice and Theory* 9 (1985): 177–260.

This series of three articles is, perhaps, the most thorough analysis of any sort of approval plan acquisitions available. Reidelbach and Shirk pulled together an enormous amount of data taken from a detailed survey of library practice. The result is an excellent overview of how approval plans are managed in libraries throughout the United States.

BB16. Rossi, Gary J. "Library Approval Plans: A Selected, Annotated Bibliography." *Library Acquisitions: Practice and Theory* 11, no. 1 (1987): 3–34.

Annotated citations to seventy-seven titles about approval plans published between 1957 and 1986; thorough, comprehensive, and well-written annotations.

BB17. Schmidt, Karen A. "Capturing the Mainstream: Publisher-Based and Subject-Based Approval Plans in Academic Libraries." *College & Research Libraries* 47, no. 4 (July 1986): 365–69.

The author looks at subject-based and publisher-based approval plans and suggests that publisher-based plans are more efficient in developing collections and in the use of subject specialists' time. Publisher-based plans are predictable, particularly with domestic publications.

BB18. St. Clair, Gloriana, and Jane Treadwell. "Science and Technology Approval Plans Compared." *Library Resources & Technical Services* 33 (Oct. 1989): 382–92.

An underlying assumption of approval plans throughout the years has been that science and technology areas are too specialized to be handled well by general approval plans. The authors test this assumption and describe difficulties that do exist for approval plans in science and technology subject areas.

BB19. Spyers-Duran, Peter, ed. *Approval and Gathering Plans in Academic Libraries: Proceedings of the International Seminar on Approval and Gathering Plans in Large and Medium Size Academic Libraries.* Littléton, Colo.: Libraries Unlimited, 1969.

From a historical point of view, these proceedings are important in establishing the issues associated with developing approval plans. The topics discussed in this first conference are of interest today and, in many instances, continue to be studied and debated. The conference went on for several years afterward, generating original research and much debate about acquisitions, collection development, and efficiency in library operations.

BB20. Warzala, Martin. "Approval Plan versus Standing Order." *Library Acquisitions: Practice and Theory* 15 (1991): 313–27.

Warzala follows somewhat the lead of Alessi and Goforth (*see* BB1) in discussing the difficulties of managing approval plans and standing orders effectively without overlap. This article is valuable for its in-depth discussion of the nature of monographic series and how vendors are equipped to handle them.

BC
Automation of Acquisitions

Acquisitions has been among the last of library processes to be automated, as perusers of this section can tell from the dates of many of the entries. There is nothing unusual about the literature of automation for acquisitions: included are the discussion of what is needed and how to choose systems, implementation descriptions, national standard efforts, and comparisons of various incarnations of systems throughout the past decade or so. Commentary by vendors, who operate in the middle between publishers and libraries, is an especially vital part of acquisitions automation and adds to this rich discussion.

BC1. American National Standards Institute, Accredited Standards Committee, X12. *ANSI ASC X12 Electronic Data Interchange X12 Draft Version 2 Release 4 Standards.* Alexandria, Va.: Data Interchange Standards Association, 1990.

This represents one of many iterations of the ANSI standard for electronic exchange of information among publishers, booksellers, and libraries. The standard spells out in minute terms the placement of specific information

about library materials that allows a sales and bibliographic transaction to be made online. There are—and will continue to be—many other publications that describe the ANSI X12 format in detail. *See,* for example, Margaret Emmenhainz's book *Electronic Data Interchange: A Total Management Guide* (New York: Van Nostrand Reinhold, 1990) or the ANSI publication *An Introduction to Electronic Data Interchange* (Alexandria, Va.: Data Interchange Standards Association, 1987).

BC2. Boissonnas, Christian M. "What Cost, Automation?" *Library Acquisitions: Practice and Theory* 10 (1986): 107–12.

This is an interesting and unusual discussion on how to determine the value of automation for the acquisitions function and how to communicate that value to the library administration. Boissonnas speaks plainly about the politics and funding of automation and how to use a system to its full advantage.

BC3. Boss, Richard W., Susan Harrison, and Hal Espo. "Automating Acquisitions." *Library Technology Reports* 22 (Sept./Oct. 1986): 479–634.

Boss is undoubtedly the king of automation, and his discussions of planning for and implementing automated systems are thorough, logical, and useful. Although somewhat out of date, this presentation continues to be valuable for its basic identification of the important elements of an automated acquisitions system and listing of questions to ask and considerations to make when choosing a vendor. It includes a good glossary and bibliography. Boss is always a good place to start.

BC4. Boss, Richard W., and Judy McQueen. "The Uses of Automation and Related Technologies by Domestic Book and Serials Jobbers." *Library Technology Reports* 25 (Mar./Apr. 1989): 125–251.

Somewhat similar in scope to the title listed above, this discussion is an additional aid in defining vendor strengths in developing automation for library services. Boss and McQueen give detailed reviews of vendors' systems. Although quickly out of date, the information is helpful in reviewing a vendor's commitment to electronic service support and allows the librarian an opportunity to look at development within a company.

BC5. Bryant, Bonita. "Automating Acquisitions: The Planning Process." *Library Resources & Technical Services* 28: (Oct. 1984): 285–98.

This article brings together a diffuse number of points raised in the literature about automation of the acquisitions function. Bryant covers the whole spectrum of automation activity from the request for proposal to staff training. The basis for the analysis is the experience at SUNY-Albany.

BC6. Bullard, Scott R. "Standards for Automated Acquisitions Systems: BISAC and SISAC Considerations." *Library Acquisitions: Practice and Theory* 11 (1987): 357–72.

Bullard provides a synopsis of presentations made at the 1987 ALA conference to the acquisitions librarians discussion group. Much of what is cutting edge in acquisitions occurs at these meetings, and these conference reviews are valuable for this reason. In this set of papers, the issues revolving around the implementation of BISAC and SISAC in automated acquisitions are discussed by many of the principals involved in their development.

BC7. Chamberlain, Carol E. "Automating Acquisitions: A Perspective from the Inside." *Library Hi Tech* 3, no. 3 (1985): 57–66.

Not all automated acquisitions systems are purchased: throughout the country, libraries are using systems developed at the local level. Chamberlain describes this process at Pennsylvania State University, and gives the reader good insight into the initial planning and final implementation of a local system. Because of the many pitfalls that can be found in local systems development, this is a particularly valuable article.

BC8. Coe, George, Virginia Gatcheff, and Ron Van-Fleet. "Book Distribution and Automation: A Complete Package." *Library Technology Reports* 26 (July/Aug. 1990): 497–50.

In order to stay competitive, book dealers have offered a wide range of automated services to library customers. These can range from online bibliographic databases to electronic ordering and claiming mechanisms to electronic invoicing. This technology update covers the many new products available from vendors and assesses product usefulness and effect on service.

BC9. Evans, E. Edward. "Acquisition—Automation." In his *Developing Library and Information Center Collections*, 275–90. 2nd ed. Littleton, Colo.: Libraries Unlimited, 1987.

A textbook approach to acquisitions automation, listing the procedures that are automated and how each can benefit the acquisitions operation. This is a good overview of the considerations that should be reviewed in automating acquisitions. It provides a useful reading list, arranged by type of library, that incorporates more than just topics in acquisitions technology.

BC10. Hawks, Carol Pitts. "The GEAC Acquisitions System as a Source of Management Information." *Library Acquisitions: Practice and Theory* 10 (1986): 245–53.

Looking at one automated acquisitions system, from Geac, Hawks describes how acquisitions management information can be obtained through careful system profiling and data manipulation. This article is the result of a paper given at an ALA conference, and provides some practical advice for planning the implementation of an automated system.

BC11. _____. "Internal Control, Auditing, and the Automated Acquisitions System." *The Journal of Academic Librarianship* 16, no. 5 (1990): 296–301.

An important aspect of acquisitions automation is fund accounting, often overlooked in the discussion of automated systems concerns. Hawks looks at crucial issues in accounting and the creation of audit trails by automated systems, and details the many considerations librarians

should keep in mind when choosing an automated acquisitions system.

BC12. Hunsberger, Barbara B. "Electronic Book Ordering." In *Operations Handbook for the Small Academic Library*, edited by Gerard B. McCabe, 199–204. New York: Greenwood Press, 1989.

The ability to order library material from a vendor or publisher is just one aspect of automated acquisitions, albeit a complicated one. This chapter describes the technological difficulties in developing systems that respond to many different kinds of libraries and library automation and talks about procedural considerations when instituting online ordering in a library.

BC13. Miller, Amy. "Automation: A Book Vendor's Perspective." *Advances in Library Automation and Networking* 3 (1989): 69–85.

With libraries purchasing or developing a myriad number of automated systems for acquisitions, vendors are faced with the problem of developing interfaces to communicate with as many systems as possible while keeping expenses down. Miller outlines some of the concerns that vendors have about automated acquisitions systems and the ways in which they respond to the call for more automation.

BC14. Mutter, John. "Parlez-Vous X12? Do You Speak EDI?" *Publishers Weekly* 237 (Nov. 9, 1990): 27–30.

An example of the accessible and up-to-date articles provided by *Publishers Weekly* (BAD9) on items of interest to acquisitions librarians. The presentation is simple and straightforward, with terms explained and discussed from a practical point of view. An update on electronic ordering systems that will be used by publishers, booksellers, and libraries is given.

BC15. Nelson, Barbara K. "Automated Acquisitions in Small Academic Libraries." *Library Acquisitions: Practice and Theory* 13 (1989): 351–59.

Automation concerns often are addressed only for the large academic library. Smaller libraries want and need to automate this part of their work, too. Nelson surveyed a number of small college libraries to seek a correlation between library size and amount of automation in acquisitions. Her findings indicate that the size of the school does not necessarily determine the amount of automation available. In addition, there are many helpful comments from smaller schools about the automated acquisitions process.

BC16. Phelps, Doug. "Cost Impact on Acquisitions in Implementing an Integrated Online System." In *Operational Costs in Acquisitions*, edited by James R. Coffey, 33–46. New York: Haworth Press, 1991. Also published as *The Acquisitions Librarian*, no. 4.

The financial impact of automating acquisitions is reported here in a case study from Vanderbilt University, where the NOTIS integrated system was installed. Results show a benefit in terms of productivity and the negative financial impact in terms of costs. This serves as an excellent model for costing out the impact of automation.

BC17. Rooks, Dana. "Implementing the Automated Acquisitions System: Perspectives of a Personnel Administrator." *Library Acquisitions: Practice and Theory* 12 (1988): 431–36.

The staff aspect of automation is often overlooked. Staff need to be involved in the transition from manual to automated systems and to be trained to use the new system to its fullest. Rooks provides an honest and useful appraisal of this transition and looks critically at the issues that acquisitions librarians have to face in the personnel management aspects of automation.

BC18. Sabosik, Patricia E. "SISAC: Standardized Formats for Serials." *Information Technology and Libraries* 5 (June 1986): 149–54.

SISAC, the Serials Industry Systems Advisory Committee, is involved in the development of a standardized computer format for the serials industry. Sabosik, who is involved in this process, offers a clear account of the work of SISAC and how it can affect the acquisition and internal handling of serials, including the bar code symbol for check-in. As with the ANSI X12 standard, there is much written about SISAC, including a newsletter, *SISAC News: A Report of the Serials Industry Systems Advisory Committee* (New York: Book Industry Study Group, 1985–), that can be read to keep current on the topic.

BC19. Schwartz, Frederick E. "The EDI Horizon: Implementing an ANSI X12 Pilot Project at the Faxon Company." *The Serials Librarian* 19, no. 3–4 (1991): 39–57.

The F. W. Faxon Company has taken a leading role in testing and bringing electronic data transfer to the library and vendor communities. Schwartz, from the Faxon Company, describes the concept of Electronic Data Interchange (EDI), the standards attached to it, and the projects in which his company has been involved to develop and implement a new technology. EDI is undoubtedly the acquisitions communicator of the future, and should be a working part of the acquisitions librarian's vocabulary.

BC20. Stankowski, Rebecca House. "Automated Acquisitions and OCLC: A Brief History, Present Concerns, Future Options." *Technical Services Quarterly* 8, no. 3 (1991): 59–68.

This is a case study of one library's experience using the OCLC automated acquisitions system. Of particular interest here are a description of a system offered by a large and successful library automation company and the discussion of electronic ordering using this system. It offers as much a review of the OCLC system as it does insight into the positive and negative aspects of handling any automated system.

BD
Out-of-Print Material

Procurement of out-of-print (o.p.) material is becoming more and more essential to the success of acquisitions departments, especially those in academic libraries. Shorter print runs make it more likely that titles will become o.p. quickly, and acquisitions librarians must know how to cope with this relatively new development in their work. Out-of-print procurement also includes antiquarian buying and selling, which is an art itself, one that many acquisitions librarians may learn through association with special collections librarians. The entries here embrace both aspects of o.p. acquisitions, as well as the movement of this specialized area into the arena of automation.

BD1. Barker, Joseph W., Rebecca A. Rottman, and Marilyn Ng. "Organizing Out-of-print and Replacement Acquisitions for Effectiveness, Efficiency, and the Future." *Library Acquisitions: Practice and Theory* 14 (1990): 137–63.

How o.p. acquisitions is organized can have a direct impact on its effectiveness. The authors argue for centralized processing of the routines associated with the difficult acquisitions: replacements and o.p. materials. Among the many advantages of their recommendation is increased staff knowledge of ephemeral materials dealers and copyright issues.

BD2. Biblarz, Dora. "The Growing Out-of-print Crisis: A Collection Development Librarian's Perspective." *Technical Services Quarterly* 7, no. 2 (1989): 3–12.

On the tenth anniversary of the Thor Power Tool Company tax decision, which affected the amount of inventory publishers could keep and still retain tax benefits, Biblarz addresses the difficulties in acquiring new and replacement scholarly titles. Her recommendation to pursue several flexible alternatives in book acquisition is timely.

BD3. Colbert, Antoinette Walton. "Sources of Back Issues of Periodicals." *Online* 13 (May 1989): 102.

This one-page listing of places to buy back issues of periodicals may become obsolete in a few years' time, but is a good example of the kinds of timely information that can be found in library literature to help the acquisitions librarian purchase hard-to-find items. Many of the dealers listed here have been in the journal replacement business for a number of years and will undoubtedly continue to thrive.

BD4. Fouts, Judi. "Library Acquisitions and the Antiquarian/OP Book Trade: Papers from a Seminar Held in Birmingham, Ala., November 1989." *Library Acquisitions: Practice and Theory* 15, no. 1 (1991): 45–83.

This is a summary article of papers delivered at a two-day seminar held at the Alabama Association of College and Research Libraries. The papers are practically oriented. While the summary is useful in itself, it is more helpful as a guide to the librarians that are actively publishing and practicing in this area.

BD5. Garnett, Anthony. "A Worm's Eye View of the Out-of-print Market." In *Acquisitions '90: Conference on Acquisitions, Budgets, and Collections, 1st: 1990: St. Louis, Mo.,* edited by David Genaway, 179–87. Canfield, Ohio: Genaway & Associates, 1990.

Garnett is a dealer in "fine books" whose observations on the book market and bookstores in general are candid and helpful. In this article, he discusses the process by which o.p. dealers manage their market and offers excellent suggestions to librarians on how to procure o.p. titles.

BD6. Kilton, Thomas D. "Out-of-print Procurement in Academic Libraries: Current Methods and Sources." *Collection Management* 5 (Fall/Winter 1983): 113–34.

Kilton's study is no longer current, but still valuable for recording the work in o.p. purchasing in academic libraries. As expected, o.p. purchases were lower in the 1980s than in previous decades, and one suspects a replication of the study would find even lower expenditures. The sources for purchase remain useful to the acquisitions librarian.

BD7. Landesman, Margaret. "Out-of-print and Secondhand Markets." In *Understanding the Business of Library Acquisitions*, edited by Karen A. Schmidt, 187–205. Chicago: American Library Association, 1990.

Landesman notes that the o.p. market ". . . tries the patience and the budget." In this highly readable chapter, she gives practical advice about types of dealers, pricing of offers, buying trips, and desiderata lists. This is a good overall discussion of the topic.

BD8. _____. "Selling Out-of-Print Books to Libraries." *AB Bookman's Weekly* 74 (5 November 1984): 3184+.

This is a short guide directed at the antiquarian dealer describing how best to interact with libraries and librarians in advertising and selling o.p. titles. The advice is practical and is, for the most part, the way that o.p. dealers do work with libraries.

BD9. Rees-Mogg, William. *How to Buy Rare Books: A Practical Guide to the Antiquarian Book Market.* Oxford: Phaidon, 1985.

Part of the Christie's *Collectors Guide*, the Rees-Mogg book is a highly readable, accessible introduction to the antiquarian market. It is well illustrated and will tell the reader everything he or she wants to know about book collecting, antique book manufacture, and care and conservation. Included are a glossary, addresses, and items for further reading.

BE
Gifts and Exchanges

Gifts are donations to the library and may be solicited or unsolicited. They may be individual items or massive collections of materials. Exchange programs are agreements between libraries to exchange materials, usually on a continuing basis and without charge, according to a prescribed plan or guidelines. Many exchange programs are between libraries in different countries.

The gifts and exchange section of a library has gained more importance in the past several years as library budgets are cut. As a result, there is a growing interest in development of this area of acquisitions, which frequently takes place within the acquisitions section of the library (although it may be found in other related areas, depending upon the organizational history of the library). The new tax laws implemented in the 1980s have prompted more writings on the subject of gifts, and the altered political scenes in many foreign countries have changed many exchange procedures, initiating a new look at this area of librarianship. The resources included here are international in scope, although written from the U.S. perspective.

BE1. Allardyce, Alex. *Letters for the International Exchange of Publications: A Guide to Their Composition in English, French, German, Russian and Spanish.* IFLA Publications 13. New York: K. G. Saur, 1978.

See also annotation under BE9. A compendium of sample letters.

BE2. Barker, Joseph W. "A Case for Exchange: The Experience of the University of California, Berkeley." *Serials Review* 12 (Spring 1986): 63–73.

Barker describes the international exchange program at the University of California, Berkeley library, which has a 100-plus–year history. He describes the administration and procedures that support this active program, and also discusses the philosophy behind maintaining exchanges. This is a good introduction to the many aspects of international exchanges, particularly in a large library setting.

BE3. _____. "Gifts and Exchanges." In *Technical Services Today and Tomorrow*, edited by Michael Gorman, 23–37. Englewood, Colo.: Libraries Unlimited, 1990.

A practical overview of gifts and exchanges, written by an acquisitions librarian. The organization of the work is covered, including staffing levels and automation and policy considerations. For academic acquisitions librarians, this is a good place to review the literature and cover the major issues in gifts and exchanges acquisitions.

BE4. Carter, Harriet. "Setting Up an Exchange Operation in the Small Special Library." *Library Resources & Technical Services* 22 (Fall 1978): 380–85.

Although this is an older publication, it remains useful for its practical description of the planning process and procedural issues that arise when an exchange operation is established.

Included is a listing of the costs associated with this aspect of acquisitions.

BE5. Clark, Mae. "Gifts and Exchanges." In *Understanding the Business of Library Acquisitions*, edited by Karen A. Schmidt, 167–85. Chicago: American Library Association, 1990.

In a somewhat similar vein to the Barker essay (BE2), Clark gives a thorough overview of gifts and exchanges. Clark goes on to explain the advantages and disadvantages of these two types of acquisition and gives an excellent review of the tax implications of gifts. Included is a summary of an internal Library of Congress memorandum citing the handling of gifts since the tax reform act.

BE6. Diodato, Louise W., and Virgil P. Diodato. "The Use of Gifts in a Medium Sized Academic Library." *Collection Management* 5 (Spring/Summer 1983): 53–69.

The University of Wisconsin–Milwaukee Library is the setting for this discussion of a gifts program. The authors look at patron use of gifts as a measure of the effectiveness of pursuing an active gifts program. They conclude that a gifts program must be extremely cost effective before it can be deemed successful in getting worthwhile books into a library. This is a good example of the blend of statistics and management issues in acquisitions.

BE7. Dole, Wanda. "Gifts and Block Purchases: Are They Profitable?" *Library Acquisitions: Practice and Theory* 7 (1983): 247–54.

Dole talks about the usefulness of treating gifts as a regular part of library collection development activities. She points out the vagaries of accepting gifts (particularly in large lots) and the difficulty of controlling what comes to a library through gifts and purchases of large lots of materials.

BE8. Galejs, John E. "Economics of Serials Exchanges." *Library Resources & Technical Services* 16 (Fall 1972): 511–20.

The article is twenty years old, but the question it addresses remains fresh: how does an acquisitions librarian cost out the economic feasibility of running a serials exchange program? This is a case study from Iowa State University Library that concludes that, especially in times of financial austerity, serials exchange benefits outweigh any staff costs.

BE9. Genzel, Peter, ed. *Studies in the International Exchange of Publications.* IFLA Publications no. 18. New York: K. G. Saur, 1981.

This represents one of many IFLA publications that address international exchange issues. Some of them seem, by date of publication, to be too old for usefulness, but this is not the case. Contains valuable information on acquisitions techniques, funding, and cost analysis. The development of international exchanges of publications in libraries takes a long time and is not likely to change nature quickly. IFLA will undoubtedly continue to publish in this important area as political realities throughout the world alter. *See also* BE1, another IFLA publication of special interest in this area.

BE10. Kovacic, Mark. "Gifts and Exchanges in U.S. Academic Libraries." *Library Resources & Technical Services* 24 (Spring 1980): 155–63.

Kovacic studied gifts and exchanges at eighteen academic libraries, looking at organization and staffing levels, as well as policies and procedures. The results of this survey, and his observations about them, continue to serve as a standard for handling these kinds of materials. Although some aspects have changed—notably due to the tax reform act and the introduction of automation—the article is still part of the basic bibliography in this section of acquisitions.

BE11. Lane, Alfred H. *Gifts and Exchange Manual.* Westport, Conn.: Greenwood Press, 1980.

Lane covers all the procedural aspects of managing a successful gifts and exchange program, including the necessary paperwork and the disposition of unwanted material. Also included are useful documents such as the Association of College and Research Libraries' policy on appraisals and sample gift policy statements. This is an excellent overview text.

BE12. Magrill, Rose Mary, and John Corbin. "Gifts and Exchanges." In their *Acquisitions Management and Collection Development in Libraries*, 216–33. 2nd ed. Chicago: American Library Association, 1989.

Along with the Clark (BE5) and Barker (BE3) chapters, this is the other contemporary textbook essay on gifts and exchanges that provides a good overview of the policies and procedures attached to this area of acquisitions. This chapter is useful for relating the gift process in particular to collection development and other areas of the library. There is an excellent bibliography included.

BE13. Nilson, Julieanne V., comp. *The Gifts and Exchange Function in ARL Libraries.* SPEC Kit, no. 117. Washington, D.C.: Association of Research Libraries, Office of Management Studies, 1985.

Eleven sample policy and procedure examples are included in this SPEC kit, including the impact of the Tax Reform Act of 1984, staffing pattern changes, and suggested trends in handling this material. This SPEC kit provides a useful overview of the current status of procedures for gifts and exchanges in the larger academic libraries. Replaces SPEC Kit no. 28 (1976).

BE14. Reid, Marion T. "The Gifts and Exchange Operations: Considerations for Review." *RTSD Newsletter* 10, no. 3 (1985): 21–24.

A practical introduction to gifts and exchange operations. Reid discusses organization and staffing, selection of gifts to be added, disposing of gifts not added, and maintaining a balanced exchange. Concludes with "relevant further readings."

BE15. Schenck, William Z. "Evaluating and Valuing Gift Materials." *Library Acquisitions: Practice and Theory* 6 (1982): 33–40.

This publication is a result of a paper presented at the acquisitions conference "Issues in Book and Serial Acquisitions: Where Is All the Money Going?" Schenck gives a practical overview of how to evaluate the worth of gifts, discusses the tax laws, and covers the impact of Library Friends groups on obtaining gift materials. For this last element especially, Schenck's article is an interesting and valuable addition to the literature of gifts and exchanges. He includes a good bibliography.

BE16. United Nations Educational, Scientific and Cultural Organization. *Handbook on the International Exchange of Publications*, edited by Frans Vanwijngaerden. 4th ed. Documentation, Libraries, and Archives: Bibliographies and Reference Works 4. Paris: UNESCO, 1978.

A guide to the methodology, organization, and management of the international exchange of publications and a directory of exchange centers with a national responsibility. Despite publication date, this remains of use to exchange librarians, librarians who want to set up an exchange center, students, and information officers and documentalists.

BE17. United States Internal Revenue Service. *Regulation 1.170A-13* and *Internal Revenue Code of 1986*, as amended, Section 170, "Charitable, Etc. Contributions and Gifts." Washington, D.C.: U.S. IRS.

These are the IRS regulations covering the tax implications of gifts to libraries. Consult the most recent code revisions.

BE18. White, Thomas C., J. Michael Morgan, and Gus A. Gordon. "Gifts—The Answer to a Problem." In *Legal and Ethical Issues in Acquisitions*, edited by Katina Strauch and Bruce Strauch, 55–61. New York: Haworth Press, 1990. Also published as *The Acquisitions Librarian*, no. 3.

This article discusses the effects of the tax codes on library collections. The authors, accounting and taxation professors, advise libraries on how to use tax laws to encourage donations to libraries. Included is practical information on appraisals and forms that support donations.

BF
Vendor Selection and
Evaluation

Perhaps the most significant contribution to library literature from acquisitions has been in the area of vendor selection and performance evaluation. Here are found the articles that use statistical analysis freely in a meaningful way, and here are seen the give-and-take discussions between the vendors and the librarians about the ethics and fallout from these kinds of studies that vendors and librarians alike have to handle. Included in this section are the best of these statistical studies, as well as some of the more fundamental, philosophical writings on conducting good vendor studies and working through the vendor selection process. Much of the seminal work in this area was done in the mid-1980s and stands today as the best in the field.

BF1. Alsbury, Donna. "Vendor Performance Evaluation as a Model for Evaluating Acquisitions." In *Evaluating Acquisitions and Collection Management*, edited by Pamela S. Cenzer and Cynthia I. Gozzi, 93–103. New York: Haworth Press, 1991. Also published as *The Acquisitions Librarian*, no. 6.

Acquisitions librarians are always evaluating the work of vendors, but too infrequently look at ways to evaluate their own work. Alsbury argues that the objectives of vendors and acquisitions librarians are very similar, and that many of the same evaluative techniques used in vendor analysis can be used for self-inspection. Included is speed, service, and fulfillment.

BF2. American Library Association, ALCTS Collection Management and Development Committee and Acquisitions Committee. *Guide to Performance Evaluation of Library Materials Vendors.* Acquisition Guidelines, no. 5. Chicago: American Library Association, 1989.

This committee-produced pamphlet describes the framework against which vendor evaluation should be made. It is not in-depth and does not provide the guidance that many articles in the literature do, but does discuss the policies and procedures that should form the underpinnings of all good vendor evaluations.

BF3. Baldwin, Jane, and Arlene Moore Sievers. "Subscription Agents and Libraries: An Inside View of What Every Serials Librarian Should Know." *Advances in Serials Management* 2 (1988): 37–45.

The authors give an in-depth description of the work of the serials vendor in filling, claiming, and paying for orders. This is an excellent account of the work of the serials middleman, and identifies a number of little-understood aspects of journal publishing and selling.

BF4. Barker, Joseph W. "Random Vendor Assignment in Vendor Performance Evaluation." *Library Acquisitions: Practice and Theory* 10 (1986): 265–80.

The methodology used in vendor evaluation has always been of paramount importance to vendors and acquisitions librarians alike. Barker describes a methodology that emphasizes good statistical techniques for determining order fulfillment rate with different types of orders. Here is a model that can be used in any type of vendor analysis, manual or automated.

BF5. Baumann, Susan. "An Application of Davis' 'Model for a Vendor Study.'" *Library Acquisitions: Practice and Theory* 8 (1984): 83–90.

For annotation, *see* BF6.

BF6. _____. "An Extended Application of Davis' 'Model for a Vendor Study.'" *Library Acquisitions: Practice and Theory* 9 (1985): 317–29.

These studies by Baumann build on Mary Byrd Davis's work (BF10) and take it into a different setting.

BF7. Brownson, Charles W. "A Method for Evaluating Vendor Performance." In *Vendors and Library Acquisitions*, edited by Bill Katz, 37–51. New York: Haworth Press, 1991. Also published as *The Acquisitions Librarian*, no. 5.

The speed with which an order is filled can form the basis for evaluating vendor performance, as well as provide information on setting up useful cancellation periods and predicting receipt patterns. The author suggests a mathematical model for determining these items, and suggests that some of the same modeling can be used to evaluate the work of the acquisitions department.

BF8. Cooper, Michael D. "Modeling Arrival Patterns of Library Book Orders." *Library & Information Science Research* 10 (1988): 237–55.

In an update to the Barker study on vendor performance evaluation (BF4), Cooper uses different statistical models to analyze the same data. He focuses on factors that determine the arrival of material and variations in arrival time. The study provides another approach to statistical analysis of vendor work.

BF9. Dannelly, Gay N. "The 'E's' of Vendor Selection: An Archetype for Selection, Evaluation, and Sustenance." In *Understanding the Business of Library Acquisitions*, edited by Karen A. Schmidt, 105–21. Chicago: American Library Association, 1990.

As the author points out, much of the writing on vendor evaluation has been on the "plumbing" and not any underlying philosophy. Dannelly talks about the theory that goes into vendor selection and evaluation, and guides the reader in asking the right questions. There is a good bibliography attached.

BF10. Davis, Mary Byrd. "Model for a Vendor Study in a Manual or Semi-Automated Acquisitions System." *Library Acquisitions: Practice and Theory* 3 (1979): 53–60.

The Davis model for vendor evaluation has become a hallmark in this area of acquisitions. Davis used good statistical sampling techniques to build her study, and many of her approaches have been incorporated into subsequent vendor analyses. It is a "must read" study before one attempts the first vendor evaluation. *See also* Susan Baumann's studies (BF5 and BF6).

BF11. Derthick, Jan and Barbara B. Moran. "Serials Agent Selection in ARL Libraries." *Advances in Serials Management* 1 (1986): 1–42.

This report of a survey of Association of Research Libraries' serials-vendor-selection practices describes the process by which large libraries choose and use serials agents or deal directly with publishers. It serves as a useful comparison tool when reviewing serial agents.

BF12. Hayes, Joan Mancell. "Acquiring Special Formats." In *Understanding the Business of Library Acquisitions*, edited by Karen A. Schmidt, 239–57. Chicago: American Library Association, 1990.

Hayes looks at nonprint materials and discusses the special problems attached to identifying and acquiring them. The chapter is especially useful for its extensive bibliography of directories that list special format items and for its discussion of acquiring computer software. If read in tandem with its companion chapter by Charles Forrest ("The Nonprint Trades," 219–37), the acquisitions librarian will have a good understanding of nonprint publishing and acquisition.

BF13. Ivins, October. "We Need Department Store *and* Boutique Serials Vendors." *The Serials Librarian* 17, nos. 3/4 (1990): 99–106.

Journal acquisitions is a major portion of most library budgets, and the selection of an agent to fill the majority of subscriptions is of serious consequence. Ivins argues convincingly here that more than one agent is a positive way to procure library subscriptions. The theory behind vendor selection is inherent in this essay.

BF14. Magrill, Rose Mary and John Corbin. "Purchasing Individual Items." In their *Acquisitions Management and Collection Development in Libraries*, 101–19. 2nd ed. Chicago: American Library Association, 1989.

For annotation, *see* BF16.

BF15. _____. "Purchasing Non-Book Materials." In their *Acquisitions Management and Collection Development in Libraries*, 165–94. 2nd ed. Chicago: American Library Association, 1989.

For annotation, *see* BF16.

BF16. _____. "Purchasing Special Types of Book Materials." In their *Acquisitions Management and Collection Development in Libraries*, 138–64. 2nd ed. Chicago: American Library Association, 1989.

The authors describe the work of jobbers, as well as methods of acquiring different types of materials (depository accounts, etc.) in these three chapters (BF14–BF16). The firm order process for obtaining individual items is outlined, and the philosophy behind vendor selection is discussed. Difficulties associated with acquiring nonbook materials are outlined. There is an excellent bibliography at the end of each of the chapters.

BF17. Price, Larry. "Book Wholesaling: Looking Toward the 21st Century." In *Vendors and Library Acquisitions*, edited by Bill Katz, 21–36. New York: Haworth Press, 1991. Also published as *The Acquisitions Librarian*, no. 5.

Written by a vice-president of a vendor company, this essay includes some old-fashioned and sensible advice about dealing with vendors. Price describes the pitfalls that occur in the interplay between the for-profit and not-for-profit sectors that the vendors and publishers and libraries represent. His advice to acquisitions librarians—to identify and speak their needs clearly—should be well-heeded.

BF18. Reid, Marion T. "Evaluating the Work of a Vendor." In *Understanding the Business of Library Acquisitions*, edited by Karen A. Schmidt, 123–35. Chicago: American Library Association, 1990.

Reid synthesizes a large body of literature about the why's and wherefore's of vendor evaluation. This is a good overview chapter on the topic, logically presented. The bibliography covers most of the highlights of the work on vendor evaluation.

BF19. Schmidt, Karen A. "Choosing a Serials Vendor." *The Serials Librarian* 14, nos. 3/4 (1988): 11–15.

Schmidt compares and contrasts the differences between choosing a serials and choosing a monograph vendor. There are fewer players in the serials vending field, and so competition can be more fierce. In addition to objective criteria, acquisitions librarians need to rely on intuition when choosing any vendor, including a serials vendor.

BF20. Vendor Study Group. "Vendor Evaluation: A Selected Annotated Bibliography, 1955-1987." *Library Acquisitions: Practice and Theory* 12 (1988): 17–28.

Covering over thirty years of writing about vendor evaluation, this annotated bibliography cites the most important works in this area. Included are methodological and case studies, as well as models for evaluation. Approval plan evaluations are not included here.

BF21. Womack, Kay, Agnes Adams, Judy L. Johnson, and Katherine Walter. "An Approval Plan Vendor Review: The Organization and Process." *Library Acquisitions: Practice and Theory* 12 (1988): 363–78.

The authors, all from one academic library, report on their review of five approval plan vendors. The study includes a literature review, as well as a discussion of the evaluation process. Analysis of approval vendors is somewhat different from evaluation of firm order vendors, and this study helps define the distinctions.

BG
Administration

BG1. Coffey, James R., ed. *Operational Costs in Acquisitions*. New York: Haworth Press, 1990. Also published as *The Acquisitions Librarian*, no. 4.

Coffey has brought together a series of essays on cost analyses in acquisitions work that cover personnel, automation, and specific procedural questions. Also included

is an annotated bibliography that is extremely useful for following this area of acquisitions. The essays routinely discuss the practical aspects of costing out the various services that an acquisitions section may provide in a library. Readers will find the realistic approach used by most of the authors to be extremely useful.

BG2. Hamilton, Marsha. *Guide to Preservation in Acquisition Processing*. Chicago: American Library Association, 1993. (Acquisitions Guidelines, no. 8.)

This brief treatise is a practical guide for all levels of acquisitions staff in handling incoming material for preservation and conservation. Included are discussions of binding requirements, printing concerns, and handling of new and out-of-print material. Hamilton brings preservation issues to the forefront of technical processing and provides basic information that should be required by all acquisitions staff.

BG3. Hardy, Eileen D., ed. *Statistics for Managing Library Acquisitions*. Chicago: American Library Association, 1989. (Acquisitions Guidelines, no. 6.)

Prepared by the Acquisitions Committee of ALA's ALCTS Resources Section, this quick guide answers the questions of why acquisitions departments should keep statistics and which statistics are useful to keep. It discusses how to quantify acquisitions work and provides some general guidance on the use of external statistics provided by vendors.

BG4. Haskell, John D., Jr. "Subject Bibliographers in Academic Libraries: An Historical and Descriptive Review." *Advances in Library Administration and Organization* 3 (1984): 73–84.

Here is a historical treatment of how the position of subject bibliographer developed in academic libraries. Haskell discusses the potential future roles of subject bibliographers as well. This does not address acquisitions issues specifically, but since many acquisitions departments deal with or include subject bibliographers, this is an important tangential area.

BG5. Henn, Barbara. "Acquisitions Management: The Infringing Roles of Acquisitions Librarians and Subject Specialists—An Historical Perspective." *Advances in Library Administration and Organization* 8 (1989): 113–29.

Henn looks at the role of the subject bibliographer in research libraries and discusses the development of both acquisitions librarians and subject specialists. How these two areas interact and sometimes clash makes for interesting historical reading and provides valuable insight into how dialogue between the two areas can be improved to further the effectiveness of the library as a whole. A good bibliography is attached.

BG6. Hirshon, Arnold, and Barbara A. Winters. *Managing the Purchasing Process: A How-to-Do-It Manual for Librarians*. New York: Neal-Schuman Publishers, 1993.

This is a useful discussion of the purchasing processes that take place in acquisitions: bidding, firm orders, approval plans, and requests for proposal are covered.

Librarians wishing to understand the mechanics of how acquisitions take place should refer to this guide.

BG7. Kohl, David F. *Acquisitions, Collection Development, and Collection Use: A Handbook for Library Management.* Santa Barbara, Calif.: ABC Clio Information Services, 1985.

See also annotation under BAA6. A useful first stop in researching administrative issues in acquisitions.

BG8. O'Neill, Ann. "Evaluating the Success of Acquisitions Departments: A Literature Review." *Library Acquisitions: Practice and Theory* 16, no. 3 (Fall 1992): 209–19.

The author looks at existing performance measures of acquisitions work, citing articles that use objective methods of measuring success in areas such as vendor evaluations, approval plans, and preorder searching. The literature review is critical, and suggests the need for more rigorous and far-ranging research in acquisitions.

BG9. Potter, William Gray. "Form or Function?: An Analysis of the Serials Department in the Modern Academic Library." *The Serials Librarian* 6 (Fall 1981): 53–60.

This is a unique discussion of the development of the serials department in academic libraries. It traces the history of the schism between acquisitions and processing of serials and monographs and investigates the rationale for separate and merged departments to handle different types of material. It also elicited some intense reactions from serials librarians in later issues of *The Serials Librarian.*

BG10. Schmidt, Karen A. "The Acquisitions Process in Research Libraries: A Survey of ARL Libraries' Acquisitions Departments." *Library Acquisitions: Practice and Theory* 11 (1987): 35–44.

This survey covers the work of acquisitions departments in large research libraries in the United States and Canada and describes the type of work that is done and which level of personnel handles it. It is one of a handful of studies that look at the professional aspects of acquisitions librarians' work, and it sets a model for deciding how many librarians are needed based on the size of department.

BH
Publishing

The literature of publishing is enormous, and much of it is of little application to library work. But acquisitions librarians in particular should make it an essential part of their continuing education to know how the publishing industry works, how production and marketing occur, and how changes in the technology used in producing books and journals affect their daily professional lives. The entries included here will help the acquisitions librarian learn the basics and remain current with the field of publishing. Many of the standard sources are older works that have stood up to time.

BH1. Bodian, Nat G. *Book Marketing Handbook.* 2 vols. New York: R. R. Bowker, 1983.

Bodian is one of the better-known authors to describe publishing for the uninitiated. This book discusses tips and techniques for promoting and selling monographs and serials. While the topic is of more immediate interest to the publishing industry, it is useful information for the acquisitions librarian as well.

BH2. *The Bowker Annual of Library and Book Trade Almanac.* New York; New Providence, N.J.: R. R. Bowker, 1956– . ISSN 0068-0540.

This covers much more than the publishing industry but is included here because of the statistical information it includes on publishing and book buying as it affects libraries. Included are national association reports from the Association of American Publishers, the American Booksellers Association, and similar groups. It is an excellent reference source for basic data on publishing. Earlier title: *The Bowker Annual of Library and Book Trade Information.*

BH3. Dessauer, John P. *Book Publishing: A Basic Introduction.* New expanded ed. New York: Continuum, 1990.

Dessauer represents the best example of a thorough and readable introduction to publishing books. He discusses the cultural and social aspects of publishing, as well as book manufacturing, and includes highly readable sections on marketing of different types of books. Acquisitions librarians who want a good guide to publishing will do well to consider spending some time with this book. Included is a glossary and a good index.

BH4. Geiser, Elizabeth A., and Arnold Dolin, with Gladys S. Topkis. *The Business of Book Publishing: Papers by Practitioners.* Boulder, Colo.: Westview Press, 1985.

Here is a practical initiation into the world of publishing. Essays by people in the publishing industry describe the nuts and bolts of the business. It is well illustrated and includes essays on specialized types of publishing.

BH5. Greenfield, Howard. *Books from Writer to Reader.* New York: Crown Publishers, 1989.

Using a popular, easy-to-read format, Greenfield—who boasts several years in the publishing industry as writer, editor, and publisher—brings the reader an interesting and focused view of the publishing industry. He covers the whole range of topics from the conception of an idea to the marketing of the finished product. The book is illustrated.

BH6. *Publishers Weekly.* New Providence, N.J.: R. R. Bowker. v. 1– , January 18, 1872– . Weekly. ISSN 0000-0019.

As mentioned in the general section of this chapter (BAD9), *Publishers Weekly* is the closest thing to a bible of the publishing industry. Acquisitions librarians should regularly read it for information on changes in publishing, controversies, and reviews.

BH7. Society for Scholarly Publishing. *Proceedings of the . . . Annual Meeting.* Washington, D.C.: Society for Scholarly Publishing, 1978– . ISSN 0734-8509; 0196-6146.

The Society for Scholarly Publishing routinely discusses cutting-edge issues that affect both the publishing world and libraries. Since the mid-1980s, librarians have become increasingly interested in SSP matters, as they address some of the pricing issues that affect library collections so heavily. It is worthwhile to attend SSP meetings, but in lieu of that, reading the *Proceedings* is a useful continuing education exercise.

BH8. Tebbel, John. *A History of Book Publishing in the United States.* 4 vols. New York: R. R. Bowker, 1972–1981.

Here is a set for the ambitious. This is a social history that covers virtually every aspect of publishing in this country, including the history of presses and imprints, fine and small presses, and the development of types of publishers. For information on the historical side of publishing in this country, Tebbel is the author of choice.

BH9. Unwin, Stanley. *The Truth about Publishing.* 8th ed. Chicago: Academy Chicago Publishers, 1982.

This is an odd and interesting introduction to the inside story of publishing. It first appeared in 1926. There is something of a bias toward publishing in Great Britain, but it is still an enjoyable and commonsensical read for librarians interested in the publishing industry.

BI
Ethics

Ethics in acquisitions librarianship is a topic that generates a lot of interest and discussion but not a lot of writing. It has defied adequate description of just what it entails and so is a very slippery issue to discuss in conferences and in the literature. Listed below are, with the exception of brief reports from meetings, most of the present writings on ethics for acquisitions librarians, although more are surely to appear as the discussion continues. As with some of the other areas of librarianship, it is a topic that brings together vendors and librarians, sometimes in intense debate, and so is a very vital part of the literature of acquisitions.

BI1. Boissonnas, Christian M. "The Cost Is More Than an Elegant Dinner: Your Ethics Are at Steak." *Library Acquisitions: Practice and Theory* 11, no. 2 (1987): 145–52.

Boissonnas' discussion of the ethical problems that can arise in library–vendor relations is probably the most commonsensical around. Using a scenario that many acquisitions librarians know, the dinner with the vendor, Boissonnas points out the pitfalls on both sides of the relationship and discusses how they can be avoided. This paper emanates from the College of Charleston Conference on Issues on Book and Serial Acquisitions held in 1987.

BI2. Bullard, Scott R. "The Ethics of Working with Vendors: A Report on the RTSD RS Acquisitions Librarians/ Vendors of Library Materials Discussion Group." (ALA Annual Conference, 1987.) *Library Acquisitions: Practice and Theory* 11, no. 4 (1987): 373–75.

There are other reports of other meetings on ethics at library conferences that could be cited here as well, but this serves as a fair example of the type of presentations and discussions that acquisitions librarians and vendors frequently have about ethics. The topic will undoubtedly continue to stimulate discussion in this branch of librarianship.

BI3. Dean, Barbara, and others. "Toward a Code of Ethics for Acquisitions Librarians." *Against the Grain* 4, no. 4 (Nov. 1992): 20–24.

Dean offers a statement of ethics that includes eight maxims that acquisitions librarians should follow. This is followed by reactions from two acquisitions librarians and one vendor, all of whom would require somewhat different statements about ethics and acquisitions. This is an excellent example of the difficulties inherent in writing an acceptable code of ethics for acquisitions work.

BI4. Goehner, Donna M. "Vendor-Library Relations: The Ethics of Working with Vendors." In *Understanding the Business of Library Acquisitions*, edited by Karen A. Schmidt, 137–51. Chicago: American Library Association, 1990.

Goehner posed a series of questions to vendors and librarians about ethical practices and recorded their responses. Her discussion covers many of the basic issues that confront vendors and acquisitions librarians as they work together: What are breaches of ethics? How should they be handled? What contributes most to a positive, ethical working relationship? This is a good introduction to the topic.

BI5. Strauch, Katina, and Bruce Strauch, eds. *Legal and Ethical Issues in Acquisitions.* New York: Haworth Press, 1990. Also published as *The Acquisitions Librarian*, no. 3.

Using authors from both the publishing and legal worlds, the editors have drawn together a number of useful articles on ethics for acquisitions librarians. Some of the highlights include discussions on acquisitions and the Federal Trade Commission, billing problems, tax issues on charitable contributions, and ethical considerations in contract negotiations. This covers the gamut of issues in ethics, the essays are well written, and the appended bibliographies are helpful.

C

Descriptive Cataloging

Janet Swan Hill

Overview

Descriptive cataloging encompasses physical description of information resources so that they can be identified usefully and uniquely, and assignment and formulation of access points to those resources based on appearance, publishing pattern and history, and intellectual responsibility for the work.

The most commonly perceived purpose of descriptive cataloging today is to provide access to information resources through a catalog or other information retrieval system. Viewed this narrowly, description serves mainly as a pointer to information resources. There are, however, other essential purposes served by descriptive cataloging. Physical description sufficient to aid in choosing among materials (e.g., Is this videotape Beta or VHS? Does this book include a bibliography?) is important to all users of library catalogs, and especially to potential users of materials that may be awkward to retrieve or use. Physical description sufficient to identify an item positively is critical to such diverse activities as acquisitions, collection development, circulation, inventory control, interlibrary loan, and rare books librarianship.

The multiple uses of description are complementary rather than conflicting, and the need to succeed

at them all has resulted in an extensive body of codes and instructions and in bibliographic records that are more detailed than some users in some constituencies need. Other factors contributing to the body of codes and complexity of records include the proliferation of physical forms of materials and the needs for standardization and for coding that arise in connection with library automation and bibliographic networks.

Perhaps because of the complexity of instructions for description and because of insufficient appreciation for the variety of challenges and constituencies served, questions often are asked about the need for certain aspects of descriptive content, the degree of education and judgment required to perform descriptive cataloging, and the possible use of technology to decrease the descriptive work load. No doubt, these questions will continue to be asked, but until they are answered well, descriptive cataloging remains to be done, and information about its theory and practice continues to be needed.

Chapter Content and Organization

The ideal structure for this chapter would probably be as a card file or database so that catalogers could rearrange the entries to suit their particular needs. The present organization is a compromise. The first section includes general and overview works. The second section includes standards, manuals of application for the standards as a whole, works related to cataloging specific types of materials, and sources of information about cataloging. The final section covers resources for the cataloging data itself.

This chapter emphasizes resources that may assist catalogers in performing descriptive cataloging. On the premise that understanding the background for rules and practices is essential to performance, some general and historical works are included. The primary aim is to identify a working reference collection and set of data resources for catalogers in the United States who wish to perform cataloging that conforms to prevailing national standards. Works that relate primarily to cataloging in other contexts and other countries generally are not included. There are many citations given to works and resources that are of primary use to catalogers of particular types or materials (e.g., audiovisual materials, serials). These works and resources should be regarded as a starting point only. Catalogers who find themselves in need of more guidance or of other reference sources that pertain to those special materials will need to look beyond the sources cited in this chapter.

A Note about Currency

The tools that govern the descriptive content of cataloging records are continually evolving. Even between formal editions or reprintings, the *Anglo-American Cataloguing Rules*, the MARC formats, and the rule interpretations issued by national libraries may be subject to substantive change. Currency is therefore an important factor in determining the usefulness of any cataloging tool. In using a particular tool, catalogers need to be alert to the effective date of its information and to understand that some examples or instructions may have been invalidated by subsequent revision or interpretation of the rule.

The need for currency means that older cataloging tools must be replaced continually. Those that include discussion of principles, historical context, etc., may not be rendered obsolete by the appearance of a more recent tool on the same topic, but if they are retained, they must be used cautiously. A number of older titles are cited in this chapter, not as suggestions for a newly assembled cataloger's reference collection (many of the titles are no longer available) but as an aid in deciding whether these titles should be retained in an existing collection.

CA
General Works

CAA
Textbooks, Guides, and Manuals

CAA1. Carpenter, Michael, and Elaine Svenonius, eds. *Foundations of Cataloging: A Source Book.* Englewood, Colo.: Libraries Unlimited, 1989.

An anthology of writings that traces the development of descriptive cataloging principles and theory over the past 150 years. Includes items by Panizzi, Cutter, Lubetsky, and others, as well as influential papers such as the Paris Principles.

CAA2. Chan, Lois Mai. *Cataloging and Classification: An Introduction.* McGraw-Hill Series in Library Education. New York: McGraw-Hill, 1981.

See also annotation under DAA1. Covers various aspects of cataloging. Includes suggested readings and references to other cataloging tools. Specific examples and bibliographies may be somewhat dated, but the general discussions remain useful.

CAA3. Clack, Doris Hargrett, ed. *The Making of a Code: The Issues Underlying AACR 2.* Chicago: American Library Association, 1980.

Papers given at the International Conference on *AACR2* (CBA4) at Tallahassee, Florida, 1979. Despite the later revisions to *AACR2*, the background perspective remains interesting.

CAA4. Downing, Mildred Harlow, and David H. Downing. *Introduction to Cataloging and Classification.* 6th ed. Jefferson, N.C.: McFarland & Co., 1992.

A basic and somewhat brief text covering various aspects of cataloging. Focused on online cataloging and aimed at beginners.

CAA5. Hunter, Eric J., and K. G. B. Bakewell. *Cataloguing.* 3rd ed. London: Library Association, 1991. Distributed by Unipub, Lanham, Md.

A general text, revised to include details on the 1988 revision of *AACR2* (CBA1) and other recent developments in cataloging. British perspective.

CAA6. Intner, Sheila S., and Jean Weihs, eds. *Standard Cataloging for School and Public Libraries.* Englewood, Colo.: Libraries Unlimited, 1990.

Includes basic discussion of cataloging principles, description of activities involved in cataloging, and a general guide to the tools that will likely be used. Addresses costs and benefits of standard cataloging. Discussions and examples refer often to the types of materials frequently encountered in school and public libraries.

CAA7. Svenonius, Elaine, ed. *The Conceptual Foundations of Descriptive Cataloging.* San Diego: Academic Press, 1989.

Papers delivered at the Conference on the Conceptual Foundations of Descriptive Cataloging, held at UCLA in 1987. Includes historical, theoretical, and speculative papers.

CAA8. Taylor, Arlene G., ed. *Introduction to Cataloging and Classification.* 8th ed. Library Science Text Series. Englewood, Colo.: Libraries Unlimited, 1992.

See also annotation under DAA7. A classic text (originally published by Bohdan Wynar in 1964), updated, covering all aspects of cataloging. A useful basic textbook for beginning librarians and library school students. Includes plentiful examples and suggested readings, including citations to other cataloging tools.

CAA9. Weinberg, Bella Hass, ed. *Cataloging Heresy: Challenging the Standard Bibliographic Product.* Medford, N.J.: Learned Information, 1992.

Proceedings of the Congress for Librarians held at St. John's University, 1991. Broad coverage, including both practical and theoretical papers on cataloging and management issues, as well as implications and applications of technological advances.

CAA10. Zuiderfeld, Sharon, ed. *Cataloging Correctly for Kids: An Introduction to the Tools.* Rev. ed. Chicago: American Library Association, 1991.

Designed to help catalogers of children's materials provide appropriate and cost-effective cataloging. Discusses special needs of users of children's cataloging, relevant standards, and shared and purchased cataloging. Covers book and nonbook materials.

CAB
Management Issues and the Role of Catalogers

The role and standing of catalogers and the nature of the work that they do has changed radically in this century. Cataloging has been perceived as a genteel and scholarly pursuit suitable for deposed royalty or introverted academics; as a complex and legalistic profession for harmless fussbudgets and persons best removed from the reference desk; or as a dull, detail-ridden, and fast-vanishing activity suitable for clerks and artificial intelligence programs. None of these characterizations comes close to describing either the occupation or its practitioners, and not all views of cataloging are unflattering. Cataloging can be seen as a vital activity and a series of intellectual puzzles requiring careful and inquisitive individuals with a service orientation.

Just as views of cataloging and catalogers differ, no single view of how cataloging fits into a library organization is correct. Catalogers may be highly

specialized, cataloging only certain types of materials or performing only certain facets of cataloging (e.g., doing only subject analysis); others may catalog all types of materials. Some handle all aspects of processing, including cataloging; some may do cataloging only rarely. Some catalogers may view their work only in terms of their local constituency, and some may catalog for a nationwide—or at least network-wide—constituency.

Despite the variety, some generalizations can be made. Widespread availability of copy for already cataloged titles has decreased the number of titles that require a high degree of professional training. Certain features of library automation have decreased the difficulty of performing certain cataloging tasks and decreased the time required to perform others. It has been increasingly possible to identify and separate the simpler aspects of cataloging from the more difficult and then to assign responsibility for each aspect to an appropriate level of staff, thus concentrating the most-complex work and assigning it to a few highly qualified cataloging librarians.

In addition, wider application of library automation and the desirability of sharing cataloging records have increased the importance of standardized practice. Extensive sharing of cataloging records leads catalogers to catalog "for the world" as opposed to cataloging for local needs only. It has also broadened the community of catalogers. All these factors have a profound effect on catalogers, on their work, on how they are perceived and how they perceive themselves, and on how they might best be educated. The following books address these topics.

CAB1. Carter, Ruth C., ed. *Education and Training for Catalogers and Classifiers.* New York: Haworth Press, 1988. Also published as *Cataloging & Classification Quarterly 7,* no. 4.

A collection of papers by different authors. Coverage includes the roles of graduate education and on-the-job training, cataloging of special types of materials, and case studies.

CAB2. Hafter, Ruth. *Academic Librarians and Cataloging Networks: Visibility, Quality Control, and Professional Status.* Contributions in Librarianship and Information Science, no. 57. New York: Greenwood Press, 1986.

An examination of the impact of bibliographic networks on catalogers, their work and status.

CAB3. Intner, Sheila S., and Janet Swan Hill. *Recruiting, Educating, and Training Cataloging Librarians: Solving the Problems.* New Directions in Information Management, no. 19. New York: Greenwood Press, 1989.

Papers presented at a symposium held at Simmons College in 1989. Divided among the topics of recruiting, education for cataloging, and training catalogers. Includes contributions from Avram, Miksa, Frost, and others.

CAB4. _____. *Cataloging: The Professional Development Cycle.* New Directions in Information Management, no. 26. New York: Greenwood Press, 1991.

A companion to the above title (CAB3). Includes transcripts of those papers presented orally that differed substantially in content or focus from the paper contributed to the formal proceedings. Also includes transcript of discussion.

CAB5. Taylor, Arlene G. *Cataloging with Copy: A Decision-Maker's Handbook.* 2nd ed. Englewood, Colo.: Libraries Unlimited, 1988. Covers cataloging and management issues that arise from use of previously existing copy, discussing the impact of alteration of copy on catalog users and on work flow. Contains numerous examples.

CAC
Local Policies

Even though the content of cataloging records and their coding may be determined by international standards and the input and display of records may be dictated by an automated system, every library is unique and needs its own policies and procedures to answer such questions as Do we revise old cataloging as a matter of course, or only when it causes a problem for retrieval? When do we not follow LC series tracing practice? What do we have to do to make sure that titles with ampersands and other symbols are retrieved in the catalog? Do we make added entries for faculty members even though the rules don't require it?

Typically, a great deal of local cataloging policy is handed down as oral tradition, but to the extent possible, it should be written down to minimize misunderstanding, inconsistent application, and "drift."

CAC1. Allen, Alice, comp. *Local Cataloging Policies.* SPEC Kit, no. 110. Washington, D.C.: Association of Research Libraries, Office of Management Studies, 1985.

Examples of local cataloging policies formulated by various ARL libraries. Topics addressed include copy editing, minimal level cataloging, quality and quantity standards, and professional responsibilities.

CAC2. Tyckoson, David A., ed. *Enhancing Access to Information: Designing Catalogs for the 21st Century.* New York: Haworth Press, 1991. Also published as *Cataloging & Classification Quarterly* 13, nos. 3/4 (1991).

See also annotation under FB31. A collection of papers by different authors relating to the general theme of the journal issue. Coverage includes increased use of contents notes; inclusion of previously uncataloged material; better integration of holdings, location, and circulation data with the bibliographic record; and accessing remote and non-traditional databases.

CAD
Cooperative Projects and Databases

Librarianship is a cooperative profession and cataloging an intensely cooperative activity within it. The works in this section describe cooperative projects in broad terms.

CAD1. Carpenter, Michael, ed. *National and International Bibliographic Databases.* New York: Haworth Press, 1989. Also published as *Cataloging & Classification Quarterly* 8, nos. 3/4.

A collection of papers by different authors. Coverage includes linked systems, cooperative cataloging activities such as Name Authority Cooperative (NACO) and Cooperative Online Serials (CONSER), descriptions of bibliographic networks, and systems and activities worldwide. This is not a manual or textbook, but the background on networks and projects may be of interest to those trying to make sense of the present and look to the future.

CAD2. Carter, Ruth C., ed. *The United States Newspaper Program.* New York: Haworth Press, 1987. Also published as *Cataloging & Classification Quarterly* 6, no. 4.

A collection of papers by different authors. Coverage includes special problems of providing, through a multiyear cooperative project, bibliographic control and holdings information for newspapers held in various libraries across the country. The Newspaper Project resulted in a number of cataloging innovations and practices, including methods for dealing with titles available in multiple versions. Problems and solutions are described.

CAD3. Mandel, Carol A. "Cooperative Cataloging: Modes, Issues, Projects." *Advances in Librarianship* 16 (1992): 33–82.

A comprehensive review of cooperative cataloging projects.

CAD4. Woodsworth, Anne, with Thomas B. Wall. *Library Cooperation and Networks: A Basic Reader.* New York: Neal-Schuman Publishers, 1991.

Not a manual. Broad coverage of networks and cooperation, including types, governance, participation, alternatives, etc.

CAE
Periodicals

With certain exceptions, e.g., *Cataloging Service Bulletin* (CAE4), cataloging standards and guides to their application usually do not appear in journals, but journal literature does form a valuable portion of the literature relating to descriptive cataloging, and especially to issues of management, work flow, and policy.

The following journals regularly or frequently contain items relating to some aspect of descriptive cataloging. Journals and serials that may only occasionally publish substantive items relating to the topic are not included.

CAE1. *ALCTS Network News.* [serial online] Chicago: Association for Library Collections and Technical Services. v. 1– , May 13, 1991– . Irregular. ISSN 1056-6694.

For annotation, *see* AF4.

CAE2. *ALCTS Newsletter.* Chicago: Association for Library Collections and Technical Services. v. 1– , 1990– . Frequency varies. ISSN 1047-949X.

For annotation, *see* AF5.

CAE3. *Cataloging & Classification Quarterly.* New York: Haworth Press. v. 1– , Fall 1980– . Quarterly. ISSN 0163-9374.

Covers a broad range of cataloging topics, including practice, theory, and management. Individual issues are often organized around a theme, with articles solicited. Theme issues are often issued simultaneously as a monograph. Edited by Ruth C. Carter.

CAE4. *Cataloging Service Bulletin.* Washington, D.C.: Library of Congress. no. 1– , Summer 1978– . Quarterly. ISSN 0160-8029.

Known as *CSB.* Includes news about cataloging projects, LC cataloging practices, Library of Congress rule interpretations, and official rule revisions. A necessary tool in all cataloging operations of any size. Continues Library of Congress Cataloging Service *Bulletin.* The older title is useful to those interested in the history of cataloging practice.

CAE5. *International Cataloguing and Bibliographic Control.* London: IFLA UBCIM Programme. v. 17– , Jan./Mar. 1985– . Quarterly. ISSN 1011-8829.

Contains reports from IFLA's Universal Bibliographic Control and International MARC Programme, papers delivered there, and announcements of progress and publications of IFLA documents, including the International Standards for Bibliographic Description (ISBDs). Papers are often descriptions of practices or projects in foreign countries.

CAE6. *LC Cataloging Newsline.* [serial online] Washington, D.C.: Library of Congress. Jan. 15, 1993– . Quarterly.

This new electronic newsletter is intended to contain information about cataloging activities at LC of interest to the library community. The first issue was posted to **AUTOCAT@UVMVM** (CAF3); LC will announce availability of the newsletter when installation of local LISTSERV software is complete.

The first issue is available to INTERNET users through anonymous FTP (the file-transfer protocol for moving files between computers) using the following commands:

1. At the system prompt, enter: **ftp seq1.loc.gov** or **ftp 140.147.3.12**
2. At the name prompt, enter your INTERNET address
3. At the name prompt, enter: **anonymous**
4. At the ftp> prompt, enter: **cd pub/coop.cataloging/ docs**
5. Request file by entering: **get lccn.news**
6. After transfer, enter: **quit**

For information about *LC Cataloging Newsline,* contact Robert M. Hiatt, Cataloging and Support Office, Library of Congress (202) 707-4380.

CAE7. *Library Hi Tech.* Ann Arbor, Mich.: Pierian Press. v. 1– , Summer 1983– . Monthly. ISSN 0737-8831.

For annotation, *see* AF12.

CAE8. *Library Hi Tech News.* Ann Arbor, Mich.: Pierian Press. v. 1– , Jan. 1984– . Ten times a year. ISSN 0741-9058.

Focus is the same as *Library Hi Tech,* but content is primarily news, reports of conferences, etc.

CAE9. *Library Resources & Technical Services.* Chicago: Association for Library Collection and Technical Services. v. 1– , Winter 1957– . Quarterly. ISSN 0024-2527.

See also annotation under AF13. Once a year includes a survey article of the year's work in descriptive cataloging.

CAE10. *Technicalities.* Lincoln, Nebr.: Media Periodicals, a division of Westport Publishers. v. 1– , Dec. 1980– . Monthly. ISSN 0272-0884.

See also annotation under AF23. Includes continuing columns, one of which, "Interfaces" by Sheila S. Intner, frequently covers issues in descriptive cataloging.

SPECIAL INTEREST JOURNALS

The following journals are focused on various aspects of specific types of materials. They are presented as being indicative of the sources that may be available to catalogers seeking additional guidance for cataloging special types of materials.

CAE11. *MOUG Newsletter.* Various places: Music OCLC Users Group. no. 1– , 1977– . Irregular. ISSN 0161-1704.

Includes news from OCLC, cataloging questions and answers, and news of the Group.

CAE12. *Music Cataloging Bulletin.* Ann Arbor, Mich.: Music Library Association. v. 1– , 1970– . Monthly. ISSN 0027-4283.

Includes coverage and discussion of rule revisions and application and notices of new reference materials.

CAE13. *OLAC Newsletter.* Various places: On-Line Audiovisual Catalogers. v. 5– , Mar. 1985– . Quarterly. ISSN 0739-1153.

Includes news and reports of OLAC and related organizations' activities, questions and answers, and some book reviews.

CAF
Sources of Expertise

PROFESSIONAL ORGANIZATIONS

A great deal of discussion, problem solving, and investigative and developmental work in cataloging is performed within professional organizations. Individuals who are involved with these organizations compose a ready-selected body of potential experts. An effort to keep abreast of developments in descriptive cataloging should include keeping abreast of activities of relevant committees and other groups.

In addition to the groups listed here, other organizations or committees within organizations have a substantial interest in cataloging or a special interest in cataloging of particular types of materials. These organizations provide a ready forum for discussion of cataloging issues and a pool of expertise upon which to draw. They may also sponsor continuing education programs or create, publish, or contribute to cataloging standards and guidelines. Some may publish journals or newsletters that contain much of interest to catalogers.

CAF1. ALA Association for Library Collections and Technical Services (ALCTS). Executive Director: Karen Muller.
    For annotation, *see* AGA3.

CAF2. ALA ALCTS Cataloging and Classification Section (CCS).
    CCS is the organization with the widest-ranging impact on descriptive cataloging. A description of ALCTS committees and discussion groups may be found in the current *ALA Handbook of Organization*. Meetings of these groups are held during the ALA Annual and Midwinter conferences. Meetings of all committees (except for awards and nominations committees) are open to interested observers. Advance notice of meetings is made available in the *ALCTS Newsletter* (CAE2) and *ALCTS Network News* (CAE1), through mailing lists, and on electronic bulletin boards. Following are some of the CCS committees most closely involved with maintenance of the *Anglo-American Cataloguing Rules*.
    ["Anglo-American Cataloguing Rules" The Joint Steering Committee for the Revision of (JSC). Membership includes one representative each from the British Library, the Library Association, the Library of Congress, the American Library Association, the Canadian Committee on Cataloging (representing both Canadian library associations and the national library), and the Australian Committee on Cataloging (representing both the library association and the national library). The JSC determines the content and direction of the code, based on advice from constituent organizations. It publishes, through the associations, the *Anglo-American Cataloguing Rules* and, as required, revisions and addenda to the rules. Meetings are held approximately annually, rotating among member countries.]

Committee on Cataloging: Description and Access (CC:DA). A committee of CCS. Membership includes nine members and thirty-five nonvoting representatives and *ex officio* members from ALA units and external organizations. Meetings are held during ALA conferences. CC:DA determines the ALA position on proposed rules changes. Proposals may emanate from any represented constituency or from members of the JSC. CC:DA occasionally publishes, through ALCTS or ALA, guidelines for application of the code.

CC:DA Task Forces. In the course of business, CC:DA encounters many questions that cannot be adequately investigated or answered at a committee meeting. When this occurs, a task force may be appointed, with a charge to report back to the Committee at a later date. In recent years, CC:DA has appointed task forces to investigate such matters as description of materials produced in multiple versions, description of interactive media, and the definition of *edition*. Task forces may work by correspondence between conferences, but meetings held at conferences are open. Reports to CC:DA are written.

ELECTRONIC DISCUSSION GROUPS

Within the past decade, electronic discussion groups (sometimes called computer conferences, lists, or bulletin boards) have emerged as another means of getting in touch with colleagues from whom to obtain advice or with whom to discuss common problems. Access to a computer conference is dependent upon having access to appropriate computer equipment and a telecommunications network, but once those hurdles are passed, participation is merely a matter of signing on and joining in. Messages sent to a conference are broadcast to all of its subscribers, who have the option of not responding, of posting a response to the whole list, or of responding to the individual.

There are many lists that may be of interest and use to catalogers. A list of current computer conferences, together with instructions on how to subscribe to them, is published from time to time on PACS-L (CAF4). Some computer conferences focus on the issues facing particular types of libraries or encountered with particular types of materials. On most of these, cataloging is only one of the topics that may arise. An increasing number of computer conferences are devoted to issues relating to use of particular library automation systems.

CAF3. AUTOCAT [electronic discussion group].

The Library Cataloging and Authorities Discussion Group is unmoderated, which means that all messages appear exactly as they are sent. The types of topics that appear on AUTOCAT vary widely, including questions of rules application, MARC tagging, work flow, and personnel management; discussions of rule revision, education for cataloging, ethics; requests for help in translating or in locating subject experts; job and meeting announcements; and conference reports. To subscribe, send a message to: **LISTSERV@UVMVM** (BITNET) or **LISTSERV%-UVMV.BITNET@VM1.NODAK.EDU** (INTERNET) with the command: **SUBSCRIBE AUTOCAT [your name].**

CAF4. PACS-L. [electronic discussion group] 1989– . Houston: University of Houston Library.

For annotation, *see* GAE2.

ADDITIONAL SOURCES OF EXPERTISE

Despite—and partly because of—the number of cataloging codes governing descriptive cataloging, along with their level of detail and the availability of rule interpretations and guides, catalogers still find themselves faced with situations in which the "right" answer eludes them. Despite the richness of reference sources available, catalogers still may not be able to find the information they need. When formulating new policy or extending old practice or policy into new areas, catalogers often find it necessary or desirable to go beyond code books, manuals, and dictionaries, and find a *person* to talk with. Hearsay or tradition do not always make reasonable foundations for correct or useful cataloging, but there are many instances in which there is no satisfactory substitute for personal expertise or joint consideration of problems. The following categories or sources of experts should not be overlooked.

SUBJECT OR LANGUAGE EXPERTS. A librarian attached to an educational institution may be able to get help from faculty in the subject or language department. From time to time various professional associations, consortia, and networks compile lists of librarians within the group who are willing to share their expertise. A "blind" letter or telephone call to a library that appears to catalog a great deal of material in the subject or language in question can also often elicit needed help.

OTHER CATALOGERS. The value of brainstorming and cooperative problem solving is well established.

Catalogers with lengthy or broad experience who may already have encountered and solved a problem that another cataloger is seeing for the first time, as well as catalogers with less experience and a fresh eye, can contribute signally to problem resolution. The expertise of catalogers who have received special training and/or "validation" of the quality of their work in connection with special cooperative projects can be especially useful: NACO (Name Authority Cooperative) catalogers have received special training sufficient to allow them to contribute authority records to the national authority database. NCCP (National Coordinated Cataloging Program) catalogers have received training in cataloging sufficient to allow them to contribute bibliographic records directly to the Library of Congress database. Catalogers at Enhance institutions are authorized to upgrade records that appear on the OCLC database. CONSER (Cooperative Online Serials) catalogers create serial records of the highest quality. There is, unfortunately, no single source to identify institutions that are participating in these programs, but a list of participants can be solicited from the sponsoring body.

USERS OF CATALOGING. It is essential to keep in touch with those who make use of cataloging in their own work (e.g., circulation, preservation, collection development) and those who help others use cataloging (e.g., reference librarians). The perspective that these individuals can bring to the usefulness and impact of certain practices and their expressions of unmet needs can be of inestimable value in formulating and modifying policies and practice.

LIBRARY OF CONGRESS. The Library of Congress will respond to cataloging-related inquiries. From time to time the *Cataloging Service Bulletin* (CAE4) publishes a list of officers at the Library of Congress to whom cataloging-related inquiries may be sent.

BIBLIOGRAPHIC NETWORKS AND VENDORS. Networks and library automation vendors often offer training programs and instructional materials to their users and customers. Much of the training materials and programs provided through networks and vendors are phrased in terms of using the particular system, but they also may contain much of general applicability. For example, a network workshop in basic cataloging will include instruction both on cataloging and on using the system. It is often possible to have network and vendor training geared toward a particular audience (e.g., basic cataloging for small libraries). Networks and vendors maintain staffs of experts whose job is to field questions about use of their systems and services. Where those services include cataloging or retrospective conversion, expertise may also extend to cataloging.

Networks and vendors may sponsor or facilitate user or interest groups. These groups constitute another source of common interest and expertise that may be consulted. Many networks and library automation vendors act as hosts to an electronic mail system by which questions and other correspondence can be sent to and received from representatives of the organization. Comments can be addressed either to individuals or to offices. Some vendors may also sponsor or facilitate electronic discussion groups or computer conferences. Though often hosted by a user's institution instead of by the vendor itself, the vendor should be able to supply information about the list.

CB
Standards and Their
Application

Descriptive cataloging is governed by, or performed in accordance with, a number of nationally or internationally accepted codes, each of which has a prescribed level of "authority" over a specified aspect of descriptive cataloging.

CBA
Standards for Descriptive Content

CBA1. Gorman, Michael, and Paul Winkler, eds. *Anglo-American Cataloguing Rules.* 2nd ed., 1988 rev. Chicago: American Library Association, 1988.

Also known as *AACR2R* and *AACR2* (1988 revision). Available in hard or paper cover or in loose-leaf binder. This is the standard in the United States, Canada, United Kingdom, and Australia that governs bibliographic description, choice and form, and nonsubject access points. It has also been adopted widely beyond these countries, often in translation. The code is intended for use in general libraries, and rules are provided for all types of materials. The code is complex and detailed. Its content is under continual review by an international committee, the Joint Steering Committee for Revision of *Anglo-American Cataloguing Rules.*

AACR2R will soon be available in electronic format. The American Library Association, acting on behalf of the publishers and copyright holders of the *Anglo-American Cataloguing Rules*, plans to release a machine-readable version of the code, formatted in Standard Generalized Mark-Up Language (SGML), in 1993. *AACRE*, as it has been nicknamed, will be an electronically formatted version of the printed code. The Joint Steering Committee and the publishers of *AACR2R* will make every effort to assure that the content remains in sync with the print version. SGML coding will support data manipulation and retrieval by various software retrieval systems. It is expected that library automation vendors and others will develop software specifically for use of this code format. While ALA is working on the SGML version of *AACR2R*, the Library of Congress is carrying out preliminary investigations aimed toward creating a MARC-type format for the code.

Although the process of revising the *Anglo-American Cataloguing Rules* is continuous, revisions are cumulated and issued in batches by the publishers to decrease disruption in the cataloging community. Until they are published, revisions are not official and are not to be implemented. The first package of rule revisions issued since the publication of the 1988 revision of the code is planned for 1993.

SUPERSEDED CODES

Superseded codes are of primarily historical interest. Although they should not be used in preparing new cataloging, they can be useful to those who deal with older cataloging records and headings. Understanding why a heading or record was formulated as it was, for example, may be helpful in record revision, retrospective conversion, or item identification. A new catalogers' reference collection might well contain no superseded codes, but as codes become superseded, one copy should be retained for historical and reference purposes. Recent superseded codes include:

CBA2. Butler, Clara, ed. *ALA Cataloging Rules for Author and Title Entries.* 2nd ed. Prepared by the Division of Cataloging and Classification of the American Library Association. Chicago: American Library Association, 1949.

Superseded by *AACR.*

CBA3. Gorman, Michael, and Paul Winkler, eds. *Anglo-American Cataloging Rules.* North American text. Chicago: American Library Association, 1967.

Known as *AACR.* Superseded by the second edition.

CBA4. _____. *Anglo-American Cataloguing Rules.* 2nd ed. Chicago: American Library Association, 1978.

Known as *AACR2.* Superseded by the 1988 revision.

UNDERLYING STANDARDS

CBA5. International Conference on Cataloguing Principles, Paris, France, 1961. *Statement of Principles: Adopted at the International Conference on Cataloguing Principles, Paris, October, 1961.* Annotated ed. with commentary and examples by Eva Verona assisted by [others]. Definitive ed. London: International Federation of Library Associations and Institutions, 1971.

Known as the "Paris Principles." Internationally agreed-to principles that provided the basis for the *Anglo-American Cataloguing Rules* and the International Standard Bibliographic Descriptions (ISBDs).

INTERNATIONAL STANDARDS FOR BIBLIOGRAPHIC DESCRIPTION (ISBD)

The ISBDs are not cataloging codes in themselves. They are internationally agreed-to "skeletons" upon which codes may be based. The *Anglo-American Cataloguing Rules*, for example, are written in basic conformity with the ISBDs. The ISBDs specify data elements to be included in bibliographic description as well as their order, presentation, and punctuation. ISBDs do not cover choice and form of access points. The ISBD (G) provides the General framework for all other ISBDs, each of which is concerned with a particular type of material. The content of ISBDs is determined as part of IFLA's UBCIM Programme. They are published in London, through IFLA, and are reviewed and updated periodically. In addition to ISBD (G), ISBDs are available for monographs—ISBD (M), antiquarian publications—ISBD (A), serials—ISBD (S), cartographic materials—ISBD (CM), nonbook materials—ISBD (NBM), printed music—ISBD (PM), computer files—ISBD (CF), and component parts—ISBD (CP). The following are included as examples of these standards.

CBA6. *ISBD (M): Description bibliographique internationale normalisie des Monographes; International Standard Bibliographic Description for Monographic Publications.* Rev. ed. Paris: Bibliotheque Nationale, 1990.

"Recommendée par le Comité de révision des ISBD, approuvée par le Bureau permanent de la Section de catalogage de IFLA."

CBA7. *ISBD (S): International Standard Bibliographic Description for Serials.* Rev. ed. London: IFLA UBCIM Programme, 1988.

"Recommended by the ISBD Review Committee, approved by the Standing Committees of the IFLA Section on Cataloguing and the IFLA Section on Serial Publications."

CBB
Standards for Content Designation

In order for cataloging records to be shared or manipulated electronically, their content must be labeled in a way that can be interpreted consistently by automated systems. Standards that define these labels or codes and describe their application to cataloging records are generically referred to as "Formats" or "Tag Charts." Both the process and the result of applying a format or tag chart to a cataloging record is called "coding," "tagging" or "content designation." It is important for catalogers to recognize that formats or tag charts dictate only how the content of a cataloging record is coded, not what the content is. In addition to providing instructions for coding data, however, formats and tag charts provide many examples of both cataloging coding and content that catalogers may find useful.

MARC FORMATS

The MARC (MAchine Readable Cataloging) format was originally developed in the United States but was so widely adopted that the general MARC record structure now is subject to an International Organization for Standardization (ISO) standard (2709). The USMARC Format is the standard in the United States and is also used in countries that have not developed MARC formats tailored to their special needs. Initially, the MARC formats were a group of separate though similar formats, each covering a particular type of material. Currently, they are published in a single sequence in which applicability of individual tags or codes to particular types of material is specified. A further process of "integration" will soon lead to a single format. For a more complete discussion of MARC, see Chapter K, Database Management.

Major bibliographic networks in North America, and most major local automation systems, use MARC-formatted records, but specific needs and capabilities of the particular networks or systems may involve local definition of MARC fields as allowed for in the formats, as well as additions to or variations from coding specified in the USMARC communications format. Networks and systems that have system-specific tagging conventions issue formats designed to meet the requirements of their users. As with the MARC formats themselves, network and system tag charts are not cataloging rules, but in illustrating how codes are to be applied, they often provide examples of cataloging practice that catalogers may find useful.

The exact form of system and format documentation varies from network to network and from system to system. Bibliographic networks and local systems may also issue other instruction manuals, such as input standards, input translations for diacritics and special characters, etc. Particular system and network manuals, code books, and tag charts are not cited here.

So long as catalogers have easy access to network and system tag charts, they have limited need to refer to the MARC communications formats themselves. Catalogers who participate in the development of an automation system, however, or in local implementation of such a system, or who are developing cataloging policy that affects manipulation or display of cataloging data sometimes need to be able to verify the intended application of particular elements of content designation. For these purposes, the MARC formats themselves may be needed.

CBB1. *USMARC Concise Formats for Bibliographic, Authority, and Holdings Data*. Washington, D.C.: Cataloging Distribution Services, Library of Congress, 1991. Base text plus updates.

Updates available individually or on standing order. Loose-leaf for easy cumulation of updates into the base text. Includes concise description of all content designators. Update no. 2 (1992) includes classification data.

CBB2. *USMARC Format for Bibliographic Data: Including Guidelines for Content Designation*. Washington, D.C.: Cataloging Distribution Service, Library of Congress, 1988. Base text plus updates through 1992.

Updates available individually or on standing order. Loose-leaf for easy cumulation of updates into the base text. Fields and tags appear in a single sequence, in which applicability for particular types of material is specified. Includes specifications for a National Level Bibliographic Record. The content of the Format is under continual review and revision by an interdivisional Committee of the American Library Association, MARBI (MAchine-Readable Bibliographic Information). Maintenance of the format is the responsibility of the Network Development and MARC Standards Office of the Library of Congress.

A number of special code lists are published separately. All are available from the Library of Congress. These include:

CBB3. *USMARC Code List for Countries*. Washington, D.C.: Library of Congress, 1988.

CBB4. *USMARC Code List for Geographic Areas*. Washington, D.C.: Library of Congress, 1988.

CBB5. *USMARC Code List for Languages*. Washington, D.C.: Library of Congress, 1989.

CBB6. *USMARC Code List for Relators, Sources, Description Conventions*. Washington, D.C.: Library of Congress, 1990.

For annotation, *see* KBB11.

CBC
Application of the Standards as a Whole

GENERAL WORKS ON APPLICATION OF THE STANDARDS FOR DESCRIPTION

CBC1. Gorman, Michael. *The Concise AACR2, 1988 Revision*. Chicago: American Library Association, 1989.

Follows the basic organization of *AACR2R* (CBA1) and adheres to its principles. Condenses *AACR2R*, simplifying expression, eliminating subrules and examples for less frequently encountered situations. Useful to students, infrequent catalogers, noncatalogers, and those who are not subject to strict network requirements for the content of records created.

CBC2. Maxwell, Margaret F. *Handbook for AACR2 1988 Revision: Explaining and Illustrating the Anglo-American Cataloguing Rules*. Chicago: American Library Association, 1989.

An introduction and guide to *AACR2R* (CBA1), containing useful and understandable explanations of and insights into the rules. Especially useful to new catalogers, library school students, and those who train catalogers. A valuable reference for experienced catalogers as well.

CBC3. Millsap, Larry, and Terry Ellen Ferl. *Descriptive Cataloging for the AACR2R and USMARC: A How-to-Do-It Workbook*. New York: Neal-Schuman Publishers, 1991.

Intended for occasional catalogers without easy access to experienced specialists. Organized as a series of "problems," consisting of title pages and other information from which to create a cataloging record, and "answers" in the form of completed records, plus explanation. Covers a variety of physical formats.

CBC4. Piggott, Mary. *The Cataloguer's Way Through AACR2: From Document Receipt to Document Retrieval*. London: Library Association, 1990.

An overview of the philosophy and methodology of *AACR2R* (CBA1) and a basic introduction to *AACR2R* as it relates to names and to certain cataloging challenges such as conference proceedings, analytics, and government publications.

CBC5. Smiraglia, Richard P., ed. *Origins, Content, and Future of AACR2 Revised*. ALCTS Papers on Library Technical Services and Collections, no. 2. Chicago: American Library Association, 1992.

Based on material presented at the Association for Library Collections and Technical Services conference program and regional institutes. Discusses the impetus and mechanism for the 1988 revision (CBA1) of *AACR2* (CBA4), with special emphasis on its content and the changes from the previous version. Also includes papers speculating on the future of the code. Topics are covered by various experts in the field.

CBC6. Swanson, Edward, comp. *Changes to the Anglo-American Cataloguing Rules, Second Edition.* Lake Crystal, Minn.: Soldier Creek Press, 1989.

Identifies and discusses differences between *AACR2* (CBA4) and its 1988 revision (CBA1).

ADJUNCTS TO THE CODE FOR DESCRIPTION

CBC7. Barry, Randall K., comp. *ALA-LC Romanization Tables: Transliteration Schemes for Non-Roman Scripts.* Washington, D.C.: Library of Congress, 1991.

Supersedes all previously published romanization tables. Includes coverage for all languages previously appearing in *Cataloging Service Bulletin* (CAE4), plus some never published in *CSB*.

CBC8. *Library of Congress Romanization Tables.*

For cataloging records created in the United States for inclusion in bibliographic networks, the standards for romanizing headings and other applicable elements are the romanization tables developed by the Library of Congress. These tables are published individually in the *Cataloging Service Bulletin* (CAE4), where they can be located via the various indexes to the *Bulletins*, as well as in cumulated forms.

CBC9. *University of Chicago Press.* The *Chicago Manual of Style.* 14th ed. Chicago: University of Chicago Press, 1993.

The *Anglo-American Cataloguing Rules* specify that the most recent edition of the *Chicago Manual of Style* is to be used to answer questions of style, punctuation, etc., that are not specifically covered by the code.

INTERPRETATIONS OF THE RULES FOR DESCRIPTION

Although the *Anglo-American Cataloguing Rules* may appear to be comprehensive and prescriptive, there are many places within the code where more than one approach to a problem is authorized and many instances where cataloger's judgment—interpretation of such terms as "predominant," "prominent," or "appropriate"—is critical to correct application of a particular rule. In addition, there are certain provisions of the code that one or more of the national libraries that share in the authorship of *Ango-American Cataloguing Rules* have chosen not to follow.

From the time that *AACR2* (CBA4) was first published, the national libraries have issued rule interpretations (RIs) to assist their own catalogers in using the code and to help increase consistency in their cataloging practice. RIs provide valuable guidance in interpretation of rules, clarification of ambiguity, and explanation of cataloging practice of the national libraries. Because major bibliographic networks in the United States define full standard cataloging as having been performed according to *AACR2R* (CBA1) "as interpreted by the Library of Congress," any library that contributes its cataloging to one of these networks needs to have ready access to the Library of Congress rule interpretations (CBC10, CBC11).

The Library of Congress implements its rule interpretations (LCRIs) as soon as it makes them, and libraries contributing to bibliographic networks are expected to implement them as soon as they are published. Currency, therefore, and a commitment to maintaining currency are critical aspects in selecting among sources of rule interpretations. Other factors include physical format and page layout, quality of indexing, method of updating, inclusion of interpretations from more than one national library, inclusion of official rule revisions published between major reprintings of the code, preservation of the history of individual rule revisions, and inclusion of other information such as romanization tables.

CBC10. *Cataloging Service Bulletin.* Washington, D.C.: Library of Congress. no. 1– , Summer 1978– . Quarterly. ISSN 0160-8029.

See also annotation under CAE4. Library of Congress rule interpretations (LCRIs) are published first here. Because *CSB* contains much more than LCRIs and because of the way in which it is printed (a new rule-number sequence in each issue), some catalogers find *CSB* awkward to use as a sole source of rule interpretations, even when used in conjunction with published indexes. Despite the currency and authoritativeness of *CSB*, therefore, catalogers sometimes create their own cumulations or interleave interpretations with *AACR2R* (CBA1) through photocopying. They may also purchase a separately published cumulation.

CBC11. *Library of Congress Rule Interpretations.* 2nd ed. Washington, D.C.: Cataloging Distribution Service, 1990– . Loose-leaf.

The Library of Congress's own cumulation of its rule interpretations. Loose-leaf to allow for easy replacement and addition of pages and incorporation of local decisions and information. Includes the most recent version of all LCRIs originally published in *Cataloging Service Bulletin* (CBC10). Those instructions intended for Library of Congress in-house use only are clearly marked. An update subscription is available.

LCRIs and other information about descriptive cataloging developments and practice, including romanization tables, are published first in the *Cataloging Service Bulletin*. Although the Library of Congress now indexes the content of *CSB*, this was not always the case, and over the years, interested individuals have prepared indexes to these journals, and made them available in various ways. Indexes currently available include:

CBC12. Olson, Nancy B., comp. *Index to the Library of Congress Cataloging Service Bulletin No. 1-120 (June 1945–Winter 1977)*. Lake Crystal, Minn.: Soldier Creek Press, 1977.

Indexes the content of the predecessor to today's *Cataloging Service Bulletin*. Information in the older titles is primarily of historical interest.

CBC13. _____. *Cataloging Service Bulletin Index. Index to Bulletins 1-56 (Summer 1978–Spring 1992)*. Lake Crystal, Minn.: Soldier Creek Press, 1992. Loose-leaf.

Annual cumulative index, available on standing order.

INDEPENDENT CUMULATIONS OF RULE INTERPRETATIONS

CBC14. Howarth, Lynne C., ed. *AACR2 Decisions & Rule Interpretations*. 5th ed. Chicago: American Library Association, 1991.

Consolidates in one two-volume loose-leaf work the official interpretations and application decisions for *AACR2R* that have been promulgated by the Library of Congress, the National Library of Canada, the British Library, or the National Library of Australia. Current to March 1991. "Ownership" of decisions is indicated.

COMPILATIONS OF EXAMPLES

Examples in *AACR2R* (CBA1) are rule specific and partial. They include only those parts of a cataloging record that illustrate the rule under which they appear, and they have no content designation (MARC coding). There are many situations, such as during training, in which catalogers find examples of *complete* catalog records helpful, and a number of manuals of examples have been produced. Such manuals are to be used in conjunction with relevant codes and standards, not as substitutes for them. As always, catalogers must remember that the rule upon which a particular data element in an example was based may have been revised or interpreted since publication of the manual. Most compilations of examples cover selected types of materials, and are included with the special materials manuals in the section following (CBD4 through CBD47). A number of general compilations of examples were published

soon after the publication of *AACR2* (CBA4) and have by now become outdated. Someone wanting a general compilation of examples reflecting *AACR2R* (CBA1) might look first at Studwell and Loerstcher's *Cataloging Books: A Workbook of Examples* (CBD4).

COMPILATIONS OF NOTES

Notes are used to amplify or extend the description of items beyond the data that appear in areas 1–6 on the catalog record (Title through Series). Unlike information contained in areas 1–6, notes are usually less structured, often being composed by the cataloger. The inclusion of many notes is optional. Special challenges in formulating notes include determining what information deserves inclusion and conveying that information succinctly and unambiguously. Although exact wording for notes is generally not prescribed, catalogers often take wording that appears in *AACR2R* (CBA1) or wording that they have seen on Library of Congress cataloging as a guide for note formulation. The evidence of records on bibliographic databases suggests that there is a certain amount of de facto standardization in note construction. Works on notes in the catalog record provide sought-after guidance on appropriate and useful expression.

Although care must be taken to discover if practice reflected in any cataloging tool has been superseded by later revisions in the rules, notes are less likely to change between versions of the code than are other elements of description. Works on notes, therefore, often remain useful for some time, although they may have few if any notes for newer forms of materials. The following works offer notes for all types of materials. Compilations of notes for selected types of materials are included in the sections following for each type of material.

CBC15. Salinger, Florence A., and Eileen Zagon. *Notes for Catalogers: A Sourcebook for Use with AACR2*. White Plains, N.Y.: Knowledge Industry Publications, 1985.

Organized by physical format and according to order of rules. Consists of examples of notes. Prepared under *AACR2* (CBA4).

CBC16. Saye, Jerry D., and Sherry L. Vellucci. *Notes in the Catalog Record: Based on AACR2 and LC Rule Interpretations*. Chicago: American Library Association, 1989.

Prepared under *AACR2R* (CBA1). Organized by type of note. Includes explanation of rules pertaining to notes, statements of Library of Congress policy, and copious examples.

CBD
Application of the Standards for Content Designation

CBD1. Beaumont, Jane. *Make Mine MARC: A Manual of Practice for Libraries.* Westport, Conn.: Meckler, 1992.

Aimed at cataloging staff of small to medium-sized libraries. Explains use of the most commonly used MARC fields, and includes numerous examples.

CBD2. Byrne, Deborah J. *MARC Manual: Understanding and Using MARC Records.* Englewood, Colo.: Libraries Unlimited, 1991.

Covers history and development, structure, and use of MARC bibliographic, authority, and holdings formats, and a field-by-field discussion of commonly used fields. *See also* annotation under KBC1.

CBD3. Crawford, Walt. *MARC for Library Use: Understanding Integrated USMARC.* 2nd ed. Boston: G. K. Hall, 1989.

See also annotation under KBC3. Covers structure of each format. Discusses extensions of USMARC used by the bibliographic utilities.

APPLICATION OF THE STANDARDS TO SPECIAL TYPES OF MATERIALS

The authors of the *Anglo-American Cataloguing Rules* acknowledge that instructions contained in the main code may not provide sufficiently detailed instruction for cataloging all types of materials, especially in libraries where significant concentrations of materials other than books are cataloged. Detailed format- or publication-type–specific instruction is left to manuals of interpretation or specialized cataloging guides. Such manuals of interpretation or guides should not be used independently, but rather must be used in conjunction with the *AACR2R* (CBA1) and any relevant rule interpretations.

Manuals of interpretation, instruction, or examples are created by individuals, associations, or institutions with an interest in cataloging the particular type of material. The manuals may be widely used, but they are not "standards" in the same sense as the *Anglo-American Cataloguing Rules* or the MARC formats upon which they may be based are standards. Because the code and the interpretations are in a constant state of evolution, any supplementary manual or set of examples must be used with caution.

Manuals of application and interpretation for cataloging particular types of materials are listed below. For many of these types of materials there also exist material-type–specific journals, glossaries, thesauri, and headings lists. Only a few such sources are included. Catalogers of such materials should be aware that special aids beyond those listed below may exist.

For convenience, types of materials are arranged in approximately the order in which they are treated in Part I (physical description) of *AACR2R*.

Books

CBD4. Studwell, William E., and David V. Loerstcher. *Cataloging Books: A Workbook of Examples.* Englewood, Colo.: Libraries Unlimited, 1989.

A practice workbook. Examples include reproduction of title page and other relevant information from the work being considered. Answers, plus additional exercises, are available separately in either print or floppy disk form.

Rare Books

CBD5. *Descriptive Cataloging of Rare Books.* 2nd ed. Washington, D.C.: Library of Congress, 1991.

To be used in conjunction with *AACR2R* (CBA1), Chapter 2. Includes rules, interpretations, guidance in cataloging, and coding instructions for USMARC field 040. Replaces *Bibliographic Description of Rare Books: Rules Formulated under AACR2 and ISBD(A) for the Descriptive Cataloging of Rare Books and Other Special Printed Materials.* Washington, D.C.: Library of Congress, 1981.

CBD6. *Printing and Publishing Evidence: Thesauri for Use in Rare Book and Special Collections Cataloguing.* Chicago: ACRL, Standards Committee of Rare Books and Manuscripts Section, 1986.

For annotation, *see* CBD8.

CBD7. *Provenance Evidence: Thesaurus for Use in Rare Book and Special Collections Cataloguing.* Chicago: ACRL, Standards Committee of Rare Books and Manuscripts Section, 1988.

For annotation, *see* CBD8.

CBD8. *Type Evidence: A Thesaurus for Use in Rare Book and Special Collections Cataloguing.* Chicago: ACRL, Standards Committee of Rare Books and Manuscripts Section, 1990.

These three (CBD6–8) are among the several pamphlets the Rare Books and Manuscripts Section of ALA's Association of College and Research Libraries has produced to aid in rare book cataloging.

CBD9. VanWingen, Peter, and Stephen Paul Davis. *Standard Citation Forms for Published Bibliographies and Catalogs Used in Rare Books Cataloging.* Washington, D.C.: Library of Congress, 1982.

Lists recommended citation forms to be used in cataloging rare books. Also serves as a guide to information sources of interest to rare books catalogers.

Cartographic Materials

CBD10. *Cartographic Materials: A Manual of Interpretation for AACR2*, edited by Hugo L. P. Stibbe. Chicago: American Library Association, 1982.

Prepared under *AACR2* (CBA4). Follows organization of Chapter 3, incorporating relevant rules from other chapters. Expands on the content of *AACR2*, including detailed instructions, illustrations, and examples, plus indication of practice at various national libraries. Although outdated by the publication of *AACR2R* (CBA1), some of the discussions remain useful and do not duplicate coverage with the LC *Map Cataloging Manual* (CBD11).

CBD11. *Map Cataloging Manual*. Washington, D.C.: Library of Congress, 1991.

Contains reference to and application of all pertinent rules in *AACR2R* (CBA1), as well as Library of Congress Rule Interpretations. Contains rules and practices used by the LC Geography and Map Division. Includes guidance for special problem types of maps, such as panoramas, and special cataloging issues, such as minimal level cataloging.

Manuscripts (Including Manuscript Collections)

CBD12. **Henson, Steven L.** *Archives, Personal Papers, and Manuscripts: A Cataloging Manual for Archival Repositories, Historical Societies, and Manuscript Libraries*. Washington, D.C.: Library of Congress, 1983.

Prepared under *AACR2* (CBA4). Somewhat dated but still useful because there is no comprehensive manual prepared under *AACR2R* (CBA1).

CBD13. **Smiraglia, Richard P.** *Describing Archival Materials: The Use of the MARC AMC Format*. New York: Haworth Press, 1991. Also published as *Cataloging & Classification Quarterly* 11, nos. 3/4.

A collection of papers by different authors, relating to the general theme of the journal issue. Coverage includes cataloging and content designation of general archival collections, as well as handling of special types of materials such as still images, sound recordings, and cartographic materials in archival collections.

Music and Sound Recordings

CBD14. **Holzberlein, Deanne.** *Cataloging Sound Recordings: A Manual with Examples*. New York: Haworth Press, 1989. Supplement no. 1 to *Cataloging & Classification Quarterly*.

Step-by-step instructions in the application of *AACR2* (CBA4) to sound recordings. Although prepared prior to publication of *AACR2R* (CBA1), the *Manual* takes into account many of the revisions that appeared in *AACR2R*. Examples include copies of title pages, labels, etc.

CBD15. *MOUG Newsletter*. Various places: Music OCLC Users Group. no. 1– , 1977– . Irregular. ISSN 0161-1704.

For annotation, *see* CAE11.

CBD16. *Music Cataloging Bulletin*. Ann Arbor, Mich.: Music Library Association. vol. 1– , 1970– . Monthly. ISSN 0027-4283.

For annotation, *see* CAE12.

CBD17. **Smiraglia, Richard P.** *Music Cataloging: The Bibliographic Control of Printed and Recorded Music in Libraries*. Englewood, Colo.: Libraries Unlimited, 1989.

A textbook. Discusses the various types of music materials, how they are used, and how they are generally collected. Cataloging issues such as description, authority control, and cataloging with copy are covered.

CBD18. **Weitz, Jay.** *Music Coding and Tagging: MARC Content Designation for Scores and Sound Recordings*. Lake Crystal, Minn.: Soldier Creek Press, 1990.

Shows and explains content designation for OCLC, RLIN, and WLN.

Motion Pictures and Videorecordings

CBD19. **Olson, Nancy B.** *Cataloging Motion Pictures and Videorecordings*. Lake Crystal, Minn.: Soldier Creek Press, 1991.

Primarily examples, consisting of title page and other information from actual items, a tagged OCLC record for the item, and the resulting catalog card format record.

CBD20. **White-Henson, Wendy, comp.** *Archival Moving Image Materials: A Cataloging Manual*. Washington, D.C.: Library of Congress, 1984.

Prepared under *AACR2* (CBA4), to be used in conjunction with Chapter 7. Provides cataloging rules and guidance, including examples. Although somewhat dated, no complete substitute based on *AACR2R* (CBA1) is yet available.

Graphic Materials and Photographs

CBD21. **Betz, Elizabeth W., comp.** *Graphic Materials: Rules for Describing Original Items and Historical Collections*. Washington, D.C.: Library of Congress, 1982.

Prepared under *AACR2* (CBA4). Contains rules and guidance for describing graphic materials both as individual items and as collections. Although somewhat dated, no substitute based on *AACR2R* (CBA1) is yet available.

Computer Files

CBD22. **Dodd, Sue A.** *Cataloging Machine-Readable Data Files: An Interpretive Manual*. Chicago: American Library Association, 1982.

An early "classic" for these materials. Discusses nature and special characteristics of computer files, interprets Chapter 9 of *AACR2* (CBA4), and includes detailed examples. Publication of *AACR2R* (CBA1) and rapid developments in the formats and characteristics of computer files have dated much of the information in this work, but much, including the historical perspective, remains useful.

CBD23. Dodd, Sue A., and Ann M. Sandberg-Fox. *Cataloging Microcomputer Files: A Manual of Interpretation for AACR2.* Chicago: American Library Association, 1985.

Prepared under *AACR2* (CBA4). Discusses nature and special characteristics of microcomputer files, and traces development of cataloging rules. Includes detailed instruction and interpretation of *AACR2* for these materials, and a number of step-by-step cataloging examples. Although some content has been outdated by publication of *AACR2R* (CBA1), this remains a useful manual.

CBD24. *Guidelines for Description of Interactive Media.* Chicago: Association of Library Collections and Technical Services, American Library Association, 1993.

Prepared by a task force of the Committee on Cataloging: Description and Access. Interactive media is a rapidly developing material type that has some of the characteristics of computer files, kits, audiovisual materials, etc. The *Guidelines* provide a definition of interactive media and guidance on deciding which materials might be cataloged under its provisions. Specific cataloging instructions are given. The *Guidelines* do not constitute official revisions to *AACR2R* (CBA1). It has been published both to meet the need for direction in cataloging these materials and to provide an opportunity to test the instructions before any formal rule revision proposals are made.

CBD25. Olson, Nancy B. *Cataloging Computer Files.* Lake Crystal, Minn.: Soldier Creek Press, 1992.

Covers a wide variety of materials, including some CD-ROMs and interactive media. Consists primarily of examples, which include reproductions of title pages, frames, boxes, and other relevant information.

Serials, Including Newspapers

CBD26. Butler, Todd. *Newspaper Cataloging and Union Listing Manual.* Washington, D.C.: Library of Congress, 1990.

The official manual for participants in the United States Newspaper Project, a national cooperative project to catalog and inventory holdings of newspapers published in the United States. Covers creation of bibliographic and holdings records according to Project standards, including instructions on use of a master record for all physical manifestations of a title. Essential for Project participants, and highly useful to all newspaper catalogers.

CBD27. *CONSER Editing Guide.* Washington, D.C.: Library of Congress, 1991. Base text plus update service. Loose-leaf.

Cooperative Online Serials is a national cooperative cataloging project in which selected libraries contribute fully authenticated serials cataloging records to OCLC. This is the official guide to content designation for CONSER participants. It includes a field-by-field guide to the USMARC format as applied to serials, plus examples illustrating cataloging and input. Also includes a description of the CONSER project. Essential to CONSER participants. Highly useful to all serials catalogers.

CBD28. Edgar, Neal, ed. *AACR2 and Serials.* New York: Haworth Press, 1983. Also published as *Cataloging & Classification Quarterly*, 3, nos. 2/3.

A collection of papers by different authors, relating to the central theme of the journal issue. Covers historical development of codes from a serials perspective, and serials management. Papers were written with reference to *AACR2* (CBA4), but the work is not a manual and much of the discussion remains useful.

CBD29. Leong, Carol L. H. *Serials Cataloging Handbook: An Illustrative Guide to the Use of AACR2 and LC Rule Interpretations.* Chicago: American Library Association, 1989.

Although this title was prepared under *AACR2* (CBA4), it takes into account most of the rule revisions that were published in the subsequent *AACR2R* (CBA1). Discusses and illustrates application of the code to serials materials, with special emphasis on problem situations. Aimed at catalogers with some experience.

CBD30. Thomas, Nancy G., and Rosanna O'Neil. *Notes for Serials Cataloging.* Littleton, Colo.: Libraries Unlimited, 1986.

Organized by MARC field number. Consists of brief explanations and copious examples.

"In" Analytics

CBD31. Swanson, Edward. *A Manual of AACR2 Examples for "In" Analytics, with MARC Tagging and Coding.* Manuals of the Minnesota AACR2 Trainers. Lake Crystal, Minn.: Soldier Creek Press, 1985.

Prepared under *AACR2* (CBA4). Because no similar manual of examples has been prepared under *AACR2R* (CBA1), it may be useful to retain this title.

Nonbook Materials

CBD32. Frost, Carolyn O. *Media Access and Organization: A Cataloging and Reference Sources Guide for Nonbook Materials.* Englewood, Colo.: Libraries Unlimited, 1989.

Covers all nonbook formats included in *AACR2R* (CBA1). Examples include MARC tagging. Discusses basic trends, issues, reference sources, etc.

CBD33. Intner, Sheila S., and Richard Smiraglia. *Policy and Practice in Bibliographic Control of Nonbook Media.* Chicago: American Library Association, 1987.

Not an instructional manual. Principles, rationale, and standards for bibliographic control and access are covered as part of a more comprehensive consideration of nonbook media.

CBD34. Rogers, JoAnn V., and Jerry D. Saye. *Nonprint Cataloging for Multimedia Collections: A Guide Based on AACR2.* 2nd ed. Littleton, Colo.: Libraries Unlimited, 1987.

Prepared under *AACR2* (CBA4). Formats are defined and illustrations of cataloging are included. Much of the content remains valid, but where coverage of this and the

Urbanski title (CBD35) coincide, prefer to use information from Urbanski.

CBD35. Urbanski, Verna, with Bao Chu Chang and Bernard L. Karon. *Cataloging Unpublished Nonprint Materials: A Manual of Suggestions, Comments, and Examples.* Lake Crystal, Minn.: Soldier Creek Press, 1992.

Examines *AACR2R* (CBA1) rules that pertain specifically to these materials. Where there are no rules specifically geared to them, suggestions are made on how rules for published nonprint materials may be used as guidance.

CBD36. Weihs, Jean, and Shirley Lewis. *Nonbook Materials: The Organization of Integrated Collections.* 3rd ed. Ottawa: Canadian Library Association, 1989.

Presupposes a knowledge of basic cataloging. Covers a wide range of nonbook materials, from art originals through videorecordings, with explanations and examples. Also covers management, policy, and storage issues.

Audiovisual Materials

CBD37. *OLAC Newsletter.* Various places: On-Line Audiovisual Catalogers, v. 5– , Mar. 1985– . Quarterly. ISSN 0739-1153.

For annotation, *see* CAE13.

CBD38. Olson, Nancy B. *Audiovisual Material Glossary.* OCLC Library Information and Computer Science Series, no. 7. Dublin, Ohio: OCLC, 1988.

Defines audiovisual material types and related terms.

CBD39. _____. *A Cataloger's Guide to MARC Coding and Tagging for Audiovisual Material.* Mankato, Minn.: Minnesota Scholarly Press, 1992.

Distributed by Media Marketing Group, De Kalb, Ill. Includes tagged OCLC worksheets for all examples contained in Olson's *Cataloging of Audiovisual Materials.*

CBD40. _____. *Cataloging of Audiovisual Materials*, edited by Sheila S. Intner and Edward Swanson. 3rd ed. Mankato, Minn.: Minnesota Scholarly Press, 1992.

Includes cataloging instruction for most audiovisual formats, including computer files. Includes LC rule interpretations and copious examples.

Special Categories of Materials Not Tied to Physical Format

For physical description, *AACR2R* (CBA1) categorizes materials primarily in terms of physical format. Some types of materials that do not constitute a separate physical category from the point of view of *AACR2R*, however, do present many of the same problems to catalogers, both in terms of physical description and in choice and form of access points. Instructional manuals have been published for several of these material types.

Reproductions (Including Multiple Versions)

CBD41. *Guidelines for Bibliographic Description of Reproductions.* Chicago: Association of Library Collections and Technical Services, 1992.

Prepared by a task force of the Committee on Cataloging: Description and Access, the *Guidelines* represent years of work and international consultation. The concept of "reproduction" is defined, and guidance is given on deciding which materials might be cataloged under the *Guidelines.* Specific instructions on cataloging works that appear in multiple versions are given. The *Guidelines* do not represent official revisions to *AACR2R* (CBA1). They have been published both to meet the need for direction in cataloging these materials and to provide ample opportunity to test the instructions before any formal rule revision proposals are made.

Legal Literature and Loose-Leaf Publications

CBD42. Enyingi, Peter, Melody Busse Lembke, and Rhonda Lawrence Mittan. *Cataloging Legal Literature: A Manual on AACR2 and Library of Congress Subject Headings for Legal Materials, With Illustrations.* 2nd ed. AALL Publication Series, no. 22. Littleton, Colo.: Rothman, 1988– .

Issued in loose-leaf, with updates in the form of replacement pages issued periodically. The most recent update pages were distributed in 1990. A standard manual for cataloging legal materials.

CBD43. Hallam, Adele. *Cataloging Rules for the Description of Looseleaf Publications, With Special Emphasis on Legal Materials.* 2nd ed. Washington, D.C.: Library of Congress, 1989.

Elucidates and expands on *AACR2R* (CBA1), as applied to loose-leaf materials.

Government Documents

CBD44. Documents Cataloging Committee, Government Documents Round Table. *Cataloging Government Documents: A Manual of Interpretation for AACR2.* Chicago: American Library Association, 1984.

Prepared under *AACR2* (CBA4), the work reproduces relevant rules verbatim, and expands or elucidates them in terms of government publications. Although general discussions remain useful, because much of the text is tightly tied to *AACR2*, specific provisions should be applied only after ascertaining that particular rules or practices have not been made obsolete by later revision of the code, the RIs, or the MARC formats.

Liturgical Works

CBD45. Kellen, James D. *A Manual of AACR2 Examples for Liturgical Works and Sacred Scriptures.* 2nd ed. Manuals of the Minnesota AACR2 Trainers. Lake Crystal, Minn.: Soldier Creek Press, 1987.

Provides guidance, through examples, for dealing with some of the special problematic characteristics of these materials. Although the work was prepared under *AACR2*

(CBA4), enough remains valid to justify retaining it until it can be replaced with a more current manual.

Technical Reports

CBD46. Swanson, Edward. *A Manual of AACR2 Examples for Technical Reports.* Manuals of the Minnesota AACR2 Trainers. Lake Crystal, Minn.: Soldier Creek Press, 1984.

This manual provides guidance through examples for dealing with some of the special problematic characteristics of these materials. Although the work was prepared under *AACR2* (CBA4), enough remains valid to justify retaining it until it can be replaced with a more current manual.

Hebraica

CBD47. Maher, Paul. *Hebraica Cataloging.* Washington, D.C.: Library of Congress, 1987.

Includes guidance on cataloging and application of LC Rule Interpretations, plus a detailed and historical guide to romanization, and a list of reference works useful in Hebraica cataloging. Although the work was prepared under *AACR2* (CBA4), there is sufficient content unaffected by the revision of the code to justify retaining it until a more current manual becomes available.

CC
Sources of Information Used in Catalog Records

CCA
Sources of Copy

Perhaps the greatest help in cataloging an item is discovering that someone else has already cataloged it. Although it may be necessary to review previously prepared bibliographic copy for accuracy and to modify it to suit local needs, the savings in both time and money that are derived from cataloging with copy are tremendous. Cataloging records once created do not remain unchanged. Rules and standards for descriptive cataloging are in a state of constant evolution. Cataloging may be modified at any time to correct errors, to reflect additional information found, or to reflect changes in cataloging practice. For these reasons, the currency of cataloging copy found is one factor in determining its usefulness or the ease with which it can be used.

Tools and services described below are those used for handling materials new to a library's collection. They also may be useful in retrospective conversion (creating machine-readable records for materials whose cataloging was previously only in manual form). See Chapter K, Database Management, for a discussion of and resources on retrospective conversion.

CARD IMAGE RESOURCES

Prior to the advent of library automation, most sources that might be used by catalogers looking for cataloging records to copy were produced in "card-image." The cataloging *looked* like catalog cards. In many instances, this cataloging actually consisted of photocopied catalog cards. Many card-image catalogs are still produced and are valuable resources for catalogers seeking copy or researching a variety of cataloging problems. The primary inconveniences of card-image resources are that records are not content designated and, thus, cannot be easily incorporated in a local automation system except through rekeying of data and addition of content designation. In addition, searching card-image resources is more cumbersome than searching in a machine-readable resource. Incorporation of card-image copy into a manual catalog requires rekeying or photocopying.

CCA1. *National Union Catalog (NUC).* New York: Roman and Littlefield, etc., 1963–1982.

Records in catalog card image produced by the Library of Congress and by cooperating libraries across the country. Ownership of individual titles is indicated by institution code. Published over time in a variety of formats and subsets, and encompassing materials of various ages. All constitute rich resources of cataloging copy. All are useful in determining predominant usage and form of names. Cumulations cover 1956–1982.

CCA2. *National Union Catalog, Pre-1956 Imprints.* 754 vol. London: Mansell, 1968–1981.

Includes items published prior to 1956. Often called "Mansell." Many items in Mansell do not appear on any bibliographic database.

CCA3. *New Serial Titles.* Washington, D.C.: Library of Congress, Jan. 1953– . Eight monthly issues, four quarterly issues, and annual cumulations. ISSN 0028-6680.

Available by subscription, with retrospective coverage from 1971. R. R. Bowker published a four-volume cumulation for 1950–1970. Duplicates titles on *CONSER Microfiche* (CCA4).

NATIONAL UNION CATALOGS ON MICROFICHE

The *NUC* (CCA1) is available separately in various sets of data from the Library of Congress on 48× microfiche, consisting of a register and index. Titles added in a single year are cumulated in a register for that year only. Each new year's register is accompanied by indexes to its contents (indexed by name, title, subject, series). Indexes are cumulated periodically.

CCA4. *CONSER Microfiche.* [microform] Ottawa: National Library of Canada; Washington, D.C.: Library of Congress, 1975/78– . ISSN 0707-3747.

Includes all records authenticated by members of the Cooperative Online Serials Program. Duplicates titles on *New Serial Titles* (CCA3). *See also* annotation for *CDMARC Serials* (CCA12).

CCA5. *The Music Catalog.* [microform] Washington, D.C.: Library of Congress, 1991– . Quarterly. ISSN 1055-5536.

Includes only Library of Congress cataloging. First issue is a cumulative for years 1980–1990. Includes scores, sound recordings, books, serials. Continues the paper version, *Music, Books on Music, and Sound Recordings*, published 1973–1989.

CCA6. *National Union Catalog. Audiovisual Materials.* [microform] Washington, D.C.: Library of Congress, 1983– . Quarterly. ISSN 0734-7669.

Coverage from Jan./Mar. 1983, with cumulated index available for 1983–1992. Continues the paper version, variously titled *Audiovisual Materials* (1979–1982), *Films and Other Materials for Projection* (1973–1978), and *Library of Congress Catalog. Motion Pictures and Filmstrips* (1954–1972).

CCA7. *National Union Catalog. Books.* [microform] Washington, D.C.: Library of Congress, 1983– . ISSN 0734-7650.

Coverage from 1983, with cumulated indexes available for 1983–1987 and 1988–1991. Includes records for books, pamphlets, manuscripts, atlases, microform masters, and monographic government publications in all languages (materials in nonroman alphabets or scripts are romanized).

CCA8. *National Union Catalog. Cartographic Materials.* [microform] Washington, D.C.: Library of Congress, 1983– . Quarterly. ISSN 0734-7634.

Coverage from 1983, with cumulated index available for 1983–1992.

CD-ROM CATALOGING COPY RESOURCES

CD-ROM resource databases generally include MARC records that can be copied or downloaded and transferred to a local library automation system at no cost beyond the cost of the subscription. Most CD-ROM resources have their own searching software. CD-ROM cataloging products are in a state of rapid development, with new products constantly added and old ones dropped or modified.

CCA9. *BiblioFile.* [database on CD-ROM] Inwood, W.Va.: The Library Corporation. Updating schedule varies with particular product.

Databases available include: LC MARC records for English language materials; LC MARC records for foreign language materials; AV Access, which includes records for the kinds of AV materials purchased by public libraries; AV Online, the NICEM (National Information Center for Educational Media) database of educational audiovisual materials; records created by academic and research library users of BiblioFile; records created by school and public libraries.

CCA10. *CD-CATSS.* [database on CD-ROM] Toronto: Utlas. Updated quarterly.

Contains MARC records distributed by National Library of Canada, and user contributed records.

CCA11. *CDMARC Bibliographic.* [database on CD-ROM] Washington, D.C.: Library of Congress. Issue 1– , 1991– . Updated quarterly. 6 disks. ISSN 1054-3996.

Includes USMARC-formatted records created by the Library of Congress and National Union Catalog cooperating institutions. Includes books, serials, maps, music, visual materials, and computer files. Retrieval software enables users to search any combination of nineteen indexes using Boolean operators.

CCA12. *CDMARC Serials.* [database on CD-ROM] Washington, D.C.: Library of Congress. 1992– . Updated quarterly. ISSN 1063-8784.

Cumulated listing of over 600,000 (in 1992) serial records—the complete CONSER database. Access is by search and browse (commands) in sixteen indexes. Subscribers are able to retain superseded discs. No extra charge for local area network (LAN) use. Discs include contributions from the U.S. Newspaper Program.

CCA13. *LaserQuest.* [database on CD-ROM] Santa Barbara, Calif.: General Research Corporation. Updated bimonthly.

MARC records including all records distributed by Library of Congress and National Library of Canada, plus records contributed by GRC customers. Includes significant number of records for audiovisual materials.

CCA14. *OCLC Cat CD 450.* [database on CD-ROM] Dublin, Ohio: OCLC Inc. Updated quarterly.

MARC records from the Online Union Catalog. Databases available include: Recent Books (imprints in the past six years), Older Books and Most-Used Nonbooks, Law Cataloging Collection, Medical Cataloging Collection, Music Cataloging Collection, LC Authorities Collection.

CCA15. *Precision One.* [database on CD-ROM] Williamsport, Pa.: Brodart. Current cataloging updated monthly.

Records for materials most often held by school and public libraries. Current cataloging contains records for materials published within the past two years. The Retrospective Conversion disc contains approximately 250,000 records with earlier imprints.

CATALOG COPY BY TAPE SUBSCRIPTION

Most libraries have only indirect access to cataloging copy distributed on magnetic tape. That is, they acquire their copy through a bibliographic network, a materials vendor, or a CD-ROM product that itself consists largely of records derived from tape subscriptions. A few libraries and consortia maintain one or more tape subscriptions of their own for use on their local system. Cataloging copy acquired from tape subscriptions is fully content designated, and records can be easily used in most local automation systems.

CCA16. *LC Cataloging Files on MARC Tape.* [database on magnetic tape] Washington, D.C.: Library of Congress.

Bibliographic records produced by, or distributed through, the Library of Congress and available from Library of Congress MARC Distribution Service on tape reels or cartridges, in USMARC communications format. Various sets and subsets of the data are available, most in two parts: a retrospective file and a subscription service. Tape subscription services offered include the following:

Complete Service	Serials CJK. Forthcoming
Books All	Books Arabic.
Books English	Forthcoming
Books U.S.	Hebrew
Maps	U.S. GPO Cataloging
Music	File
Serials	British National Bibliog-
Visual Materials	raphy Records in
Books CJK	USMARC Format

FOREIGN NATIONAL LIBRARY CATALOGING FILES. Either available currently, or forthcoming, are tape subscription services including cataloging produced by the national cataloging agencies of the United Kingdom, Canada, Australia, New Zealand, Germany, Japan, France, and Russia.

SELECT—NATIONAL PROFILES. Records selected according to purchaser's requirements based on country of publication and/or language. Roman alphabet languages. Records cataloged by the Library of Congress and through NCCP.

CATALOG CARD SERVICES

For some libraries, purchasing catalog cards remains the easiest way to acquire bibliographic copy for items being added to their collections. The Library of Congress began selling catalog cards for the materials it cataloged in 1901. From that time, LC has been the largest supplier of catalog cards in this country, but there are still a number of commercial firms from which libraries can acquire cataloging in card form. Commercial firms may derive most of their cataloging copy from LC MARC tapes, but their service may also include some "value added" features such as Sears subject headings or accompanying labels and circulation slips.

BIBLIOGRAPHIC NETWORKS

"MEMBER" NETWORKS. Perhaps the predominant source of bibliographic copy today is the bibliographic networks (also called bibliographic utilities), such as OCLC, RLIN, Utlas, and WLN. Records available on bibliographic networks generally include those loaded from Library of Congress and other resource tapes plus original records contributed by members. "Member" networks are focused on the creation and use of the database. Database size, available search techniques, ease of record modification, ability to customize records to local needs, and methods of incorporation of copy into local catalogs vary from network to network. Cataloging copy acquired through a bibliographic network is fully content designated, and records can be easily used in most local automation systems.

"VENDOR" NETWORKS. A second type of bibliographic network is beginning to emerge. In this model, vendors of library automation maintain a central resource file of LC MARC records that can be used by commercial subscribers to the service. In some cases, original cataloging created by users of the vendor network also may be maintained on the network. In contrast to a "member" network, the resource database is an adjunct to the automation vendor's other business, even though a customer may contract to use the resource database without using the particular vendor's library automation system. Data Research Associates' DRANET is an example of one such vendor network. *See also* the following section on vendor-supplied cataloging copy.

VENDOR-SUPPLIED CATALOGING COPY

COPY VENDORS. A number of companies offer services to supply specific MARC records on tape or disk. Selection of records for the database, ordering, and delivery mechanisms vary from vendor to vendor. Among commercial vendors currently offering cataloging copy in this way are Marcive and Card Catalog Company. Marcive records may be ordered on disk, through Marcive's own cataloging software, by typed list, through a participating integrated system vendor, or through participating book jobbers. Card Catalog Company specializes in children's book collections for school and public libraries. Records are available in MS-DOS and Macintosh formats.

MATERIALS VENDORS. It is not uncommon for major materials vendors to offer to supply bibliographic copy for materials that may be or have been purchased from them. Selection of records for the database, fullness of copy, and delivery mechanisms vary from vendor to vendor. Among vendors currently offering such an option are Blackwell North America, and Baker and Taylor.

SYSTEM VENDORS. Some library automation vendors maintain a database of bibliographic records for use by users of their automation system. Records may be selected or modified in ways that suit the vendor's primary market. Among vendors currently offering such an option are Follett, for its Alliance Plus system, and Auto Graphics. *See also* the previous section on vendor networks.

CCB
Sources of Headings

Formulation of access points related to the creation or publication of a work is an important part of descriptive cataloging that is covered by *AACR2R* (CBA1) Chapters 21–26. Uniformity of application of these rules is critical to the usability of a catalog or database and to the accessibility of information and materials represented in that catalog or database. As noted previously, application of *AACR2R* is subject to interpretation and to choices for implementation of certain of its provisions. For headings, application of the rules may also be influenced by the particular catalog or database into which the resulting record will be incorporated.

The process of determining the correct form for a given access point and determining any references that may need to be made to that access point is ac-

knowledged to be the most expensive part of the cataloging process. Finding an authoritative form of a heading already in use, therefore, affords significant savings in time, money, and retrievability of information, even though it may be necessary to review headings found in authoritative sources for suitability for local needs. Any resource for bibliographic copy is also a prime resource for headings.

Neither headings nor their authority records necessarily remain unchanged. Rules and standards for descriptive cataloging are in a state of constant evolution. Headings are modified as errors are found or as conflicts arise or to reflect changes in cataloging practice. For these reasons, the currency of a heading resource is an important factor in determining its usefulness, as is the ease with which it can be used.

Headings that appear on bibliographic records may often be used as indications of the authorized form of heading. Local library policies may determine how readily a heading is accepted, depending on factors such as the source of the copy and the age and fullness of the cataloging.

Most bibliographic networks and many consortial databases maintain files of authority records that may be consulted by users of those networks. These files are usually based on the Library of Congress authorities databases. They also may include records contributed by members. Some library or consortial databases also may include records that are created by the particular automation system—if that system automatically creates authority records for headings in bibliographic records not previously represented by an authority record. Smaller databases may include subsets of authority records selected on some inclusion/exclusion mechanism, such as language or date, or based on whether the headings in question are represented in an entry field in the associated bibliographic database. The ability to download, modify, or add records to a local database varies from system to system and depends on such factors as ability to accommodate MARC authority records.

A number of companies will supply authority records to libraries, selecting records based on the library's own bibliographic database. This service often is combined with a database "clean-up," in which the vendor compares the library's bibliographic records to a master authority file and corrects bibliographic records to reflect authority-authorized headings. Some vendors also offer update services in which new cataloging is sent to the vendor in batches and "clean-up" is performed, and relevant authority records are returned along with newly cleaned bibliographic records. The fullness of records supplied varies from vendor to vendor.

Among companies currently offering an authority record service are Blackwell North America and Utlas.

See also Chapter E, Authority Control.

SEPARATELY PUBLISHED HEADING RESOURCES

The most commonly used source of headings for descriptive cataloging is the Library of Congress Name Authority File. Although most catalogers access the file through a bibliographic network or vendor database, it is also available separately as a tape subscription or in the following two forms.

CCB1. Library of Congress, Catalog Publication Division. *CD-MARC Names.* [database on CD-ROM] Washington, D.C.: Catalog Distribution Service, LC. Quarterly, with each issue cumulative. ISSN 1041-2964.

See also annotation under EAC1. Full file of LC MARC format name and uniform title authority records. Includes sophisticated searching and display software.

CCB2. _____. *Name Authorities.* Cumulative Microform Edition. [microform] Washington, D.C.: Cataloging Distribution Service, LC. 1979– . Quarterly, with each issue cumulative. ISSN 0195-9093.

See also annotation under EAC3. Cumulative microform edition of all name authority records in the computerized master file at LC. 48 × microform of full file of LC MARC format name and uniform title authority records. Cumulations for 1977–1986, 1987–1991, plus current subscription.

HEADING SOURCES FOR SPECIAL CATEGORIES OF MATERIALS

There are numerous sources of headings that have been compiled for various special types of materials. The following two titles are intended only to be indicative of the sorts of sources that may be available.

CCB3. International Federation of Library Associations, Working Group on Uniform Headings for Liturgical Works. *List of Uniform Titles for Liturgical Works of the Latin Rites of the Catholic Church.* London: The Working Group, 1975.

Recommended by The Working Group. Any such list may become outdated by revisions in the cataloging rules but may, nevertheless, be useful in helping catalogers identify the works in question and begin to formulate appropriate headings.

CCB4. Weidow, Judy. *The Music OCLC Users Group Presents the Best of MOUG.* 4th ed., rev. and expanded. Austin, Tex.: MOUG, 1991.

Contains Library of Congress name authority file headings for prominent composers.

General Reference Materials

Reference sources cited so far have pertained largely to the standards that govern the content of descriptive cataloging records or to organizational or policy issues that surround descriptive cataloging. Not all questions that a cataloger may need to answer, however, have to do with rules or standards, or even with cataloging policies or practices. In order to formulate headings, for example, or to determine responsibility for a work or its relationship to other works, catalogers must often learn something about a particular person, body, or work. Preparation of an appropriate description or correct tagging of a bibliographic record often depends on whether a cataloger understands a particular word or is familiar with the characteristics of a particular type of material. To obtain this information, catalogers frequently need to refer to general (i.e., non–librarianship-specific) reference tools. Some of these tools are referred to often enough and are affordable enough that they belong in the catalogers' reference collection. For others, having them in the library's general collections may be sufficient.

The following sections contain general indications of the types of materials that may be useful to catalogers. Some specific sources are cited, but they should not be regarded as the only sources that might be useful.

Topical Glossaries and Dictionaries

The Glossary in the *Anglo-American Cataloguing Rules* second edition, 1988 revision (CBA1) contains only terms that cannot be found in more general glossaries or dictionaries or those whose meanings for the purposes of cataloging differ from the meanings that might be found in a more general reference source. Glossaries in format-specific manuals of interpretation have similar criteria for inclusion. Because an accurate or context-specific understanding of particular terms is sometimes essential to understanding the materials being cataloged and to applying descriptive cataloging rules correctly, catalogers must often refer to subject-specific glossaries or dictionaries. The collecting patterns of a particular library will influence what sorts of subject dictionaries and glossaries may be of greatest use. Some glossaries of librarianship and publishing are cited below.

CCB5. Allen, C. G. *A Manual of European Languages for Librarians.* London: Bowker, 1975.

Not a dictionary per se. Organized by language group. Discusses general language characteristics such as inflection, word order, articles, plurals, etc., as well as matters of special interest to librarians, such as names, titles, imprints, volume numbering. Can assist catalogers not familiar with a particular language to interpret data present on the item being cataloged and to use a dictionary of the language effectively for translation.

CCB6. Orne, Jerrold. *The Language of the Foreign Book Trade: Abbreviations, Terms, Phrases.* 2nd ed. Chicago: American Library Association, 1962.

Not a dictionary per se. Covers eleven European languages, including Russian. Organized by language. Entries consist of synonyms, e.g. (under Dano-Norwegian), "under trykken: in press."

CCB7. Room, Adrian. *Dictionary of Translated Names and Titles.* London: Routledge & Kegan Paul, 1986.

Includes English, French, German, Spanish, Italian, and Russian equivalents for major geographic and personal names, historical events, and international bodies, as well as for major literary and musical works. Cross-indexed for all languages included.

CCB8. Young, Heartsill, ed. *The ALA Glossary of Library and Information Science.* Chicago: American Library Association, 1983.

A general glossary of terms relevant to libraries, librarianship, and publishing. The *ALA Glossary* is a good "first stop" for such terms. As a new edition is being planned, this one is becoming somewhat outdated for terms relating to new and evolving types of library materials and to automation.

FOREIGN LANGUAGE DICTIONARIES. Correct and effective cataloging requires an understanding of the information appearing on items being cataloged. Because catalogers often have to catalog materials published in languages in which they are not knowledgeable, bilingual or multilingual dictionaries covering the languages most commonly handled are a necessary part of a cataloging reference collection.

Gazetteers and Atlases

Determination of geographic locations, jurisdictional units, and commonly used forms of place names is a commonplace need in description and heading formulation. No cataloger should be without easy access to recent gazetteers and atlases, including an atlas of the United States, an atlas of the world, and a historical atlas. Because atlases are often quite expensive, catalogers may need to rely primarily on atlases in the general reference collection and keep mainly smaller atlases, or previous editions that have been weeded from the general reference collection, in the catalogers' reference collec-

tion. Paper-bound road atlases of the United States (or the United States and Canada) are frequently published by various map publishers, automobile clubs, gasoline companies, etc. While not so detailed as other atlases, they are more affordable. Some commonly used atlases and gazetteers are listed below. Because of changes in governments, etc., atlases and gazetteers should be replaced as frequently as economically feasible.

The United States Board on Geographic Names (BGN) is the U.S. government agency responsible for determining the official name, nature, and location of geographic places worldwide. BGN publishes gazetteers for individual countries and Antarctica, with new editions published as needed. More recent gazetteers are on microfiche. Entries consist of name, nature (e.g., PPL = populated place), latitude, longitude, and various locator codes. BGN is the source that the Library of Congress uses in establishing place names.

The resources cited here are representative of these important tools.

CCB9. *Cambridge World Gazetteer.* Cambridge, Eng.: Cambridge University Press, 1990.

CCB10. *Goode's World Atlas,* edited by Edward B. Espenshade. 18th ed. Chicago: Rand McNally, 1990. World coverage.

Indexed for cities, jurisdictions, and physical features.

CCB11. *Rand McNally Commercial Atlas and Marketing Guide.* New York: Rand McNally, 1876– . Annual.

Detailed maps and indexes of the United States.

CCB12. *Times Atlas of World History,* edited by Geoffrey Barrachough. Rev. ed. Maplewood, N.J.: Hammond, 1984.

Useful in tracing the history or determining status of cities, countries, former cities, etc.

CCB13. *Webster's New Geographical Dictionary.* Springfield, Mass.: Merriam-Webster, 1984.

Government Handbooks and Handbooks of International Organizations

Headings for governmental agencies and international organizations are among the most difficult to establish. Intellectual responsibility for government and organization-published documents is among the most difficult to assess. Government and organizational handbooks are invaluable in helping a cataloger to determine the official name, organizational structure, and history of these agencies, both to formulate the proper heading and to decide an agency's degree of responsibility for a work. The handbooks most needed will depend on the materials collected in a given library. In addition to the handbooks cited below, catalogers may also need to consult handbooks of state and foreign governments.

CCB14. *United States Government Manual*. Washington, D.C.: U.S. Office of the Federal Register. 1973/74– . Annual. ISSN 0092-1904.

Describes individual government agencies, covering their role and organization, as well as current officeholders and phone numbers. Includes organization charts. A valuable resource for current agencies.

CCB15. *Yearbook of International Organizations*. Brussels: Union of International Associations; New York: Saur. 1966/67– . Annual. ISSN 0084-3814.

Gives brief history, structure, membership, etc., of international organizations, from professional to commercial to intergovernmental, including organizations formed specifically to oversee treaties.

Biographical Dictionaries

Establishing the identity of persons, determining their correct and full names, etc., are essential to the process of formulating headings and providing references to persons. Catalogers need to have ready access to a current general biographical dictionary and may also often need biographical dictionaries covering nationalities, subjects, professions, and so on. The following is a general resource.

CCB16. *Webster's New Biographical Dictionary*. Springfield, Mass.: Merriam-Webster, 1988.

Other Tools

Many other tools provide useful information. The following is one example.

CCB17. *Publisher's International ISBN Directory*. 19th ed. New York: Saur, 1992.

Includes alphabetical and geographical index to publishers and numerical index to ISBNs (International Standard Book Numbers) assigned to publishers. Useful in verifying ISBNs and publishers.

D

Subject Analysis Systems

Nancy J. Williamson

Overview

In the most comprehensive sense, the literature of subject analysis encompasses any resources that aid in the analysis, representation, and retrieval of recorded information *about* persons, places, events, and topical subjects. More specifically, it includes all of the literature that supports the three basic processes of information handling—the content analysis of documents and information, the categorization and representation of that content, and the access and retrieval of documents and information from both manual and automated systems. The literature forms part of both library science and information science and is growing rapidly.

To deal with all three aspects of this topic in a single chapter would be a very difficult task. Moreover, to do so would be to risk superficial coverage of the field with possible omission of important and useful items. Therefore, the coverage of this topic has been limited to the literature related to "subject analysis systems," that is, the systems that are used to analyze and represent documents by their subjects. No attempt has been made to include the vast literature of "subject access" to these systems.

As defined here, subject analysis systems are of two types: alphabetical systems (e.g., subject headings, most thesauri, and PRECIS, the Preserved

Context Indexing System) and systematic or classificatory systems (e.g., Library of Congress Classification, Dewey Decimal Classification, and some thesauri). *See also* Chapter F, Filing and Indexing, for further treatment of thesauri and PRECIS. Both types of systems—alphabetical and systematic—are used to analyze and categorize recorded information according to its subject(s). These two types of systems supplement and complement each other and together provide for different kinds of access to document collections and information.

Chapter Content and Organization

Several criteria were followed in selecting the contents of this chapter. Coverage includes both printed and machine-readable sources, and the majority of items have been published during the last five years. However, it was important to not rule out important resources published earlier and essential to pursue a well-rounded coverage of the subject; indeed, the items selected also include several important manuals and standards still in process at this writing but expected to be published in the near future.

Inclusions focus primarily on subject analysis systems needed for effective subject cataloging in academic, public, and special libraries in North

America. For the most part, the intended audience includes subject catalogers, students, and library and information science educators. Some publications will also be of interest to systems librarians and technical services administrators. The majority of the publications emanate from the United States. A limited number of Canadian resources have been included because, in some cases, they have been designed to be used along with the American publications and/or they may have special use in American libraries. Moreover, it seemed important to include materials that could have some bearing on future developments in the evolution of subject analysis systems on the North American library and information science scene. For example, few, if any, libraries and information agencies on this continent are using faceted classification systems, although the principles of faceting are becoming increasingly important in thesaurus construction, knowledge-based systems, and hypermedia. Hence, the works included take this trend into consideration.

With respect to the types of publications included, priority has been given to the tools used in the process of analysis and representation of documents, that is, the classification schemes, subject heading lists, and thesauri together with the textbooks and manuals that support them and that aid subject catalogers in interpreting and applying them. Some works dealing with the history of the various systems have been included as background, as well as a selection of reports and articles on research into ways and means of improving subject analysis systems.

The contents of this chapter are divided into four categories: general works; management and organization in subject analysis; classification systems; and subject headings, thesauri, and related systems. The general works section includes general textbooks of an introductory nature that are suitable for students and beginners. Most of these tend to combine descriptive cataloging with subject cataloging and, therefore, are also appropriate to the chapter on cataloging. However, they are included here because of their importance to subject analysis. Some major bibliographical sources have been included to aid subject catalogers and others in quick and effective access to the vast amount of literature being published in this field. Several major periodicals support this subject area, and a number of national and international organizations have mandates to deal with subject analysis problems, develop guidelines and standards, and inform their members of innovative developments in the field. Together these organizations represent a nucleus of experts who can be called upon to aid in solving problems and developing subject analysis systems.

The section on management and organization in subject analysis is small. Management includes subject authority control, which is covered at the end of the chapter in a separate section under subject headings, thesauri, and related systems. Also because of economic constraints, very little redevelopment is taking place except in the implementation of online catalogs. There have been some recent reclassification activities in conjunction with catalog conversion projects and a few cases of reclassification as a result of the publication of the latest edition of the *Dewey Decimal Classification* (DC11).

The third section on classification systems is primarily devoted to the two major classification systems used in North America, the Dewey Decimal (DDC) and Library of Congress (LCC) classification systems. Here an atttempt has been made to be as complete as possible with respect to schedules, guides, and manuals. A selection of the most useful textbooks for beginners has been included. As a result of the recent publication of *DDC 20* (DC11), the workbooks and manuals on this system are particularly numerous. Another major classification system, used widely outside North America, is the Universal Decimal Classification (UDC). The most recent English edition (DC28) and a forthcoming guide to the use of UDC (DC29) have been included here because recent developments are bringing about administrative and editorial changes that could have a significant impact on the future of this system and its use. After some thought, it was decided not to include Ranganathan's Colon Classification in this bibliography. However, it was considered important to recognize the Indian librarian's unique contribution to the development of modern information retrieval systems. Therefore, the second edition of the *Bliss Bibliographic Classification* (DC30) has been included together with two articles on faceted classification and its application in the contemporary setting. In the subsection on design and development of classification systems, the only item (DC6) is a brief description of the process of developing a faceted classification.

Not surprisingly, there is very little activity in the construction of new classification systems, particularly in North America, although some such projects were located in articles from Japan, Germany, and countries in Eastern Europe. In contrast, there is a great deal of activity taking place in research and application of expert systems to classification.

The final section of the bibliography deals with five distinct areas: subject headings, subject authority control, thesauri, PRECIS, and expert systems applications. Subject headings dominate the section, partly because *Library of Congress Subject Head-*

ings (LCSH) are available in several formats and numerous manuals and indexes are required to support their application. *Medical Subject Headings* (MeSH) has been included as a major list in a special subject area. A number of other lists supplement and complement LCSH.

Subject authority control is an important process that supports the analysis and representation process and is considered appropriate to this chapter, as are the MARC (MAchine Readable Cataloging) formats for subject authorities and classification and forthcoming international guidelines for subject authority and reference entries. *See also* Chapter E for in-depth treatment of authority control.

With the increasing development and use of online systems, thesauri become more and more important as the basis for representation of topics in catalogs and bibliographies. Coverage has been given to the various standards, guides, and directories. Many thesauri exist in a wide range of disciplines and subject areas, and it would be impossible to include even all of the most useful lists here. Instead, three thesauri that should be of interest to the users of this guide have been included. A selection of the best manuals on thesaurus construction has also been given. PRECIS is represented here as an alternative to LCSH. Some expert systems applications have been included.

As was noted earlier, the literature of subject analysis is vast. Certainly, not everything that would aid practicing subject catalogers, students, library and information science educators, researchers, and other interested professionals can be covered here. However, the author hopes this is a reasonable start on a useful list of subject analysis systems resources.

DA
General Works

DAA
Textbooks, Guides, and Manuals

DAA1. Chan, Lois Mai. *Cataloging and Classification: An Introduction.* New York: McGraw-Hill, 1981.

See also annotation under CAA2. One of the best basic textbooks on all aspects of descriptive and subject cataloging. Part 3 on subject cataloging covers the basics of *Library of Congress Subject Headings* (DD15), *Sears List of Sub-*

ject Headings (DD24), and *PRECIS* (DD45). Part 4 includes general principles of classification, the Dewey Decimal Classification, the Library of Congress classification, and brief introductions to five other general classification systems, including the Universal Decimal Classification, the Colon Classification, and the Bibliographic Classification of Henry Bliss. An important introductory text for students and beginning subject catalogers. Though publication was more than ten years ago, the basic content is still sound and the author is presently working on a new edition.

DAA2. Chan, Lois Mai, Phyllis A. Richmond, and Elaine Svenonius, eds. *Theory of Subject Analysis: A Sourcebook.* Littleton, Colo.: Libraries Unlimited, 1985.

See also annotation under FAD6. A selection of the major contributions throughout the history of subject analysis principles and theory, by three experts in the field. Assembles writings that are "classics" and considered by the editors to "contain the thoughts and ideas that best illustrate the course which subject analysis has taken over the years and that shed light on future directions." Brings together sources that might not otherwise be readily available and charts the development of the most significant ideas in the field. Writings have been chosen for their theoretical emphasis rather than for practical and technical considerations, for their significance and impact on the field, and for their comprehensibility and clarity of style. The contributions range from Charles Amni Cutter's nineteenth-century principles of "Subjects" (FAB5) to Derek Austin's PRECIS system (DD45) and are arranged in chronological order to reflect the development of the field.

DAA3. Coates, E. J. *Subject Catalogues: Headings and Structure.* Reissued with a new preface. London: Library Association, 1988.

Originally published in 1960, this theoretical analysis of subject catalogs was considered important enough to be reissued in 1988 with a preface relating this work to computerization. Looks at developments in subject cataloging principles and the nature of catalogs since Cutter's work. Emphasizes term relationships in compound headings, chain indexing, and the contribution of classification to subject cataloging. Builds on and develops the principles first set out by Ranganathan and describes contributions to subject cataloging between Cutter and the advent of PRECIS. Could be described as a companion volume to Francis Miksa's *The Subject in the Dictionary Catalog from Cutter to the Present* (DD1). Most useful to advanced students and to subject catalogers with an interest in the background and development of subject analysis systems.

DAA4. Dym, Elinor D, ed. *Subject and Information Analysis.* New York and Basel: Marcel Dekker, 1985.

See also annotation under FAD9. A collection of articles on various aspects of subject analysis selected from the *Encyclopedia of Library and Information Science.* Includes groups of articles on topics such as natural language text processing, indexing, terminology control, classification, and abstracting. Useful background reading in a range of areas. Most useful for students in courses in subject analysis.

DAA5. Foskett, Anthony Charles. *The Subject Approach to Information.* 4th ed. London: Clive Bingley, 1982.

See also annotation under FAD10. Broad overview of subject access to information retrieval systems. A classic in the field. Includes a general description of the theory of information retrieval systems; provides useful background on both precoordinate and postcoordinate indexing languages. The major classification and subject heading systems are described, and a chapter on the evaluation of information retrieval systems is included. A basic source for further investigation of the subject. Has good bibliographies and will be most useful to students.

DAA6. Langridge, D. W. *Subject Analysis: Principles and Procedures.* London and New York: Bowker-Saur, 1989.

Describes principles and the process for analyzing documents to determine their subject content in preparation for the assigning of classification numbers, subject headings, or thesaurus descriptors to represent them in catalogs and other information systems. Emphasizes the nature of knowledge and documents and the theoretical and practical aspects of determining document content. Includes examples of analysis and provides an index to the authors and titles of books analyzed. One of very few sources on the "analysis" of document content. Useful for students and beginning subject catalogers.

DAA7. Taylor, Arlene G., ed. *Introduction to Cataloging and Classification.* 8th ed. Library Science Text Series. Englewood, Colo.: Libraries Unlimited, 1992.

See also annotation under CAA8. A useful basic text. Part III, Subject Analysis, includes sections on the principles of classification and verbal subject analysis, general and technical descriptions of the Dewey Decimal and Library of Congress classifications, and Library of Congress and Sears subject headings. Also describes the creation of complete call numbers. Introductory material on other classification systems, such as the *Bliss Bibliographic Classification* (DC30), and other types of verbal subject analysis such as PRECIS. A brief introduction to automatic and machine-aided indexing also included. Generous examples support the text, and suggestions for further reading are provided. An alternative to Lois Chan's *Cataloging and Classification: An Introduction* (DAA1).

DAB
Bibliographies and Catalogs

DAB1. *Annual Review of Information Science and Technology.* Medford, N.J.: Published on behalf of the American Society for Information Science by Learned Information. v. 1– , 1966– . Annual. ISSN 0066-4200.

Substantial bibliographic essays on the topic provide excellent overviews of current issues. The review articles relate to a variety of issues in library and information science and technology. From its inception has contained articles dealing with content analysis, including some aspects of classification and indexing languages in general. Articles on "subject analysis" in its broad sense have been published in volumes 9 (1974), 12 (1977), 17 (1982), 21 (1986), and 24 (1989). Supplements and complements the "Year's Work" articles (DAB3) in *Library Resources & Technical Services* (AF13). More information science–oriented than *LRTS*.

DAB2. University of Toronto, Faculty of Library and Information Science Library, Subject Analysis Systems Collection.

The major North American collection of classification systems, thesauri, and subject heading lists and the primary world collection in the English language. Also contains French-Canadian and some French resources. The collection is a practical resource for library and information science professionals who are designing, or applying, subject analysis systems in specialized subject areas. Also a research resource for students and researchers.

This collection was established in 1924 by the Special Libraries Association and was later administered by the Bibliographic Systems Center and School of Library Science, Case Western Reserve University, until 1976 when it was moved to the University of Toronto. Contains approximately 2,500 items and is growing rapidly. The Faculty's library provides a search and interlibrary loan service. Inquiries and requests should be addressed to: Subject Analysis Systems; Faculty of Library and Information Science Library, University of Toronto, 140 St. George Street, Room 404, Toronto, Canada, M5S 1A1. Tel.: (416) 978-7060; fax: (416) 978-5762. Individual titles may also be searched in the UTCat database, which is part of UTLink (the University of Toronto Libraries Information System), which in turn may be accessed through the INTERNET.

DAB3. "Year's Work in Subject Analysis." *Library Resources & Technical Services.* Chicago: Association for Library Collections and Technical Services, American Library Association.

A series of review articles, usually in bibliographic essay form, that have appeared annually since 1958 in issues of *Library Resources & Technical Services* (AF13). The titles of the articles vary. Between 1958 and 1978 the material on subject analysis was combined with descriptive cataloging under the title "Year's Work in Cataloging and Classification." Beginning with the "Year's Work" for 1979, published in 1980, subject analysis was separated from descriptive cataloging and published under the title "Year's Work in Subject Analysis." This latter title also varies slightly over the years.

The coverage is relatively complete for the output of a given year, and the content and organization of the articles vary depending on the nature of the publishing output for a particular year. The emphasis is on library practice and library science research including subject cataloging, indexing, thesaurus construction, and subject analysis tools, as well as the nature and characteristics of users and subject searching in catalogs and databases. These articles are objective in nature and provide an excellent comprehensive survey of the vast annual output on this aspect of technical services for technical services librarians, library educators, and students. Also, they supplement and complement review articles that appear infrequently in the *Annual Review of Information Science and Technology* (DAB1), but the coverage is not mutually exclusive.

DAC
Periodicals

DAC1. *Cataloging & Classification Quarterly*. New York: Haworth Press. v. 1– , Fall 1980– . Quarterly. ISSN 0163-9374.

See also annotation under CAE3. Classification, subject headings, authority control, and online catalogs are among the topics covered.

DAC2. *Cataloging Service Bulletin*. Washington, D.C.: Library of Congress. no. 1– , Summer 1978– . Quarterly. ISSN 0160-8029.

See also annotation under CAE4. Announces changes in policies and procedures at the Library of Congress with respect to descriptive cataloging and subject cataloging, including the LC classification. Some subject cataloging topics appear on a regular basis. For example, most issues include lists of "Subject Headings of Current Interest," "Revised LC Subject Headings," and "Subject Headings Replaced by Name Headings." An essential tool for subject catalogers in North American libraries.

DAC3. *International Classification*. Frankfurt am Main, Ger.: International Society for Knowledge Organization. v. 1– , 1974– . Quarterly. ISSN 0340-0050.

Broader in coverage than its name suggests, this journal is devoted to "concept theory, systematic terminology and organization of knowledge." Its invited papers cover a broad range of topics including classification, thesauri, knowledge-based systems, and standards for subject analysis systems. Theoretical in its approach, but documents practical research projects and conference papers. Also contains news items on conferences and the activities of various organizations in the field, including committees and sections of American Library Association, American Society for Information Science (ASIS), International Federation for Information and Documentation (FID), and International Federation of Library Associations and Institutions (IFLA). International bibliographic coverage of subject analysis literature. Important source for students, library and information science professionals, and researchers. Title change to *Knowledge Organization* scheduled for 1993.

DAC4. *Library Resources & Technical Services*. Chicago: Association for Library Collections and Technical Services. v. 1– , 1957– . Quarterly. ISSN 0024-2527.

For annotation, *see* AF13.

DAC5. *Technicalities*. Lincoln, Nebr.: Media Periodicals, a division of Westport Publishers. v. 1– , Dec. 1980– . Monthly. ISSN 0272-0884.

See also annotation under AF23. A resource that endeavors to present innovative and challenging ideas as alternatives to traditional methods and tools. Contains frequent articles on subject analysis issues, such as the need for a subject cataloging code and nature and application of Library of Congress subject headings.

DAD
Sources of Expertise

DAD1. American Society for Information Science (ASIS). Headquarters: 8720 Georgia Avenue, Suite 501, Silver Spring, MD 20910. Executive Director: Richard B. Hill.

See also annotation under AGA1. Within ASIS, the *Special Interest Group on Classification Research* (SIG/CR) is of particular interest. SIG/CR is the ASIS counterpart of the ALA Subject Analysis Committee. Its mandate is to study fundamental principles, processes, and analytical constructs of bibliographic and information systems. Its concerns include organizing information, indexing, thesaurus construction, and the development and application of indexing languages and classification systems. It publishes a newsletter (*SIG/CR News*) and offers programs and workshops at the ASIS conferences.

DAD2. ALA Association for Library Collections and Technical Services (ALCTS). Executive Director: Karen Muller.

For annotation, *see* AGA3.

DAD3. ALA ALCTS Cataloging and Classification Section (CCS).

See also annotation under CAF2. Within CCS, the Subject Analysis Committee (SAC) is of particular interest.

This is the major national organization in the United States with a mandate "to study problems and recommend improvements in patterns, methods, and tools for subject analysis and the organization of library materials, including particularly classification and subject headings systems." SAC acts as a forum for discussion of issues concerning subject cataloging and provides liaison with other groups and organizations with similar concerns, including the Library of Congress and Decimal Classification Division of LC. It establishes ad-hoc subcommittees to study specific issues related to special subjects and special materials, and it prepares and reviews standards.

DAD4. INFOTERM (International Information Centre for Terminology). Headquarters: Österreichisches Normungsinstitut (ON) Postfach 130, A-1021 Vienna, Austria. Director: Christian Galinski.

Established in 1971, INFOTERM is sponsored by UNESCO within the framework of UNISIST (United Nations Intergovernmental Programme for Co-operation in the Field of Scientific and Technical Information) and works in liaison with the Technical Committee 37 "Terminology (principles and coordination)" of the International Organization for Standardization (ISO). It has a major role in the development of standards related to terminology and has a particular interest in thesauri, thesaurus construction, and standards.

DAD5. International Federation for Information and Documentation (FID). Headquarters: POB 90402, 2509LK, The Hague, The Netherlands. Executive Director: Ben G. Goedegebuure.

Within FID, the following committee is of interest: Committee on Classification Research (FID/CR). FID/CR is interested in both the theoretical and practical aspects of the organization of knowledge. It has two primary mandates: support for, and participation in, the ongoing development and revision of the Universal Decimal Classification (UDC) and the support and fostering of research in the broader context of the organization of knowledge. Its newsletter, *FID/CR News*, is published in *International Classification* and in *FID News Bulletin*.

DAD6. International Federation of Library Associations and Institutions (IFLA). Headquarters: POB 95312, 2509CH, The Hague, The Netherlands. Secretary General: Paul Nauta.

See also annotation under AGA4. Within IFLA, the following is of interest: Division of Bibliographic Control, Section on Classification and Indexing.

An organization with interests in classification and indexing at the international level. Oriented primarily to library and information science, it encourages research and establishes working groups on standards and other issues of concern on various aspects of subject cataloging. It is involved in the development of "Guidelines for Subject Authority and Reference Entries" and in the development of "Subject Heading Principles." The Standing Committee of the Section presents programs and workshops at annual conferences of IFLA and endeavors to foster cooperation and exchange of information with respect to subject cataloging systems worldwide. It publishes a brief newsletter.

DB
Management and Organization in Subject Analysis

DB1. Beatty, Sue. "DDC to LCC in Eight Weeks." *Cataloguing Australia* 13 (Sept. 1987): 92–100.

Description of a project to convert the collection of the Australian Defence Force Academy Library from the Dewey Decimal Classification to the Library of Congress Classification, December 1985 to February 1986. Sixty-six percent of the LCC numbers were obtained via a retrospective conversion project and the remainder of the class numbers were assigned by a team of casuals. Reasons for and effects of the changeover are discussed.

DB2. Berman, Sanford. "To *Change* Headings: Documentation." *Technical Services Quarterly* 2 (Fall/Winter 1984): 155–65.

Contribution to a special theme issue of *Technical Services Quarterly* devoted to critiques and innovations in subject cataloging. Documents how and why the Hennepin County Library dealt with changes to a series of conventional headings through discussions among subject catalogers and nonlibrarians, such as editors, in order to provide more appropriate headings for the catalog.

DB3. Dean, Barbara C. "Reclassification in an Automated Environment." *Cataloging & Classification Quarterly* 5 (Winter 1984): 1–11.

Compares the procedures needed for reclassifying in a manual environment with those required when the library has an in-house computer system. Describes how computer assistance makes a reclassification project more feasible than it would be in a completely manual library. Also considers the relationship between reclassification and catalog-conversion projects. Of interest to technical services administrators and subject catalogers who are planning to embark on such projects.

DB4. Massonneau, Suzanne. "Reclassification and Barcoding: A Unique Opportunity." *Collection Management* 13, nos. 1/2 (1990): 15–37.

Describes the experience of the University of Vermont Library in carrying out a two-year computer-based reclassification of its collections from the Dewey Decimal Classification to the Library of Congress Classification. Covers planning, costs, personnel, work flow, and procedures as well as an integration of bar coding with the reclassification process. Of interest to library and information science professionals who are embarking on reclassification projects.

DB5. Schroeder, Carolyn D. "Digital Warrant: Revised DDC 004-006 in a Public Library." *Library Resources & Technical Services* 32 (Oct. 1988): 367–77.

Describes the application of the Dewey Decimal Classification phoenix schedules for data processing, computer science, and computer engineering to a selection of materials previously classified according to older schedules in a Boston public library. Useful to subject catalogers who are considering reclassification to update their collections to the latest DDC schedules.

DC
Classification Systems

GENERAL WORKS

DC1. *Classification Theory in the Computer Age: Conversations Across Disciplines*. Produced by the School of Science and Policy and the Professional Development Program. Albany, N.Y.: Nelson A. Rockefeller College of Public Affairs and Policy, University of Albany, State University of New York, 1989.

The proceedings of a conference held in Albany, New York, November 18–19, 1988. While the title of this publication suggests ''theory,'' it contains papers that will be of interest to practicing subject catalogers on such topics as the future of DDC, subject headings and searching online, and Library of Congress Classification, as well as a section on the implications of the computer age for classification theory and practice.

DC2. Humphrey, Susanne M., and Barbara H. Kwasnik, eds. *Advances in Classification Research: Proceedings of the 1st ASIS SIG/CR Classification Research Workshop*. Medford, N.J.: Learned Information for the American Society for Information Science, 1991.

Contains papers on projects, proposals, systems, and other work recently undertaken in classification research. Topics include faceted indexing and the use of faceted classification in thesauri, classification of images, possibilities for linking classification and subject headings in online catalogs, and frame-based systems. A useful update on recent research in the field of classification and its application in online systems.

DC3. Nitecki, Andre, and Tony Fell, eds. *International Conference on Library Classification and Its Functions, Edmonton, Alberta, June 20-21, 1989*. [Edmonton]: Faculty of Extension, University of Alberta, 1989.

Includes papers on the bibliothecal, bibliographical, and cognitive functions of classification and addresses major theoretical and practical issues in the development and use of classification systems in general and a comparison of the major classification systems.

STANDARDS

DC4. Guenther, Rebecca S. ''The USMARC Format for Classification Data: Development and Implementation.'' In *Classification Research for Knowledge Representation and Organization: Proceedings of the 5th International Study Conference on Classification Research, Toronto, Canada, June 24–28, 1991*, edited by Nancy J. Williamson and Michele

Hudon, 235–46. FID Publication, no. 698. Amsterdam: Elsevier Science Publishers, 1992.

Discusses the *USMARC Format for Classification Data* (DC5). It reviews the potential uses of the format within an online system and discusses its development as a USMARC standard. Includes a summary of the fields in the format, and discusses the prospects for its implementation. Of interest to technical services, systems personnel, and subject catalogers who may be using an online version of the LCC schedules in the future.

DC5. USMARC Format for Classification Data: Including Guidelines for Content Designation. Washington, D.C.: Cataloging Distribution Service, Library of Congress, 1990. Loose-leaf.

The most recent addition to the family of USMARC formats. Approved in 1990 as a provisional format for the conversion of Library of Congress and Dewey Decimal Classification schedules to machine-readable form. After review and possible modification, the format will be submitted for final approval. Intended for use in the creation and maintenance of classification records and the design and maintenance of systems for the communication and processing of classification records. Where possible, the format has been designed to accommodate other classification systems such as the National Library of Medicine and the Universal Decimal Classification systems.

Ultimately the format will be useful both to Library of Congress staff in maintaining the LCC system and to classifiers at LC and in other libraries in understanding and applying the machine-readable schedules.

DESIGN AND DEVELOPMENT OF CLASSIFICATION SYSTEMS

DC6. Vickery, B. C. *Faceted Classification: A Guide to Construction and Use of Special Schemes*. London: Aslib, 1960.

An older publication, but gives a brief and relatively simple explanation of faceted classification and a procedure for constructing such a system. Based on the approach to faceted systems taken by the Classification Research Group (UK). Useful for library and information professionals who have an interest in faceted classification or in the development of thesauri based on faceted classification principles.

DEWEY DECIMAL CLASSIFICATION

General Works

DC7. Beall, Julianne. ''Editing the Dewey Decimal Classification Online: The Evolution of the DDC Database and Editorial Support System.'' In *Classification Research for Knowledge Representation and Organization: Proceedings of the 5th International Study Conference on Classification Research, Toronto, Canada, June 24–28, 199*, edited by Nancy J. Williamson and Michele Hudon, 29–38. FID Publication, no. 698. Amsterdam: Elsevier Science Publishers, 1992.

Describes the database and Editorial Support System (ESS) used to publish the twentieth edition of the *Dewey Decimal Classification and Related Index* (DDC) (DC11). Records in the database are in a format designed for the ESS system, which was developed before the USMARC format for classification was available. This paper looks toward the twenty-first edition of DDC and emphasizes the problems relevant to the conversion of the ESS records to USMARC format; the searching of component parts of, and the analysis of, synthesized DDC numbers; and the tracking of hierarchical relationships not expressed by the DDC notation. This database is a forerunner of the *Electronic Dewey* (DC14) and will be of interest to subject catalogers and other technical services librarians who are concerned with new developments in DDC in relation to new technologies.

DC8. Comaromi, John P. *The Eighteen Editions of the Dewey Decimal Classification.* Albany, N.Y.: Forest Press Division, Lake Placid Education Foundation, 1976.

The definitive history and development of this major classification system. Useful for students, subject catalogers, and researchers who have an interest in this scheme.

DC9. Holley, Robert P., ed. *Dewey: An International Perspective; Papers from a Workshop on the Dewey Decimal Classification and DDC 20.* UBCIM Publications, New Series, V4. London: K. G. Saur, 1991.

A collection of papers presented at the General Conference of the International Federation of Library Associations and Institutions (IFLA), August 24, 1989. Designed to be of interest to an international audience, it includes papers on the international use of Dewey, the international aspects of *DDC 20*, and an overview of the changes as well as a critical review of *DDC 20*. Provides an unusual profile of the latest edition.

Schedules

DC10. Dewey, Melvil. *Abridged Dewey Decimal Classification and Relative Index.* 12th ed. Edited by John P. Comaromi and assistant eds. Julianne Beall, Winton E. Matthews, Jr., and Gregory R. New. Albany, N.Y.: Forest Press, a Division of OCLC, Inc., 1990.

An abridged version of *Dewey Decimal Classification and Relative Index*, 20th ed. (DC11). Primarily intended for small public and school libraries. Based on the same principles and uses the same technical devices as the full edition. Contains an informative introduction to the use of the schedules and a glossary of terms used in the schedules. Incorporates a "Manual on the Use of the Dewey Decimal Classification." Abridged editions are developed and derived from the schedules of each full edition following its publication. The class numbers from the abridged *DDC* are represented in Library of Congress records by that part of the class number preceding the first prime mark or indicator in class numbers assigned to the items described in the records.

DC11. _____. *Dewey Decimal Classification and Relative Index.* 20th ed. Edited by John P. Comaromi and assistant eds. Julianne Beall, Winton E. Matthews, Jr., and Gregory R. New. 4 vols. Albany, N.Y.: Forest Press, a Division of OCLC, Inc., 1989.

The major classification system in use in public and school libraries in North America and in libraries worldwide. This edition is known as *DDC 20*. Has been translated into thirty-five languages. The system consists of an extensive introduction to the characteristics and use of the schedules, the schedules themselves, tables of subdivisions to be applied in extending the class numbers, a comprehensive relative index to the schedules and tables, and a "Manual on the Use of the Dewey Decimal Classification." The system is continuously revised with new editions appearing at five- to ten-year intervals. Between editions, changes in policy and revisions of the schedules are published annually in *Dewey Decimal Classification: Additions, Notes and Decisions* (DC12), also known as *DC&*. Major revisions of whole classes or parts of classes sometimes appear as separate publications between editions, are implemented, and later become incorporated into the next edition. The Dewey Decimal Classification is applied to catalog records produced by the Library of Congress and in national bibliographies such as *Canadiana*, *British National Bibliography*, and the *Australian National Bibliography*. In applying the system to library collections, these agencies always use the latest edition of the classification system. Also available on CD-ROM as *Electronic Dewey: DDC 20* (DC14).

DC12. *Dewey Decimal Classification: Additions, Notes and Decisions.* Albany, N.Y.: Forest Press, a Division of OCLC, Inc. v. 5– , March 1990– . Annual.

Popularly known as *DC&*. Functions as a supplement to the *Dewey Decimal Classification and Relative Index* (DC11), covering news of policy decisions, changes, and revisions to the schedules. Supplements both the full and abridged editions. An important update to the printed schedules and an essential tool for Dewey Decimal Classification subject catalogers. Sent free of charge to purchasers of the abridged (DC10) and full editions (DC11) of *DDC* who return the postcard located in the front of each edition. Also sent free of charge to library and information science educators listed in the "classification," "subject cataloging," and "technical services" sections of the current directory of the Association of Library and Information Science Educators (AGA2).

DC13. *Dewey Decimal Classification: 200 Religion Class; Reprinted from Edition 20.* Edited by John P. Comaromi, Julianne Beall, Winton E. Matthews, Jr., Gregory New, and Michael B. Cantlon. Albany, N.Y.: Forest Press, 1989.

Reprinted from the twentieth unabridged edition of the *Dewey Decimal Classification* (DC11). Includes a revised and expanded index and "Manual" notes from the twentieth edition. This reprint is designed to meet the needs of libraries with "in-depth religious collections and smaller general collections where the *DDC Abridged 12* (DC10) and this reprint might serve such a library's needs."

DC14. *Electronic Dewey: DDC 20.* [database on CD-ROM] Albany, N.Y.: Forest Press, a Division of OCLC, Inc., 1993.

The *Dewey Decimal Classification*, 20th ed. (DC11), in CD-ROM format. A database that includes the *DDC 20* schedules, tables, index, and manual including changes through March 1993. The system has advanced online searching and windowing techniques, full-text indexing, a personal notepad, and Library of Congress subject headings linked to Dewey Decimal Classification numbers. The package includes the database, the system software, and a users' guide. The database operates on an IBM PC 386SX computer or compatible (with 640K RAM and a hard disk) and a CD-ROM drive. A color monitor and printer are recommended. Because of its sophisticated search capabilities, this tool will be of major interest to all Dewey Decimal Classification catalogers.

Textbooks, Guides, and Manuals

DC15. Batty, David. *An Introduction to the Twentieth Edition of the Dewey Decimal Classification.* Albany, N.Y.: Forest Press, a Division of OCLC, Inc., 1992.

A programmed text designed for library school students and beginning classifiers in learning and understanding the Dewey Decimal Classification. Structured textbook for self-instruction.

DC16. Davis, Sydney W. *DDC 20 Workbook.* Albany, N.Y.: Forest Press, a Division of OCLC, Inc. 1992; Occasional Monographs, no. 10. Wagga Wagga, N.S.W. [Australia]: Centre for Information Studies, Charles Sturt University–Riverina, 1990.

Introduces students and beginning classifiers to the use of the Dewey Decimal Classification and provides the opportunity for practical application of the schedules. Includes chapters on number building, citation and precedence order, and the use of tables. Generous use of examples; includes exercises with answers. Approaches the topic at a more advanced level than the Sifton and Dragani *Workbook for DDC 20* (DC18). Useful for library school students, workshops, and continuing education programs.

DC17. Osborn, Jeanne. *Dewey Decimal Classification, 20th Edition: A Study Manual.* Revised and edited by John Comaromi. Englewood, Colo.: Libraries Unlimited, 1991.

Traces recent developments in the Dewey Decimal Classification and is primarily concerned with the differences between DDC 19 and DDC 20. Number building, well taken care of in the schedules themselves, receives some limited attention. A very useful tool for libraries making the transition to the latest edition of the DDC system.

DC18. Sifton, Pat, and Noreen Dragani. *Workbook for DDC 20.* Ottawa: Canadian Library Association, 1989.

Designed to introduce classifiers to the Dewey Decimal Classification system. An elementary, practical introduction and "a starting point for further study and practice." Contains a brief introduction followed by chapters on the application of the standard subdivisions and other tables in the DDC system. Each section is accompanied by exercises with classification topics to be worked out in applying the schedules. Answers to the questions in exercises are provided. Could be used in training sessions or for independent study.

LIBRARY OF CONGRESS CLASSIFICATION

General Works

DC19. Larson, Ray R. "Experiments in Automatic Library of Congress Classification." *Journal of the American Society for Information Science* 43 (Mar. 1992): 130–48.

The results of research into the automatic selection of Library of Congress Classification numbers based on titles and subject headings in MARC records. Uses partial match retrieval techniques utilizing various elements of the records as "queries." Tested sixty individual methods using four different partial match methods, five query types, and three representations of search terms. The database consisted of 283 MARC records. Results predicted that if the "best" method for each individual case could be determined, "up to 86 percent" of new records could be correctly classified. In the experiment, the best single method yielded 46 percent success. This article breaks new ground in LCC research and raises interesting possibilities for classification in computerized systems.

Schedules

DC20. Library of Congress. *Library of Congress Classification Schedules Combined with Additions and Changes through 1991.* Detroit, Mich.: Gale Research Company, 1992.

Published annually, this edition of the *Library of Congress Classification* (DC22) schedules integrates the latest editions of the LC schedules with all changes found in LC's quarterly publication *Library of Congress Classification—Additions and Changes* (DC23). For each schedule, it brings together in one volume all schedule information for the particular class or subclass, making it unnecessary for the classifier to have to look in at least two places to find the required classification information.

DC21. Library of Congress, Office for Subject Cataloging Policy. *LC Classification Outline.* 6th ed. Washington, D.C.: LC, 1990.

Provides an outline of the LC classification schedules as of September 1990. Presents an overview of the arrangement of the classification system, showing the major divisions of the topics in each of its classes and subclasses. Helpful to the classifier in selecting the appropriate schedule for classifying a particular item and serves as a buying guide in purchasing individual schedules.

DC22. Library of Congress, Subject Cataloging Division. *Library of Congress Classification.* 47 vols. Washington, D.C.: Cataloging Distribution Service, LC.

The major classification system used in North American academic libraries. Continuously updated through its

Additions and Changes (DC23), which are issued each year as four numbered lists. The number of volumes varies as revision takes place and some classes are split into two or more volumes. New editions of the individual schedules are published as they are completed. Individual schedules have detailed indexes, but there is no LC official overall index to the system as a whole. Several unofficial indexes have been published in the past but these would now be considered too old to be useful as a means of accessing the schedules. The *LC Classification Outline* (DC21) and *Library of Congress Subject Headings* (DD15) are both helpful to the classifier in locating appropriate schedules in the classification process.

DC23. Library of Congress, Subject Cataloging Division. *Library of Congress Classification—Additions and Changes.* Washington, D.C.: Cataloging Distribution Service, LC, 1992– . Quarterly. ISSN 0041-7912.

Contains the updates of changes made to the *Library of Congress Classification* schedules (DC22). An important supplement to the schedules themselves. Four numbered lists of the *Additions and Changes* are issued each year to notify users of new and changed classification numbers that may be expected to appear on LC bibliographic records. Primary users will be subject catalogers working with the LC classification.

Textbooks, Guides, and Manuals

DC24. Chan, Lois Mai. *Immroth's Guide to the Library of Congress Classification.* 4th ed. Library Science Text Series. Englewood, Colo.: Libraries Unlimited, 1990.

The major guide to the interpretation of the Library of Congress Classification (LCC) system. Intended as an introduction to LCC and designed to provide a "basic understanding" of the characteristics of the system, its arrangement, schedules, and tables. Interprets Library of Congress policies with respect to the application of LCC. A general description rather than a detailed treatment of individual classes, subclasses, and tables. Background reading for students and a reference resource for practicing classifiers.

DC25. Library of Congress, Subject Cataloging Division. *Subject Cataloging Manual: Classification.* 1 vol. Washington, D.C.: Cataloging Distribution Services, LC, 1992. Loose-leaf.

Explains LC policy and standards on the application of the Library of Congress Classification. Accumulates guidelines dealing with recurring questions on the LCC system. Designed for use by the LC cataloging staff, but also functions as a practical how-to manual for subject catalogers in individual libraries in formulating classification numbers. Its companion volume is the *Subject Cataloging Manual: Shelflisting* (DC26), which sets out the policies on assigning Cutter numbers and aids subject catalogers in completing call numbers. Examples included are based on LC's MARC record database. This is the first edition of this manual, and its loose-leaf format suggests that additions and changes will be forthcoming and the possibility that there will be further editions.

DC26. _____. *Subject Cataloging Manual: Shelflisting.* Washington, D.C.: Subject Cataloging Division, LC, 1989. Loose-leaf.

Documents the shelflisting policies and procedures used at the Library of Congress to complete LC call numbers in the classification process. While the policies and procedures are developed for LC's own use, they are also important to other subject catalogers in interpreting LC call numbers and in establishing call numbers for their own libraries' collections. Functions as an important companion volume to the LC classification schedules themselves.

UNIVERSAL DECIMAL CLASSIFICATION

General Works

DC27. Gilchrist, Alan, and David Strachan, eds. *The UDC: Essays for the New Decade.* London: Aslib, 1990.

A collection of papers on the Universal Decimal Classification. Gathered together from a number of sources describing the current status of UDC, it points to new directions for this classification system in terms of automated systems. Included are suggestions for the revision and redevelopment of UDC, including the "The aurification of UDC," "Expert Systems for Automatic UDC Number Assignment," and a summary article on the work of the UDC "Task Force on UDC System Development" that established new directions for the future of UDC. International in its coverage, this overview provides some insight into recent thinking about future directions for this classification, which is still used by a large number of libraries and information agencies throughout the world.

Schedules

DC28. *Universal Decimal Classification.* International Medium Edition, English Text. 2 vols. FID Publication, No. 571. London: British Standards Institution, 1985–1988.

The Universal Decimal Classification is used by numerous libraries throughout the world and has been translated into many languages. Originally based on the Dewey Decimal Classification, it has evolved as a distinct classification system in its own right. It is a very important tool for libraries and information agencies requiring great depth of analysis in a classification system. It is particularly useful where classified catalogs are in use and has particular potential for online systems. Problems in using the schedules are caused by the lack of detailed explanation of how to use the system and by the inadequacy of the index, which was computer produced from the systematic schedules. An important supporting resource will be the *Guide to the Use of the UDC* (DC29). Editions in the various languages have been published in one or more full, medium, and abridged editions. This International Medium Edition consists of Part 1, systematic tables, and Part 2, the alphabetical index. As a result of recent policy changes in the development and revision of UDC, this particular edition is expected to become the basis for the development of a "standard edition," which in future will be the basis for all other editions published.

Textbooks, Guides, and Manuals

DC29. McIlwaine, I. C. *Guide to the Use of the UDC*. The Hague, Netherlands: International Federation for Information and Documentation [publication forthcoming; ca. 1993–94].

A guide to the practical application of the Universal Decimal Classification system. Based primarily on the International Medium Edition, English Text, but contains examples from editions in other languages where appropriate. In part replaces the now outdated *Guide to the Universal Decimal Classification (UDC)*, published by the British Standards Institution in 1963. Emphasis is on the practical application of UDC, and less attention is given to theory than in the earlier "guide." An important tool for classifiers in understanding and applying UDC. Publication in progress at this writing.

FACETED CLASSIFICATION SYSTEMS

DC30. *Bliss Bibliographic Classification*. 2nd ed. [Revised and prepared] by J. Mills and Vanda Broughton, with the assistance of Valerie Lang. 2nd ed. London: Butterworths, 1977– .

A new and completely restructured edition of a general classification system developed by Henry Bliss and originally published in 1935. The original scheme was described by many as one of the best organized systems of its time. The only example of a general enumerative classification system that has been redeveloped and modernized into a fully faceted classification system. Well documented as to its theoretical background, the organization of the disciplines, and the use of the schedules. Volume 1 contains an excellent glossary of classification terminology. Still in progress, the following schedules have been published: the "Introduction," classes H (Anthropology, Human Biology, Health Sciences), I (Psychology and Psychiatry), J (Education), K (Society), P (Religion, The Occult, Morals and Ethics), Q (Social Welfare), and T (Economics, Management of Economic Enterprises).

DC31. Coates, E. J. "The Role of Classification in Information Retrieval: Action and Thought in the Contribution of Brian Vickery." *Journal of Documentation* 44 (Sept. 1988): 216–25.

An assessment of Brian Vickery's contribution to the development of classification in information retrieval. Emphasizes his contribution to the work of the Classification Research Group (UK), in particular his work with faceted classification and his elaboration and development of S. R. Ranganathan's facet categories for application to special classification systems in the Western world. Also discusses some remaining "gray areas" in faceted classification and classificatory fragments present in many thesauri. The principles of faceted classification are fundamental to the design of modern subject analysis systems

such as thesauri and to development of frame-based systems, hypertext, and artificial intelligence. This paper provides an insight into faceted classification for subject catalogers and compilers of thesauri; it is perhaps less cumbersome and more easily understood than Ranganathan's Colon Classification itself.

DC32. Whitehead, Cathleen. "Faceted Classification in the Art and Architecture Thesaurus." *Art Documentation* 8 (Winter 1989): 175–77.

A recent application of faceted classification in the development of a thesaurus. Describes what it means to classify terminology, and explains how the *Art & Architecture Thesaurus* (DD39) hierarchies function as a classification system for subject cataloging. Of interest to library and information science professionals who are developing thesauri using faceted classification as a basis.

DD
Subject Headings, Thesauri, and Related Systems

SUBJECT HEADINGS

General Works

DD1. Miksa, Francis. *The Subject in the Dictionary Catalog from Cutter to the Present*. Chicago: American Library Association, 1983.

See also annotation under FB26. An extensive history of the influence of Charles A. Cutter's impact on subject cataloging in North American libraries. Endeavors to address the rationality of subject heading work. A definitive analysis and insight into the subject.

Subject Cataloging Codes

DD2. Chan, Lois Mai. "A Subject Cataloging Code?" *Cataloging & Classification Quarterly* 10, nos. 1/2 (1989): 199-202.

In the context of online catalogs, examines whether a subject cataloging code is, "at this point in time, necessary or economically feasible" and raises questions as to who would develop such a code encompassing both practical problems and philosophical issues. Chan recognizes a number of serious problems in developing such a code, including the lack of consensus on the objectives of the subject catalog, the problems of subject analysis, and subject specificity. Offers some practical suggestions for improving subject cataloging without the development of a theoretical code. The issues raised should be of interest to all subject catalogers.

DD3. Reynolds, Sally Jo. "In Theory There Is No Solution: The Impediments to a Subject Cataloging Code." *Library Quarterly* 59 (July 1989): 223–38.

Focuses on the need for a subject cataloging code as a basis for evaluating the effectiveness of the subject catalog in order to take advantage of online technology and to enable non–Library of Congress subject catalogers to establish their own headings as needed. Like Chan (DD2), Reynolds points out the issues of lack of consensus on the objectives of the subject catalog, the importance of dealing with philosophical issues as well as practical problems, and the difficulties presented by the inability to define specificity and relevance and to develop the principles of intellectual analysis. The author also suggests that effort should be focused on the improvement of subject cataloging even without a theoretical code. An important issue that will be of interest to all subject catalogers.

DD4. Studwell, William E., and Paule Roland-Thomas. "The Form and Structure of a Subject Heading Code." *Library Resources & Technical Services* 32 (Apr. 1988): 167–69.

Presents a case for a theoretical code for the development of Library of Congress subject headings. The issue is discussed with a review of past endeavors in this direction. Presents a position opposite to the views of Lois Mai Chan (DD2) and Sally Jo Reynolds (DD3).

Standards

DD5. International Federation of Library Associations and Institutions, Division of Bibliographic Control, Section on Classification and Indexing, Working Group on Guidelines for Subject Authority Files. *Guidelines for Subject Authority Files and Reference Entries.* Frankfurt am Main, Ger.: IFLA, Universal Bibliographic Control and International MARC Programme [publication forthcoming, ca. 1993–94].

International guidelines for subject authority control and the development of subject authority records developed by an international committee of experts. Parallels the *Guidelines for Authority and Reference Entries* (EAB3), another IFLA publication that provides international guidance on the control of names. A worldwide review has been held, and the text is in final form. Final approval by IFLA and publication of the guidelines were expected to take place in 1993. An important tool for subject catalogers in libraries involved in the international exchange of subject authority data.

DD6. National Library of Canada, Canadian MARC Office. *Canadian MARC Communication Format: Authorities.* 3rd ed. Ottawa: Canadian MARC Office, 1988– . Loose-leaf.

Includes specifications for subject, name, and authority data. Conforms with the international standard format for bibliographic information interchange on magnetic tape (ISO 2709-1981) and with the American standard ANSI Z39.2-1979. An essential manual for users of CAN/MARC authorities.

DD7. USMARC Format for Authority Data: Including Guidelines for Content Designation. Washington, D.C.: Cataloging Distribution Service, LC, 1987– . Loose-leaf.

Official manual for USMARC authority formats. Includes both subject authority data and name authority data. Subject authority data is based on *Library of Congress Subject Headings* (LCSH). With respect to subject authority records, the format deals with fields and content designators relevant to topical subject terms, geographic names, names with subject subdivisions and terms and names used as subject subdivisions as well as the appropriate reference structure. Continuously updated by periodic issuing of new and replacement pages. An essential manual for libraries maintaining and developing authority control systems using USMARC.

DD8. Utlas MARC Coding Manual for Authorities. 1st ed. Compiled and edited by Elizabeth Black. Toronto: Utlas International Canada, a Division of International Thomson Limited, 1987– . Loose-leaf.

Includes MARC format for authority data for both subject and name authorities. Reflects the USMARC and CAN/MARC formats and deals with fields and content designators relevant to subject authorities and the appropriate reference structure. An essential tool for libraries using the Utlas authorities system. Periodic updates in loose-leaf format.

Library of Congress Subject Headings

Lists and Files

DD9. Library of Congress, Office for Subject Cataloging Policy. *LC Period Subdivisions under Names of Places.* 4th ed. Washington, D.C.: Cataloging Distribution Service, LC, 1990.

A compact, easy-to-consult list of subject headings for place names with date divisions. Lists date subdivisions under each place name in chronological order and covers all LCSH headings through December 1989. An important supporting tool in assigning LC subject headings.

DD10. ———. *LC Subject Headings: Weekly Lists.* Washington, D.C.: Cataloging Distribution Service, LC, 1993– .

Weekly list of new and altered subject headings reviewed and approved by the Office of Subject Cataloging Policy. Distributed to libraries monthly. Up-to-date printed source of the latest new, changed, and deleted headings. Essential for subject catalogers assigning Library of Congress subject headings.

DD11. Library of Congress, Subject Cataloging Division. *CD MARC Subjects.* [database on CD-ROM] Washington, D.C.: Cataloging Distribution Service, LC. Issue 1– , June 1988– . Quarterly, with each issue cumulative.

Library of Congress subject headings in CD-ROM format. Provides a sophisticated search mode, facilitating keyword searching using Boolean logic and processing based on six indexes. Headings are present in both thesauruslike and MARC record displays. Subscription includes appropriate retrieval software, a reference manual, and a ready reference card and keyboard template. Records can be written to a disk file or to a printer. Useful for subject catalogers in assigning subject headings. Also helpful to reference librarians and researchers as an aid in subject searching. Has search capabilities not possible with the printed volumes and brings together in one file the contents of the printed volumes and the weekly lists.

DD12. _____. *Library of Congress Subject Headings.* Cumulative Microform Edition. [microform] Washington, D.C.: Cataloging Distribution Service, LC. Jan./Mar. 1976– . Quarterly, with each issue cumulative. ISSN 0361-5243.

Library of Congress subject headings on microfiche. Includes separate fiche for "Subject Headings for Children's Literature." Also includes the authority record number for each heading. These numbers, important for easy checking of records in the online system, are not included in the printed version of LCSH. The microfiche have a reduction ratio of 48×. This edition provides an important backup source for the computerized version. Useful for students, subject catalogers, reference librarians, and researchers.

DD13. _____. *Revised Library of Congress Subject Headings: Cross References from Former to Current Subject Headings.* Washington, D.C.: Cataloging Distribution Service, LC, 1991.

A list of Library of Congress subject headings that have been canceled and/or replaced by subsequent headings. Through a "search under" instruction, identifies previously valid headings and their current counterparts, 1976 to 1990. All cross-references also appear in LCSH. A ready reference resource to historical changes in LCSH. An aid to subject catalogers in identifying, editing and correcting, and updating obsolete headings in local authority files and bibliographic records.

DD14. _____. *Subject Authorities.* [database on magnetic tape] Washington, D.C.: Cataloging Distribution Service, 1992– .

Library of Congress Subject Headings (DD15) in USMARC record format. Each tape contains approximately 19,000 records, of which 6,000 will be new records. Retrospective files for 1986–1991 consisting of approximately 192,000 records are also available from LC.

DD15. _____. *Library of Congress Subject Headings.* 4 vols. Washington, D.C.: Cataloging Distribution Service, LC, 1990– . Annual. ISSN 1048-9711.

Often called simply LCSH or "The Red Book," this is a comprehensive list of subject headings covering a broad spectrum of subjects about which books have been written. The list contains the subject headings prepared by the Library of Congress for its collections and used as the basis for the development of LC's subject authority files. The major subject heading tool applied to a majority of general collections in public, university, and some special libraries in North America. In its application it must be supported by tools listed in a following section under the subheading "Textbooks, Guides, and Manuals." Published annually and kept up to date by weekly lists. Avail-

able in four physical formats—print, CD-ROM (DD11), microfiche (DD12), magnetic tape (DD14), and in the databases of bibliographic utilities.

Textbooks, Guides, and Manuals

DD16. Chan, Lois Mai. *Library of Congress Subject Headings: Principles and Application.* 2nd ed. Littleton, Colo.: Libraries Unlimited, 1986.

A basic comprehensive examination of LCSH in all its aspects. Part 1 discusses principles, form, and structure with specific reference to basic principles, forms of headings, subdivisions, cross-references, proper names, and subject heading control. Part 2 describes the application of LCSH, including its use for special types of materials and special subjects; Part 3 addresses LCSH in the online environment. Parts 1 and 2 are still sound in principle, but it should be noted that this work was written before the change in the relational symbols in LCSH from "see, see also, x," and "xx" to "BT, NT, RT," and "SA." Part 3 is still relevant, but changes are occurring in the relationship between LCSH and online systems. Has a useful glossary of terms and helpful appendixes. An important text for beginning subject catalogers and library science students and a reference resource for other professionals.

DD17. _____. *Library of Congress Subject Headings: Principles of Structure and Policies for Application.* Annotated version. Washington, D.C.: Cataloging Distribution Service, LC, 1990.

For efficiency and ease of use, the basic principles and policies involved in the application of Library of Congress subject headings have been derived from the *Subject Cataloging Manual: Subject Headings* (DD20) and LCSH itself and set out in a convenient and concise form for use by subject catalogers. The text is generously supported by examples. This is the most useful and up-to-date discussion of this topic available and should be considered essential support for the application of LCSH.

DD18. Conway, Martha O'Hara, ed. *The Future of Subdivisions in the Library of Congress Subject Headings System: Report from the Subject Subdivisions Conference Sponsored by the Library of Congress, May 9–12, 1991.* Washington, D.C.: Cataloging Distribution Service, LC, 1992.

Contains sixteen papers that address four proposals for change in the LCSH subdivision practice. Prepared by experts from the United States and Canada, these proposals were entitled "Machine Validation of Subdivided Headings, Especially Headings with Free-Floating Subdivisions," "Order and Display of Subdivided Headings," "Simplification of Rules for Assigning Subdivisions," and "The Creation of a National Subject Authority File." Includes an overview of the conference, its recommendations, and current subdivision practices, as well as an annotated bibliography. An important document for subject catalogers in understanding LCSH subdivision practices and the direction in which they are evolving.

DD19. Library of Congress, Office for Subject Cataloging Policy. *Free-Floating Subdivisions: An Alphabetical Index.*

4th ed. Washington, D.C.: Cataloging Distribution Service, LC, 1992.

Brings together in one alphabetical list the free-floating subdivisions in the separate lists contained in the *Subject Cataloging Manual: Subject Headings* (SCM) (DD20). For each subdivision, the index locates it in the manual, identifies it by category, and as appropriate indicates whether usage guidelines are provided in the SCM. It is an essential aid to the use of the SCM. New editions are published to coincide with new editions of the SCM.

DD20. _____. *Subject Cataloging Manual: Subject Headings*. 4th ed. 2 vols. Washington, D.C: Cataloging Distribution Service, LC, 1991. Loose-leaf.

Sets out the policies and procedures used at the Library of Congress in applying *Library of Congress Subject Headings* (LCSH) to its collections and is an important working tool for all libraries using LCSH. It is particularly important for its sections on formulating subject headings, handling references, and for the application of subdivisions and the development of pattern headings. Designed to be used with LCSH, it is published annually and updated with supplementary and replacement pages between editions.

Medical Subject Headings

DD21. *Medical Subject Headings: Annotated Alphabetical List.* Bethesda, Md.: Library Operations, Medical Subject Headings, National Library of Medicine, 197?– . Annual. ISSN 0147-5711.

Popularly referred to as *MeSH*, or the *Annotated MeSH*. The most comprehensive and important list of terms used in catalogs and databases in the medical field. Designed particularly for use in the online system MEDLINE, this edition contains information "not available in the edition designed for *Index Medicus* users." A comprehensive list, liberally annotated as to the nature, scope, and use of individual descriptors, together with their cross-references and their tree numbers, which link the descriptors to the hierarchical classification in the *Medical Subject Headings: Tree Structures* (DD22). Contains separate lists of new headings added since the last edition and supporting documentation on the application of the list. An essential tool for medical subject catalogers and for searchers of the MEDLINE system. Complemented and supplemented by MeSH *Tree Structures* and the *Permuted Subject Headings* (DD23).

DD22. *Medical Subject Headings: Tree Structures.* Bethesda, Md.: Library Operations, Medical Subject Headings, National Library of Medicine, 1969– . Annual. ISSN 0147-099X.

A companion volume to the *Annotated MeSH* (DD21), the *Permuted MeSH* (DD23), and the online MeSH vocabulary file. Organizes the MeSH terms into fifteen categories and their subcategories, for example, Diseases, Chemicals and Drugs, and Anatomy. Within categories, subcategories of descriptors are structured into hierarchies for purposes of browsing the subject area. An essential tool for medical subject catalogers and searchers of the MEDLINE system.

DD23. *Permuted Medical Subject Headings.* Bethesda, Md.: Library Operations, Medical Subject Headings, National Library of Medicine, 197?– . Annual. ISSN 1045-2338.

Referred to as *Permuted MeSH*. A computer-generated display of all descriptors and cross-references contained in the alphabetical list of MeSH headings, as well as all check tag and geographic descriptors from the annotated alphabetical MeSH. Each significant term appears, and listed under it are all the headings in which that term appears. It also extracts selected word roots and lists all MeSH descriptors containing that particular root. Provides another way of searching topics and subtopics in addition to the approaches found in the *Annotated Alphabetical List* (DD21) and the *Tree Structures* (DD22). For purposes of locating descriptors either for subject cataloging and online searching, *Permuted MeSH* is supplementary and complementary to these other publications.

Sears List of Subject Headings

DD24. *Sears List of Subject Headings*. 14th ed. Edited by Martha T. Mooney. New York: H. W. Wilson, 1991.

A general list of subject headings and their cross-references, intended for use by small public and school libraries. Resembles *Library of Congress Subject Headings* (DD15) in structure, although the use of the thesaurus symbols *NT, BT, RT, USE,* and *UF* has not been adopted by Sears. Less complex than LCSH, with fewer basic terms and less frequent use of subdivisions. Contains an excellent section, "Principles of the Sears List of Subject Headings," which is useful not only to understand Sears and its application but also to help beginning subject catalogers to understand the principles and application of LCSH as well as Sears. The subject headings are accompanied by the appropriate Dewey Decimal Classification number in many cases. Particularly useful for beginning catalogers, students in beginning cataloging courses, and library and information science educators. A new edition appears approximately every five years.

DD25. *Sears List of Subject Headings: Canadian Companion.* 2nd ed. Compiled by Ken Haycock and Lynne Isberg Lighthall. New York: H. W. Wilson, 1992.

A list of Canadian subject headings, designed to supplement the 14th edition of Sears. Intended for use in small Canadian libraries or in libraries with special collections of Canadian materials. Particularly useful for historical and geographical materials. Its relationship to Sears is similar to the relationship of *Canadian Subject Headings* (DD28) to LCSH (DD15).

Other Subject Heading Lists

DD26. *Guidelines on Subject Access to Individual Works of Fiction, Drama, etc.* Chicago: Resources and Technical Services Division, Cataloging and Classification Section, Subject Analysis Committee, Subcommittee on Subject Access to Individual Works of Fiction, Drama, etc., American Library Association, 1990.

While the title of this work describes it as "guidelines," this publication is primarily a list of subject headings derived from LCSH with some exceptions to headings used by LC. It follows the LCSH format and structure and describes the handling of special problems in providing subject access to individual works of fiction. In particular, there are brief chapters on the handling of the names of characters in works of fiction and the handling of "settings," real and imaginary, and topical subjects in fiction. Designed to be used with LCSH, it will be a very useful resource for any library with a policy of providing subject access to these materials.

DD27. Intner, Sheila S., and William E. Studwell. *Subject Access to Films and Videos.* Lake Crystal, Minn.: Soldier Creek Press, 1992.

A list of Library of Congress subject headings and cross-references pertaining to motion pictures and video recordings. Genre terms taken from the Library of Congress publication *Moving Image Materials* have been included in the list. The introduction discusses general principles of subject access and LC policies and practices in handling these materials. Material on the development of video collections and a bibliography of sources are also included. A specialized list for libraries with collections of motion picture and video recordings.

DD28. National Library of Canada. *Canadian Subject Headings.* 3rd ed. Edited by Alina Schweitzer. Ottawa: National Library of Canada, 1992.

A list of subject headings pertaining to subjects peculiar to the economic, political, social, and historical aspects of the Canadian scene and designed for use in conjunction with the *Library of Congress Subject Headings* (DD15) in Canadian libraries or libraries with special collections in Canadian studies. Provides for terminology peculiar to Canada and is designed to be integrated into the same catalog with LC's subject headings. The list is in English, but English-to-French and French-to-English indexes link *Canadian Subject Headings* with the French-language headings of the *Repertoire de vedettes-matiere* (RVM) (tenth edition, Quebec: Bibliothèque de l'Université Laval, 1988). *Canadian Subject Headings* is used in catalog records published in the national bibliography *Canadiana* and Canadian MARC records. It contains an excellent introduction describing the nature of the list and its relationship to LCSH. It could serve as a model for other libraries wishing to develop headings for special collections of a similar nature that need to be integrated and used in conjunction with LCSH.

DD29. Olderr, Steven. *Olderr's Fiction Subject Headings: A Supplement and Guide to the LC Thesaurus.* Chicago: American Library Association, 1991.

Intended to assist in the use of Library of Congress subject headings so that they can be applied specifically to fiction. Builds on LCSH, and additional scope notes and cross-references have been supplied where appropriate. Designed to be fully compatible with LCSH and used in conjunction with it, because the LCSH reference structure is not reproduced in full. An important supplement to LCSH for libraries that wish to provide subject headings for fiction.

SUBJECT AUTHORITY CONTROL

DD30. Drabenstott, Karen Markey, ed. *Subject Authorities in the Online Environment.* ALCTS Papers on Library Technical Services and Collections, no. 1. Chicago, London: American Library Association, 1991.

A collection of papers from a conference program held during the ALA Annual Conference in San Francisco, June 29, 1987. Contains papers on the functions of a subject authority file, practical considerations in dealing with LCSH, and the problems of handling multiple vocabularies in an authority control system. Important because it brings together a number of papers on *subject* authority control, where much of the literature tends to focus on name authorities. Covers technical details of the MARC authority format, and some of the papers include useful bibliographies. A good overview for beginners in the area of authority control.

DD31. Frost, Carolyn O., and Bonnie A. Dede. "Subject Heading Compatibility Between LCSH and Catalog Files of a Large Research Library." *Information Technology and Libraries* 7 (Sept. 1988): 288–99.

A research study in which assigned topical and geographic subject headings from a sample of bibliographic records from the University of Michigan's library catalog were analyzed to determine the degree of match in headings found in Library of Congress subject headings, to identify types of heading conflicts that lend themselves to automated authority control. A high degree of match was found, particularly in headings without subdivisions. Lack of match could frequently be attributed to free-floating subdivisions. On the basis of findings the authors recommended that a machine-readable file of LCSH free-floating subdivisions be developed. Of interest to practicing library and information professionals who are developing automated authority control systems and those with a general interest in the practice of using LCSH.

DD32. Krieger, Michael T. "Subject Authority Control on the Dynix System," *Cataloging & Classification Quarterly* 12, no. 1 (1990): 103–15.

See also annotation under EE16. The Dynix system's subject authority control is examined using the implementation at Dayton University, Dayton, Ohio, as an example. Discusses features of the system and its structure, as well as its impact on the subject authority control process. Of particular interest to technical services librarians considering the implementation of authority control systems in general and the Dynix system in particular.

DD33. Palmer, Joseph W. "Subject Authority Control and Syndetic Structure—Myths and Realities," *Cataloging & Classification Quarterly* 7, no. 2 (Winter 1986): 71–95.

See also annotation under EC15. Examines subject heading practices in a selected number of card catalogs and addresses the question, "What libraries include references in their catalogs?" Findings indicated that only the largest libraries provided any type of reference, and not even those libraries included "see also" references in most cases. Of interest in light of the development of online catalogs where, in many cases, there is still no authority control and where linkage between subject authority records and bibliographic records would be beneficial in maintenance and updating of subject heading terminology.

THESAURI

Directories and Databases

DD34. Gesellschaft für Information und Dokumentation. *Thesaurus Guide: Analytical Directory of Selected Vocabularies for Information Retrieval, 1985*. Prepared for the Commission of the European Communities. Amsterdam: North-Holland, 1985.

See also annotation under FAE3. Part of an action plan prepared by the Commission of the European Communities to facilitate the exchange of data among information systems through the use of suitable monolingual and multilingual search aids, particularly thesauri. Compiled from a broad spectrum of source materials, this guide contains bibliographical and factual information on all thesauri available at the time of publication that were available in at least one of the official European Communities' languages. The guide arranges the thesauri alphabetically within ten broad disciplines and subject fields. It includes indexes to organizations and persons and three trilingual subject indexes in English, French, and German. The preface states that the directory "will also be made available to the user in the form of a data bank." This resource is a useful starting place in searching for an appropriate thesaurus in a specialized subject area in numerous European languages as well as in English.

DD35. *Thesaurus Database*. [online database] Amsterdam: Commission of European Communities. 1985– .

A database of published thesauri that have appeared "in at least one of the official languages of the European Communities." Also includes thesauri from the United States and Canada. Records contain bibliographic data and details of the structure of each thesaurus, including subject coverage, term relationships, language(s) of the thesaurus, display and implementation. Machine-readable version of the *Thesaurus Guide* (DD34). Updated and maintained by Eurobrokers of Luxembourg. Currently resides in ECHO, the official host database of the European Communities. Further information may be obtained from J. M. Leick, CEC DG XIII, L-2920 Luxembourg. Tel.: (352) 4301-4595; FAX: (352) 4301-2354.

Standards

DD36. International Organization for Standardization. *Documentation: Guidelines for the Establishment and Development of Monolingual Thesauri*. 2nd ed. [Geneva]: International Organization for Standardization, 1986. ISO 2788-1986.

An internationally accepted set of standards for the construction, development, and maintenance of monolingual thesauri. Includes rules for the development of thesaurus descriptors, the determination of relationships among terms, and their display. An essential tool for library and information professionals who are planning, developing, and maintaining thesauri.

DD37. _____. *Documentation: Guidelines for the Establishment and Development of Multilingual Thesauri*. Geneva: International Organization for Standardization, 1985. ISO 5964-1985.

A companion standard to ISO 2788-1986 (DD36) for the planning, development, and maintenance of thesauri in multiple languages.

DD38. National Information Standards Organization. *Proposed American National Standard Guidelines for the Construction, Format, and Management of Monolingual Thesauri*. Bethesda, Md.: National Information Standards Organization, 1991. ANSI/NISO Z39.19-199x.

Provides guidelines for constructing monolingual thesauri. Includes rules for formulating descriptors, displaying relationships among terms, and functional specifications for thesaurus management systems. Is a much improved and extensive revision of *Guidelines for Thesaurus Structure, Construction and Use* (ANSI Z39.19 1980). An important tool for librarians and information professionals who are planning, developing, and maintaining thesauri.

Lists

DD39. *Art & Architecture Thesaurus*. Toni Petersen, Director. 3 vols. plus supplement. New York: Oxford University Press, 1990–1992.

Popularly known as *AAT*, and published on behalf of the Getty Art History Information Program. Consisting of three volumes together with its first supplement, this is the most comprehensive terminology list of descriptors on art and architecture ever published. A scholarly work that drew its terminology from many sources, it is structured according to the basic principles of faceted classification. Volume 1 contains a detailed introduction that includes the background and history of the thesaurus, a guide to its use, and an extensive bibliography of sources. The remainder of Volume 1 covers the hierarchical displays of descriptors organized into nine facets. Volumes 2 and 3 contain the alphabetical display of the terms in the hierarchies. The hierarchical structure is modeled on the tree structures in MeSH (DD22). The alphabetical display is organized in the traditional thesaurus form with Broader Term (BT), Narrower Term (NT), Related Term (RT), and Use/UF relationships. It contains carefully developed scope notes, and each term is accompanied by a unique identifier referred to as a "classification number" (CN), which may be substituted for the descriptor in an automated database. A line number also accompanies each descriptor, linking the descriptors in the alphabetical display with their location in the hierarchical display. *AAT* is an important contribution to the terminology of the art world. At the same time, it is innovative in its design and makes an important contribution to the future design and development of thesauri in other disciplines and subject areas. The printed thesaurus has been prepared from an online database.

DD40. *ROOT Thesaurus.* 3rd ed. 2 vols. Milton Keynes, Bucks, Eng.: British Standards Institution, 1988.

A general thesaurus with an unusual format. Covers a number of subject areas in science and technology, including medical sciences, environmental and safety engineering, energy technology, transport engineering, and consumer goods and services and includes a small section on the social sciences and humanities. Important for its format, which is a combined faceted classification system and thesaurus, sometimes described by the term "thesaurofacet." It is multilingual, in that versions of this thesaurus have been produced in French and German, with versions in Arabic, Chinese, Czech, Japanese, and Portuguese in preparation. Further language versions will be undertaken in due course. Because of its multilingual nature, symbols that are independent of language have been used to show relationships among terms; for example, < is used for broader term, > for narrower term, and = for nonpreferred synonyms or quasi synonyms. This thesaurus is included here because it is recognized as a model in thesaurus construction and has been described by reviewers as "the Rolls Royce of thesauri."

DD41. *Thesaurus of ERIC Descriptors.* 12th ed. Phoenix: Oryx Press, 1990.

This thesaurus, developed under the auspices of the Education Resources Information Center (ERIC) of the U.S. Department of Education's Office of Educational Research and Improvement (OERI), enhances access to one of the most frequently used bibliographic databases accessed through DIALOG, BRS, and ORBIT. An introduction explains its use in ERIC database and in the printed versions of *Resources in Education* (*RIE*) and *Current Index to Journals in Education* (*CIJE*). The thesaurus contains an alphabetical list of descriptors in the traditional thesaurus format, a rotated display of descriptors, a two-way hierarchical term display, and a display of descriptor groups. The thesaurus is continuously revised as the ERIC database grows and is published in printed form every four to five years. An important resource for the majority of libraries.

Thesaurus Design and Construction

DD42. Aitchison, Jean, and Alan Gilchrist. *Thesaurus Construction: A Practical Manual.* 2nd ed. London: Aslib, 1987.

A concise manual on all aspects of thesaurus construction prepared by experts in the field. Designed as a practical guide, it can serve as a companion to F. W. Lancaster's *Vocabulary Control for Information Retrieval* (DD43). It is designed to support step-by-step construction techniques and contains many examples, including illustrations from

published thesauri. Useful in teaching courses in thesaurus construction and in the actual construction of thesauri.

DD43. Lancaster, F. W. *Vocabulary Control for Information Retrieval.* 2nd ed. Arlington, Va.: Information Resources Press, 1986.

See also annotations under EC10 and FE5. Within the context of the general topic of design and development of controlled vocabulary, concentrates almost exclusively on the design and development of thesauri and on thesauruslike aids to natural language searching. Among the topics covered are development, organization, and display of thesaural systems; standards for thesauri; and evaluation. Scope differs from the first edition of this work, which was more concerned with vocabulary control in general. Useful in teaching and construction.

DD44. Mandel, Carol A. *Multiple Thesauri in Online Library Bibliographic Systems: A Report Prepared for the Library of Congress Processing Services.* Washington, D.C.: Cataloging Distribution Service, Library of Congress, 1987.

See also annotation under EC11. The author explores the prospect of bringing multiple controlled vocabularies online. Analyzes the problems of developing an online system that would accommodate multiple thesauri, including LCSH. Covers thesaurus management, subject authority control, and subject searching. Describes the cutting edge of future systems. Of interest to technical services and systems personnel, subject catalogers, and library and information science students and educators.

PRECIS

DD45. Austin, Derek, and Mary Dykstra. *PRECIS: A Manual of Concept Analysis and Subject Indexing.* 2nd ed. London: Bibliographic Services Division, British Library, 1984.

See also annotation under FH2. PRECIS (Preserved Context Indexing System), a string indexing system, was developed in the 1970s for purposes of providing subject access to the *British National Bibliography*. The system is taught in library schools and used to provide subject access in specialized bibliographies and catalogs (e.g., catalogs of audiovisual materials) throughout the world. It is a system that has been strongly recommended as an alternative to *Library of Congress Subject Headings* (DD15) and has potential for use in both manual and online catalogs. This is the latest edition of the primary manual for development and implementation of the PRECIS system.

DD46. Dykstra, Mary. *PRECIS: A Primer.* Metuchen, N.J.: Scarecrow Press, 1987.

See also annotation under FH5. This manual is intended to provide students, information specialists, and beginning catalogers or indexers with an introduction to the PRECIS system. Useful in courses and workshops or for independent study. It has been prepared as a "companion volume" to the more "advanced" *PRECIS: A Manual of Concept Analysis and Subject Indexing* (DD45) and serves as a beginning textbook. The author describes it as "relevant to American, Canadian, British, and other students internationally" as well as to users in the United Kingdom. It is very useful in training courses in the application of PRECIS and provides a good resource for information professionals interested in understanding PRECIS, while not necessarily applying it.

EXPERT SYSTEMS APPLICATIONS

DD47. Drabenstott, Karen Markey, Leslie C. Reister, and Bonnie Dede. "Shelflisting Using Expert Systems." In *Classification Research for Knowledge Representation and Organization: Proceedings of the 5th International Study Conference, Toronto, Canada, June 21–24, 1991,* edited by Nancy J. Williamson and Michele Hudon, 199–208. FID Publication, no. 698. Amsterdam: Elsevier Science Publishers, 1992.

Discusses research that tests the viability of an expert system for the Library of Congress Classification (LCC). Applied to a portion of the QA schedules, a prototype system was used to assign topical and author Cutter numbers devised from the Cutter-Sanborn tables to classification numbers assigned to documents. The system, called "ShelfPro," can also be used to assign translation Cutter numbers, dates for conference and congress proceedings, and dates for versions of originals, reprints, etc. The experiment indicated promise for automated shelflisting in the future, but the authors stressed the need for the shelflisting process to be integrated with other cataloging functions. Such a system would need to be integrated into the online cataloging system, and the best use of this kind of system would require the classification schedules to be in machine-readable form.

DD48. Endres-Niggemeyer, Brigitte, and Bettina Schmidt. "Knowledge Based Classification Systems: Basic Issues, a Toy System and Further Prospects." *International Classification* 16, no. 3 (1989): 146–56.

Examines the potential for expert systems for classification by discussing the affinity between faceted classification systems and frame-based knowledge representation, using a simple example and a model system as an illustration. As background, the authors examine several approaches to knowledge classification from artificial intelligence, classification research, and information science in preparing the ground for the development of more comprehensive systems in the future.

DD49. Fenly, Charles, and Howard Harris. *Expert Systems: Concepts and Applications.* Advances in Library Information Technology, no. 1. Washington, D.C.: Cataloging Distribution Service, Library of Congress, 1988.

See also annotation under AHC8. A concise overview of expert systems for shelflisting, subject cataloging, and serials work. Important for systems design of subject cataloging systems using advanced technological methods.

DD50. Gilroy, Joyce. "An Expert System for Classification." *ITS News* 22 (Aug. 1990): 39–40.

Reports briefly on a project that examines the feasibility of using an expert system shell (Crystal) as a tool in applying the Dewey Decimal Classification. Of interest to those who are looking for innovative ideas in handling classification systems.

DD51. Humphrey, Susanne M. "Use and Management of Classification Systems for Knowledge-Based Indexing." In *Classification Research for Knowledge Representation and Organization: Proceedings of the 5th International Study Conference on Classification Research, Toronto, Canada, June 24–28, 1991,* edited by Nancy J. Williamson and Michele Hudon, 89–100. FID Publication, no. 698. Amsterdam: Elsevier Science Publishers, 1992.

Describes a research project at the National Library of Medicine that combines artificial intelligence and information retrieval in the development and testing of the MedIndEx (Medical Indexing Expert) System. This system is an interactive knowledge-based prototype for computer assisted indexing of the MEDLINE database. For use by indexers in a workstation environment to facilitate "expert indexing" at the National Library of Medicine. Of interest to users of the MEDLINE system and *Medical Subject Headings* (DD21) and to information professionals considering the development of frame-based subject heading or descriptor systems

DD52. Sharif, Carolyn A. *Developing an Expert System for Classification of Books Using Micro-Based Expert Systems Shells.* British Library Research Report, no. 32. London: British Library, 1988.

Report of an investigation into the feasibility of using commercially available expert systems shells to develop an expert system for classification of monographs. Three microcomputer-based shells were examined, and their methods of representing and manipulating classification schedules were implemented as knowledge bases. Both enumerative and faceted classification systems were used. While these systems are suggested as alternatives to developing expert systems from the ground up, as could be expected, they were demonstrated to have limitations that could have an impact on the efficiency of the classification system. Nevertheless, the study did show that such expert systems shells could be used in other library functions.

E

Authority Control

Stephen Hearn

Overview

Authority work, as defined in much of the literature covered in this chapter, generally emphasizes the process by which libraries ensure that the headings in their catalogs are consistent and that access is provided through cross-references to variant forms and related headings (e.g., Avram, EAD3; Clack, EAA2; Tillett, EAD20). Such a broad definition can result in a blurring of the distinction between authority work and cataloging, since simply formulating a heading according to cataloging rules such as *Anglo-American Cataloguing Rules*, second edition, revised 1988 (CBA1) often accomplishes the goal of providing unique and consistent access.

A more-specific definition of authority work and authority control has been adopted for the purposes of this chapter: the use of authority records and an authority file to control the form and definition of headings and multiply access to them. By this definition, formulating a heading for a bibliographic record does not by itself constitute authority work. Verifying a heading in an authority file marks the beginning of true authority work, while establishing and managing headings with authority records in an authority file becomes the central task of authority. This is not the only means by which authority control can be achieved; however, it is the method

that has been most fully developed and implemented in modern libraries.

The shared nature of cataloging explains the need for authority control to standardize headings. Catalogers sharing a file with each other and with users soon find that individuals cannot be relied on to use the same terms for their headings and searches. The authority file was developed to record and authorize the forms of headings used in a library's bibliographic records. Authority files have been developed at both the national and local levels. By making its cataloging available to smaller libraries, the Library of Congress (LC) encouraged widespread use of its authorized name and subject headings. At the same time, local libraries encountered the need for headings and decisions in their own catalogs for which no LC authority work was available and so found it necessary to maintain local authority files as well.

For years, the card file was the primary technology of authority control. However, managing authority work in a card environment proved more and more difficult over time, as the rate at which headings were added and modified increased (*see* Palmer, EC15). The development of online systems led to renewed interest in authority control, with its promise of swifter and far less cumbersome data-management techniques. However, with this increase in efficiency came a greater need for data

86

quality. Machine filing is more efficient and consistent than human filing but far less intelligent and forgiving. Online systems require much greater control of data quality to yield consistent indexes. Furthermore, the MARC formats were developed to permit better automated data transfer and management. These formats analyzed bibliographic data more finely and explicitly than had previously been the case, resulting in many new occasions for error. Thus, automated authority work has proved both more efficient and more demanding of data quality and consistency.

Various approaches have been taken to organizing and managing authority work in library catalogs. Some libraries mount significant in-house authority control efforts, while others rely on outside vendors to revise their headings and supply authority records for current cataloging. In-house authority work may be the task of a specialized unit or may be included in the work of cataloging unit staff. Vendors are often used to provide authority processing of files compiled during retrospective conversion, though usually with room for significant local decisions about the extent of that processing. No one approach to managing authority work is best for all libraries or for all situations.

Underlying these differences, the current cataloging environment depends on shared rules, standards, and records. The *Anglo-American Cataloguing Rules*, second edition, revised 1988 (CBA1) and *Library of Congress Rule Interpretations* (CBC11) standardize the form of name and title headings and references in most American libraries. Library of Congress Subject Headings (DD15) and LC's *Subject Cataloging Manual: Subject Headings* (DD20) are widely used to provide controlled subject access. LC's authority records are available on microfiche (EAC3 and EAC6) and in MARC format from major bibliographic utilities (OCLC, RLIN, WLN, Utlas), from authority processing vendors, and from LC's recent CD-ROM releases (EAC1 and EAC5). Some libraries purchase LC's MARC authority files (EAC2 and EAC7) directly from LC, with subscriptions to tape updates, for mounting directly on their online systems.

Despite this underlying standardization, utilities and local systems manipulate standard formats and data in diverse ways and offer significant differences in their handling and presentation of authority-controlled data. One major difference in approach is between linked and unlinked authority systems. In the former, authority-controlled headings are not stored in bibliographic records; instead, links are created between the bibliographic heading field and the corresponding authority record. Controlled heading searches are done in the authority file, and when a bibliographic record is displayed, the system reconstructs it from the linked authority data. WLN and Utlas use linked authority files. OCLC and RLIN use unlinked files; bibliographic and authority records are stored intact in separate files and must be searched independently. Some systems (e.g., NOTIS) offer a middle ground between these two structures by integrating entries from bibliographic and authority records into a single, merged index, without explicitly linking the records. Each approach has advantages and disadvantages, and recent vendor surveys indicate that new approaches and features are constantly being developed (Grady [EE13], Johnston [EE15]). This volatile area of system design promises continued innovation and increasing sophistication in the use of catalog data.

The underlying standards also are not fixed but continue to evolve. In its June 1992 meeting, the American Library Association's Machine-Readable Bibliographic Information Committee (MARBI) (KAB4), which is responsible for overseeing the development of the MARC formats, significantly expanded the number of fields in the MARC authorities format to accommodate subdivision records and different authorized vocabularies. ALA's Cataloging Committee: Description and Access (CC:DA) reviews proposed changes to the Anglo-American cataloging rules and forwards its comments to the Joint Steering Committee for revision of Anglo-American cataloging rules. The Library of Congress, in consultation with ALA's Subject Analysis Committee and other groups, is currently engaged in a major effort to simplify its subject headings and subdivisions and the rules governing them (*see The Future of Subdivisions in the Library of Congress Subject Headings System*, 1992, EC5; *Cataloging Service Bulletin*, CBC10, numbers 54 and following). In short, it is not enough to adopt current standards; libraries also must be committed to keeping up with them.

Driving many of the changes in both systems and standards are emerging needs for new kinds of authority control and new uses of authority data. Recent changes to the MARC authorities format are designed to accommodate better linkages among headings in different subject systems and among headings in different languages and written in different characters. Much of the recent research in authority control has been devoted to techniques for making library catalogs more responsive to user searching vocabularies. Improved data-manipulation techniques using authority records hold out the promise of more efficient, timely, and accurate validation and revision of controlled headings and subdivisions. And always, librarians and library users look for more sophisticated access to the highly encoded data in MARC bibliographic and authority records.

In their search for more efficient cataloging and searching methodologies, some librarians have raised questions about the value of authority work, particularly for names. A number of research studies have concluded that modern name authority work adds few useful cross-references to the catalog and that its purposes could be better served by search manipulation techniques such as automatic right truncation and keyword searching (Taylor, EB15 and EE30; Thomas, EB18; Weintraub, EB23). However, as Wajenberg (EE32) and Thomas observe, a change in the rules for constructing cross-references that presumes the availability of these techniques would require a greater standardization of the searching capabilities of online systems than has emerged thus far. In any case, it is important to remember that many of problems that result in failed searches (searching the wrong index, searching with an initial article, searching names in direct order, typographical errors, etc.) are not problems that authority control is intended to address. New system-design strategies are clearly needed to address these other problems, but such strategies should not be seen as competing alternatives to authority control. Both are necessary to provide library users with precise, comprehensive, and reliable information retrieval.

In addition to changes in systems and technical standards, changes in institutional relationships may also be necessary. The ever-increasing volume of cataloging data threatens to become unmanageable. The Name Authority Cooperative program, or NACO, was begun by the Library of Congress as a way of sharing the burden of authority work with the library community. The NACO acronym has since been inherited by LC's NAtional Coordinated Cataloging Operations. The Library of Congress is currently exploring changes to the NACO program to increase its flexibility and is engaged in projects to solicit greater participation from the library community in building its name and subject authority files ("Meetings," *Library of Congress Information Bulletin*, 1992, EG3).

In the future, new organizational structures may emerge to manage a shared national authority file that has outgrown LC's own file. The result will be broader participation than is currently possible but without sacrificing the quality control that LC's presence as gatekeeper has provided. International efforts also face obstacles that are more organizational than technical as librarians pursue the goal of an international clearinghouse for authority data and a mechanism for linking the authority records of different national libraries (Bourdon, EB2).

Still, the goals of authority control are worth striving for. Authority work can ensure consistent access to library materials, but it can also do much more. Authority records can define the terms that they establish with scope and usage notes; they can enrich the available searching vocabulary by multiplying the access to a term through cross-references from variant forms; and they can make explicit the diverse relationships between personal names, corporate bodies, series, topical concepts, etc., for the catalog user. When authority records are integrated with bibliographic records and formatted for public display, the result is a metacatalog. The library catalog is transformed from an alphabetical list into a complex semantic web providing the intellectual structure and connections necessary for efficient access to the bibliographic universe.

Chapter Content and Organization

The bibliography that follows is selective and limited in scope. Its primary foci are on automated authority control in the North American context and on articles and tools of practical use to librarians charged with planning and carrying out authority work. Consequently, it does not attempt to cover the significant body of theoretical and experimental literature related to indexing vocabularies or the many valuable authority systems that have found only limited or specialized use in North American libraries. The author hopes that the sources included will help librarians make decisions, assign priorities to tasks, plan procedures, and carry out the work necessary to achieving authority control in their catalogs.

EA
General Works

EAA
Textbooks, Guides, and Manuals

EAA1. Burger, Robert H. *Authority Work: The Creation, Use, Maintenance, and Evaluation of Authority Records and Files.* Littleton, Colo.: Libraries Unlimited, 1985.

A thoughtful and readable introduction to authority control principles and decision making, the creation and maintenance of authority files, and the evaluation of different authority control systems. Includes an appendix on the MARC authorities format and a bibliography.

EAA2. Clack, Doris H. *Authority Control: Principles, Applications, and Instructions.* Chicago: American Library Association, 1990.

Discusses many aspects of authority control, with emphasis on practical guidance in the construction of authority records and references. Most examples are in card format, but the book includes a chapter on the MARC authorities. Other chapters focus on general principles, on the structure of the authority record, and on different types of headings. The book concludes with a brief guide to reference sources useful for doing authority work and an extensive bibliography. A generally helpful guide, though suffering a certain number of errors in the examples and tables.

EAA3. Library of Congress, Office of Subject Cataloging Policy. *Subject Cataloging Manual: Subject Headings.* 4th ed. 2 vols. Washington, D.C.: Government Printing Office, 1991. Loose-leaf.

See also annotation under DD20. The primary source for rules governing the form of subject headings and the use of subject subdivisions.

EAA4. Miller, R. Bruce. *Name Authority Control for Card Catalogs in the General Library.* Austin, Tex.: General Libraries, University of Texas at Austin, 1981.

A technical manual for card-based authority control in a large university library system, highly prescriptive but grounded in national standards and conventions. Includes detailed instructions for preparing authority card sets, for maintaining central control over branch catalogs, and for dealing with split files with minimal revision of bibliographic headings. The most thorough handbook available for card-based authority control.

EAA5. Taylor, Arlene G. *Cataloging with Copy: A Decision-Maker's Handbook.* 2nd ed. Englewood, Colo.: Libraries Unlimited, 1988.

See also annotation under CAB5. Though not exclusively about authority control, Taylor's book makes numerous valuable points about the challenges of maintaining authority control in a copy cataloging environment. Includes a helpful summary of LC MARC authority records (311–327) and many examples of card and MARC format authorities to clarify specific points in the discussion.

EAA6. *Utlas MARC Coding Manual for Authorities.* 1st ed. Compiled and edited by Elizabeth Black. Toronto: Utlas International Canada, a Division of International Thomson Limited, 1987– . Loose-leaf.

For annotation, *see* DD8.

EAB
Codes and Standards

EAB1. *Anglo-American Cataloguing Rules.* 2nd ed., 1988 rev. Edited by Michael Gorman and Paul Winkler. Chicago: American Library Association, 1988.

See also annotation under CBA1. Chapters 22–26 are the primary source for rules governing the form of name and uniform title headings and references.

EAB2. International Federation of Library Associations and Institutions, Division of Bibliographic Control, Section on Classification and Indexing, Working Group on Guidelines for Subject Authority Files. *Guidelines for Subject Authority Files and Reference Entries.* Frankfurt am Main, Ger.: IFLA, Universal Bibliographic Control and International MARC Programme [publication forthcoming, ca. 1993–94].

For annotation, *see* DD5.

EAB3. International Federation of Library Associations and Institutions, Working Group on an International Authority System. *Guidelines for Authority and Reference Entries.* London: IFLA International Programme for UBC, 1984.

International guidelines for name authority control and the development of name authority records developed by an international committee of experts. Known as *GARE.*

EAB4. National Library of Canada, Canadian MARC Office. *Canadian MARC Communication Format: Authorities.* 3rd ed. Ottawa: Canadian MARC Office. 1988– . Loose-leaf.

See also annotation under DD6. An essential tool for users of CAN/MARC authorities.

EAB5. *UNIMARC/Authorities: Universal Format for Authorities.* Munich; New York: K. G. Saur, 1991.

The UNIMARC authorities format is related to the bibliographic format in much the same way that the two US-MARC formats are related. Though the format is designed to carry data based on a variety of cataloging rules, in this case a specific set of rules—the IFLA *Guidelines for Authority and Reference Entries* (EAB3)—serves as the foundation for the format.

EAB6. *USMARC Format for Authority Data: Including Guidelines for Content Designation.* Washington, D.C.: Cataloging Distribution Service, Library of Congress. 1987– . Loose-leaf.

See also annotation under DD7. The primary source for MARC authority record structure, definitions of fields and subfields, and instructions in their use. Accompanying blue pages record LC and NACO usage guidelines.

EAC
Sources for Authorized Headings

NAMES

EAC1. Library of Congress, Catalog Publication Division. *CD MARC Names.* [database on CD-ROM] Washington, D.C.: Cataloging Distribution Service, LC, 1988– .

Quarterly, with each issue cumulative. ISSN 1041-2964. 3 discs.

See also annotation under CCB1. Contains the entire LC name authority file of approximately three million records in CD-ROM format. Includes authority records for personal, corporate, and geographic names; uniform titles; and series. Provides a sophisticated search mode, facilitating keyword searching using Boolean logic. Subscription includes retrieval software, a reference manual, a ready-reference card, and a keyboard template.

EAC2. _____. *Name Authorities.* [database on magnetic tape] Washington, D.C.: Cataloging Distribution Service, LC, 1988– . Weekly.

MARC records for personal, corporate, conference, and geographic name headings, uniform titles, and series established by LC and cooperating libraries under the NAtional Coordinated Cataloging Operations (NACO) program. Names written in non-Roman script appear in romanized form only. Retrospective (1977–1991) file available.

EAC3. _____. *Name Authorities.* Cumulative Microform Edition. [microform] Washington, D.C.: Cataloging Distribution Service, LC. 1979– . Quarterly, with each issue cumulative. ISSN 0195-9093.

See also annotation under CCB2. A single source in microfiche for all LC name and series authority records, including personal and corporate names, conference headings, uniform titles, and series. Also lists geographic names of political and civil jurisdictions. Useful for all catalogers responsible for assigning name headings and uniform titles. Available also in CD-ROM (EAC1) and magnetic tape (EAC2) formats and through the bibliographic utilities. The microfiche have a reduction ratio of 48 ×. Began with 1977/Sept. 1979. The 1992 subscription consists of four quarterly issues cumulating for the year, as well as a cumulative fifth issue for the period 1987-1992. Supersedes the book format *Library of Congress Name Headings with References* (1974–1980).

SUBJECTS

EAC4. Library of Congress, Office for Subject Cataloging Policy. *LC Subject Headings: Weekly Lists.* Washington, D.C.: Cataloging Distribution Service, LC. 1993– .

For annotation, *see* DD10.

EAC5. Library of Congress, Subject Cataloging Division. *CDMARC Subjects.* [database on CD-ROM] Washington, D.C.: Cataloging Distribution Service, LC. Issue 1– , June 1988– . Quarterly, with each issue cumulative.

For annotation, *see* DD11.

EAC6. _____. *Library of Congress Subject Headings.* Cumulative Microform Edition. [microform] Washington, D.C.: Cataloging Distribution Service, LC. Jan./Mar. 1976– . Quarterly, with each issue cumulative. ISSN 0361-5243.

For annotation, *see* DD12.

EAC7. _____. *Subject Authorities.* [database on magnetic tape] Washington, D.C: Cataloging Distribution Service, 1992– .

For annotation, *see* DD14.

EAC8. _____. *Library of Congress Subject Headings.* 4 vols. Washington, D.C.: Cataloging Distribution Service, LC, 1990– . Annual. ISSN 1048-9711.

See also annotation under DD15. Contains the subject headings prepared by the Library of Congress for its collections and used as the basis for the development of LC's subject authority files. Available in four physical formats—print, CD-ROM (DD11), microform (DD12), magnetic tape (DD14), and in the databases of bibliographic utilities (OCLC, RLIN, WLN, etc.).

EAD
General Resources

EAD1. "Archives and Authority Control: Proceedings of a Seminar Sponsored by the Smithsonian Institution, October 27, 1987." Edited by Avra Michelson. *Archival Informatics Technical Report* 2, no. 2 (Summer 1988).

Includes papers from the seminar, several of which (by Jackie M. Dooley, Thomas Garnett, Marion Matters, and Richard V. Szary) are cited separately below, as well as an introduction by the editor, transcripts of panel discussions, and a bibliography. Of interest to both librarians and archivists.

EAD2. Auld, Larry. "Authority Control: An Eighty-Year Review." *Library Resources & Technical Services* 26 (Oct./Dec. 1982): 319–30.

Traces the development of authority control principles and practices from files kept for catalogers' convenience to an essential element of national and international shared cataloging. Includes a brief bibliography.

EAD3. Avram, Henriette D. "Authority Control and Its Place." *The Journal of Academic Librarianship* 9, no. 6 (Jan. 1984): 331–35.

A clear presentation of the purpose of authority control, its role in library operations and benefits to library users, and the advantages of centralizing authority control efforts.

EAD4. Baer, Nadine, and Karl E. Johnson. "The State of Authority." *Information Technology and Libraries* 7, no. 2 (June 1985): 139–53.

A three-part article, including a valuable review of authority control literature from 1972 to 1986, the results of a survey of authority control functions and activities in academic libraries, and an analysis of new personal and corporate name entries added to the University of Rhode Island catalog. The authors conclude that authority control is essential in online catalogs and that without it any catalog suffers increasing heading inconsistencies over time.

EAD5. Bearman, David. "Authority Control Issues and Prospects." *American Archivist* 52, no. 3 (Summer 1989): 286–99.

Explores the need of archives for different types of authority control, discounting the value of traditional subject authority work in favor of standardized data for geography, chronology, form, and function; and informational name authority records containing history, affiliations, and other data. Though the means of coordinating and relating the multiple specialized authority files called for are not clearly addressed, and the implicit notion that explicit access can be provided to all aspects of a collection or entity is utopian, the ideas presented are provocative and of general interest.

EAD6. Bulaong, Grace. "Authorities and Standards in a Changing World. Parts 1-2." *International Cataloguing* 11, no. 3 (July/Sept. 1982): 35-36; 11, no. 4 (Oct./Dec. 1982): 41-44.

Describes the impact of changing standards and technologies on library cataloging and authority work. Concludes that the use of records from multiple databases with varying degrees of authority control requires renewed authority work efforts to ensure collocation of entries and comprehensive searching for users of the catalog.

EAD7. Burns, Barrie A. F. "Authority Control in Two Languages." In *Authority Control: The Key to Tomorrow's Catalog: Proceedings of the 1979 Library and Information Technology Association Institutes*, edited by Mary W. Ghikas, 128–57. Phoenix: Oryx Press, 1982.

Discusses problems encountered by the National Library of Canada in attempting to provide bilingual library cataloging and authority control, and some solutions. Though the solutions may be somewhat dated, the discussion of problems and policy options is still useful and relevant.

EAD8. Calhoun, Karen, and Mike Oskins. "Rates and Types of Changes to LC Authority Files." *Information Technology and Libraries* 11, no. 2 (June 1992): 132–36.

Reports on a study of updates to LC's name and subject authority files that found that 60 percent of name file updates are new records, while 60 percent of subject file updates are changed records. A closer analysis of name file changes found an average of sixty significant 1XX heading changes per production day. Concludes that local system files need regular updating to stay consistent with LC's dynamic authority files.

EAD9. Delsey, Tom. "Authority Control in an International Context." *Cataloging & Classification Quarterly* 9, no. 3 (1989): 13–28.

Charts the progress of the International Federation of Library Associations (IFLA) toward the development of international standards for the structure and elements of name headings and of the UNIMARC/Authorities format. Differing national conventions have led planners to propose a clearinghouse model for assigning standard numbers to established named entities to be used for linking different versions of a record and distributing them to their appropriate users. A clear account of a complex, ongoing, international effort.

EAD10. Dooley, Jackie M. "An Introduction to Authority Control for Archivists." *Archival Informatics Technical Report* 2, no. 2 (Summer 1988): 5–18.

Presents the purposes, methods, and standards of authority control from an archival perspective. A useful introduction for both archivists and librarians.

EAD11. Dwyer, James R. "The Road to Access & the Road to Entropy." *Library Journal* 112, no. 14 (1 Sept. 1987): 131–36.

Discusses factors that diminish catalog access to library materials, including incomplete retrospective conversion, lack of authority control, poor copy cataloging records, and inadequate systems. Calls for improvements in all these areas to improve catalog consistency and better serve catalog users.

EAD12. Evans, Max J. "Authority Control: An Alternative to the Record Group Concept." *American Archivist* 49, no. 3 (Summer 1986): 249–61.

Advocates the use of enhanced corporate name authority records rather than record group hierarchies to organize access to archival series and record groups, stressing the flexibility with which an authority file can relate different agencies and series and accommodate new information and relationships. Valuable for the emphasis the author places on the authority file as an informational database in its own right.

EAD13. Gregor, Dorothy. "Creating Authority Records at the Library of Congress: LC's Assumptions." In *Authority Control in Music Libraries: Proceedings of the Music Library Association Preconference, March 5, 1985*, edited by Ruth Tucker, 35–43. Canton, Mass.: Music Library Association, 1989.

Presents the assumptions underlying LC's approach to name and series authority work—that authority work is worth doing, that it is most cost effective to do it at the highest level of the network hierarchy, and that the task of creating authority records should be shared. Describes the long review process that LC authority records must undergo. Questions whether name authority records are needed in all cases, with a suggestion from LC's Lucia Rather that computer-generated authority records might better suffice for some names.

EAD14. Jaramillo, George R. "Authority Control: Is It Needed for the 80's?" *Colorado Libraries* 11 (Spring 1985): 24–27.

Discusses the need for authority control in light of user studies. Concludes that authority control is needed to provide reliable, comprehensive search results and predicts that online subject control may result in increased use of subject searching.

EAD15. Matters, Marion. ''Authority Files in an Archival Setting.'' *Archival Informatics Technical Report* 2, no. 2 (Summer 1988): 29–33.

Describes authority control procedures developed by the Minnesota Historical Society's Division of Archives and Manuscripts. Useful to both archivists and librarians for its discussion of the problems of finding compromises between national authority standards and local access needs.

EAD16. _____. ''Authority Work for Transitional Catalogs.'' In *Describing Archival Materials: The Use of the MARC AMC Format*, edited by Richard Smiraglia, 91–115. New York: Haworth Press, 1990.

Discusses the use of authority records in archives for both the management of headings and the recording of historical and contextual information about the entity named. Recommends adherence to national standards and calls for the development of authority records capable of enhanced information storage and retrieval. The author's comments are clear, forward-looking, and applicable to bibliographic as well as archival authority work.

EAD17. Miller, R. Bruce. ''Authority Control in the Network Environment.'' In *Authority Control: The Key to Tomorrow's Catalog: Proceedings of the 1979 Library Information and Technology Association Institutes*, edited by Mary W. Ghikas, 36–52. Phoenix: Oryx Press, 1982.

Useful if somewhat dated discussion of costs associated with doing and not doing authority work. Uses cost figures to argue that individual library resources should be pooled to support network-level authority control research and development.

EAD18. Schmierer, Helen F. ''The Relationship of Authority Control to the Library Catalog.'' *Illinois Libraries* 62, no. 7 (Sept. 1980): 599–603.

Describes the purpose and process of authority control. Argues for authority control as essential to fulfilling the gathering function of library catalogs.

EAD19. Taylor, Arlene G. ''Research and Theoretical Considerations in Authority Control.'' *Cataloging & Classification Quarterly* 9, no. 3 (1989): 29–56.

Summarizes recent research into the necessity, techniques, and effectiveness of authority control. A thoughtful, well-organized bibliographic essay.

EAD20. Tillett, Barbara B. ''Authority Control: An Overview.'' In *Authority Control in Music Libraries: Proceedings of the Music Library Association Preconference, March 5, 1985*, edited by Ruth Tucker, 4–14. Canton, Mass.: Music Library Association, 1989.

Discusses definitions of authority work and authority control and potential applications of computers to authority work. Stresses the need for authority control in library catalogs and the need for shared standards and automation to reduce the costs of authority work.

EAD21. Truitt, Marc. ''USMARC to UNIMARC/Authorities: A Qualitative Evaluation of USMARC Data Ele-

ments.'' *Library Resources & Technical Services* 36, no. 1 (Jan. 1992): 37–58.

See also annotation under KBD4. Compares the US-MARC and UNIMARC authorities formats to explore the possibilities of translating data from one to the other. The author notes differences between the formats (e.g., use of explicit interrecord links and language codes in UNIMARC) that would pose problems for translation and that suggest modifications the USMARC format may need to undergo.

EAD22. Udoh, D. J. E., and M. R. Aderibigbe. ''The Problems of Development, Maintenance, and Automation of Authority Files in Nigeria.'' *Cataloging & Classification Quarterly* 8, no. 1 (1987): 93–103.

Discusses the need both for local adaptation of LCSH and cataloging rules in the Nigerian context and for standardization of headings and cataloging practice among Nigerian libraries. The authors caution against adopting automation when technical support is uncertain, calling instead for greater attention to the coordinated building of a national authority file.

EAE
Periodicals

At this writing, no serial publication devotes itself exclusively to authority control. New developments are often covered in more general cataloging journals, such as the following.

EAE1. *Annual Review of Information Science and Technology*. Medford, N.J.: Learned Information. v. 1– , 1966– . Annual. ISSN 0066-4200.

For annotation, *see* DAB1.

EAE2. *Cataloging & Classification Quarterly*. New York: Haworth Press. v. 1– , Fall 1980– . Quarterly. ISSN 0163-9374.

For annotation, *see* CAE3.

EAE3. *Cataloging Service Bulletin*. Washington, D.C.: Library of Congress, Cataloging Distribution Service. no. 1– , Summer 1978– . Quarterly. ISSN 0160-8029.

For annotation, *see* CAE4.

EAE4. *Information Technology and Libraries*. Chicago: Library and Information Technology Association. v. 1– , March 1982– . Quarterly. ISSN 0730-9295. Continues *Journal of Library Automation*.

For annotation, *see* AF10.

EAE5. *Library of Congress Rule Interpretations*. 2nd ed. Washington, D.C.: Cataloging Distribution Services, 1990– .

For annotation, *see* CBC11.

EAE6. *Library Resources & Technical Services*. Chicago: Association for Library Collections and Technical Services. v. 1– . 1957– . Quarterly. ISSN 0024-2527.

For annotation, *see* AF13.

Three additional sources that often include reports of conference sessions and other authority-related events follow.

EAE7. *ALCTS Newsletter*. Chicago: Association for Library Collections and Technical Services. v. 1– , 1990– . Frequency varies. ISSN 1047-949X.

For annotation, *see* AF5.

EAE8. *Library of Congress Information Bulletin*. Washington, D.C: Library of Congress. v. 31– , Jan. 6, 1972– . Biweekly. ISSN 0041-7904.

General information newsletter of the Library of Congress.

EAE9. *LITA Newsletter*. Chicago: Library and Information Technology Association. no. 1– , Winter 1980– . Quarterly. ISSN 0196-1799.

For annotation, *see* AF17.

EAF
Sources of Expertise

There are several professional groups devoted to authority control. In addition, many automated systems vendors have organized interest groups devoted to cataloging and authorities; contact the system vendor or user group for more information. The professional-association group of particular interest follows.

PROFESSIONAL ASSOCIATIONS

EAF1. ALA LITA/ALCTS CCS Authority Control in the Online Environment Interest Group.

This in an interdivisional group that provides a forum for discussion of issues related to authority control for online catalogs and for international sharing of authority of data. *See also* annotations for ALA's Library and Information Technology Association (LITA) (AGA5) and Association for Library Collection and Technical Services (ALCTS) (AGA3).

ELECTRONIC DISCUSSION GROUPS

A growing number of electronic mail lists (also called electronic discussion groups or LISTSERVs) devoted to library topics have emerged in the last few years. Each list functions both as a bulletin board for announcements and as a forum for posing questions and discussing issues. The two lists of most immediate relevance to authority control follow.

EAF2. AUTOCAT [electronic discussion group].

For annotation, *see* CAF3.

EAF3. USMARC-L [electronic discussion group].

USMARC-L, USMARC Advisory Group Forum, is a moderated forum operated on behalf of the USMARC Advisory Group by the Library of Congress Network Development and MARC Standards Office in cooperation with the University of Maine System Libraries and Computer and Data Processing Services. Intended for the discussion of issues related to the development, maintenance, and implementation of the MARC formats. Subscribers may also retrieve all proposals for changes to the MARC formats and MARBI discussion papers from the list. The forum is open to anyone interested in its topics. To subscribe, send a message to: **USMARC@SUN7.LOC.GOV** (INTERNET) with the command: **SUBSCRIBE USMARC-L [your name]**.

EB
Name and Uniform Title
Authority Control

EB1. Anderson, Douglas. "Automatically Generated References in Minimal-Level Authority Records." *Information Technology and Libraries* 10, no. 4 (Dec. 1991): 251–62.

Proposes a number of ways in which data in bibliographic and minimal authority records could be used to generate references from variant forms automatically for name and name/title headings. Also notes numerous complications and exceptions that would have to be taken into account.

EB2. Bourdon, Francoise. "How Can IFLA Contribute to Solving Problems in Name Authority Control at the International Level?" *International Cataloguing and Bibliographic Control* 20, no. 4 (Oct./Dec. 1991): 54–55.

Summarizes the author's original French report, "La coopération internationale en matière de données d'autorité auteurs: constats, refléxions, recommandations," inquiring into problems facing international exchange of authority data. Identifies lack of definitions for international authority goals and data types and the varieties of cataloging agency goals and systems as problems. Calls for renewed commitment to establishing names nationally and sharing name authority data internationally and for a concerted effort to overcome organizational obstacles to the use of an ISADN (International Standard Authority Data Number) to facilitate exchange.

EB3. Dickson, Jean, and Patricia Zadner. "Authority Control and the Authority File: A Functional Evaluation of LCNAF on RLIN." *Cataloging & Classification Quarterly* 9, no. 3 (1989): 57–71.

Finds that catalogers' use of LC's name authority file to verify headings rarely uses references and that bibliographic records often contain more complete information for this purpose than authority records. Argues for the value of indexes integrating bibliographic and authority records and against the need for many personal name authorities.

EB4. Dixson, Larry E. "Creating Authority Records for Music Materials Cataloged at the Library of Congress." In *Authority Control in Music Libraries: Proceedings of the Music Library Association Preconference, March 5, 1985,* edited by Ruth Tucker, 44–54. Canton, Mass.: Music Library Association, 1989.

Describes rules used by LC's Music Section for determining name and uniform title headings and references, with examples. Also presents data comparing MARC record length and field occurrence frequencies in book and music format records in LC's online file.

EB5. Elias, Cathy Ann, and C. James Fair. "Name Authority Control in a Communication System." *Special Libraries* 74 (July 1983): 289–96.

Reports the experience of a Standard Oil public relations office that found that a lack of authority control in its media queries database resulted in variant entries and potentially costly retrieval problems, though only three staff were involved in creating the records. The solution cited consists of a simple set of rules for formulating entries.

EB6. Fuller, Elizabeth E. "Variation in Personal Names in Works Represented in the Catalog." *Cataloging & Classification Quarterly* 9, no. 3 (1989): 75–95.

Finds that 80 percent of personal author names in the study sample appear in only one form and analyzes patterns of variation in the remaining 20 percent. Argues against the need for full MARC authority records for the majority of personal names.

EB7. Houissa, Ali. "Arabic Personal Names: Their Components and Rendering in Catalog Entries." *Cataloging & Classification Quarterly* 13, no. 2 (1991): 3–22.

Explains the various elements of Arabic names, explores the difficulties of establishing them under *AACR2R* (CBA1), and offers advice on the choice of references. Includes an annotated bibliography of selected reference sources for Arabic personal names.

EB8. Lao, Shuk-fong, and Vicky Yang. "Chinese Personal Names and Titles: Problems in Cataloging and Retrieval." *Cataloging & Classification Quarterly* 13, no. 2 (1991): 45–65.

Discusses the variations commonly found in the romanization of Chinese names and the need for authority control and references in the public catalog to ensure good retrieval.

EB9. Maccaferri, James Tilio. "Cataloging Ottoman Turkish Personal Names." *Library Resources & Technical Services* 34, no. 1 (Jan. 1990): 62–78.

Discusses the history and unique aspects of Ottoman Turkish personal names and proposes a series of rules based on *AACR2R* (CBA1) for achieving greater consistency in headings of this type. A clear presentation of a complex subject.

EB10. Nagy, Karen. "Music Authority Control: A Public Service Perspective." In *Authority Control in Music Libraries: Proceedings of the Music Library Association Preconference, March 5, 1985,* edited by Ruth Tucker, 15–34. Canton, Mass.: Music Library Association, 1989.

Reports on a survey exploring the impact of *AACR2R* (CBA1) heading changes on music libraries. Notes that "those most satisfied with the current state of affairs almost always cited effective cross-references." Also includes a list of problematic composer names and titles developed at Northwestern University.

EB11. Ralli, Tony. "Cleaning Up the ABN Database." *Cataloguing Australia* 15, no. 2 (June 1989): 35–39.

Analyzes the problems of heading discrepancies and duplicate records found in the Australian Bibliographic Network that make searching the ABN more costly and inefficient. Cites a renewed commitment to, and better incentives for, doing authority work as essential to resolve the problems.

EB12. Roughton, Karen G., and David A. Tyckoson. "Browsing with Sound: Sound-Based Codes and Automated Authority Control." *Information Technology and Libraries* 4, no. 2 (June 1985): 130–37.

Discusses the use of SOUNDEX and Davidson's Consonant Code, two algorithms for reducing names to compressed coded forms of entry, to enhance retrieval in online catalogs. Proposes that sound-based codes be generated by computer and added as references to authority records and that searches yielding zero hits be passed through a similar process and matched with the authority references to provide additional options to the user.

EB13. Smiraglia, Richard P. "Authority Control and Uniform Titles for Music: Some Implications of Research." In *Authority Control in Music Libraries: Proceedings of the Music Library Association Preconference, March 5, 1985,* edited by Ruth Tucker, 63–70. Canton, Mass.: Music Library Association, 1989.

Reports on a study of music uniform titles based on a sample drawn from OCLC and the *National Union Catalog* (CCA1). Results show that LC's cataloged collection contains only a small proportion of the physical manifestations of music works identified elsewhere and that titles do vary significantly among the many manifestations of most musical works. Concludes that uniform titles are necessary to collocate music entries and that more references are needed on music uniform title authority records, along with a simpler process for creating such records.

EB14. _____. "Uniform Titles for Music: An Exercise in Collocating Works." *Cataloging & Classification Quarterly* 9, no. 3 (1989): 97–113.

Finds that musical works appear in multiple manifestations and with many title variations. Argues that authority control is needed both to standardize varying titles and to provide a logical organization for specific types of compositions.

EB15. Taylor, Arlene G. "Authority Files in Online Catalogs: An Investigation of Their Value." *Cataloging & Classification Quarterly* 4, no. 3 (Spring 1984): 1–17.

Reports on a study of no-hit name searches sampled from Northwestern's NOTIS system. Finds that references on authority records created according to LC rules and practice would have helped in only 6.4 percent of the cases, while automatic right hand truncation and term flipping would have helped in 40 percent of cases. Argues for rethinking the need to establish every name and for finding other ways to mediate between user search vocabulary and bibliographic headings.

EB16. _____. "Responding to User Needs: The Complementary Roles of Authority Control and System Design." In *Authority Control in Music Libraries: Proceedings of the Music Library Association Preconference, March 5, 1985*, edited by Ruth Tucker, 71–91. Canton, Mass.: Music Library Association, 1989.

Discusses linked and unlinked authority systems and examines author and title searches done at the Music Library at Northwestern to determine the usefulness of authority references. Concludes that many searches fail for reasons that can be better addressed through search processing functions (truncating, reversing search terms, checking for initial articles) rather than through explicit references and that the rules for formulating references should be reexamined. Includes a thoughtful analysis of detailed transaction logs.

EB17. _____. "Variations in Personal Name Access Points in OCLC Bibliographic Records." *Library Resources & Technical Services* 35, no. 2 (Apr. 1992): 224–41.

Reports on a study of the frequency and kinds of variation that occur in name headings found in a sample of OCLC records. Results of the study suggest that variant name headings occur on 18 to 24 percent of records in OCLC and other catalogs. Taylor also reports a decline in the frequency of variants over time for names with LC authority records and proposes machine-assisted solutions for dealing with certain types of variants.

EB18. Thomas, Catherine M. "Authority Control in Manual vs. Online Catalogs: An Examination of 'See' References." *Information Technology and Libraries* 3, no. 4 (Dec. 1984): 393–98.

Reports on a study that determined that keyword access to headings provided by University of California's MELVYL system obviates the need for references from inverted and less-than-full forms of names. Proposes that by adopting similar searching strategies and establishing

all names in their fullest form, the library community could simplify name authority work and shift the burden of enhancing retrieval to the automated system.

EB19. Tull, Laura, Norma Velez-Vendrell, and Jacque A. Halverson. "Establishing Geographic Names." *Cataloging & Classification Quarterly* 10, no. 3 (1990): 3–17.

Describes the process of creating authority records for geographic names in accordance with LC practice and gives examples of such records detailing the rules and decisions involved. Includes an annotated bibliography of selected reference sources for geographic names.

EB20. Vassie, Roderic. "A Reflection of Reality—Authority Control of Muslim Personal Names." *International Cataloguing and Bibliographic Control* 19, no. 1 (Jan./Mar. 1990): 3–6.

Describes the rich variety of Muslim naming conventions in different parts of the world and the inadequacies of current authority control efforts to encompass them. Calls for more informed, detailed research in establishing Muslim names.

EB21. Walfish, Barry. "Hebrew and Yiddish Personal Name Authorities under AACR2." *Cataloging & Classification Quarterly* 3, no. 4 (Summer 1983): 51–64.

Outlines a procedure for verifying and establishing Hebrew names based on LC guidelines. Describes the difficulties presented by differing transliteration systems and calls for the development of vernacular non-Roman records.

EB22. Watson, Mark R., and Arlene G. Taylor. "Implications of Current Reference Structures for Authority Work in Online Environments." *Information Technology and Libraries* 6, no. 1 (Mar. 1987): 10–19.

Reports on a study that finds that 83 percent of personal name authority records in LC's file contain no references, or no references that would be necessary in a system equipped with keyword searching and right-hand truncation. Findings are similar for 34 percent of corporate name authority records. Makes the point that the need for and utility of authority records and references can depend on searching capabilities of specific systems and calls for wider use of such searching features as a means of reducing authority work without sacrificing authority control.

EB23. Weintraub, Tamara S. "Personal Name Variations: Implications for Authority Control in Computerized Catalogs." *Library Resources & Technical Services* 35, no. 2 (Apr. 1991): 217–28.

Compares transcribed forms of names on bibliographic records and established name headings and references on authority records from the University of California at San Diego libraries to measure how often personal names vary, and in what ways. Concludes that 82 percent of the names show no variations in transcription, and that many of the references found would be unnecessary in catalogs with keyword searching and truncation capabilities.

EC
Subject Authority Control

EC1. American Library Association, Subject Analysis Committee, Ad Hoc Subcommittee on Library of Congress Subject Authority Control: Scope, Format, and Distribution. *Library of Congress Subject Authority Control: Scope, Format, and Distribution: A Final Report.* 1982. (Unpublished report.)

Presents recommendations to Library of Congress, some of which have been implemented (e.g., distribution of LCSH in MARC format), while others are still under discussion (e.g., creation of MARC authorities for all LC subject headings on LC records).

EC2. Bishoff, Liz. "Public Access to the Library of Congress Subject Headings Online." In *Subject Authorities in the Online Environment: Papers from a Conference Program Held in San Francisco, June 29, 1987*, edited by Karen Markey Drabenstott, 57–65. Chicago: American Library Association, 1991.

Reports on a series of focus group interviews with technical and public services staff indicating public services interest in accessing and using subject authority records. Also compares the advantages and disadvantages of controlled vs. keyword searching as viewed by both groups.

EC3. Chan, Lois Mai. "Functions of a Subject Authority File." In *Subject Authorities in the Online Environment: Papers from a Conference Program Held in San Francisco, June 29, 1987*, edited by Karen Markey Drabenstott, 9–30. Chicago: American Library Association, 1991.

Analyzes the dual function of LCSH as both an authority list and a thesaurus, and its usefulness for cataloging, database maintenance, thesaurus development, and retrieval. Insightful and well reasoned. Chan proposes a list of all subject headings used on LC records, though this chapter editor would question its value; even LC's headings are not uniformly valid, and many valid headings in use in other catalogs would not be represented. Maintaining such a list would also be a serious consideration.

EC4. Conway, Martha O'Hara. "Characteristics of Subject Headings in the Library of Congress BOOKSM Database." *Library Resources & Technical Services* 37, no. 1 (Jan. 1993): 47–58.

Analyzes a sample of LC-generated MARC records to determine patterns of subject heading and subdivision use practiced at LC. Concludes that subdivisions are heavily used, noting further that their use is largely rule-governed rather than specifically authorized by authority records. Recommends development of more sophisticated validation methods capable of coding and comparing categories of headings and subdivisions.

EC5. _____, ed. *The Future of Subdivisions in the Library of Congress Subject Headings System: Report from the Subject Subdivisions Conference Sponsored by the Library of Congress, May 9-12, 1991.* Washington, D.C.: Cataloging Distribution Service, Library of Congress, 1992.

See also annotation under DD18. An in-depth analysis of LC's subject subdivisions with papers arguing for and against four different options for revising LC's policies and practices, the conference's recommendations, and supporting documents. Progress on implementing the recommendations has been reported in LC's *Cataloging Service Bulletin* (CAE4), numbers 54 and following.

EC6. Dalrymple, Prudence W., and Jennifer A. Younger. "From Authority Control to Informed Retrieval: Framing the Expanded Domain of Subject Access." *College & Research Libraries* 52, no. 2 (Mar. 1991): 139–49.

Calls for a concerted effort by catalogers, bibliographic instruction librarians, and system designers to produce systems that incorporate controlled vocabulary and keyword searching techniques and the use of feedback to provide users with a better array of search assistance options. A valuable corrective to the mistake of regarding controlled vocabulary and keyword searching as exclusive, competing alternatives.

EC7. Drabenstott, Karen M. "Facilitating Geographic Subdivision Assignment in Subject Headings." *Library Resources & Technical Services* 36, no. 4 (Oct. 1992): 411–25.

Examines geographic subdivisions appearing in a sample of assigned subject headings drawn from OCLC, dividing valid and invalid geographic subdivisions into various categories. Recommends that (1) additional coding be authorized in the MARC authorities format to record indirect subdivision forms, (2) "SUBJECT USAGE" notes be made more consistent, and (3) the Direct/Indirect Geographic Subdivision Code be explicitly coded in MARC authority records for topical subdivisions. These changes would enable catalogers and system developers to do more machine validation and manipulation of geographic subdivision data.

EC8. _____. "The Need for Machine-Readable Authority Records for Topical Subdivisions." *Information Technology and Libraries* 11, no. 2 (June 1992): 91–104.

Presents the results of a study of LCSH subdivision usage as reflected in a sample of OCLC bibliographic records. Argues persuasively for the creation of subject subdivision authority records and for the inclusion in subject authority records of the categories in LC's *Subject Cataloging Manual: Subject Headings* (DD20) to which main headings and subdivisions are assigned in order to permit machine validation of subdivided headings.

EC9. Garrison, William A. "Practical Considerations in Using the Machine-readable LCSH." In *Subject Authorities in the Online Environment: Papers from a Conference Program Held in San Francisco, June 29, 1987*, edited by Karen Markey Drabenstott, 41–55. Chicago: American Library Association, 1991.

Discusses various aspects of LC's MARC subject heading file, including updated and deleted records, general explanatory references and notes, and problems with the use of pattern headings to verify headings and provide references. Also discusses Northwestern University's use of NOTIS to process and index subject authority records.

EC10. Lancaster, F. W. *Vocabulary Control for Information Retrieval.* 2nd ed. Arlington, Va.: Information Resources Press, 1986.

See also annotations under DD43 and FE5. A detailed analysis of the purposes and methods of vocabulary control and thesaurus construction, maintenance, and use. A clear exposition of the theories that underlie much subject authority work.

EC11. Mandel, Carol A. *Multiple Thesauri in Online Library Bibliographic Systems: A Report Prepared for Library of Congress Processing Services.* Washington, D.C.: Cataloging Distribution Service, Library of Congress, 1987.

See also annotation under DD44. A detailed survey and analysis of current developments in the use of multiple subject thesauri in online systems. Examines the searching and maintenance aspects of subject authority control in seven systems (ORION, WLN, DOBIS at the National Library of Canada, Utlas, Geac, NOTIS, and Carlyle's TOMUS), defines four approaches to managing access to files with multiple subject systems (segregated files, mixed vocabularies, integrated vocabularies, and front-end navigation), and discusses the use of multiple thesauri at LC. A thorough examination of a cutting-edge issue in online subject access.

EC12. ———. "Multiple Vocabularies in Subject Authority Control." In *Subject Authorities in the Online Environment: Papers from a Conference Program Held in San Francisco, June 29, 1987,* edited by Karen Markey Drabenstott, 67–81. Chicago: American Library Association, 1991.

Discusses different approaches to managing multiple subject vocabularies online, including segregated files, mixed files, intellectually integrated files, and front-end navigation. An excellent, concise analysis.

EC13. Markey, Karen, and Diane Vizine-Goetz. *Characteristics of Subject Authority Records in the Machine-Readable Library of Congress Subject Headings.* Dublin, Ohio: OCLC, Inc., 1988.

Presents a thorough, detailed analysis of LC's machine-readable subject authority file, including number of records in various categories, average and maximum record and field length, frequency of occurrence of various field tags, etc. A valuable resource for anyone planning to load and maintain LCSH online.

EC14. O'Neill, Edward T. "Interactive Authority Control." *The Bookmark* 47 (Spring 1989): 173–75.

Proposes drawing on developments in spelling checkers and user interface design to provide interactive help to catalogers dealing with erroneous subject entries and users getting no results from erroneous subject searches. The authority file would be used as the dictionary from which suggested alternate "spellings" would be retrieved.

EC15. Palmer, Joseph W. "Subject Authority Control and Syndetic Structure—Myths and Realities: An Inquiry into Certain Subject Heading Practices and Some Questions about Their Implications." *Cataloging & Classification Quarterly* 7, no. 2 (Winter 1986): 71–95.

See also annotation under DD33. Reports on a survey of subject authority control in the card catalogs of nine Erie County (N.Y.) libraries, which found limited use of "see" references, no use of "see also" references, and only occasional correction of obsolete headings. Though the author's data do not seem to justify his conclusion that syndetic structure in the catalog is "a complete myth," his study does demonstrate the serious erosion of subject authority control in many card catalogs, an erosion to which automated catalogs are also vulnerable if not maintained.

EC16. Pietris, Mary K. D. "Characteristics of LC Subject Headings That Should Be Taken into Account When Designing On-Line Catalogues." *Cataloguing Australia* 13, no. 3 (Sept. 1987): 70–80.

Explains various cases in which LC subject heading policy and practice result in unnatural forms of entry and omitted cross-references, as well as cases in which authorized LC subject headings are not found in LC's MARC records and legitimate headings are not authorized in LCSH. Encourages system designers to find ways to compensate for discrepancies between uncontrolled searcher vocabulary and the structured headings and references of LCSH.

EC17. ———. "Library of Congress Subject Headings: Past Imperfect, Future Indicative." *Cataloguing Australia* 13, no. 3 (Sept. 1987): 8–19.

Describes trends at LC toward simpler, more direct subject headings, clearer hierarchical structure, use of free-floating subdivisions, and better documentation. Also discusses projects to update classification numbers in subject authorities, revise scope notes and cross-references, and eliminate name headings from the subject file. A helpful explanation of problems with LCSH and LC's efforts to resolve them.

EC18. Randtke, Angela W. "Automated Pre-Coding of Free-Floating Subdivisions in Subject Authority Control at the University of North Florida Libraries." *Cataloging & Classification Quarterly* 15, no. 1 (1992): 27–48.

Describes programs that extend the processing of NOTIS new and dropped subject headings lists to indicate whether subject subdivisions are verified and appropriate for use under given types of headings. Single letter codes representing categories of main headings under which a subdivision is appropriate are added to a locally maintained list of free-floating subdivisions. The local list is then used to verify subdivisions in new headings and to report out the code letters to assist human review of the new headings. Also calls for changes to the MARC authority format to permit coding of heading types and the creation of subdivision records with complementary coding.

EC19. Schauder, Cherry. "Library of Congress Subject Heading Reference Structure and OPACS." *Cataloguing Australia* 17, no. 3/4 (Sept./Dec. 1991): 44–64.

Presents the results of a survey of LCSH references in Australian academic library online public access catalogs (OPACs), that generally found high levels of interest but limited staff and funding for implementation of such references. Systems capable of loading and displaying MARC authority records are offered as the most hopeful solution to the problem. Includes a bibliography.

EC20. Vizine-Goetz, Diane, and Karen Markey. "Characteristics of Subject Heading Records in the Machine-Readable Library of Congress Subject Headings." *Information Technology and Libraries* 8, no. 2 (June 1989): 203–9.

Presents data from a statistical analysis of LC's MARC subject authority file as of July 1987, measuring characteristics such as record length, field length, and frequency of occurrence for various MARC tags. Also presents statistics for records enhanced by the addition of narrower term references.

ED
Series Authority Control

ED1. Botero, Cecilia, Colleen Thorburn, and Nancy Williams. "Series in an Online Integrated System: An Option beyond the MARC Authority Record." *Cataloging & Classification Quarterly* 11, no. 2 (1990): 49–67.

Describes the University of Florida Libraries' use of serial bibliographic records as substitutes for series authority records in its NOTIS system. Could also be useful to libraries whose systems lack an authority file.

ED2. Santizo, Nedria A., and Charlene S. Rezabek. "Series Authority Control: Report of a Survey." *Cataloging & Classification Quarterly* 15, no. 1 (1992): 75–81.

Reports on a survey of NOTIS libraries that found a general reliance on vendors for the creation of authority files, use of both professional and paraprofessional staff in authority control units, and a continuing commitment to series authority control. Exceptions are noted to each trend. University of Oklahoma used the survey results to design its own series authority work flow.

ED3. Wilson, Mary Dabney. "Back to the Concept: Perspectives on Series Authorities." *Information Technology and Libraries* 7, no. 1 (Mar. 1988): 79–83.

Recounts the history of cataloging rules regarding series description and access. A blurring of the distinction

between these two functions in previous and current rules created negative consequences for automated authority control. A careful analysis, which resulted in a redefinition of the USMARC series fields.

EE
Automated Systems

The works cited in this section are intended to represent the range of automated techniques that librarians and system designers have employed to manage authority control data. Though an effort has been made to avoid accounts of outmoded approaches, features described do not necessarily reflect the current state of the systems discussed.

EE1. Brandt, Scott. "Authority Files for Microcomputer Databases." *Special Libraries* 79, no. 4 (Fall 1988): 296–301.

Describes the use of CODEN data (unique identification numbers assigned to scientific and technical materials) to link latest issue information with an authority file of journal titles in a microcomputer database. Notes that this local solution resulted in lower input costs and greater file consistency and accuracy.

EE2. Burger, Robert H. "Artificial Intelligence and Authority Control." *Library Resources & Technical Services* 28, no. 4 (Oct./Dec. 1984): 337–45.

Uses AI concepts to describe the functional differences between linked and unlinked authority control systems and to argue that linked systems may dispense with the concept of a single authorized form, relying instead on record number links for collocation. The problem of exporting records from a linked system without unique authorized headings is not addressed.

EE3. Clack, Doris H. "Authority Control and Linked Bibliographic Databases." *Cataloging & Classification Quarterly* 8, nos. 3/4 (1988): 35–46.

Notes the evolution of library catalogs from manual card files to online systems linked in various networks. Stresses the need for standards, cooperation, and authority control to facilitate intersystem searching and communication.

EE4. Coyne, Fumiko H., and Ingrid Mifflin. "Shared Authority Control at the Western Library Network." *Library Resources & Technical Services* 34, no. 4 (Oct. 1990): 493–503.

Describes local and network procedures for maintaining authorized headings at Washington State University using WLN's linked authority file. Argues for the advantages of a shared linked authority system for verifying and revising bibliographic headings.

EE5. Drabenstott, Karen M. ''The Need for Machine-Readable Authority Records for Topical Subdivisions.'' *Information Technology and Libraries* 11, no. 2 (June 1992): 91–104.

For annotation, *see* EC8.

EE6. Epstein, Susan Baerg. ''Automated Authority Control: A Hidden Time Bomb? Parts 1–2.'' *Library Journal* 110, no. 18 (1 Nov. 1985): 36–37; 111, no. 1 (Jan. 1986): 55–56.

A cautionary essay that points out problems of access to current authority data, conflicting subject heading systems, increased data storage demands, updating of headings used for shelving, blind references, and the continuing need for human review and decision making.

EE7. Fox, Judith A., and Kay Kanafani. ''Global Change Capabilities to Improve Authority Control in an Online Catalog.'' *Information Technology and Libraries* 8, no. 3 (Sept. 1989): 273–83.

Describes local global change programs developed at Washington University to work with its NOTIS system. Includes a useful discussion of the involved processing sequence used and pitfalls to be avoided when changing geographic subdivisions.

EE8. Garnett, Thomas. ''Development of an Authority Control System for the Smithsonian Institution Libraries.'' *Archival Informatics Technical Report* 2, no. 2 (Summer 1988): 21–27.

Describes the process of working with Geac to develop and implement an authority control system. Provides a detailed analysis of the insights and problems encountered in this process, which should be of interest to any library undertaking such a project.

EE9. Gibbs, George E., and Diane Bisom. ''Creating an Interactive Authority File for Names in the UCLA ORION System: Specifications and Decisions.'' *Cataloging & Classification Quarterly* 9, no. 3 (1989): 153–69.

Describes the process and specifications used for building ORION's linked authority file; problems encountered with filing indicators, series, and uniform titles; and solutions to the latter.

EE10. Goldman, Helen, and Carolyn Havens. ''Authority Control Efficiency Increase: NOTIS Online Authority and Merged Headings.'' *Cataloging & Classification Quarterly* 12, no. 2 (1990): 27–45.

Reports statistical evidence that Auburn University managed to increase the number of name headings corrected with fewer staff by switching from its card authority file to NOTIS online authorities. Also discusses Auburn's organization of authority work and procedures for verifying and establishing headings.

EE11. Goldman, Helen, and David M. Smith. ''Name Authority in a NOTIS Environment—Auburn University

Libraries.'' *Cataloging & Classification Quarterly* 9, no. 3 (1989): 121–31.

Describes planning for and implementing online name authority control. Useful discussion of the issues faced during a transition from a card to an online authority file.

EE12. Gorman, Michael. ''Authority Control in the Prospective Catalog.'' In *Authority Control: The Key to Tomorrow's Catalog: Proceedings of the 1979 Library and Information Technology Association Institutes*, edited by Mary W. Ghikas, 155–80. Phoenix: Oryx Press, 1982.

Gorman envisions an online catalog in which authority records, via linkages to each other and to descriptive records for items, become the primary tools for managing access to library materials. Though change has not proceeded as rapidly or uniformly as Gorman predicted, this is still a valuable contribution to the linked approach to authority control.

EE13. Grady, Agnes M. ''Online Maintenance Features of Authority Files: Survey of Vendors and In-House Systems.'' *Information Technology and Libraries* 7, no. 1 (Mar. 1988): 51–55.

Reports on a survey of libraries and vendors regarding automated maintenance of authority records. Useful for its enumeration of features to be noted in different systems: global updates; uniqueness, hierarchical, and reciprocity checks; human review and editing; record and field validation; and file updating.

EE14. Hunn, Nancy O., and Jean Acker Wright. ''The Implementation of ACORN Authority Control at Vanderbilt University Library.'' *Cataloging & Classification Quarterly* 8, no. 1 (1987): 79–91.

Describes policies and procedures developed during the implementation of Vanderbilt's NOTIS system, ACORN, to coordinate online authority control efforts among three cataloging units.

EE15. Johnston, Sarah Hager. ''Current Offerings in Automated Authority Control: A Survey of Vendors.'' *Information Technology and Libraries* 8, no. 3 (Sept. 1989): 236–54.

Reports on survey responses from eighteen vendors to questions regarding authority control features of their systems. The survey points up significant differences between systems but also notes increasing sophistication in the functions available for providing online authority control. Useful for gauging the emphasis given to authority control by different systems.

EE16. Krieger, Michael T. ''Subject Authority Control on the Dynix System.'' *Cataloging & Classification Quarterly* 12, no. 1 (1990): 103–15.

See also annotation under DD32. Details the process of maintaining subject authority control at the University of Dayton using Dynix (release 112). The process is complicated by the Dynix system's inability to report which parts of a new subdivided heading need establishing and by its difficulty in moving between different editing procedures.

RASMUSON LIBRARY
UNIVERSITY OF ALASKA-FAIRBANKS

EE17. Lowchy, Gregory. "The Hidden Structures of Research: The Problem of Authority Control in an Online Catalog." *Advances in Library Automation and Networking: A Research Annual* 4 (1991): 93–120.

Reviews recent definitions of authority control and research into its value and argues that the library literature on authority control shows a bias in favor of serving the fact-oriented information needs of the sciences over those of the humanities, where meanings and relationships are often more highly valued than hard data.

EE18. Ludy, Lorene E. "LC Name Authority Tapes Used by Ohio State University Libraries." *Information Technology and Libraries* 3, no. 1 (Mar. 1984): 69–71.

Describes the successful loading of LC's name authorities into Ohio State's Library Control System (LCS). LC authority records were used to validate and update heading records in LCS, including many changes resulting from *AACR2* (CBA4), and to add cross-references to the file.

EE19. _____. "OSU Libraries' Use of Library of Congress Subject Authorities File." *Information Technology and Libraries* 4, no. 2 (June 1985): 155–60.

Describes Ohio State University Libraries' integration of LC's MARC subject authorities into its catalog (Library Control System, LCS). LCS's headings file was compared with the LCSH file and with a list of common subdivisions to verify headings, integrate cross-references with the online catalog, and correct headings matching on LCSH "see" references.

EE20. Malinconico, S. Michael. "Bibliographic Data Base Organization and Authority File Control." *Wilson Library Bulletin* 54, no. 1 (Sept. 1979): 36–45. Reprinted in *Authority Control: The Key to Tomorrow's Catalog: Proceedings of the 1979 Library Information and Technology Association Institutes,* edited by Mary W. Ghikas, 1–18. Phoenix: Oryx Press, 1982.

Presents a strong case for the value of authority control. Controlled headings ensure the collocation of like entries. Authority records establish the form of headings, clarify their meaning, and indicate the relationships between headings with cross-references. In linked systems, authority records also simplify the process of updating headings.

EE21. _____. "The Role of a Machine Based Authority File in an Automated Bibliographic System." In *Automation in Libraries: Papers Presented at the CACUL Workshop on Library Automation, Winnipeg, June 22–23, 1974.* Ottawa: Canadian Library Association, 1975. Reprinted in *Foundations of Cataloging: A Sourcebook,* edited by Michael Carpenter and Elaine Svenonius, 211–33. Littleton, Colo.: Libraries Unlimited, 1985.

A still-cogent statement of the need for authority control in an automated environment, with clear examples of what can and will go wrong without it. Also describes the linked authority control system developed at New York Public Library.

EE22. McDonald, David R. "Data Dictionaries, Authority Control, and Online Catalogs: A New Perspective." *The Journal of Academic Librarianship* 11, no. 4 (Sept. 1985): 219–22.

Compares the management of automated library catalogs with nonlibrary databases, noting that the latter routinely employ data dictionaries to provide the structured control that library authority records offer. Concludes that authority files can ensure an online catalog's consistency, provide it with a logical structure and cross-references, and extend its searching capabilities beyond those found in card catalogs.

EE23. Meernik, Mary. "Controlled or Controlling—Authority Work in the NOTIS Online Environment." *Technicalities* 11 (Sept. 1991): 9–15.

An excellent account of NOTIS authority control and how its evolution has affected library decision making and work flow as reflected in the experience of Eastern Michigan University. Includes a careful analysis of the problems of deblinding "search also under" references in NOTIS and of the use of multiple subject systems.

EE24. Nye, Julie Blume. "User Interaction with the Authority Structure of the Online Catalog: Results of a Survey." *Information Technology and Libraries* 7, no. 3 (Sept. 1988): 313–16.

Presents results of a 1987 survey of authority data displays in vendor and in-house systems. Useful for considering the range of options employed to represent authority-controlled headings and references online.

EE25. Page, Mary. "Authority Control in the Online Environment, or, Now That We Can Access the World, How Do We Look up What's 'er Name?" *Computers in Libraries* 11, no. 3 (Mar. 1991): 8–12.

Reports on presentations by Arlene G. Taylor, Barbara B. Tillett, and James D. Anderson at a forum sponsored by Rutgers University Libraries. All three speakers encourage forward-looking approaches to authority control, such as systems that will link equivalent terms without preferring one over another, link names and concepts in authority records, and make greater use of searcher terminology to better facilitate access.

EE26. Ridgeway, Michael. "Authority Control on the Geac Bibliographic Processing System." *Cataloging & Classification Quarterly* 9, no. 3 (1989): 133–52.

Describes Geac's approach to building a linked authority file via batch processing and online operations. Also includes printouts of online public access catalog search results making use of authority references.

EE27. Rood, Joanna. "Practical Considerations in Dealing with LCSH-mr." In *Subject Authorities in the Online Environment: Papers from a Conference Program Held in San Francisco, June 29, 1987,* edited by Karen Markey Drabenstott, 31–40. Chicago: American Library Association, 1991.

Recounts Utlas's efforts to construct and maintain a linked online subject authority file, including the problems that resulted from Utlas's decision to undertake local initiatives in advance of LC's development and release of its machine-readable (mr) file.

EE28. Slater, Ron. "Authority Control in a Bilingual OPAC: MultiLIS at Laurentian." *Library Resources & Technical Services* 34 (Oct. 1991): 422–58.

Describes the use of the MultiLIS authority control system at Laurentian University for English and French bilingual access. MultiLIS uses 9XX fields in the authority record to add "equivalent" headings and automatically generates reciprocal authority records when equivalent headings are added. The Laurentian OPAC displays hits for both a term and its equivalent when either is searched. Also discusses maintenance features of MultiLIS and describes possible improvements.

EE29. Szary, Richard V. "Technical Requirements and Prospects for Authority Control in the SIBIS-Archives Database." *Archival Informatics Technical Report* 2, no. 2 (Summer 1988): 41–44.

Discusses authority control capabilities of the Smithsonian Institution's Geac-based SIBIS system, including a provision for up to ten thousand independent authority files to store records separately for different types of headings (personal name, corporate name, title, form, genre, function, etc.) and for different holding agencies.

EE30. Taylor, Arlene G., Margaret F. Maxwell, and Carolyn O. Frost. "Network and Vendor Authority Systems." *Library Resources & Technical Services* 29, no. 2 (Apr./June 1985): 195–205.

Examines the approaches to authority control taken by networks and system vendors in the first half of the 1980s. The advantages and disadvantages of linked and unlinked systems are considered, and a list of questions to guide evaluation of online authority control options is provided.

EE31. Tillett, Barbara B. "Considerations for Authority Control in the Online Environment." In *Authority Control in the Online Environment: Considerations and Practices*, edited by Barbara B. Tillett, 1–11. New York: Haworth Press, 1990.

An overview of authority control issues, introducing a collection of articles on the topic. Tillett discusses the definition and purpose of authority control, the differences between national and local authority files, cost and labor issues, and the need for cooperation and the creative use of new technologies.

EE32. Wajenberg, Arnold S. "Authority Work, Authority Records, and Authority Files." In *Technical Services Today and Tomorrow*, edited by Michael Gorman, 86–94. Englewood, Colo.: Libraries Unlimited, 1990.

Examines the complex impact that automation is having on authority control practice. The use of networks encourages the adoption of national standards for authority work; yet the searching capabilities of some automated systems (e.g., automatic right truncation and inversion of terms) make much current authority work unnecessary.

Argues that authority record standards could change if online system searching capabilities become more standardized.

EF
Management and Organization of Work

EF1. Anderson, Barbara. "Authority Control: Whose Pain Is It?" *Library Acquisitions: Practice and Theory* 16, no. 1 (1992): 63–66.

Notes that automated systems have dissolved the distinction between catalog records and acquisitions records and describes Virginia Commonwealth University's approach to authority control, which skips locally entered name headings on order records. Calls for better prepublication cataloging and authority records to be provided by a national cataloging agency in cooperation with publishers and vendors.

EF2. Bennett, Lee L. "Authority Control at the Order Process: What Do Catalogers Want, and Do We Care? The NOTIS Environment/Loyola Perspective." (Presented at ALA 1991 Midwinter meeting.) *Library Acquisitions: Practice and Theory* 16, no. 1 (1992): 71–74.

Discusses Loyola's decision to use full bibliographic records from OCLC as the basis for orders, to have acquisitions staff select the records, and to have authority control unit staff promptly review and establish new headings on order records. Acquisitions staff verify entries on locally created order records, but leave other work to authority control staff.

EF3. Brugger, Judith M. "Automated Acquisitions and the Quality Database: A Response." (Presented at ALA 1991 Midwinter meeting.) *Library Acquisitions: Practice and Theory* 16, no. 1 (1992): 79–83.

Summarizes papers presented at the program on authority control and proposes that adoption by vendors and libraries of electronic data interchange based on X12 formats may permit acquisitions staff to devote more time to database quality control.

EF4. Fahy, Terry W. "Authority Control in the Acquisitions Process: What Do Catalogers Want, and Do We Care?" (Presented at ALA 1991 Midwinter meeting.) *Library Acquisitions: Practice and Theory* 16, no. 1 (1992): 75–78.

Analyzes various factors affecting decisions regarding acquisitions and authority work at the University of Arizona, including the availability of vendors able to transmit full MARC records with orders, the ability of local systems to accept them, and the decisions made by the library regarding which records in the in-process file to display to the public.

EF5. Fiegen, Ann M., Sara C. Heitshu, and Edward P. Miller. "The Effect of the LASS Microcomputer Software on the Cost of Authority Work in Cataloging." *Information Technology and Libraries* 9, no. 3 (Sept. 1990): 253–57.

Details a study conducted at the University of Arizona Library measuring the costs associated with moving from typed authority cards to cards produced using LASS. Useful for demonstrating the worth of even relatively simple automation of authority work.

EF6. Glazier, Ed. "Bibliographic Utilities and the Automation of Authority Files." In *Authority Control in Music Libraries: Proceedings of the Music Library Association Preconference, March 5, 1985,* edited by Ruth Tucker, 92–109. Canton, Mass.: Music Library Association, 1989.

Defines authority work options—how much to do and when to do it—in terms of pros and cons and discusses the approaches to automated authority control taken by WLN, OCLC, and RLIN. Useful for clarifying the differences among these approaches and for framing local system and procedure decisions.

EF7. Henigman, Barbara. "Networking and Authority Control: Online Catalog Authority Control in Illinois." *Information Technology and Libraries* 10, no. 1 (Mar. 1991): 47–54.

Describes the development of shared authority control policies and procedures for maintaining ILLINET Online, a WLN-based statewide online catalog. Stresses the need for training, communication, and adherence to standards to ensure the success of cooperative efforts at authority control.

EF8. Ludy, Lorene E. "LC Name Authority Tapes Used by Ohio State University Libraries." *Information Technology and Libraries* 3, no. 3 (Sept. 1984): 262–66.

Analyzes changes in the management of authority control tasks resulting from automation, including greater dependence on national authority files and more postcataloging authority work. Notes that a library's original cataloging still requires local authority control, which must now be integrated with national as well as local headings.

EF9. Maccaferri, James Tilio. "Managing Authority Control in a Retrospective Conversion Project." *Cataloging & Classification Quarterly* 14, no. 3/4 (1992): 145–67.

Discusses choosing a source for retrospective conversion records, setting standards for consistency in a converted database, and deciding between in-house and vendor-supplied authority control processing or on a combination of the two. Vendor processing proves less expensive but imprecise, while in-house work is more accurate but labor intensive. Includes an account of UCLA's four-year in-house project to bring retrospective headings under authority control.

EF10. Miller, Dan. "Authority Control in the Retrospective Conversion Process." *Information Technology and Libraries* 3, no. 3 (Sept. 1984): 286–92.

A basic description of Blackwell North America's tape processing service to update authority-controlled headings in a library's retrospective database and provide a base file of authority records for loading into an automated system. Useful for libraries starting to consider loading retrospective tapes into a new system.

EF11. Peterson, Elaine, and Bonnie Johnson. "Is Authority Updating Worth the Price?" *Technicalities* 10, no. 5 (May 1990): 1, 15.

Describes Montana State University's experience loading a three-year-old tape of authority records into its Inlex online catalog. Based on the number of authority records not loaded because the corresponding heading no longer appeared in the bibliographic file, the authors calculate an annual rate of change of 8 percent for their authority file, highlighting the importance of budgeting for regular authority updating.

EF12. Webster, Judy. "Authority Control for Acquisitions." (Presented at ALA 1991 Midwinter meeting.) *Library Acquisitions: Practice and Theory* 16, no. 1 (1992): 67–69.

Discusses the problems at the University of Tennessee, Knoxville, of integrating practices used to manage order file entries when these practices conflict with cataloging rules, e.g., name main entry for serials, special codes, set order records for items to be cataloged separately, etc. Notes that acquisitions staff using the Geac system try to use established names and series but do not create authority records.

EF13. Wittenbach, Stephanie A. *Automated Authority Control in ARL Libraries.* SPEC Kit, no. 156; SPEC Flyer, no. 156. Washington, D.C.: Office of Management Services, Association of Research Libraries, 1989.

SPEC Flyer presents the result of a brief survey of authority control activity and staffing. SPEC Kit includes job descriptions, procedural documents, work forms, and sample system reports relating to authority work submitted by various university libraries. Includes bibliography.

EG
Name Authority Cooperative Project (NACO)

EG1. Burger, Robert H. "NACO at the University of Illinois at U-C: A Narrative Case Study." *Cataloging & Classification Quarterly* 7, no. 2 (Winter 1986): 19–28.

Discusses involvement with NACO from a participating library's perspective. Burger describes his NACO training at LC and the adjustments needed to incorporate NACO work and LC standards into the library's procedures, stressing the need for cooperation, trust, and mutual understanding between the library and LC.

EG2. Fenly, Judith G., and Sarah D. Irvine. "The Name Authority Co-op (NACO) Project at the Library of Congress: Present and Future." *Cataloging & Classification Quarterly* 7, no. 2 (Winter 1986): 7–18.

Recounts the history of the NACO Project and describes the procedure by which NACO records are submitted to LC and approved. Also discusses bibliographic records submitted through NACO and the transmission of records via the Linked Systems Project.

EG3. "Meetings." *Library of Congress Information Bulletin* 51, no. 21 (2 Nov. 1992): 474–75.

Reports on two meetings, one aimed at mapping out new directions for NACO with the help of NACO participants and the other at identifying procedural, technical, and governance issues relating to the growth of cooperative authority control. Proposals from the two meetings include revising documentation to be less LC-centric, accepting OCLC and RLIN as databases against which new headings may be searched, and including more member participation in the governance of NACO along the lines of the CONSER (Cooperative Online Serials) Program.

EG4. Papakhian, A. Ralph. "NACO-Music Project Update." In *Authority Control in Music Libraries: Proceedings of the Music Library Association Preconference, March 5, 1985,* edited by Ruth Tucker, 60–62. Canton, Mass.: Music Library Association, 1989.

Reports on the emergence of the NACO Music Project (NMP) from the earlier Retrospective Music Project (RE-MUS). Describes the review procedure that authority records contributed through NMP undergo to ensure quality control.

F

Filing and Indexing

Sarah E. Thomas
and
Anne Blankenbaker

Overview

This chapter covers filing (the arrangement of bibliographic records in a catalog) and the creation of indexes, an index being "a list of bibliographic information or citations to a body of literature, usually arranged in alphabetical order and based on some specified datum, such as author, subject, or keyword." (*Introduction to Indexing and Abstracting* by Donald and Ann Cleveland, Englewood, Colo.: Libraries Unlimited, 1990, 17 [FD2].) Each of these topics could be addressed logically in a separate chapter; they have been combined in one chapter on the premise that both filing and indexing are mechanisms for organizing information for retrieval.

Since the ascendancy of the online catalog in the last several years, the emphasis on filing of cataloging cards has greatly diminished. Gone are the days when every new library staff member knew the basic principles of filing, such as "nothing comes before something." Yet, catalog cards are still produced in the millions, primarily shelflist cards for research libraries and large public libraries and full sets for smaller public institutions, school libraries, and international repositories that continue the century-old practice of filing.

The faltering economy, with retrenchment hitting public and private institutions alike, virtually guar-

antees that catalog cards will be produced into the twenty-first century, as some libraries will be unable to make the capital investment in an online catalog. Consequently, filing rules remain an essential component of the librarian's bibliographic tool kit. Adherence to standard filing rules is a basic underpinning in the provision of materials to the reader. Charles Cutter set the standard for filing rules in his *Rules for a Printed Dictionary Catalog* in 1876, and he subsequently elaborated on filing in the fourth edition of the work published in 1904 (FAB5). The essence of filing as expressed by Cutter is to file word by word and within a word, letter by letter. Cutter's rules for filing began to break down under the weight of exceptions as the size of manual catalogs expanded, and they are also not inherently transferable into a computer program. Even before the advent of machine-readable catalogs, however, librarians struggled with the transition from Cutter's nineteenth-century rules to the complexities of large manual files of the mid-twentieth century.

The American Library Association first published the *ALA Rules for Filing Catalog Cards* (FAB3) in 1942. A revision was published in 1968 (FAB2) to coincide with the publication of the *Anglo-American Cataloging Rules* (CBA3), known as *AACR*, in 1967. ALA's Editorial Committee's Subcommittee on Filing was responsible for preparing rules for filing in a manual catalog. The Subcommittee focused chiefly on rules for a dictionary catalog, although shelflist arrangement was also considered.

In 1978, the *Anglo-American Cataloguing Rules*, second edition (known as *AACR2*) (CBA4), was published, incorporating substantial revisions. A parallel revision of the filing rules occurred. The ALA Resources and Technical Services Division, now called the Association for Library Collections and Technical Services (ALCTS), established a Filing Committee in the 1970s to consider the extension of filing rules to the automated environment. The result of the committee's efforts culminated in the publication of a new text, the *ALA Filing Rules* (FAB1), in 1980, which accommodated changes introduced under *AACR2* and which presented rules suited to the display of bibliographic records in databases in addition to filing in manual card catalogs. In the last few years, revisions have been infrequent, owing to decreased emphasis on manual filing. The ALA Committee on Filing Rules no longer exists; filing order is one of many issues subsumed under the charge of the ALCTS Committee on Catalog Form and Function.

As the card catalog has been gradually superseded by online files, interest in filing has shifted to indexing. Database retrieval is heavily dependent on the degree to which data elements in the file are indexed. In the MARC format, filing indicators are employed in the title fields to allow the computer to simulate manual filing practice as well as to aid in the production of cards in filing order from online records. Most online catalogs duplicate card catalogs in filing by the first significant word of the title, after initial articles in all languages are ignored. Increasingly, however, there is a movement away from this practice as libraries move toward the next generation of online catalogs. These catalogs are more forgiving. They can compensate for the patron's lack of precision in specifying a title or inaccurate spelling through keyword access, tables, or algorithms that supply the correct information in a manner that had been unthinkable in the manual catalog. The power of an intelligent front end lessens the reliance on traditional filing. Nonetheless, individual words and strings must be indexed to be searchable.

Indexing in library terminology has multiple meanings. First, there is the keyword access provided in the back-of-the-book indexes. Secondly, there is the automated process described above, in which computer programs list words or series of words, i.e., strings, contained in a data element for retrieval purposes. Another type of indexing is the detailed subject analysis offered by indexing and abstracting services in which the intellectual assessment of information is performed by highly trained specialists.

In recent years, there has been considerable experimentation with automated indexing, in which machine-readable full-text is analyzed via computer programs. Using algorithms based on frequency of use of vocabulary and relevance of terms to those contained in a thesaurus, the program suggests subject index terms. Automated indexing systems exist chiefly as prototypes, but some variations have been operational for several years. For example, PRECIS, Preserved Context Indexing System, is a string indexing system designed to provide subject index data for UK/MARC records and to generate an alphabetical subject index for the British National Bibliography. Thesauri and PRECIS are also treated in Chapter D, Subject Analysis Systems.

Chapter Content and Organization

The sources selected for this chapter reflect the criteria followed throughout the *Guide to Technical Services Resources*. The intent is to provide the basic tools for filing and indexing and relevant, current information about both activities. Some earlier publications are included because the results of filing and indexing are almost always integrated into files (and databases) that have evolved under successive generations of rules, standards, and guidelines.

The first three subsections of the chapter (FAA through FAC) present general tools for filing. The next two subsections (FAD and FAE) address indexing and list dictionaries and glossaries. The subsections FAF through FAJ list other general resources, including directories, and conclude with sources of expertise. Following these are sections on indexing and the library catalog, indexing special formats, indexing and abstracting, thesauri, automated indexing, indexing software, and PRECIS.

FA
General Works

FAA
Filing: General Works

FAA1. Booth, Pat F. "Finding Your Way Around." *Library Work* 3 (Jan. 1989): 10–11.

Describes problems presented by the alphabetical order of headings in catalogs and subject indexes. References.

FAA2. Boyce, Bert R., and Mary Stowe. "A Brief Investigation of U.S. Superintendent of Documents Filing Practice." *Government Publications Review* 18 (1991): 347–52.

Reports on the results of a questionnaire that found wide variation in filing procedures in eighty-seven government document libraries. The data could be applied to the creation of a program for sorting by SuDoc number. References.

FAA3. Daily, Jay E. "Filing." In vol. 8, *Encyclopedia of Library and Information Science*, 405–31. New York: Marcel Dekker, 1972.

Provides an excellent conceptual and historical discussion of filing, including the iron laws of filing, library filing rules, and the Mandalay rules, which the author characterizes as the simplest filing rules. Includes bibliography and appendix on metalanguage.

FAA4. Wynar, Bohdan S. *Introduction to Cataloging and Classification*. 8th ed. Revised by Arlene G. Taylor. Littleton, Colo.: Libraries Unlimited, 1992.

Provides an excellent overview of the history of the development of filing rules as well as a thorough discussion of the basic principles of current filing practice with illustrative examples. Briefly covers alternative filing rules for shelflists. Includes bibliographical references.

FAB
Filing: Rules

FAB1. American Library Association, Filing Committee, Resources and Technical Services Division. *ALA Filing Rules*. Chicago: ALA, 1980.

Brief overview of filing rules offering succinct description of general and special rules. Useful appendixes contain lists of modified letters and special characters and articles in the nominative case in various foreign languages.

FAB2. American Library Association, Editorial Committee, Subcommittee on the ALA Rules for Filing Catalog Cards. *ALA Rules for Filing Catalog Cards*. 2nd ed., abridged. Chicago: ALA, 1968.

Rules largely intended for manual filing in a dictionary card catalog. Basic rules are given with many examples. Specialized and explanatory material will be found in the full filing code, the nonabridged edition of the same title. Index.

FAB3. American Library Association, Subcommittee on the Filing Code. *ALA Rules for Filing Catalog Cards*. Chicago: ALA, 1942.

An effort to provide a set of rules in accord with generally accepted practice in large- and medium-sized libraries. Appendixes include rules for small libraries. The bibliography affords an interesting historical perspective on

the numerous and diverse filing codes in use prior to ALA's publishing a uniform standard.

FAB4. Anderson, James D. "Catalog File Display: Principles and the New Filing Rules." *Cataloging & Classification Quarterly* 1, no. 4 (1982): 3–23.

The 1980 *ALA Filing Rules* (FAB1) and the 1980 *Library of Congress Filing Rules* (FAB9) are compared with each other and with their earlier versions. Illustrates the different sequences that result from application of each code. References.

FAB5. Cutter, Charles A. *Rules for a Dictionary Catalog*. 4th ed. Washington, D.C.: Government Printing Office, 1904.

Cutter's principles of the construction of the catalog are the basis of most of what the United States knows as cataloging. He emphasized using accepted natural language phrases as subjects, assigning "specific" subject terms rather than broad classes, and maintaining a syndetic structure of references.

FAB6. Gatenby, J. "An Analysis of the Justification for New Filing Rules." *Cataloguing Australia* 8, no. 3 (1982): 16–24.

The 1980 *ALA Filing Rules* (FAB1) and *Library of Congress Filing Rules* (FAB9) are examined in terms of their impact on the creation of online catalogs and searching behavior. References.

FAB7. Gorman, Michael. "Fear of Filing: Daunted Librarians Have Ally in New Rules." *American Libraries* 12 (Feb. 1981): 71–72.

Gorman cites examples to suggest that the simpler approach of the 1980 *ALA Filing Rules* (FAB1)—particularly their emphasis on "file-as-is"—benefits both staff and users.

FAB8. Hoffman, Herbert H. "A Review of the New ALA Filing Rules." *Technicalities* 1, no. 6 (1981): 5, 7, 15.

Identifies problems in the 1980 *ALA Filing Rules* (FAB1), particularly needless complexity and a lack of clarity in the exposition.

FAB9. Library of Congress, Processing Services. *Library of Congress Filing Rules*. Prepared by John C. Rather and Susan C. Biebel. Washington, D.C.: Library of Congress, 1980.

Rules developed and adopted to arrange LC's large bibliographic files, in both card and automated forms. The rules apply to headings formulated under various cataloging rules and practices. The authors provide many examples and offer clear and succinct instruction in the approximately 100-page volume.

FAB10. Rather, John C. "Filing Arrangement in the Library of Congress Catalogs." *Library Resources & Technical Services* 16 (Spring 1972): 240–61.

Discusses filing rules in relation to the functions of large bibliographic files and in terms of the "uses" of the catalog as opposed to the "users." An abridged version of the LC rules (FAB9), a glossary, and an extended example are included.

FAB11. Seely, Pauline. "ALA Filing Rules: New Edition." *Library Resources & Technical Services* 11 (Summer 1967): 377–79.

A summary of the 1968 *ALA Rules for Filing Catalog Cards* (FAB2) and the principles on which changes were made. Primarily, entries are largely to be filed "as is," without mental transpositions or insertions.

FAB12. ———. "ALA Rules for Filing Catalog Cards: Differences between 2d and 1st Editions (Arranged by Rule Numbers)." *Library Resources & Technical Services* 13 (Spring 1969): 291–94.

A concise, point-by-point comparison of FAB1 and FAB2.

FAB13. Wellisch, Hans H. "The ALA Filing Rules: Flowcharts Illustrating Their Application, with a Critique and Suggestions for Improvement." *Journal of the American Society for Information Science* 34 (1983): 313–30.

A flowchart analysis of the 1980 *ALA Filing Rules* (FAB1). The issues brought out are relevant to the design of bibliographic databases and to the construction of a filing manual. References.

FAC
Filing: Handbooks, Manuals, and Guides

FAC1. Akhtar, Nasreen. "Indexing Asian Names." *The Indexer* 16 (1989): 157–58.

Akhtar gives general guidelines for alphabetizing Muslim, Arabic, Indian, and Chinese names.

FAC2. Bidlack, Russell E. *Typewritten Catalog Cards: A Manual of Procedures and Forms with 300 Sample Cards.* 2nd ed. Revised and expanded by Constance Rinehart. Ann Arbor, Mich.: Campus Publishers, 1970.

A manual based on the first edition of *AACR* (CBA3), intended for library science students.

FAC3. Carothers, Diane Foxhill. *Self-instruction Manual for Filing Catalog Cards.* Chicago: American Library Association, 1981.

A self-contained program based on the 1980 *ALA Filing Rules* (FAB1), by which filers can learn with minimal supervision. Includes a glossary of terms.

FAC4. Elrod, J. McRee. *Filing in the Public Catalog and Shelflist.* Metuchen, N.J.: Scarecrow Press, 1980.

A self-guided instruction program for nonprofessional library staff, with sample cards, based on the 1980 *ALA Filing Rules* (FAB1).

FAC5. Gupta, Sushma. "Cataloging Ethiopian Personal Names." *Cataloging & Classification Quarterly* 14, no. 2 (1991): 81–92.

Provides solutions for transliteration, filing, and retrieval not supplied by *AACR2R* (CBA1) or the International Federation of Library Associations and Institution's document on personal names.

FAC6. Johnson, C. M. *Filer's Guide for Looseleaf Services in a Law Library.* Milwaukee, Wis.: Knier Associates, 1979.

Essentially a training aid for new filers, this manual also covers procedures for managing the subscriptions.

FAC7. Moore, Donald. "The Indexing of Welsh Personal Names." *The Indexer* 17 (1990): 12–20.

A guide to dealing with the patronymic system and with spelling variations (which occur depending on linguistic context). References.

FAC8. ———. "The Indexing of Welsh Place-names." *The Indexer* 15 (1986): 3–8.

Presents solutions to two difficulties: variations in the use of hyphens and spelling variations (which occur depending on linguistic context). References.

FAC9. O'Deirg, Iosold. " 'Her Infinite Variety'—On the Ordering of Irish Surnames with Prefixes, Especially Those of Women." *An Leabharlann. The Irish Library* 10, no. 1 (1981): 14–16.

Describes the unique linguistic problems presented for filing order and indexing by Irish names and argues that filing Irish surnames by prefix optimizes retrieval.

FAC10. Wellisch, Hans H. "The Arrangement of Entries in Non-Roman Scripts in Multiscript Catalogs and Bibliographies." *International Forum on Information and Documentation* 3, no. 3 (1978): 18–24.

Suggests a filing order encompassing all scripts now used in publication based on two criteria: family affinity of scripts and the volume of book production.

FAC11. Werking, Richard Hume, Jay Whaley, and Ruby Miller. "Rearranging the Subject Catalog at Trinity University." *College & Research Libraries News* 47 (Jan. 1986): 7–9.

Describes a change in filing rules at a university library in order to improve access: subject cards were arranged by imprint date in reverse chronological order.

FAD
Indexing: General Works

FAD1. Aluri, Rao, D. Alasdair Kemp, and John Boll. *Subject Analysis in Online Catalogs.* Englewood, Colo.: Libraries Unlimited, 1991.

Several chapters provide an up-to-date, lucid introduction to major issues in indexing. Topics include the structure of the database, language in information retrieval, subject indexing, and keyword subject access. Extensive bibliography and index.

FAD2. Bell, Hazel K. "Bias in Indexing and Loaded Language." *The Indexer* 17 (1991): 173–77.

Bell cautions against introducing bias while representing the subject of a work and describes pitfalls such as choosing loaded terms and suppressing ideas.

FAD3. Booth, Pat F., and M. L. South. *Information Filing and Finding.* Cambridgeshire, Eng.: ELM Publications, 1982.

A theoretical overview of information storage and retrieval: the organization, design, and evaluation of files; searching files; and constructing indexes for documents. Extensive references and index.

FAD4. Borko, Harold, and Charles L. Bernier. *Indexing Concepts and Methods.* New York: Academic Press, 1978.

The discussion of "concepts" is more useful now than the outdated explanation of "methods." Sections are titled Structure, Indexing and Editing Procedures, Types of Indexes, Index Evaluation, and Professionalism. Extensive bibliography and index.

FAD5. Brown, A. G. *An Introduction to Subject Indexing.* 2nd ed. London: Clive Bingley, 1982.

Programmed self-instruction presenting basic principles and practices of subject indexing rather than a particular system of subject analysis. The Colon Classification and *Universal Decimal Classification* (DC28) systems are used as illustrations.

FAD6. Chan, Lois Mai, Phyllis Richmond, and Elaine Svenonius, eds. *Theory of Subject Analysis: A Source Book.* Littleton, Colo.: Libraries Unlimited, 1985.

See also annotation under DAA2. Seminal writings from 1876 to the 1980s on the theory of subject analysis, including a dozen selections on indexing. Authors include Charles Cutter, Julia Pettee, Hans Luhn, F. W. Lancaster, and others. A resource for introductions to specialized aspects of indexing. Original references are reproduced. Subject and name indexes.

FAD7. Chandler, Helen E., and Vincent de Paul Roper. "Citation Indexing: Uses and Limitations." *The Indexer* 17 (1991): 243–49.

"Outlines the principles, uses and limitations of citation indexing. . . . Discusses them in relation to their online counterparts." Indicates how to use citation indexes for more general reference information.

FAD8. Craven, Timothy C. *String Indexing.* Orlando, Fla.: Academic Press, 1986.

An introduction to the principles and attributes of string indexing systems, focusing on the 1980s. Appendixes include a case study, a manual for composition of NEPHIS input strings, and a list of organizations involved in string indexing. Bibliography and index.

FAD9. Dym, Eleanor D., ed. *Subject and Information Analysis.* New York and Basel: Marcel Dekker, 1985.

See also annotation under DAA4. Extracts from the Dekker *Encyclopedia of Library and Information Science* and *Encyclopedia of Computer Science and Technology*, intended for students. Indexing (including automated), classifying, and abstracting are among topics covered. Original references are reproduced.

FAD10. Foskett, Anthony Charles. *The Subject Approach to Information.* 4th ed. London: Clive Bingley, 1982.

See also annotation under DAA5. Includes a theoretical, detailed discussion of the major precoordinate indexing systems and languages. A scholarly, yet readable, introduction to information retrieval. Extensive references and index.

FAD11. *Freelancers on Indexing.* Washington, D.C.: American Society of Indexers, 1989.

A transcription of an ASI panel discussion. The four panelists discuss how to start, what to charge, computer-assisted indexing, relations with publishers, and the future of indexing.

FAD12. Garfield, Eugene. *Citation Indexing: Its Theory and Application in Science, Technology, and Humanities.* New York: Wiley, 1979.

The inventor of citation indexing details its conceptual basis, its historical development, and the process of production. He deals at length with its wide-ranging applications in historical research, bibliometrics, science management, etc. Extensive references and index.

FAD13. Gill, Suzanne L. *File Management and Information Retrieval Systems: A Manual for Managers and Technicians.* Englewood, Colo.: Libraries Unlimited, 1988.

Emphasizes the creation of procedures for a records and information management program. Explains how to apply indexing and classification methods developed in libraries to business needs. Bibliography and index.

FAD14. Harrod, L. M., ed. *Indexers on Indexing: A Selection of Articles Published in The Indexer.* New York: R. R. Bowker, 1978.

A collection from the 1950s to the 1970s on widely divergent topics. Of interest to librarians may be sections on the application of modern technology to indexing and on comparative indexing systems. Index.

FAD15. Horowitz, Roberta S., Larry Latinwo, and John M. Weiner. "Building Your Own Database: Potentials for Creativity." In *ASIS '87: Proceedings of the 50th Annual ASIS Annual Meeting,* 106–10. Medford, N.J.: Learned Information, 1987.

Discusses methods of construction of three types of database: bibliographic with indexing terms, bibliographic with enriched access, and an "idea database" with citation information. References.

FAD16. Jackson, E. B. "Indexing: A Review Essay." *Journal of Library History* 15 (1980): 320–25.

Compares the subject coverage of four monographs on indexing published 1969 through 1979 by G. Norman Knight, L. M. Harrod, and Borko and Bernier.

FAD17. Kesselman, Martin, and Irene Perry. "What On-line Searchers Should Know about Indexing and What Indexers Should Know about Online Searching." In *National Online Meeting: Proceedings, 1984*, compiled by Martha E. Williams and Thomas H. Hogan, 141–48. Medford, N.J.: Learned Information, 1984.

Summarizes the indexing qualities that facilitate efficient subject access to a database and suggests features needed for end-users unfamiliar with indexing policies.

FAD18. Knight, G. Norman. *Indexing, The Art of: A Guide to the Indexing of Books and Periodicals.* London: George Allen and Unwin, 1979.

Written in a conversational style, this volume by the dean of British indexing covers the basics of indexing, including indexing of periodicals, newspaper indexing, and cumulative indexing. Emphasis is on manual indexing with no reference to automation. There is a small section on humor in indexing.

FAD19. Lipetz, Ben-Ami. "The Usefulness of Indexes." *The Indexer* 16 (1989): 173–76.

Argues that "usefulness" is a subjective concept dependent upon each user. Suggests that book indexes be input into online databases to increase demand for titles.

FAD20. Milstead, Jessica L., ed. *Subject Access Systems: Alternatives in Design.* Orlando, Fla.: Academic Press, 1984.

Examines the design of subject access systems as a series of choices. Considers the trade-offs of various policies in the construction of the file, the choice of indexing terms, and the treatment of items in a collection. References and index.

FAD21. Pao, Miranda Lee. *Concepts of Information Retrieval.* Englewood, Colo.: Libraries Unlimited, 1989.

Emphasizes concepts over specific technologies. Pao includes chapters on information representation (which covers abstracts, indexes, vocabulary control, and automatic indexing) and file organization. References and index.

FAD22. Piggott, Mary. *A Topography of Cataloguing.* London: Library Association, 1988.

An introduction to the "intellectual environment" of cataloging. Includes chapters on the subject catalogs, the dictionary catalog, the arrangement of catalogs and indexes, and the transcriptions of non-Roman alphabets. Emphasizes definitions of terms and the basic principles. References and indexes.

FAD23. Prasher, R. G. "Index and Indexing." In *Tools for Knowledge Organization and the Human Interface: Proceedings of the 1st International ISKO Conference, Darmstadt, 14–17 August 1990*, edited by Robert Fugmann, 239–49. Frankfurt am Main, Ger.: Indeks-Verlag, 1990.

Describes the development of major types of subject indexes (including PRECIS, chain indexing, keyword indexing, and citation indexing), with particular attention to innovations in India. References.

FAD24. Pritchard, J. A. T. *Electronic Indexing and Hardcopy Management.* Manchester, Eng.: National Computing Centre, 1983.

A practical discussion of indexing paper and electronic files in an integrated office information system.

FAD25. Soergel, D. *Organizing Information: Principles of Data Base and Retrieval Systems.* Orlando, Fla.: Academic Press, 1988.

Offers a complex, theoretical base for the analysis, design, and operation of information systems, with a focus on information storage and retrieval. Contains a substantial bibliography organized by subject.

FAD26. Vickery, Brian C., and Alina Vickery. *Information Science in Theory and Practice.* Rev. ed. London: Bowker-Saur, 1992.

Discusses the principles of information science in the context of experimental research and the practical tasks of information provision. The relation between the design of information systems and communication in society is explored. References and index.

FAD27. Weinberg, Bella H., ed. *Indexing: The State of Our Knowledge and the State of Our Ignorance.* Medford, N.J.: Learned Information, 1989.

"A distillation of the key ideas on the art of indexing." Topics include the literature of indexing (H. Wellisch), file organization and retrieval (J. Anderson), database design (J. Milstead), indexing and relevance (T. Saracevic), and others. References and index.

FAE
Indexing: Dictionaries and Glossaries

FAE1. Buchanan, Brian. *Glossary of Indexing Terms.* London: Clive Bingley, 1976.

More than fifteen years old, this glossary holds up as a basic definition of terms. Some bias toward British usage can be seen, but overall, a useful reference or textbook supplement.

FAE2. Chan, Lois Mai, and Richard Pollard. *Thesauri Used in Online Databases: An Analytical Guide.* New York: Greenwood Press, 1988.

Descriptions of 122 widely used thesauri. Includes bibliographic information, scope and usage of the thesauri, characteristics of descriptors, types of cross-references, and examples of descriptors. Indexed by personal name, subject, database, and organization.

FAE3. Gesellschaft für Information und Dokumentation. *Thesaurus Guide: Analytical Directory of Selected Vocabularies for Information Retrieval, 1985.* Prepared for the

Commission of the European Communities. Amsterdam: North-Holland, 1985.

See also annotation under DD34. A directory of thesauri, subject heading lists, and abstracting/indexing services, giving bibliographical and technical details (e.g., content, structure, size). Terms used by various thesauri to denote relationships between terms are defined uniformly. The emphasis is on thesauri from countries of the European Community, the United States, and Canada.

FAE4. Peniston, Silvina. *Thesaurus of Information Technology Terms.* London: T. Graham, 1988.

A thesaurus of information science and its related technology, including American and British terms. In addition to print, it is available online; the software runs on IBM-compatible personal computers with a 10MB hard disk.

FAE5. Wellisch, Hans H. *Indexing from A to Z.* Bronx, N.Y.: H. W. Wilson, 1991.

Covers the gamut of terms related to indexing in an alphabetical arrangement. Offers substantive discussion and definition of terms such as "filing" and "indexing" in a section on "Indexing: The Process and Its Techniques." Bibliography.

FAF
Directories

FAF1. Dahlberg, Ingetraut. *Who Is Who in Classification and Indexing.* Frankfurt am Main, Ger.: Indeks-Verlag, 1983.

Addresses of some 700 members of classification and indexing organizations in forty-five countries.

FAF2. *Gale Directory of Databases.* Detroit: Gale Research. 1993– . Semiannual. ISSN 1066-9834.

Comprises three (now defunct) Gale directories: *Computer-Readable Data Bases*, *Directory of Online Databases*, and *Directory of Portable Databases*. Describes and indexes a broad range of databases, many of which are indexes to publications in all formats. The directory is also available electronically through these online services: Data-Star, ORBIT, and Questel.

FAF3. *The Index and Abstract Directory: An International Guide to Services and Serials Coverage.* 2nd ed. Birmingham, Ala.: EBSCO, 1990.

Lists 30,000 serial titles, indicating their coverage by abstracting and indexing services. Lists indexing and abstracting services with information about price, publisher, formats, etc., with a list of serials covered.

FAF4. *Information Industry Directory.* 11th ed. Detroit: Gale Research. 1991– . Annual. ISSN 1051-6239.

A "comprehensive guide to the organizations, systems, products, and services of the worldwide information and publishing industries." Includes (but is not limited to) abstracting and indexing services and products, associations involved in indexing, and software products

for indexing. Includes description, scope, address, publications, contact people, etc. Indexes.

FAF5. *Register of Indexers.* Port Aransas, Tex.: American Society of Indexers, 197?– . Annual. ISSN 0149-4694.

Directory of professional indexers available for freelance work.

FAG
Bibliographies

FAG1. Bakewell, K. G. B. "Reference Books for Indexers." *The Indexer* 15 (1987): 131–40.

A bibliographical essay, with a strongly British orientation, on 197 works useful to the indexer: textbooks, guides to microcomputers, guides to organizations and libraries, etc. Additions supplied by readers appear in volume 15, 1987 (195–96).

FAG2. Bakewell, K. G. B., and G. Rowland. "Indexing and Abstracting." In Vol. 2, *British Librarianship and Information Work, 1981–1985*, 207–26. London: Library Association, 1988.

Notes significant developments in indexing during 1981 through 1985, including bibliographies published, the role of the computer, changes in thesauri, and changes in indexing and abstracting services. Essentially a review essay with 130 references.

FAG3. Burton, Paul F. *Microcomputers in Library and Information Services: An Annotated Bibliography.* Aldershot, Eng.: Gower, 1986.

Six hundred citations of journal articles, conference proceedings, and monographs, covering both general guides to hardware and software and specific applications. Four-fifths of the citations are from 1981 through 1985. Subject and author indexes.

FAG4. Desmond, Winifred F., and Lester A. Barrer. *Indexing and Classification: A Selected and Annotated Bibliography.* Oak Ridge, Tenn.: Special Libraries Association, 1966.

Covers primarily English-language articles, monographs, and papers from 1960 through 1964. The emphasis is on indexing scientific materials and the origins of automated indexing.

FAG5. Lancaster, F. W., Calvin Elliker, and Tschera Harkness Connell. "Subject Analysis." *Annual Review of Information Science and Technology* 23 (1989): 35–84.

A review of some 300 citations, largely from the mid- to late 1980s, in these categories: indexing theory and practice, controlled vocabularies, search strategies and methods, natural language searching, classification, subject headings, automatic indexing, and citation relationships in information retrieval.

FAG6. Robertson, Carolyn. *A Bibliography of Standards Relevant to Indexing and Abstracting and the Presentation of*

Information. Ottawa: Library Documentation Center, National Library of Ottawa, 1980.

The standards listed are those of the American National Standards Institute, the Association Française de Normalisation, the British Standards Institution, the International Federation of Library Associations and Institutions, and the International Organization for Standardization. Notes and index in French and English.

FAG7. Wellisch, Hans H. *Indexing: A Basic Reading List.* 2nd ed. Port Aransas, Tex.: American Society of Indexers, 1992.

An annotated thirty-page guide covering technical aspects of indexing books and periodicals.

FAG8. _____. "Indexing and Abstracting: A Current-awareness Bibliography." *The Indexer* 15 (1986–1987): 29–36, 95–98, 159–62, 219–56; 16 (1988–1989): 33–39, 107–10, 181–88, 255–67.

An annotated list of about 500 items in English, covering 1984–1989, to update the author's monograph bibliographies (FAG9, FAG10). Published in parts in each issue of volumes 15 and 16. The author/title/subject indexes appear in the last issue of each volume. Its one drawback as a reference source is that articles published in *The Indexer* are not included.

FAG9. _____. *Indexing and Abstracting: An International Bibliography.* Santa Barbara, Calif.: ABC Clio Information Services, 1980.

A major research guide to verbal indexing. Includes lengthy annotations for nearly 2,400 items in twenty-five languages, covering 1856–1980. Eighty percent of the items are in English; the title is translated for non-English items. Wellisch selected only those items that made an original contribution to the literature. Arranged by subject; index.

FAG10. _____. *Indexing and Abstracting, 1977–1981: An International Bibliography.* Santa Barbara, Calif.: ABC Clio Information Services, 1984.

Continues the 1980 *Indexing and Abstracting* (FAG9) on an enlarged international scale. Lists 1,426 new items, with 220 new items for the period of the previous volume. Items are in twenty-six languages; two-thirds are in English. The subject arrangement and annotations are similar to those of the previous volume.

FAH
Standards

FAH1. American National Standards Institute. *American National Standard for Library and Information Sciences and Related Publishing Practices: Basic Criteria for Indexes.* New York: ANSI, 1984. (ANSI Z39.4-1984)

Addresses indexes used for information retrieval for all types of documents and media. Sets standards for methods of compilation, indexing languages, display media, and search procedures. Describes principles of syntax and

vocabulary linking. Includes a glossary, descriptions of index features, and a classification of types of indexes.

FAH2. _____. *American National Standard Guidelines for Thesaurus Structure, Construction, and Use.* New York: ANSI, 1980. (ANSI Z39.19-1980)

Defines terms, outlines the structure of thesauri, and gives the principles of their construction. Includes a sample form for review of a thesaurus term. *See* FAH4 for edition in progress.

FAH3. Highsmith, Anne L. "Fulfilling the Paris Principles in the Online Catalog Indexing, Display, and Referencing of Automated Records." In *National Online Meeting: Proceedings, 1984*, compiled by Martha E. Williams and Thomas H. Hogan, 97–113. Medford, N.J.: Learned Information, 1984.

Suggests standards for the indexing and display of bibliographic records based on the Paris Principles, formulated in 1961 at an international conference on cataloging principles. Unfortunately, the original references were apparently not reproduced.

FAH4. National Information Standards Organization. *Guidelines for Thesaurus Construction and Maintenance.* New Brunswick, N.J.: Transaction Publications (forthcoming, ca. 1993–1994).

A major revision of the 1980 ANSI standards (FAH2), in progress in 1993. (For information about its status, fax NISO at [301] 869-8071.)

FAI
Periodicals

FAI1. *Annual Review of OCLC Research.* Dublin, Ohio: OCLC. July 1985/June 1986– . Annual. ISSN 0894-198X.

Brief reports of research funded at least partially by OCLC. Areas of emphasis are the enhanced use of the OCLC catalog, improving cataloging productivity, investigating the library of the future, and the digitization of documents. Typical summaries of research are "A Syntactic Approach to Automatic Book Indexing" (G. Salton) and "Enhanced Bibliographic Retrieval" (M. Dillon), both from 1988/89. Some articles include references.

FAI2. *The Indexer.* Northampton, Eng.: Society of Indexers. v. 1– , Mar. 1958– . Biannual. ISSN 0019-4143.

Published by the Society of Indexers (Great Britain), the American Society of Indexers, and the Australian Society of Indexers. Concerned with the role of indexers in the advancement of knowledge and with standards and techniques of all forms of indexing. Articles cover the creation and use of indexes from practical, theoretical, and historical perspectives. Book and software reviews.

FAI3. *KEY WORDS.* Port Aransas, Tex.: American Society of Indexers. v. 1– , July/Aug. 1992– . Bimonthly. ISSN 1064-1211.

Newsletter featuring articles of interest to professional indexers on methods, standards, working conditions, etc. Reports on activities to raise awareness of indexing in publishing, and on the activities of national chapters. Reviews software and utilities. Addresses practical problems of indexing.

FAI4. *Library and Information Services Today.* Chicago: American Library Association. 1991– . Annual. ISSN 1055-3665. Continues *ALA Yearbook of Library and Information Services.*

See 1991 articles on "Abstracting and Indexing Services" and index entries on "filing," "MARC format," etc. [Annual publication was being reconsidered as of 1993.—Ed.]

FAI5. *Library Software Review.* Westport, Conn.: Meckler. v. 3– , Mar. 1984– . Bimonthly. ISSN 0742-5759. Continues *Software Review.*

See also annotation under AF14. Articles generally focus on a single software package or compare several packages with similar applications. Particular attention is given to library applications (in contrast to more general information science periodicals). Indexing, document organization and retrieval, and cataloging are frequently covered functions.

FAI6. *Library Technology Reports.* Chicago: American Library Association. v. 12– , 1976– . Bimonthly. ISSN 0024-2586.

See also annotation under AF16. Offers an objective basis for comparison among current library technologies by testing products and reporting results. Two recent reports relevant to indexing are "Optical Character Recognition Software for IBM-Compatible Microcomputers" (27 [May–June 1990]: 569–750) and "Microcomputer-Based Library Systems" (26 [Mar.–Apr. 1990]: 131–291; 26 [May–June 1990]: 295–444; and 27 [May–June 1991]: 217–398).

FAJ
Sources of Expertise

FAJ1. ALA Association for Library Collections and Technical Services (ALCTS). Executive Director: Karen Muller.

For annotation, *see* AGA3. Of particular interest is the Committee on Catalog Form and Function, which is concerned with the structure of catalogs, filing order, record content, record display, and other issues regarding the form and function of catalogs in all formats. Studies issues, coordinates discussion, and issues guidelines. Meets annually at ALA conferences.

FAJ2. American Society of Indexers (ASI). Headquarters: P.O. Box 386; Port Aransas, TX 78373.

An organization of some 1,000 members, including indexers, librarians, editors, publishers, and organizations employing indexers. Promotes high standards and improvements in indexing; advises individuals and organizations on qualifications and remuneration; sponsors workshops and seminars; fosters communication in the field. Holds annual conferences. Publishes *KEY WORDS* (FAI3), *Register of Indexers* (FAF5), *Guide to Indexing Software* (FG1), conference proceedings, and occasional books, articles, and guidelines.

FAJ3. Indexing and Abstracting Society of Canada/Société canadienne pour l'analyse de documents (SCAD). Headquarters: P.O. Box 744; Sta. F; Toronto, ON M4Y 2N6 Canada.

Promotes the production and use of indexes and abstracts and improvement in methods. Conducts workshops and seminars. Holds annual conferences. Publishes guides, bibliographies, and its own quarterly, *IASC/SCAD Bulletin.*

FAJ4. International Council for Scientific and Technical Information/Conseil internationale pour l'information scientifique et technique. Headquarters: 51 Blvd. de Montmorency; F-75016 Paris, France. Executive Secretary: Marthe Orfus.

Aims to increase accessibility to scientific and technical information, including the improvement of abstracting and indexing in scientific disciplines.

FAJ5. National Federation of Abstracting and Information Services. Headquarters: 1429 Walnut Street; Philadelphia, PA 12102. Executive Director: Ann Marie Cunningham.

Essentially a federation of firms in the information industry. Among other activities, NFAIS promotes improved documentation of the world's literature. Publishes *Abstracting and Indexing Career Guide, Indexing and Searching in Perspective* (a history of indexing in the United States), and the NFAIS *Directory of Consultants and Contractors.*

FAJ6. Project SMART. Cornell University; Computer Science Department; Upson Hall, Ithaca, NY 14853.

Experiments with automatic methods for text analysis, automatic indexing, automatic classification of documents, automatic thesaurus preparation, and related activities. Can provide advisory and consulting services in documentation and automation areas. Contact Dr. Gerald Salton at **GS@GVAX.CS.CORNELL.EDU** (ARPNET).

FAJ7. The Society of Indexers. Headquarters: 38 Rochester Road, London NW1 9JJ England. Secretary: Mrs. C. Troughton.

An international organization of individuals and institutions promoting high standards and new techniques of indexing, particularly in book and periodical indexing. Maintains a list of qualified indexers and provides professional advice. Organizes training courses and discussions. Publishes *The Indexer* (FAI2), *The Microindexer, Training in Indexing,* and occasional publications on various topics.

FB
Indexing and the Library Catalog

FB1. Bakewell, K. G. B. "Access to Information Via the Index." *Catalogue & Index* 71 (Winter 1983): 1–4.

Argues that subject access may be more effectively improved by consulting published bibliographies than by adding terms to the MARC record.

FB2. Bates, Marcia. "Rethinking Subject Cataloguing in the Online Environment." *Library Resources & Technical Services* 33 (1989): 400–12.

In light of new capabilities of online catalogs, "describes the design of a 'superthesaurus' geared to the needs of users rather than indexers." References.

FB3. Berg, Øivind. "Current Problems with the MARC/ISBD Formats in Relation to Online Public Access of Bibliographic Information." *International Cataloguing and Bibliographic Control* 20, no. 1 (Jan./Mar. 1991): 12–14.

Argues that reducing processing time in cataloging should be a top priority and that formats must, therefore, be simplified. Describes two projects in simplifying the cataloging process.

FB4. Bland, Robert N. "Toward the Catalog as a Tutorial Guide to the Literature." *Cataloging & Classification Quarterly* 11, no. 1 (1990): 71–82.

Explores ways in which indexing in the online catalog may provide innovative avenues of access to the intellectual content of the collection. The concept of intellectual level may be one such guide to the collection. Responses in same issue.

FB5. Byrne, Alex, and Mary Micco. "Improving OPAC Subject Access: The ADFA Experiment." *College & Research Libraries* 49 (1988): 432–47.

A description of a project to enhance bibliographic records at a small academic library. Keywords from chapter headings and indexes were added to MARC records. Analyzes the impact on work load and resources and the impact on information retrieval. References.

FB6. Carr, Angela R., and N. Strachan. "Development of a System for Treatment of Bible Headings in an OPAC System." *Catalogue & Index* 95 (Winter 1989): 5–6.

Describes a coding process used in addition to MARC tagging to create a logical display of Bible headings. The system can be used for anonymous classics and works of prolific authors.

FB7. Chan, Lois Mai. "The Library of Congress Classification System in an Online Environment." *Cataloging & Classification Quarterly* 11, no. 1 (1990): 7–25.

Explores LC classification as an online access point: as a search enhancement for subject browsing, as a method for known-item searching, and as a limiting feature on other types of searching. References. Responses in same issue.

FB8. Cochrane, Pauline A. *Redesign of Catalogs and Indexes for Improved Online Subject Access.* Phoenix: Oryx Press, 1985.

Selected papers of Cochrane from 1961 through 1984. "Redesign" means making new use of data already present in the bibliographic record and adding further information. Extensive references to research. Index.

FB9. Cochrane, Pauline A., and Karen Markey. "Preparing for the Use of Classification in Online Cataloging Systems and in Online Catalogs." *Information Technology and Libraries* 4 (June 1985): 91–111.

Considers how the machine-readable versions of LC and Dewey Decimal Classification schedules and index record files should be constructed to take advantage of their multiple potential uses. References.

FB10. Comaromi, John P. "Summation of Classification as an Enhancement of Intellectual Access to Information in an Online Environment." *Cataloging & Classification Quarterly* 11, no. 1 (1990): 99–102.

Maintains that classification structure and indexes to classification need to be better understood at a theoretical level before classification will become an effective online-access point.

FB11. DeHart, Florence E., and Karen Matthews. "Subject Enhancements and OPACs: Planning Ahead." *Technical Services Quarterly* 7 (1990): 35–52.

Reports on research exploring the implications, for OPAC searching, of displaying tables of contents, abstracts, and reviews, or terms from these sources. References.

FB12. DeHart, Florence E., and Richard Reitsma. "Subject Searching and Tables of Contents in Single-Work Titles." *Technical Services Quarterly* 7 (1989): 33–51.

Reports on research that examined the effect on subject access of including table of contents terms in the MARC record. Concludes that such inclusion may improve subject access more than increasing the number of subject headings assigned to each record. References.

FB13. Diodato, Virgil P. "Table of Contents and Book Indexes: How Well Do They Match Readers' Descriptions of Books?" *Library Resources & Technical Services* 30 (1986): 402–12.

Reports on research that compared readers' descriptions of books to terms in the indexes and tables of contents and also to the LC subject headings assigned to the books. Concludes that using terms from a book as access points would improve subject retrieval.

FB14. Frantz, Paul. "A Gaping Black Hole in the Bibliographic Universe." *American Libraries* 21, no. 7 (July/Aug. 1990): 632–33.

Faults Library of Congress subject cataloging policy for aiming to summarize the contents of a book and suggests that indexing should provide more specific access to a book's parts.

FB15. Fugmann, Robert. "Unusual Possibilities in Indexing and Classification." In *Tools for Knowledge Organization and the Human Interface: Proceedings of the 1st International ISKO Conference, Darmstadt, 14–17 August 1990*, edited by Robert Fugmann, 65–77. Frankfurt am Main, Ger.: Indeks-Verlag, 1990.

Proposes that information retrieval may be improved by combining indexing and classification with vocabulary categorization. References.

FB16. Furniss, P. "A Proposed Methodology for Examining the Provision of Subject Access in the OPAC." *International Classification* 17, no. 2 (1990): 85–90.

Suggests that revived interest in subject access online should call for reexamination of underlying theory. References.

FB17. High, Walter H. "Library of Congress Classification Numbers as Subject Access Points in Computer-based Retrieval." *Cataloging & Classification Quarterly* 11, no. 1 (1990): 37–43.

Considers the advantages of using classification as an online access point and concludes that librarians are the group most likely to benefit.

FB18. Holley, Robert P., ed. *Subject Control in Online Catalogs.* New York: Haworth Press, 1989.

Essays on the relationship between indexing design and the performance of the OPAC; the role of classification in the OPAC, the implementation of keyword searching, and PRECIS in the online catalog are among topics covered. An annotated bibliography of some fifty items is included.

FB19. Larson, Ray R. "Subject Searching Online." *Advances in Librarianship* 15 (1991): 175–236.

An excellent overview of the literature on enhancing subject information in the MARC record. Treats classification enhancements, subject heading enhancements, keyword searching enhancements, and special indexes that work in conjunction with a bibliographic database. Extensive references.

FB20. Library of Congress, Network Development and MARC Standards Office. *Content-Enriched and Enhanced Subject Access in USMARC Records.* MARBI Discussion Paper no. 42 (7 Feb. 1991).

In this four-page paper, issues for the enhancement of USMARC records are outlined in terms of specific fields. The possibilities of adding terms from tables of contents, indexes, abstracts, and book reviews are mentioned.

FB21. _____. *Enhancing USMARC Records with Table of Contents.* MARBI Discussion Paper no. 46 (16 Oct. 1991).

This eight-page paper "explores how USMARC currently accommodates contents information and offers several approaches for adding content designation to field 505 in the USMARC bibliographic format" (summary).

FB22. McTeigue, Bernard. "Indexing Journal Articles Directly into the Classified Catalogue." *Library Association Record* 89 (1987): 402.

A thumbnail sketch of a card-based method for integrating the indexing of journals into the main subject catalog.

FB23. Markey, Karen, and Karen S. Calhoun. "Unique Words Contributed by MARC Records with Summary and/or Contents Notes." In *ASIS '87: Proceedings of the 50th Annual ASIS Annual Meeting*, 153–62. Medford, N.J.: Learned Information, 1987.

Reports on research that explored whether summary and/or contents notes in MARC records contain terms that would enhance subject access. Such notes fields were found to be a significant source of subject terms. References.

FB24. Martin, Dillon, and Patrick Wenzel. "Retrieval Effectiveness of Enhanced Bibliographic Records." *Library Hi Tech* 8, no. 3 (1990): 43–46.

Reports on a research project on the effect on retrieval of adding abstracts and tables of contents to bibliographic records. Recall was improved.

FB25. Michalak, Thomas J. "An Experiment in Enhancing Catalog Records at Carnegie Mellon University." *Library Hi Tech* 8, no. 3 (1990): 33–41.

Outlines the initial stages of an experiment in enhancing bibliographic records with contents notes, terms from the table of contents, and abstracts. References.

FB26. Miksa, Francis. *The Subject in the Dictionary Catalog from Cutter to the Present.* Chicago: American Library Association, 1983.

See also annotation under DD1. A historical approach to the question How does the dictionary subject catalog function? Looks for the underlying rationality in the modern subject access system. References and index.

FB27. Parker, Lorraine M. Purgailis, and Robert E. Johnson. "Does Order of Presentation Affect Users' Judgment of Documents?" *Journal of the American Society for Information Science* 41 (1990): 493–94.

Reports on research examining whether the order in which citations are presented affects a user's perception of their relevance. Significant differences were found for groups of more than fifteen documents. References.

FB28. Saye, Jerry D. " 'The Library of Congress Classification System in an Online Environment': A Reaction." *Cataloging & Classification Quarterly* 11, no. 1 (1990): 27–35.

A response to Lois M. Chan's article in the same issue (FB7). Saye accepts that LC classification could be a useful access point but questions whether the needs of the typical library user justify developing the tools to make it possible.

FB29. Summerville, Lovenia. "Cataloging, Classification and Pedagogy: Toward the Catalog as a Guide to the Literature: Reaction." *Cataloging & Classification Quarterly* 11, no. 1 (1990): 83–88.

A response to Robert N. Bland's article in the same issue (FB4). Discusses indexing as an indication of intellectual level in relation to minimal-level cataloging, retrospective conversion projects, and the limitations of certain formats.

FB30. Takawashi, Tadayoshi, Tsutomu Shihota, and Zensei Oshiro. "The No-main-entry Principle: The Historical Background of the Nippon Cataloging Rules." *Cataloging & Classification Quarterly* 9 (1989): 67–77.

The historical development of the no-main-entry rule, with a justification of its aptness for the online catalog. References.

FB31. Tyckoson, David A., ed. *Enhancing Access to Information: Designing Catalogs for the 21st Century.* New York: Haworth Press, 1991.

Essays by Tyckoson and others on the state of the art in the design of online catalogs. Topics include the process of enhancing bibliographic records, the indexing of journals in an OPAC, and novel ways to manipulate LC subject headings and call numbers. References, but no index.

FB32. Van Orden, Richard. "Content-Enriched Access to Electronic Information: Summaries of Selected Research." *Library Hi Tech* 8, no. 3 (1990): 27–32.

A review essay listing research on the topic of subject access and the inclusion of terms from tables of contents, abstracts, summaries, and index entries in MARC records. References.

FB33. Vasiljev, Anatol. "Enhancement of the Subject Access Vocabulary in an Online Catalogue." In *Tools for Knowledge Organization and the Human Interface: Proceedings of the 1st International ISKO Conference, Darmstadt, 14–17 August 1990,* edited by Robert Fugmann, 163–70. Frankfurt am Main, Ger.: Indeks-Verlag, 1990.

Describes the integration of thesauri with the OPAC at a Netherlands university library. References.

FB34. Weinberg, Bella Hass. "Why Indexing Fails the Researcher." *The Indexer* 16 (1988): 3–6.

Argues that major subject access systems neglect the aspect of a document of greatest interest to researchers: the document's point of view. References.

FB35. Wilkinson, Catherine L. "Intellectual Level as a Search Enhancement in the Online Environment: Summation and Implications." *Cataloging & Classification Quarterly* 11, no. 1 (1990): 89–97.

Argues that to index intellectual level as a search enhancement would be costly and would hamper patrons' searches. Bibliography.

FB36. Williamson, Nancy J. "The Library of Congress Classification and the Computer: Research in Progress." *International Cataloguing and Bibliographic Control* 18 (1989): 8–12.

Reports on research on the feasibility of the computerization of LCC and the possible benefits of indexing LCC in interactive online systems. References.

FB37. Wyllie, Jan. "Concept Indexing: The World Beyond the Windows." *Aslib Proceedings* 42 (1990): 153–59.

"The realization of the electronic hypermedia of the future depends on integrating the technology of free text retrieval with the classification-based discipline of content analysis."

FC
Indexing Special Formats

FC1. Besser, Howard. "Visual Access to Visual Images: The UC Berkeley Image Database Project." *Library Trends* 38, no. 4 (Spring 1990): 787–98.

Describes an image database (while still in development) that allows patrons to search a catalog of graphic materials with verbal queries, then to browse electronic surrogates to identify specific items. References.

FC2. Bottoms, John W. "Full Text Indexed Retrieval Systems." In *The CD ROM Handbook,* edited by Chris Sherman, 309–28. New York: Intertext Publishers, 1988.

A basic description, for nontechnical readers, of the mechanics of indexing text and multimedia documents on CD-ROM.

FC3. Feinberg, Hilda, ed. *Indexing Specialized Formats and Subjects.* Metuchen, N.J.: Scarecrow Press, 1983.

Essays on the methods of several well-known indexes in biomedical literature, chemical literature, education, newspapers, and other areas. Several essays address general issues: keyword and free text indexing, index design, the use of the thesaurus. References and index.

FC4. Hill, Linda L. "Geographic Indexing for Bibliographic Databases." *Resource Sharing and Information Networks* 4 (1989): 1–12.

Describes geographic indexing methods other than controlled vocabulary, including map reference points (e.g., latitude and longitude) and the use of computer graphic display. References.

FC5. Keefe, Jeanne M. "The Image as Document: Descriptive Programs at Rensselaer." *Library Trends* 38, no. 4 (Spring 1990): 659–81.

Describes the design and implementation of a MARC-based online catalog of visual images and its integration with the primary OPAC.

FC6. Leung, C. H. C. "Architecture of an Image Database System." *Information Services & Use* 10, no. 6 (1990): 391–97.

Describes the essential elements of a system for machine processing of pictorial data: picture description, picture indexing and filing, and picture retrieval. References.

FC7. Leung, C. H. C., and others. "Retrieval by Content in an Image Database." *ITS News* 22 (Aug. 1990): 41–46.

Describes a prototype of an information retrieval system that responds to content-based queries to locate images from a pictorial database.

FC8. *Library Trends* 38 (Spring 1990): 4.

See also annotations under FC1 and FC5. Special issue on intellectual access to graphic information. Topics covered include the development of the *Art & Architecture Thesaurus* (DD39), the NASA image archives, preparing a catalog for textile art, electronic imaging at the National Library of Medicine, indexing of heraldry, the ArchiVISTA system of the National Archives of Canada, and the impact of standards developed by the Department of Defense on the electronic publishing industry.

FC9. Thiel, Thomas J., Cathy M. McConnahey, and Scott A. Gielda. "Document Indexing for Image-based Optical Information Systems." *Document Image Automation* 11, no. 2 (Mar./Apr. 1991): 82–88.

Discusses problems inherent in image-based information retrieval and describes the systems and tools available. Describes a CD-ROM indexing project undertaken for the Pentagon library. References.

FC10. Thom, William. "The Status of Imaging." *ITS News* 22 (Aug. 1990): 25–30.

A review of current work in document imaging and information retrieval from document images. Describes the STATUS system for computerized processing of images.

FD
Indexing and Abstracting

FD1. Clark, Katie. "To Cancel or Not to Cancel." *CD-ROM Professional* 5, no. 4 (1992): 126–28.

Outlines factors to consider before replacing print versions of abstracting and indexing services with their CD-ROM counterparts.

FD2. Cleveland, Donald B., and Ana D. Cleveland. *Introduction to Indexing and Abstracting*. 2nd ed. Englewood, Colo.: Libraries Unlimited, 1990.

Contains detailed information on indexing, including a discussion of types of indexes and methodologies. One chapter is devoted to automated indexing. Other topics addressed in depth are vocabulary control, abstracting, book indexes, and indexing and abstracting services. Includes a comprehensive bibliography.

FD3. Fay, Catherine H. "Off-site Indexing: A Cottage Industry." *Information Services & Use* 4 (1984): 299–304.

A short look at the administrative issues for off-site indexing and abstracting periodicals, including quality control and costs.

FD4. Grimwood-Jones, Diana. "Abstracting and Indexing Journals: The Unkindest Cut?" *Serials* 4 (1991): 12–13.

Deals with the choice between reducing subscriptions to journals and dropping abstracting and indexing journals. Suggests methods of evaluating abstracting and indexing journals.

FD5. Harris, Colin, and J. Blunden-Ellis. "Services." In *Librarianship and Information Work Worldwide, 1991*, edited by Maurice Line, Graham Mackenzie, and Ray Prytherch, 145–63. London: Bowker-Saur, 1991.

Reviews the year's activity through writings on the topic, which the authors admit is nebulous. Focuses on information technology, user services in two subject areas (agriculture and business), and public libraries.

FD6. Kinyon, William R., and others. "Producing In-house Indexes at Texas A & M." *RQ* 30, no. 1 (Fall 1990): 51–59.

A step-by-step guide to the production of in-house indexes to local materials and collections. Discusses time and cost factors.

FD7. Lancaster, F. W. *Indexing and Abstracting in Theory and Practice*. Champaign, Ill.: University of Illinois Graduate School of Library and Information Science, 1991.

Examines the theory and practice of indexing and abstracting in a thorough, scholarly manner. Copious examples illustrate aspects of indexing ranging from principles and practices, quality, and consistency to automated indexing and the future of indexing and abstracting services. Actual indexing and abstracting exercises compose the second section of the book. A lengthy list of references covers several decades of research.

FD8. Neufeld, M. Lynne, and Martha Cornog. *Abstracting and Indexing Career Guide*. 2nd ed. Philadelphia: NIS, 1986.

Rapidly covers the field of abstracting and indexing skills and education needed to succeed, organizations that hire indexers, how to establish a professional network, etc. An appendix lists professional organizations. References and index.

FD9. Rowley, Jennifer E. *Abstracting and Indexing.* 2nd ed. London: Clive Bingley, 1988.

A basic guide to indexing and abstracting from the British perspective. Includes a short bibliography.

FD10. Shroyer, Andrew, and Laura Nanna. "Serial Services 1992." *Library Journal* 117, no. 7 (15 Apr. 1992): 63–64.

Twenty-ninth in an annual survey (by various authors) of prices of periodical abstracting and indexing services. Indicates average prices and rate of increase.

FE
Thesauri

FE1. Dykstra, Mary. "Can Subject Headings Be Changed?" *Library Journal* 113, no. 15 (15 Sept. 1988): 55–58.

In a follow-up to an earlier article (FE2), Dykstra proposes that a thesaurus could be created from the LC subject headings list to be used in conjunction with it. References.

FE2. _____. "LC Subject Headings Disguised as a Thesaurus." *Library Journal* 113, no. 4 (1 Mar. 1988): 42–46.

Criticizes the eleventh edition of LCSH, which replaced "see" and "see also" references with "UF," "RT," etc. Argues that this change violates standards for thesaurus construction. References. Continued by FE1.

FE3. Foskett, Douglas J. "Thesaurus." In Vol. 30, *Encyclopedia of Library and Information Science,* 416–63. New York: Marcel Dekker, 1980.

A well-illustrated overview that emphasizes theoretical similarities across international boundaries. Covers the thesaurus's historical development, the nature and format of terms, the range of relationships between terms, layout and graphic display, machine compilation, revision and currency, and relations between thesauri. Includes a bibliography of eighteen items from the mid-1970s.

FE4. Ganzmann, Joachen. "Criteria for the Evaluation of Thesaurus Software." *International Classification* 17, nos. 3/4 (1990): 148–57.

Outlines criteria for tools to construct, apply, and maintain a thesaurus on a microcomputer. Includes checklist. References.

FE5. Lancaster, F. W. *Vocabulary Control for Information Retrieval.* 2nd ed. Arlington, Va.: Information Resources Press, 1986.

See also annotations under DD43 and EC10. A detailed, theoretical, close analysis of the role of vocabulary control in information retrieval. Addresses the influence of system vocabulary on the performance of a retrieval system, creating index languages automatically, and cost-effectiveness aspects of vocabulary control. References and index.

FE6. Milstead, Jessica L. "Specifications for Thesaurus Software." *Information Processing & Management* 27, nos. 3/4 (1991): 165–75.

Outlines criteria for software designed to aid the development and maintenance of thesauri.

FE7. Rada, Roy. "Connecting and Evaluating Thesauri: Issues and Cases." *International Classification* 14 (1987): 63–69.

Presents issues in evaluating thesauri, including the ability to support automatic indexing. Describes experiments in linking MeSH to other medical thesauri to create a more powerful information retrieval system. References.

FE8. Schmitz-Esser, Winfried. "New Approaches in Thesaurus Application." *International Classification* 18, no. 3 (1991): 143–47.

Discusses new approaches to the use of thesauri in expert systems, interface systems, hypertext systems, machine translation, and machine abstracting. References.

FF
Automated Indexing

See also section on expert systems applications in Chapter D.

FF1. Anderson, Barbara. "Expert Systems for Cataloging: Will They Accomplish Tomorrow the Cataloging of Today?" *Cataloging & Classification Quarterly* 11, no. 2 (1990): 33–48.

Assesses the state of expert systems that aid in descriptive cataloging. Suggests that the emphasis on title page information will change as cataloging moves toward accessing the full text. References.

FF2. Anderson, James D., and Gary Radford. "Back-of-the-Book Indexing with the Nested Phrase Indexing System: NEPHIS." *The Indexer* 16 (Oct. 1988): 79–84.

A description of Timothy Craven's semiautomatic, PC-based indexing system. The human indexer codes statements to indicate major and subordinate concepts. The computer creates grammatical index entries. References.

FF3. Deerwester, Scott, and others. "Indexing by Latent Semantic Analysis." *Journal of the American Society for Information Science* 41 (1990): 391–407.

Describes a new method for automatic indexing and retrieval in which the variation between terms in queries and terms occurring in a document is treated as a statistical problem.

FF4. Driscoll, James R., and others. "The Operation and Performance of an Artificially Intelligent Keywording System." *Information Processing & Management* 27, no. 1 (1991): 43–54.

An approach to automated indexing based on mimicking the behavior of subject experts. Rules generated by subject experts tell the system to add new terms to a document that are conceptually related to those already present and to ignore terms whose context in the document is ambiguous.

FF5. Enser, P. G. B. "Automatic Classification of Book Material Represented by Back-of-the-Book Index." *Journal of Documentation* 41 (Sept. 1985): 135–55.

Describes research in which automatic classification is applied to book indexes (as surrogates for books). Results are compared to conventional library classification. Includes references.

FF6. Humphrey, Susanne M., and De-Chih Chien. *The MedIndEx System: Research on Interactive Knowledge-based Indexing and Knowledge Management.* Bethesda, Md.: Lister Hill National Center for Biomedical Communications, National Library of Medicine, 1990. (NTIS: PB90-234964/AS)

Describes an interactive, knowledge-based prototype for computer-assisted indexing of the biomedical literature developed at the National Library of Medicine. Details the software development and conceptual underpinning of the system. References.

FF7. Humphrey, Susanne M., and Nancy E. Miller. "Knowledge-based Indexing of the Medical Literature: The Indexing Aid Project." *Journal of the American Society for Information Science* 38 (Mar. 1987): 184–96.

The Indexing Aid Project conducts research "in the areas of knowledge representation and indexing for information retrieval in order to develop interactive knowledge-based systems for computer-assisted indexing of the periodical medical literature." References.

FF8. Jeng, Ling Hwey. "Knowledge Representation of the Visual Image of a Title Page." *Journal of the American Society for Information Science* 42 (Mar. 1991): 99–109.

Reports on a study of title pages considered as visual objects with characteristics indicative of specific bibliographic elements. Proposes that this data is the potential basis of an expert system in descriptive cataloging.

FF9. Jones, Kevin P. "Getting Started in Computerized Indexing." *The Indexer* 15 (1986): 9-14.

Jones discusses which indexing tasks can be currently automated (i.e., clerical tasks) and how more conceptual tasks may be handled by machine in the future. References.

FF10. Jones, Leslie P., Edward W. Gassie, Jr., and Sridhar Radhakrishnan. "INDEX: The Statistical Basis for an Automatic Conceptual Phrase-indexing System." *Journal of the American Society for Information Science* 41 (1990): 87–97.

Describes two programs, INDEX and INDEXD, that count repeated phrases in a document and rank them according to their value as index phrases. Programs are described as the basis of an automatic conceptual indexing system. References.

FF11. Kuntz, Robert. "The Application of Expert Systems to Indexing." *Current Studies in Librarianship* 15 (1991): 3–26.

Examines the potential role of expert systems in indexing, which have already been studied for use in online searching and cataloging.

FF12. Molto, Mavis, and Elaine Svenonius. "Automatic Recognition of Title Page Names." *Information Processing & Management* 27 (1991): 83–95.

Reports on research concerning the feasibility of developing algorithms to distinguish character strings representing names from other character strings on English-language title pages. References.

FF13. Purcell, Royal. "Wanted: Fully Automated Indexing." *Library Software Review* 10 (1991): 390–95.

Describes an algorithm for automated indexing and the necessary conditions for an expert system in indexing. Distinguishes between automated and computer-aided indexing.

FF14. Schwarz, Christoph. "Automatic Syntactic Analysis of Free Text." *Journal of the American Society for Information Science* 41 (1990): 408–17.

Describes COPSY (context operator syntax) that "uses natural language processing techniques during fully automatic syntactic analysis (indexing and search) of free text documents." References.

FF15. Vleduts-Stokolov, Natasha. "Concept Recognition in an Automatic Text-Processing System for the Life Sciences." *Journal of the American Society for Information Science* 38 (1987): 269–87.

A technical discussion of an aid to assigning subject headings to life sciences literature based on article titles. Problems of ambiguity and the system's algorithms for dealing with ambiguity are described. References.

FF16. Weibel, Stuart, Mike Oskins, and Diane Vizine-Goetz. "Automated Title-Page Indexing." In *ASIS '87: Proceedings of the 50th Annual ASIS Annual Meeting*, 234–40. Medford, N.J.: Learned Information, 1987.

A report on an experimental rule-based system that captures bibliographic elements from machine-readable facsimiles of title pages. References.

FF17. Zimmermann, Harald H. "Language and Language Technology." *International Classification* 18, no. 4 (1991): 196–99.

Deals with several aspects of machine processing of language, including word processing, communication between humans and machine, spoken language–machine interfaces, automatic indexing, and machine translation. References.

FG
Indexing Software

FG1. *Guide to Indexing Software.* Port Aransas, Tex.: American Society of Indexers. Annual.

The most complete review of indexing software. Draws in part on reviews published in the Society's newsletter, *KEY WORDS* (FAI3). *See also* the annotations for *The Indexer* (FAI2); *Library Software Review* (FAI5); and *Library Technology Reports* (FAI6).

FH
PRECIS

FH1. Austin, Derek. "The Development of PRECIS: A Theoretical and Technical History." *The Journal of Documentation* 30 (1974): 47–102.

An overview of the principles of the system, together with the details of its theoretical basis and its historical development. An important article for understanding the rationale behind PRECIS. References.

FH2. Austin, Derek, and Mary Dykstra. *PRECIS: A Manual of Concept Analysis and Subject Indexing.* 2nd ed. London: Bibliographic Services Division, British Library, 1984.

See also annotation under DD45. A technical manual with diagrams, examples, and exercises. Appendixes include PRECIS operators and codes and algorithms for entry construction and validation of strings. Includes a chapter on management aspects of PRECIS. A less technical introduction is *PRECIS: A Primer* (FH5).

FH3. Biswas, Subal C., and Fred Smith. "Efficiency and Effectiveness of Deep Structure Based Subject Indexing Languages: PRECIS vs. DSIS." *International Forum on Information and Documentation* 16 (July 1991): 6–21.

A comparison of PRECIS and DSIS (a version of POPSI) from the searcher's viewpoint. Systems are compared for predictability, collocation, clarity, succinctness, and eliminability. PRECIS is favored. Seventy-one references.

FH4. Calderon, F. "Library of Congress Subject Headings: Vested Interest Versus the Real Needs of the Information Society." *Cataloging & Classification Quarterly* 11, no. 2 (1990): 85–94.

Argues that the library community should move beyond LCSH despite its current investment in that system. The bibliography represents both sides of the issue.

FH5. Dykstra, Mary. *PRECIS: A Primer.* Metuchen, N.J.: Scarecrow Press, 1987.

See also annotation under DD46. An introduction in a more manageable size than the manual (FH2). Its emphasis is PRECIS procedures for analysis of subject statements. Includes exercises. Index.

FH6. _____. "PRECIS in the Online Catalog." *Cataloging & Classification Quarterly* 10 (1989): 81–94.

Argues that PRECIS has been successful in online catalogs because the strings of terms can be easily manipulated. PRECIS conforms to international standards for thesaurus design and construction. References.

FH7. Kohli, B. L., and K. Bedi. "Index and Indexing System." *Herald of Library Science* 27 (1988): 195–202.

This brief article includes a bibliography of eighty-seven items, largely on PRECIS, and to a lesser extent on other indexing systems.

FH8. Krarup, Karl, and Ivan Boserup. *Reader-Oriented Indexing.* Copenhagen: The Royal Library, 1982.

Reports on research in which PRECIS indexers analyzed summaries of documents created by subject specialists rather than analyzing the documents themselves. Concludes that indexers need to collaborate closely with subject specialists.

FH9. Richmond, Phyllis A. *Introduction to PRECIS for North American Usage.* Littleton, Colo.: Libraries Unlimited, 1981.

An introduction to the techniques and methods of PRECIS, using North American idioms. The first two chapters explain its history and relationship to the universe of information retrieval.

FH10. Tonta, Yasar. "LCSH and PRECIS in Library and Information Science: A Comparative Study." *Occasional Papers* 194 (May 1992): 1–68.

A description of LCSH and PRECIS subject analysis of eighty-two titles in the field of library science: the number of entries provided, the depth of analysis, and the role of subdivisions. References.

FH11. Wellisch, Hans H., ed. *The PRECIS Index System: Principles, Applications, and Prospects.* New York: H. W. Wilson, 1977.

Papers from a 1976 workshop by Derek Austin and others on the principles of the system, comparative studies of other indexing systems, and practical applications. References are few. Index.

G

Serials Management

Marcia Tuttle

Overview

Serials management developed as a specialty within librarianship in the mid-1930s when J. Harris Gable's *Library Journal* article advocated the "integrated serials department" ("The New Serials Department," volume 60, 1935, 867–71). His thesis was that serials could best be processed and made accessible by persons familiar with their idiosyncrasies. These persons would be situated in the same administrative unit. Others supported Gable's position, and grouping by format remained popular until the mid-1970s, when libraries began to automate their technical services processes. At that time, function began to take priority over format as the basis for library administrative structure, and the trend continues today. With automation, many believe that the special qualities of serials—continuing nature, constant change, long-term commitment of resources—do not require processing by specialists. The concept of the integrated serials department is in jeopardy.

No matter where their place on the organizational chart, librarians working with serials are in the forefront of our profession because of the serious pricing situation. With the combination of publishers' inflation and the fluctuating U.S. dollar, librarians can no longer afford to purchase all journals consid-

ered necessary to support their institutions' mission. In addition to being a primary concern, serials pricing affects other matters of current interest.

Organization of serials management functions is still in flux. Separate serials units appear, disappear, and reappear regularly. Not all serials functions have been successfully automated, nor have all libraries converted their manual receipt records to computer. The pricing issue occupies serials managers with regard to acquisitions and to overall funding priorities.

Serials publishing is much on the minds of serials specialists, and the 1990s are a time of learning. Librarians are learning about publishing, and publishers are learning about library needs and constraints. We are trying to understand why journal prices keep rising steeply, and publishers are trying to determine why librarians do not simply get more money for journals. Together with the concern over serials pricing is the interest in the development of electronic publishing. Will electronic journals have a significant place in the library?

Expense is again a concern in serials processing, specifically the cost of electronic technology. In traditionally understaffed serials units, will automation permit staff members to give more time to their nonroutine responsibilities? Will it provide reasonable shortcuts to enable fewer staff members to do more processing?

By the early 1990s there were a number of good serials management systems or serials modules within integrated systems; no longer were serials considered too difficult to automate. Many a large library's serials collection had become literally unmanageable in a manual situation because staff members could not keep up with claiming, invoice posting, title changes, and problem solving. With automation librarians are more likely to stay current with these chores and to produce reports examining the collection from many aspects. Some libraries manipulate data on a personal computer, while others receive the information directly from their management system. Automation permits us to know far more about our serials collections and obligations than we have known before.

A further concern for serials acquisitions librarians is the changing role of subscription agents. In the past decade the largest domestic agents have grown through purchasing smaller companies and through expanding the scope of their services. These vendors consider themselves international agents, capable of supplying serials of all types from throughout the world. This effort has cut into the American libraries' business with foreign subscription agents.

However, the market for journal supply has become saturated within the past few years and is even shrinking with library journal cancellations. At the same time, international publishers have decreased their discounts to the subscription agents, seriously reducing subscription agents' revenue even further. Competition is fierce among the American vendors. Thus, the large agencies have turned their efforts away from the traditional supply of subscriptions toward the marketing of their online systems and, most recently, document delivery. With the end user a primary target of the latter effort, some librarians perceive a decline in service in the traditional role of the agent.

But it is the subscription price of journals, especially scientific journals, that is the greatest concern in serials management today. The profile of the library budget has been altered by the necessity of transferring funds from other lines into serials. Collection development personnel, traditionally book specialists, have had to become expert in evaluating serials in preparation for cancellation projects. While most of the blame for what is generally known as a crisis has been placed on the publishers and has given rise to charges of price gouging, the recent poor performance of the U.S. dollar has had a severe impact on prices.

Another significant factor is the mushrooming of the amount of scholarly information worthy of publication. More scholars plus larger and faster computers equals more articles. Even when a journal's price per page (a favorite measure of value) remains virtually the same, the subscription rate will increase because the journal's size has grown, perhaps doubled, in a short time.

Serials holdings lists and union lists of serials have changed within the last decade from being print products to electronic, specifically online, resources. The growth of OCLC, the tremendous success of the CONSER project, and—again—technology have enabled library patrons and staff members to have unsurpassed bibliographic access to materials. The challenge is now for physical access to catch up; the telefacsimile machine is helping librarians to meet that challenge, and electronic transmission of data is beginning to be a factor.

Serials management is a library specialty in which some feel that change is the only constant. Two areas, in addition to pricing, are in the midst of possibly severe change and are frequent topics of conversation in print, in person, and in electronic discussion groups. These concerns are the evolving format of scholarly information and the future role of the serials specialist. How much of the dissemination of scholarly information will shift to electronic format? How large a share of journal article-type information will be acquired "on demand," electronically? What effect will these changes have on pricing? Will libraries continue to acquire any information at all by means of journal subscriptions? While pricing has thrust serials librarianship into the professional spotlight, electronic technology is likely to keep it there. At the same time, both these issues may hasten the demise of the serials specialist.

Chapter Content and Organization

Most of the resources in this chapter have appeared since 1985 and reflect current practice in serials management. A few older works are included—even one published in 1937—because they set trends, nothing better has been published on the topics, or they represent ideas whose time has perhaps come again. I have sought to provide the practical tools a serials manager needs to consult and have emphasized electronic resources where they exist. Arrangement of the bibliography follows the major points identified in the introduction above.

Descriptions of commercial system features do not necessarily represent the latest versions. Users of this guide should check with vendors for updated information.

GA
General Works

GAA
Textbooks, Guides, and Manuals

GAA1. Brown, Clara D., and Lynn S. Smith. *Serials: Past, Present and Future.* 2nd ed., rev. Birmingham, Ala.: EBSCO Industries, Inc., 1980.

Although the procedures recommended in this very practical treatment of serials management are long outdated, Brown and Smith's situational checklists are worth remembering. For example, "Items to keep in mind when paying invoices," and "What may happen to mail." The book is also full of such nuggets as: "There is no use setting up a claiming project while there is unchecked material sitting around on the shelves." Disregard the illustrations of forms.

GAA2. Graham, Margaret E., and Fiona Buettel. *Serials Management: A Practical Handbook.* London: Aslib, 1990.

This British collection of essays on serials management is one of the more recent publications in the field. Some of the discussions and conclusions do not apply to American library situations, but on the whole the work is valuable because of the quality of its content and its publication date. Nine chapters, written by British specialists, are grouped within three categories. "Collection Development" consists of selection/deselection, acquisitions, and financial control and budgeting; "Collection Management" consists of housekeeping routines, cataloging/classification, storage/preservation, and user services. "Automation" and "Standards" comprise one chapter each.

GAA3. *Guidelines for Handling Library Orders for Serials and Periodicals.* Rev. ed. Chicago: American Library Association, 1992.

Updated by the Serials Section Acquisitions Committee of the Association for Library Collections and Technical Services, this manual consists of three sections, one each for librarians, subscription agents, and publishers. Within each section are guides for efficient handling of serials orders. This edition reflects changes in procedures resulting from increased automation and standardization.

GAA4. Osborn, Andrew D. *Serial Publications: Their Place and Treatment in Libraries.* 3rd ed. Chicago: American Library Association, 1980.

Despite its age and scant treatment of serials automation, Osborn's book remains a useful resource for serials managers because of its comprehensive scope, its historical perspective, and the principles imparted by the author. Highlights include the twenty-one-page first chapter on "Definition of a Serial" and the chapter titled "Principles of Selection."

GAA5. Taylor, David C. *Managing the Serials Explosion: The Issues for Publishers and Libraries.* White Plains, N.Y.: Knowledge Industry Publications, Inc., 1982.

What was a problem in 1982 is still a problem in the mid-1990s, and Taylor's very readable and sensible effort to "make a contribution toward finding those answers [to volume and cost problems] by analyzing the problems from the perspective of both librarians and publishers" is valid today.

GAA6. Tuttle, Marcia. *Introduction to Serials Management.* Foundations in Library and Information Science, 11. Greenwich Conn.: JAI Press, 1983.

More recent than Osborn (GAA4) or Brown (GAA1), this American work covers collection development (by Luke Swindler), acquisitions, cataloging (by Nancy I. White), preservation, public service, and resource sharing/standards. The book needs to be revised, in part because it does not consider automated serials systems. A strong feature is an annotated bibliography.

GAB
Directories

GAB1. "Directory of Union Lists of Serials: Second Edition." *Serials Review* 14, nos. 1/2 (1988): 115–59.

Compiled by the Union List of Serials Committee of the Serials Section of ALA/ALCTS, this guide is based on 1986 information. The 137 entries are arranged geographically. Features include a matrix section with "over 60 columns of detailed information," statistics, a listing of nine union list vendors, and an index of union lists by producer.

GAB2. *Gale Directory of Publications and Broadcast Media.* Detroit: Gale Research, Inc. v. 1– , 1869– . Annual. ISSN 1048-7972.

Arranged by state or province, then town. This directory, formerly known as "Ayer's," has had several titles during its publication. It is the best source for information about newspapers. Subject indexes include agricultural, ethnic, and fraternal publications. Entries include, besides the usual data, size, number of columns, key personnel, advertising rates, and paid circulation. Information included about some towns.

GAB3. Holley, Beth, comp. *Directory of Back Issue Dealers.* New York: North American Serials Interest Group, 1992.

This directory, originally prepared as a handout for a North American Serials Interest Group (NASIG) workshop, is based on surveys of back issue dealers. Ninety-six vendors are included. In addition to address and telephone and fax numbers, entries give scope of service, whether a catalog is available, and contact person, among other data. The list is international in its coverage.

GAB4. *International Directory of Little Magazines and Small Presses.* Paradise, Calif.: Dustbooks. First– , 1965– . Annual. ISSN 0092-3974.

Long edited by Len Fulton, presents magazine titles, presses, and cross-references (imprints) in a single alphabetical arrangement. Entries for magazines include subscription and publication information and recent publication pattern; for publishers entries include address, scope with quotes from publishers, editorial slant, titles listed in directory, discounts, and payment policies.

GAB5. Katz, Bill, and Linda Sternberg Katz, eds. *Magazines for Libraries.* 7th ed. New Providence, N.J.: Bowker, 1992. ISSN 0000-0914.

This irregularly published directory uses *Ulrich's* (GAB12) subject arrangement and lists 6,600 annotated citations of magazines suitable for school, public, academic, and special libraries. A symbol notes appropriate audience. Titles selected by 140-plus subject specialists. Each section is compiled by named consultant(s) and has a brief narrative introduction and a list of basic periodicals and indexes/abstracting journals.

GAB6. *MLA Directory of Periodicals: A Guide to Journals and Series in Languages and Literatures.* 1978/79– . New York: Modern Language Association of America. Biennial. ISSN 0197-0380.

This is a companion to the *MLA International Bibliography of Books and Articles on the Modern Languages and Literatures.* More than 3,000 entries comprise journals that print articles on language, literature, and folklore. Series are also included. Arrangement is alphabetical by title with a subject index. Entries include editorial information, sponsor, subject information, advertising information, editorial description, and submission requirements.

GAB7. *Monthly Catalog of United States Government Publications.* Washington, D.C.: Cataloging Branch, Library Division, Library Programs Service, Superintendent of Documents, U.S. Government Printing Office no. 1– , 1895– . Monthly. ISSN 0362-6830.

Title has varied slightly over the years. Since 1977, the *Monthly Catalog* has issued an *Annual Periodicals Supplement*; before 1977 data were included in the February issue in an appendix: "Directory of United States Government Publications and Subscription Publications." A work must be issued three or more times a year to be included; less-frequently published serials are listed in the main body of the *Monthly Catalog.* Arrangement is by Superintendent of Documents number. Indexes include author, title, subject, series/report, stock number, and title keyword. There are also sections listing title changes and discontinued publications.

GAB8. Perryman, Wayne, and Lenore Wilkas, eds. *International Subscription Agents: An Annotated Directory.* 5th ed. Chicago: American Library Association, 1986.

In an alphabetical arrangement are 319 entries including address, date service began, area covered, type of material supplied, services offered, catalogs and lists issued, and notes. Data are based on questionnaire responses from agents. Sixth edition projected in late 1993 or early 1994.

GAB9. *The Serials Directory: An International Reference Book.* Birmingham, Ala.: EBSCO Publishing. v. 1– , 1986– . Annual. ISSN 0886-4179.

This directory is based on the CONSER tapes, enhanced by data from EBSCO's title information file. Arrangement is by subject, then by key title. Indexes include title, new title, ceased title, ISSN, and others. New features for 1993 include ISI Impact Factor and Copyright Clearance Center information. Also available on CD-ROM.

GAB10. *Serials for Libraries: An Annotated Guide to Continuations, Annuals, Yearbooks, Almanacs, Transactions, Proceedings, Directories, Services.* 2nd ed. New York: Neal-Schuman Publishers, 1985.

Serials are listed in a subject arrangement with a title index. A special feature is "When to Buy What List" in which 800 entries are arranged by title with a month/season index.

GAB11. *Standard Periodical Directory.* New York: Oxbridge Publishing Company. 1st– , 1964/65– . Annual. ISSN 0085-6630.

Arranged by subject with a title index, *SPD*'s scope is United States and Canadian serials that are published at least twice a year. It includes some newspapers. It is particularly valuable for small-circulation, ephemeral, and processed publications. Some entries are annotated, and advertising rates are given.

GAB12. *Ulrich's International Periodicals Directory.* New Providence, N.J.: R. R. Bowker. v. 1– , 1932– . Quarterly. ISSN 0000-0175.

This annual directory is the standard listing of currently published serials. It now incorporates *Irregular Serials and Annuals*, which covered nonperiodical serials. The work is arranged by subject and has liberal indexes and cross-references. In addition to editorial and subscription data, entries may include notice of availability online, former titles, and a publisher-supplied annotation. Also available on CD-ROM as *Ulrich's Plus.*

GAC
Bibliographies

GAC1. Ginneken, Jos van. *770 Articles and Books on Serials: An Annotated Bibliography 1983–1989.* Wageningen, Netherlands: Library Agricultural University, 1991.

The bibliography is divided into five subject categories: general, acquisitions and collection development, technical services (e.g., standards, binding, etc.), finance, and automation. The last category is subdivided into general, subscription agents, serials control, applications and experiences, and microcomputers. Scope is international, with most citations and all annotations in English. Article titles in other languages are translated into English.

GAC2. Tuttle, Marcia. "Annotated Bibliography of 1982–85 Books and Articles on Serials." *Advances in Serials Management* 1 (1986): 135–230.

Continues the annotated bibliography published in the author's monograph *Introduction to Serials Management*(GAA6), and arranged virtually the same as that one. Many of the 625 entries were published before 1982.

GAC3. _____. [Bibliography] in her *Introduction to Serials Management*, 213–306. Greenwich, Conn.: JAI Press, 1983.

A 649-item annotated bibliography of research tools and books and articles, arranged according to the chapters of the book. Index to bibliography. Covers materials published prior to 1982.

GAC4. "Year's Work in Serials." In *Library Resources & Technical Services*. Chicago: Association for Library Collections and Technical Services, American Library Association.

LRTS publishes an annual bibliographic essay covering "the year's work in serials." In 1991, Jana Lonberger wrote a nine-page essay covering the major issues and trends of 1990, to which she appended a five-page bibliography. Over the years noted serials specialists have been selected as authors, and all have accomplished this difficult task well. Titles of articles vary.

GAD
Periodicals

GAD1. *ACQNET.* [serial online] Ithaca, N.Y.: Cornell University Library. no. 1– , 1990– . Irregular. ISSN 1057-5308.

For annotation, *see* BAD1.

GAD2. *Advances in Serials Management.* Greenwich, Conn.: JAI Press. v. 1– , 1986– . Annual. ISSN 1040-4384.

Published approximately every two years, this series contains substantial articles on all aspects of serials management. It is not peer reviewed, but most articles are invited.

GAD3. *Australian & New Zealand Journal of Serials Librarianship.* Binghamton, N.Y.: Haworth Press. v. 1– , 1990– . Quarterly. ISSN 0898-3283.

This quarterly journal concentrates on articles by Australians and New Zealanders and on subjects reflecting conditions in those countries.

GAD4. *Citations for Serial Literature.* [serial online] Cambridge, Mass.: Massachusetts Institute of Technology. no. 1– , 1992– . Irregular. ISSN 1061-7434.

SERCITES lists the contents and abstracts, when available, for articles related to the serials information chain. It covers journals about library serials and serials work and journals carrying frequent articles on serials. To subscribe, send a message to **LISTSERV@MITVMA** (BITNET) or

LISTSERV@MITVMA.MIT.EDU (INTERNET) with the command: **SUBSCRIBE SERCITES [your name].**

GAD5. *Library Resources & Technical Services.* Chicago: Association for Library Collections and Technical Services. v. 1– , 1957– . Quarterly. ISSN 0024-2527.

See also annotation under AF13. *LRTS* contains, in addition to articles on the technical services aspects of serials work, an annual review of serials librarianship, listing publications and discussing new developments. Serials concerns also are a part of the annual reviews of cataloging, preservation, resources, and reprographics.

GAD6. *Newsletter on Serials Pricing Issues.* [serial online] Chapel Hill, N.C.: Marcia Tuttle. no. 1– , Feb. 1989– . Irregular. ISSN 1046-3410.

Formerly a publication of ALA/ALCTS, this electronic newsletter is now privately edited and published by Marcia Tuttle. It contains brief articles, reports, and news notes about serials pricing. Contributors and audience are primarily librarians, publishers, subscription agents, and scholars. The newsletter appears irregularly, but at least once every two or three weeks. To subscribe, send a message to **LISTSERV@GIBBS.OIT.UNC.EDU** (INTERNET) with the command: **SUBSCRIBE PRICES [your name].**

GAD7. *Public Access Computer Systems Review.* [serial online] University Park: University Libraries, University of Houston. Jan. 1990– . Irregular. ISSN 1048-6452.

A peer-reviewed electronic journal associated with the moderated PACS-L electronic discussion group (GAE2). *PACS Review* articles are stored as individual files on the list server, and a table of contents message for each issue is sent out to all PACS-L users. Articles may then be retrieved individually. *PACS Review* is also available in paper format (on a delayed basis) from ALA's Library and Information Technology Association. To retrieve the table of contents file for an issue of the *PACS Review*, send an E-mail message to **LISTSERV@UHUPVM1** (BITNET) or **LISTSERV@UHUPVM1.UH.EDU** (INTERNET) that contains the appropiate command based on the issue's volume and number: **GET CONTENTS PRV1N1 F=MAIL, GET CONTENTS PRV1N2 F=MAIL,** etc.

GAD8. *Rights: Copyright and Related Rights in the Service of Creativity.* Geneva, Switz.: International Publishers Association. v. 1– , Spring 1987– . Quarterly. ISSN 1011-0240.

This newsletter is published in sixteen-page issues by the International Publishers Association and the International Group of Scientific, Technical and Medical Publishers. It reflects the publishing industry's views on copyright. Includes reports of relevant international conferences and occasional full texts of talks.

GAD9. *Serials: The Journal of the United Kingdom Serials Group.* Bradford, Eng.: United Kingdom Serials Group. v. 1– , 1988– . Three times a year. ISSN 0953-0460.

Serials continues *UKSG Newsletter*, which ceased publication after the December 1987 issue, and the proceedings of the UKSG conferences, which were discontinued after the 1987 conference. Published three times a year, *Serials* contains both conference presentations and other articles on the topic, along with news from libraries, publishers, and vendors.

GAD10. *The Serials Librarian: The International Quarterly of Serials Management.* Binghamton, N.Y.: Haworth Press. v. 1– , 1976– . Quarterly. ISSN 0361-526X.

This journal covers all aspects of serials work in both scholarly, theoretical articles and in more practical contributions. There are occasional reviews of books related to serials work and a regular section of news reports (although the "news" is always several months late). Occasional separately priced monograph supplements.

GAD11. *Serials Review.* Ann Arbor, Mich.: Pierian Press, Inc. v. 1– , 1975– . Quarterly. ISSN 0098-7913.

Serials Review contains both reviews of serials and serials management resources and articles about serials management. It features an array of regular columns on specific aspects of serials (e.g., Serials Pricing, Tools of the Serials Trade), which have column editors. *Serials Review* is a good place to find conference reports.

GAD12. *STM Newsletter.* Amsterdam, The Netherlands: International Group of Scientific, Technical & Medical Publishers. no. 1– , 19??– . Irregular. ISSN 0165-0408. Continues *STM Book News*.

This newsletter is the organ of the group consisting of the heads of houses of the leading scientific publishers. It contains news of the organization and the meetings it sponsors, as well as relevant news reports from around the world.

GAE
Sources of Expertise

ELECTRONIC DISCUSSION GROUPS

In addition to the discussion groups listed, there are many related to specific automated library systems (e.g., INNOPAC and NOTIS-L).

GAE1. CNI-Copyright. [electronic discussion group] Washington, D.C.: Center for Networked Information, 1992– .

Moderated by Mary Brandt Jensen and Chet Grycz, the objective of this discussion group is to bring together network commentary on all aspects of copyright, including serials. To subscribe, send a message to **LISTSERV@CNI.ORG** (INTERNET) with the command: **SUBSCRIBE CNI-COPYRIGHT [your name]**.

GAE2. PACS-L. [electronic discussion group] Houston, Tex.: University of Houston Library, 1989– .

Public Access Computer Systems List, begun by Charles W. Bailey, Jr., is one of the oldest and most general library-related online discussion groups; it deals with all computer systems that libraries make available to their patrons. It is now moderated by Dana Rooks. Many of the messages and responses concern serials matters. To subscribe, send a message to **LISTSERV@UHUPVM1** (BITNET) or **LISTSERV@UHUPVM1.UH.EDU** (INTERNET) with the command: **SUBSCRIBE PACS-L [your name]**.

GAE3. SERIALST. [electronic discussion group] Burlington, Vt.: University of Vermont Library, 1991– .

SERIALST is owned by Birdie MacLennan and is a moderated discussion group on BITNET, covering all aspects of serials management. To subscribe, send a message to **LISTSERV@UVMVM** (BITNET) or **LISTSERV @UVMVM.UVM.EDU** (INTERNET) with the command: **SUBSCRIBE SERIALST [your name]**.

GAE4. VPIEJ-L. [electronic discussion group] Blacksburg, Va.: Virginia Polytechnic Institute and State University, 1992– .

This list, owned by James Powell, is devoted to the more technical (and bibliographic) aspects of electronic publications. To subscribe, send a message to **LISTSERV@VTVM1** (BITNET) with the command: **SUBSCRIBE VPIEJ-L [your name]**.

PROFESSIONAL ASSOCIATIONS

Before the mid-1980s the only formal organization for serials specialists was the Serials Section of the Resources and Technical Services Division (now the Association for Library Collections and Technical Services, AGA3) of the American Library Association. The structure of committees and the annual program within the Serials Section drew far more serials librarians than could hold offices and appointments. As library travel funds have stretched thinner, the lack of a committee appointment might keep serials personnel from getting financial support for the annual conference and midwinter meeting.

In 1986 the North American Serials Interest Group (NASIG) (GAE7) held its first annual conference on the campus of Bryn Mawr College. Serials librarians and appropriate representatives of the commercial sector joined the new organization and attended the conference. Use of dormitories and college dining halls enabled the group to keep registration costs low and all-inclusive. Many people interested in serials have found a home within NASIG with its workshops, newsletter, and most recently, online discussion group. The organization has thrived and has passed 1,000 in membership.

NASIG is modeled on the United Kingdom Serials Group, the first of several national and international organizations whose mission is to bring together all parties involved in producing and making available library serials. Other groups have formed in Australia, China, Europe, and South Africa.

The Society for Scholarly Publishing (GAE8) is a small association whose membership consists of publishers (especially societies and university presses), subscription agents and booksellers, librarians, and others involved in scholarly publishing. The annual meeting and other SSP programs have gone far to facilitate communication among all members and have proved to be a place where librarians can come to know their commercial partners in the dissemination of scholarly information.

Other opportunities exist for association with one's colleagues, both librarian and otherwise. Certain annual conferences, such as those at the College of Charleston (BAE6) and the University of Oklahoma (BAE5), are not devoted entirely to serials matters but include serials in their programming on acquisitions and collection development. State and regional library associations also have occasional workshops or meetings that cover serials topics. Serials conferences are low-risk meetings for organizers because serials librarians attend such meetings seeking every opportunity to meet and talk with one another.

Among the several divisions of ALA, the Association of College & Research Libraries and the Association of Library Collections and Technical Services are most useful to serials specialists.

GAE5. ALA Association of College and Research Libraries (ACRL). Executive Director: Althea Jenkins.

Within ACRL are, among others of interest to serial librarians, the Science and Technology Section's Publisher/Vendor Relations Committee and the ACRL Journal Prices in Academic Libraries Discussion Group.

GAE6. ALA Association for Library Collections and Technical Services (ALCTS). Executive Director: Karen Muller.

See also annotation under AGA3. Within ALCTS, the sections of particular interest to serials librarians are the Serials Section, the Cataloging and Classification Section, and the Acquisition Section. Each section has an executive committee and a full range of committees and discussion groups.

GAE7. North American Serials Interest Group (NASIG). No permanent address. Secretary: Susan Davis, Head, Periodicals Section; Lockwood Library; State University of New York at Buffalo; Buffalo, NY 14260-2200; phone: (716) 645-2784; fax: (716) 645-5955; INTERNET: **UNLSDB@UBVM.CC.BUFFALO.EDU.**

Modeled after the United Kingdom Serials Group, NASIG was established in 1986. It is composed of librarians, publishers, subscription agents, binders, library science students and faculty members, and others interested in library serials. An annual conference, held on a college or university campus, consists of plenary sessions, workshops, discussion groups, and social events. NASIG membership is more than 1,000, and 1992 conference registration exceeded 500. Publications include conference *Proceedings*, the NASIG *Newsletter*, *Directory of Back Issues Dealers* (1992), and an online discussion group for members (NASIG-L). The group also sponsors occasional continuing education events. The low cost of dues ($20 at this writing), the concentration on matters of interest to serials specialists, and the opportunity to network with colleagues make NASIG a prime continuing education opportunity. Individual memberships only.

GAE8. Society for Scholarly Publishing. Headquarters: 10200 West 44th Ave., #304, Wheat Ridge, CO 80033.

Membership in SSP is predominantly publishers (especially society and university press publishers), but many librarians, subscription agents, binders, printers, and others also belong. Activities include an annual meeting attended by several hundred members, seminars, workshops, and an annual Top Management Roundtable. The seminars and roundtable are particularly good for publishers, agents, and librarians to interact in small groups. Society programs are more expensive than most library meetings, perhaps because publishers and others of the commercial sector have their expenses totally paid by their companies, while librarians usually do not. Institutional or individual membership. Individual dues are $50.

GB
Management of Serials Units

ORGANIZATION

GB1. Boissonnas, Christian. " 'But Serials Are Different!' " *Advances in Serials Management* 4 (1992): 171–92.

Boissonnas examines the differences between serials and monographs in terms of information transmittal devices, procurement, access, and impact on the professional culture. He also discusses automation as an agent of change in librarianship.

GB2. Carter, Ruth C. "Decentralization of Serials Functions." *Advances in Serials Management* 1 (1986): 83–99.

After reviewing the literature and stating her conviction that there is no best organizational approach for serials, the author takes the side of decentralized functions, giving advantages and disadvantages and noting the impact of automation on organization.

GB3. Collver, Mitsuko. "Organization of Serials Work for Manual and Automated Systems." *Library Resources & Technical Services* 24 (Fall 1980): 307–16.

Collver applies James D. Thompson's principle of "reciprocal interdependence" to a newly automated serials unit. She shows that the changeable nature of serials requires interaction among the various functions, and that serials management works best when these functions are grouped administratively.

GB4. Cook, Jean G. "Serials' Place in the Organizational Chart: A Historical Perspective." *Advances in Serials Management* 1 (1986): 53–66.

Cook, showing a love for serials librarianship, traces the history of the controversy over administrative organization of serials functions as expressed in the professional literature from Ralph Munn through Michael Gorman.

GB5. Ezzell, Joline R. "The Integrated Serials Department." *Advances in Serials Management* 1 (1986): 67–82.

Basing conclusions on her questionnaire on organization, sent to Association of Research Libraries members, Ezzell justifies centralizing serials functions in academic libraries.

GB6. Gellatly, Peter, ed. *The Good Serials Department.* New York: Haworth Press, 1990. Also published as *The Serials Librarian,* 19, nos. 1/2, (1990).

Contains articles by serials managers at thirteen academic libraries, including two foreign libraries, describing the organization, history, and functions of their departments (or parts of departments). Illustrates well the diversity among libraries in treating serials.

GB7. McKinley, Margaret. "Serials Departments: Doomed to Extinction?" *The Serials Librarian* 5, no. 2 (Winter 1980): 15–24.

Responding to a perceived trend toward decentralization of serials functions, McKinley points out that informal communication systems exist now and will continue to exist among serials specialists, even though they may cross organizational lines.

GB8. Presley, Roger L., and Carolyn L. Robison. "Changing Roles of Support Staff in an Online Environment." *Technical Services Quarterly* 4 (Fall 1986): 25–39.

For annotation, *see* AHD13.

RELATIONS WITH EXTERNAL AGENCIES

GB9. Cox, John. "Subscription Agents: Why Librarians Love Them and Publishers Take Them for Granted." *Logos* 2 (1991): 154–58.

Librarians realize that they need subscription agents for ordering, invoicing, claiming, and the like. But publishers are not aware of the services agents provide librar-

ies. It is the agents' responsibility to inform publishers and to market their services to journal publishers.

GB10. Ivins, October, ed. "Do Serials Vendor Policies Affect Serials Pricing?" *Serials Review* 16, no. 2 (Summer 1990): 7–27.

Responding to subscription agents' practice of delaying renewal payments to publishers, Ivins introduces and presents statements on the topic by three publishers, three librarians, and five agents. A major contribution to the effort to learn more about our mutual interdependence.

GB11. Manoff, Marlene, and others. "Report of the Electronic Journals Task Force, MIT Libraries." *Serials Review* 18, nos. 1/2 (Spring/Summer 1992): 113–30.

This report is an overview of issues on all aspects of the management of electronic journals. Written for the MIT libraries, it covers selection, acquisition, cataloging, access, indexing, archiving, and copyright. The task force presents both an aggressive scenario for its library system and a conservative one, stating that reality is probably somewhere in between. A significant and valuable document.

GB12. Tuttle, Marcia. "The Serials Manager's Obligation." *Library Resources & Technical Services* 31 (Apr. 1987): 135–47.

Serials managers have an obligation to learn about serials publishing and supply, to take advantage of the continuing education opportunities available, and to participate actively in professional activities.

GC
Serials Publishing

PRINTED SERIALS

GC1. Curtis, Mary E. "Financial Management in Publishing Journals." *Scholarly Publishing* 17 (Oct. 1985): 65–72.

Curtis explains the three levels of financial management of journals: the single journal, all journals issued by the publisher, and "the organizational or environmental context" in which the program operates. She then adds a fourth level: what is right for the organization.

GC2. Graham, Gordon. "Reflections on the Origins of European Journals." *Advances in Serials Management* 4 (1992): 1–14.

Graham, former chairman of Butterworths, documents the development of the large international scientific publishers from their origin (or rebirth) just after the Second World War.

GC3. Page, Gillian, Robert Campbell, and Jack Meadows. *Journal Publishing: Principles and Practice.* London: Butterworths, 1987.

The primary audience for this book is "people concerned with journal publishing throughout the world but whose experience of it is necessarily limited." Librarians working with serials can benefit as well, for the work covers journal editing, production, distribution, and finances. The authors have written a "library-friendly" book. Revision in progress.

ELECTRONIC SERIALS

GC4. Amiran, Eyal, and John Unsworth. "Postmodern Culture: Publishing in the Electronic Medium." *The Public Access Computer Systems Review.* [serial online] 2, no. 1 (1991): 67–76.

The authors founded one of the earliest and most popular refereed electronic journals. The article discusses prepublication considerations and the use of the flexibility of electronic technology to add such features as a related discussion group for reaction to published articles.

GC5. Bailey, Charles W., Jr. "The Coalition for Networked Information's Acquisition-on-Demand Model: An Exploration and Critique." *Serials Review* 18, nos. 1/2 (Spring/Summer 1992): 78–81.

Bailey lists options within ten qualities of electronic journals of the future and charges librarians "to identify desirable futures from the many potential futures and to work toward making these outcomes a reality."

GC6. Barschall, H. H. "Electronic Version of Printed Journals." *Serials Review* 18, nos. 1/2 (Spring/Summer 1992): 49–51.

The electronic version of choice in Barschall's scenario is CD-ROM. He considers advantages and disadvantages of this format and discusses the economics of CD-ROM production and acquisition. Advances in electronic technology will make CD-ROM journals more affordable and easier to use than they are now.

GC7. Drake, Miriam A. "Buying Articles in the Future." *Serials Review* 18, nos. 1/2 (Spring/Summer 1992): 75–77.

Electronic production and distribution of articles will bring not only change but also choices. Drake discusses some of the choices librarians, researchers, and publishers will have to make, e.g., format, source, copyright.

GC8. Getz, Malcolm. "Electronic Publishing: An Economic View." *Serials Review* 18, nos. 1/2 (Spring/Summer 1992): 25–31.

Getz looks at the economics of the coming electronic scientific publishing industry from the perspectives of costs of publication, values to scientists, market prices, and the role of government and its policies.

GC9. Grycz, Czeslaw Jan, ed. "Economic Models for Networked Information." Special issue of *Serials Review* 18, nos. 1/2 (Spring/Summer 1992).

This special issue contains twenty-seven articles discussing models of electronic publishing and the economics of scholarly communication. Several of the articles are listed separately in this chapter.

GC10. Harrison, Teresa M., Timothy Stephen, and James Winter. "Online Journals: Disciplinary Designs for Electronic Scholarship." *The Public Access Computer Systems Review.* [serial online] 2, no. 1 (1991): 25–38.

Uses *Electronic Journal of Communication/La Revue Electronique de Communication* as a case study in a discussion of the design of online journals. *EJC/REC* is distributed through a preexisting electronic service, Comserve.

GC11. Hugo, Jane, and Linda Newell. "New Horizons in Adult Education: The First Five Years (1987–1991)." *The Public Access Computer Systems Review.* [serial online] 2, no. 1 (1991): 77–90.

Graduate students at Syracuse University, determined to publish an electronic journal in the field of adult education, had to learn not only how to produce a refereed journal but also how to communicate with each other and to distribute the journal over BITNET. This is one of the earliest efforts in scholarly electronic publishing.

GC12. Jennings, Edward M. "EJournal: An Account of the First Two Years." *The Public Access Computer Systems Review.* [serial online] 2, no. 1 (1991): 91–110.

An account of the day-to-day frustrations and small victories in planning, producing, and distributing an electronic journal on electronic networking. Stresses the importance of a good relationship with someone in the institution's computing center.

GC13. Kaufman, Paula, and Angie LeClercq. "Archiving Electronic Journals: Who's Responsible for What." *Library Issues* 11 (July 1991): 1–4.

A plea for libraries to take responsibility for acquiring electronic journals, making them accessible bibliographically, and archiving them for future readers. The authors discuss the need for standards and the question of format for archiving.

GC14. King, Timothy B. "The Impact of Electronic and Networking Technologies on the Delivery of Scholarly Information." *The Serials Librarian* 21, nos. 2/3 (1991): 5–13.

Speaking at the 1991 NASIG (North American Serials Interest Group) Conference, King projects changes in four aspects of scholarly communication: "finding out what's going on, but not yet published; staying current with what has just been published; searching the literature; [and] collaborating on research at a distance." He sees least change in "searching the [retrospective] literature."

GC15. McMillan, Gail. "Embracing the Electronic Journal: One Library's Plan." *The Serials Librarian* 21, nos. 2/3 (1991): 97–108.

The library at Virginia Tech was one of the first to develop a comprehensive plan for offering access to electronic publications. McMillan, a member of the committee drawing up the plan, explains their options, their decisions, and their unanswered questions.

GC16. Okerson, Ann. "Back to Academia? The Case for American Universities to Publish Their Own Research." *Logos* 2 (1991): 106–12.

Okerson bases her argument for electronic self-publishing on economics, "a burgeoning literature," and changing information technology. She touches on the copyright implications of this system.

GC17. Piternick, Anne B. "Serials and New Technology: The State of the 'Electronic Journal.'" *Canadian Library Journal* 46 (Apr. 1989): 93–97.

Electronic technology offers new methods of access to and storage of journals. Piternick discusses the benefits of the new technology with respect to serials acquisition and retention, then she takes a brief look at the future.

GC18. Savage, Lon. "The Journal of the International Academy of Hospitality Research." *The Public-Access Computer Systems Review.* [serial online] 2, no. 1 (1991): 54–66.

Savage, director of Virginia Tech's Scholarly Communications Project, discusses the planning and decision making that resulted in what is probably the first electronic journal for which a subscription fee is charged. He also covers the process of resolving problems related to subscribers' unfamiliarity with the networks.

GC19. Smith, Eldred. "Resolving the Acquisitions Dilemma: Into the Electronic Information Environment." *College & Research Libraries* 52 (May 1991): 231–40.

Smith analyzes the reasons for the crisis in serials pricing and the problems with strategies libraries are using to resolve the crisis. He then proposes an electronic solution akin to the once-proposed national periodicals center and investigates potential obstacles to this system for distributing the results of scholarly research.

GC20. Stern, Barrie. "The New ADONIS." *Serials: The Journal of the United Kingdom Serials Group* 5 (Nov. 1992): 37–43.

In 1991 ADONIS progressed from a test to a commercial enterprise, a publisher-backed electronic document delivery system, directed toward the pharmaceuticals industry. Stern discusses the transition.

GC21. Stern, Barrie, and Robert M. Campbell. "ADONIS—Publishing Journal Articles on CD-ROM." *Advances in Serials Management* 3 (1989): 1–60.

The ADONIS director and board chairman explain the planning and testing phase of this international document delivery and resource-sharing project. The article offers suggestions for enhancements and discusses problems yet to be resolved. List of the 219 original biomedical titles included in the project.

COPYRIGHT AND LICENSING

GC22. Hunter, Karen. "The National Site License Model." *Serials Review* 18, nos. 1/2 (Spring/Summer 1992): 71–72.

Examines the problems that must be resolved in national (or regional) site licenses for access to electronic journals. This article is written from the publisher's perspective but with consideration for the library and the user.

GC23. Jensen, Mary Brandt. "Making Copyright Work in Electronic Publishing Models." *Serials Review* 18, nos. 1/2 (Spring/Summer 1992): 62–65.

Drawing from policy governing live performance, jukeboxes, and cable television, Jensen advocates a "hybrid negotiated compulsory license" model for electronic copying as fairest to all parties.

GC24. Lesk, Michael. "Pricing Electronic Information." *Serials Review* 18, nos. 1/2 (Spring/Summer 1992): 38–40.

Lesk considers three means of pricing electronic information: page charges to the author, tax on blank media, and site licenses. He forms no conclusion as to the best way to price, but he warns that publishers must avoid the extremely high charges that are pricing many paper journals out of the library market.

GC25. Okerson, Ann. "With Feathers: Effects of Copyright and Ownership on Scholarly Publishing." *College & Research Libraries* 52 (Sept. 1991): 425–38.

The present copyright law does not address the needs of scholarly publishing, thus creating a barrier to the sharing of ideas. Okerson proposes that scholars work within the law by changing the ownership of scholarly ideas. Instead of transferring copyright to the commercial publisher, authors or their institutions should retain rights to scholarly works.

GC26. Parkhurst, Todd S. "Serial Pricing and Copyrights: Prophecies, Strategies and Fallacies." *Library Acquisitions: Practice and Theory* 14 (1990): 223–26.

A lawyer's comments on the copyright law regarding librarians' photocopying of journal articles.

GC27. Peters, Paul Evan. "Making the Market for Networked Information: An Introduction to a Proposed Program for Licensing Electronic Uses." *Serials Review* 18, nos. 1/2 (Spring/Summer 1992): 19–24.

On behalf of the Coalition for Networked Information (CNI), Peters presents the Rights for Electronic Access to and Delivery of Information (READI) Program. This introductory document, designed to stimulate discussion, envisions flow of permissions/authorizations and of money between a rights brokering organization representing subscribers and a rights holders organization representing commercial and noncommercial publishers and other rights holders.

GC28. Sabosik, Patricia E. "Electronic Subscriptions." *The Serials Librarian* 19, nos. 3/4 (1991): 59–70.

Electronic technology has changed the terms of the traditional subscription agreement between library and publisher into a licensing agreement. Sabosik explores the implications of this change.

GD
Serials Processing

MANAGEMENT OF SERIALS PROCESSING

GD1. Kruger, Betsy. "Serials Acquisitions: Trends and Prospects." In *Technical Services Today and Tomorrow*, edited by Michael Gorman, 38–49. Littleton, Colo.: Libraries Unlimited, 1990.

Kruger gives an overview of serials acquisitions, with an emphasis on automation, at the threshold of the 1990s.

GD2. Paul, Huibert. "Serials Processing: Manual Control vs. Automation." *Library Resources & Technical Services* 21, no. 4 (Fall 1977): 345–53.

Paul writes in defense of the manual serials check-in system, but there is food for thought for those planning to convert to an automated system. He shows how eight problem areas in serials control can be resolved manually, whereas shifting to an automated system because of these problems would be a mistake. A discussion-provoking article.

GD3. Tuttle, Marcia. "Magazine Fulfillment Centers: What They Are, How They Operate, and What We Can Do about Them." *Library Acquisitions: Practice and Theory* 9 (1985): 41–49.

Investigates the automated fulfillment center and its impact on libraries; gives guidelines to assist libraries in their acquisition of mass-circulation magazines. Since 1985, the distributors' automation has become more sophisticated, and more journals than mass-circulation titles come from fulfillment centers. The problems remain.

GD4. _____. "Serials Control, from an Acquisitions Perspective." *Advances in Serials Management* 2 (1988): 63–94.

Discussion of serials acquisitions functions in the context of serials management in general. Emphasizes interaction with other librarians, subscription agents, and publishers. Practical treatment.

SUBSCRIPTION AGENT SELECTION AND EVALUATION

GD5. Anderson, Jan. "Challenging the 'Good Buddies' Factor' in Vendor Selection." *Advances in Serials Management* 3 (1989): 153–71.

Anderson gives Utah State University's reasons for wanting to consolidate serial orders with a single vendor and describes the process of determining that vendor. Throughout, the goal was to be as objective as possible in coming to the decision. The excellent and detailed request for proposal is included.

GD6. Barker, Joseph W. "Unbundling Serials Vendors' Service Charges: Are We Ready?" *Serials Review* 16, no. 2 (Summer 1990): 33–43.

Barker investigates the possibilities and the hazards of subscription agents charging libraries separately for certain services. He sees the advantage of open communication about vendor costs, but he also warns of confusion among both librarians and vendors.

GD7. Basch, N. Bernard, and Judy McQueen. *Buying Serials: A How-to-Do-It Manual for Librarians*. New York: Neal-Schuman Publishers, 1990.

Basch and McQueen have written primarily for librarians, but they also see subscription agents and serials publishers as a secondary audience. The book describes subscription agencies and the work they do, and then it teaches librarians how to work with the agencies to the library's best advantage. Basch's years as a subscription agent give the book authority.

GD8. Cowan, Cynthia D., and Michael Markwith. "Coffee at the Carolina Inn: The Discussion to End All Discussions." *Advances in Serials Management* 4 (1992): 91–122.

A serials acquisitions supervisor and a subscription agent representative discuss the relationship between the librarian and the agency. The question and answer format covers what the agency can do for the library and how the librarian can make the most of agency services.

GD9. Derthick, Jan, and Barbara B. Moran. "Serials Agent Selection in ARL Libraries." *Advances in Serials Management* 1 (1986): 1–42.

For annotation, *see* BF11.

GD10. Ivins, October. "Do Subscription Agents Earn Their Service Charges and How Can We Tell?" *Library Acquisitions: Practice and Theory* 13 (1989): 143–47.

Ivins comments on ten assumptions librarians commonly make about journal vendors and suggests reasonable methods for busy librarians to use in evaluating these vendors. A very practical article.

GD11. McKinley, Margaret. "Vendor Selection: Strategic Choices." *Serials Review* 16, no. 2 (Summer 1990): 49–53+.

Practical advice on matching subscription agent to the type of order. Careful vendor' selection creates financial economies for the library.

SUBSCRIPTION AGENTS' DATABASES

GD12. *CONNECT.* [database online] B. H. Blackwell.

CONNECT is B. H. Blackwell's new (at this writing) online information and ordering system, available over the INTERNET at a one-time charge based on the amount of business the library does with the company. In addition to online ordering and claiming, librarians can access bibliographic files and send electronic mail messages to Blackwell personnel.

GD13. *DataLinx.* [database online] Faxon Company.

DataLinx is the Faxon Company's online system, consisting of bibliographic and publisher files, a library's payment history, the SC-10 mainframe-based check-in system, and the MARC-S files. The electronic mail function, COURIER, allows electronic ordering, claiming, and other messaging. It is available through INTERNET and by other means, by subscription.

GD14. *EBSCONET.* [database online] EBSCO Subscription Services.

EBSCONET is the online bibliographic and communications system of EBSCO Subscription Services. It can be accessed through TYMNET, the INTERNET, and various commercial serials systems. Title, publisher, and pricing files are available, as well as the CARL system and its UNCOVER service. Check-in records for certain CARL titles are available. The system provides online ordering, claiming, and other communication between the librarian and the vendor. Back issues/volumes may be ordered from Kraus Reprint & Periodicals, Alfred Jaeger, Inc., and the EBSCO Missing Copy Bank. There is a charge for access.

GD15. *ROSS.* [database online] Readmore Academic Subscription services.

ROSS permits the librarian to order titles and place claims online, using the title database and formatted screens. Both orders and claims are forwarded by the agent without editing. There is no subscription fee. *ROSS* is available on the INTERNET at no charge to the Readmore customer.

CLAIMING AND OTHER ACQUISITIONS PROCESSES

GD16. Carlson, Barbara A. "Claiming Periodicals: The 'Trembling Balance' in the 'Feud of Want and Have.'" In *Legal and Ethical Issues in Acquisitions*, edited by Katina Strauch and Bruce Strauch, 119–27. Binghamton, N.Y.: Haworth Press, 1990.

A balanced look, by a librarian, at the stresses that threaten an effective claiming system. Carlson urges both librarians and publishers to view the system from the other's perspective and "work together to devise appropriate checks and balances."

GD17. _____. "Guilt-Free Automated Claiming." *Serials Review* 15, no. 4 (Winter 1989): 33–42.

Responding to generalized charges of excessive claiming by libraries with automated serials management systems, Carlson analyzes the results of a study done at the Medical University of South Carolina and shows that at her library claiming actually declined after automating.

GD18. Fairbanks, Deborah. "Claim Rates for Exchanges and Subscriptions." *Serials Review* 16, no. 3 (Fall 1990): 55–59.

The University of Florida Library acquired materials by subscription when possible, using exchange only when necessary because of the perception that exchange titles require more claiming than paid titles. Fairbanks's study found no basis for this perception, particularly for domestic exchanges.

GD19. Kruse, Ted. "Cutting Periodical Costs without Dropping Subscriptions." *Special Libraries* 82 (Winter 1991): 69–71.

Periodicals costs can be reduced in several ways. Those discussed here are substituting controlled free subscriptions, buying groups of titles from one publisher, using air freight instead of air mail for overseas titles, negotiating vendor service charges, seeking the best rate, using institutional memberships, and placing multiyear subscriptions.

GD20. Leach, J. Travis, and Karen Dalziel Tallman. "The Claim Function in Serials Management." *Advances in Serials Management* 4 (1992): 149–69.

The authors discuss the serials claiming function in the context of library/vendor/publisher interaction. They cover the frustrations encountered by each party and give general guidelines for improving this most important and least supported process.

GD21. Pionessa, Geraldine F. "Serials Replacement Orders: A Closer Look." *Serials Review* 16, no. 1 (Spring 1990): 65–73+.

Replacement orders require different procedures than regular continuing orders, and this process has policy implications for managers. Pionessa uses the University of Arizona Library's procedure to investigate the questions a library must confront in filling missing issue requests.

GD22. Schmidt, Karen A. "Distributed Check-In of Serials: A Case Study of the University of Illinois–Urbana Library." In *Projects and Procedures for Serials Administration*, edited by Diane Stine, 219–26. Ann Arbor, Mich.: Pierian Press, 1985.

With automation of serials processing, departmental library journals' bypassing of centralized check-in becomes more feasible. Schmidt describes the procedures used by Illinois in changing to distributed check-in and discusses the problems (most related to publishers' address changes) and benefits (getting most-needed journals to their readers as quickly as possible).

GE
Automation of Serials Processing

GE1. Cady, Susan A. "Creating a Serial Database Using Subscription Agency Files." *The Serials Librarian* 14, nos. 3/4 (1988): 99–111.

Lehigh University Library loaded disk copies of EBSCO invoice files into database management software to produce a quick, low-cost, very useful serials database. Cady gives step-by-step instructions for loading data into dBASE III and PC-File III. She also describes several applications of the file and tells how to merge disk-format data from several subscription agencies.

GE2. Hawks, Carol Pitts. "Automated Library Systems: What's Next?" *The Serials Librarian* 21, nos. 2/3 (1991): 87–96.

Most of the growing pains of automating serials management are behind us. Hawks discusses five areas in which major improvements should come in this decade: enhanced management reports, improved mechanisms for migration from one system to another, introduction of expert systems and artificial intelligence, external interfaces to vendor/publisher databases, and enhanced serials check-in.

GE3. Hayman, Lynne Myers. "Serials Budget Management Using a Microcomputer." *The Serials Librarian* 21, no. 1 (1991): 13–27.

A small library can make good use of dBASE III + for a serials management system. Hayman describes the system designed and programmed at Beaver College. The article includes file structures, a sample periodicals list, and a sample budget report. An appendix gives the procedure for transferring data from EBSCO invoice disks to the local system.

GE4. Shuster, Helen M. "Fiscal Control of Serials Using dBase III + ." *Serials Review* 15, no. 1 (Spring 1989): 7–20.

A small college library uses dBASE III + , Lotus 1–2–3, and Faxon's FI$CAL software to create an in-house fiscal control system. Heavily illustrated.

GF
Serials Pricing

GF1. Astle, Deana L. "The Scholarly Journal: Whence or Wither?" *The Journal of Academic Librarianship* 15 (July 1989): 151–56.

See annotation under GF2.

GF2. ———. "Suicide Squeeze: The Escalating Cost of Scholarly Journals." *Academe* 75 (July-Aug. 1989): 13–17.

Astle, in two highly recommended articles (GF1 is directed toward librarians; GF2 is written for scholars), documents with statistics the library crisis in serials pricing.

GF3. ———. "With Sci/Tech Journals, Hidden Costs Cost a Lot." *Library Acquisitions: Practice and Theory* 12 (1988): 163–67.

Increased journal costs come partly from a larger number of pages and issues. Astle questions whether researchers need all that is being published or whether many articles benefit only the author and the publisher. She encourages librarians to work with scholars to evaluate the content of expensive sci/tech journals in light of their own research needs.

GF4. Astle, Deana L., and Charles Hamaker. "Journal Publishing: Pricing and Structural Issues in the 1930s and the 1980s." *Advances in Serials Management* 2 (1988): 1–36.

A study of the journals pricing issue in Germany between the world wars demonstrates that the current situation is not new. Activist librarians were able to force changes then and could well do so today. The authors offer a list of recommendations for action.

GF5. Byrd, Gary D. "An Economic 'Commons' Tragedy for Research Libraries: Scholarly Journal Publishing and Pricing Trends." *College & Research Libraries* 51 (May 1990): 184–95.

Byrd develops his theme of the coming breakdown of the scholarly communication system in economic terms. He then reviews strategies to combat "spiraling quantities and costs of scholarly information," including reshaping the research library's mission, government regulation of the scientific information industry, and reducing the role of the commercial publisher. Neither the publisher nor the scholar has incentive to change the situation; research librarians must do it.

GF6. Dow, Ronald F., Karen Hunter, and G. Gregory Lozier. "Commentaries on Serials Publishing." *College & Research Libraries* 52 (Nov. 1991): 521–27.

A librarian, a publisher, and a university scholar comment from their own perspectives on four articles previously published on the topic of scholarly communication and serials prices. The articles, by Marks (GF12), E. Smith (GC19), Metz and Gherman (GF13), and Okerson (GC25), are listed in this chapter.

GF7. Gilman, Lelde B. "The Scholarly Publishing Imbroglio: A Personal View." *Bulletin of the Medical Library Association* 79 (Jan. 1991): 88–92.

Gilman responds to Gary Byrd's article, "An Economic 'Commons' Tragedy for Research Libraries" (GF5), by challenging his assumption that the current scientific publishing situation is responsible for the impending tragedy. She describes the motives of publisher, scientist, and librarian, showing that each group has a different goal. In conclusion, Gilman invites all parties to share the commitment to and the cost of access to knowledge.

GF8. Hafner, Arthur Wayne, Thomas J. Podsadecki, and William P. Whitely. "Journal Pricing Issues: An Economic Perspective." *Bulletin of the Medical Library Association* 78 (July 1990): 217–23.

The publisher's and librarian's positions on the journal pricing issue are presented from a general perspective. The faculty member's position is related to health science libraries. Suggested action includes government support for publication of research results, cost-effective means of editing and producing journals, reviews of journals, selective page charges, and refusal by all parties to participate in publication of duplicate information.

GF9. Haley, Jean Walstrom, and James Talaga. "Academic Library Responses to Journal Price Discrimination." *College & Research Libraries* 53 (Jan. 1992): 61–70.

A survey of 213 academic libraries documents strategies used to counteract journal publishers' price discrimination. The authors analyze survey results and list strategies they consider the most successful. These are not necessarily the most-used responses. "References" lists additional articles on price discrimination.

GF10. Ivins, October. "Serials Prices." [column in] *Serials Review* 14, no. 3– (1988–).

Ivins' quarterly column not only covers obvious price fluctuations but also reports on conferences and relevant material in other publications. She has special columns in which publishers, vendors, and librarians contribute to the discussion of a "hot" topic (e.g., the impact of subscription agents' holding the libraries' renewal payments for a long period before paying the publisher).

GF11. Kingma, Bruce R., and Philip B. Eppard. "Journal Price Escalation and the Market for Information: The Librarians' Solution." *College & Research Libraries* 53 (Nov. 1992): 523–35.

The authors attribute price escalation to increased volume and better quality of photocopying, resulting in fewer individual subscriptions to journals. To restore the balance between individual and institutional subscriptions, they recommend that libraries restore the demand for individual subscriptions by restricting journal use to the library and raising the cost of photocopying.

GF12. Marks, Kenneth E., and Steven P. Nielsen. "A Longitudinal Study of Journal Prices in a Research Library." *The Serials Librarian* 19, nos. 3/4 (1991): 105–35.

Report of a major investigation of prices of 370 STM journals in the Utah State University Library. Using price per page, the prices of these journals were tracked over 20 years and analyzed in several ways. The authors give plans for application of the data. Heavily supported by graphs of varying print quality. Virtually the same article was published as Marks, Kenneth E., and others, "Longitudinal Study of Scientific Journal Prices in a Research Library," in *College & Research Libraries* volume 52, Mar. 1991 (125–38).

GF13. Metz, Paul, and Paul M. Gherman. "Serials Pricing and the Role of the Electronic Journal." *College & Research Libraries* 52 (July 1991): 315–27.

This article first reviews the current "dilemma of serials pricing" and the status and promise of electronic publishing. It then proposes that universities cooperate in promoting the issuing of research in electronic format, retaining copyright, and accepting the responsibility of archiving. The library's role is to convince faculty that such a system is in their best interest.

GF14. Milne, Dorothy, and Bill Tiffany. "A Cost-per-Use Method for Evaluating the Cost-Effectiveness of Serials: A Detailed Discussion of Methodology." *Serials Review* 17, no. 2 (Summer 1991): 7–19.

See annotation under GF15.

GF15. _____. "A Survey of the Cost-Effectiveness of Serials: A Cost-per-Use Method and Its Results." *The Serials Librarian* 19, nos. 3/4 (1991): 137–49.

Faced with the need to reduce its serials expenditures, the library at Memorial University of Newfoundland conducted a journal use study. Staff members calculated the cost per use and compared the results with the cost of interlibrary loan required to accommodate patrons' need for the journal. Titles found not to be cost effective were considered candidates for cancellation. GF14 presents a detailed report of the methodology used in this study.

GF16. Noll, Roger, and W. Edward Steinmueller. "An Economic Analysis of Scientific Journal Prices: Preliminary Results." *Serials Review* 18, nos. 1/2 (Spring/Summer 1992): 32–37.

Two Stanford economists report on data collection methods for and indicate preliminary results of a study of the causes of subscription price increases of scientific journals. Initial economic analysis supports the authors' hypothesis that circulation is the most important source of price variation.

GF17. Okerson, Ann. "Periodical Prices: A History and Discussion." *Advances in Serials Management* 1 (1986): 101–38.

In this award-winning article, Okerson does much more than review the history of periodical prices. She introduces and assesses the several price indexes available annually, and she discusses the role of the publisher and the subscription agent in price increases.

GF18. Pascarelli, Anne M. "Coping Strategies for Libraries Facing the Serials Pricing Crisis." *Serials Review* 16, no. 1 (Spring 1990): 75–80.

After reviewing the serials pricing crisis and its probable causes, Pascarelli urges librarians to act to educate themselves and their users about the situation, to be assertive in dealing with publishers, and to prepare reliable management data about their collections.

GF19. Petersen, H. Craig. "The Economics of Economics Journals: A Statistical Analysis of Pricing Practices by Publishers." *College & Research Libraries* 53 (Mar. 1992): 176–81.

Petersen, an economics professor, uses multiple regression analysis to study noncost pricing variations of economics journals. His investigation showed that for-profit and European publishers charge U.S. libraries highest prices. Peterson also found a strong positive correlation between a journal's impact and its price.

GF20. _____. "Variations in Journal Prices: A Statistical Analysis." *The Serials Librarian* 17, nos. 1/2 (1989): 1–9.

A study of 439 journals using multiple regression analysis indicates that titles in the physical sciences and from European for-profit publishers have higher prices in the United States than can be accounted for by cost of production and distribution.

GF21. Talaga, James A., and Jean Walstrom Haley. "Marketing Theory Applied to Price Discrimination in Journals." *The Journal of Academic Librarianship* 16 (Jan. 1991): 348–51.

Talaga and Haley examine each of "six prerequisites for successful discriminatory pricing." They conclude that each is currently being met in the journal pricing situation. The authors suggest strategies that might be successful in reducing discrimination, especially the strategy of involving library users in helping to find a solution.

GF22. Thompson, James C. "Confronting the Serials Cost Problem." *Serials Review* 15, no. 1 (Spring 1989): 41–47.

Adapted from a background paper prepared for University of California system administrators, this article is one of the best statements of the "nature and magnitude of the problem of rising serials costs." Included are suggestions made for short-term relief for the University of California system.

GG
Resource Sharing, Union Listing, and Serials Holdings

GG1. Baker, Barry B., ed. *USMARC Format for Holdings and Locations: Development, Implementation and Use.* Technical Services Quarterly. Monograph Supplement, no. 2. New York: Haworth Press, 1988.

A collection of essays written during "final draft" stage of the format by persons using it in their work or with experience in developing holdings standards. The latter group includes "Developing a Format for Holdings and Location Data," by Nolan F. Pope; "The Display of Serial Holdings Statements," by Marjorie E. Bloss; and "SISAC: The Serials Industry Systems Advisory Committee," by Minna C. Saxe. Other articles discuss implementation of the format by librarians at Harvard and the universities of Georgia, Kansas, and Florida, and by managers of SOLINET and of VTLS, NOTIS, and Faxon automated serials systems.

GG2. Brugger, Judith M. "How the NISO Holdings Standard Works: The Findings of an Investigation at CUNY, 1989." *The Serials Librarian* 20, nos. 2/3 (1991): 17–30.

When the City University of New York changed from OCLC to NOTIS, it decided to enter serials holdings data according to the NISO standard Z39.44. This article covers problems encountered and decisions that had to be made during the conversion.

GG3. CDMARC Serials. [database on CD-ROM] Washington, D.C.: Library of Congress. 1992– . Updated quarterly. ISSN 1063-7784.

For annotation, *see* CCA12.

GG4. Clack, Mary Elizabeth, and others. "The Balance Point: The National Shared Pattern Database." *Serials Review* 17, no. 3 (Fall 1991): 67–76.

See also annotation under KBE14. Contributions from four librarians and one subscription agent discuss the possibility of creating a centralized database of serials publication data. The contributors view the project objectively, from different perspectives.

GG5. Coty, Patricia Ann. "Reflections on Grant Writing for Union Lists." *Serials Review* 14, nos. 1/2 (1988): 89–93.

An experienced grant author and administrator, Coty covers identifying funding sources, tailoring the proposal to the funding agency, budgeting, and scheduling. She also presents several examples of union listing projects.

GG6. Council on Library Resources. *A National Periodicals Center: Technical Development Plan.* Washington, D.C.: Council on Library Resources, Inc., 1978.

This pre-INTERNET, pre–CD-ROM plan was developed for the Library of Congress by CLR. The plan proposes a means of improving access to periodical literature for libraries and their patrons. It includes a document delivery system, a way of working with publishers, and the creation of a national library system. The study was a basis for discussions in Congress, but the Center was never funded, in part because of less than full support by the library community. (Readers may consult Mary Biggs' article, "The Proposed National Periodicals Center, 1973–1980: Study, Dissension, and Retreat," *Resource Sharing and Information Networks* 1 [Spring/Summer 1984]: 1–22, for an analysis of the Center.) The report is included here because the need for efficient, centralized document delivery remains.

GG7. Kim, Sook-Hyun. "Application of the USMARC Format for Holdings and Locations." *The Serials Librarian* 16, nos. 3/4 (1989): 21–31.

In ten months the University of Tennessee Library, Knoxville, staff coded 12,000 holdings records in the USMARC Format. Kim explains the decisions that had to be made and the adaptations chosen by the library.

GG8. Kutz, Myer. "Distributing the Costs of Scholarly Journals: Should Readers Contribute?" *Serials Review* 18, nos. 1/2 (1992): 73–74.

Kutz discusses a site license model in which libraries (or a single national site) would receive journals in either paper or electronic form and resell articles to libraries and end users. He sees this scenario as fairest to all parties.

GG9. McKay, Sharon Cline, and Betty Landesman. "The SISAC Bar Code Symbol." *Serials Review* 17, no. 2 (1991): 47–51.

Describes the symbol for serial issue identification, which has become ANSI/NISO Z39.56-1991, and justifies its choice over the already heavily used Universal Product Code. The article explains benefits for publishers, system vendors, and libraries. The authors ask for librarians' help in promoting widespread use of this bar code.

GG10. O'Neil, Rosanna M., with contributions from Ron Watson and others. "CONSER: Cons . . . and Pros, or, What's in It for Me?" *Serials Review* 17, no. 2 (1991): 53–62.

O'Neil introduces the topic, discussing the database, its development, and its members' current activities. In addition, brief reports cover a positive view of CONSER, the reasons one library decided not to join, OCLC's perspective, and the Center for Research Libraries' approach.

GG11. Postlethwaite, Bonnie S. "Publication Patterns, the USMARC Holdings Format, and the Opportunity for Sharing." *Information Technology and Libraries* 9 (Mar. 1990): 80–88.

See also annotation under KBE19. The author explains library uses of a publication pattern database, then turns to potential stumbling blocks to this resource. She suggests possible parent agencies to house and manage the database. A set of recommendations concludes the article.

GG12. Striedieck, Suzanne. "CONSER and the National Database." *Advances in Serials Management* 3 (1989): 81–109.

After giving a brief history of the CONSER project, Striedieck emphasizes the impact of CONSER on serials librarianship and discusses cooperative efforts with other agencies to construct a true national database.

H

Collection Management

Peggy Johnson

Overview

As the library environment changes, so does the area of technical services we call "collection management." Perhaps instead of attempting to define the term, we can understand it best by the tasks, functions, and responsibilities that fall within it. This chapter addresses materials selection, collection policies, collection maintenance (selection for weeding and storage, preservation, and serials cancellation), budget and finance, assessment and evaluation, cooperation and resource sharing. Also included are sources that address organization and assignment of responsibilities for collection management. The acquisition—ordering, claiming, and receiving—of materials in a library is covered in Chapter B.

I have chosen collection management for the title of this chapter as a more inclusive term than collection development, which implies collection building and is often associated with an increasing collection and resource base. The present emphasis is on decisions that are made within the context of all library operations and reflect the pressures of shrinking budgets, new formats, deteriorating collections, increased accountability, changing user expectations, and forces for cooperation and resource sharing.

This understanding is much broader than the early emphasis of the theory and practice of collection development on selection and evaluation of individual titles. Many of the works of that era concentrated on the difficulties public libraries faced balancing public demands for materials versus their perceived value. Academic libraries and school libraries also focused on the criteria for selecting among individual publications. Though narrower in focus, this period of collection management laid the groundwork for theories about quality and discrimination in the selection of items for library collections.

Following the Second World War, increased funding for education and for public libraries led to a period of unparalleled expansion in library collections. The seemingly endless possibilities for collection growth broadened the librarian's responsibilities. Moving beyond individual book evaluation, librarians began to view building the collection as an important responsibility. Theory looked at who should be selecting materials for the library, at how selection decisions were made, and at alternatives for building collections. The emphasis during this period was on growth and how to handle it effectively.

By the mid-1970s, budgets began to hold steady or to shrink. Libraries were unable to keep pace with increasing costs and growing numbers of publications; thus, they started to look at making do with less. Interest in downsizing serials collections and increasing cooperation grew. Collection development policy statements became more common as libraries sought guidance in managing limited financial resources amid conflicting demands. Concerns about deteriorating collections and assigning priorities for use of funds troubled the profession. As austerity became more pronounced in the 1980s, the term "collection management" became more meaningful as a way to describe the broader responsibilities of collection development librarians. Nevertheless, collection development and collection management often continue to be used interchangeably in much of the literature referenced in this chapter.

Chapter Content and Organization

The literature on collection management published since 1970 is voluminous. The annual "Year's Work" review articles in *Library Resources & Technical Services* often cite more than 200 publications on collection management. I have sought to present the most useful, practical, and current tools for performing the tasks of selection and deselection, budgeting, assessment and measurement, policy preparation, and preparing bibliographies. Some theoretical works provide the context in which tasks are performed and responsibilities executed. I have concentrated on works that present original results, methods, or perceptions that are informative for the practitioner. Though much of the literature on collection development continues to be written by library educators and academic librarians, I have sought a balance between resources that addresses collection management in academic, research, special, school, and public libraries. I have not included dissertations, theses, unpublished materials, or inhouse documents. This chapter does not contain recommended lists of titles that should be acquired to build collections in specific disciplines or subject areas. Resources and tools published before 1985 have been excluded, with some exceptions. Readers may consult the bibliographies cited here for earlier publications.

As collection management responsibilities have increased and become more complex, librarians have turned to information resources outside those prepared by and for the library profession. This chapter excludes references to that literature, useful as it is. Practitioners should be aware, however, of the valuable information available in the professional literature on organizational behavior, management, public affairs, organizational change, finance, and communication.

The interconnected nature of collection management activities makes any organization of resources and tools a compromise. The chapter begins with works on collection management in the broadest understanding of that term. Section HB addresses organization and staffing. HC covers collection policies. HD covers collection building. HE includes resources on collection managment (including selection) in specific subject areas, types of libraries, and collections. HF is devoted to collection maintenance—decisions about weeding and storage, preservation, and cancellation. The final three sections are HG, budget and finance; HH, assessment and evaluation; and HI, cooperative collection management and resource sharing.

HA
General Works

Practitioners and students of collection development are fortunate to have available several excellent textbooks, many of which have been issued in revised editions to reflect the changing conditions of libraries. These texts provide an overview of collection management and usually address the major functions and activities of a collection management program and a librarian with collection management responsibilities. As such, they are a good beginning point for a librarian new to the practice of collection management.

The first collection of essays that presented practice and theory by experts, *Collection Development in Libraries: A Treatise* (HAF10), appeared in 1980. This two-volume set remains a valuable guide to the field. *Collection Management: A New Treatise* (HAF6) was published in 1991. This work supplements and builds on the earlier collection. Each of these is cited in the general works section along with other compendiums, since they provide an overview of the field when read in total. Individual essays may be cited separately according to subject.

The Collection Management and Development Section of the American Library Association's Association of Library Collections and Technical Services (ALCTS) is issuing a series of guides on specific topics in collection development. The several guides replace the broader *Guidelines for Collection Management*, published in 1979 by Resources and Technical Services Division (RTSD) and now outdated. These are basic tools for anyone involved in collection management, especially those new to the field. Each guide is listed according to the subject covered in later sections of this chapter.

HAA
Textbooks, Guides, and Manuals

HAA1. Curley, Arthur, and Dorothy Broderick. *Building Library Collections.* 6th ed. Metuchen, N.J.: Scarecrow Press, 1985.

One of the standard texts on collection development since the first edition (by Mary Duncan Carter and Wallace J. Bonk) appeared in 1959. Extensive bibliographies with each chapter. Includes a list of selection sources.

HAA2. Evans, G. Edward. *Developing Library and Information Center Collections.* 2nd ed. Littleton, Colo.: Libraries Unlimited, 1987.

A comprehensive introduction to and state-of-the-art survey of the field, intended to give students an overall understanding of what is involved in building a collection for a library. Covers different types of libraries.

HAA3. Gorman, G. E., and B. R. Howes. *Collection Development for Libraries.* London: Bowker-Saur, 1989.

Designed to convince librarians and students in the Anglophone world of the value of collection development and to train them in its techniques. Covers collection development policies, evaluation and use studies, and weeding. Australian slant, but universal application. Includes reprints of important collection management articles. Bibliography of more than 700 resources arranged by subject. Chapter 8 lists selection sources.

HAA4. Magrill, Rose Mary, and John Corbin. *Acquisitions Management and Collection Development in Libraries.* 2nd ed. Chicago: American Library Association, 1989.

For annotation, *see* BAA7.

HAA5. Spiller, David. *Book Selection: An Introduction to Principles and Practice.* 5th ed. London: Clive Bingley, 1991.

An introduction to materials selection and provision. Includes information on database and computer software selection. Discusses matters of policy and management, selection sources, and how the selection process varies according to type of material and library. Intended for both students and practitioners.

HAA6. Wortman, William A. *Collection Management: Background and Principles.* Chicago: American Library Association, 1989.

This practical book is for experienced librarians, newcomers to the profession, and library administrators. Wortman's stated intention is to describe the best way to manage the library collection. He covers the standard topics of an introductory text and includes a useful bibliography. Discusses precisely and thoroughly the issues,

methods, and procedures of a collection management program.

HAB
Bibliographies

The following are general bibliographies; bibliographies on specific topics are found with other tools on that topic in subsequent sections.

HAB1. Chapman, L. "Collection Management and Development in Libraries: Some Recent Books: A Review Essay." *Journal of Library and Information Science* 23 (Dec. 1991): 222–24.

Review of recent monographs on collection management.

HAB2. Clark, Lenore. "Acquisitions, Budgets, and Materials Costs: A Selected Bibliography." In *Acquisitions, Budgets and Material Costs: Issues and Approaches*, edited by Sul H. Lee, 145–62. New York: Haworth Press, 1988.

Broader in coverage than the title suggests, this bibliography lists publications on approval plans, impact and management of rising materials costs, discriminatory pricing, and the acquisition of materials in new formats.

HAB3. Godden, Irene P., Karen W. Fachan, and Patricia Smith, comps.; with the assistance of Sandra Brug. *Collection Development and Acquisitions 1970–1980: An Annotated Critical Bibliography.* Metuchen, N.J.: Scarecrow Press, 1982.

Compilers have annotated citations to 345 sources published between 1970 and 1980 reflecting trends in acquisitions and collection development. Has author, title, and subject indexes. An extremely comprehensive bibliography.

HAB4. Kohl, David F. *Acquisitions, Collection Development, and Collection Use: A Handbook for Library Management.* Santa Barbara, Calif.: ABC Clio Information Services, 1985.

For annotation, *see* BAA6.

HAC
Standards

HAC1. American Association of School Librarians. *Planning Guide for Information Power: Guidelines for School Library Media Programs.* Chicago: American Library Association, 1988.

A useful, brief (32 pages) guide that serves as a companion piece to *Information Power: Guidelines for School Library Media Programs* (HAC2). Designed as a guide through the planning process outlined in Chapter 4, "Leadership, Planning, and Management."

HAC2. American Association of School Librarians and Association for Educational Communications and Technology. *Information Power: Guidelines for School Library Media Programs.* Chicago: American Library Association, 1988.

Revises the 1975 *Media Programs: District and School.* Intended to aid the school library media program professional in decision making. Sets forth guidelines for developing school library media programs. Specifically addresses collections in a chapter called "Resources and Equipment" and an appendix of budget formulas for materials and equipment.

HAC3. Association for Educational Communications and Technology/Association of College and Research Libraries Joint Committee. "Standards for Two-Year College Learning Resources Programs: A Draft." *College & Research Libraries News* 50, no. 6 (June 1989): 496–505.

Replaces *Guidelines for Two-Year College Learning Resources Programs (Revised)* and *Quantitative Standards for Two-Year Learning Resources Programs.* Standard 6 specifically deals with collections.

HAC4. Association of College & Research Libraries. "An Evaluative Checklist for Reviewing a College Library Program." *College & Research Libraries News* no. 10 (Nov. 1979): 305–16.

Developed by the ACRL Standards and Accreditation Committee to supplement the "Standards for College Libraries." Checklist follows the outline of the standards. Standard 2, which addresses the collections, covers availability, accessibility, selection, withdrawal, and quantity of library materials.

HAC5. _____. "Guidelines for Audio Visual Services in Academic Libraries." *College & Research Libraries News* 48, no. 9 (Oct. 1987): 533–36.

Section 6 addresses collection development, and section 9 covers collection maintenance.

HAC6. _____. "Guidelines for Branch Libraries in Colleges and Universities." *College & Research Libraries News* no. 9 (Oct. 1975): 281–83.

Includes sections on "Collections Development" and "Collection Organization."

HAC7. _____. "Guidelines for Extended Library Services." *College & Research Libraries News* 51, no. 4 (Apr. 1990): 353–55.

Revises the 1981 document. Includes a section on resources that addresses library materials.

HAC8. _____. "Information Services for Information Consumers: Guidelines for Providers." *RQ* 30, no. 2 (Winter 1990): 262–65.

Prepared by the Standards and Guidelines Committee, Reference and Adult Services Division, ALA, and adopted by RASD in 1990. Includes standards for resources.

HAC9. _____. "Mission of an Undergraduate Library: Model Statement." *College & Research Libraries News* 48, no. 9 (Oct. 1987): 542–44.

Prepared by the ACRL Undergraduate Librarians Discussion Group and the University Libraries Section Steering Committee. Devotes one section to collection.

HAC10. _____. "Standards for College Libraries, 1986." *College & Research Libraries News* 37, no. 3 (Mar. 1986): 189–200.

Prepared by ACRL's Ad Hoc College Library Standards Committee; revises the 1975 version. Standard 2 deals with library collections, including print and audiovisual resources and resource sharing.

HAC11. _____. "Standards for University Libraries." *College & Research Libraries News* 50, no. 8 (Sept. 1989): 679–91.

Revises the 1979 document. Prepared by the ACRL Ad Hoc University Library Standards Review Committee. Addresses collection management and collection preservation as factors to be considered in developing goals. Discusses collection adequacy under the criteria for evaluation.

HAC12. Association of College & Research Libraries and Association for Educational Communications and Technology. "Standards for Community, Junior and Technical College Learning Resources Programs." *College & Research Libraries News* 51, no. 8 (Sept. 1990): 757–67.

Standard 6 addresses collections and is a lengthy treatment, as far as standards go.

HAC13. Krueger, Karen J. "Guidelines for Collection Management." in *Collection Management in Public Libraries,* edited by Judith Serebnick, 13–26. Chicago: American Library Association, 1986.

Differentiates guidelines appropriate for public libraries from inappropriate guidelines. Discusses collection-centered and client-centered guidelines. Presents information about written guidelines that have been developed nationally and regionally to assist public librarians in evaluating their collections.

HAC14. McClure, Charles R., and others. *Planning and Role Setting for Public Libraries: A Manual of Options and Procedures.* Chicago: American Library Association, 1987.

See also annotation under AHA5. One component of the Public Library Development Program, developed to assist public libraries in the areas of planning, measurement, and evaluation. Intended to be used with *Output Measures for Public Libraries* (HAC17). The work describes a step-by-step planning process. The manual guides the library as it reviews existing conditions and services, defines the library's mission, sets goals and objectives, chooses strategies for achieving objectives, and evaluates the results of the process.

HAC15. Public Library Association. Goals, Guidelines, and Standards Committee. *Public Library Mission Statement* *and Its Imperatives for Service.* Chicago: American Library Association, 1979.

Addresses library resources in the section "Imperatives for Services."

HAC16. Van House, Nancy A., Beth Weil, and Charles R. McClure. *Measuring Academic Library Performance: A Practical Approach.* Chicago: American Library Association, 1990.

See also annotation under AHA8. A manual similar to *Output Measures for Public Libraries: A Manual of Standardized Procedures* (HAC17) prepared for the ACRL Ad Hoc Committee on Performance Measures. Includes a chapter on materials availability and use. Provides practical advice. Includes forms and worksheets.

HAC17. Van House, Nancy A., and others. *Output Measures for Public Libraries: A Manual of Standardized Procedures.* 2nd ed. Chicago: American Library Association, 1987.

See also annotation under AHA7. Not a standard or guideline, but one component of the Public Libraries Development Program, a combination of activities and products developed by the Public Library Association to assist public libraries in the areas of planning, measurement, and evaluation. Intended to be used with *Planning and Role Setting for Public Libraries* (HAC14), this publication describes a set of measures to assess common public library services. Instructions are included for collecting, analyzing, and interpreting data.

HAD
Periodicals

HAD1. *The Acquisitions Librarian.* New York: Haworth Press. no. 1– , 1989– . Irregular. ISSN 0896-3576.
For annotation, *see* BAD2.

HAD2. *Against the Grain.* Charleston, S.C.: Katina Strauch. v. 1– , 1989– . Five times a year. ISSN 1043-2094.
For annotation, *see* BAD3.

HAD3. *ALCTS Newsletter.* Chicago: Association for Library Collections and Technical Services. v. 1– , 1990– . Frequency varies. ISSN 1047-949X. Continues *RTSD Newsletter.*
For annotation, *see* AF5.

HAD4. *Collection Building.* Syracuse, N.Y.: Gaylord Professional Publications. v. 1– , 1978– . Quarterly. ISSN 0160-4953.
Intended as a forum for discussion and debate on all aspects of collection development.

HAD5. *Collection Management.* New York: Haworth Press. v. 1– , 1976– . Quarterly. ISSN 0146-2679.
See also annotation under BAD5. Devoted to problems facing libraries in the efficient management of their collections. Includes research of interest to librarians responsi-

ble for all phases of developing and maintaining collections within all types of libraries. Covers collection management, resource sharing, weeding, no-growth collections, storage, and budget allocation and development.

HAD6. *Librarians Collection Letter: A Monthly Newsletter for Collection Development Staff.* Keller, Wash.: Regan Robinson. v. 1– , 1991– . Monthly. ISSN 1063-5386.
Provides an informal forum for collection development issues and serves as an alternative to the more academic journals. Covers a wide range of topics, including information on specialty publishers and distributors, reviews of professional books, and reports on recent news and developments.

HAD7. *Library Acquisitions: Practice and Theory.* New York: Pergamon Press, v. 1– , 1977– . Quarterly. ISSN 0364-6408.
See also annotation under BAD6. Contains many articles of interest to collection management librarians.

HAD8. *Library Resources & Technical Services.* Chicago: Association for Library Collections and Technical Services. v. 1– , 1957– . Quarterly. ISSN 0024-2527.
For annotation, *see* AF13.

ELECTRONIC JOURNALS

HAD9. *ACQNET.* [serial online] Ithaca, N.Y.: Cornell University Library, Christian Boissonnas. no. 1– , 1990– . Irregular. ISSN 1057-5308.
See also annotation under BAD1. Covers many topics of interest to collection management librarians.

HAD10. *ALCTS Network News.* [serial online] Chicago: Association of Library Collections and Technical Services, American Library Association. v. 1– , 13 May 1991– . Irregular. ISSN 1056-6694.
For annotation, *see* AF4.

HAD11. *Newsletter on Serials Pricing Issues.* [serial online] Chapel Hill, N.C.: Marcia Tuttle. no. 1– , Feb. 1989– . Irregular. ISSN 1046-3410.
For annotation, *see* GAD5.

HAE
Sources of Expertise

Collection management librarians have many sources of expertise available. These include professional associations, special interest groups, conferences, and continuing education institutes, all of which draw together knowledgeable professionals for presentations and discussion. Particularly useful are a series of regional institutes sponsored by ALA's Association for Library Collections and Technical Services Collection Management and Development Section (CMDS), held irregularly since 1981.

PROFESSIONAL ASSOCIATIONS

HAE1. ALA Association for Library Collections and Technical Services (ALCTS). Executive Director: Karen Muller.

For annotation, *see* AGA3.

HAE2. ALA ALCTS Collection Management and Development Section (CMDS).

This group is charged with contributing to library service and librarianship through encouragement of, promotion of, and responsibility for activities relating to collection management and development, selection, and evaluation of library materials in all types of institutions. Committees and discussion groups address specific topics. These include:

Administration of Collection Development Committee
Collection Development and Electronic Media Committee
Collection Development Practice in a Changing Environment Committee
Continuing Education Committee
Education for Collection Development Committee
Quantitative Measures for Collection Management Committee
Chief Collection Development Officers of Large Research Libraries Discussion Group
Collection Development Librarians of Academic Libraries Discussion Group
Collection Management/Selection for Public Libraries Discussion Group

HAE3. ALA Reference and Adult Services Division (RASD). Executive Director: Andrew M. Hansen.

RASD is responsible for stimulating and supporting the delivery of reference/information service to all groups in every type of library.

HAE4. ALA RASD Collection Development and Evaluation Section (CODES).

CODES seeks to develop the professional skills and knowledge of reference and adult services librarians who are involved in collection development and evaluation. It is also responsible for liaison with related groups in ALCTS. The several committees and discussion groups include:

Adult Library Materials Committee
Bibliography Committee
Collection Development Policies Committee
Collection Evaluation Techniques Committee
Computer-based Methods and Resources Committee
Continuing Education Committee
Liaison with Users Committee
Notable Books Council

Reference Collection Development and Evaluation Committee
Reference Sources Committee
Materials Reviewing Committee
Staffing and Organization of Collection Development/Organization Committee
Collection Development and Evaluation in Public Libraries Discussion Group
Dual Assignments Discussion Group

HAE5. ALA Ethnic Materials and Information Exchange Round Table. Collection Development Task Force.

This EMIERT task force specifically addresses collection development issues in the area of ethnic materials.

HAE6. *CMDS Guide.* [database online] Chicago: ALA/ALCTS, 1992– .

A finding guide designed to help librarians identify groups within ALA concerned with collection management. The guide was prepared by the ALA ALCTS CMDS Collection Development Practice in a Changing Environment Committee. This list has been published on ALCTSERV, the ALCTS fileserver, under the name *CMDS Guide.* To obtain a copy, send a message to **LISTSERV-@UICVM** with the command: **SEND CMDS GUIDE.**

CONFERENCES

HAE7. Acquisitions, Budgets and Material Costs: Issues and Approaches. Once a year; spring.

See also annotation under BAE5. Papers presented at this conference cover many topics of interest to collection management librarians.

HAE8. The College of Charleston Conference: Issues in Book and Serial Acquisitions. Once a year; November.

See also annotation under BAE6. Another conference at which many of the speakers are collection management librarians and many of the papers are on topics of interest to collection management librarians.

HAE9. The Feather River Institute on Acquisitions and Collection Development. Once a year; May.

For annotation, *see* BAE7.

ELECTRONIC DISCUSSION LISTS

HAE10. *COLLDV-L.* [electronic discussion group] Los Angeles: University of Southern California, August 1991– .

A moderated discussion list directed primarily to library collection development officers, bibliographers, and selectors plus others involved with library collection development, including interested publishers and vendors. Topics on the list cover the broad range of collection development and management concerns, including access/ownership issues, approval plans, collection assessment, budgeting, cooperation, collection formats, organization, planning, policies, pricing, publisher and vendor relations, resource sharing, selection, and storage. COLLDV-L is moderated by Lynn F. Sipe, Assistant University Librarian for Collection Development, University of Southern California, who can be reached at **LSIPE@USCVM** (BITNET) or **LSIPE@VM.USC.EDU** (INTERNET).

To join COLLDV-L, send a message to **LISTSERV@USCVM** (BITNET) with the command: **SUBSCRIBE COLLDV-L [your name]**.

HAE11. CONSPECTUSNET. [electronic discussion group] Lacey, Wash.: WLN, Inc., 1993– .

For users of WLN Conspectus and other interested persons. Intended to provide a convenient means for current WLN Conspectus users and those interested in learning about the conspectus process to communicate and exchange information. A forum for discussion of both theoretical issues and practical applications. To join CONSPECTUSNET, send a message to **LISTSERV @WLN.COM** (INTERNET) with the command: **SUBSCRIBE CONSPECTUSNET [your name].**

Questions or concerns about the list should be sent to Mary Bushing, Chair of the WLN Conspectus User Group: **BUSHING/LIB@RENNE.LIB.MONTANA.EDU** (INTERNET).

HAF
Overview of Collection Management

HAF1. Atkinson, Ross. "Conditions of Collection Development." In *Collection Management: A New Treatise,* edited by Charles B. Osburn and Ross Atkinson, 29–44. Greenwich, Conn.: JAI Press, 1991.

Atkinson describes the current process of collection development by defining four concepts: combination, locality, temporality, and focus. He interprets "collection" in a manner that is applicable to both traditional and online environments.

HAF2. _____. "Old Forms, New Forms: The Challenge of Collection Development." *College & Research Libraries* 50, no. 5 (Sept. 1989): 507–20.

Atkinson recommends that collection development adapt to rapidly changing technical and economic conditions and suggests steps to achieve greater control over scholarly and education information. Provocative paper.

HAF3. Branin, Joseph J., ed. *Collection Management for the 1990s: Proceedings of the Midwest Collection Management and Development Institute, University of Illinois at Chicago, August 17–20, 1989.* ALCTS Papers on Library Technical Services and Collections, no. 3. Chicago: American Library Association, 1993.

Papers from the Institute emphasize trends and issues for the future of collection management and range from keynote speeches to practical workshop presentations.

HAF4. Broadhus, Robert N. "History of Collection Development." In *Collection Management: A New Treatise,* ed-

ited by Charles B. Osburn and Ross Atkinson, 3–28. Greenwich, Conn.: JAI Press, 1991.

Comprehensive history of collection development, with discussion of theory and practice; extensive notes and references.

HAF5. Johnson, Peggy. "Dollars and Sense." [column in] *Technicalities* 8, no. 9 (Sept. 1988–).

A bimonthly column devoted to issues of interest to collection management librarians. Topics include selection policies, collection evaluation and assessment, electronic media, collection depreciation, budgeting and allocation, etc.

HAF6. Osburn, Charles B. "Collection Development and Management." In *Academic Libraries: Research Perspectives,* edited by Mary Jo Lynch and Arthur P. Young, assoc. ed, 1–37. Chicago: American Library Association, 1990.

Thorough and concise historical review of the methodological and intellectual milestones of collection development.

HAF7. _____. "Toward a Reconceptualization of Collection Development." *Advances in Library Administration and Organization* 2 (1983): 175–98.

An important piece, in which Osburn suggests that collection development should be reconceptualized in order to respond to the changes occurring in libraries. Recommends that collection development librarians expand their position to become more active proponents of the library. Collection development should be seen as "a communications process driving an integral system of library, information universe, and community."

HAF8. Osburn, Charles B., and Ross Atkinson, eds. *Collection Management: A New Treatise.* 2 vols. Foundations in Library and Information Science, vol. 26. Greenwich, Conn.: JAI Press, 1991.

A notable collection of essays, intended to "capture the dynamism, the diversity, and the evolutionary character" of collection development. Twenty-three experts address many aspects of the field.

HAF9. Pankake, Marcia. "From Book Selection to Collection Management: Continuity and Advances in an Unending Work." *Advances in Librarianship* 13 (1984): 185–210.

Pankake explains that collection management is a broader term than collection development, encompassing additional areas such as maintenance and preservation. Collection management decisions must be viewed within the perspective of the collections as whole and within the same value system.

HAF10. Stueart, Robert D., and George B. Miller, eds. *Collection Development in Libraries: A Treatise.* 2 vols. Foundations in Library and Information Sciences, vol. 10. Greenwich, Conn.: JAI Press, 1980.

A landmark contribution to collection management, this work consists of twenty-four papers written by specialists. It presents theories, techniques, and analyses that have application to academic, research, public, school, and special libraries. An essential source of information that has remained an important tool since its publication.

HAG
Automation and the Practice of Collection Management

Automation affects collection management in two ways: automated or electronic resources are changing the nature and meaning of collections, and automation is changing the processes and decisions of managing collections. The following section addresses application of automation to the practice of collection management.

HAG1. Atkinson, Ross. "Text Mutability and Collection Administration." *Library Acquisitions: Practice and Theory* 14, no. 4 (1990): 355–58.

Atkinson differentiates information in electronic form from that in printed books, because electronic information is mutable. He warns libraries must not become merely a switching point, but must fulfill their traditional role of stabilizing a selected body of information. Describes major functions for the library in the online setting.

HAG2. DeBrower, Amy M., and DeAnna T. Jones. "Application of an Expert System to Collection Development: Donation Processing in a Special Library." *Library Software Review* 10, no. 6 (Nov./Dec. 1991): 385–89.

Authors describe a successful pilot project that developed an expert system to conserve professional staff time and reduce processing costs. The expert system guides gift materials processing by support staff.

HAG3. Getz, Malcolm. "The Electronic Library: Analysis and Decentralization in Collection Decisions." In *Budgets for Acquisitions: Strategies for Serials, Monographs, and Electronic Formats,* edited by Sul H. Lee, 71–84. New York: Haworth Press, 1991.

Getz describes electronic tools that have become available to support collection development and their impact upon information acquisition, drawing from his experience at Vanderbilt University.

HAG4. Johnston, Mark, and John Weckert. "Selection Advisor: An Expert System for Collection Development." *Information Technology and Libraries* 9 (1990): 219–25.

Authors report a nonworking expert system model that might provide a framework for selection decision making. They base the system on six criteria: subject, intellectual content, potential use, relation to collection, bibliographical considerations, and language.

HAG5. Loertscher, David V., and May Lein Ho. *Computerized Collection Development for School Library Media Centers.* Excellence in School Media Programs, no. 2. Fayette-

ville, Ark.: Hi Willow Research and Publishing, 1986. Includes two discs.

Authors present a method of collection building that matches the collection in a school with curricular targets. They provide step-by-step instructions for creating a complete collection development system on an Apple computer using the program *Appleworks*. Covers collection mapping, computerized acquisition, and collection evaluation. Includes sample forms.

HAG6. Sanders, Nancy P. "The Automation of Academic Library Collection Management: From Fragmentation to Integration." In *Collection Management for the 1990s,* edited by Joseph J. Branin, 50–62. Chicago: American Library Association, 1993.

Sanders describes the automated support for collection management now available and discusses the ideal automated collection management system.

HAG7. Sasse, Margo, and Patricia A. Smith. "Automated Acquisitions: The Future of Collection Development." *Library Acquisitions: Practice and Theory* 16 (1992): 135–43.

Authors examine how library automation is changing the processes of collection development and the role of the collection developer. An in-depth analysis of present and future changes in responsibilities, work flow, and cooperative activities.

HAG8. Welsch, Erwin K. "Back to the Future: A Personal Statement on Collection Development in an Information Culture." *Library Resources & Technical Services* 33, no. 1 (Jan. 1989): 29–36.

Welsch suggests ways in which computer technology can have important effects on collection development and enable selectors to take advantage of new opportunities. He proposes a "Selector's Workstation," a microcomputer linked with a local computer center and external databases, as one way in which collection development librarians can be proactive in the future.

HB
Organization and Staffing

Collection management activities vary from library to library. Consequently, no organizational structure predominates and no single definition of a collection management librarian exists. Staff members who work within collection management may be called bibliographers, selectors, subject specialists, or collection development librarians. They may devote all their time to selection and collection management decisions, or they may have additional service responsibilities, depending on the size, type, and organizational structure of their library. Multiple responsibilities and their effect on collection management is an important topic.

Within the academic library community, debate continues over the role teaching faculty should have in selection decisions. The question is no longer primarily who (librarian or professor?) should make the collection decision but how to open communication so that teaching faculty are involved in setting priorities and developing policies and plans for the library. This becomes a particularly volatile issue as libraries look at journal cancellation projects.

Broadening responsibilities have led to increasing concern about the education and training of collection management librarians. Some of the practical matters addressed are how to prepare documents and orientation programs for new staff members; what skills and expertise are necessary; how knowledge about formats, disciplines, budgeting, etc., can be gained; and how collection management librarians interact with others in the library.

ORGANIZATION

HB1. Bobick, James E. *Collection Development Organization and Staffing in ARL Libraries.* SPEC Kit, no. 131. Washington, D.C.: Office of Management Studies, Association of Research Libraries, 1987.

Bobick identifies continuing changes in the organization and staffing of collection development. Kit contains organization charts and descriptions, positions announcements, orientation and training aids for bibliographers, and task force reports. Revises SPEC Kit no. 11 (1974).

HB2. Bryant, Bonita. "Allocation of Human Resources for Collection Development." *Library Resources & Technical Services* 30, no. 2 (Apr./June 1986): 149–62.

Bryant presents a quantitative model that identifies elements that must be included in a consideration of workload measurement and subject responsibility allocation.

HB3. _____. "The Organizational Structure of Collection Development." *Library Resources & Technical Services* 31, no. 2 (Apr./June 1987): 111–22.

This article reviews the influences of organizational evolution and intentional change, library posture toward collection development, personnel management, and human perspectives upon the establishment of an administrative framework for achieving collection development goals. Explores the role of collection development officers.

HB4. Cogswell, James A. "The Organization of Collection Management Functions in Academic Research Libraries." *The Journal of Academic Librarianship* 13, no. 5 (1987): 268–76.

Author identifies eight functions of collection management: planning and policy making, collection analysis, materials selection, collection maintenance, fiscal management, user liaison, resource sharing, and program evaluation. Suggests three models for the organization of collection management functions and evaluates their effectiveness.

HB5. Creth, Sheila D. "The Organization of Collection Development: A Shift in the Organization Paradigm." *Journal of Library Administration* 14, no. 1 (1991): 67–85.

Creth proposes a revised organizational structure based on the functional and the team design for collection management.

HB6. Pitschmann, Louis A. "Organization and Staffing." In *Collection Management: A New Treatise*, edited by Charles B. Osburn and Ross Atkinson, 125–43. Greenwich, Conn.: JAI Press, 1991.

Pitschmann provides historical background in organization and staffing and describes current methods of organization, role of the collection development officer, and future influences on organizational methods.

RESPONSIBILITIES OF BIBLIOGRAPHERS AND COLLECTION DEVELOPMENT LIBRARIANS

HB7. *Guide for Writing a Bibliographer's Manual.* Collection Management and Development Guides, no. 1. Chicago: American Library Association, 1987.

Covers construction and scope of a bibliographer's manual and provides a guide to terminology. Guide presents points for possible inclusion in a bibliographer's manual. A particularly useful section looks at the bibliographer's job, duties, and responsibilities.

HB8. Hay, Fred J. "The Subject Specialist in the Academic Library: A Review Article." *The Journal of Academic Librarianship* 16, no. 1 (1990): 11–17.

Hay cites thirty-one sources in his review of the literature on subject specialists. He recommends giving greater organizational emphasis to subject specialization: "It is an egregious error to leave collection development to non-subject librarians, or worse, to vendors whose sole purpose for being is to maximize profits."

HB9. Johnson, Peggy. "Collection Development Officer, a Reality Check: A Personal View." *Library Resources & Technical Services* 33, no. 2 (Apr. 1989): 153–60.

Author describes expanding role of academic collection officer and offers checklist of competencies that are needed beyond subject and selection expertise for successful job performance.

HB10. Metz, Paul. "Quantifying the Workload of Subject Bibliographers in Collection Development." *The Journal of Academic Librarianship* 17, no. 5 (1991): 284–87.

Suggests quantifying the workload of subject bibliographers by devising a locally applicable formula with five input parameters measuring client- and literature-based job elements. The formula is useful both to evaluate personnel and to adjust and review workloads.

HB11. Schad, Jasper G. "Managing Collection Development in University Libraries That Utilize Librarians with Dual-Responsibility Assignments." *Library Acquisitions: Practice and Theory* 14, no. 2 (1990): 165–71.

Notes that collection development integrates work and staff across functional boundaries and advocates the use of matrix management, in which the traditional hierarchy is overlaid by explicit lateral lines of authority. Schad offers a plan for action to overcome inherent inefficiencies of matrix structure.

HB12. Siggins, Jack. *Performance Appraisal of Collection Development Librarians.* SPEC Kit, no. 181. Washington, D.C.: Office of Management Services, Association of Research Libraries, 1992.

Kit reports the results of a survey on how collection development librarians are evaluated and how the selection aspects of the duties of librarians with multiple assignments are evaluated. Sample documents are performance criteria for selectors, policy statements, performance review models, job descriptions, and other reports and forms.

ETHICS

HB13. Bullard, Scott R. "Tribes and Tribulations: Ethical Snares in the Organization of the Collection Management Units." In *Acquisitions '90*, edited by David C. Genaway, 17–23. Canfield, Ohio: Genaway & Associates, 1990.

Bullard suggests that some collection management organizational structures lend themselves to deceit and duplicity. He focuses on specific ethical lapses within the organization rather than those that occur in dealings with outside agents, i.e., vendors or publishers.

HB14. Hannaford, William E., Jr. "Ethics and Collection Development." In *Collection Development in College Libraries*, edited by Joanne Schneider Hill, William E. Hannaford, Jr., and Ronald H. Epp, 55–60. Chicago: American Library Association, 1991.

Calls for the application of ethics to collection development, which he suggests may be dominated by expediency or self-interest.

EDUCATION AND TRAINING

HB15. Brooks, Terrence A. "The Education of Collection Developers." In *Collection Management: A New Treatise*, edited by Charles B. Osburn and Ross Atkinson, 145–58. Greenwich, Conn.: JAI Press, 1991.

Examines the practice of collection development and suggests a new educational program for collection development.

HB16. D'Aniello, Charles. "Bibliography and the Beginning Bibliographer." *Collection Building* 6, no. 2 (Summer 1984): 11–19.

Advice directed to those who are considering becoming or have recently become bibliographers. Author presents a description of responsibilities and educative sources for selectors. Lengthy list of references, including selection tools.

HB17. Gleason, Maureen L. "Training Collection Development Librarians." *Collection Management* 4, no. 4 (Winter 1982): 1–8.

A practical article that describes an ideal training program for collection development librarians. Identifies objectives of a training program and specific methods for achieving them.

HB18. Intner, Sheila S., and Peggy Johnson, eds. *Recruiting, Educating, and Training Librarians for Collection Development.* Westport, Conn.: Greenwood, ca. 1993.

A collection of essays by educators and practitioners that lays out practical steps to recruit, educate, and train librarians for collection development responsibilities.

HB19. Williams, Lynn B. "Subject Knowledge for Subject Specialists: What the Novice Bibliographer Needs to Know." *Collection Management* 14, nos. 3/4 (1991): 31–47.

Williams seeks to define the minimum level of subject knowledge a subject specialist selector should have, while providing methods of gaining or strengthening such knowledge short of formal education. Extensive list of references.

HC
Policies

A collection development policy is a plan that provides guidelines about the appropriateness of various types of materials for a particular collection. A policy may address only selection decisions for acquisition or may present criteria to guide all manner of collection management activities. Policies establish goals and priorities for the collection and for use of fiscal resources. Policies reflect the institutional context or community setting of the library.

OVERVIEW

HC1. Bryant, Bonnie, ed. *Guide for Written Collection Policy Statements.* Collection Management and Development Guides, no. 3. Chicago: American Library Association, 1989.

Identifies the essential elements of a written statement of policy for collection management and development and establishes a standard terminology and structure for use in preparing comparable policies. Addresses the planning, informational, administrative, and technical functions served by policies. Includes bibliography and glossary. (Revision, scheduled for 1993, will address the inclusion of electronic publications.)

HC2. Cassell, Kay Ann, and Elizabeth Futas. "Collection Development Policies." *Collection Building* 11, no. 2 (1991): 26–29.

Practical presentation, in outline form, of the steps to take to begin the process of developing a collection policy for a specific library in a particular community.

HC3. Farrell, David. "Policy and Planning." In *Collection Management: A New Treatise*, edited by Charles B. Osburn and Ross Atkinson, 51– 65. Greenwich, Conn.: JAI Press, 1991.

Farrell looks at collection policy and collection planning. He presents a historical and managerial context for collection development policy statements and looks to the future.

PREPARING POLICIES, INCLUDING MODEL POLICY STATEMENTS

HC4. Adams, Helen R. *School Media Policy Development: A Practical Process for Small Districts*. Littleton, Colo.: Libraries Unlimited, 1986.

Intended as a guide for school media professionals working in small districts and planning to initiate media policy development. Author presents the argument for policies, basic principles for effective policy making, and a detailed description of the process of preparing a policy. Appendixes include sample policies. Notes and suggested readings with most chapters.

HC5. Anderson, R. Joseph. "Managing Change and Chance: Collecting Policies in Social History Archives." *American Archivist* 48 (Summer 1985): 296–303.

Anderson states that traditional methods for developing collecting policies do not work well in social history archives. He recommends coherent guidance, flexibility, and a means for ongoing reassessment.

HC6. Brancolini, Kristine R. *Audiovisual Policies in ARL Libraries*. SPEC Kit, no. 162. Washington, D.C.: Association of Research Libraries, Office of Management Studies, 1990.

This kit provides examples for developing audiovisual policies or revising existing policies and identifies factors related to the development of audiovisual collections and services. "Audiovisual" covers audiocassettes, audio compact discs, computer software, films, phonodiscs, slides, videocassettes, and videodiscs. Contains sample brochures, fact sheets, and policies for circulation, fines, collection development, selection, and reserves.

HC7. _____. *Audiovisual Policies in College Libraries*. CLIP Note, no. 14. Chicago: Association of College & Research Libraries, 1991.

Reports a survey on audiovisual collections and policies in college libraries, paralleling the ARL survey above. Sample documents are brochures, user guides, and various policies.

HC8. Callison, Daniel. "The Evolution of School Library Collection Development Policies, 1975–1995." *School Library Media Quarterly* 19 (Fall 1990): 27–34.

Examines past, current, and probable future states of school library collection policies; identifies minor and major issues.

HC9. Cassell, Kay Ann, and Elizabeth Futas. *Developing Public Library Collections, Policies, and Procedures: A How-to-Do-It Manual for Small and Medium-Sized Public Libraries*. New York: Neal-Schuman Publishers, 1991.

A useful step-by-step guide to planning and writing public library collection development policies. Begins with advice on assessing institutional goals, objectives, and priorities. Includes sample forms, a model collection development policy, an extensive bibliography of selection aids, and a list of additional information sources.

HC10. Phillips, Faye. "Developing Collecting Policies for Manuscript Collections." *American Archivist* 47 (Winter 1984): 30–42.

Phillips presents a concise model outline for a collecting policy for manuscript collections. Includes a review of policy development and a synopsis of archival literature relating to policy development.

HC11. *Reference Collection Development: A Manual*. RASD Occasional Papers, no. 13. Chicago: Reference and Adult Services Division, American Library Association, 1992.

Intended to serve as a guide for writing collection development policies for reference collections serving adults in academic and public libraries. Contains a checklist, outline of a model policy with examples, and two sample policies. Useful list of sources for other sample policies.

HC12. Taborsky, Theresa, and Patricia Lenkowski, comps., with assistance of Anne Webb and Lisa Lewis. *Collection Development Policies for College Libraries*. CLIP Note, no. 11. Chicago: College Library Section, Association of College and Research Libraries, American Library Association, 1989.

Report of a survey of collection development policies in small college and university libraries. Includes six complete policy documents as well as selected policies for separate collections and special formats. Replaces CLIP Note no. 2 (1981).

HC13. *Women's Studies Collection Development Policies*. Chicago: Women's Studies Section, Association of College and Research Libraries, American Library Association, 1992.

A project of the Collection Development and Bibliography Committee of the Women's Studies Section of ACRL. Provides, as models, sixteen women's studies policy statements, two cooperative agreements, and the Women's Studies section of the RLG Conspectus (see conspectus discussion under HH, Assessment and Evaluation).

HD
Collection Building

Collection building covers the process of first identifying (individually or en bloc) appropriate materials and then deciding which to acquire for the library. This selection responsibility is often the function first considered when reviewing the tasks of collection development librarians and the first skill covered in library school courses on collection management. Keyes Metcalf wrote in 1940 that "the most important single task that any librarian can perform is to build up the collection." ("The Essentials of an Acquisitions Program" in *The Acquisition and Cataloging of Books*, edited by William M. Randall, Chicago: University of Chicago Press, 1940, 77.) Selection becomes increasingly complex as the volume of publications increases and formats proliferate, while budgets fail to keep pace. In addition, the communities being served are changing while selectors seek to build collections that meet expanding and evolving needs. Some client groups are becoming more vocal in what they want and don't want in their libraries and school media centers.

Resources identified in this section address the theory and practice of selecting both current and retrospective materials. The activities of selection and acquisition are always intertwined, especially in the areas of mass buying (gathering plans, approval plans, blanket orders, and standing orders) and gifts and exchange arrangements. These topics are covered in depth in Chapter B, Acquisitions, and not repeated here. I have included tools that focus on building collections to serve diverse populations and on censorship and intellectual freedom, increasingly important concerns. Additional subsections deal with selection of serials and nonprint materials. This section concludes with literature that examines how collection management librarians use selection tools.

I have not listed individual selection tools and review sources; a comprehensive list of these resources would extend far beyond the size limits of this chapter. However, several of the tools cited in this chapter do include selection sources, which are noted in the annotations. The most comprehensive guides to selection tools have been published by ALA's Association of Library Collections and Technical Services (formerly Resources and Technical Services Division) and its Collection Management and Development Section (formerly Committee).

The field of publishing is as important an area for collection management librarians as it is for acquisitions librarians. Since the topic is well covered in Chapter B, resources are not repeated here.

THEORIES OF SELECTION

HD1. Atkinson, Ross. "The Citation as Intertext: Toward a Theory of the Selection Process." *Library Resources & Technical Services* 28, no. 2 (Apr./June 1984): 109–19.

Unique analysis of the intellectual processes that determine the selection of library materials. Presents a hypothetical model of how individual selection decisions are made. Applies concepts of linguistic theory to the process of selecting library materials.

HD2. Harloe, Bart. "Achieving Client-Centered Collection Development in Small and Medium-Sized Academic Libraries." *College & Research Libraries* 50, no. 3 (May 1989): 344–53.

Harloe presents a model for client-centered collection development. Though directed to libraries primarily supporting undergraduate education, the model is of value to academic libraries regardless of size and clientele.

HD3. Hazen, Dan C. "Selection: Function, Models, Theory." In *Collection Management: A New Treatise*, edited by Charles B. Osburn and Ross Atkinson, 273–300. Greenwich, Conn.: JAI Press, 1991.

Addresses theoretical speculation concerning the process of selecting materials for library collections.

HD4. Losee, Robert M., Jr. "Optimality and the Best Collection: The Goals and Rules of Selection and Collection Managers." *Collection Management* 14, nos. 3/4 (1991): 21–30.

Losee presents selection and evaluation criteria and suggests rules that describe what should be done to yield superior collections.

HD5. Rutledge, John, and Luke Swindler. "The Selection Decision: Defining Criteria and Establishing Priorities." *College & Research Libraries* 48, no. 2 (Mar. 1987): 123–31.

An important contribution to selection theory. Authors arrange selection criteria in six categories to illustrate their interrelationship. The categories can be ranked by priority, so the influence of the criteria can be adjusted by priority to conform with fiscal resources.

HD6. Shapiro, Beth J. "Categories of Resources." In *Collection Management: A New Treatise*, edited by Charles B. Osburn and Ross Atkinson, 161–72. Greenwich, Conn.: JAI Press, 1991.

Review of various typologies of categories of materials/resources and discussion of their utility for collection development activities now and in the future.

RETROSPECTIVE SELECTION

See also the section on out-of-print materials in Chapter B, Acquisitions.

HD7. Bryant, Bonita, and Barbara Van Deventer. "Retrospective Selection." In *Collection Management: A New Treatise*, edited by Charles B. Osburn and Ross Atkinson, 313–35. Greenwich, Conn.: JAI Press, 1991.

Authors present selection principles, discuss funding for retrospective selection, and suggest methods for locating and acquiring retrospective materials. Directed primarily to academic libraries, but useful for anyone interested in retrospective selection.

MASS BUYING

See also the section on approval plans in Chapter B, Acquisitions.

HD8. Bucknall, Carolyn. "Mass Buying Programs." In *Collection Management: A New Treatise*, edited by Charles B. Osburn and Ross Atkinson, 337–49. Greenwich, Conn.: JAI Press, 1991.

Bucknall focuses primarily on approval plans. She lists pros and cons, plus issues to be considered when selecting and implementing an approval plan.

DIVERSE LITERATURES AND COMMUNITIES

HD9. Cornog, Martha, ed. *Libraries, Erotica, Pornography.* Phoenix: Oryx Press, 1991.

Essays on the conflict for librarians in collecting what is representative of variety and plurality. Pro and con arguments on collecting pornography in libraries, as well as a brief history of erotica and its collecting in libraries.

HD10. Danky, James I., and Elliot Shores, eds. *Alternative Materials in Libraries.* Metuchen, N.J.: Scarecrow Press, 1982.

A collection of essays by activist librarians and alternative press individuals, discussing practical issues associated with selection, acquisition, and cataloging of alternative materials. Includes a list of small press distributors.

HD11. Gough, Cal, and Ellen Greenblatt, eds. *Gay and Lesbian Library Service.* Jefferson, N.C.: McFarland & Co., 1990.

An important work that examines libraries' accountability in providing collections and service to the gay and lesbian population. Suggests what can be done to improve the situation and proposes the means of accomplishing this objective. Sections on collection development, special collections of gay and lesbian materials, bibliographic access, service issues. Extensive appendixes including core collections, bibliographies, filmography, discography, publishers, and sources for materials.

HD12. Josey, E. J., and M. L. DeLoach. *Ethnic Collections in Libraries.* New York: Neal-Schuman Publishers, 1983.

Useful social synthesis of the issues and trends in ethnic collection development. Deals with diversity of ethnic collections, major collections on ethnic minorities, and archives, programming, federal policy, and linkages.

HD13. Scarborough, Katharine T. A., ed. *Developing Library Collections for California's Emerging Majority: A Manual of Resources for Ethnic Collection Development.* San Francisco: Bay Area Library and Information System, 1990.

Essays discuss the theoretical, administrative, and practical issues differentiating collection building for ethnically diverse clienteles from the standard model; considers African American, Native American, Asian/Southeast Asian, Chicano/Latino collections. Intended for all types of libraries developing relevant collections for increasingly diverse communities. Concludes with useful lists of sources of ethnic materials and information.

HD14. Whitaker, Cathy Seitz. *Alternative Publications: A Guide to Directories, Indexes, Bibliographies and Other Sources.* Jefferson, N.C.: McFarland & Co., 1990.

A selective bibliography intended as an introduction to alternative media. Annotated bibliography of indexes and abstracts useful for identifying sources in the alternative press.

GREY LITERATURE

Grey literature, sometimes called fugitive literature, is the material not available through normal bookselling channels. Typically, it addresses practical problems and contemporary issues.

HD15. Allison, Peter. "Stalking the Elusive Grey Literature." *College & Research Libraries News* 48, no. 5 (May 1987): 244–46.

Allison discusses the importance of grey literature and suggests ways to make identification and acquisition easier.

HD16. Wood, D. N. "The Collection, Bibliographic Control and Accessibility of Grey Literature." *IFLA Journal* 10 (1984): 278–82.

Wood calls grey literature a "costly public asset going largely to waste" (p. 278). Offers estimates of numbers of materials and agencies producing grey literature and provides recommendations for the producers and for librarians.

CENSORSHIP AND INTELLECTUAL FREEDOM

HD17. American Library Association. *Intellectual Freedom Manual.* 4th ed. Chicago: ALA, 1992.

Intended to answer practical questions that confront librarians in applying the principles of intellectual freedom to library services. Sections cover the history and interpretation of the Library Bill of Rights and Freedom to Read, intellectual freedom and the law, dealing with censorship, assistance from ALA, and an annotated reading list. Practical and useful tool.

HD18. Branin, Joseph J. "Collection Management and Intellectual Freedom." In *Collection Management for the 1990s,* edited by Joseph J. Branin, 148–55. Chicago: American Library Association, 1993.

Discusses the influence of intellectual freedom on collection management. Addresses self-censorship as well as external attempts at censorship. Bibliography.

HD19. Osburn, Charles B. "Impact of Collection Management Practices on Intellectual Freedom. *Library Trends* 39, nos. 1/2 (Summer/Fall 1990): 168–82.

Osburn identifies collection management practices that have the potential to impede freedom of access to information.

HD20. Reichman, Henry. *Censorship and Selection: Issues and Answers for Schools.* Chicago: American Library Association, 1988.

A joint publication of the ALA and the American Association of School Administrators. Includes a chapter on establishing selection policies. Appendixes of sample letters, statements, guidelines, tips on preparing selections policies, etc. No index.

NONPRINT MEDIA, INCLUDING COMPUTER FILES

Nonprint media, for the purposes of this chapter, include materials such as audio and video recordings, slides, films, photos, drawings, filmstrips, computer software, computer files, CD-ROM, and realia. Several terms are often used interchangeably with nonprint media; they include nonbook media, multimedia, audiovisual media, and even media (as a term for everything except conventional print materials). The selection of computer files is a topic of great interest among collection development librarians; sources listed here explore their importance along with associated problems.

HD21. Brady, Mary Louise, Ilene F. Rockman, and David B. Walch. "Audio and Visual Materials." In *Collection Management: A New Treatise,* edited by Charles B. Osburn and Ross Atkinson, 223–54. Greenwich, Conn.: JAI Press, 1991.

A review of the changes in audiovisual librarianship over the last several years and a look to the future. Authors consider budget and focus on the selection and management of the major types of audiovisual materials (visuals, audio, realia, film/video/television, satellite technology, hypercard, and optical media). Lists of selected reviewing resources.

HD22. Clark, Katie. *Management of CD-ROM Databases in ARL Libraries.* SPEC Kit, no. 169. Washington, D.C.: Office of Management Services, Association of Research Libraries, 1990.

Kit looks at funding, instruction, publicity, organization, equipment, security, staffing, and selection of CD-ROM databases in ARL libraries. Includes six CD-ROM selection policies.

HD23. Demas, Sam. "Mainstreaming Electronic Formats." *Library Acquisitions: Practice and Theory* 13, no. 3 (1989): 227–32.

Demas offers three strategic questions to ask when formulating collection policy on electronic publications: criteria, service implications, and the skills necessary to select and manage electronic information.

HD24. Ellison, John W., and Patricia Ann Coty, eds. *Nonbook Media: Collection Management and User Services.* Chicago: American Library Association, 1987.

Chapters on twenty-two different media, ranging from film and microformats to holographs and computer files. Each chapter defines the medium and presents a brief history, unique characteristics, advantages and disadvantages, selection criteria, and maintenance and management advice. Bibliographies with each chapter. Does not include CD-ROM or mixed media; concluding bibliography of evaluative and nonevaluative periodicals.

HD25. Ferguson, Anthony W. "Assessing the Collection Development Need for CD-ROM Products." *Library Acquisitions: Practice and Theory* 12, nos. 3/4 (1988): 325–32.

Ferguson provides eight criteria for determining which CD-ROMs should be acquired. These can serve as useful reminders for any library evaluating nontraditional formats.

HD26. Fothergill, Richard, and Ian Butchart. *Non-Book Materials in Libraries: A Practical Manual.* 3rd ed. London: Clive Bingley, 1990.

A definitive work on nonbook materials. British slant, but valuable for all readers. Manual begins with historical overview of the evolution of nonbook materials (visual materials, sound recordings, computer files, laser disks, CDs, etc.). Includes definitions. Concludes with useful bibliography.

HD27. Gaunt, Marianne I. "Machine-Readable Literary Texts: Collection Development Issues." *Collection Management* 13, nos. 1/2 (1990): 87–99.

Gaunt identifies the specific problems surrounding the acquisition and use of machine-readable literary texts in libraries. She advises librarians to become actively involved in scholarly networks and discussions in order to address scholars' concerns and to play a role in the future development of machine-readable literary texts.

HD28. *Guide to the Acquisition of CD-ROMs, Software, and Similar Materials Published in Electronic Format.* Chicago: American Library Association, 1993 (forthcoming).

Prepared by the Acquisitions Section of ALCTS, this guide will cover both the selection and acquisition of electronic formats, addressing technological and service concerns along with copyright, licensing, leasing and rental agreements, and the importance of standards. (Note: Title may vary.)

HD29. Intner, Sheila S. "Selecting Software." *Library Acquisitions: Practice and Theory* 13, no. 3 (1989): 233–40.

Intner enumerates the important considerations to be made in selecting software. She suggests selection tools and criteria.

HD30. Jascó, Péter. *CD-ROM Software, Dataware, and Hardware: Evaluation, Selection, and Installation.* Database Searching Series, no. 4. Englewood, Colo.: Libraries Unlimited, 1992.

Author reviews the most characteristic features of CD-ROM databases and the computer facilities required to use them. Intent is to help librarians evaluate, compare, select, install, and operate CD-ROM products. A comprehensive, thorough tool, complete with sources of information for selection and purchase and sample evaluation forms. Lists directories and catalogs.

HD31. Johnson, Margaret. "Adding Computer Files to the Research Library: Issues in Collection Management and Development." In *Computer Files and the Research Library*, edited by Constance C. Gould, 3–13. Mountain View, Calif.: Research Libraries Group, 1990.

Author introduces computer files as an increasingly important resource and discusses whether collection development should treat computer files differently from other formats. She suggests that they will need special attention until they are as familiar as standard print sources and identifies the specific areas that need consideration.

HD32. LaGuardia, Cheryl, and Stella Bentley. "Electronic Databases: Will Old Collection Development Policies Still Work?" *ONLINE* 16, no. 4 (July 1992): 60–63.

Authors advise that the collections criteria in most libraries have failed to anticipate fully the implications of buying decisions for CD-ROMs and computer files. Authors identify eleven questions that should be asked when selecting these formats and suggest other related issues that need attention.

HD33. Metz, Paul. "Software and Nonbibliographic Databases." In *Collection Management: A New Treatise*, edited by Charles B. Osburn and Ross Atkinson, 255–70. Greenwich, Conn.: JAI Press, 1991.

Metz introduces fundamental differences among the wide range of products accessible through the personal computer. Lists selection tools for software.

HD34. Scholtz, James C. *Developing and Maintaining Video Collections in Libraries.* Santa Barbara, Calif.: ABC Clio Information Services, 1989.

See also annotation under IIF6. A how-to manual for video collections and service development for public libraries, useful also for library systems and school libraries. Covers establishing a collection development rationale, setting goals, community surveys, developing selection policies, and collection evaluation. Scope limited to the ½-inch videocassette, but application to other video formats. Includes sample collection development policy and list of video selection sources.

HD35. Shreeves, Edward. "Between the Visionaries and the Luddites: Collection Development and Electronic Resources in the Humanities." *Library Trends* 40 (Spring 1992): 579–95.

Shreeves identifies issues that should concern collection development librarians in determining the role of computer files in building collections in the humanities as well as making particular purchase decisions. Addresses standards, software, and selection criteria.

SERIALS

Serials, because of title proliferation and rapid cost increases, are an area of primary concern to collection management librarians. Serials pricing is treated in depth in Chapter G, Serials Management. Serials cancellation is covered in HF, following.

HD36. Hastreiter, Jamie, Larry Hardesty, and David Henderson, comps. *Periodicals in College Libraries.* CLIP Notes, no. 8. Chicago: College Library Information Packet Committee, College Libraries Section, Association of College & Research Libraries, 1987.

Reports results of survey of college libraries. Includes sections on guidelines for selection of periodicals, collection development policies, evaluation, retention and storage policies, and weeding policies.

HD37. Heitshu, Sara C., and J. Travis Leach. "Developing Serial Collections in the 1990s." In *Collection Management: Current Issues*, edited by Sarah Shoemaker, 53–59. New York: Neal-Schuman Publishers, 1989.

Authors discuss the range of issues associated with developing serial collections and provide a literature review. They describe the economic problems associated with serials collections.

USING SELECTION TOOLS

HD38. Gorman, G. E., and J. J. Mills. "Evaluating Third World National Bibliographies as Selection Resources."

Library Acquisitions: Practice and Theory 12, no. 1 (1988): 29–42.

A careful evaluation of national bibliographies as selection tools that considers currency, comprehensiveness, and accuracy; includes tables.

HD39. Parker, Jean McGruer. "Scholarly Book Reviews in Literature Journals as Collection Development Sources for Librarians." *Collection Management* 11, nos. 1/2 (1989): 41–57.

Parker looks at how reviews affect selection; notes that scholarly journals are a major source for selection in large libraries, despite drawbacks in timeliness.

HD40. Reed-Scott, Jutta. "Typology of Selection Tools." In *Collection Management: A New Treatise*, edited by Charles B. Osburn and Ross Atkinson, 301–11. Greenwich, Conn.: JAI Press, 1991.

Reed-Scott offers a taxonomy of selection sources and overview of type of tools; does not list specific titles.

HE
Collection Management in Specific Subject Areas, Collections, and Types of Libraries

While much of the practice of collection management remains constant across disciplines and throughout libraries, much depends also on the specific subject area, collection, or type of library in which the librarian is working. The following sources can provide guidance for those working or interested in working in each specialty.

ACADEMIC AND RESEARCH LIBRARIES

HE1. Hill, Joanne Schneider, William E. Hannaford, Jr., and Ronald H. Epp, eds. *Collection Development in College Libraries*. Chicago: American Library Association, 1991.

Designed to compensate for the emphasis in the literature on collection development in university libraries. Papers address differences of college libraries, emerging issues, effective collection development, role of faculty, and trends in collection development; includes bibliographic essay on collection development in academic libraries since 1940.

HE2. Jenkins, Clare, and Mary Morley, eds. *Collection Management in Academic Libraries*. Aldershot, Eng., and Brookfield, Vt.: Gower Publishing Co., 1991.

Intended to add to the limited UK professional literature on collection development in academic libraries. Articles on finance and budgeting, performance measurement, impact of automation, influence of the library user, serials, nonbook materials, and cooperative collection development. Useful glossary. Intended for the academic library administrator and secondarily for library science students.

HE3. Johnson, Richard D. "The College Library Collection." *Advances in Librarianship* 14 (1986): 143–74.

Comprehensive overview of collection management in college and undergraduate libraries. Johnson includes practical discussion of standards for the college library collection, selection of the collection, components of the collection, acquisition, resource sharing. Extensive bibliography.

HE4. Miller, Arthur H., Jr. "Small Academic Libraries." In *Collection Management: A New Treatise*, edited by Charles B. Osburn and Ross Atkinson, 417–43. Greenwich, Conn.: JAI Press, 1991.

Miller looks at the environmental backgrounds of small academic libraries at the end of this century—factors external to the institution along with trends on campus. He relates these to changes emerging overall in the small academic library and draws conclusions for collection development.

APPLIED AND INTERDISCIPLINARY FIELDS

HE5. Metz, Paul, and Bela Foltin, Jr. "A *Social History of Madness*—or, Who's Buying This Round? Anticipating and Avoiding Gaps in Collection Development." *College & Research Libraries* 51 (1990): 33–39.

Authors suggest that the internal organization of collection development and the nature of science and scholarship lead to inevitable gaps in collection development in academic libraries. They identify seven nondisciplinary and interdisciplinary areas especially vulnerable to oversight and suggest remedies to prevent their perpetuation.

HE6. Shapiro, Beth J., and John Whaley, eds. *Selection of Library Materials in Applied and Interdisciplinary Fields*. Chicago: American Library Association, 1987.

A guidebook of practical information for new selectors, who have little knowledge of the subjects, and of value as a useful refresher for experienced bibliographers. Sections are agriculture, business and management, communication arts and sciences, criminal justice, education, engineering, environmental studies, geography and maps, health sciences, home economics, law, public administration and policy sciences, race and ethnic studies, the radical left and right, social work, sports and recreation, urban planning, and women's studies. Each chapter concludes with a list of selection sources.

AREA STUDIES AND FOREIGN MATERIALS

HE7. Johns, Cecily A., ed. *Selection of Library Materials for Area Studies.* Chicago: American Library Association, 1990– .

Planned as a multivolume set. An invaluable resource addressed to the novice area-studies librarian who has to identify and select materials to support the curricular and research needs of an academic institution or to satisfy the needs of immigrants who patronize the local public library. Each essay describes current and retrospective sources for identifying materials and includes names and addresses of local book dealers. Vol. 1, edited by David Block, covers Asia, Iberia, the Caribbean and Latin America, Eastern Europe and the Soviet Union, and the South Pacific. (Note: The essays on Eastern Europe and the Soviet Union were written before the political and economic changes that began in the early 1990s.)

HE8. Pritchard, Sarah M. "Foreign Acquisitions." In *Collection Management: A New Treatise*, edited by Charles B. Osburn and Ross Atkinson, 351–72. Greenwich, Conn.: JAI Press, 1991.

A survey of the collection development issues surrounding the demand for and acquisition of foreign materials, and a review of the historical background and current trends in the publishing industry and in library collecting. Directed primarily to academic and research libraries.

GOVERNMENT PUBLICATIONS

HE9. Ekhaml, Leticia T., and Alice J. Wittig. *U.S. Government Publications for the School Library Media Center.* 2nd ed. Englewood, Colo.: Libraries Unlimited, 1991.

An annotated bibliography of more than 500 current federal publications useful in school library media centers. Includes brief review of U.S. government information collecting and disseminating activities.

HE10. Hernon, Peter, and Gary R. Purcell. *Developing Collections of U.S. Government Publications.* Foundations of Library and Information Science, vol. 12. Greenwich, Conn.: JAI Press, 1982.

Comprehensive overview of collection development as applied to federal government publications, concentrating on selection of Government Printing Office (GPO) depository titles. Includes literature survey on government publications collection development and a model collection development policy. Appendix contains reprints of sample collection development policies for government publications.

HE11. Lane, Margaret T. *Selecting and Organizing State Government Publications.* Chicago: American Library Association, 1987.

Useful guide for selection and acquisition of state government publications. Valuable for all librarians working with government documents.

HE12. Rozkuszka, W. David. "Government Publications." In *Collection Management: A New Treatise*, edited by Charles B. Osburn and Ross Atkinson, 207–22. Greenwich, Conn.: JAI Press, 1991.

Rozkuszka looks at document bibliography and resulting collection management in a global and philosophical sense. Useful selected bibliography.

HE13. Williams, Wiley J. *Subject Guide to Major United States Government Publications.* 2nd ed. Chicago: American Library Association, 1987.

Selectively identifies federal publications of permanent importance published between 1789 and 1986. Annotated citations, arranged by subject. Intended for documents and reference librarians and for library science students.

HUMANITIES, SOCIAL SCIENCES, AND SCIENCES

HE14. Gould, Constance C. *Information Needs in the Humanities: An Assessment.* Stanford, Calif.: Research Libraries Group, 1988.

One of the series by RLG prepared for the Program for Information Management (PRIMA). Provides a broad view of the shape of each of eight humanities disciplines and explores the relationship between trends and data requirements. Covers classical studies, history, history of art, literature, philosophy, religion, music, and linguistics.

HE15. Gould, Constance C., and Karla Pearce. *Information Needs in the Sciences: An Assessment.* Mountain View, Calif.: Research Libraries Group, 1991.

Another publication in the RLG PRIMA series, this discusses the nature of research and information in the fields of physics, chemistry, biology, geosciences, astronomy, engineering, mathematics, and computer science. Observations of the information that educators and researchers value can provide guidance to collection development librarians.

HE16. Gould, Constance C., and Mark Handler. *Information Needs in the Social Sciences: An Assessment.* Mountain View, Calif.: Research Libraries Group, 1989.

Another in RLG's PRIMA series. Disciplines addressed are economics, political science, sociology, psychology, and anthropology. Intended as an information needs assessment that can help determine future collection and information management for libraries. Stresses the interdisciplinary nature of the social sciences, importance of government documents, access to current research, and dependence on computer files of all types.

HE17. McClung, Patricia A., ed. *Selection of Library Materials in the Humanities, Social Sciences, and Sciences.* Chicago: American Library Association, 1985.

Collection of essays introducing specific sources for selecting materials in the humanities, social sciences, and sciences. Chapters cover general considerations, selection sources and strategies, buying out-of-print books, serials,

English and American literature, history, philosophy and religion, art and architectural history, music, sociology, anthropology, economics and political science, psychology, scientific and technical materials, biology, computer science, mathematics, physics and astronomy, government publications, small presses, microforms, nonprint media, machine-readable data files. Most essays include a general overview of the literature; a section on selection methodology; and a list of selection sources. Nearly nine hundred references to reviewing media and selection sources.

HE18. McPheron, William, general ed., with Stephen Lehmann, Craig S. Likness, and Marcia J. Pankake, eds. *English and American Literature: Sources and Strategies for Collection Development.* ACRL Publications in Librarianship, no. 45. Chicago: American Library Association, 1987.

Essays on building collections of English and American literature for academic libraries. Each essay contains detailed bibliographies and presents a practical approach to each of the areas. The overview includes an excellent statement of how to write a collection development policy. Addresses acquisitions, selection tools, retrospective collection development, serials and selection of editions, nonprint media resources, reference collections, and special collections.

PUBLIC LIBRARIES

HE19. Baker, Sharon L. "Public Libraries." In *Collection Management: A New Treatise*, edited by Charles B. Osburn and Ross Atkinson, 395–416. Greenwich, Conn.: JAI Press, 1991.

Baker identifies marketing as extremely important for public libraries. She explores the effects of two trends (in-depth community analysis and the growing perception of collection management as an integrated three-step cycle) on collection management in public libraries.

HE20. Serebnick, Judith, ed. *Collection Management in Public Libraries; Proceedings of a Preconference to the 1984 ALA Annual Conference, June 21-22, 1984, Dallas, Texas.* Chicago: American Library Association, 1986.

Papers intended to address the limited attention given to public libraries in much of the literature of collection development. Authors examine collection management functions, guidelines, budgeting, and organizational patterns from a public library point of view and investigate how automation can aid collection management.

REFERENCE COLLECTIONS

HE21. Haar, John M. "The Reference Collection Development Decision: Will New Information Technologies Influence Libraries' Collecting Patterns?" *The Reference Librarian* 22 (1988): 113–24.

Haar discusses the new generation of automated reference tools and developing selection criteria.

HE22. Katz, William A. "Evaluating Reference Sources." In *Introduction to Reference Work.* vol. 1, Basic Information Sources, 23–30. 5th ed. New York: McGraw-Hill, 1987.

Covers the selection of individual reference works and discusses criteria: purpose, authority, scope, audience, and format.

HE23. Neeley, Jim, ed. *Reference Collection Development: A Bibliography.* RASD Occasional Paper, no. 11. Chicago: Reference and Adult Services Division, American Library Association, 1991.

A bibliography of materials published between 1977 and the end of 1989 on the development, evaluation, and management of reference collections serving adults in academic and public libraries. Includes publications treating CD-ROM in reference collections.

SCHOOL LIBRARY MEDIA CENTERS

HE24. Callison, Daniel. "A Review of the Research Related to School Library Media Collections: Part I" and "Part II." *School Library Media Quarterly* 19 (Fall 1990): 57–62; (Winter 1990/1991): 117–21.

Comprehensive review of research related to library media collection management. Callison addresses budgets and collection size, selection process, collection policies, evaluation, networking and collection mapping, student preference, and special collections. Extensive references.

HE25. Kemp, Betty, ed. *School Library and Media Center Acquisitions Policies and Procedures.* 2nd ed. Phoenix: Oryx Press, 1986.

Kemp has compiled policies, procedures, and forms used for collections building by schools and media centers. She begins with a useful review of the literature on selection and acquisitions processes that affect school libraries. Discusses the impact of microcomputers on school library media centers.

HE26. Van Orden, Phyllis J. *The Collection Program in Schools: Concepts, Practices, and Information Sources.* Englewood, Colo.: Libraries Unlimited, 1988.

An introductory text that provides an overview of the processes and procedures associated with developing, maintaining, and evaluating a collection at the building level; covers the school media program setting, materials selection (including visual materials), and administrative concerns. Bibliographies with each chapter. Appendixes list selection tools, plus associations and agencies offering services and/or publications of interest to media specialists.

HE27. _____. "School Libraries." In *Collection Management: A New Treatise*, edited by Charles B. Osburn and

Ross Atkinson, 445–67. Greenwich, Conn.: JAI Press, 1991.

Van Orden examines the evolution of the collection in school library media centers. Considers concerns with censorship and reviews, plus contemporary issues of networking, resource sharing, technology, and evaluation. Lengthy bibliography.

HE28. White, Brenda H., ed. *Collection Management for School Library Media Centers.* New York: Haworth Press, 1986. Also published as *Collection Management* 7, nos. 3/4 (Fall/Winter 1985–86).

A collection of theoretical and practical articles by library media specialists and library educators. Covers collection development, networking and collection development, school and public library cooperation, collections management in specific areas and formats, and intellectual freedom. Contains a selected and partially annotated bibliography.

SMALL LIBRARIES

HE29. Cassell, Marianne K., and Grace W. Greene. *Collection Development in the Small Library.* LAMA Small Libraries Publications, no.17. Chicago: Library Administration and Management Association, American Library Association, 1991.

Small practical guide, written exclusively for the small library. Addresses policy making and planning, selecting books and other media, weeding, using statistics. Reviews general collection principles and then applies them to specific collecting activities.

SPECIAL COLLECTIONS, ARCHIVES, AND SPECIAL LIBRARIES

HE30. Abraham, Terry. "Collection Policy or Documentation Strategy: Theory and Practice." *American Archivist* 54 (Winter 1991): 44–53.

An informative paper that compares and contrasts documentation strategy and collection development. Defines documentation strategy as understood by the archivist. Author reviews thirty years of archival literature.

HE31. Erdman, Christine, comp. *Special Collections in College Libraries.* CLIP Note, no. 6. Chicago: Association of College & Research Libraries, American Library Association, 1986.

Designed to assist librarians who are considering expanding or refining special collections, this work presents the results of a survey on special collections and contains documents from libraries on projects and activities, publicity, financial support, archives, preservation and security, and use policies.

HE32. Grabowski, John J. "Fragments or Components: Theme Collections in a Local Setting." *American Archivist* 48 (Summer 1985): 304–14.

Description of collecting policy at the Western Reserve Historical Society. Identifies three factors that have contributed to its success.

HE33. Reed-Scott, Jutta. "Collection Management Strategies for Archivists." *American Archivist* 47, no. 1 (Winter 1984): 23–29.

Reed-Scott suggests how the functions of collection management (planning, efficient selection, evaluation and analysis, and cooperative collection development and resource sharing) can assist archivists in effectively carrying out their responsibilities.

HE34. Ryan, Michael T. "Developing Special Collections in the 90s: A fin-de-siecle Perspective." *The Journal of Academic Librarianship* 17 (1991): 288–93.

Ryan calls for a reevaluation of what special collections should be about. He stresses the need to pay attention to what is being collected and how it fits into the institution and the national collection.

HE35. _____. "Special Collections." In *Collection Management: A New Treatise,* edited by Charles B. Osburn and Ross Atkinson, 173–206. Greenwich, Conn.: JAI Press, 1991.

Ryan provides a comprehensive view of an overall program for developing and managing special collections. He looks at selection policies, acquisition of special collections, the marketplace for rare books and manuscripts, and the antiquarian book trade, and examines programmatic aspects of special collections management. Useful notes and references, including lists of reference tools and catalogs for special collections development.

HE36. Sullivan, Michele. "Special Libraries." In *Collection Management: A New Treatise,* edited by Charles B. Osburn and Ross Atkinson, 469–76. Greenwich, Conn.: JAI Press, 1991.

Sullivan identifies factors affecting collection development in special libraries and briefly discusses selection processes. Examines new technologies in the special library.

WOMEN'S STUDIES

HE37. Ariel, Joan, ed. *Building Women's Studies Collections: A Resource Guide.* Bibliographic Essay Series, no. 8. Chicago: American Library Association, 1987.

A guide intended to assist selectors in academic libraries in identifying and obtaining women's studies materials. Contains eighteen categories of published materials or sources for women's studies including print, audiovisual, and electronic media. All references are annotated. Includes information on publishers, organizations, review media, bookstores, and book dealers.

HF
Collection Maintenance

Collection maintenance is an umbrella term covering the decisions collection management librarians make and the processes they initiate to deal with materials already in the collection. These decisions and processes should be a regular part of an effective collection management program, but often become critical because of budget, condition, or space limitations. Maintenance decisions are also made when materials are no longer relevant to the user population and when materials in a general collection need special handling for security and other reasons. Decisions about which materials to replace, duplicate, preserve, and move to storage are part of the maintenance process. Preservation involves its own complex choices among various treatments.

Since so much emphasis traditionally has been placed on collection building, collection development librarians are often less comfortable removing materials. They use several terms to talk about their responsibilities when the topic is taking items out of the collection and canceling journal subscriptions. The sources cited here discuss weeding, pruning, withdrawal, deselection, deaccession, and bookstock control.

WEEDING AND STORAGE

HF1. Association of College & Research Libraries Rare Books and Manuscripts Section Ad Hoc Committee for Developing Transfer Guidelines. "Guidelines on the Selection of General Collection Materials for Transfer to Special Collections." *College & Research Libraries News* 46, no. 7 (July/Aug. 1985): 349–52.

These guidelines address librarians' responsibility to identify rare and valuable materials in general and open stack collections and to arrange for their transfer to the greater security of special collections departments.

HF2. Bellanti, Claire Q. "Implementing the Decision: The Mechanics of Selecting Materials to Store and Changing Their Records." In *The Great Divide: Challenges in Remote Storage*, edited by James R. Kennedy and Gloria J. Stockton, 17–24. Chicago: American Library Association, 1991.

Author discusses the nitty-gritty work of selecting specific titles for storage after criteria have been decided and identifies processes for changing the appropriate bibliographic records.

HF3. Clark, Lenore, ed. *Guide to Review of Library Collections: Preservation, Storage, and Withdrawal.* Collection Management and Development Guides, no. 5. Chicago: American Library Association, 1991.

Intended to assist librarians and others who are involved in reviewing materials for preservation, storage, or withdrawal. It identifies various elements of the review process and describes goals, criteria, and methods for making decisions about physical disposition of materials. Lengthy bibliography and glossary.

HF4. Lucker, Jay K., Kate S. Herzog, and Sydney J. Owens. "Weeding Collections in an Academic Library System: Massachusetts Institute of Technology." *Science & Technology Libraries* 6, no. 3 (Spring 1986): 11–23.

Practical advice on weeding—an excellent analysis of a successful weeding program at MIT, a zero-growth institution. Weeding includes decisions to store, convert print to microform, and discard, as well as careful selection and a willingness to discard purchased materials prior to cataloging if examination shows an item is outside scope.

HF5. Mosher, Paul H. "Reviewing for Preservation, Storage, and Weeding." In *Collection Management: A New Treatise*, edited by Charles B. Osburn and Ross Atkinson, 373–91. Greenwich, Conn.: JAI Press, 1991.

Covers benefits and problems of weeding. Mosher provides historical background, plus methods. Sample form.

HF6. Paquette, Judith. "What Goes to the Storage Facility: Options and Consequences." In *The Great Divide*, edited by James R. Kennedy and Gloria J. Stockton, 3–16. Chicago: American Library Association, 1991.

Paquette presents issues in the political process of deciding what goes into remote storage. She considers selection criteria for storage of dead or little-used materials.

HF7. Pierce, Sydney J., ed. *Weeding and Maintenance of Reference Collections.* New York: Haworth Press, 1990. Also published as *The Reference Librarian* no. 29 (1990).

Thirteen articles dealing with institutional context, policy decisions, and programs for evaluating and weeding. Several authors examine impact of CD-ROM services.

HF8. Slote, Stanley J. *Weeding Library Collections: Library Weeding Methods.* 3rd ed. Littleton, Colo.: Libraries Unlimited, 1989.

A useful tool that combines principles with practical techniques. Describes four methods of weeding in detail. Describes arguments for and against weeding. Thorough literature review.

HF9. Streit, Samuel A. "Transfer of Materials from General Stacks to Special Collections." *Collection Management* 7, no. 2 (Summer 1985): 33–46.

Examines transfers of materials to special collections as part of collection management in light of concerns with collection development policies, preservation, and security. Describes methods for a successful transfer program.

PRESERVATION

See also Chapters I, Preservation, and J, Reproduction of Library Materials.

HF10. Atkinson, Ross. "Selection for Preservation: A Materialistic Approach." *Library Resources & Technical Services* 30 (Oct./Dec. 1986): 341–53.

Author examines theoretical strategies of individual libraries when choosing priorities for preservation and conservation. Introduces a typology of preservation consisting of three classes of preservation priorities and actions.

HF11. Kwater, Elizabeth. "Preservation Issues: How to Achieve More with Less." In *Acquisitions '91*, edited by David C. Genaway, 169–87. Canfield, Ohio: Genaway and Associates, 1991.

Short overview of library preservation, placing it within the context of collection management. Useful for anyone new to collection development. Kwater defines terms and presents a practical summary of preservation problems and possible solutions.

HF12. Mareck, Robert. "Practicum on Preservation." In *Collection Management for the 1990s*, edited by Joseph J. Branin, 114–26. Chicago: American Library Association, 1993.

Provides a framework for the preservation selection process and discusses decision making. Defines treatment options and their pros and cons. Includes sample evaluation form.

HF13. *Selection for Preservation of Research Library Materials.* Washington, D.C.: Commission on Preservation and Access, 1989.

Brief summary of the factors that should affect selection of library items and subcollections for preservation microfilming. Considers disciplinary differences, approaches to selection, and factors affecting the choice of approach.

HF14. Williams, Lisa B. "Selecting Rare Books for Physical Conservation: Guidelines for Decision Making." *College & Research Libraries* 46, no. 2 (Mar. 1985): 153–59.

Williams discusses the rationale for, and possible uses of, a decision-making model to guide conservation decisions. The model systematically weighs such factors as monetary, intellectual, and aesthetic value; projected use; and usability.

SERIALS CANCELLATION

See also Chapter G, Serials Management.

HF15. Degener, Christie T., and Marjory A. Waite. "Using an Automated Serials System to Assist with Collection Review and Cancellations." *Serials Review* 17, no. 1 (Spring 1991): 13–20.

Authors describe an evaluation methodology using criteria, weights, options, and values developed in the

Health Sciences Library, University of North Carolina/ Chapel Hill. This methodology uses an automated serials control system to store the data, assist with serials collection review, and guide cancellation decisions. Includes tables.

HF16. Farrell, David. *Serials Control and Deselection Projects.* SPEC Kit, no. 147. Washington, D.C.: Office of Management Studies, Association of Research Libraries, 1988.

Kit contains documents collected from ARL libraries who were conducting or had recently conducted serials review and cancellation projects in mid-1988. Sample reports, instructions, appeals, lists of canceled titles, and articles from campus and library newsletters.

HF17. Hunt, Richard K. "Journal Deselection in a Biomedical Research Library: A Mediated Mathematical Approach." *Bulletin of the Medical Library Association* 78 (Jan. 1990): 45–48.

Suggests a formula that calculates an institutional cost ratio for titles, based on factors such as local use, costs for subscription, interlibrary loans, and staffing.

HF18. Metz, Paul. "Thirteen Steps to Avoiding Bad Luck in a Serial Cancellation Project." *The Journal of Academic Librarianship* 18, no. 2 (1992): 76–82.

Metz recommends thirteen steps to ensure a successful cancellation project based on experience canceling $300,000 worth of journals in the University Libraries, Virginia Tech. Practical, down-to-earth approach.

HF19. Miller, Edward P., and Ann L. O'Neill. "Journal Deselection and Costing." *Library Acquisitions: Practice and Theory* 14, no. 2 (1990): 173–78.

Authors review earlier attempts to quantify the deselection process and propose a flexible model, incorporating several elements, including the opinion of local experts on the quality of journals.

HF20. Ventress, Alan. "Use Surveys and Collection Analysis: A Prelude to Serials Rationalization." *Library Acquisitions: Practice and Theory* 15, no. 1 (1991): 109–18.

Examines the evaluation of a serials collection in a large research library (State Library of New South Wales) prior to a cancellation program. Ventress describes surveys of use and collection analyses, plus the use of microcomputer software to do statistical analysis.

HG
Budget and Finance

The materials budget may take a variety of forms and be called the book budget, materials budget, resources budget, or information budget. Effective budgets serve as tools for planning, monitoring, and communicating collection management activities.

ALLOCATION

Allocation is the process of distributing monies or funds among different subject areas, collections, and formats. Because of competing needs and limited funds, this is one of the more troubling areas. Much has been and continues to be written about the pros and cons of various allocation approaches, particularly about formula-based allocation.

HG1. Budd, John M. "Allocation Formulas in the Literature: A Review." *Library Acquisitions: Practice and Theory* 15, no. 1 (1991): 95–107.

Helpful historical review of allocation formulas. Author ties together the concerns about formulas that various authors have articulated.

HG2. Freeman, Michael S. "Allocation Formulas as Management Tools in College Libraries: Useful or Misapplied?" In *Collection Development in College Libraries*, edited by Joanne Schneider Hill, William E. Hannaford, Jr., and Ronald H. Epp, 71–77. Chicago: American Library Association, 1991.

A critical assessment of use of formula allocation in college libraries; provides sample formulas.

HG3. Genaway, David C. "Administering the Allocated Acquisitions Budget: Achieving a Balanced Matrix." In *The Acquisitions Budget*, edited by Bill Katz, 145–67. New York: Haworth Press, 1989.

Outlines the problems of administering a systematically allocated library acquisitions budget in an academic environment in the context of multiple formats and fund accounts. Suggests guidelines for working with an allocated budget.

HG4. Lowry, Charles B. "Reconciling Pragmatism, Equity, and Need in the Formula Allocation of Book and Serials Funds." *College & Research Libraries* 53, no. 4 (Mar. 1992): 121–38.

Comprehensive introduction to a matrix formula for allocating funds used at the University of Texas at Arlington. This formula provides a method for determining the variables that best represent institutional goals, normalizing them, and explicitly determining the percent of funds allocated by the individual variable. Includes tables generated using the matrix formula.

HG5. Packer, Donna. "Acquisitions Allocations: Equity, Politics, and Formulas." *The Journal of Academic Librarianship* 14, no. 5 (Nov. 1988): 276–86.

Useful summaries and comparisons of twelve formula approaches for allocation. Packer describes successful

process used at Western Washington University Libraries to combine mathematical formulas with the reality of local campus politics in guiding allocation.

HG6. Schad, Jasper G. "Fairness in Book Fund Allocation." *College & Research Libraries* 48 (Nov. 1987): 479–86.

Highly original article in which Schad considers the issue of equity in budget allocation, drawing on research in social psychology. He identifies environmental factors affecting equitable allocation, principles that serve as a basis for equity in allocation, measures in applying those principles, and procedural rules of allocation.

HG7. Shreeves, Edward, ed. *Guide to Budget Allocation for Information Resources.* Collection Management and Development Guides, no. 4. Chicago: American Library Association, 1991.

Intended to assist librarians making information resources budget allocations by describing the character and function of the budget document, stating allocation principles, presenting an array of considerations and options for application to the local budget allocation process, and enumerating sources of information helpful to that process. A hands-on tool. Includes bibliography and glossary, plus appendix of "Sources of price information about library materials."

HG8. Werking, Richard Hume. "Allocating the Academic Library's Book Budget: Historical Perspective and Current Reflections." *The Journal of Academic Librarianship* 14 (July 1990): 140–44.

Werking examines major allocation issues and cautions against relying solely on formulas for allocation. A concise historical review of the process of allocation resources going back to 1908.

BUDGETING

Budgeting covers all aspects of working with a library's materials budget. It is a process rather than a product. Budgeting looks at need and demand, priorities and possibilities. Budgeting covers preparing the desired budget, presenting it to the funding arm of the parent institution, distributing funds, monitoring expenditures and balances, being accountable, and revising the budget in light of these areas.

HG9. Blake, Virgil L. P., and Renee Tjoumas. "Determining Budgets for School Library Media Centers." *Collection Building* 9, no. 2 (1989): 12–18.

Authors summarize the approaches used by school and academic librarians, indicate similarities, and identify elements contained in academic library methodologies that might apply to school library media centers. Useful bibliography.

HG10. Brownson, Charles W. "Modeling Library Materials Expenditure: Initial Experiments of Arizona State University.'' *Library Resources & Technical Services* 35, no. 1 (Jan. 1991): 87–103.

Examines a quantitative model that attempts to explain variation in expenditure by subject in terms understandable as selection policy. Brownson proposes this model as a management tool that explicates the link between policy and selection practice while avoiding the controlled environment of allocation formulas.

HG11. Houbeck, Robert L., Jr. "Who Gets What: Allocating the Library's Materials Budget." In *Budgets for Acquisitions: Strategies for Serials, Monographs, and Electronic Formats*, edited by Sul H. Lee, 99–119. New York: Haworth Press, 1991.

Suggests possibilities for enhancing the library's profile on campus and opportunities for increased internal funding. Warns against allocating materials budgets according to simple perceived demand, especially in research collections.

HG12. Johnson, Peggy. *Materials Budgets in ARL Libraries.* SPEC Kit, no. 166. Washington, D.C.: Association of Research Libraries, Office of Management Studies, 1990.

Reports results of survey of ARL libraries regarding processes for budgeting, allocation of funds, personnel involved with allocation, impact of computer files on financial planning, and sources of funding. Includes sample documents on budgeting and allocation practices and policies.

HG13. Moskowitz, Mickey, and Joanne Schmidt. "Managing the College Library's Acquisitions Budget." In *The Acquisitions Budget*, edited by Bill Katz, 49–68. New York: Haworth Press, 1989.

Moskowitz and Schmidt examine the day-to-day monitoring of the acquisitions budget in a small to medium-sized college library. They consider the budget process, monitoring the budget and its divisions, define terms, present a timetable. Authors address books, approval plans, standing orders, and periodicals within the budgeting process. An excellent introduction to budgeting applicable to most libraries.

HG14. Wiemers, Eugene L., Jr. "Budget." In *Collection Management: A New Treatise*, edited by Charles B. Osburn and Ross Atkinson, 67–79. Greenwich, Conn.: JAI Press, 1991.

Looks at the materials budget as a tool that affects distribution of resources, reflects distribution of decision-making power over use of funds, and implies distribution of accountability and autonomy related to decision making.

HG15. _____. "Budgeting Methods for Collection Management." In *Collection Management for the 1990s*, edited by Joseph J. Branin, 105–13. Chicago: American Library Association, 1993.

Discusses library, institutional, and personal goals in budgeting. Defines types of budgets and their pros and cons.

USING COST AND PRICE INFORMATION

Most aspects of the budgeting process depend, to some extent, on cost and price information drawn from published sources. No single source provides all relevant information, and sources vary in the frequency with which they present updated information. Some librarians have created their own price indexes to compensate for the problems with external sources. This section will not list the sources for cost and price; such publications are too volatile. Instead, the following resources suggest the information that is necessary and appropriate ways in which to use it.

HG16. Carpenter, Kathryn Hammell. "Forecasting Expenditures for Library Materials: Approaches and Techniques." In *The Acquisitions Budget*, edited by Bill Katz, 31–48. New York: Haworth Press, 1989.

Identifies the competencies needed to forecast expenditures. Author considers economic factors, national price indexes, local cost studies, publishing industry and pricing, collection development practices, and techniques for money management. Extensive references.

HG17. Lynden, Fred C. "Cost Analysis of Monographs and Serials." *Journal of Library Administration* 12, no. 3 (1990): 19–40.

Lynden identifies categories of data to collect, appropriate methodology for analyzing the data, and how to present it, drawing from his experience at Brown University, Providence, Rhode Island.

HG18. Smith, Dennis. "Forecasting Price Increase Needs for Library Materials: The University of California Experience." *Library Resources & Technical Services* 28, no. 2 (Apr./June 1984): 136–48.

Presents the Voigt/Susskind acquisitions model, developed to assist with establishing adequate base book budgets and to measure price increase needs to maintain budgeted acquisition rates. Stresses the need to relate book fund needs to academic and research programs. Concludes with cautionary note that no method or model will work forever and requestors need to be prepared for change.

HG19. Welsch, Erwin K. "Price Versus Coverage: Calculating the Impact on Collection Development." *Library Research & Technical Services* 32, no. 2 (Apr. 1988): 159–63.

Proposes a formula that factors the change in percent of literature coverage and in size of the literature into funding cost to project financial need. Offers explanation and sample statistics.

DEVELOPMENT, GRANTS, AND FUND RAISING

The role of the collection management librarian in development activities and for raising funds and securing grants varies greatly between libraries. This is, however, becoming an increasingly important area in many institutions and one with which the collection development librarian should be familiar.

HG20. "Library Development: A Future Imperative." Edited by Dwight Burlingame. *Journal of Library Administration* 12, no. 4 (1990).

A special issue devoted to development and fund raising. Directed to library leaders, librarians, board members, and friends currently involved in fund raising; to those who are planning to get involved; and to academics and students of librarianship. Looks at philanthropy, public relations, special events, major donors, capital campaigns, endowment campaigns, planned giving.

HG21. Steele, Victoria, and Stephen D. Elder. *Becoming a Fundraiser: The Principles and Practice of Library Development.* Chicago: American Library Association, 1992.

Intended as a handbook for librarians engaged in or embarking on fundraising. Though primarily for library directors, includes advice useful to anyone involved in fund raising, soliciting gifts, and obtaining money from external agencies. Includes list of recommended readings.

HG22. Thompson, Ronelle K. H. "Supplementing Library Budgets Through Grants and Gifts." In *Acquisitions '91*, edited by David C. Genaway, 327–36. Canfield, Ohio: Genaway & Associates, 1991.

Author discusses grant opportunities and donors as possible sources of additional funding. Includes checklist for libraries exploring these avenues. Brief, but useful, list of sources for further information.

HH
Assessment and Evaluation

More has been published on how to analyze a collection than on any other topic in collection management—more than 700 articles since 1970. The terms *evaluation* and *assessment* have been used interchangeably by some authors; others distinguish between the two. Usually, the aim of evaluation is to determine how well the collection supports the goals, needs, and curriculum of the parent organization. Assessment seeks to examine or describe collections either in their own terms or relative to other collections and checklists. Both evaluation and assessment provide a better understanding of the collection and the community and so allow librarians to adjust the direction of library growth systematically in relation to the institution's needs.

Collection analysis is becoming an increasingly significant area as the benefits of and need for resource sharing have pointed out the need for more systematic techniques. Many of the tools developed over the last ten to twenty years have grown out of the need to compare and contrast collections systematically as part of cooperative or collaborative collection development. Sharing information in consistent format can lead to sharing collecting responsibilities as well. The Association of Research Libraries' Collection Analysis Project (CAP) was begun in the 1970s to analyze collections within institutional contexts and with hopes for increasing cooperative collection development.

Collection analysis techniques range from impressionistic, descriptive assessments to complex statistical analysis. Two topologies are used in discussing the various approaches to analysis. Techniques usually can be considered either use- or collection-based and either quantitative or qualitative. Use- and user-based approaches look at who is using materials, how often, and what their expectations are. Collection-based techniques examine the size, growth, and coverage of library materials. Quantitative analysis measures such finite areas as titles, circulation transactions, and dollars spent. Qualitative analysis considers the strengths and weaknesses of collections and user perceptions in more subjective ways and is dependent on personal opinion or the use of external lists.

The resources following offer guidelines for planning evaluation and assessment programs and projects, selecting and combining appropriate methodologies, reporting the results, and following the analysis with appropriate action. Most identify the benefits and disadvantages of each technique.

OVERVIEW

HH1. Doll, Carol A., and Pamela Petrick Barron. *Collection Analysis for the School Library Media Center: A Practical Approach.* Chicago: American Library Association, 1991.

Doll and Barron introduce a technique for gathering and analyzing information for decision making, measuring quality, and presenting fiscal needs. They discuss management objectives, weeding, communication with teachers, and library automation. Work defines terms, provides sample forms, has bibliographies. An extremely useful and practical guide for school media centers.

HH2. Endelman, Judith. "Looking Backward to Plan for the Future: Collection Analysis for Manuscript Depositories." *American Archivist* 50 (Summer 1987): 340–53.

Author describes three collection analysis projects that led to the development of new collecting priorities and strategies. Examines collection analysis as a useful managerial tool.

HH3. Hall, Blaine H. *Collection Assessment Manual for College and University Libraries.* Phoenix: Oryx Press, 1985.

This manual provides practical information to plan a collection assessment, select and apply appropriate measurement techniques, analyze the results, and report the findings. Many of the recommendations can be adopted by any library. Particularly useful appendixes: statistical aids, a list of accrediting groups, sample survey instruments, and reprints of five ACRL academic library standards documents.

HH4. Henige, David. "Value and Evaluation." In *Collection Management: A New Treatise*, edited by Charles B. Osburn and Ross Atkinson, 111–24. Greenwich, Conn.: JAI Press, 1991.

Henige looks at value, evaluation, and verification and discusses the daily, reflexive nature of evaluation.

HH5. Lockett, Barbara, ed. *Guide to the Evaluation of Library Collections.* Collection Management and Development Guides, no. 2. Chicago: American Library Association, 1989.

Practical tool, intended to provide a statement of principles and methods to guide in determining the extent to which a library acquires the books, journals, and other materials needed in order to satisfy users and fulfill the library's stated mission. Extensive bibliography.

HH6. Loertscher, David V. "The Elephant Technique of Collection Management." In *Collection Management for School Library Media Centers*, edited by Brenda H. White, 45–54. New York: Haworth Press, 1986.

Author presents an evaluation technique for school library media centers called collection mapping in which three collection segments are charted. Includes recommendations on how to use a collection map for evaluating and improving the collection.

HH7. MacEwan, Bonnie. "An Overview of Collection Assessment and Evaluation." In *Collection Management for the 1990s*, edited by Joseph J. Branin, 95–104. Chicago: American Library Association, 1993.

Brief descriptions of collection evaluation methods. Useful because of lengthy bibliography.

HH8. Nutter, Susan K. "Online Systems and the Management of Collections: Use and Implications." *Advances in Library Automation and Networking* 1 (1987): 125–49.

Covers the possibilities and problems of using statistics generated by automated library systems for collection evaluation.

HH9. Sandler, Mark. "Quantitative Approaches to Qualitative Collection Assessment." *Collection Building* 8, no. 4 (1988): 12–17.

Sandler explains that assessment can provide library and campus administrators more and better information on which to base decisions about funding and collection

management. Offers practical recommendations for conducting a collection evaluation and identifies seven questions that should be answered in the process of an evaluation project. Includes advice on data analysis.

HH10. Stielow, Frederick J., and Helen R. Tibbo. "Collection Analysis in Modern Librarianship: A Stratified, Multidimensional Model." *Collection Management* 11, nos. 3/4 (1989): 73–91.

Authors' model builds on the conspectus (see discussion of the conspectus preceding HH26). Accommodates a variety of analysis strategies and offers flexibility and tolerance for a variety of evaluative measures at the local and national levels; includes historical review of collection evaluation.

BIBLIOGRAPHIES

HH11. Kaag, Cynthia Stewart, comp., with the assistance of Sharon Lee Cann, and others. *Collection Evaluation Techniques: A Short, Selective, Practical, Current, Annotated Bibliography 1980–1990.* RASD Occasional Papers, no. 10. Chicago: Reference and Adult Services Division, American Library Association, 1991.

Designed to assist the planner/evaluator in choosing and implementing techniques for collection evaluation. Emphasizes practical goals and results. Brief glossary.

HH12. Nisonger, Thomas E. "An Annotated Bibliography of Items Relating to Collection Evaluation in Academic Libraries, 1969–1981." *College & Research Libraries* 43, no. 4 (July 1982): 300–11.

Approximately 100 annotated references that focus on case studies of evaluation projects, techniques, attempts to define adequacy in a collection, and overviews of the evaluation process.

HH13. _____. *Collection Evaluation in Academic Libraries: A Literature Guide and Annotated Bibliography.* Englewood, Colo.: Libraries Unlimited, 1992.

Contains more than 600 annotations to the literature of collection analysis, most published since 1980. Covers all forms of analysis, organized by broad subject. Author/title and subject indexes. Includes glossary.

QUANTITATIVE METHODS

Quantitative methods demonstrate growth and use of collections by looking at collection and circulation statistics, interlibrary loan requests, and budget information. Once a baseline is established, the size and growth (by title and volume counts) of a collection can be measured. The North American Title Count project (formerly the National Shelf List Count), sponsored by the ALA ALCTS Collection Management and Development Section, provides objective, comparative information about subject collections and rates of growth at participating institutions by counting titles in more than 600 Library of Congress (LC) classifications. Collection size formulas have been developed that use local variables to calculate the number of volumes needed to meet local need. The Clapp-Jordan formula (HH17) is one model for this approach. Existing collections then can be compared to that ideal specified by the formula. Some library standards provide formulas for deciding optimum collection size.

Circulation analysis or collection use study produced one of the more controversial statistical studies—that conducted at the University of Pittsburgh in the 1970s. This study (reported by Allen Kent and others in *Use of Library Materials: The University of Pittsburgh Study.* New York: Dekker, 1979) suggested that much of the collection in the University of Pittsburgh Library was not being used and implications were seen for past and future collection management practices. The 80/20 ratio, considered by several authors, suggests that 20 percent of a collection accounts for 80 percent of circulation. Questions remain whether frequency of book and journal circulation is an appropriate measure of academic library effectiveness. Circulation studies can provide guidance about which parts of the collection can be put in storage or withdrawn, as well as which areas need to be developed.

Other quantitative use studies examine in-library use, shelf availability, document delivery, and interlibrary lending and borrowing statistics. Measuring growth of the materials budget, changes in the ratio of expenditures for serials to those for monographs, and comparing allocations between subject areas are additional quantitative techniques for evaluating the relation of library operations to its goals and long-term mission.

HH14. Brancolini, Kristine R. "Use and User Studies for Collection Evaluation." In *Collection Management for the 1990s*, edited by Joseph J. Branin, 63–94. Chicago: American Library Association, 1993.

Describes and defines use and user studies for collection evaluation. Includes a questionnaire employed in a user survey at Indiana University. Bibliography.

HH15. Britten, William A. "A Use Statistic for Collection Management: The 80/20 Rule Revisited." *Library Acquisitions: Practice and Theory* 14, no. 2 (1990): 183–88.

Suggests validity of using circulation statistics as a guide in assessing a collection when used to quantify relative uses among the LC classes; reports study at the University of Tennessee, Knoxville.

HH16. Christiansen, Dorothy E., Roger C. Davis, and Jutta Reed-Scott. "Guide to Collection Evaluation through Use and User Studies." *Library Resources & Technical Services* 27, no. 4 (Oct./Dec. 1983): 432–40.

Prepared by members of the Subcommittee on Use and User Studies of ALA's RTSD Resources Section and approved by the Resources Section in 1983. Provides a summary of the types of methods available to determine the extent to which library materials are used. Intended to assist librarians in identifying the kind of use or user studies best suited to their needs.

HH17. Clapp, Verner W., and Robert T. Jordan. "Quantitative Criteria for Adequacy of Academic Library Collections." *College & Research Libraries* 50, no. 3 (Mar. 1989): 153–63.

This is a reprint of a classic, originally published in 1965. Clapp and Jordan state that pure numbers aren't sufficient. They seek to develop formulas to find a method for establishing size for minimum adequacy in academic library collections. Their goal is to identify and weigh principal factors that affect the need for books and to assign weights to each.

HH18. Dannelly, Gay N. "The National Shelflist Count: A Tool for Collection Management." *Library Acquisitions: Practice and Theory* 13, no. 3 (1989): 241–50.

Describes the national shelflist count, its history, and uses; includes example tables from the 1985 count, in which forty-eight libraries participated, plus examples from the reports generated annually at Ohio State University. Reviews the limitations and value of the count.

HH19. Lee, Dae Choon, and Larry A. Lockway. "Using an Online Comprehensive Library Management System in Collection Development." *Collection Management* 14, nos. 3/4 (1991): 61–73.

Authors demonstrate the possibilities of using circulation statistics provided by an automated system to evaluate collections and suggest future collection development strategies. Includes tables.

QUALITATIVE METHODS

Qualitative studies seek to evaluate the intrinsic worth of the collection and are, by nature, subjective. They depend in large part on the perceptions of librarians and library users. Some studies compare a library's holdings with a standard list or bibliography, such as ALA's *Books for College Libraries* (HH25), and depend on the assumption that those titles in the resource list are worthy and that the library needs them to satisfy patrons and support programs. The collection is studied by finding the percentage of the titles on the list that are owned by the library. Verification studies are a variation on list checking. Two or more libraries carry out a collection analysis by checking their collections against a specially prepared list of titles. These lists are designed to verify that the libraries understand their collections' strength and that they have correctly and consistently reported it on a shared analysis instrument.

Citation studies are sometimes called bibliometrics or statistical bibliography. Source publications are searched for bibliographic references, and these citations then are used to analyze the collection. Citation studies assume that the more frequently cited publications are the more valuable, will continue to be heavily used, and, consequently, are more important to have in the library collections. In times of tight budgets and increasing serials costs, citation studies can provide guidance in choosing among titles to retain and to cancel. Comparison and overlap studies examine collection duplication among several libraries. They also may be used to identify unique resources. The *OCLC/ AMIGOS Collection Analysis CD-ROM* (HH40) constructs individual databases for libraries wishing to compare their collections with those of peer institutions.

HH20. Childress, Boyd, and Nancy Gibbs. "Collection Assessment and Development Using B/NA Approval Plan Referral Slips." *Collection Management* 11, nos. 1/2 (1989): 137–43.

Explains how Auburn University Libraries have assessed and evaluated collections and strengthened existing collections through the use of Blackwell/North America approval plan slips in a retrospective buying project.

HH21. Lundin, Anne H. "List-Checking in Collection Development: An Imprecise Art." *Collection Management* 11, nos. 3/4 (1989): 103–12.

Examines list checking as a guide to selection and to evaluation of collections; identifies problems and benefits.

HH22. Sanders, Nancy P., Edward O'Neill, and Stuart Weibel. "Automated Collection Analysis Using the OCLC and RLG Bibliographic Databases." *College & Research Libraries* 49 (1988): 305–14.

Authors show how to use both OCLC and RLG databases to analyze collections and to compare holdings, noting that local cataloging differences and priorities may affect the reliability of the results.

HH23. White, Howard D. "Computer Techniques for Studying Coverage, Overlaps and Gaps in Collections." *The Journal of Academic Librarianship* 12, no. 2 (1987): 365–71.

Explores computerized techniques for collection evaluation, especially the Statistical Package for the Social Sciences.

Books for College Libraries

HH24. Budd, John M. "The Utility of a Recommended Core List: An Examination of *Books for College Libraries*, 3rd ed." *The Journal of Academic Librarianship* 17, no. 3 (July 1991): 140–44.

Budd looks at the utility of BCL3 as an evaluation and collection development tool, comparing the titles in BCL3 against actual holdings and against a list of books in print. Identifies problems with BCL3.

HH25. Clark, Virginia, ed. *Books for College Libraries: A Core Collection of 50,000 Titles.* 3rd ed. 6 vols. Chicago: American Library Association, 1988. [also available in machine-readable format]

This tool, despite some criticisms, continues to be an important tool for collection assessment. BCL3, limited primarily to English-language materials, is used for measuring and evaluating college library collections. The work is divided into six volumes based on broad subject areas: humanities; language and literature; history; social sciences; psychology, science, technology, bibliography; and index. Commercial vendors will provide services through which a library's collection is compared with the BCL3 file and missing titles are identified.

Conspectus

The conspectus is a comprehensive collection assessment tool that provides an overview or summary of collection size and collecting intensities arranged by subject, classification scheme, or a combination of either. The conspectus grew out of the Research Libraries Group's interest in a tool for mapping collection depths of its members. Ideally, the conspectus provides a standardized procedure and terminology for sharing detailed descriptions of research collections. Using the Library of Congress classification scheme as a structure, librarians apply numerical codes to identify six levels of collection strength and alphabetical codes to describe language coverage.

Participants in the RLG Conspectus project have entered their detailed descriptions of collections in an online database, the *RLG Conspectus On-Line* (HH32), and offline products. Other groups have adapted the conspectus for their own use, both for individual library collection analysis and to provide a synopsis of a consortium's or network's coordinated collection development. The Canadian Conspectus project began in 1985. The WLN, Inc., Conspectus project, formerly called the Pacific Northwest Conspectus project, provides an online database, the *WLN Collection Assessments Database* (HH35); a PC-based product, the *WLN Conspectus Software* (HH36); and offline collection analysis products. There are many evaluation initiatives involving conspectus adaptations in Europe and the South Pacific.

The conspectus approach to collection assessment, though challenged by some as too dependent on individual perceptions, has become accepted as a tool that is both adaptable and widely applicable. The Association of Research Libraries, working with RLG, began the North American Collections Inventory Project (NCIP) in 1983 as a cooperative effort involving research libraries throughout the United States and Canada. The project's long-term goal is to describe collections and develop an online North American inventory, using the structure of the conspectus. The result is aimed at facilitating resource sharing and assisting scholars in locating materials needed to support their research.

HH26. Ferguson, Anthony W., Joan Grant, and Joel Rutstein. "The RLG Conspectus: Its Uses and Benefits." *College & Research Libraries* 49, no. 3 (May 1988): 197–206.

Authors give a ten-year review of the conspectus, describing its structure and operation. They explain its use as a major tool of evaluation, communication, and cooperation between and within libraries.

HH27. Jakubs, Deborah. *Qualitative Collection Analysis: The Conspectus Methodology.* SPEC Kit, no. 151. Washington, D.C.: Office of Management Services, Association of Research Libraries, 1989.

Kit addresses the assessment of collections through use of the RLG Conspectus, including advantages and disadvantages. Contains report of survey and sample planning documents, methodologies, uses of assessment data, and reports. Useful to anyone involved in assessment.

HH28. _____. *The RLG Conspectus On-Line: User's Manual.* Stanford, Calif.: Research Libraries Group, 1982– . Updated irregularly. Loose-leaf.

Describes the *RLG Conspectus On-Line* database (HH32) and its uses.

HH29. Johnson, Susan. "The WLN Conspectus Service and Collection Assessment." *Information Retrieval and Library Automation* 26, no. 11 (Apr. 1991): 1–4.

Presents possible uses of a completed assessment, done using the WLN Conspectus; detailed description of the WLN project and products.

HH30. Reed-Scott, Jutta. *Manual for the North American Inventory of Research Library Collections.* rev. ed. Washington, D.C.: Association of Research Libraries, Office of Management Services, 1988.

Designed to guide libraries undertaking conspectus-based collection assessment, the manual serves as a reference tool and a handbook for planning and organizing assessment within the framework of the North American Collections Inventory Project.

HH31. *RLG Conspectus.* Mountain View, Calif.: Research Libraries Group, 1990– . Loose-leaf.

Twenty-two volumes of printed worksheets for the RLG Conspectus.

HH32. *RLG Conspectus On-Line.* [database online] Mountain View, Calif.: Research Libraries Group, 1982– .

One of RLG's special centrally mounted databases available for search to all Research Libraries Information Network (RLIN) users under contractual agreement. A remotely searchable tool for comparing and analyzing the existing collection strengths and current collecting policies of member libraries and for distributing primary collecting responsibilities among members. Updated at RLG when members submit revised or new worksheets.

HH33. Oberg, Larry R. "Evaluating the Conspectus Approach for Smaller Library Collections." *College & Research Libraries* 49, no. 3 (May 1988): 187–96.

Reviews the Library and Information Resources for the Northwest (LIRN) project—a conspectus-based collection assessment project. Discusses conspectus methodology problems, staff-time costs, and the value of the complete conspectus to an individual library or group of libraries. Includes sample work sheets.

HH34. Powell, Nancy, and Mary Bushing. *WLN Collection Assessment Manual.* 4th ed. Lacey, Wash.: WLN, Inc., 1992.

A reference tool for people trained in the conspectus assessment methodology and using the WLN (previously Pacific Northwest) Conspectus. Also intended as a beginning point for people who are considering doing assessments. Includes work sheets for gathering collection and user statistics and an outline for writing a collection development policy. Particularly valuable list of bibliographies for use in list checking.

HH35. *WLN Collection Assessments Database.* [database online] Lacey, Wash.: WLN, Inc., 1990– .

A centralized online database that includes collection assessments using the conspectus model from more than 230 libraries of all types and sizes in North America.

HH36. *WLN Conspectus Software.* [database on disk] Release 4.15. Lacey, Wash.: WLN, Inc., 1992.

A microcomputer-based method for assessing both Dewey and LC classified collections. A library or consortium can enter collection information from conspectus work sheets into a local collection assessment database and update records at any time. New versions released irregularly.

HH37. *WLN/RLG Conspectus Software.* [database on disk] Lacey, Wash.: WLN, Inc., 1993– .

A version of the WLN Conspectus microcomputer software that supports the RLG Conspectus. Designed to support downloading from the *RLG Conspectus On-Line* (HH32) into local assessment files and uploading of locally maintained assessment data into the *RLG Conspectus On-Line*.

HH38. Wood, Richard. "The Conspectus as a Collection Development Tool for College Library and Consortia." In *Acquisitions '90*, edited by David C. Genaway, 413–34. Canfield, Ohio: Genaway & Associates, 1990.

Wood explains how and why The Citadel and Charleston Academic Libraries Consortium have adapted the conspectus to the smaller academic library and the consortium setting. Describes the process and identifies concerns and benefits. Also briefly addresses other assessment techniques.

OCLC/AMIGOS Collection Analysis

HH39. Gyeszly, Suzanne D., Gary Smith, and Charles R. Smith. "Achieving Academic Excellence in Higher Education through Improved Research Library Collections: Using OCLC/AMIGOS Collection Analysis for Collection Building." In *Academic Libraries: Achieving Excellence in Higher Education*, edited by Thomas Kirk, 197–206. Chicago: Association of College and Research Libraries, American Library Association, 1992.

Authors describe a project at Texas A & M that surveyed academic departments to learn about current and projected curriculum and research directions. Areas of emphasis were converted to LC call number ranges and then analyzed by the *OCLC/AMIGOS Collection Analysis CD-ROM* (HH40). An evaluation model for other libraries that relates collection analysis to institutional priorities.

HH40. *OCLC/AMIGOS Collection Analysis CD-ROM.* [database on CD-ROM] Dallas: AMIGOS Bibliographic Council, 1989– .

Version 2.0. A compact disc–based collection analysis tool, designed to allow OCLC member academic libraries to compare their collection development activity against that of predetermined peer institutions, as reflected in a database derived from the OCLC Online Union Catalog. Accompanied by users manuals. A similar product is available from OCLC/AMIGOS through tape analysis. This product compares the portion of a library collection represented on OCLC archival tapes with that of one or more cooperating libraries. Provides collection counts within specified classification areas and an analysis of overlap and uniqueness.

HI
Cooperative Collection
Management and Resource
Sharing

Most librarians will agree that no library can meet its users' needs without the cooperation of others. This is the premise of interlibrary loan—borrowing and lending to supplement local collections. ILL has a

long history of support and success among libraries. Another facet of cooperation is coordinated or cooperative collection management in which two or more libraries enter into an agreement for the purpose of sharing the management and development of library collections. Shrinking budgets, expanding numbers of publications, and increasing materials costs provide impetus for cooperation in collection management. There are several models for cooperative collection management, but this area has seen more support in theory than in practice.

The Center for Research Libraries, begun in 1949, now has more than one hundred members who participate by paying dues, sending materials to the Center, and recommending materials for purchase. Some networks and regional consortia have been successful in distributing responsibilities for collecting specified categories of materials and avoiding duplication of resources among the consortium members. As noted earlier, the RLG Conspectus and other assessment tools were developed to facilitate coordinated collection management as well as to evaluate collections. Nevertheless, local priorities continue to dominate collection activities, and coordination usually is assigned a secondary importance.

HI1. *Cooperative Collection Development.* SPEC Kit, no. 111. Washington, D.C.: Association of Research Libraries, Office of Management Studies, 1985.

Sample documents on cooperative activities, including guidelines, plans, task-force reports, work sheets, and program descriptions. Documents address programs that extend beyond the ARL libraries.

HI2. Branin, Joseph J. "Cooperative Collection Development." In *Collection Management: A New Treatise*, edited by Charles B. Osburn and Ross Atkinson, 81–101. Greenwich, Conn.: JAI Press, 1991.

Branin discusses forces for and against cooperative collection development and examines implications of electronic access, national centers for providing resources, and local, regional, and national responsibilities. Lengthy notes and references.

HI3. Erickson, Rodney. "*Choice* for Cooperative Collection Development." *Library Acquisitions: Practice and Theory* 16, no. 1 (1992): 43–49.

Reports on a program using reviews from *Choice*, proximity, automation, and committed personnel to manage a cooperative collection development and resource sharing project among the Tri-College University Consortium at Moorhead, Minnesota, and Fargo, North Dakota. Identifies benefits and problems.

HI4. Farrell, David, and Jutta Reed-Scott. "The North American Collections Inventory Project: Implications for the Future of Coordinated Management of Research Collections.'' *Library Resources & Technical Services* 33, no. 1 (Jan. 1989): 15–28.

Authors evaluate the NCIP project and describe regional and international uses of the conspectus. They look at accomplishments, strengths and weaknesses, and implications for the future of coordinated management of research collections.

HI5. Jaffe, Lawrence Lewis. ''Collection Development and Resource Sharing in the Combined School/Public Library.'' In *Collection Management for School Library Media Centers*, edited by Brenda H. White, 205–15. New York: Haworth Press, 1986.

Takes a favorable look at several combined school and public libraries in which collection appropriateness, use, size, and accessibility have been enhanced by cooperation.

HI6. Mosher, Paul H., and Marcia Pankake. ''A Guide to Coordinated and Cooperative Collection Development.'' *Library Resources & Technical Services* 27 (Oct./Dec. 1983): 417–31.

An important guide to the topic, prepared by members of the Subcommittee on Guidelines for Coordinated Collection Development of the ALA RTSD Resources Section Collection Management and Development Committee and approved by the Resources Section in 1983. Defines terms and concepts essential to understanding cooperative collection development. (Revision projected for 1994.)

HI7. Stephens, Dennis. ''A Stitch in Time: The Alaska Cooperative Collection Development Project.'' In *Coordinating Cooperative Collection Development: A National Perspective*, edited by Wilson Luquire, 173–84. New York: Haworth Press, 1986.

Stephens relates a project that links public, special, academic, and school libraries for optimizing collection development. Project trains librarians and staff for collection development policy formulation, collection assessment, and the use of the conspectus in Alaska. A model for coordinated statewide collection development initiatives.

I

Preservation

Wesley L. Boomgaarden

Overview

Not that many years ago, the bulk of the literature about the preservation and conservation of library materials could be described as a dichotomy: on the one hand, a very technical literature; and on the other, a literature of cheerleading and of hyperbole about preservation crises and the potential loss of humanity's memory.

Today the literature of preservation and conservation is vastly different and greatly expanded and improved, reflecting the maturation of the field and its considerable experience. Nevertheless, in many areas the literature still reflects, as one reviewer wrote in 1991, "a profession where fundamental operating assumptions are not yet agreed upon and basic research is not complete" (Lynn Jones, "More Than Ten Years After: Identity and Direction in Library Preservation," *Library Resources & Technical Services*, volume 35, [July 1991]: 294).

Chapter Content and Organization

The literature on preservation is very large and is growing rapidly. Selecting entries for this section of the *GTSR* has been, therefore, an interesting challenge. As in the *Guide*'s other chapters, the selections were made with an eye to the entries' accu-

racy, currency, availability, and usefulness. The chapter reflects the attempt to be comprehensive in scope without being exhaustive. The time is upon us when preparing exhaustive bibliographies in this part of librarianship is, well, foolish if not impossible.

"Preservation" is defined here as any "action taken to retard, stop, or prevent deterioration by providing a proper storage environment, policies for handling and use of library materials, conservation treatment for damaged or deteriorated items, and selective transfer of deteriorated items to an alternative format such as microfilm" (Carolyn Morrow, ICA4, 218). This broad definition is the focus of this chapter.

The organization of this chapter is somewhat problematic but reflects, I hope, a topical arrangement logical to both the preservation specialist and the generalist. Some general comments about its contents:

"IA General Works" includes a wide variety of general (background) readings, reference sources, periodicals, online resources, and sources of expertise. Standards are addressed in this section through a number of secondary sources that explicate and point to the actual standards related to preservation.

"IB Commercial Library Binding" cites the key sources in a library function that continues to be the largest preservation line in most library budgets.

"IC Conservation (Books and Paper)" is broken into those sources related to either general or "collections" conservation, or to single-item treatments of books and paper as artifacts in their original format.

"ID Cooperative Preservation" attempts to cover how libraries and agencies collaborate with one another in the preservation enterprise.

"IE Paper Deacidification and Quality" considers the most up-to-date library literature related to mass deacidification technology and includes important works relating to the history and technology of papermaking.

"IF Disaster Control, Recovery, and Insurance" includes the most important in a mushrooming literature that discusses anticipating, preventing, and coping with catastrophes.

"IG Environmental Control and Pest Management" identifies the core collection related to the physical environment, the crucial front line of defense in preservation, including library building design.

"IH Preservation Administration" attempts to describe the most important literature in the growth and development of preservation administration and management.

"II Nonbook and Nonpaper Media" considers some of the best works related to preservation in the rapid growth and proliferation of physical formats in modern libraries.

"IJ Decision Making for Preservation" lists the key literature in selecting, reformatting, and replacing brittle, damaged, or deteriorated books. However, most of the literature of the actual reformatting techniques and technologies is covered in Chapter J, Reproduction of Library Materials.

"IK Staff Training and User Awareness" attempts to compile the best of a relatively short list of good literature in this difficult area of mitigating the effects of handling and using collections.

Our perception of preservation in librarianship is that preservation is a set of *technical* problems, with social and economic complications, that are solved only by workable *management* solutions. The problems are everywhere in library collections and are becoming more complex each year as libraries expand their collections beyond traditional paper sources. Our management solutions depend upon

access to the technical information and upon sound approaches. The literature cited here, with critical annotations, attempts to assist both the specialist and nonspecialist in both areas. We as librarians live by Samuel Johnson's observation that knowledge is of two kinds: we know a subject ourselves, or we know where we can find information upon it. The pace of change in this field and in its literature stretches even Dr. Johnson's dictum.

IA
General Works

The sources listed in this section constitute a wide variety of materials covering very different, but essential, aspects of the literature of preservation. Included are general sources that should be considered for introductory or background reading, for historical perspective, or for reference. The sections on periodicals; indexes, abstracts, and databases; and electronic newsletters and listservers identify essential resources for keeping up with the subject's literature and current practice.

IAA
General and Introductory Works

IAA1. Banks, Paul N. "Preservation of Library Materials." In vol. 23, *Encyclopedia of Library and Information Science*, edited by Allen Kent, Harold Lancour, and Jay E. Daily, 180–222. New York: Marcel Dekker, 1978.

A fine overview of library materials preservation. In addition to emphasizing the importance of the proper physical environment, Banks suggests philosophical, ethical, technical, and practical problems requiring resolution. Books and paper are the clear focus. Contains some outdated information. Good illustrations of, for example, an "ideal book packaging" for shipment.

IAA2. Billington, James H. "The Moral Imperative of Conservation." In *Meeting the Preservation Challenge*, edited by Jan Merrill-Oldham, 5–12. Washington, D.C.: Association of Research Libraries, 1988.

Presented at "Invest in the American Collection," a regional forum on the conservation of cultural property at the Art Institute of Chicago, June 16, 1987. An eloquent and erudite justification of the conservation of cultural property.

IAA3. Higginbotham, Barbra Buckner. *Our Past Preserved: A History of American Library Preservation, 1876–1910.* Boston: G. K. Hall, 1990.

A well-documented history of library preservation theory and practice that "explores the circumstances and forces that stimulated awareness of a significant library problem and led eventually to conscious, organized efforts to address it" in the 1876–1910 period. Detailed history of concerns, plans, actions, and practices in that era related to the physical library environment, influence over reader behavior, bookbinding, cleaning, repair, paper, ink, etc. Includes a preservation timeline, 1842–1910. Extensive bibliography includes other key works related to preservation's history in the United States before and after 1910. Indexed.

IAA4. Morrow, Carolyn Clark, with Gay Walker. *The Preservation Challenge: A Guide to Conserving Library Materials.* White Plains, N.Y.: Knowledge Industry Publications, 1983.

An excellent and well-written overview of library materials preservation. Although portions of the book have become dated, the substance of the work remains accurate and valuable. For example, it contains an excellent overview of deterioration of organic material and the composition and preservation of library materials. In addition, the case studies of conservation treatment of artifactually valuable library materials still read well. Bibliography and index.

IAA5. *Nature of Things: Turning to Dust.* [videorecording] A Canadian Broadcasting Corporation Production. Toronto: CBC, 1990. One-hour videocassette.

Part of the CBC's Nature of Things series. Covers a great deal of ground, although its initial minutes include what some might consider dramatic overstatement. Features U.S. and Canadian libraries. When used in segments, can be a very good vehicle for teaching in preservation courses. Usage for general audience depends upon time available and attention span of that audience.

IAA6. *Preservation of Library Materials.* Edited by Merrily A. Smith. Conference held at the National Library of Austria. Vienna, April 7–10, 1986. IFLA Publications 40 & 41. 2 vols. Munich: K. G. Saur, 1987.

Volume 1 consists of remarks made by the administrators of several of the world's largest libraries about preservation policies, preservation planning, interinstitutional cooperation, and "emerging technologies" (in 1986). These are of interest primarily in their international and rhetorical context. Volume 2, "Technical Presentations," has more information of practical and long-term value to preservation managers. The second volume consists of authoritative papers on policy and training; reproduction and copyright concerns; storage and handling of bound materials, photographic materials, and audio/magnetic media; and treatments and environment, including conservation of rare books/paper, disaster control, pest management, and climate control.

IAA7. Shahani, Chandru, and William K. Wilson. "Preservation of Libraries and Archives." *American Scientist* 75 (May/June 1987): 240–51.

Nicely illustrated general history and overview of the challenges of preserving nineteenth- and twentieth-century papers, with discussion of solutions found and sought.

IAA8. *Slow Fires: On the Preservation of the Human Record.* [videorecording] A presentation of American Film Foundation. Sponsored by Council on Library Resources, Library of Congress, National Endowment for the Humanities. A Terry Sanders Film, written by Ben Maddow and Terry Sanders. Santa Monica, Calif.: American Film Foundation, 1987. Video (VHS, 3/4") and 16mm film formats, 58- and 33-minute versions.

Highly effective film that outlines the key issues in the preservation of library and archives collections, using the talents of Robert MacNeil as narrator. Featuring the great libraries and articulate representatives of those libraries, captures the essence of the problems caused by brittle paper. Excellent introduction to the subject of preservation for general audiences and students. The shorter version is considered superior by most. Note: Because some of the information has become outdated, a sequel is being developed to focus on issues related to preservation and access in the era of electronic data.

IAB
Dictionaries and Glossaries

IAB1. DePew, John N., with C. Lee Jones. *A Library, Media, and Archival Preservation Glossary.* Santa Barbara, Calif.: ABC Clio Information Services, 1992.

Fills a gap in the literature by providing, in one source, definitions of more than 1,500 preservation-related terms from the paper industry, bookbinding, micrographics, magnetic imaging, and other technologies. Source for nonspecialists seeking meaning of technical terms. Most definitions refer to a fifty-five–item bibliography for authority.

IAB2. Lynn, M. Stuart, and the Technology Assessment Advisory Committee to the Commission on Preservation and Access. *Preservation and Access Technology: The Relationship between Digital and Other Media Conversion Processes: A Structured Glossary of Technical Terms.* Washington, D.C.: The Commission, 1990.

This volume's structured glossary organization provides a unique approach in the preservation literature. Arranged in three broad segments: the original document (medium, format, condition, etc.), the selection process, and the preserved copy (conversion, capture, storage, access, distribution, and presentation technologies). An important source. Bibliographical references; indexed.

IAB3. Roberts, Matt T., and Don Etherington. *Bookbinding and the Conservation of Books: A Dictionary of Descriptive*

Terminology. Washington, D.C.: Preservation Office, Library of Congress, 1982.

A handsome and excellent dictionary of bookbinding and book structure, with illustrations. Of interest to preservation administrators, conservators, bibliophiles, and curators.

IAC
Directories

IAC1. American Institute for Conservation of Historic and Artistic Works. *Directory*. Washington, D.C.: The Institute, 1992– . Annual. Continues *AIC Directory*.

An annual publication of the AIC listing the names, addresses, and specialties of its members (conservators).

IAC2. Coleman, Christopher D. G., comp. *Preservation Education Directory*. 6th ed. Chicago: Association for Library Collections and Technical Services, American Library Association, 1990. ISSN 1049-619X.

Lists preservation programs, courses, and workshops in library schools; includes training in conservation and programs offered abroad. Written to answer the query "Where can one learn more about preservation and conservation?" A new edition always seems to be needed to keep up with changes in educational opportunities.

IAC3. Commission on Preservation and Access. *Directory: Information Sources on Scientific Research Related to the Preservation of Books, Paper, and Adhesives*. Commission on Preservation and Access. Report. Washington, D.C.: The Commission, 1990.

A handy summary listing of laboratories and organizations such as the Canadian Conservation Institute, Smithsonian Institution, Getty Conservation Institute, Image Permanence Institute, Library of Congress, etc., involved in preservation and conservation research, with comments on projects in progress. Summarizes the scope of indexes, abstracts, and databases available.

IAC4. DeCandido, Robert, and Cheryl Shackelton. *Who Ya Gonna Call? A Preservation Services Sourcebook for Libraries and Archives*. Prepared for METRO, the New York Metropolitan Reference and Research Library Agency, in conjunction with METRO's Conservation/Preservation Advisory Council. New York: METRO, 1992.

A listing of preservation resources available to libraries and archives in the New York metropolitan area. Although most valuable for those in that geographic area, this sourcebook is handy for those outside that region seeking preservation service providers. Alphabetical arrangement of providers, with subject and personal name indexes. A good annotated bibliography of preservation literature.

IAD
Bibliographies, Bibliographic Essays, and Indexes

IAD1. Banks, Paul N. *A Selective Bibliography on the Conservation of Research Library Materials*. Chicago: Newberry Library, 1981.

Despite its age, this fine bibliography has value in its organizational approach and its excellent sources relating to historical issues such as conservation ethics, bookbinding, materials of manufacture, and so on. The arrangement is by subject with full author index.

IAD2. Crawford-de Sa, Elizabeth, and Michele Valerie Cloonan. "The Preservation of Archival and Library Materials: Part I: A Bibliography of Government Publications." *Conservation Administration News* 46 (July 1991): 16–17, 30–31; and "The Preservation of Archival and Library Materials: Part II: A Bibliography of Government Publications." *Conservation Administration News* 47 (Oct. 1991): 12–13.

An annotated bibliography of government agency publications related to preservation of library and archives collections. Brief background information is provided on the many agencies whose publications are included. Lists publications of at least eighteen U.S. agencies and UNESCO.

IAD3. Cunha, George M., and Dorothy G. Cunha. *Conservation of Library Materials; A Manual and Bibliography on the Care, Repair and Restoration of Library Materials*. 2nd ed. 2 vols. Metuchen, N.J.: Scarecrow Press, 1972. (Volume II: Bibliography)

For annotation, *see* 1AD4.

IAD4. Cunha, George M., and Dorothy G. Cunha, assisted by Suzanne E. Henderson. *Library and Archives Conservation: 1980s and Beyond*. 2 vols. Metuchen, N.J.: Scarecrow Press, 1983. (Volume II: Bibliography)

Together, the 1972 (IAD3) and 1983 bibliographies offer nearly 11,000 entries in nine sections from the very general to the very specific. Entries not annotated. Author index. Note: Volume I in each set is generally outdated.

IAD5. Morrow, Carolyn Clark, and Steven B. Schoenly. *A Conservation Bibliography for Librarians, Archivists, and Administrators*. Troy, N.Y.: Whitston, 1979.

An impressive subject bibliography of sources dated from 1966 through the late 1970s; includes nearly 1,400 entries. In two parts; subject index.

IAD6. Sitts, Maxine K. *A Practical Guide to Preservation in School and Public Libraries*. Syracuse, N.Y.: ERIC Clearinghouse on Information Resources, 1990.

A bibliographic essay aimed at school and public libraries, an audience largely ignored in the literature. Arranged in three broad categories: awareness, judgment, and advocacy. Cites and provides annotations on a number of sources not often found relating to public libraries, audiovisual media, and local history. Some references are to specific persons, addresses, or presentations not always easy to locate.

IAD7. Thompson, Don K., and Joan ten Hoor. *A Core Collection in Preservation.* 2nd ed. Edited by Lisa Fox. Chicago: Association for Library Collections and Technical Services, American Library Association, 1992.

This annotated listing of just over one hundred "books, reports, periodicals, and major articles that are likely to be most useful in preservation planning and administration" is now in its revised second edition. A very good single source of information on the "core" collection, especially for the nonspecialist. Order information is provided.

IAD8. "Year's Work in Preservation." In *Library Resources & Technical Services.* Chicago: Association of Library Collections and Technical Services, American Library Association.

A bibliographic essay on preservation literature that appears annually in *LRTS,* often listing from seventy-five to more than 150 important resources. Titles of articles vary. Recent authors have included Maralyn Jones (1991), Karl E. Longstreth (1989, 1990) with Carla J. Montori (1988), and Marcia A. Watt (1992).

IAD9. Zimmermann, Carole. *Bibliography on Mass Deacidification.* Washington, D.C.: Preservation Office, Library of Congress, 1991.

See also annotation under IE13. An unannotated bibliography of 259 citations related to mass deacidification.

IAE
Handbooks and Manuals

IAE1. DePew, John N. *A Library, Media, and Archival Preservation Handbook.* Santa Barbara, Calif.: ABC Clio Information Services, 1991.

This handbook's preface states that it is "designed to introduce those who have little knowledge of the preservation of library materials to the basic environmental controls, materials, processes, and techniques that are required to house and preserve library materials in all types and sizes of collections." Brings together a great deal of information; can be useful as a textbook for a course in preservation, meeting a real need in the education and training of librarians. Also a good reference book for the specialist or nonspecialist. Appendixes, glossary, index.

IAE2. Ogden, Sherelyn, ed. *Preservation of Library and Archival Materials: A Manual.* Andover, Mass.: Northeast Document Conservation Center, 1992.

A compilation and expansion of Northeast Document Conservation Center's (NEDCC) technical leaflet series available in an updatable notebook format. The series has existed for years and has proved to be very helpful to the nonspecialist needing accurate and practical information

about collection care. First issue of this *Manual* contains thirty-seven technical leaflets.

IAE3. *Preservation Planning Program: An Assisted Self-Study Manual for Libraries.* Developed by Pamela W. Darling with Duane E. Webster. Revised by Jan Merrill-Oldham and Jutta Reed-Scott. Rev. 1993 ed. Washington, D.C.: Office of Management Services, Association of Research Libraries, 1993.

See also annotation under IH12. Methodology developed by Darling and others to assist libraries in evaluating their preservation situation and needs. The basis for the study and establishment of many library preservation programs.

IAE4. Ritzenthaler, Mary Lynn. *Archives & Manuscripts: Conservation. A Manual on Physical Care and Management.* SAA Basic Manual Series. Chicago: Society of American Archivists, 1983.

An excellent starting point for understanding the basics of preservation and conservation in archives and manuscript collections. Appendixes include a glossary, basic conservation procedures, literature review, and lists of supplies and equipment. A great deal of practical information, well presented.

IAE5. Thackery, David, and Edward Meachen. *Local History in the Library: A Manual for Assessment and Preservation.* Bloomington, Ill.: Bloomington Public Library, 1989.

A good tool for the librarian with responsibility for the local history collection. In three parts: a review of the published and manuscript sources and types in local history, a cogent bibliographic essay of recent preservation and conservation literature of interest to local history collections, and a collection assessment instrument/form to be adapted on site. When published it was available for $1, a great bargain.

IAF
Standards (Secondary Sources)

Although many standards exist that relate directly or indirectly to the preservation of library collections, preservation as a component of librarianship lacks published standards in many important areas. This is being remedied by the National Information Standards Organization (NISO) and other standards development organizations, but a great deal of work remains to be done, especially in areas of rapid technological change. The following sources handle the subject in a variety of ways but should be considered only introductory sources and sources for locating specific published standards. *See also* "Standards" in Chapter J, Reproduction of Library Materials.

IAF1. Crawford, Walt. *Technical Standards: An Introduction for Librarians.* 2nd ed. Boston: G. K. Hall, 1991.

For annotation, *see* AA3.

IAF2. *Index and Directory of Industry Standards.* Englewood, Colo.: Information Handling Services, 1989– . Irregular.

An annual multivolume reference publication that has value for one trying to stay up to date with standards in different industries and fields. Continues *Index and Directory of U.S. Industry Standards.*

IAF3. *Information Standards Quarterly.* Bethesda, Md.: National Information Standards Organization, 1989– . v. 1– . Quarterly. ISSN 1041-0031.

ISQ provides updates on the progress and status of standards development and revision. Covers a wide variety of standards of interest and importance to libraries and archives. Includes information about ordering NISO standards.

IAF4. Walch, Victoria Irons. "Checklist of Standards Applicable to the Preservation of Archives and Manuscripts." *American Archivist* 53 (Spring 1990): 324–38.

Excellent overview and listing of published standards related to preservation. Includes a long list of pertinent International Organization for Standardization (ISO) and American National Standards Institute (ANSI) standards (and specifications) and many from other technical and professional associations such as ALA, the Research Libraries Group (RLG), Society of American Archivists (SAA), Technical Association of the Pulp and Paper Industry (TAPPI), the Library of Congress (LC), and the National Institute for Standards and Technology (NIST).

IAG
Periodicals

Following are the primary periodicals dealing with preservation and conservation. There are many other periodical titles that have regular or occasional content of direct interest to preservation and conservation professionals. Most are indexed or abstracted in the sources following. Some additional periodicals are listed in other subsections of this chapter.

IAG1. *The Abbey Newsletter: Bookbinding and Conservation.* Austin, Tex.: Abbey Publications. v. 1– , 1975– . Eight times a year. ISSN 0276-8291.

AN is a very important source of news, current issues, reprinted articles, conference listings and summaries, position offerings, products and services, new publication listings and reviews, and editorial opinion—all related to preservation and conservation of library and archival materials. Has great value to conservation and preservation professionals largely because of its scope, the editor's interpretation of technical issues related to preservation, and the listing and review of a wide range of published materials.

IAG2. *Advances in Preservation and Access.* Westport, Conn.: Meckler. v. 1– , 1992– . Annual. ISSN 1063-2263.

Inaugural volume included nineteen papers covering a wide variety of current topics among preservation and conservation administrative issues. Has promise to be a very important annual publication for library preservation administration and good reading for library preservation education.

IAG3. *AIC Newsletter.* Washington, D.C.: American Institute for Conservation of Historic and Artistic Works. v. 1– , 1975– . Bimonthly. ISSN 0887-705X.

News for members of the AIC, covering information relating to the several specialty groups within the organization. Lists recent publications, position postings, conference details, etc.

IAG4. *ALCTS Newsletter.* Chicago: Association for Library Collections and Technical Services. v. 1– , 1990– . Frequency varies. ISSN 1047-949X. Continues *RTSD Newsletter.*

For annotation, *see* AF5.

IAG5. *Alkaline Paper Advocate.* Austin, Tex.: Abbey Publications. v. 1– , 1988– . Six times a year. ISSN 0897-2524.

"An interdisciplinary forum" whose "chief function . . . [is] to provide a forum for producers and consumers, who now find communication difficult because of the complexity of the marketplace" (volume 1, number 1). Provides current information on issues related to the production and availability of alkaline ("acid-free"), permanent/durable paper for books, records, and copiers. Of interest to manufacturers, distributors, and consumers of alkaline, permanent papers.

IAG6. *The American Archivist.* Chicago: Society of American Archivists. v. 1– , 1938– . Quarterly. ISSN 0360-9081.

Official publication of the SAA. Contains well-researched articles, news, reviews, and other information of interest (including preservation and conservation) to the archival profession.

IAG7. *Book and Paper Group Annual.* Washington, D.C.: Book and Paper Group, American Institute for Conservation of Historic and Artistic Works. v. 1– , 1982– . Annual. ISSN 0887-8978.

The annual papers compiled by the AIC's Book and Paper Group (BPG), the division that includes library and archival conservators. A nonjuried anthology representing the research and documentation of many of North America's conservators. (The BPG also produces the *Paper Conservation Catalog* [ICB7] and the *Book Conservation Catalog*, forthcoming.)

IAG8. Commission on Preservation and Access. *Annual Report.* Washington, D.C.: The Commission. 1988/89– . Annual. ISSN 1057-8064.

These reports summarize the Commission's extensive national and international projects and activities, providing a summary of background information and work-in-progress.

IAG9. _____. *Newsletter.* Washington, D.C.: The Commission. no. 1– , 1988– . Monthly. ISSN 1045-1919.

Produced "to provide a direct, regular information flow among individuals actively concerned with preservation issues." Covers issues of interest to preservation professionals, library administrators, university administrators, scholars, and other individuals. Information on task forces, workshops, legislation, cooperative projects, and consortial issues related to the Commission's national and international efforts. Heavy emphasis on selection strategies, preservation reformatting, bibliographic control, and new preservation technologies.

IAG10. *Conservation Administration News.* Tulsa, Okla.: University of Tulsa. no. 1– , 1979– . Quarterly. ISSN 0192-2912.

CAN offers a mixture of news, feature articles, book/media reviews, grants updates, products/services, conference announcements/summaries, position announcements, regular columns, and a bit of humor, all related to preservation, conservation, disaster control, security, and other preservation topics. Editorial practice has been to feature nearly every preservation program in the United States and abroad at one time or another, providing the opportunity to read about a wide range of approaches. Provides extensive coverage of disaster control and security issues, from an "I survived" and "our experience" perspective.

IAG11. *Conservation: The GCI Newsletter.* Marina del Rey, Calif.: Getty Conservation Institute. v. 1– , Winter 1986– . Irregular. ISSN 0898-4808.

Formerly titled *The Getty Conservation Institute Newsletter*, this publication includes information about the Getty's research interests and projects related to the preservation of cultural property around the globe. A source for keeping informed about the GCI's research publications and educational opportunities.

IAG12. *Disaster Recovery Journal.* St. Louis, Mo.: Systems Support. v. 1– , 1988– . Quarterly.

Although aimed at contingency planners and risk management personnel, the journal has value for library professionals. Most of the brief articles are in an informal, reportorial style, without footnotes or other documentation. The major value to library professionals lies in the extensive advertising by "hot-site" and "cold-site" vendors, other electronic data and service salvage and recovery vendors, and document recovery applications.

IAG13. *International Preservation News.* Washington, D.C.: Library of Congress. no. 1– , 1987– . Occasional. ISSN 0890-4960.

Newsletter of the International Federation of Library Associations (IFLA) Programme on Preservation and Conservation. Formerly edited at the Library of Congress for the IFLA Core Programme on Preservation and Conservation (PAC). Covers preservation and conservation activities of libraries and archives worldwide. It is expected that in the future this publication will be edited and distributed from the Bibliothèque Nationale in Paris.

IAG14. *Journal of the American Institute for Conservation.* Washington, D.C.: American Institute for Conservation of Historic and Artistic Works. v. 1– , 1960– . Semiannual. ISSN 0196-0075.

The official journal of the AIC, containing well-researched and well-documented articles relating to the conservation of cultural property of all types and formats. The conservation of library and archival materials is covered irregularly; e.g., volume 31, number 1, Spring 1992, is focused upon library and archival materials.

IAG15. *Library & Archival Security.* New York: Haworth Press. v. 2– , 1978– . Quarterly. ISSN 0196-0075. Continues *Library Security Newsletter*.

See also annotation under LAB3. Because security is a crucial issue in the preservation of and continued access to library collections, this journal's coverage is of interest to preservation professionals. High-quality articles cover collection mutilation/defacement, fire protection, pest infestations, general and specific security concerns, and others.

IAG16. *Library Conservation News.* London: British Library Preservation Service. v. 1– , 1983– . Quarterly. ISSN 0265-041X.

Newsletter of the British Library's preservation office.

IAG17. *Library Resources & Technical Services.* Chicago: Association for Library Collections and Technical Services, American Library Association. v. 1– , Winter 1957– . Quarterly. ISSN 0024-2527.

For annotation, *see* AF13.

IAG18. *Microform Review.* Westport, Conn.: Meckler. v. 1– , 1972– . Bimonthly. ISSN 0002-6530.

For annotation, *see* JAF14.

IAG19. *The New Library Scene.* Edina, Minn.: Library Binding Institute. v. 1– , 1982– . Bimonthly. ISSN 0735-8571.

Organ of the North American library binderies' trade association, the Library Binding Institute (LBI). Though published by an industry group, the publication nevertheless has value to librarians in management of preservation programs and activities. Articles are often written by library preservation specialists on specific topics directly or indirectly related to commercial library binding in particular or on preservation and conservation of collections in general. Content of the articles is generally good. News and advertising copy is of interest, as well.

IAG20. *Paper Conservation News.* Leigh, Worcester, Eng.: Institute for Paper Conservation. no. 1– , 1976– . Quarterly. ISSN 0140-1033.

Official newsletter of the IPC.

IAG21. *The Paper Conservator.* Leigh, Worcester, Eng.: Institute for Paper Conservation. v. 1– , 1976– . Annual. ISSN 0309-4227.

Covers research in paper conservation for works of art on paper and for library and archives materials. Highly technical for the conservator as scientist and craftsperson.

IAG22. *Restaurator: International Journal for the Preservation of Library and Archival Materials.* Copenhagen: Munksgaard International. v. 1– , 1969– . Quarterly. ISSN 0034-5806.

One of the premier journals in conservation and preservation and an important source for conservators and preservation administrators. The journal's approach and coverage are scholarly, and research is well-documented.

IAG23. *Studies in Conservation.* London: International Institute for Conservation of Historic and Artistic Works. v. 1– , 1952– . Quarterly. ISSN 0039-3630.

Publishes scholarly articles (mostly in English) and book reviews reflecting the constituency of the world's conservators.

IAG24. *Technology & Conservation.* Boston: Technology Organization. v. 1– , 1976– . Irregular. ISSN 0146-1214.

Covers issues of concern to the preservation and conservation of cultural property in general. Of interest to library and archives preservation because it covers related issues of direct or indirect interest and often prepares profiles of conservation facilities in the United States.

IAH
Indexes, Abstracts, and Databases

IAH1. *Art and Archaeology Technical Abstracts.* Marina del Rey, Calif.: The Getty Conservation Institute. v. 6– , 1966– . ISSN 0004-2994.

The *AATA* indexes and abstracts a wide variety of journal and technical literature mostly related to museum conservation research but including significant topics of interest to libraries and archives. Continues *I.I.C. Abstracts.*

IAH2. *Conservation Information Network.* [database online] Marina del Rey, Calif.: Getty Conservation Institute, 198?– .

Includes a conservation bibliographic database, a conservation materials database, and a product/supplier directory. The bibliographic database is an online information resource for the conservation and preservation of cultural property that includes more than 100,000 citations (including the *AATA* abstracts of the holdings of the International Centre for the Study of the Preservation and the Restoration of Cultural Property [ICCROM] library in Rome; and other sources).

IAI
Anthologies

IAI1. Darling, Pamela W., comp. *Preservation Planning Program: Resource Notebook.* Expanded 1987 ed. Edited by Wesley L. Boomgaarden. Washington, D.C.: Office of Management Studies, Association of Research Libraries, 1987.

To address the paucity of general textbooks and anthologies in the field of preservation management, ARL's Office of Management Studies (now Office of Management Services) published this compilation of basic readings, hard-to-find technical sources, bibliographies, in-house guides, and lists. It was created by ARL/OMS to support the ARL Preservation Planning Program (*see* IAE3 for the companion *Manual*). ARL allowed this item to go out of print in 1992, to be replaced with a series of "Resource Guides" covering most of the subjects included in this 1987 *Resource Notebook* compilation. (For three of these "resource guides" *see* Byrne, ICA1; Cloonan, IH3; and Boomgaarden, IK1.)

IAI2. *Library Conservation: Preservation in Perspective.* Edited by John P. Baker and Marguerite C. Soroka. Stroudsburg, Pa.: Dowden, Hutchinson & Ross, 1978.

This work brings together thirty-four reprinted articles, most of which are considered classics of library and archival preservation and conservation from the 1940s through the 1970s. The entries' references and bibliographies point to other seminal works in the field.

IAJ
Electronic Resources

IAJ1. Conservation DistList. [electronic discussion group] 1987– .

A LISTSERV for preservation administrators, conservators, curators, and scientists, moderated by Walter Henry, Stanford University Libraries. A source of timely news and a vehicle for information sharing among subscribers, it works in three online forms: (1) a moderated online forum, the ConsDistList, on technical issues, announcements, and news (back issues are available); (2) a directory of electronic mail addresses for preservation/conservation professionals, updated and distributed regularly; and (3) FileList of text files available via ConsDistList and the INTERNET. To join, send a message to the moderator at **CONSDIST-REQUEST@ LINDY.STANFORD.EDU** (INTERNET).

IAJ2. *FLIPPER: The Electronic Library.* [database online] Gainesville, Fla.: University of Florida, 1992– .

A library of electronic documents associated with the FLIPPER listserv, "Florida Libraries Interested in Preservation Programs, Education and Resources." The library is a collection of documents, most in the public domain, dealing with a wide variety of preservation concerns, including the reproduction of library materials. Documents include policies, procedures, studies, etc., from print publications and institutions active in preservation. Most documents, to date, originate from the University of Florida Libraries. Has great promise for preservation practitioners at all levels of experience and expertise. Access is free and available through electronic mail. For more information, contact: **ERIKESS@NERVM** (BITNET) or **ERIKESS @NERVM.NERDC.UFL.EDU** (INTERNET).

IAK
Sources of Expertise

Preservation activities in libraries grew tremendously in the 1980s, and library positions with preservation responsibility continue to increase in number in the early 1990s. Individual librarians are prepared for these positions in a wide variety of programs and opportunities. They range from the formal University of Texas (formerly at Columbia University) library school program to formal internships such as those supported by the Mellon Foundation or the Johns Hopkins University Library; to other internships, workshops, or on-the-job opportunities; and to any variety of other informal training.

With the increase in the numbers of professionals who have specialized in preservation has come a very considerable increase in the number of meetings, conferences, workshops, and other activities related to the preservation and conservation of library materials. Keeping up with new approaches and the pace of change is essential but not at all easy. This brief section gives an overview of how librarians can maintain currency in this continually changing area.

PROFESSIONAL ASSOCIATIONS AND CONFERENCE OPPORTUNITIES

IAK1. American Institute for Conservation of Historic and Artistic Works (AIC). Headquarters: 1200 16th Street N.W., Suite 340, Washington, DC 20036. Executive Director: Sarah Rosenberg.

Librarians with preservation expertise and responsibility may find it useful and informative to join this organization. AIC conferences are generally held in the late spring of each year. The AIC Book and Paper Group (BPG) is of particular interest to librarians and, of course, to conservators, who make up most of the active BPG membership.

IAK2. ALA Association for Library Collections and Technical Services (ALCTS). Executive Director: Karen Muller.

For annotation, *see* AGA3.

IAK3. ALA ALCTS Preservation of Library Materials Section (PLMS).

The primary location of preservation discussion in ALA, although preservation-related topics may be discussed in other sections of ALCTS and within other ALA divisions. PLMS committees and discussion groups (as of early 1993) are as follows:

Education Committee
Physical Quality and Treatment of Library Materials Committee
Policy and Planning Committee
Preservation Management Committee

Publications Committee
Cooperative Preservation Programs Discussion Group
Library Binding Discussion Group
Library-Vendor Relations Discussion Group
Physical Quality and Treatment Discussion Group
PLMS-RLMS (Reproduction of Library Materials) Joint Reporting Session Discussion Group
Preservation Administrators Discussion Group
Preservation Course and Workshop Discussion Group
Preservation Education and Outreach Discussion Group
Preservation of Library Materials Discussion Group

For those unable to attend the ALA annual and midwinter conferences, preservation-related news is generally summarized in at least three sources, *Abbey Newsletter* (IAG1), *ALCTS Newsletter* (AF5), and *Conservation Administration News* (IAG10).

In addition to the ALA annual and midwinter conferences, many opportunities for continuing education exist in the form of national, regional, or local conferences or institutes. ALA's ALCTS sponsors or cosponsors a number of them. For example, in 1992–1993 PLMS committees have formed the following groups to discuss, plan, or execute regional programs and institutes.

Management Strategies for Disaster Preparedness
Preservation and Technical Services Program Planning
Preservation of Magnetic Media Institute Planning
Public Libraries Program Planning
Library Binding Regional Institutes

Other conference opportunities for continuing education and professional development cover many aspects of preservation and conservation. These are too numerous to list here and go far beyond ALA and AIC conferences and institutes. Such conference opportunities include the Rochester Institute of Technology/Image Permanence Institute–sponsored photograph preservation seminars, special conferences held at the National Archives, Commission on Preservation and Access–sponsored seminars, disaster preparedness workshops, and so on. The best advice is to read *Abbey Newsletter* (IAG1), *CAN* (IAG10), Commission on Preservation and Access Newsletter (IAG9), and the electronic sources *AN2* (AF4) and ConsDistList (IAJ1) to stay informed about the opportunities. State and local opportunities not listed in these sources may also be available.

SOURCES TO READ ON A REGULAR BASIS

In a library specialization as multidisciplinary and diverse in scope as preservation is, one cannot read too much or too far afield. There is great merit in reading *each* of the sources included in this chapter, including and especially the periodical sources that provide the news, trends, and lists of new publications of potential interest to each preservation professional. At minimum, one should receive and read regularly

Abbey Newsletter (IAG1), *CAN* (IAG10), the Commission's *Newsletter* (IAG9) and each of its special reports, and *Library Resources & Technical Services* (AF13) to become aware of the other articles, books, and reports published or available more informally. A periodic review of *Library Literature* is, of course, indispensable. In addition, one should subscribe to the ConsDistList (IAJ1), an increasingly valuable source for news, discussion, and awareness of other electronic discussion groups and electronic text files.

IB
Commercial Library Binding

Library binding, a very traditional library function, has undergone considerable and positive changes in the past decade and continues to be among the largest budget lines in most library preservation budgets. High-quality commercial bookbinding is a crucial line of protection for books inside the library and out, making communication between the librarian and the commercial library binder as important today as it ever was. Quality assurance and cost containment are often competing interests in an industry squeezed by static or shrinking library binding budgets and bindery operating costs. The sources listed here cover most of the issues, but readers should be alert to continuing changes in the industry.

IB1. *Commercial Library Binding: The Librarian's View.* [slide-tape] New Haven, Conn.: Yale University Library, 1982. 76 35mm slides and one 28-minute audiocassette, with printed script.

This slide-tape program is straightforward and full of information. For staff training or in library education, it makes a fine companion piece to the Library of Congress's video on library binding (IB4).

IB2. DePew, John N. "Binding and In-house Repair." In his *A Library, Media, and Archival Preservation Handbook*, 109–33. Santa Barbara, Calif.: ABC Clio Information Services, 1991.

This chapter compresses much of the literature of library binding and book structure in a good overview of the topic. Covers structure, leaf attachment, quality control, binder selection, and contracts. Good illustrations have been reproduced from other sources.

IB3. Lanier, Don, comp. *Binding Operations in ARL Libraries.* SPEC Kit, no. 114. Washington, D.C.: Office of Management Studies, Association of Research Libraries, 1985.

Combines the responses from eighteen ARL libraries related to organization/administration, contracts/specifications, automated systems, and binding treatments/guidelines/flowcharts. This snapshot of binding in 1985 is not the most up-to-date source, but is worth reviewing because some of the material included still has use and is difficult to find elsewhere.

IB4. *Library Binding: A Collaborative Process, A Shared Responsibility.* [videorecording] Washington, D.C.: Library of Congress, 1990. Videocassette, 26 minutes, VHS-SP.

Excellent for staff orientation/training and for library education related to preservation in general and commercial library binding in particular. Focus is on the value of library binding for continued access to library collections. The approach is a very effective video tour of the binding facility, narrated in the words and voices of bindery employees. Clear communication between library and binder is the message.

IB5. Merrill-Oldham, Jan. "Binding for Research Libraries." *The New Library Scene* 3 (August 1984): 4–6.
For annotation, *see* IB7.

IB6. ———. "Flow Charts of Library Binding: A Reassessment." *The New Library Scene* 8 (Feb. 1989): 7–9.
For annotation, *see* IB7.

IB7. ———. "Method of Leaf Attachment: A Decision Tree for Library Binding. University of Connecticut at Storrs." *The New Library Scene* 4 (August 1985): 16.

These three articles (IB5, IB6, and IB7) lay out a flowchart of analysis and action in binding and rebinding materials of permanent research value.

IB8. Merrill-Oldham, Jan, and Paul A. Parisi. *Guide to the Library Binding Institute Standard for Library Binding.* Chicago: American Library Association, 1990.

This *Guide* was written to explicate, interpret, and expand upon the eighth edition of the *LBI Standard* (IB9). Offers the reader additional guidance in choosing binding options and methods. The *Guide* and the *Standard* both should be consulted when preparing library binding specifications and contracts.

IB9. Parisi, Paul A., and Jan Merrill-Oldham, eds. *Library Binding Institute Standard for Library Binding.* 8th ed. Rochester, N.Y.: Library Binding Institute, 1986.

This edition of the *LBI Standard* greatly improved the documentation of conservation-related commercial library binding. It is arranged as an introduction followed by technical specifications, materials specifications, and a glossary all within seventeen pages. The *Standard* allows those drafting binding contracts to cite sections in a shorthand reference where most appropriate. An essential source until a new and improved (ninth) edition is prepared. A National Information Standards Organization (NISO) standard is being developed and can be expected in the next two to five years. See also Merrill-Oldham and Parisi (IB8) for the companion to the current (eighth) edition.

IC
Conservation
(Books and Paper)

This section lists the most important works on the physical treatment or conservation of books and paper by conservators and conservation technicians. It has been divided into two subsections that deal separately with general and special collections materials. The general collections literature—related to "collection conservation," as it is called now—includes those reflecting some generally accepted practices (usually of academic and research libraries) on materials of permanent research value. The section on special collections includes sources about conservation of rare books and works of art on paper. Also included are important citations about curator-conservator communication. The literature of conservation is in itself very extensive; this section is a mere sampling.

ICA
General Collections

ICA1. Byrne, Sherry. *Collection Maintenance and Improvement Program.* Washington, D.C.: Association of Research Libraries, 1993.

One of a series of brief monographs ("resource guides") written for ARL and libraries that are undertaking reviews of their preservation programs. This guide defines collections maintenance and outlines the elements of such a program, reviews how a library can investigate its current situation for improvement, and includes an annotated bibliography and reprints from the most germane sources. Includes guidelines and recommendations for nonbook, nonpaper media as well as for books.

ICA2. Milevski, Robert J., and Linda Nainis. "Implementing a Book Repair and Treatment Program." *Library Resources & Technical Services* 31 (Apr./June 1987): 159–76.

Presents "a workable design for establishing an in-house repair unit that will be a complementary component in the library's overall preservation program." Advice on justifying a repair facility, planning for and acquiring space and equipment, defining personnel requirements, and selecting for preservation or repair. Costs of various components discussed.

ICA3. Morrow, Carolyn Clark, and Carole Dyal. *Conservation Treatment Procedures: A Manual of Step-by-Step Proce-*

dures for the Maintenance and Repair of Library Materials. 2nd ed. Littleton, Colo.: Libraries Unlimited, 1986.

A popular general collections conservation manual that takes a systems approach to conservation and preservation in the library. The bulk of the volume is a step-by-step approach to analyzing book structure and condition, followed by treatment procedures. Of value are the many photographs that illustrate the procedures and a good annotated, selected bibliography.

ICA4. Morrow, Carolyn Clark, and Roy Weinstock, eds. *Library Preservation: Fundamental Techniques.* [videorecording] Washington, D.C.: Library of Congress, 1986. Six videocassettes in VHS or 3/4″ format.

Excellent set of videos accompanied by printed instructions and supplemental materials to make the package a particularly good way in which to gain familiarity with six procedures in house. Conservation professionals demonstrate the following: No. 1: "Surface Cleaning, Encapsulation, and Jacket-making"; No. 2: "Books in General Collections: Paper Repair and Pockets"; No. 3: "Pamphlet Binding"; No. 4: "Books in General Collections: Recasing"; No. 5: "Protective Enclosures: Simple Wrappers"; No. 6: "Protective Enclosures."

ICA5. *Polyester Film Encapsulation.* Illustrated by Margaret R. Brown. Washington, D.C.: Library of Congress, Preservation Office, Research Services, 1980.

This widely distributed pamphlet explains the properties, advantages, and disadvantages of polyester film encapsulation for physical support of flat paper-based materials. Step-by-step approaches to encapsulations are explained and illustrated. Recommends deacidification of documents prior to encapsulation. Pamphlet was written prior to the widespread availability of ultrasonic welding equipment.

ICA6. *Preservation and Conservation: Basic Preservation Techniques for Libraries and Archives.* Baltimore, Md.: Milton S. Eisenhower Library, Johns Hopkins University, 1987. 67-minute videotape (VHS, Beta, 3/4″) with accompanying manual.

A well-executed video with spiral-bound manual that can serve as an excellent teaching tool for staff and student assistants involved with conservation in the library or archive. Preservation principles and concepts are clearly outlined first. This is followed by step-by-step routine conservation actions: cleaning, mending, housing, pamphlet binding, protective enclosures, exhibit cradles, and in-house book repair.

ICB
Special Collections

ICB1. Brown, Margaret R., comp., with the assistance of Don Etherington and Linda McWilliams. *Boxes for the Protection of Rare Books: Their Design and Construction.* Washington, D.C.: Preservation Office, Library of Congress, 1982.

The standard manual for fabrication of protective boxes for rare materials requiring effective primary protection, usually drop-spine book boxes, phase boxes, and portfolios.

ICB2. Clapp, Anne E. *Curatorial Care of Works of Art on Paper*. 4th ed., rev. New York: Nick Lyons Books, 1987.

Excellent manual describing the procedures for protection and repair of works of art on paper, intended for the curator and conservation technician. Much of the work has application to library and archives materials. Bibliography and index.

ICB3. *Code of Ethics and Standards of Practice.* Amended May 24, 1985. Washington, D.C.: American Institute for Conservation of Historic and Artistic Works, 1985.

Statement of ethics and standards by the membership of the AIC, updated on occasion by AIC membership.

ICB4. Ellis, Margaret Holben. *The Care of Prints and Drawings*. Nashville: American Association for State & Local History Press, 1988.

Excellent source of practical information and advice; a complement to Clapp (ICB2). Arranged in five parts: support; media; matting, hinging, and framing; storage and environment; and basic preservation procedures. Appendixes, annotated bibliography, and index.

ICB5. Greenfield, Jane. *The Care and Repair of Fine Books*. New York: Nick Lyons Books, 1988.

A manual describing the general and specific in caring for book collections. Good title to recommend to private collectors as well as curators and conservators.

ICB6. Middleton, Bernard C. *The Restoration of Leather Bindings*. Rev. ed. Drawings by Aldren A. Watson. Library Technology Reports, Publication No. 18. Chicago: American Library Association, 1984.

A most important work on the subject, a manual describing the techniques of restoring leather bindings. Bibliographic references.

ICB7. *Paper Conservation Catalog.* Washington, D.C.: Book and Paper Group, American Institute for the Conservation of Historic and Artistic Works, 1984– . Looseleaf.

The *Catalog's* "statement of purpose" says that the intention of this ambitious tool is "to record a variety of treatment procedures in current use or with a history of use. Not intended to establish definitive procedures nor provide step-by-step recipes for the untrained." A reference work in progress distributed several chapters per year. Written by and for AIC Book & Paper Group (BPG) members. A remarkable resource in the making.

ICB8. Paris, Jan. *Choosing and Working with a Conservator*. Atlanta, Ga.: SOLINET Preservation Program, Southeastern Library Network, Inc., 1990.

Intended for curators, librarians, and collectors interested in selecting a professional to conserve their most valuable artifacts. Written by a trained conservator, the manual describes briefly what conservation is and what conservators are, how to find a conservator, suggested interview questions to pose to a conservator, and what to expect in a course of treatment. Additional resources and lists of regional conservation centers are given, along with a brief bibliography of further readings.

ICB9. Pilette, Roberta, and Carolyn Harris. "It Takes Two to Tango: A Conservator's View of Curator/Conservator Relations." *Rare Books and Manuscripts Librarianship* 4 (Fall 1989): 103–11.

Discusses the importance of good communication between curatorial and conservatorial professionals. Includes discussion of the dialogue necessary between the curator and the in-house or contractually secured conservator.

ICB10. Roberts, Matt T., and Don Etherington. *Bookbinding and the Conservation of Books: A Dictionary of Descriptive Terminology*. Washington, D.C.: Preservation Office, Library of Congress, 1982.

For annotation, *see* IAB3.

ICB11. Smith, Merrily A., comp. *Matting and Hinging of Works of Art on Paper*. Illustrations by Margaret R. Brown. Washington, D.C.: Library of Congress, 1981.

Introduces to the nonspecialist the techniques of matting and hinging developed and used by the Library of Congress. Well illustrated, clearly written, and contains a glossary and a list of needed supplies.

ICB12. Waters, Peter. "Phased Preservation: A Philosophical Concept and Practical Approach to Preservation." *Special Libraries* 81 (Winter 1990): 35–43.

An essay on the history, principles, and practices of phased preservation—actions that meet the short-term needs of items that eventually might require full conservation treatment, especially in large collections. Waters discusses a number of phased approaches not limited to the fabrication of phase boxes, and he outlines the point/quota system used at the Library of Congress and elsewhere for allocating conservation resources.

ICB13. Young, Laura A. *Bookbinding & Conservation by Hand: A Working Guide*. New York: R. R. Bowker, 1981.

Thorough coverage by an authority on hand bookbinding. Illustrated, with bibliography and index.

ID
Cooperative Preservation

An early assumption by library administrators was that preservation of library collections was too vast a task for any one library. Cooperative or collaborative approaches for preservation have a long history going back at least to the 1930s for cooperative preservation microfilming. The literature in this section includes the important resources about the national and international brittle books effort and how regional centers, states, national organizations, and international cooperation benefit the tasks at hand.

ID1. *Access to Library Resources through Technology and Preservation.* Edited by Robert P. Doyle. Proceedings of the 1988 U.S.–U.S.S.R. Seminar, July 5–8, 1988, Washington, D.C. Chicago: American Library Association, 1989.

General Session IV is concerned specifically with the current status of preservation programs in the two countries and intersperses Soviet and U.S. descriptions of existing programs and efforts. An example of a hopeful exchange of information and a cooperative spirit before the collapse of the Soviet Union.

ID2. *Brittle Books: Reports of the Committee on Preservation and Access.* Washington, D.C.: Council on Library Resources, 1986.

A compilation of reports from CLR's Committee on Preservation and Access related to the brittle books challenge as a cooperative endeavor. One of the first appearances in print of the mission of the Commission on Preservation and Access. Enhanced access is a clear focus of the reports. Important background document.

ID3. **Fox, Lisa L.** "The SOLINET Preservation Program: Building a Preservation Network in the Southeast." *The New Library Scene* 7 (Aug. 1988): 1, 5–9.

A profile of the successful SOLINET Preservation Program, from the perspective of a member of its staff.

ID4. **Gwinn, Nancy E.** "CLR and Preservation." *College & Research Libraries* 42 (Mar. 1981): 104–26.

Lest the immense positive impact of Verner Clapp and Jim Haas on cooperative library preservation efforts be forgotten, Gwinn's article provides a succinct history of the Council on Library Resources' (CLR) influence from its formation by the Ford Foundation in 1956. Includes a bibliography of items resulting from or related to CLR-supported programs, covering 1956–1980.

ID5. _____. "The Rise and Fall and Rise of Cooperative Projects." *Library Resources & Technical Services* 29 (Jan./Mar. 1985): 80–86.

A concise history of cooperative preservation microfilming efforts among U.S. and some foreign agencies and libraries from 1938 into the 1980s. Important source for historical perspective. Refers to several important cooperative projects.

ID6. **Harris, Carolyn.** "Cooperative Approaches to Preservation Microfilming." In *Preservation Microfilming: Planning & Production,* 55–65. Papers from the RTSD Preservation Microfilming Institute, New Haven, Conn., Apr. 21–23, 1988. Chicago: Association for Library Collections and Technical Services, American Library Association, 1989.

Clear discussion of the realities of library involvement in cooperative preservation microfilming projects and programs. Review of advantages, issues to be considered, models of such programs, local issues related to participation, and a set of axioms for successful cooperative projects.

ID7. **Hayes, Robert.** *The Magnitude, Costs and Benefits of the Preservation of Brittle Books.* Washington, D.C.: Council on Library Resources, 1987.

Originally prepared in some haste for the Committee on Preservation and Access in 1984–1985, this more-refined edition from the Council characterizes the magnitude and costs of the brittle books problem in the nation's largest research libraries. It provided the basis for the estimates of numbers of unique embrittled volumes to be preserved in the nationwide preservation microfilming effort. An important document in its approach and findings. Bibliography.

ID8. **Miller, J. Hillis.** *Preserving the Literary Heritage.* Commission on Preservation and Access. Report. Washington, D.C.: The Commission, 1991.

Final report of the Scholarly Advisory Committee on Modern Language and Literature of the Commission on Preservation and Access. Briefly (seven pages) summarizes the basic considerations of a committee of scholars and their recommendations for action by professional organizations and individuals within the discipline.

ID9. *National Conference on the Development of Statewide Preservation Programs.* Edited by Carolyn Clark Morrow. Sponsored by the Library of Congress, and others. Washington, D.C.: Distributed by the Commission on Preservation and Access, 1991.

Papers from the 1989 conference "on the current status and future directions of statewide programs for the preservation of our intellectual heritage" at which nearly all states were represented. A number of nationwide, statewide, and local efforts are showcased, including the exemplary programs. Brief bibliography.

ID10. *Our Memory at Risk: Preserving New York's Unique Research Resources.* Albany, N.Y.: New York State Education Department, 1988.

A report and recommendations to the citizens of New York by the New York Document Conservation Advisory Council. New York was among the first of a growing number of states that have studied and documented the needs of preservation and access in the state, done with assistance from the National Endowment for the Humanities (Division of Preservation and Access). This widely distributed and widely cited 1988 report is the result of intensive study and consensus building among state archivists, librarians, educators, and others. Recommendations identify the recommended action, initiators, and resources. Note: other states' preservation studies and plans are also available.

ID11. **Russell, Ann, Karen Motylewski, and Gay Tracy.** "Northeast Document Conservation Center: A Leader in Preservation." *Library Resources & Technical Services* 32 (Jan. 1988): 43–47.

A profile of the successful and influential NEDCC from the perspective of three members of its staff.

ID12. Stevenson, Condict Gaye. *Working Together: Case Studies in Cooperative Preservation.* Commission on Preservation and Access. Report. Washington, D.C.: The Commission, 1991.

Profiles in six cooperative preservation programs including those in Connecticut, Los Angeles, Nebraska, New York (an audiovisual preservation program), Oklahoma, and Pittsburgh. Lists three additional start-up programs in North Carolina, New York, and Amigos Bibliographic Council. A convenient source of locating lists of cooperating agencies in preservation. Bibliography.

ID13. Welsh, William J. "The Library of Congress: A More-Than-Equal Partner." *Library Resources & Technical Services* 29 (Jan./Mar. 1985): 87–93.

A perspective of the nation's largest library as a participant in nationwide and international cooperative preservation efforts and initiatives. Of historical and continuing interest for LC's role.

IE
Paper Deacidification and Quality

With the enthusiasm that electronic information resources have created in librarianship, one might forget that paper has been and can continue to be in the future an "archival" medium, with life expectancies in the hundreds of years. However, most of the vast collections of paper-based materials held in the nation's libraries have much shorter expected shelf lives because their papers are acidic. Although the technology is encouraging for the mass "deacidification" of book and record papers, there appears no certainty or assurance that such technologies will find the market necessary to become commercially viable. Many issues still need sorting out before mass deacidification is a routine in any library; these issues include costs per volume, capitalization costs, and labor costs for selection and processing books treated in the deacidification process. The resources here include descriptions of processes and of management issues to be considered when preparing for collection treatment. A few sources about paper manufacturing also are included. This is an area that is changing rapidly.

IE1. Clapp, Verner W. "The Story of Permanent/Durable Book Paper, 1115-1970." *Scholarly Publishing* 2 (Jan. 1971): 107–24; 2 (Apr. 1971): 229–45; and 2 (July 1971): 353–67.

Delightfully readable history of the decline of paper permanence (shelf life) and durability (ability to withstand usage) from the Middle Ages through the mid-twentieth century. Points to residual paper acidity as the largely ignored cause of paper deterioration from the early 1800s. Penned by the late, venerable preservation advocate and change agent Verner W. Clapp of the Council on Library Resources. Bibliographic references.

IE2. Committee on Institutional Cooperation, Task Force on Mass Deacidification. *Mass Deacidification: A Report to the Library Directors.* Champaign, Ill.: CIC, 1992.

In 1989 the library directors of the Committee on Institutional Cooperation (CIC, which consists of the Big Ten universities plus the University of Chicago) charged a Task Force on Mass Deacidification "to pursue activities towards positioning the CIC Libraries to take timely and responsible action on mass deacidification." This report is a result of that study and represents the most serious effort to date rationally to choose a mass deacidification vendor and to consider the logistical in-house implications of such a program. The report itself consists of a series of justified recommendations to the library directors. The appendixes are of equal or greater interest because of the documentation of surveys, selection issues, treatment records, contracts, quality control, toxicology review, in-house processing, and correspondence. Two vendors, Akzo Chemical (DEZ process) and FMC Corporation (Lithco process), are the focus of the process discussions.

IE3. Cunha, George M. "Mass Deacidification for Libraries." *Library Technology Reports* 23 (May/June 1987): 359–472.

For annotation, *see* IE4.

IE4. ———. "Mass Deacidification for Libraries: 1989 Update." *Library Technology Reports* 25 (Jan./Feb. 1989): 5–81.

The publication of this and the previous source (IE3) is indicative of the pace of development and change in mass deacidification technology and marketing. The American Library Association's *Library Technology Reports* commissioned Cunha to do the 1987 study (IE3), which contains a broad overview of paper preservation and considerable technical detail on the diethyl zinc (DEZ) and Wei T'o mass deacidification systems. Also includes the Austrian National Library's system for conserving newsprint. The 1989 update was produced to add several additional mass deacidification companies and processes that became, at least for a time, contenders in the slowly developing market for deacidification services. Bibliography.

IE5. *Paper Preservation: Current Issues and Recent Developments.* Edited by Philip Luner. Atlanta: TAPPI Press, 1990.

This book contains primarily the papers from the Technical Association for the Pulp and Paper Industry (TAPPI) Paper Preservation Symposium held in 1988 in Washington, D.C. It is divided into five parts, including congressional voices, preservation concerns, testing and monitoring of paper aging, alkaline papers, and book preservation technologies. The last section is a review of the state of thinking about the science of mass paper preservation as of late 1988. Since then, many changes and important marketplace developments have occurred. Bibliographic references.

IE6. *Permanence/Durability of the Book.* 7 vols. Richmond, Va.: W. J. Barrow Research Laboratory, 1963–74.

Landmark studies by William Barrow and his laboratory investigating and documenting a number of book/paper permanence and durability issues: the shelf-life expectancy of book papers, especially those from acidic post-1800 books; spray deacidification; polyvinyl acetate (pva) adhesives for library binding; and spot testing for paper quality. Very influential, historic studies sponsored by the Council on Library Resources.

IE7. *Preserving Knowledge: The Case for Alkaline Paper.* Rev. ed. Washington, D.C.: Association for Research Libraries, 1990.

A compilation of twenty-seven items "to highlight progress and considerable success in promoting the use of alkaline paper in book production." Organized into seven sections: background articles, paper industry developments, library community initiatives, author and publisher support, federal and state government responses, standards, and fact sheets from the four organizations that assisted in the compilation. Predicts and documents the rapid changeover from acid to alkaline papermaking in the United States. Handy source for text of federal legislation to establish a national policy on permanent paper and for text of legislation adopted or drafted in six states.

IE8. *A Roundtable on Mass Deacidification: Report on a Meeting Held September 12-13, 1991 in Andover, Massachusetts.* Edited by Peter G. Sparks. Sponsored by the Association of Research Libraries and the Northeast Document Conservation Center. Washington, D.C.: Association of Research Libraries, 1992.

The papers from this conference represent a meeting of the minds on the subject. They cover the subject with authority, including issues related to administration and management, collection development, funding, cooperative approaches, special collections, toxicology, laboratory tests, technical evaluation of processes, and experiences with trial treatments. Highly recommended in preparing for mass deacidification of collections.

IE9. **Sparks, Peter G.** *Technical Considerations in Choosing Mass Deacidification Processes.* Commission on Preservation and Access; Report. Washington: Commission on Preservation and Access, 1990.

An important source for library administrators considering mass deacidification. Introduces the topic in the context of library preservation, briefly outlines what is known about mass deacidification, explains the differences between mass- and single-item treatment strategies, states the difficulties in choosing a process, and discusses the technical evaluation factors in mass deacidification.

The technical evaluation also describes administrative issues: effectiveness, process engineering, toxicity, costs, vendor performance, liability, and other considerations.

IE10. **Turko, Karen.** *Mass Deacidification Systems: Planning and Managerial Decision Making.* Washington, D.C.: Association of Research Libraries, 1990.

Administrators would do well to read this report in conjunction with Sparks (IE8 and IE9) and the CIC report (IE2) because the four cover most if not all the pertinent issues of mass deacidification. Turko's work is the most introductory of the four but provides comparative information on competing processes. In-house operational issues and implementation models are covered briefly.

IE11. **U.S. Congress, Office of Technology Assessment.** *Book Preservation Technologies.* Washington, D.C.: U.S. Government Printing Office, 1988. OTA-0-375.

For annotation, *see* IE12.

IE12. _____. *Book Preservation Technologies Summary.* Washington, D.C.: U.S. Government Printing Office, 1988. OTA-0-376.

Detailed review by the congressional technology analytical unit of the diethyl zinc (DEZ) mass deacidification process in the context of the Library of Congress's situation and needs. Provides details of the DEZ process development, effectiveness, costs, safety, and health and environmental effects. Comparisons are made with other mass deacidification processes that were available in late 1987. Appendixes provide brief definitions of terms used and estimated operating and capital cost estimates (as of November 1987). Bibliographic references.

IE13. **Zimmermann, Carole.** *Bibliography on Mass Deacidification.* Washington, D.C.: Preservation Office, Library of Congress, 1991.

Arranged in chronological segments, this unannotated bibliography of 259 entries up through 1990 includes citations from scientific, library science, and popular works. The arrangement makes the bibliography more useful, especially since it also has an author index. Preface suggests updates may be forthcoming.

IF

Disaster Control, Recovery, and Insurance

Librarians fool themselves if they assume they can move through their careers without experiencing a major disaster or catastrophe that affects collections and services. Preparation is the only hedge against the destruction and disruption caused by fire, flood, and other calamities. The literature of library disaster control is huge and never ending. (*See* Toby Murray's 700-plus bibliography [IF11] as an example.) Included here are sources that should provide all one needs to get a good grasp of the issues of prevention, preparation, and response. *See also* section LG on "Security, Theft, and Mutilation" in Chapter L, Access Services.

IF1. Barton, John P., and Johanna G. Wellheiser, eds. *An Ounce of Prevention: A Handbook on Disaster Contingency Planning for Archives, Libraries, and Record Centres.* Toronto: Toronto Area Archivists Group Education Foundation, 1985.

An outstanding resource for disaster contingency planning, full of information and advice of value to preservation administrators and those involved in risk management in libraries and archives. Coverage, as comprehensive as any source on the subject, includes general planning considerations, prevention strategies, checklists in handling specific disasters, salvage operations, and recovery. Large bibliography and other appendixes of interest, including a good index. Focus on suppliers, services, and materials is largely Canadian.

IF2. Buchanan, Sally A., with bibliography by Toby Murray. *Disaster Planning, Preparedness and Recovery for Libraries and Archives: A RAMP Study with Guidelines.* Paris: UNESCO, 1988.

One of a series of internationally distributed preservation tools, this was put together by an expert in preparation, salvage, and recovery. Coverage includes planning, preparation, prevention, response, and recovery. A practical approach, with a real-world perspective. Appendixes and large bibliography.

IF3. *Disaster Preparedness: Planning Resource Packet.* New York State Program for the Conservation and Preservation of Library Research Materials. Albany, N.Y.: University of the State of New York, State Education Department [and] New York State Library, Division of Library Development, 1989. 1 packet with 9 pieces.

A packet of nine items of value for disaster preparedness and planning. They are "Hell and High Water: A Disaster Information Sourcebook"; Mildred O'Connell's "Disaster Planning: Writing and Implementing Plans for Collections-holding Institutions"; Sally Buchanan's "Disaster Prevention, Preparedness and Action" and "Resource Materials for Disaster Planning in New York Institutions"; "Statewide Disaster Planning and Recovery Volunteers for Library and Archival Collections in New York"; "Publications Available from the National Fire Protection Association"; Betty Walsh's "Salvage Operations for Water-damaged Collections"; "Salvage of Water-damaged Archival Collections: Salvage at a Glance"; and Peter Waters's "Procedures for Salvage of Water-damaged Library Materials."

IF4. Fortson, Judith. *Disaster Planning and Recovery: A How-to-Do-It Manual for Librarians and Archivists.* How-to-Do-It Manuals for Libraries, no. 21. New York: Neal-Schuman Publishers, 1992.

This is a much-welcomed recent addition to the extensive literature in disaster control and recovery. A clearly written how-to approach that nicely complements *An Ounce of Prevention* (IF1) for libraries in the United States. Chapters on fire, water/wind, earthquakes, recovery, developing a plan, and managing the risk. A good bibliography and seven appendixes: vendors of supplies and services, useful addresses, National Fire Protection Association (NFPA) documentation, and other sources of interest.

IF5. Hendriks, Klaus B., and Brian Lesser. "Disaster Preparedness and Recovery: Photographic Materials." *American Archivist* 46 (Winter 1983): 52–68.

Report about experiments done with recovery of water-damaged, still photographic images. Pages 64–68 summarize findings and recommendations in handling this sensitive medium after water damage. Reel formats (motion picture and microfilm) not included in study.

IF6. *Library and Archival Disaster: Preparedness and Recovery.* [videorecording] Oakton, Va.: BiblioPrep, 1986. VHS videocassette, 21 minutes, with manual. Also titled *Library Disaster: Prevention & Recovery.*

Excellent orientation video for a disaster preparedness effort (if it is shown well before the catastrophe occurs). Step-by-step approach to preparation for a major disaster. Sobering and effective.

IF7. Matthews, Fred W. "Sorting a Mountain of Books." *Library Resources & Technical Services* 31 (Jan./Mar. 1987): 88–94.

An account of the process of sorting and reshelving 100,000 volumes removed from the Halifax, Nova Scotia, Dalhousie University fire and water damage of 1985. This article details a computer-assisted approach to a real problem not addressed much in the literature.

IF8. Morris, John. *The Library Disaster Preparedness Handbook.* Chicago: American Library Association, 1986.

The title of this work is not as descriptive as it might have been since it covers other issues not directly related to disasters, such as basic building security, problem patrons, theft/mutilation of library materials, and preservation/conservation. The work has been criticized for this; nevertheless, it provides an authoritative view of fire protection, water damage, safety and security, planning and design, and insurance and risk management. Also, the glossary, bibliography, and index make this source a valuable contribution.

IF9. _____. *Managing the Library Fire Risk.* 2nd ed. Berkeley: University of California, 1979.

A seminal work in the literature of disaster control. It has informed a whole generation of librarians and archivists of the vulnerability of their collections, the value in contingency planning, and the wisdom of fire suppressant systems.

IF10. ———. "Fire Protection for the Library." *The Construction Specifier* 42, no. 10 (Oct. 1989): 133–41.

Written for nonlibrarians, it considers the history of some famous library fires and relates them to architecture, design, and materials used in construction. Gives a brief overview of current thinking about planning for fire protection in new and renovated facilities. Discusses compartmentalization, currently available fire suppression systems, book-return design, fire-retardant paint, and other factors. References.

IF11. Murray, Toby, comp. *Bibliography on Disaster, Disaster Preparedness, and Disaster Recovery.* Tulsa, Okla.: Oklahoma Conservation Congress, Feb. 1991.

An extensive unannotated bibliography, updated occasionally. Available from the Preservation Officer at the Oklahoma Department of Libraries. The current bibliography contains over 700 citations covering the gamut from an article on "roach-proof book varnish" (from a 1913 Philippine journal) to articles on floods in the 1990s. Includes citations of current and lasting value alongside those of ephemeral value.

IF12. Myers, Marcia J. *Insuring Library Collections and Buildings.* SPEC Kit, no. 178. Washington, D.C.: Office of Management Services, Association of Research Libraries, 1991.

Results of a survey of insurance practices and coverage by ARL libraries. Reproduces documents about insurance coverage, collection valuation, and losses/claims. A valuable contribution because these documents are not easily obtainable elsewhere.

IF13. National Fire Protection Association (NFPA). [*Codes and Standards*] Quincy, Mass.: NFPA, various dates.

The following codes and standards are important in a collection of materials related to disaster prevention and control. They are arranged alphabetically with date of latest issue or update. Librarians and archivists are not the primary readers and users of all these codes and standards; however, it is important that they be aware of their contents.

Automatic Fire Detectors. NFPA 72E. 135 pp., 1990.
Cellulose Nitrate Motion Picture Film. NFPA 40. 18 pp., 1988.
Fire Prevention Code. NFPA 1. 33 pp., 1987.
Halon 1211 Fire Extinguishing Systems. NFPA 12B. 45 pp., 1990.
Halon 1301 Fire Extinguishing Systems. NFPA 12A. 61 pp., 1989.
Inspection, Testing and Maintenance of Sprinkler Systems. NFPA 13A. 27 pp., 1987.
Inspection, Testing and Maintenance of Water-Based Fire Protection Systems. NFPA 25. 90 pp., 1992.
Installation of Sprinkler Systems. NFPA 13. 130 pp., 1991.
Libraries and Library Collections. NFPA 910. 45 pp., 1991.
Life Safety Code. NFPA 101. 327 pp., 1992.
Museums and Museum Collections. NFPA 911. 38 pp., 1992.
Portable Fire Extinguishers. NFPA 10. 53 pp., 1990.
Protection of Records. NFPA 232. 18 pp., 1991.

IF14. New York University Libraries, Preservation Committee. *Disaster Plan Workbook.* New York: New York University Libraries, 1984.

A workbook used by many libraries to avoid reinventing the disaster contingency planning wheel. The looseleaf, fill-in format can assist the local disaster contingency plan writers by saving time in creating a unique organization for a written plan. In any situation, variations will be necessary to meet the local need, but this may be just the ticket for many libraries looking for an organization for their written plan. Other supporting literature such as Barton and Wellheiser (IF1), Fortson (IF4), and Morris (IF8) should be consulted in the process, however.

IF15. *Recovery of Water-damaged Library Materials.* [slide-tape] A workshop sponsored by the Illinois Cooperative Conservation Program. Carbondale, Ill.: Illinois Cooperative Conservation Program, Morris Library, Southern Illinois University, 1986. Slides, audiotape, and printed script.

A good audiovisual tool for beginning to train staff or volunteers for salvage of water-damaged books, paper, catalog cards, photographs, and some audiovisual materials. Toby Murray, well-known library and archives disaster control expert, leads the workshop.

IF16. Shelton, John A. *Seismic Safety Standards for Library Shelving: California State Library Manual of Recommended Practice.* Sacramento: California State Library Foundation, 1990.

Published earthquake safety standards for library shelving in California. Information in the standard would be valuable anywhere seismic activity is a threat.

IF17. Ungarelli, Donald L. "Insurance and Preservation: Why and How?" *Library Trends* 33 (Summer 1984): 57–67.

A brief overview of insurance for libraries, with discussion of insurance history, the modern insurance industry, loss factors, examples of losses, prevention and preparedness, risk management, appraisals and valuations of property, insurance options, and lack of recognition of protective and preventative measures. This issue of *Library Trends* is entitled "Protecting the Library" and has additional articles of interest to disaster control, protection, and security.

IG

Environmental Control and Pest Management

The library building is truly the first line of defense for its collections. The quality of the storage environment and its ability to protect its contents from fire and other calamities can hardly be overestimated. Preservation specialists have increasingly familiarized themselves with the details of and have become advocates for controlling temperature, relative humidity, lighting, and related components of the library's physical environment. Also, a knowledge of pest control can be critical, especially in a time when chemicals for the control of insects and fungi are under increased scrutiny. This section includes sources for the study of the indoor environment.

IG1. American Society of Heating, Refrigerating and Air-Conditioning Engineers (ASHRAE). *Handbook of Fundamentals.* Atlanta: ASHRAE, 1991.

One of a series of publications published by ASHRAE. Covers the basics of controlling the indoor environment. Physical plant personnel and architects refer to the ASHRAE guides regularly. Bibliography and index.

IG2. Banks, Paul N. "Environmental Standards for Storage of Books and Manuscripts." *Library Journal* 99 (1 Feb. 1974): 339–43.

Although not recent, still a good introduction to the subject of the conservation environment, providing an excellent rationale for the effort. Some of the particulars relating to temperature and relative humidity will need to be checked with current guidelines for specific types of library materials. This article was distributed in the early 1990s as part of an "environmental controls resource packet" by the New York State Program for the Conservation and Preservation of Library Research Materials. Bibliographic references.

IG3. *Building Air Quality: A Guide for Building Owners and Facility Managers.* U.S. Environmental Protection Agency, Office of Air and Radiation, Office of Atmospheric and Indoor Air Programs, Indoor Air Division; U.S. Department of Health and Human Services, Public Health Service, Centers for Disease Control, National Institute for Occupational Safety and Health. (DHHS NIOSH Publication no. 91–114.) Washington, D.C.: Superintendent of Documents, Government Printing Office, 1991.

The focus of this volume is not specifically the preservation of library and archives materials, but it does contain helpful, up-to-date background information for those concerned with the indoor environment. Bibliography and index.

IG4. Canadian Conservation Institute. *Technical Bulletins.* Ottawa: Canadian Conservation Institute, 1978– . ISSN 0706-4152.

A series of authoritative guidelines for libraries, museums, and archives. Readers should check for the latest revision available.

Lafontaine, Raymond H.
Environmental Norms for Canadian Museums, Art Galleries and Archives. Technical Bulletin 5. 1981.
Fluorescent Lamps. Technical Bulletin 7. 1982.

Recommended Environmental Monitors for Museums, Galleries and Archives. Technical Bulletin 3. 1980.
Silica Gel. Technical Bulletin 10. 1984.

Macleod, K. J.
Museum Lighting. Technical Bulletin 2. 1978.
Relative Humidity: Its Importance, Measurement, and Control in Museums. Technical Bulletin 1. 1978.

Strang, Thomas J. K., and John E. Dawson.
Controlling Museum Fungal Problems. Technical Bulletin 12. 1991.
Controlling Vertebrate Pests in Museums. Technical Bulletin 13. 1991.

IG5. *Hold Everything! A Storage and Housing Information Sourcebook for Libraries and Archives.* New York: New York Metropolitan Reference and Research Library Agency (METRO), 1990.

A practical source whose title is descriptive. Covers the physical environment, monitoring, shelving/storage furniture, housekeeping, moving, suppliers, services, consultants, and professional organizations. Each section contains brief and basic information, but the value of the work lies in the lists of sources for supplies and services, which are generally companies with nationwide distribution systems.

IG6. Lee, Mary Wood. *Prevention and Treatment of Mold in Library Collections with Emphasis on Tropical Climates: A RAMP Study.* Paris: UNESCO, 1988.

RAMP is the Records and Archives Management Programme of UNESCO. Respected source of advice on the very difficult challenge of controlling fungal growth in warm, damp environments.

IG7. Lull, William P., with the assistance of Paul N. Banks. *Conservation Environment Guidelines for Libraries and Archives.* Albany, N.Y.: University of the State of New York, 1991.

By far the best single source for technical information for librarians and archivists concerned with the physical environment in their collections. Filled with accurate information about the conservation environment and how to assess, monitor, and achieve it. Well designed and well written for clarity in describing such things as heating, ventilating, air-conditioning systems; lighting; fire protection; design/conservation processes; and more. Appendixes include an explication of abbreviations and terms, a brief annotated bibliography, and one page on selecting manufacturers. Indexed.

IG8. Metcalf, Keyes D. *Planning Academic and Research Libraries.* 2nd ed. Revised by Philip D. Leighton and David C. Weber. Chicago: American Library Association, 1986.

An essential work for planning new or renovated academic library facilities. Not organized as a reference book and thus is best read cover-to-cover. Focus is on the planning process. The original 1966 edition is also recommended.

IG9. Nyberg, Sandra. *The Invasion of the Giant Spore.* SOLINET Preservation Program, Leaflet Number 5. Atlanta: Southeastern Library Network, Inc., 1987.

Covers the mold-preventive environment and mold eradication, with plenty of caveats regarding health and safety. Additional concerns and controls over pesticides have been raised since the publication of this leaflet, so check with local authorities before moving ahead with fumigation. Bibliography.

IG10. Padfield, Timothy. "Climate Control in Libraries and Archives." In *Preservation of Library Materials: Conference Held at the National Library of Austria, Vienna, April 7–10, 1986,* edited by Merrily A. Smith, 124–38. Vol. 2, IFLA Publications 41. Munich: K. G. Saur, 1987.

A good place to begin with the basic principles of indoor climate control of repositories. Written for the nonspecialist and very readable. Covers relative humidity and dew point, technology of climate control, air pollution, controls and calibration, specific needs of readers and collections, effects of controls on the building itself, passive climate control, and indoor air pollution. Bibliographic references indicate a few standard industry (nonlibrary) indoor climate control sources.

IG11. Parker, Thomas A. "Integrated Pest Management for Libraries." In *Preservation of Library Materials: Conference Held at the National Library of Austria, Vienna, April 7–10, 1986,* edited by Merrily A. Smith, 103–23. Vol. 2, IFLA Publications 41. Munich: K. G. Saur, 1987.

Parker, a noted expert on pest management, covers insects (cockroaches, silverfish, carpet beetles, cigarette beetles, drugstore beetles, psocids), rodents, mold, mildew, and fumigation. Includes straightforward and practical guidelines on how to control the pests. The audience for Parker's paper at this IFLA-sponsored conference included many from the tropics, librarians and archivists who face very serious pest control problems. Additional references cite other important sources.

IG12. *Preservation of Historical Records.* Committee on Preservation of Historical Records, National Materials Advisory Board, Commission on Engineering and Technical Systems, National Research Council. Washington, D.C.: National Academy Press, 1986.

See also annotation under IIA5. Chapter 3, "Environmental Criteria" provides well-documented recommendations for indoor environments, taking into consideration paper and nonpaper formats. They form the basis for the environmental standards for the new National Archives building.

IG13. Sebera, Donald K. "A Graphical Representation of the Relationship of Environmental Conditions to the Permanence of Hygroscopic Materials and Composites." In *Proceedings of Conservation in Archives: International Symposium, Ottawa, Canada, May 10–12, 1988,* 51–57. Ottawa: National Archives of Canada, 1989.

A very important study of the combined effects of temperature and relative humidity on hygroscopic materials (especially paper) by a Library of Congress Preservation

Office scientist. Includes and describes an isoperm: "a simple graphical representation of the relationship of environmental factors to the permanence" of paper, wood, canvas, and other similar materials. The graphs and accompanying text are remarkable in their straightforward but dramatic depiction of the preservation enhancements that result from lowered temperatures and relative humidity levels in storage environments. Now being adapted by some libraries to justify lowered temperature and relative humidity specifications for off-site storage facilities and depositories. References.

IG14. Stolow, Nathan. *Conservation and Exhibitions: Packing, Transport, Storage, and Environmental Considerations.* London: Butterworths, 1987.

The textbook by the authority on the subject. Largely related to museum objects but has definite library applications. Bibliography. Index.

IG15. Story, Keith O. *Approaches to Pest Management in Museums.* Suitland, Md.: Smithsonian Institution Conservation Analytical Laboratory, 1985.

A good source of information for librarians. Divided into two distinct parts: an illustrated biology and outline control measures for a dozen common insect pests, and pest management approaches (e.g., using containers, heat, low temperature, nonchemical methods, conventional insecticides, etc.). Good source for identifying pests and learning what can be done. Each option is accompanied by an extensive bibliography, much of which may be too detailed or outdated to be of value to the librarian. Appendixes include index of chemical pesticide names, glossary of terms, and criteria for choosing pesticides.

IG16. Swartzburg, Susan Garretson, and Holly Bussey, with Frank Garretson. *Libraries and Archives: Design and Renovation with a Preservation Perspective.* Metuchen, N.J.: Scarecrow Press, 1991.

In two parts: part one provides a summary history of library design and preservation of books. Part two is a large bibliography of hundreds of sources, with one-sentence annotations, each section preceded by a brief introductory essay. An important addition to the literature. Indexed.

IG17. Thomson, Garry. *The Museum Environment.* 2nd ed. London: Butterworths, 1986.

As the title suggests, this work is written from the museum point of view. A widely cited source, especially for the bases of the concerns about temperature, relative humidity, light, and air pollution from the conservation science perspective. Considerable coverage about exhibition environments. Bibliography and index.

IG18. Wellheiser, Johanna G. *Nonchemical Treatment Processes for Disinfestation of Insects and Fungi in Library Collections.* IFLA Publications 60. Munich: K. G. Saur, 1992.

A timely and important addition to the literature. Reviews and describes current commonly used chemical treatments (such as ethylene oxide, methyl bromide, ortho-phenyl phenol, thymol, etc.) as well as nonchemical treatments such as freezing, gamma ray and microwave irradiation, and modified atmospheres. Includes section on other nonchemical treatment, control, and prevention methods that covers general environmental controls and facilities maintenance. Large bibliography. Index.

IH
Preservation Administration

Preservation management or "preservation administration," the term more often used, has been a growth field in the 1980s and early 1990s. This section includes resources on the day-to-day management of the preservation department and the overarching library preservation program. Costs for treatments and condition of collections are addressed, as are organizational issues and funding.

IH1. Association of Research Libraries. *ARL Preservation Statistics.* Washington, D.C.: Association of Research Libraries, 1988– . Annual. ISSN 1050-7442.

Compilation of preservation data from ARL libraries. An analysis of the figures helps document trends in the national preservation effort and assists ARL libraries in comparing and contrasting figures among similarly sized institutions.

IH2. Buchanan, Sarah, and Sandra Coleman. "Deterioration Survey of the Stanford University Libraries Green Library Stack Collection." *Preservation Planning Program: Resource Notebook,* rev. ed. by Wesley L. Boomgaarden, 189–221. Washington, D.C.: Office of Management Studies, Association of Research Libraries, 1987.

Published methodology and results of a book-condition survey at Stanford. Most subsequent library condition surveys have followed either this influential model or the methodology of the Yale Survey (IH17). Bibliography.

IH3. Cloonan, Michele Valerie. *Planning for Preservation.* Washington, D.C.: Office of Management Services, Association of Research Libraries, 1993.

One of a series of brief monographs ("resource guides") written for libraries reviewing their preservation programs or needs. Discusses various administrative contexts for organizing preservation programs. Also considers the process of change in the implementation of preservation policies and procedures. Bibliography.

IH4. Darling, Pamela W., comp. *Preservation Planning Program: Resource Notebook.* Expanded 1987 ed. edited by Wesley L. Boomgaarden. Washington, D.C.: Office of

Management Studies, Association of Research Libraries, 1987.

For annotation, *see* IAI1.

IH5. DeCandido, Robert, and GraceAnne A. De-Candido. "Micro-Preservation: Conserving the Small Library." *Library Resources & Technical Services* 29 (Apr./June 1985): 151–60.

Straightforward advice for preserving library collections. Details provided on environment, bookbinding, repair, other protection, unique items, and disaster control. Bibliography.

IH6. Harris, Carolyn, Carol Mandel, and Robert Wolven. "A Cost Model for Preservation: The Columbia University Libraries' Approach." *Library Resources & Technical Services* 35 (Jan. 1991): 33–54.

A detailed review of the cost components in routine library preservation functions, such as repair, rebinding, purchased replacement, photocopying, microfilming, etc. Documents staffing levels required for each function, time spent per function, percentage of costs by the dozen or so units involved, etc. Although results are specific to Columbia University Libraries, approach can be applied at other institutions. Fills a huge gap in cost model projections in the field.

IH7. Larsen, A. Dean, and Randy H. Silverman. "Preservation." In *Library Technical Services: Operations and Management,* edited by Irene P. Godden, 205–69. 2nd ed. San Diego: Academic Press, 1991.

Practical and sensible introduction and overview of preservation management in the context of both library technical services and library administration as a whole. Notable is this chapter's section on relationship to other departments, which covers in some way nearly every aspect of preservation management that is of concern in the 1990s. Glossary and bibliography.

IH8. Merrill-Oldham, Jan, ed. *Meeting the Preservation Challenge.* Washington, D.C.: Association of Research Libraries, 1988. Originally published as *Preservation: A Research Library Priority for the 1990s: Minutes of the 111th Membership Meeting of the Association of Research Libraries.*

Twelve papers written for an audience of research library directors (presented first at the ARL membership meeting in October 1987). Papers discuss a rationale for well-funded, comprehensive preservation programs. In addition to the perspectives on program development, this book is a source for James Billington's paper, "The Moral Imperative of Conservation" (IAA2).

IH9. Merrill-Oldham, Jan, Carolyn Clark Morrow, and Mark Roosa. *Preservation Program Models: A Study Project and Report.* Washington, D.C.: Committee on Preservation of Research Library Materials, Association of Research Libraries, 1991.

A brief monograph written for the ARL membership to identify and rationalize the components of research library preservation programs, providing models and benchmarks for their growth and development based upon collection size. Well written and clearly organized with four case histories for examples.

IH10. Merrill-Oldham, Jan, and Merrily A. Smith, eds. *The Library Preservation Program: Models, Priorities, Possibilities.* Chicago: American Library Association, 1985.

Papers from a conference in 1983 whose audience was primarily research library directors. The papers are excellent and cover organizational models; needs, priorities, and options; and fiscal concerns. Index.

IH11. *Preservation Guidelines in ARL Libraries.* SPEC Kit, no. 137. Washington, D.C.: Office of Management Studies, Association of Research Libraries, 1987.

The results of a survey of ARL statements of preservation policy and priorities, preservation decision-making documentation, and brittle-books programs. Includes "Guidelines for Minimum Preservation Efforts in ARL Libraries," approved by the ARL membership in 1984.

IH12. *Preservation Planning Program: An Assisted Self-Study Manual for Libraries.* Rev. 1993 ed. Developed by Pamela W. Darling with Duane E. Webster. Revised by Jan Merrill-Oldham and Jutta Reed-Scott. Washington, D.C.: Office of Management Services, Association of Research Libraries, 1993.

See also annotation under IAE3. The manual used by ARL and other libraries systematically to identify and address preservation problems. Organized to fit a formal ARL OMS Preservation Planning Program format, which is designed to put self-help tools into the hands of people responsible for developing plans and procedures for preserving library materials. Aims to assist libraries in developing local preservation programs.

IH13. *Preserving Harvard's Retrospective Collections.* Report of the Harvard University Library Task Group on Collection Preservation Priorities. Cambridge, Mass.: Harvard University Library, 1991.

A handsomely produced in-house report on the preservation needs and priorities in Harvard's vast collections of materials in many different physical formats. Outlines an overview and background of Harvard's collections and preservation issues, reviews selection criteria, outlines "umbrella" preservation programs in place or needed, and recommends additional strategies for preservation action and access. Four appendixes; of special interest are the preservation priority inventories completed and the funds listed as designated for preservation purposes.

IH14. Reed-Scott, Jutta, comp. *Preservation Organization and Staffing.* SPEC Kit, no. 160. Washington, D.C.: Office of Management Studies, Association of Research Libraries, 1990.

Through a review of the ARL Preservation Statistics surveys and through contact with several of the larger programs, the compiler documents major trends in preservation program management in the ARL. Reproduces organization charts, position descriptions, and planning documents (some from Preservation Planning Program efforts).

IH15. *Report on the Preservation Planning Project, University of Pennsylvania Libraries.* Washington, D.C.: Commission on Preservation and Access, 1991.

An institutional study on preservation needs and recommended actions that points to the use of contractual arrangements for most preservation and conservation services.

IH16. *Supporting Preservation and Access: Ideas for Preservation Fund Raising.* Washington, D.C.: Commission on Preservation and Access, 1991.

A fundraising support package, composed of a number of samples, available from the Commission on Preservation and Access.

IH17. Walker, Gay, Jane Greenfield, John Fox, and Jeffrey S. Simonoff. "The Yale Survey: A Large-Scale Study of Book Deterioration in The Yale University Library." *College & Research Libraries* 46 (Mar. 1985): 111–32.

Among the first published research reports about the physical conditions of books in large libraries. Methodology, scope, and conclusions of the study have been very influential in subsequent studies. Findings have been widely cited and discussed and have influenced management of preservation programs. Approach should be compared with Buchanan and Coleman (IH2) above.

II
Nonbook and Nonpaper Media

Libraries have acquired and continue to acquire for their permanent collections huge quantities of nonbook and nonpaper media. Each medium has its own complex chemistry and physical characteristics. Each has great variations in life expectancy. Text mutability and concern with long-term availability of playback equipment can further complicate handling. This section includes a sampling from an extensive literature in each format. It is a growing literature, reflecting new knowledge and new applications every year.

IIA
General Works and Bibliographies

IIA1. Bowling, Mary B. "Literature on the Preservation of Nonpaper Materials." *American Archivist* 53 (Winter 1990): 340–48.

A bibliographic essay and critical review that covers sound recordings, moving images, photographs, microforms, and magnetic/optical media in addition to general works and periodicals available on the subject.

IIA2. Cohen-Stratyner, Barbara, and Brigitte Kueppers, eds. *Preserving America's Performing Arts.* Papers from the Conference on Preservation Management for Performing Arts Collections, April 28–May 1, 1982, Washington, D.C. New York: Theatre Library Association, 1985.

Brief articles by knowledgeable professionals covering preservation concerns and actions related to the many diverse formats held in performing arts libraries. Includes music library materials, scrapbooks, playbills and programs, labanotation, film, videotape, sound recordings, costumes, photographs, and others. Bibliographic references in some chapters.

IIA3. Ellison, John W., and Patricia Ann Coty, eds. *Nonbook Media: Collection Management and User Services.* Chicago: American Library Association, 1987.

See also annotation under HD24. Section on maintenance and management (storage and care, management problems/solutions) of particular interest to preservation librarians.

IIA4. Henderson, Kathryn Luther, and William T. Henderson, eds. *Conserving and Preserving Materials in Nonbook Formats.* Allerton Park Institute, no. 30. Urbana-Champaign, Ill.: Graduate School of Library and Information Science, University of Illinois, 1991.

Papers from the 1988 Allerton Park Institute feature experts discussing preservation concerns and actions for the following media: sound recordings, computer records, motion pictures, newspapers, photographs, color images, textiles, archives, and maps. Additional papers cover planning and the role of vendors. Contains bibliographies and is indexed.

IIA5. *Preservation of Historical Records.* Committee on Preservation of Historical Records, National Materials Advisory Board, Commission on Engineering and Technical Systems, National Research Council. Washington, D.C.: National Academy Press, 1986.

Detailed technical discussions of the properties and preservation requirements of paper, photographic film, magnetic recording media, and optical disks. Frequent references to accepted standards for those materials and to environmental conditions. Specific focus of this volume is the National Archives. Bibliographies, glossary, index.

IIA6. Saffady, William. *Stability, Care and Handling of Microforms, Magnetic Media and Optical Disks.* Westport, Conn.: Meckler, 1991. Also published as *Library Technology Reports* 27, no. 1 (Jan./Feb. 1991).

See also annotation under JE12. Three major categories of nonbook/nonpaper media (microforms, magnetic media, and optical disks) are examined in detail.

IIA7. Swartzburg, Susan G., ed. *Conservation in the Library: A Handbook of Use and Care of Traditional and Non-Traditional Materials.* Westport, Conn.: Greenwood Press, 1983.

Chapters written by experts on various formats, including paper, books/bindings, photographs, slides, microforms, motion picture film, videotape, sound recordings, videodiscs, and the computer. Good background information, but in need of an update for the newer formats, such as video and computer media. Bibliographic references and index.

IIB
Archives and Manuscripts

IIB1. Calmes, Alan, Ralph Schofer, and Keith R. Eberhardt. *National Archives and Records Service (NARS) Twenty Year Preservation Plan.* Gaithersburg, Md.: National Bureau of Standards, 1985. NBSIR 85-2999.

Published preservation plan of the National Archives. Documents the magnitude of preservation need through the results of an extensive collections condition survey undertaken by the National Bureau of Standards in early 1980s. Outlines a plan emphasizing four points: perform maintenance systematically, intercept and assess documents at point of usage, systematically duplicate rapidly deteriorating copies, and conserve national treasures and records of intrinsic value (for which, *see* IJ6, *Intrinsic Value in Archival Material*).

IIB2. Casterline, Gail Farr. *Archives & Manuscripts: Exhibits.* SAA Basic Manual Series. Chicago: Society of American Archivists, 1980.

A manual covering all aspects of exhibition, including planning and development, conservation, design and technique, program coordination, and administrative considerations. Appendixes on additional sources for assistance, supplies and equipment, and report forms for facilities and loans. Extensive bibliography.

IIB3. O'Toole, James M. "On the Idea of Permanence." *American Archivist* 52 (Winter 1989): 10–25.

A well-documented essay that considers the relative or absolute meaning of the term "permanent" in archives. Bibliographic references.

IIB4. Ritzenthaler, Mary Lynn. *Archives & Manuscripts: Conservation. A Manual on Physical Care and Management.* SAA Basic Manual Series. Chicago: Society of American Archivists, 1983.

For annotation, *see* IAE4.

IIC
Cartographic Materials

IIC1. Cruse, Larry. "Storage of Maps on Paper, Microforms, Optical Disks, Digital Disks and Magnetic Memories." *Science & Technology Libraries* 5 (Spring 1985): 45–57.

Published long ago (relative to the scale of change in the digital world), this article nevertheless covers the basic issues still germane to storage of maps. Brief bibliography.

IIC2. Ehrenberg, Ralph E. *Archives & Manuscripts: Maps and Architectural Drawings.* SAA Basic Manual Series. Chicago: Society of American Archivists, 1982.

A general reference work for the archivist (or librarian), with two chapters devoted to conservation and storage. The conservation section covers inspection, flattening, surface cleaning, neutralizing and buffering, mending tears, reinforcement, and preservation photocopying. Guidelines for storage discuss maps and drawings in single, bound, and rolled formats. Bibliography.

IIC3. Larsgaard, Mary Lynette. *Map Librarianship: An Introduction.* 2nd ed. Littleton, Colo.: Libraries Unlimited, 1987.

Chapter 4 discusses storage, care, and repair with a well-documented historical perspective. Begins with general preservation and historical background on inherent flaws in paper and ink permanence, and the effects of the general environment. This is followed by one of the best and most in-depth writings available about map storage, handling, and conservation. Widely cited. Very extensive bibliography.

IIC4. Scott, Mary W. "Digital Imagery: Here Today but What about Tomorrow?" *Proceedings of the Geoscience Information Society* 23 (1993): 1–4.

Paper presented at the Geoscience Information Society Symposium: Preserving Geoscience Imagery, October 27, 1992, Geological Society of America 1992 Annual Meeting. An overview of several of the problems inherent in the mutability of mapping information: How are we to preserve the variant versions of maps stored only in electronic formats? Bibliography. Other papers related to cartographic materials preservation appear in this number of the *Proceedings.*

IIC5. *Western Association of Map Libraries Information Bulletin.* Sacramento, Calif.: The Association. v. 1– , 1970– . Three nos. per year. ISSN 0049-7982.

Includes information and updates related to preservation and conservation of cartographic materials.

IID
Computer-Based, Computer-Generated Records

IID1. Beaubien, Denise M., Bruce Emerton, Alice L. Primack, and Erich Kesse. "Patron-use Software in Academic Library Collections." *College & Research Libraries News* 49 (Nov. 1988): 661–67.

Thoughtful policy and practical approaches to the issues of purchasing, cataloging, circulating, preserving, and protecting software in an academic library. Preservation issues discussed include location of an archival copy, license or agreement restrictions on copying, storage, protective packaging, and protection from electronic security systems' sensitizing equipment. Bibliography.

IID2. DeWhitt, Benjamin L. "Long-Term Preservation of Data on Computer Magnetic Media." *Conservation Administration News* no. 29 (Apr. 1987): 7, 19, 28; and no. 30 (July 1987): 4, 24.

Brief, straightforward introduction to computer magnetic tape, its inherent characteristics, recording modes, handling, storage environment, long-term retention issues, and remedial measures for damaged tapes.

IID3. Geller, Sidney B. *Care and Handling of Computer Magnetic Storage Media.* NBS Special Publication 500-101. Washington, D.C.: Institute for Computer Science and Technology, National Bureau of Standards, 1983.

A widely cited source for the physical and chemical preservation of computer magnetic storage media—largely focused upon computer magnetic tapes and the data stored therein—by using proper care, storage, and handling methods. Essentially a detailed manual intended for data processing unit managers and their technical staffs. In addition to storage and handling guidelines, includes schedule maintenance of tapes, use of tape management system software, and operation of clean room. Bibliography.

IID4. Lesk, Michael. *Preservation of New Technology. A Report of the Technology Assessment Advisory Committee to the Commission on Preservation and Access.* Washington, D.C.: Commission on Preservation and Access, 1992.

A brief paper written about the nature of much nonbook, nonpaper library media acquired by libraries. These materials (analog video and audio media, obsolete computer media) are inherently impermanent, and their playback equipment becomes obsolete rather quickly. Provides technical background, discusses file conversion and computer-based archives, notes the copyright dilemma, and makes recommendations. The conclusions: preservation means copying, which must be budgeted; cooperation is important because of the technical expertise required; coordinated computer-based archives, conversion research, and standards activities should be encouraged; coordination among librarians, computing centers, and records managers is encouraged. References. Appendix of examples of computer archives now in existence in North America.

IID5. *Research Issues in Electronic Records.* Report of the Working Meeting. St. Paul: Published for the National Historic Publications and Records Commission, Washington, D.C., by the Minnesota Historical Society, 1991.

Summary report of a conference held with key archives personnel to discuss the issues, research necessities, and priorities as they relate to the long-term preservation of and access to archival information in computer-readable, machine-readable, and electronic forms. Bulk of text is in a series of similarly formatted questions-with-answers that cover research area, purpose, background, possible approaches, potential results, resources, and expected results. References.

IIE
Microforms

IIE1. Calmes, Alan. "New Confidence in Microfilm." *Library Journal* 111 (15 Sept. 1986): 38–42.

A relatively early review of the film vs. disk discussion, in which black-and-white microfilm gets good marks as a permanent imaging and preservation medium based upon research and upon the unknowns of digital media. Bibliographic references.

IIE2. *Caring for Your Microform Collection: The Next Step in Preservation.* [videorecording] Ann Arbor, Mich.: University Microfilms, Inc., 1991. 12-minute videocassette.

Reviews the basic concerns and issues in storing and handling microforms to maximize their useful lives. Good audio and visual discussion of the master negative, especially related to inspection of aged film for problems such as mirroring and redox blemishing. Equally good discussion of the care and handling of use ("distribution" or "service") copies of film and fiche, a demonstration of cleaning techniques, and a graphic demonstration of the value of polysulfide treatment. Distributed with a paper insert with additional information and a brief bibliography.

IIE3. Dodson, Suzanne Cates. "Microfilm Types: There Really Is a Choice." *Library Resources & Technical Services* 30 (Jan./Mar. 1986): 84–90.

A brief review of the permanence and durability characteristics of silver gelatin, diazo, and vesicular microfilms. Sensible treatment of the debates over which film types to employ for service copies in libraries, based upon shelf-life, scratch- and fade-resistance, and other life-expectancy issues in the microform reading room. References.

IIE4. Reilly, James M., Douglas W. Nishimura, Kaspars M. Cupriks, and Peter Z. Adelstein. "Stability of Black-and-White Photographic Images, with Special References to Microfilm." *Abbey Newsletter* 12 (July 1988): 83–88.

Report of research done at the Image Permanence Institute with specific reference to oxidation of image silver in photographic materials and responses to the redox blemish problems in film (especially microfilm) repositories. Discusses factors that cause redox, with an emphasis on the effects of improper processing (residual thiosulfate in the wash) and of subsequent film storage environments (temperature, humidity, and pollutants' effects). Concludes that sulfiding treatment (to the films) is an effective protection against the redox oxidation. References.

IIE5. Rouyer, Philippe. "Humidity Control and the Preservation of Silver Gelatin Microfilm." *Microform Review* 21 (Spring 1992): 74–76.

A brief discussion of the revised ANSI standard (IT9.11-1991) that covers, among other aspects of processed safety film, the relative humidity (RH) in storage of silver films on both cellulose acetate and polyester bases.

RH is recommended within the 30 to 40 percent range for both; this article explains why RH is so important (and also difficult) to control. References.

IIE6. *Storage and Preservation of Microfilms.* Rev. ed. Kodak Publication D-31. Rochester, N.Y.: Eastman Kodak, 1988.

Good coverage of the topic. Bibliography.

IIF
Moving Images

IIF1. Calmes, Alan. "New Preservation Concern: Video Recordings." (Commission on Preservation and Access) *Newsletter* no. 22 (April 1990): 5–6.

Matter-of-fact statement by the National Archives' preservation officer of the relative impermanence of a common and popular (but fugitive) medium. Technical alternatives for preservation for the long haul proposed.

IIF2. *Conference on the Cold Storage of Motion Picture Films.* Edited by Lawrence F. Karr. Washington, D.C.: American Film Institute, 1980.

Includes information about film cold storage facilities in the United States, Canada, Norway, and the United Kingdom. Reviews technical specifications related to storage facilities and color film restoration. Lists institutions involved and their addresses.

IIF3. Gordon, Paul L., ed. *The Book of Film Care.* Rev. ed. Kodak Publication H-23. Rochester, N.Y.: Eastman Kodak Co., 1992.

A manual with information on the physical nature and properties of motion pictures, with additional information on housing, maintenance, duplication, projection, and other handling. Illustrated. Bibliography.

IIF4. Kuiper, John B. "Preserving Our Moving Image Heritage: A Conspiracy of Facts." *Conservation Administration News* no. 44 (Jan. 1991): 4–5, 29–30.

A call for support for the preservation of and enhanced access to endangered motion pictures in the nation's archives and film libraries. Reprinted from conference remarks, it is an effective mixture of fact and editorial style but has no references or bibliography.

IIF5. Sargent, Ralph N. *Preserving the Moving Image.* Edited by Glen Fleck. Washington, D.C.: Corporation for Public Broadcasting, 1974.

Although not recent, this publication provides valuable background in the art and technology of moving image preservation. It is presented in the format of a survey of opinions about issues by representatives from the manufacturers in the field (in the early 1970s). Bibliographic references and index. Two much more up-to-date and complete sources—which are not so easily found—are Federation Internationale des Archives du Film, *Preservation and Restoration of Moving Images and Sound*, Brussels: FIAF, 1986 (new edition expected); and Stiftung Deutsche

Kinemathek, *Archiving the Audio-Visual Heritage: A Joint Technical Symposium*. West Berlin: SDK, 1988.

IIF6. Scholtz, James C. *Developing and Maintaining Video Collections in Libraries*. Santa Barbara, Calif.: ABC Clio Information Services, 1989.

See also annotation under HD34. Brief review of the technology of video (VHS and Beta) and its playback equipment. Section on videotape repair and maintenance covers testing, cleaning, storing of videos; reviews longevity issues; suggests guidelines for preservation; and discusses video repair and VCR maintenance. Bibliographies and index.

IIG
Miscellaneous Print and Paper

NEWSPAPERS AND NEWSPRINT

IIG1. Mills, T. F. "Preserving Yesterday's News for Today's Historian: A Brief History of Newspaper Preservation, Bibliography and Indexing." *Journal of Library History* 16 (Summer 1981): 463–87.

Historical perspective on the preservation, bibliography, and indexing of newspapers in the United States. For coverage of the National Endowment for the Humanities–sponsored U.S. Newspaper Project, *see* Jeffrey Field's "The U.S. Newspaper Program" in *Newspaper Preservation and Access*, 356–66 (IIG2).

IIG2. *Newspaper Preservation and Access*. Proceedings of the Symposium Held in London, August 12–15, 1987. Edited for the Section on Serial Publications and the Working Group on Newspapers by Ian P. Gibb. 2 vols. Munich and New York: K. G. Saur, 1988.

An extensive coverage of the challenges of preserving newspapers in the original and on microfilm. Volume One is a historical perspective on the press, the management of newspaper collections, microfilming, and the contents of a series of workshops. Volume Two contains a section on "national approaches to newspaper preservation," representing nineteen nations. Also includes a chapter of four papers entitled "Elements of a Newspaper Preservation Policy Worldwide." An appendix of particular interest is the draft policy statement on the retention or disposal of newspapers after microfilming. Bibliographic references.

COMIC BOOKS

IIG3. Scott, Randall W. *Comics Librarianship: A Handbook*. Jefferson, N.C.: McFarland, 1990.

The third chapter of this informal, colloquial treatise on comics librarianship is entitled "Storing and Preserving Comics." It contains a small amount of practical advice and plenty of commentary on the comparisons and contrasts between private and public collections. More an insight into comics collectors than a valuable addition to the technical, how-to, or scholarly literature.

SCRAPBOOKS

IIG4. Zucker, Barbara. "Scrapbooks and Albums: Their Care and Conservation." *Illinois Libraries* 67 (Oct. 1985): 695–99.

A brief overview of the concerns of preserving and conserving scrapbooks and albums including accession and disposition; environmental considerations; handling, treatment, and reformatting; and physical storage and shelving. Bibliographic references.

THESES AND DISSERTATIONS

IIG5. Boyd, Jane, and Don Etherington. *Preparation of Archival Copies of Theses and Dissertations*. Chicago: American Library Association, 1986.

Prepared in the mid-1980s when a primary concern was paper quality and binding in the archival copy of college and university theses and dissertations. Covers paper quality, typing, margins, corrections, illustrations, photographs, oversized materials, plication, use of computers, music/recorded sound, binding, and sources of supply. Has met a need for model guidelines but now requires an update that gives more emphasis to nonpaper and nonbook issues. A National Information Standards Organization (NISO) standards committee has been formed to write such a national standard.

PAPER EPHEMERA

IIG6. Makepeace, Chris E. *Ephemera: Its Collection, Conservation and Use*. Brookfield, Vt.: Gower, 1985.

A practical guide to collecting and handling materials that can be problematic for long-term preservation. The chapter "Storage and Conservation" is of interest here. Appendixes, bibliography, index. One might consider examining Sitter, Clara L., *The Vertical File and Its Alternatives: A Handbook*, Englewood, Colo.: Libraries Unlimited, 1992, although its approaches to preservation, protection, and housing suggest practices for materials of short-term or current value only.

IIG7. Smith, Demaris C. *Preserving Your Paper Collectibles*. Crozet, Va.: Betterway Publications, 1989.

Prepared for the collector rather than the preservation specialist. Although neither scholarly nor technical, communicates basic information. A guidebook of interest, too, for the background and history it provides on a number of types of paper collectibles. Extensive coverage, including postal formats; posters, maps, photographs; cards; commercial paper; currency; sheet music and playbills; newspapers and magazines; books and manuscripts; puzzles and games; and other ephemera. Bibliography is largely about collecting, not preservation. Index.

PHOTOCOPIES

IIG8. Jones, Norvell M. M. *Archival Copies of Thermofax, Verifax, and Other Unstable Records.* National Archives Technical Information Paper No. 5. Washington, D.C.: National Archives and Records Administration, 1990.

A brief report with conclusions about the stability of electrostatic copying methodologies. Refers to the specifications for archival quality electrostatic photocopying. Of particular interest is the specification (materials and procedures) for the "peel test" to check for archival quality in copying. Appended to this report is the "Archival Xerographic Copying Technical Report" (GPO Jacket No. 484-988, 1987), a study commissioned by NARA.

IIH
Photographs

IIH1. Barger, M. Susan, and William B. White. *The Daguerreotype: Nineteenth-Century Technology and Modern Science.* Washington, D.C.: Smithsonian University Press, 1991.

Very impressive work to document Barger's extensive research on the conservation of this early photographic medium. Covers history, technical aspects, and conservation of daguerreotypes better than any other source. Bibliography. Index.

IIH2. Eaton, George T. *Conservation of Photographs.* Kodak Publication F-40. Rochester, N.Y.: Eastman Kodak Co., 1985.

A great deal of information well-presented and well-illustrated with particular value to twentieth-century collections. Chapters on collection management, early photographic processes, photographic image structure, technical standards, processing for black-and-white stability, color images, deterioration, storage and display, reproduction as a preservation alternative, and restoration. Glossary. Bibliography includes many Kodak publications related to photographic preservation.

IIH3. Fenstermann, Duane W. "Recommendations for the Preservation of Photographic Slides." *Conservation Administration News* 31 (Oct. 1987): 7.

A one-page summary of preventative preservation for slides and slide collections. Brief bibliography.

IIH4. Hendriks, Klaus B., with Brian Thurgood, Joe Iraci, Brian Lesser, and Greg Hill. *Fundamentals of Photograph Conservation: A Study Guide.* Toronto: Lugus Productions Ltd., 1991.

The most comprehensive single source in the photographic conservation literature. Created for use as a training textbook for photographic conservators but also a valuable volume for others such as curators, archivists, and preservation officers. Covers all aspects of the subject: equipment, procedures, processing, photographic paper conservation treatments, storage, image stability testing,

condition reports, surveys, etc. Extensive bibliography of more than 500 items. Indexed.

IIH5. Keefe, Lawrence E., Jr., and Dennis Inch. *The Life of a Photograph.* 2nd ed. Stoneham, Mass.: Focal Press, 1990.

Updated edition of a valuable contribution to the literature of photographic conservation, especially from the preventative perspective. Information and advice on processing for permanence, mounting and matting, framing, display, storage, color materials, copying, old and antique photographs, etc. Well-illustrated. Bibliography. Index.

IIH6. *Photograph Preservation and the Research Library.* Edited by Jennifer Porro. Mountain View, Calif.: Research Libraries Group, 1991.

Five papers from an RLG symposium by experts in their fields provide a good start for study of photographic preservation management in research libraries. Covers an overview of the state of the art in photographic preservation, needs assessment and program implementation, techniques and programs for duplication, and access and bibliographic control of photographic collections. Illustrated; not indexed; few bibliographic citations.

IIH7. *Picturescope.* Washington, D.C.: Picture Division, Special Libraries Association. v. 1– , 1953– . Quarterly. ISSN 0031-9694.

Contains occasional articles and news about photographic preservation and conservation.

IIH8. Reilly, James M. *Care and Identification of 19th-Century Photographic Prints.* Kodak Publication G-2S. Rochester, N.Y.: Photographic Products Group, Eastman Kodak Company, 1986.

A highly regarded manual essential to the study of nineteenth-century photographic collections. Covers history; component materials and their forms of deterioration; stability of specific print materials; a system of identification of processes; preservation and collection management; storage; and handling, display, and care. Includes a flowchart for identification guide within the volume and as a full-sized pull-out for reference. Bibliography. Index.

IIH9. Reilly, James M., Peter Z. Adelstein, and Douglas W. Nishimura. *Preservation of Safety Film.* Rochester, N.Y.: Image Permanence Institute, Rochester Institute of Technology, 1991.

Final report to the Office of Preservation, National Endowment for the Humanities (Grant #PS-20159-88). An important research study that indicates some necessary shifts in thinking about the keeping of permanently valuable photographic films. Storage at lowered relative humidity levels (to 20 percent RH) is recommended, although this generally will mean an increased cost. Polyester based films have superior chemical stability over cellulose ester base films. And some cellulose ester based films may have less stability than some cellulose nitrate films. Important reading for the preservation administrator or archivist in charge of monitoring film degradation and film storage.

IIH10. Ritzenthaler, Mary Lynn, Gerald J. Munoff, and Margery S. Long. *Archives & Manuscripts: Administration of Photographic Collections.* SAA Basic Manual Series. Chicago: Society of American Archivists, 1984.

An outstanding source on photographic collections. The chapter on photographic materials preservation was written by Ritzenthaler, a well-respected authority on the subject. Reviews basic preventative preservation (environmental controls and storage practices). Includes section on storage requirements of specific formats and processes from cased photographs through color images. Accessible and practical information. Excellent bibliography. Index.

IIH11. *Storing, Handling, and Preserving Polaroid Photographs: A Guide.* Polaroid Instant Photography. Boston: Focal Press, 1983.

Brief set of do's and don'ts in handling, using, storing, and preserving Polaroid photographs, a medium that can be a distinct preservation challenge in many of its types and varieties. Advice and technical descriptions on various Polaroid-Land film types covering storage, handling and use, preservation, additional protection, and restoring damaged photographs.

IIH12. Wilhelm, Henry. "Color Print Instability." *Modern Photography* 43 (February 1979): 92 ff.

For annotation, *see* IIH13.

IIH13. _____. "Storing Color Materials; Frost-Free Refrigerators Offer a Low Cost Solution." *Industrial Photographer* 27 (Oct. 1978): 32–35.

Two articles written for photographic journals by one who has brought the issues of color dye instability a great deal of attention.

III
Sound Recordings

III1. *ARSC Journal.* Albuquerque: Association for Recorded Sound Collections. v. 1– , 1967/68– . Semiannual. ISSN 0004-5438.

Periodical of interest to sound archivists, collectors, audio technicians, and others, including preservation specialists. Often includes book reviews and articles of interest to preservation of recorded sound collections.

III2. Association for Recorded Sound Collections, Associated Audio Archives Committee. *Audio Preservation: A Planning Study.* Final Performance Report. Prepared by the Committee, for the National Endowment for the Humanities. Silver Spring, Md.: The Association, 1988.

A huge report with value for research into the practice of U.S. sound archives, especially because of the comparable information among institutions in the areas of housing, preservation actions, condition survey reports, and more. Extensive bibliography, with its own index.

III3. Bolnick, Doreen, and Bruce Johnson. "Audiocassette Repair." *Library Journal* 114 (15 Nov. 1989): 43–46.

A how-to for in-house audiocassette repairs, with illustrations and diagrams.

III4. McWilliams, Jerry. *The Preservation and Restoration of Sound Recordings.* Nashville, Tenn.: The American Association for State and Local History, 1979.

Addresses preservation and conservation of sound recording media common prior to 1979. For these media (disc/cylinder recording and tape recording), it remains a good reference and provides good historical background. Arranged in four sections: history, preservation, restoration, and preservation policy. Includes directories of manufacturers/suppliers, and of North American Sound Archives; bibliography; index.

III5. Paton, Christopher Ann. "Whispers in the Stacks: The Problem of Sound Recordings in Archives." *American Archivist* 53 (Spring 1990): 274–80.

An essay that asks and answers the question of why traditional archives have largely ignored the medium of audio recordings. Of general interest is the review of some important audio preservation technical literature. Bibliographic references.

III6. Pickett, A. G., and M. M. Lemcoe. *Preservation and Storage of Sound Recordings.* Washington, D.C.: Library of Congress, 1959.

Still a very good source of basic information about the older disc formats such as shellac 78 rpm recordings, early vinyl LP recordings, and even early magnetic tape. Recently reissued and available from the Association for Recorded Sound Collections.

III7. St.-Laurent, Giles. *The Care and Handling of Recorded Sound Materials.* Commission on Preservation and Access. Report. Washington, D.C.: The Commission, 1991.

A brief technical overview and summary of sound; recorded sound media technology; degradation of sound recordings; and preservation, including handling, playback, and storage. Sound recording media covered include acetate discs, shellac discs, vinyl discs, magnetic tape, and compact discs (CDs). Practical advice. Bibliography of twenty-three sources from the technical literature.

III8. Smolian, Steven. "Preservation, Deterioration and Restoration of Recording Tape." *ARSC Journal* 19, no. 2 (1987): 37–53.

Good coverage of the issues of preservation of acetate and polyester recording tape. Describes a set of forty-one recommendations for the storage, care, handling, and general preservation of tape. Bibliographic references.

IJ
Decision Making for Preservation

Selection of the most important materials for the most appropriate preservation or conservation options is the crux of the issue in managing a preservation program. Reformatting to a more stable medium (such as microfilm, alkaline paper, or more sophisticated technology) is one of the most important options. Copyright issues cannot be ignored. These three areas—selection, reformatting, and copyright—are well covered in the following resources by thoughtful professionals. *See also* Chapter H, Collection Management, and Chapter J, Reproduction of Library Materials.

IJ1. Atkinson, Ross. "Selection for Preservation: A Materialistic Approach." *Library Resources & Technical Services* 30 (Oct./Dec. 1986): 341–53.

For annotation, *see* HF10.

IJ2. Bagnall, Roger S., and Carolyn L. Harris. "Involving Scholars in Preservation Decisions: The Case of the Classicists." *The Journal of Academic Librarianship* 13 (July 1987): 140–46.

Discusses approaches to preservation decision making and scholar involvement in the context of the American Philological Association's preservation microfilming project in classical studies. Authors' conclusions point to the value of microfiche over microfilm, enhanced bibliographic control in decision making, and communicating clearly to scholars the implications of such preservation projects in their disciplines. Bibliographic references.

IJ3. Child, Margaret S. "Further Thoughts on 'Selection for Preservation.' " *Library Resources & Technical Services* 30 (Oct./Dec. 1986): 354–62.

A discussion of the Atkinson paper (IJ1). Continues the discussion of selecting for preservation in a national and international context, including archival as well as library collections. Further discussion about assumption in collection strengths and about intrinsic or artifactual value. (Includes a reprint of the text of the National Archives' *Intrinsic Value in Archival Material* [IJ6] as an appendix.) Bibliographic references.

IJ4. Hazen, Dan C. "Collection Development, Collection Management and Preservation." *Library Resources & Technical Services* 26 (Jan./Mar. 1982): 3–11.

A thorough discussion of decision making for preservation in library collections, outlining close parallels in the criteria for collection management and development. An oft-cited paper presenting important considerations in selecting for preservation that also closely affect collection management and development decisions. Bibliographic references.

IJ5. _____. "Preservation in Poverty and Plenty: Policy Issues for the 1990s." *The Journal of Academic Librarianship* 15 (Jan. 1990): 344–51.

A call for a renewed look at the assumptions that have placed preservation microfilming (too) high in the priorities of preservation efforts at the local and national level. Bibliographic references.

IJ6. *Intrinsic Value in Archival Material.* Staff Information Paper 21. Washington, D.C.: National Archives and Records Service, 1982.

A six-page pamphlet listing nine qualities and characteristics of records with defined intrinsic value. Gives examples in application of the concepts. Although addressed to archivists and records managers, it is very instructive for review and retention of published library materials in their original formats.

IJ7. Merrill-Oldham, Jan, and Gay Walker, comps. *Brittle Book Programs.* SPEC Kit, no. 152. Washington, D.C.: Association of Research Libraries, Office of Management Studies, 1989.

Documents gathered from a survey of ARL libraries involved with brittle-books selection and processing. A unique source of internal memoranda, procedures, policies, guidelines, and work forms from ARL libraries.

IJ8. Miller, J. Hillis. *Preserving the Literary Heritage.* Commission on Preservation and Access. Report. Washington, D.C.: The Commission, 1991.

For annotation, *see* ID8.

IJ9. Ogden, Barclay. *On the Preservation of Books and Documents in Original Form.* Washington, D.C.: Commission on Preservation and Access, 1989.

Brief paper expressing thoughts about the preservation and conservation of books and documents of intrinsic value as artifacts, rather than for their informational contents only. Created a lively discussion.

IJ10. _____. "Preservation Selection and Treatment Options." In *Meeting the Preservation Challenge,* edited by Jan Merrill-Oldham, 38–42. Washington, D.C.: Association of Research Libraries, 1988.

A brief essay (delivered first to an audience of research library directors) about approaches that might be taken to decide which materials in collections should be selected for preservation and how such selected materials should be preserved. Cogent and compelling.

IJ11. *Preserving the Illustrated Text.* Report of the Joint Task Force on Text and Image. Washington, D.C.: The Commission on Preservation and Access, 1992.

An examination of the special preservation challenges posed by images found in embrittled texts, studied under the assumption that "present preservation practices are relatively insensitive to the vast majority of these images and fail to capture them with sufficient fidelity to be useful." Reviews image attributes, image distribution in (embrittled) texts, use implications, conservation versus preservation, alternative technologies for preservation, and recommendations. Important reading for those involved in reformatting programs.

IJ12. *Selection for Preservation of Research Library Materials.* Commission on Preservation and Access. Report. Washington, D.C.: The Commission, 1989.

For annotation, *see* HF13.

IJ13. Willis, Don. *A Hybrid Systems Approach to Preservation of Printed Materials.* Washington, D.C.: Commission on Preservation and Access, 1992.

For annotation, *see* JH4.

IK
Staff Training and User Awareness

The list of good literature on this subject is too short. It is true that training and workshop opportunities for library staff exist in much greater numbers than they did only a decade ago, and formal training programs have succeeded in training preservation and conservation specialists. However, reaching our library clientele with an effective, behavior-modifying preservation message continues to meet with mixed results. The literature that follows provides some approaches, including audiovisual programs for staff. Readers are advised to examine the bibliographic instruction, personnel management, training, and public relations literature, too.

IK1. Boomgaarden, Wesley L. *Staff Training and User Awareness in Preservation Management.* Washington, D.C.: Office of Management Services, Association of Research Libraries, 1993.

One of a series of brief monographs ("resource guides") written for ARL and other libraries that are undertaking reviews of their preservation programs. This one justifies a staff training and user awareness effort, outlines what is needed to get started, describes well-developed staff training and user awareness programs, suggests specific concepts to impart, includes a selection of current materials in use in other libraries, and provides a brief bibliography. Addresses a subject not well covered in the professional literature.

IK2. Coleman, Christopher D. G., comp. *Preservation Education Directory.* 6th ed. Chicago: Association for Library Collections and Technical Services, American Library Association, 1990.

For annotation, *see* IAC2.

IK3. Columbia University Libraries Preservation Department. *The Preservation of Library Materials: A CUL Handbook.* 5th ed. New York: Columbia University Libraries, 1991.

A good resource for staff training and awareness in addition to its value as an internal policy and procedures manual. Outlines general and specific handling of commercial library binding and replacement options including microfilming, conservation, and disaster control.

IK4. Fang, Josephine Riss, and Ann Russell, eds. *Education and Training for Preservation and Conservation.* Papers of an International Seminar on "The Teaching of Preservation Management for Librarians, Archivists and Information Scientists," sponsored by IFLA, FID, and ICA, Vienna, April 11–13, 1986, with additional information sources. Munich: K. G. Saur, 1991.

Slim volume of sixteen conference papers. An international perspective on education and training needs. Bibliographies.

IK5. *Handling Books in General Collections: Guidelines for Readers and Library Staff Members.* [slide-tape] Washington, D.C.: National Preservation Program Office, Library of Congress, 1984. Audiocassette with slides and booklet.

Informs viewers of the effects of cumulative handling on book collections and offers realistic, appropriate alternatives to daily routines in shelving, use of book trucks, photocopying, etc. An effective, professional production.

IK6. *Materials at Risk: The Preservation Challenge.* [slide-tape] Produced by Karen Garlick and Merrily A. Smith. Washington, D.C.: Library of Congress, 1990. Audiocassette, slides, and printed script, 10 minutes.

Well-paced and well-selected slides with good narration on tape to introduce the topic of preservation of all kinds of library and archival materials to a general audience.

IK7. Merrill-Oldham, Jan. *Preservation Education in ARL Libraries.* SPEC Kit, no. 113. Washington, D.C.: Office of Management Studies, Association of Research Libraries, 1986.

The results of a survey of ARL policies, procedures, and graphics from those libraries that have developed user/staff/donor preservation education efforts. A snapshot of libraries' activities with system-wide policies, staff training, reader awareness, donor relations, and exhibitions related to reaching staff, patrons, and potential donors with preservation messages. Some dated information but still valuable because not much has been published in this area.

IK8. Merrill-Oldham, Jan, ed. *Conservation and Preservation of Library Materials: A Program for the University of Connecticut Libraries.* Storrs, Conn.: University Library, 1984.

An in-house publication of interest to libraries undertaking internal preservation studies. Report of a study done at Connecticut with significant content of interest in the subject of staff training and user awareness.

IK9. *Murder in the Stacks.* [videorecording] New York: Columbia University Libraries, 1987. 1 videocassette (VHS), 15 minutes.

Sherlock Holmes "mystery" approach to staff and patron care-and-handling issues. Clever approach that may be the perfect medium for some audiences but not so perfect for certain other audiences.

IK10. Pederson, Terri L. "Theft and Mutilation of Library Materials." *College & Research Libraries* 51 (Mar. 1990): 120–28.

Results of research done on the motivation of students related to periodical and book theft and mutilation in academic libraries. A review of the recent literature on the subject is included.

IK11. Pence, Cheryl. "Audiovisual Resources on Preservation Topics." *American Archivist* 53 (Spring 1990): 350–54.

A brief review article of AV sources for awareness and training, concentrating on those issued between 1985 and 1990. Critical comments on the value and quality of videotapes, slide/audiotapes, and other productions are of interest.

IK12. *Shedding Light on the Case.* [videorecording] New York: Center for Biomedical Communications, Columbia University, 1991. 1 videocassette (VHS), 18 minutes, with pamphlet.

Video and step-by-step instruction pamphlet that discuss preservation guidelines for exhibiting library and archival materials. Sherlock Holmes-Dr. Watson characters are used to deliver the message about temperature, relative humidity, light levels, etc. (Other exhibition preparation-related citations are included in section IG.)

IK13. *Slow Fires: On the Preservation of the Human Record.* [videorecording] A presentation of American Film Foundation. Sponsored by Council on Library Resources, Library of Congress, National Endowment for the Humanities. A Terry Sanders Film, written by Ben Maddow and Terry Sanders. Santa Monica, Calif.: American Film Foundation, 1987. Video (VHS, 3/4") and 16mm film formats, 58- and 33-minute versions.

For annotation, *see* IAA8.

IK14. "Task Force F—Staff and User Education." In *Preservation Planning Program: An Assisted Self-Study Manual for Libraries.* Expanded 1987 ed. Developed by Pamela W. Darling with Duane E. Webster. Washington, D.C.: Office of Management Services, Association of Research Libraries, 1987. 105–22.

An excellent introduction to and rationale for staff and user preservation awareness and training efforts. Outlines a course of action for observing the current library situation, assessing its needs, and making realistic recommendations for action. For an updated version of this chapter *see also* the 1993 forthcoming edition of this work, IAE3.

IK15. Swartzburg, Susan G. "Audiovisual Aids on the Preservation and Conservation of Library and Archival Materials." *Conservation Administration News* No. 49 (Apr. 1992): 8–13.

A selected listing of more than sixty audiovisual aides that may prove useful for classroom and workshop instruction in conservation, preservation, disaster control, traditional book arts, security, exhibition, and some related subjects. Content of each alphabetical listing is helpful: title, running time, format, producer/distributor, and summary. A number of the entries are included in this chapter. An earlier comprehensive effort (for the period 1955–1980) is Harrison, Alice W., Edward A. Collister, and R. Ellen Willis, *The Conservation of Archival and Library Materials: A Resource Guide to Audiovisual Aids*, Metuchen, N.J.: Scarecrow Press, 1982.

J

Reproduction of Library Materials

Erich J. Kesse

Overview

Reproduction of library materials is the process by which library materials are transferred from one medium to another. Reproduction employs an array of technologies, many new and changing rapidly. More diverse than printing technologies, the reproduction technologies are increasingly described as "imaging technologies." While microform is the most familiar reproduction medium, imaging technologies encompass the following: photocopying and xerography, photography, microphotography, magnetic analog technologies (such as audiotape and videotape recording), and electronic or digital imaging and scanning technologies.

Reproduction technologies serve many functions. They are used to preserve the intellectual content of library materials when those materials cannot be bound or when they require a level of conservation treatment that exceeds their value. These materials may be deteriorating, already deteriorated, or unwieldy items. To save space and provide a more enduring medium, libraries use reproduction technologies as an alternative to retaining and binding serial back files. Commercial publishers reproduce selected current publications simultaneously in various media, providing libraries with choices among format options. New electronic formats offer the potential for improved access. Patrons have come to depend on photocopying as an alternative to borrowing materials.

The commercial application of micrographic imaging for libraries dates from the 1930s. Newspapers were among the first items microfilmed both because the paper is highly acidic and because newspapers are, by their nature, difficult to bind. Because of micrographics' long history of application for and by libraries, techniques, standards, and micrographic preservation project guidelines have received comprehensive treatment in the literature. Recent micrographic-imaging literature discusses optimum use of the technology, the longevity of its medium, and techniques for moving from micrographic images to digitized images and vice versa. Resources on these topics are cited extensively in this chapter.

The pace of change—the advance of ever newer technologies, applications, and products—is tremendous in many areas of reproduction technology. Developments ceaselessly continue in the newer technologies, affecting library applications. The literature describing these new technologies is enormous, but the definitive works cannot be discerned easily or may be displaced soon; electronic imaging literature is abundant, yet somewhat cloudy. On the other hand, new scholarship among the older technologies proceeds along recognized agendas and tends to refine rather than break new ground.

The character and condition of materials to be reproduced, as well as their projected use, determine the form of reproduction selected. No matter the particular technology or its stage of development, all reproduction technologies are standards-based. Standards for consistency, durability, and permanence inform the literature. Because technology is engineered, the literature about reproduction technologies tends to describe engineering and operational principles or the constraints of particular technologies and media. Standards delimit and optimize application for each technology within that technology's engineering, whether the engineering depends on mechanics or programming. The literature of preservation microfilming, for example, informed and infused with standards, seeks to optimize micrographic applications for preservation of library materials.

Chapter Content and Organization

This chapter deals with the broad area of reprographics/imaging. It culls works from the literature of audio and video recording, electronic imaging, micrographics, photocopying, and other technologies. In addition, sources compiled here describe copyright, management, and publishing concerns. Special consideration is also given to standards. Technology, standards, and laws affecting the topics covered in this chapter are changing rapidly. Readers are advised to seek the most current information and the most recent revisions and editions of publications.

The first section covers general works, including the usual guides, manuals, directories, etc. The periodicals subsection is subdivided by method of reprographic imaging. Subsequent sections cover copyright; imaging (micrographic and electronic); management and organization of reproduction activities; media; micrographic, optical, and electronic image publishing; photocopies and photocopying; and preservation reproduction. Standards, a compelling force in the reproduction of library materials, are covered in a substantial final section.

JA
General Works

JAA
Textbooks, Guides, and Manuals

Textbooks, guides, and manuals concerned with the reproduction of library materials—when specific to a particular technology, application, or medium—are described elsewhere in this resource list. Guides used in preservation microfilming, for example, are found under that heading.

JAA1. Hiser, Susan. *All About Microfilm Cameras.* Silver Spring, Md.: Association for Information and Image Management, 1976. AIIM CS6-1976.

A basic text describing microfilm cameras, optics, etc.

JAA2. Hoover Sung, Carolyn. *Archives & Manuscripts: Reprography.* Chicago: The Society of American Archivists, 1982.

A guide to reproduction in archives. Published as part of the SAA Basic Manual Series, it serves as a general introduction to archival, technical, and management considerations of photography, microphotography, and photocopying. The work is useful, but out of date in regard to electronic imaging.

JAA3. McWilliams, Jerry. *The Preservation and Restoration of Sound Recordings.* Nashville: American Association for State and Local History, 1979.

See also annotation under III4. This publication is a guide to cylinder, disc, tape, and digital sound recording. Though not detailed and somewhat dated, it remains the only comprehensive source on sound recording and reproduction of recorded sound.

JAB
Dictionaries

JAB1. Association for Information and Image Management. *Glossary of Imaging Technology.* Silver Spring, Md.: AIIM, 1992. AIIM TR2-1992.

An expanded revision of the earlier *Glossary of Micrographics* (AIIM TR2-1980), which defines and effectively standardizes terms used in the micrographics and electronic imaging management (EIM) industries. The glossary is designed to provide customers and suppliers of imaging technologies and products with a common language for negotiating projects, understanding and implementing standards, etc.

JAB2. Canada, Translation Bureau. *Reprography.* Ottawa, Ont.: Canadian Government Publication Centre, 1988.

This glossary of reprographic terms, compiled by the Canadian Translation Bureau's Terminology and Linguistic Services Branch, had its foundation in the Canadian General Standards Board's provisional glossary of micrographic terms issued in 1983. It is most important for its translation of English and French terms used in micrographics and electronic image management. Combined with AIIM's *Glossary of Imaging Technology* (JAB1), these terms facilitate advancement of imaging and preservation microfilming in Canada and the Caribbean basin.

JAB3. Technical Association of the Pulp and Paper Industry, Printing and Imaging Committee. *Glossary of Reprography and Non-impact Printing Terms for the Paper and Printing Industries.* Atlanta, Ga.: TAPPI, 1989.

Compiled for use among those involved in paper and printing industries, this glossary defines reprographic and primarily electronic imaging terms used to describe (hard-copy) off-printing from images using nonimpact printing techniques.

JAC
Directories

Professional associations publish the most comprehensive directories of services, professionals, etc., for particular reproduction technologies. Users will benefit most if they have developed product or service specifications before contacting or conducting business with those listed herein. Selected directories follow. In particular, U.S. researchers are advised to contact

Association for Information and Image
Management (JAH7)
Association for Recorded Sound Collections
Association of Reproduction Materials
Manufacturers (JAH8)
Audio Engineering Society
Image Permanence Institute (JAH10)
National Association of Photographic
Manufacturers (JAH13)
Society for Imaging Science and Technology
(JAH16)
Society of Motion Picture and Television
Engineers (JAH17)

JAC1. Association for Information and Image Management. *Information Management Sourcebook: The AIIM Buying Guide and Membership Directory.* Silver Spring, Md.: AIIM, 1987– . Annual. ISSN 0897-3199. Continues *The AIIM Buying Guide.*

A directory of equipment, products, and services available from AIIM members. AIIM is the professional and trade organization of the information and image manage-

ment industry. The directory is strong in micrographics and EIM systems. Information compiled in this sourcebook is of use to a variety of purchasers.

JAC2. *International Imaging Source Book: Including Micrographics and Optical Imaging.* Larchmont, N.Y.: Microfilm Publishing, 1992– . Annual. ISSN 1053-8291.

Formerly published under the title *International Micrographics Source Book,* this sourcebook contains guides and indexes to imaging equipment, products, and services and provides a directory of the micrographics EIM industries.

JAC3. *The Mix Annual Directory of Recording Industry Facilities and Services.* Berkeley, Calif.: Mix Publications, 1987– . Annual.

Compiled from information published in *The Mix* (JAF6), this directory lists sound recording facilities available to libraries considering or planning library applications or projects for the preservation of recorded sound. Information in this sourcebook is of use to a variety of purchasers.

JAC4. Nitecki, Joseph Z., comp. *Directory of Library Reprographic Services: A World Guide.* 8th ed. Westport, Conn.: Meckler, 1982.

Though much of the information is dated, this remains the only comprehensive directory of reproduction services available from libraries. The directory lists institutions engaged in reproduction of library materials, the type and extent of services offered, prices, contacts, and so on.

JAD
Bibliographies

Bibliographies dealing with the reproduction of library materials are few, and the literature referenced often is dated. Bibliographies of current literature tend to focus on publications dealing with new technologies. Bibliographic references for most reproduction technologies are given as part of standards and scholarly publications.

JAD1. Elshami, Ahmed M. *CD-ROM: An Annotated Bibliography.* Englewood, Colo.: Libraries Unlimited, 1988.

Though dated, this bibliography of articles, monographs, and other materials on CD-ROMs and optical disks is annotated specifically for librarians interested in the application of these technologies in libraries or for the reproduction of library materials.

JAD2. Hendriks, Klaus B., and Anne Whitehurst, comps. *Conservation of Photographic Materials: A Basic Reading List.* Ottawa, Ont.: National Archives of Canada, 1988.

This bibliography lists titles dealing with photographic technologies, materials, standards, and related topics, some of which have bearing upon the reproduction of library materials.

JAD3. Saffady, William. *Optical Storage Technology: A Bibliography.* Westport, Conn.: Meckler, 1989.

A listing of articles, monographs, and other materials dealing with optical storage devices, technology, and applications. Though dated, this bibliography affords the most comprehensive review of optical storage technology as of this writing. Entries pertain to various applications and may be more suited to the needs of records managers than those of librarians.

JAE
Handbooks

JAE1. Association for Information and Image Management. *Micrographic Film Technology.* 4th ed. Silver Spring, Md.: AIIM, 1992.

A basic guide to micrographic film technologies, including diazo, silver, and vesicular film technologies. Could be used in short courses or as an overview of micrographics emphasizing principles and films.

JAE2. Bensen, Blair, ed. *Audio Engineering Handbook.* New York: McGraw-Hill, 1988.

Slightly out of date, this handbook discusses analog and digital engineering of sound for recording and reproduction and describes audio-reproduction techniques. Targeted toward technicians with frequent access to state-of-the-art facilities, the handbook may be used by librarians to write requests for proposals, specifying methods of reproduction.

JAE3. Desmarais, Norman. *The Librarian's CD-ROM Handbook.* Westport, Conn.: Meckler, 1989.

Published as part of the series "Supplements to Optical Information Systems." Concerned with library applications for the reproduction of library materials using CD-ROMs and optical disks.

JAE4. Eastman Kodak Company. *Basic Photographic Sensitometry Workbook.* Rochester, N.Y.: Eastman Kodak Company, 1977. Publication Z22-ED.

Provides for a basic understanding of sensitometry and the principles of photographic imaging.

JAF
Periodicals

GENERAL PERIODICALS

JAF1. Commission on Preservation and Access. *Newsletter.* Washington, D.C.: The Commission, no. 1– , 1988– . Monthly. ISSN 1045-1919.

See also annotation under IAG9. The official newsletter of the Commission. Often contains information concerning the reproduction of library materials, notes on new technologies, and reviews of relevant publications.

JAF2. *IMC Journal.* Minneapolis: International Management Congress. v. 1– , Fall 1967– . Bimonthly. ISSN 0019-0012.

The official publication of the Congress; publishes special reports and application studies in micrographics and EIM systems.

JAF3. *Inform.* Silver Spring, Md.: Association for Information and Image Management. v. 1, no. 1– , 1987– . Monthly. ISSN 0892-3876.

AIIM's official magazine. Features special reports and application studies in micrographics and, increasingly, EIM systems, in addition to regular columns on technology and management. Targeted to management professionals in the imaging industry and to others interested in various imaging applications, it supersedes the Association's *Journal of Micrographics* and *Journal of Information and Image Management.*

JAF4. *Information & Image Management: State of the Industry.* Silver Spring, Md.: Association for Information and Image Management, 1st ed., 1986– . Annual.

The Association's industry profile, containing information on industry size, market forecast, technology usage, and attitudes about micrographics and electronic information management systems. A key indicator of future growth in the information and image management industry, useful to librarians considering or planning EIM system design or purchase. Sometimes published as *Information & Image Management: The Industry & the Technologies.*

AUDIO-RECORDING AND REPRODUCTION PERIODICALS

JAF5. *Journal of the Audio Engineering Society.* New York: Audio Engineering Society. v. 1– , 1953– . Monthly. ISSN 0004-7554.

Official organ of the Audio Engineering Society. Targeted toward technicians, articles deal with engineering for recording and reproduction of both previously recorded and original sound.

JAF6. *The Mix.* Berkeley, Calif.: Mix Publications. 1978– . Quarterly. ISSN 0164-9957.

Describing itself as "the recording industry magazine," this publication may be of some interest in the reproduction of library audio recordings. Items on the sound-recording and audio-equipment industries may be helpful to those considering or planning library applications or projects for the preservation of recorded sound.

ELECTRONIC IMAGING PERIODICALS

JAF7. *Electronic Document Imaging Systems: User Evaluations.* Silver Spring, Md.: Association for Information and Image Management. 1990– . Annual.

Responses to and analyses of survey of EIM systems, with vendor and system profiles and critiques.

JAF8. *Information Technology and Libraries*. Chicago: American Library Association. v. 1– , March 1982– . Quarterly. ISSN 0730-9295. Continues *Journal of Library Automation*.

See also annotation under AF10. Includes articles documenting the management, design, and use of electronic technologies for reproduction of library materials.

JAF9. *Journal of Electronic Imaging*. Springfield, Va.: Society of Imaging Science & Technology. v. 1– , 1992– . Quarterly. ISSN 1017-9909.

Published in association with the Society of Photo-Optical Instrumentation Engineers. Articles are most useful to those consulting in or considering technical aspects of implementing, operating, or refining electronic imaging systems.

JAF10. *Journal of Imaging Science and Technology*. Springfield, Va.: Society of Imaging Science & Technology. v. 36– , Jan./Feb. 1992– . Bimonthly. ISSN 1062-3701.

This title succeeds the *Journal of Imaging Technology* and the *Journal of Imaging Science*. Articles discuss imaging systems and image processing of analog and digital images, often with scientific applications. Provides advanced background in technical discussions but may not be readily useful to librarians or for library applications.

JAF11. *Optical Storage Technology: A State of the Art Review*. Westport, Conn.: Meckler, 1985– . Annual. ISSN 1047-3505.

An assessment of optical storage devices and their use, geared toward those planning use of the technology. Published under various titles, including *Optical Disks: A State of the Art Review*. Edited by William Saffady.

MICROGRAPHIC IMAGING PERIODICALS

JAF12. *Fyi/im: A Newsletter for the Information Professional*. Silver Spring, Md.: Association for Information and Image Management. v. 1– , no. 1– , 1985– . Bi-weekly. ISSN 1055-1743.

The newsletter of the Association's Technology and Standards Division; publishes information about new technology and standards in micrographics and, more and more, electronic image management systems.

JAF13. *International Journal of Micrographics & Optical Technology*. New York: Pergamon Press. v. 7– , 1989– . Quarterly. ISSN 0958-9961.

Continues *International Journal of Micrographics and Video Technology*. Resulting from a merger of the Microfilm Association of Great Britain's *Microdoc* and Pergamon's *Micropublishing of Current Periodicals*, this publication includes articles on the micrographic and video-recording publishing industries, geared largely toward industry personnel.

JAF14. *Microform Review*. Westport, Conn.: Meckler. v. 1– , 1972– . Bimonthly. ISSN 0002-6530.

Aimed at the library community. Contains reviews of microforms and microform sets of interest to collection development librarians. Articles treat topics of interest to managers of library microform service centers, microfilming operations, acquisitions, and cataloging. Material concerning library applications of electronic imaging systems and products now appears along with items on more traditional technologies. Meckler publishes indexes covering 1972 through 1976 (edited by Jeanne Short) and 1972 through 1981 (edited by John Wellington). Also available: *Cumulative Microform Reviews, 1977-1984*, Westport, Conn.: Meckler, 1986.

JAG
Electronic Resources

The following resources represent a new and growing area of publication dealing at least partly with the reproduction of library materials. Electronic document resources, often as a matter of economics or audience interests, cover a broad range of topics. Electronic databases often include information on the reproduction of library materials, but at this writing none are dedicated solely or principally to this topic.

JAG1. *Conservation OnLine (CoOL)*. [database online] Stanford, Calif.: Stanford University Libraries, Preservation Department, 1993– .

An electronic library built on a Wide Area Information Server (WAIS), this resource provides INTERNET access to a full-text database of conservation and preservation information. The most comprehensive of electronic document resources, *CoOL* is actually several databases including full-text information files; an electronic mail directory; lexical and classification materials, including thesauri, glossaries, and classification schemes; and complete bibliographies. Like other electronic document resources, its files are the products of institutions active in conservation and preservation. Due to the user-friendliness of WAIS, *CoOL* surpasses other electronic resources; queries may be phrased in natural English, masking technical protocols including the file transfer protocols (FTP) required by other electronic resources. For more information, contact: **WHENRY@LINDY.STANFORD.EDU** (INTERNET).

JAG2. *FLIPPER: The Electronic Library*. [database online] Gainesville, Fla.: University of Florida, 1992– .

For annotation, *see* IAJ2.

JAG3. *PREFIS*. [electronic discussion group] Mountain View, Calif.: Research Libraries Group, Inc., 1992– .

The Preservation Reference Information Service offered by RLG to its member subscribers. The service includes both a query structure typical of LISTSERVs and a growing library of electronic documents, many of which deal with reproduction of library materials. Subscribers must be members of the Research Libraries Group. For further information, contact the Preservation Program at RLG (JAH15).

JAH
Sources of Expertise

As with the literature of preservation, reprographics literature originates as much with constituencies outside librarianship as within the profession. Research into the reproduction of library materials is facilitated by contact with specialists in both constituencies. Current developments in reprographics are discussed in the proceedings and other publications of specialized groups.

JAH1. ALA Association for Library Collections and Technical Services (ALCTS). Executive Director: Karen Muller.

See also annotation under AGA3. Several groups within ALCTS deal with topics of interest to those who work with reproduction of library materials. These include

Audiovisual Committee (AV) and its Standards
    Subcommittee
Preservation Microfilming Committee (which deals
    with issues that cross Sections or require
    cooperative approaches)
Computer Files Discussion Group
Electronic Publishing Discussion Group

JAH2. ALA ALCTS Preservation of Library Materials Section (PLMS).

See also annotation under IAK3. This Section addresses reproduction of library materials with regard to specific preservation applications.

JAH3. ALA ALCTS Reproduction of Library Materials Section (RLMS).

RLMS addresses reproduction of library materials broadly, from reprographic technology and methods to storage and use of reproductions. Its committees include

Copying Committee
Education Committee
Electronic Imaging Committee
Micropublishing Committee
Policy and Planning Committee
Public Service Managers of Microform Facilities
    Discussion Group
Publications Committee
Reproduction of Library Materials Discussion Group
Standards Committee

JAH4. ALA Library and Information Technology Association (LITA). Executive Director: Linda J. Knutson.

See also annotation under AGA5. Committees of interest include the following:

Emerging Technologies Committee
Optical Information Systems Committee

JAH5. ALA Video Round Table.

A broad-based group bringing together ALA members who have an interest in and/or responsibilities for video collections. Provides a unified voice for video advocacy in legislation, collection guidelines, and other pertinent issues.

JAH6. American National Standards Institute (ANSI). 11 W. 42nd St., New York, NY 10036. President: Manuel Peralta.

Standards coordinating and approval organization. Does not develop standards, which are developed by other groups and submitted to ANSI for approval. The U.S. member of ISO (JAH12).

JAH7. Association for Information and Image Management (AIIM). Headquarters: 1100 Wayne Ave., Suite 1100, Silver Spring, MD 20910. Executive Director: Sue Wolk.

The Standards and Technology Division of AIIM is responsible to the American National Standards Institute (JAH6). This Division defines standard materials, practice, etc., for reprographic technologies, both micrographic and electronic. The Division actively invites the involvement of archivists, librarians, and records managers. Some of its committees include

Archives and Library Applications Committee
Document Quality Control Committee
Electronic Imaging Input Committee
Electronic Imaging Output Committee
Electronic Imaging Software and Systems Committee
Image Encoding Techniques
Imaging Equipment Committee
Microform Formats Committee

JAH8. Association for Reproduction Materials Manufacturers. Headquarters: 901 N. Washington Street, Suite 509, Alexandria, VA 22314. Executive Director: Philip Nowers.

Association for manufacturers of blueprints, paper, cloth, and other materials used in reproduction; reproduction machines; and engineering graphics supplies and materials.

JAH9. Commission on Preservation and Access (CPA). 1400 16th Street, NW, Suite 740, Washington, DC 20036. President: Patricia Battin.

The Commission was established to foster and support collaboration among libraries and allied organizations to ensure the preservation of the published and documentary record in all formats. It sponsors research into library applications of reprographic technologies, both micrographic and electronic. Its publications are often studies of the state of the art and the state of applications, implementation studies, or thought pieces that attempt to define applications.

JAH10. Image Permanence Institute. Rochester Institute of Technology, City Center, 50 W. Main Street, Rochester, NY 14614. Director: James M. Reilly.

Research institute on photographic preservation and stability characteristics of various imaging media, especially cellulose acetate film.

JAH11. International Federation of Library Associations and Institutions (IFLA). Headquarters: c/o The Royal Library POB 95312, 2509CH, The Hague, The Netherlands. Secretary General: Paul Nauta.

For annotation, *see* AGA4. Within IFLA, the Section on Information Technology is of interest.

JAH12. International Organization for Standardization (ISO). 1 rue de Varembé, Case postale 56, CH-1211, Geneva 20, Switzerland.

ISO serves as the specialized international agency for standardization and seeks to promote worldwide agreement on international standards. It comprises national standards bodies in eighty-nine countries.

ISO's Library and Publishing Applications, Working Group 3, is the international equivalent of AIIM's Standards and Technology Division (JAH7). This Working Group oversees development of reprographic standards, both micrographic and electronic.

JAH13. National Association of Photographic Manufacturers (NAPM). Headquarters: 550 Mamaroneck Avenue, Harrison, NY 10528. Executive Vice President: Thomas J. Dufficy.

Association for manufacturers of photographic and other imaging equipment, supplies, films, and chemicals. Responsible to the American National Standards Institute (JAH6), this division defines standard manufacture, use, storage, etc., for photographic and micrographic materials.

JAH14. National Information Standards Organization (NISO). Headquarters: P.O. Box 1056, Bethesda, MD 20827.

For annotation, *see* AGA6.

JAH15. Research Libraries Group (RLG). 1200 Villa Street, Mountain View, CA 94041. President: James Michalko.

RLG's Preservation Program brings together expertise from across the Group's membership of research and special libraries. It deals with reprographic technologies, primarily microfilming, most often in the context of preservation applications.

JAH16. Society for Imaging Science and Technology. 7003 Kilworth Lane, Springfield, VA 22151. Executive Director: Calva Lotridge.

Composed of individuals who apply photography and imaging to science, engineering, and industry.

JAH17. Society of American Archivists (SAA). 600 S. Federal St., Suite 504, Chicago, IL 60605. Executive Director: Anne P. Diffendal.

A professional association of individuals and institutions concerned with the management of current records, archival administration, and custody of historical manuscripts.

SAA's Conservation Program draws on expertise from across the Society's membership of academic and special archives, historical societies, etc. Focuses on the preserva-

tion applications of reprographic technologies, primarily microfilming.

JAH18. Society of Motion Picture and Television Engineers (SMPTE). Headquarters: 595 W. Hartsdale Avenue, White Plains, NY 10607. Executive Director: Lynette H. Robinson.

Society of professional engineers and technicians in motion pictures, television, and allied arts and sciences. SMPTE develops standards and organizes technical courses in sound techniques, laboratory processing, and film handling.

JAH19. U.S. National Institute for Standards and Technology. Gaithersburg, MD 20899.

Previously the National Bureau of Standards. Assists industry in developing technology to improve product quality and modernize manufacturing. Research and testing facility in Boulder, Colorado.

JB
Copyright

Copyright is a principal and developing concern of librarians involved in the reproduction of library materials. Interpretations of copyright law continue to affect copying and reproduction of materials in and by libraries. The language of copyright legislation and its interpretations can be complex, even Byzantine at times. Publications listed here offer general orientation and only some procedural guidance; they may be used to seek further assistance from counsel as well as to grasp the fundamental precepts of fair use in preservation reproduction.

JB1. Association of Research Libraries, Office of Management Studies. *University Copyright Policies in ARL Libraries.* SPEC Kit, no. 138. Washington, D.C.: ARL, 1987.

A compilation of copyright policies and procedural documents from ARL's member libraries. Designed as a resource tool for libraries developing or reviewing copyright procedures.

JB2. Clark, Charles. *Photo-Copying: Photocopying from Books and Journals: A Guide for All Users of Copyright Literary Works.* London: British Copyright Council, 1990.

A brief examination of fair-use provisions in British copyright legislation. Summarizes copyright for librarians and library patrons, much as do the Library of Congress Copyright Office Circulars in the United States. An early version was published under the title *Reprographic Copying of Books and Journals* in 1985.

JB3. *Copyright and the Librarian*. Washington, D.C.: Copyright Office, Library of Congress, 1977.

Issued as "Circular R21," this publication summarizes the provisions for library reproduction of copyright protected works. It should be read by those engaged in reproduction activities, but, because it is dated, additional sources should be consulted.

JB4. *Copyright Basics*. Circular 1. Washington, D.C.: Copyright Office, Library of Congress, 1992.

This summary of U.S. copyright legislation should be mandatory for those engaged in any reproduction of library materials. It reviews the basics in straightforward language. Researchers are advised to seek the most recent edition, since this publication is periodically revised.

JB5. *Copyright Law of the United States of America Contained in Title 17 of the United States Code*. Circular 92. Washington, D.C.: U.S. Government Printing Office, 1991.

See also annotation under JB7. This government publication, "revised to March 1, 1991," contains the text of the copyright law of the United States with reference to amendments and without interpretation. Interpretations written for librarians or specific to library applications are few. Researchers are advised to seek the most recent revision.

JB6. Koenigsberg, I. Fred. *Examining the Implications of the Feist and Kinko's Decisions*. New York: Practicing Law Institute, 1991.

This monograph includes discussions of the fair-use provisions of U.S. copyright legislation and copyright infringement in light of educational and library photocopying.

JB7. Oakley, Robert L. *Copyright and Preservation: A Serious Problem in Need of a Thoughtful Solution*. Washington, D.C.: Commission on Preservation and Access, 1990.

Written specifically for preservation librarians, this report reviews U.S. copyright legislation and the related challenges and possible solutions for libraries using reproduction as a form of preservation. This work should be read by all engaged in brittle-book and preservation-reproduction programs. It contains an excellent summary of copyright history plus interpretations of current legislation and its implications for the production and sale of micrographic, xerographic, and electronic copies. Numerous bibliographic references.

JB8. Reed, Mary Hutchings. *The Copyright Primer for Librarians and Educators*. Chicago: American Library Association; Washington, D.C.: National Education Association, 1987.

Though now dated in some areas, this primer discusses the pertinent basics of U.S. copyright legislation. It should be regarded as an introduction to the complex and often confusing world of reproduction within the provisions of copyright.

JC
Imaging: Micrographic and Electronic

"Imaging" is the broad term for image-reproduction technologies, analog and digital, and their applications. In reproduction of library materials, imaging is generally understood to include microfilming and scanning/digitizing. Libraries are seeking models and developing applications for new technologies while maintaining older technologies and, often, integrating them with the new.

GENERAL IMAGING SYSTEMS AND IMAGE MANAGEMENT

JC1. *Micrographics and Optical Storage Equipment Review*. Westport, Conn.: Meckler. 1988– . Annual. ISSN 0882-3294.

Written specifically for library applications, this annual evaluates new micrographic and optical storage equipment.

JC2. Otten, Klaus. *Integrated Document and Image Management*. Silver Spring, Md.: Association for Information and Image Management, 1987.

Written primarily for records-management and business applications, this title addresses integrated image management systems that capitalize on the advantages of both micrographic and electronic imaging systems.

MICROGRAPHIC IMAGING AND MICROGRAPHIC SYSTEMS

JC3. Saffady, William. *Micrographic Systems*. 3rd ed. Silver Spring, Md.: Association for Information and Image Management, 1990.

An examination of micrographics technology and applications. Explores the characteristics and advantages of various micrographic systems and the relationship of this technology with other imaging technologies, equipment, and costs. An excellent introduction to micrographics. Revises a 1980 edition by Daniel M. Costigan.

JC4. Vilhauer, Jerry. *Introduction to Micrographics*. Silver Spring, Md.: Association for Information and Image Management, 1991.

Provides an overview of both source document (i.e., book and paper) and computer-output microfilming. Introduces microfilm types, equipment, processing, and duplication; and storage and access. This volume should be regarded as a source of sound, basic information, although not all of it applies to preservation microfilming or other library applications.

DIGITIZED TEXTS AND ELECTRONIC IMAGING

Electronic technologies and information being published about them are in constant development. Current information often augments or replaces yesterday's published information. Information seekers in this area will turn to the authors, publishers, and professional associations of the following titles for updates. Few of the currently available publications address library applications; researchers will generally need to extrapolate, though they may expect to find a few significant library-related case studies.

JC5. Avedon, Don M. *Introduction to Electronic Imaging.* Silver Spring, Md.: Association for Information and Image Management, 1991.

A primer on electronic image management systems, their advantages, use, and standards, as well as systems selection ratio considerations.

JC6. Black, David B. *Document Capture for Document Imaging Systems.* Silver Spring, Md.: Association for Information and Image Management, 1992.

A detailed, comprehensive discussion of image-capture systems. Prior background reading on image scanning, indexing, storage, and retrieval would be useful.

JC7. Chen, Ching-chih. *Optical Discs in Libraries: Use & Trends.* Medford, N.J.: Learned Information, 1991.

Examines library applications of optical discs in North America and Europe, as well as the impact of optical discs upon information delivery (results of a comprehensive survey of optical-product users). Includes a large bibliography of relevant resources.

JC8. *Datapro Reports on Document Imaging Systems: Product Evaluations, User Perspectives, Management Issues.* Delran, N.J.: Datapro Information Service Group. 1991– . Loose-leaf.

Provides user evaluations of a wide variety of imaging systems available from a comprehensive list of suppliers, together with discussion of management issues relating to their use. Periodically updated, this is a type of *Consumer Reports* magazine for purchasers of imaging systems.

JC9. Helgerson, Linda. *Introduction to Scanning.* Silver Spring, Md.: Association for Information and Image Management, 1987.

A basic collection of information about scanning, including its history, techniques, and devices, and scanner-performance specifications. A good introduction to scanning itself.

JC10. Waegermann, C. Peter. *Handbook of Optical Memory Systems.* Newton, Mass.: Optical Disk Institute, 1989.

Written as a reference guide for those considering or implementing optical systems, this handbook is updated periodically. Topics and updates address the latest in feasibility and case studies, design and systems preparations, and vendor selection. Includes lists of vendors, equipment, and training opportunities.

JC11. Walker, Terri C., and Richard K. Miller. *Electronic Imaging and Image Processing.* 3 vols. Madison, Ga.: SEAI Technical Publications, 1990.

This work describes imaging technologies and imaging products, provides a vendor list, and presents case studies, implementation guidelines, and market assessments and forecasts. Though the information (particularly case studies) may not describe library applications, much of it (especially descriptions of system capabilities in Volume 2) represents a sourcebook for understanding uses to which imaging systems may be put in library settings. Those planning library applications of electronic imaging systems should review Volume 2.

JD
Management and Organization

Most library applications of reproduction technologies have been developed for use in preservation activities. Management and organization of these activities often is discussed in the literature of preservation in general and of preservation microfilming in particular. See Chapter I, Preservation of Library Resources, for additional resources.

JD1. Spreitzer, Francis, ed. *Microforms in Libraries: A Manual for Evaluation and Management.* Chicago: American Library Association, 1985.

A review of microform evaluation, collection management, and facility operations for libraries.

JD2. Starbird, Robert W., and Gerald C. Vilhauer. *A Manager's Guide to Electronic Imaging.* Silver Spring, Md.: Association for Information and Image Management, 1992.

Discussion of electronic image management systems applications and management considerations from an implementation and management perspective. Preparation for EIM and work flows are among topics considered. Publication was written specifically for those who work with records management; this emphasis requires adaptation for library applications.

JD3. Waters, Donald J. "Electronic Technologies and Preservation: A Talk Presented to the Annual Meeting of the Research Libraries Group." 1992. (unpublished paper distributed electronically by the Research Libraries Group)

Suggesting a vision for the libraries of the future, Waters discusses the incorporation of new electronic technologies into libraries. He outlines several necessary management considerations and suggests areas of cooperative or consortial action.

JE
Media

In looking at reproduction of library materials, it's as important to focus discussion on media as on technologies. Media include photographic films and microfilms; electronic media, specifically, magnetic tape and disks; and optical media and compact discs. Each medium is read by different means and should be maintained under different conditions.

MICROFORMS

JE1. Adelstein, P. Z., and others. "Stability of Cellulose Ester Base Photographic Film: Part 1—Laboratory Testing Procedures." *SMPTE Journal* 101 (May 1992): 336–46; and "Part 2—Practical Storage Conditions." *SMPTE Journal* 101 (May 1992): 347–53.

Part 1 examines the chemical stability of cellulose ester-based film (used in microfilming from 1948 through the present) when maintained at room temperature. Part 2 examines methods of increasing the chemical stability of such film when maintained at 21°C 50 percent relative humidity (RH) and below.

JE2. Association for Information and Image Management. *Color Microforms.* Silver Spring, Md.: AIIM, 1989. AIIM TR9-1989.

This technical report compiles articles and references published in the professional literature on the use and longevity of color microforms. A sound beginning for research into the use, storage, and longevity of color microforms. *See also* American National Standards Institute, *American National Standard for Imaging Media—Stability of Color Photographic Images—Methods for Measuring.* ANSI IT9.9-1990 (JI8).

JE3. ———, comp. *Microspots and Aging Blemishes.* Silver Spring, Md.: AIIM, 1987.

This compilation of articles from a variety of sources presents discussion of microspots and aging blemishes, including redox blemishes. The compilation should be read by those preparing to undertake a condition survey of microform collections, as well as those seeking to identify or inhibit blemishing.

JE4. Brown, Daniel W., Robert E. Lowry, and Leslie E. Smith. *Prediction of the Long Term Stability of Polyester-Based Recording Media.* Washington, D.C.: Center for Materials Science, National Bureau of Standards, 1982.

This pamphlet, prepared as a report for the National Archives, examines storage and stability of polyester-based films as a medium for the reproduction of archival and library materials.

JE5. Reilly, James M. *Polysulfide Treatment of Microfilm Using IPI SilverLock™.* Rochester, N.Y.: Image Permanence Institute, 1991.

A catechism of questions and answers regarding the use of polysulfide treatments to protect silver gelatin emulsion microforms from the deleterious effects of oxidation and atmospheric pollutants. Offers succinct response to commonly posed questions: What does polysulfide treatment do? How does it work? Will its use be required by standards? Is it safe for older film? And so on.

JE6. Reilly, James M., Peter Z. Adelstein, and Douglas W. Nishimura. *Preservation of Safety Film.* Rochester, N.Y.: Image Permanence Institute, Rochester Institute of Technology, 1991.

For annotation, *see* IIH9.

JE7. Reilly, James M., and Kaspars M. Cupriks. *Sulfiding Protection for Silver Images.* Rochester, N.Y.: Image Permanence Institute, Rochester Institute of Technology, 1991.

This final report to the National Endowment for the Humanities' Office of Preservation (Grant PS-20152-87) details data resulting from tests to determine the viability of using polysulfiding treatment to protect preservation microforms from oxidation and subsequent deterioration.

JE8. Saffady, William. *Micrographics.* 2nd ed. Littleton, Colo.: Libraries Unlimited, 1985.

A comprehensive examination of micrographics, its applications and uses in libraries. This volume is often used as an introductory text in library schools.

ELECTRONIC, OPTICAL, AND OTHER MEDIA

Electronic and optical media are the tablets of new technologies. Compared with paper and films, the media of older technologies, they are more readily and accurately copied but less permanent.

JE9. Hendley, A. M. *The Archival Storage Potential of Microfilm, Magnetic Media and Optical Data Discs: A Comparison Based on a Literature Review.* British National Bibliography Research Fund Report, No. 10. Hertford, Hertfordshire, Eng.: National Reprographic Centre for Documentation, distributed in the United States by International Information Management Congress, Bethesda, Md., 1983.

A comparative study of various media for preservation reproduction. It serves as an introduction for further investigation.

JE10. Saffady, William. *Optical Disks vs. Magnetic Storage.* Westport, Conn.: Meckler, 1990.

A detailed examination of the storage capabilities and potential of optical disks as compared to those of magnetic media. Discusses systems and media use by each technology, similarities and advantages, and hierarchical storage configurations that integrate components of both technologies. Written for systems analysts and managers of imaging technologies.

JE11. _____. *Optical Disks vs. Micrographics as Document Storage and Retrieval Technology.* Westport, Conn.: Meckler, 1988.

An examination of the capabilities and potential of optical imaging systems compared with the capabilities and use of micrographic technologies for storage and retrieval of information. Emphasizes the power and advantages of optical imaging systems.

JE12. _____. *Stability, Care and Handling of Microforms, Magnetic Media and Optical Disks.* Westport, Conn.: Meckler, 1991. Also published as *Library Technology Reports* 27, no. 1 (Jan./Feb. 1991).

This report, which includes an extensive bibliography, examines the stability of various reprographic media and discusses handling and storage considerations. Each medium is described in four sections: media overview, technology overview, stability of recorded information, and library guidelines. A well-researched, clearly written, authoritative source prepared specifically for librarians.

JE13. Winterbottom, D. R., and R. G. Fiddes. *Life Expectancy of Write Once Digital Optical Discs.* British Library Research Paper, no. 66. London: British Library, Research and Development Department, 1989.

This report examines the life expectancy of optical disks under storage conditions.

JF
Micrographic, Optical, and Electronic Image Publishing

CATALOGS, DIRECTORIES, AND REGISTERS

JF1. *CD-ROMs in Print: An International Guide to CD-ROM, CD-I, CDTV and Electronic Book Products.* Westport, Conn.: Meckler. 1987– . Annual. ISSN 0891-8198.

This publication, developed for use by libraries, contains directories of CD-ROMs, compact discs, and similar products and optical storage devices for library application. As more electronic book products become available, this publication may serve much as *Books in Print* or *Guide to Microforms in Print* (JF2) now do in helping preservation librarians to identify materials that have been reproduced. Also available in CD-ROM format.

JF2. *Guide to Microforms in Print: Author, Title.* Munich: K. G. Saur. 1978– . Annual. ISSN 0164-0747.

A commercial catalog of microforms available from commercial and institutional micropublishers. This publication is used in preservation microfilming projects and by acquisitions and collection development librarians to ascertain the existence of microforms not cited in the bibliographic databases.

JF3. *Microform Market Place: An International Directory of Micropublishing.* Westport, Conn.: Meckler. 1982– . ISSN 0362-0999.

A sourcebook on microform publishing; primarily covers micropublishers in North America and Europe. Like the above title (JF2), this publication is used in preservation microfilming projects and by acquisitions and collection development librarians to track major microform programs not cited in the bibliographic databases. Entries furnish detailed information about publishers.

JF4. *National Register of Microform Masters.* Washington, D.C.: Library of Congress. 1965-1983. ISSN 0090-3299.

Compiled by the Library of Congress with the cooperation of the American Library Association and the Association of Research Libraries, this is a main-entry catalog of master microforms created by commercial and institutional micropublishers and reported on a voluntary basis since 1965. Publication was discontinued in the mid-1980s as the use of automated databases for searching became widespread. Retrospective projects are adding bibliographic records for these masters to the national online databases.

JF5. New York Public Library. *New York Public Library Register of Microform Masters.* Bellevue, Wash.: Commercial Microfilm Service, 1984.

Published in microfiche, this register represents microform masters filmed by the Research Libraries of the New York Public Library circa 1938–1983. Only a portion of the bibliographic records for approximately 200,000 titles registered here have been added to the national databases. It is intended for use in preservation microfilming and collection development programs, and is most often used in conjunction with the OCLC or RLIN databases to verify that the New York Public Library has not microfilmed specific titles.

JF6. Research Libraries Group. *RLIN Register of Microform Masters.* 4th ed. Mountain View, Calif.: RLG, 1988.

Published in microfiche, with a fifth edition anticipated in CD-ROM format, this register includes preservation-microfilmed titles in the RLIN catalog. It is intended for use in preservation microfilming and collection development programs without access to the RLIN database and is most often used to verify the nonexistence of microfilmed titles prior to filming. Earlier editions were published under the title *RLG Preservation Union List*.

PUBLISHING ACTIVITY

JF7. Bourke, Thomas A. "Scholarly Micropublishing, Preservation Microfilming, and the National Preservation Effort in the Last Two Decades of the Twentieth Century: History and Prognosis." *Microform Review* 19, no. 1 (Winter 1990): 4-16.

An analytical history of commercial and educational micropublishing activity since 1979, continuing where Meckler's history of micropublishing (JF10) ends. Covers a period of volatile change, including the introduction of national preservation programs.

JF8. Hendley, A. M. *CD-ROM and Optical Publishing Systems*. British National Bibliography Research Fund Report, no. 25. Hertford, Hertfordshire, Eng.: Cimtech; Westport, Conn.: Meckler, 1987.

This monograph assesses the impact of optical read-only memory systems on the information industry. It is written as a comparison between these systems and traditional paper, microfilm, and online publishing systems.

JF9. Kesse, Erich J. *The Survey of Micropublishers*. Washington, D.C.: Commission on Preservation and Access, 1992.

This report studies the adherence of micropublishers in North America and the United Kingdom to micrographic standards and their application. "Micropublisher" is defined broadly to include associations, commercial publishers, and educational and governmental institutions that micropublish. Supplementary materials—survey results and a *Directory of Micropublishers*—were published separately by the Commission on Preservation and Access. Both *The Survey of Micropublishers* and supplementary materials are also available through *FLIPPER: The Electronic Library* (IAJ2).

JF10. Meckler, Alan M. *Micropublishing: A History of Scholarly Micropublishing in America, 1938-1980*. Westport, Conn.: Greenwood Press, 1982.

A history of micropublishing in the United States from its commercial beginnings through 1980, providing insights into micropublishing ventures, mergers, etc. Originally written in 1980 as Meckler's thesis at Columbia University.

JF11. *The Use of Optical Media for Publication of Full Text*. Amsterdam: International Group of Scientific, Technical and Medical Publishers, 1987.

A joint statement on cooperation in use of optical media for full text image capture and publication of information. Issued by publishers and librarians in Europe, it charts a course of development and may serve as a model for future cooperation elsewhere.

JG
Photocopiers and Photocopying

JG1. Association for Library Collections and Technical Services. *Guidelines for Preservation Photocopying of Replacement Pages*. Chicago: ALCTS, American Library Association, 1990.

Prepared for conservation or repair technicians by the Association's Reproduction of Library Materials Section, this title details the requirements of pages copied for purposes of preservation replacement. The guidelines outline specifications for paper, image quality, placement, and other factors.

JG2. Association of Research Libraries, Office of Management Studies. *Photocopy Services in ARL Libraries*. SPEC Kit, no. 115. Washington, D.C.: ARL, 1985.

A compilation of procedural documents and organizational models for administration of photocopy services in the Association's member libraries. Still helpful to libraries considering organizational models for implementation or review of such services.

JG3. *Catalog of Publisher Information*. Salem, Mass.: Copyright Clearance Center. 1989– . Annual. ISSN 1065-7916.

Describes royalties to be paid for photocopying of published materials. Anyone responsible for administration of photocopy services in libraries (other than preservation reproduction) should be familiar with this publication and the Center, as well as the "fair use" provisions of U.S. and international copyright legislation under which the Center operates. Continues the Center's *Publishers' Photo-Copy Fee Catalog*.

JG4. *Copier Specification Guide*. Hackensack, N.J.: Buyers Laboratory. 1989– . Semiannual. ISSN 1050-978X.

This publication provides critical evaluations of photocopiers together with some basic information about copying processes. A type of *Consumer Reports* magazine for purchasers of photocopiers and related equipment, it evaluates a wide variety of photocopiers available from a comprehensive list of manufacturers.

JG5. *Copying and Duplicating Industry Service.* Cupertino, Calif.: Dataquest. 1982– . Annual.

An annual market survey and analysis of the copying-equipment industry. Libraries considering purchase of copying equipment can find evaluations and trends here.

JG6. Jones, Norvell M. M. *Archival Copies of Thermofax, Verifax, and Other Unstable Records.* National Archives Technical Information Paper, No. 5. Washington, D.C.: National Archives and Records Administration, 1990.

For annotation, *see* IIG8.

JG7. Walker, Gay. "Preservation Decision-Making and Archival Photocopying." *Restaurator* 8(1987): 40–51.

An overview of Yale University Library's practice of using preservation photocopying for out-of-print, brittle books. Discussion of Yale's criteria for consideration of such copies as replacements for originals. Review of advantages and disadvantages of photocopying versus microfilming.

JH
Preservation Reproduction

JH1. Lesk, Michael. *Image Formats for Preservation and Access: A Report to the Technology and Assessment Advisory Committee to the Commission on Preservation and Access.* Washington, D.C.: Commission on Preservation and Access, 1990.

This report suggests a variety of alternatives for preservation of brittle books and other deteriorating library materials, including microfilming and digital imaging. Also looks at storage (e.g., magnetic and optical disks, digital audio and video tape, CD-ROM, etc.), conversion and transmission considerations, and maintenance costs. The report is a brief overview written largely to take stock of available preservation options.

JH2. Tanselle, G. Thomas. "Reproductions and Scholarship." *Studies in Bibliography* 42 (1989): 25–54.

A textual scholar's perspective on the value of originals, reproducing book texts in general, and the large-scale preservation microfilming of brittle books in particular. A very critical and unsympathetic view of libraries' transfer of books to microfilm with subsequent disposal of the originals. This and other Tanselle writings should be read by all library professionals involved in preservation selection and reformatting. Bibliographic references.

JH3. Walker, Gay. "Preserving the Intellectual Content of Deteriorated Library Materials." In *The Preservation Challenge: A Guide to Conserving Library Materials*, edited by

Carolyn Clark Morrow, 93–113. White Plains, N.Y.: Knowledge Industry, 1983.

A clear and concise overview of the issues and processes involved in preservation reformatting. Although the bibliographic-search segment requires an update, the remainder of this chapter makes a very good first source when educating oneself about the topic.

JH4. Willis, Don. *A Hybrid Systems Approach to Preservation of Printed Materials.* Washington, D.C.: Commission on Preservation and Access, 1992.

A welcome analysis of the many interrelationships between microform and digital technologies as they are applied to brittle-paper reformatting, preservation, and enhanced access. Suggests the benefits of a hybrid approach combining both film and digital imaging systems for long-term preservation and flexibility for future access to and use of converted texts. Reviews the issues, compares costs, and provides recommendations in readable language. Appendixes and figures supplement text.

PRESERVATION MICROFILMING

JH5. American Library Association, Resources and Technical Services Division. *Preservation Microfilming: Planning and Production.* Chicago: RTSD, ALA, 1988.

A compilation of addresses and papers from the RTSD Preservation Microfilming Regional Institute (New Haven, Conn., April 21–23, 1988) on planning and production issues related to preservation microfilming. Aimed at administrators of preservation microfilming projects.

JH6. Byrne, Sherry. "Guidelines for Contracting Microfilming Services." *Microform Review* 15 (Fall 1986): 253–64.

Generic guidelines for contracting preservation microfilming services. Written to serve librarians developing projects using commercial microfilming services.

JH7. Elkington, Nancy E., ed. *Preservation Microfilming Handbook.* Mountain View, Calif.: Research Libraries Group, 1992.

A valuable addition to the literature available for assisting libraries and archives in managing the many details involved in preservation microfilming activities. This 204-page spiral-bound volume supersedes and updates the earlier *RLG Preservation Manual*, second edition, 1986. Uniform guidelines for the practice of preservation microfilming in RLG projects, which touch on preparation, targeting, technical issues, and quality control. Certain to be *the* reference source on this subject.

JH8. Gwinn, Nancy E., ed. *Preservation Microfilming: A Guide for Librarians and Archivists.* Chicago: American Library Association, 1987.

One of the best sources for librarians, archivists, and staffs involved with reformatting paper-based materials to preservation microfilm. A comprehensive manual of preservation microfilming practice and techniques; includes a glossary, standards and specifications, and sample contracts for preservation microfilming. Compiled for the Association of Research Libraries to assist librarians in preservation microfilming program management and the creation of archival quality microforms.

JH9. Kanto, Paul B. *Costs of Preservation Microfilming at Research Libraries: A Study of Four Institutions.* Washington, D.C.: Council on Library Resources, 1986.

A study of preservation microfilming costs incurred by four research libraries in the United States, this pamphlet provides information to compare with that reported by Patricia A. McClung in her "Costs Associated with Preservation Microfilming: Results of the Research Libraries Group Study" (JH10).

JH10. McClung, Patricia A. "Costs Associated with Preservation Microfilming: Results of the Research Libraries Group Study." *Library Resources & Technical Services* 30 (Oct./Dec. 1986): 364–74.

A study of costs involved in RLG's Cooperative Preservation Microfilming Project, "Great Collections Microfilming Project: Phase One," including analysis of costs associated with identification, preparation, filming, and inspection. Though dated, this article outlines types of expenditures incurred through the identification, filming, quality control, and cataloging of preservation project materials. Because GCMP1 was a cooperative effort, with participants from across the United States, the study could examine regional variants.

JH11. Mid-Atlantic Preservation Service. *The Real Final Report to the Commission on Preservation and Access (Project No. CPA 7501) and the Andrew W. Mellon Foundation on Step & Repeat Camera (105mm) Operating Strategies and Applications of Archival Standards to the Fiche Production Process.* Washington, D.C.: Commission on Preservation and Access, 1989.

A study of step & repeat camera operations designed to test the application of technical standards commonly cited in 105mm roll film preservation microfilming, this report examines the use of microfiche as a preservation format. Resolution and reduction ratio were two areas of concern.

OTHER MEDIA FOR PRESERVATION REPRODUCTION

JH12. Fischer, Audrey, and Tamara Swora. *Library of Congress Optical Disk Pilot Program, Optical Disk Print Pilot Project . . . Phase I.* Washington, D.C.: Library of Congress, 1986; and *Phase II.* Washington, D.C.: LC, 1987.

Both reports document the experimentation with optical disks for the reproduction of library materials at the Library of Congress, including document preparation and imaging procedures.

JH13. Kenney, Anne R., and Lynne K. Personius. *Joint Study in Digital Preservation, Phase 1.* Washington, D.C.: Commission on Preservation and Access, 1992.

A report on a joint project by Cornell University, Xerox, and the Commission on Preservation and Access, this publication discusses digital image capture, generation of paper facsimiles, and networked access to digitized texts. The report clearly defines the project's guiding principles and products (e.g., bibliographic access, networked scanning, and paper facsimiles), processes (e.g., selection, preparation, scanning, and quality control), and findings, including cost analyses. This work, together with those authored by Donald J. Waters (JH16 and JH17), is likely to be used as a model for library applications of digital imaging technologies.

JH14. National Library of Medicine, Lister Hill National Center for Biomedical Communications, Communications Engineering Branch. *Document Preservation by Electronic Imaging.* 3 vols. Available from National Technical Information Service, Springfield, Va. Internal report, dated April 1989.

This title details experimentation done with electronic imaging of library materials at the National Library of Medicine. Volume 1 offers a synopsis of the imaging system and experiments described in Volume 2. Volume 3 contains appendixes. While the content, particularly in the second and third volumes, may be technical, it depicts a model for the use of electronic imaging for library preservation and describes some of the problems and solutions encountered.

JH15. Puglia, Steven T. "Duplication Options for Deteriorating Photo Collections." In *Photograph Preservation and the Research Library*, edited by Jennifer Porro, 29–35. Mountain View, Calif.: Research Libraries Group, 1991.

Briefly discusses an array of reproduction options, including photography, photocopy, microphotography, and electronic imaging for preservation of photograph collections.

JH16. Waters, Donald J. *From Microfilm to Digital Imagery: On the Feasibility of a Project to Study the Means, Costs and Benefits of Converting Large Quantities of Preserved Library Materials from Microfilm to Digital Images.* Washington, D.C.: Commission on Preservation and Access, 1991.

A planning report prepared by the Yale University Library and commissioned by the Commission on Preservation and Access, this report details the feasibility of converting preservation microfilm to digital imagery. The report clearly defines how such a method should work; the economic factors associated with implementation of desired storage, maintenance, and access features; systems architecture and configuration related to conversion, reproduction, storage, and access; and an implementation plan. This work will be useful to those constructing library applications for digital imaging. Appendix of examples of computer archives now in existence in North America. Supplemented by Waters's more recent reports, including JH17, following.

JH17. Waters, Donald J., and Shari Weaver. *The Organizational Phase of Project Open Book.* Washington, D.C.: Commission on Preservation and Access, 1992.

A status report on Project Open Book, a project in the Yale University Library to explore the usefulness of digital technologies for preserving and improving access to deteriorating works. This report is the second in a series commissioned by the Commission on Preservation and Access. The report defines technical components and design principles of the project and discusses key issues, particularly image quality.

JI
Standards, Specifications, and Guidelines

Standards are under constant review. Depending upon the issuing body, they may be revised, reasserted, or withdrawn periodically. In some cases, standards are replaced entirely. Readers are advised to contact the issuing body regarding availability of the latest version.

GENERAL

JI1. *AIIM Standards Activity Report*. Silver Spring, Md: Association for Information and Image Management. 1983– . Irregular.

Available from the Association's headquarters (JAH7), this report lists standards currently being written or under review together with the contact names, action dates, and actions required or taken. Sections for micrographic, electronic, and other imaging concerns are clearly delineated. The report should be reviewed periodically by those responsible for overseeing implementation of imaging standards.

JI2. *Information Standards Quarterly*. Bethesda, Md: National Information Standards Organization. v. 1, no. 1– , 1989– . Quarterly. ISSN 1041–0031.

See also annotation under IAF3. Updates NISO and other standards development activities and includes both summaries and implementation strategies. While not restricted to reproduction standards, many of the standards summarized govern micrographics, electronic image management, and information management.

MICROGRAPHICS

The following represents only the most commonly referenced standards. Each standard makes reference to other standards that also must be read to fully comprehend the subject of the standard in hand. Both Elkington's *Preservation Microfilming Handbook* (JH7) and Gwinn's *Preservation Microfilming* (JH8) list additional standards necessary to meet the requirements of preservation microfilming.

JI3. American National Standards Institute. *American National Standard for Imaging Media (Film): Ammonia-Processed Diazo Films: Specifications for Stability.* Rev. ed. New York: ANSI, 1992. ANSI IT9.5-1992.

Developed by the National Association of Photographic Manufacturers to replace ANSI PH1.5-1988, this technical standard defines the characteristics of ammonia-processed diazo films. These specifications detail processing methods and storage conditions necessary to ensure the stability of the product. This standard should be cited in contracts requiring the production of diazo films, and librarians administering these contracts should be familiar with it.

JI4. _____. *American National Standard for Imaging Media (Film)—Silver-Gelatin Type—Specifications for Stability.* New York: ANSI, 1992. ANSI IT9.1-1992.

Developed by the National Association of Photographic Manufacturers, this technical standard defines the characteristics of silver-gelatin type film used in preservation microfilming and describes processing methods and storage conditions that ensure the stability of processed films. This standard should be cited in all contracts for preservation microfilming projects; those administering such projects should be familiar with it. Replaces ANSI IT9.1-1989.

JI5. _____. *American National Standard for Imaging Media—Photographic Films and Papers—Methods for Determining Dimensional Change Characteristics.* New York: ANSI, 1989. ANSI IT9.3-1989.

A revision of standard ANSI PH1.32-1973, similar to international standard ISO 6221-1980, this standard provides uniform methods for testing and expressing dimension changes in photographic films that occur as a result of climate conditions. The standard should be consulted by librarians evaluating the condition of stored film. Test methods described may be beyond the capabilities of libraries but should be cited in requests for proposals for evaluation of stored films.

JI6. _____. *American National Standard for Imaging Media: Photographic Processed Films, Plates, and Papers—Filing Enclosures and Storage Containers.* New York: ANSI, 1991. ANSI IT9.2-1991.

This standard, replacing ANSI IT9.2-1988, describes material specifications and practice for use of filing enclosures (e.g., reel string ties) and containers (e.g., microfilm reel boxes, microfiche envelopes) that extend the life expectancy of stored microfilms.

JI7. _____. *American National Standard for Imaging Media: Processed Safety Photographic Film: Storage.* New York: ANSI, 1991. ANSI IT9.11-1991.

Defines requirements for storage of silver-gelatin type film used in preservation microfilming. Revision and redesignation of ANSI PH1.43-1985.

JI8. _____. *American National Standard for Imaging Media—Stability of Color Photographic Images—Methods for Measuring.* New York: ANSI, 1990. ANSI IT9.9-1990.

Developed by the National Association of Photographic Manufacturers, this technical standard addresses the stability of color photographic methods. It should be read by those considering the use of color photography to capture color source documents. This standard does not address the stabilization of color photographic films or storage environments for those films.

JI9. _____. *American National Standard for Photography (Chemicals)—Residual Thiosulfate and Other Chemicals in Films, Plates, and Papers—Determination and Measurement.* New York: ANSI, 1985. ANSI PH4.8-1985.

Standard for measuring residual processing chemicals that, over time, may advance the deterioration of processed microfilm. Revision of ANSI PH4.8-1978.

JI10. _____. *American National Standard for Photography: Photographic Films: Specifications for Safety Films.* New York: ANSI, 1992. ANSI/ISO #543-1990, ANSI IT9.6-1991.

A material specification for microfilm base, this standard defines the material substrate of photographic films. It is generally cited in requests for proposals for microfilming and in preservation microfilming contracts. Revision of ANSI PH1.25-1984, R1989.

JI11. _____. *American National Standard for Photography (Sensitometry)—Density Measurements—Terms, Symbols, and Notations.* New York: ANSI, 1984. ANSI PH2.16-1984; ISO 5/1-1984.

A fundamental standard, accepted in the United States and internationally, this document describes the principles and practice of density measurement in photography (and microphotography). It should be used by librarians, if for nothing else, to gain an understanding of density. It should be consulted and comprehended by librarians charged with assuring the quality of preservation microforms.

JI12. _____. *Standard for Information and Image Management: Micrographics—ISO Resolution Test Chart No. 2: Description and Use.* Silver Spring, Md: American National Standards Institute, 1991. ANSI/ISO 3334-1991, ANSI/AIIM MS51-1991.

The principal resolution test target required for preservation microfilming; use allows measurement and quality control inspection of photographically reduced images. Revises ANSI/ISO 3334-1978.

JI13. Association for Information and Image Management. *Micrographics—Microfiche.* Silver Spring, Md: AIIM, 1991. ANSI/AIIM MS5-1991.

Defines the characteristics and composition of microfiche; does not address specific topics, e.g., target-

ing, and refers back to ANSI/AIIM MS23 for discussion of resolution, reduction ratios, quality control, etc.

JI14. _____. *Practice for Operational Procedures/Inspection and Quality Control of First-Generation Silver-Gelatin Microfilm of Documents.* Silver Spring, Md: AIIM, 1991. ANSI/AIIM MS23-1991.

This standard details procedures governing production and inspection, specifically quality control, of microforms. The basic standard for all microfilming; it should be cited in contracts for preservation microfilming projects. Library project administrators should be familiar with it. A revision of this standard practice is anticipated for approximately 1994.

JI15. _____. *Recommended Practice for Identification of Microforms.* Silver Spring, Md: AIIM, 1987. ANSI/AIIM MS19-1987.

Defines practice for targeting and marking of microforms for bibliographic identification and inventory control. For library practice, this standard may be superseded by ANSI/NISO Z39.62, currently available in draft as *Proposed American National Standards for Eye-Legible Information on Microfilm Leaders and Trailers and on Containers of Processed Microfilm on Open Reels,* Bethesda, Md: National Information Standards Organization, 1992.

JI16. _____. *Recommended Practice for Microfilming Printed Newspapers on 35-mm Roll Microfilm.* Silver Spring, Md: AIIM, 1987. ANSI/AIIM MS111-1987.

In large part, a standardized version of *Specifications for Microfilming of Newspapers in the Library of Congress,* Washington, D.C.: Library of Congress, 1971. A specification for resolution, reduction ratio, and other technical factors in newspaper microfilming, this recommended practice is required for those filming newspapers as part of the United States Newspaper Project (USNP).

JI17. _____. *Recommended Practice for the Requirements and Characteristics of Original Documents That May Be Microfilmed.* Silver Spring, Md: AIIM, 1990. ANSI/AIIM MS35-1990.

Describes the optimal characteristics of documents for microfilming.

JI18. _____. *Splices for Imaged Film—Dimensions and Operational Constraints.* Silver Spring, Md: AIIM, 1987. AIIM MS18-1987.

Characterizes splices and their use with microfilm; does not differentiate splice method for preservation microfilming in 1987 publication. Under review at this writing, with anticipated revision date of 1993 or 1994.

JI19. _____. *Standard for Information and Image Management: Recommended Practice for Inspection of Stored Silver-Gelatin Microforms for Evidence of Deterioration.* Silver Spring, Md: AIIM, 1990. ANSI/AIIM MS45-1990.

Codifies a practice for evaluation of attributes of stored microfilm for evidence of deterioration.

JI20. ———. *Standard for Information and Image Management: Recommended Practice for Microphotography of Cartographic Materials.* Silver Spring, Md: AIIM, 1989. ANSI/AIIM MS37-1988.

Describes the optimal characteristics of maps and other cartographic materials for microfilming.

JI21. *Basic U.S. Government Micrographics Standards and Specifications.* 6th ed. Silver Spring, Md: Association for Information and Image Management, 1983. AIIM RS1-1983.

A compilation of standards and specifications created by various U.S. government agencies for technical aspects of microform production and quality control, some of which have been superseded or made obsolete by ANSI standards published since 1983.

JI22. Chase, Myron. "Standards and Specifications." In *Preservation Microfilming: Planning and Production,* 16–31. Papers from the RTSD Preservation Microfilming Institute, New Haven, Connecticut, April 21–23, 1988. Chicago: Association for Library Collections and Technical Services, American Library Association, 1989.

A review of the key standards related to preservation microfilming, including processing, inspection, editing, duplication, and storage. Includes brief list of standards to which reference is made. Also includes an example of the camera resolution test chart and the quality index graph.

JI23. Library of Congress, Photoduplication Service. *Specifications for Microfilming Manuscripts.* Washington, D.C.: LC, 1980.

Though now largely replaced by more general preservation microfilming guidelines, these specifications are the only authoritative guidelines for microfilming manuscripts.

JI24. ———. *Specifications for Microfilming of Books and Pamphlets in the Library of Congress.* Rev. ed. Silver Spring, Md: National Micrographics Association, 1983.

This publication was one of the first in the United States to set out specifications for preservation microfilming of monographic materials. Though superseded—in many areas by Elkington's *Preservation Microfilming Handbook* (JH7)—these specifications remain important to understanding the development of current RLG guidelines.

JI25. McKern, Debra, and Sherry Byrne. *ALA Target Packet for Use in Preservation Microfilming.* Chicago: American Library Association, 1991.

This packet includes a compilation of camera-ready targets together with a standard practice for their use. The packet was specifically designed for commercial and institution micropublishers who produce preservation microfilm.

JI26. National Information Standards Organization. *Information on Microfiche Headings.* New Brunswick, N.J.: Transaction Publishers, 1981. ANSI/NISO Z39.32-1981.

Defines the composition and format of microfiche headings.

OTHER MEDIA

JI27. Association for Information and Image Management. *Technical Report for Information and Image Management: Electronic Imaging Request for Proposal (RFP) Guidelines.* Silver Spring, Md: AIIM, 1991. AIIM TR27-1991.

This report offers a suggested model for Request for Proposal (RFP) for libraries seeking electronic imaging services. The model attempts to define the structure of an imaging RFP and the areas that respondents should address.

JI28. Mier, Michael, and Marilyn Courtot, eds. *Standards for Electronic Imaging Systems.* Bellingham, Wash.: SPIE Optical Engineering Press, 1991.

Proceedings from a Feb. 28–Mar. 1, 1991, conference sponsored by the Society of Photo-optical Instrumentation Engineers (SPIE) and Society for Imaging Science and Technology (IS&T) in cooperation with the Rochester Institute of Technology's Center for Imaging Science. A primarily technical elucidation of imaging standards, dealing with optics and engineering principles. Of interest to systems librarians engaged in the implementation of imaging systems.

JI29. National Information Standards Organization (U.S.). *Volume and File Structure of CD-ROM for Information Exchange.* New Brunswick, N.J.: Transaction Publishers, 1992. ANSI/NISO/ISO 9960.

Standard for the format and placement of data on CD-ROMs, defining volume and file structures.

EQUIPMENT

JI30. Association for Information and Image Management. *Recommended Practice for Quality Control of Image Scanners.* Silver Spring, Md: AIIM, 1988. ANSI/AIIM MS44-1988.

This standard defines practice for measuring and describing quality of scanned images. Its use is recommended in electronic imaging systems applications to assure that image scanners operate within accepted tolerances.

JI31. ———. *Standard for Information and Image Management: Readers for Transparent Microforms—Methods for Measuring Performance.* Silver Spring, Md: AIIM, 1990. ANSI/AIIM MS12-1990; ISO 7565.

This standard, accepted in the United States and internationally, defines methods for measuring the performance of microform readers. Combined with the standard for performance characteristics (ANSI/AIIM MS20-1990) (JI32), the standard provides managers of microform facilities and purchasers of microform readers with means of uniform evaluation of readers.

JI32. ———. *Standard for Information and Image Management: Readers for Transparent Microforms—Performance Char-*

acteristics. Silver Spring, Md: AIIM, 1990. ANSI/AIIM MS20-1990; ISO 6198.

This standard, accepted in the United States and internationally, describes performance characteristics of microform readers. Combined with the standard for methods for measuring performance (ANSI/AIIM MS12-1990) (JI31), it provides managers of microform facilities and purchasers of microform readers with means of uniform evaluation of readers.

JI33. _____. *Standard for Information and Image Management: Reader-Printers for Transparent Microforms—Performance Characteristics*. Silver Spring, Md: AIIM, 1990. ANSI/AIIM MS36-1990; ISO 10197.

This standard defines the function of reader-printers and recommends operational characteristics and performance. It provides managers of microform facilities and purchasers of microform readers with means of uniform evaluation of reader-printers.

K

Database Management

Christina Perkins Meyer

Overview

In the computing world, database management systems are software packages that allow users to define the structure of a database, access it, and administer it. In library technical services, human database managers perform analogous tasks: Though they do not define the structure of the records, they must be thoroughly conversant with it. The overall goal of their administration is certainly access—both to the library database and, by extension, to library collections.

Since the position of database manager has been defined relatively recently at most institutions, its boundaries are still unclear. Some database managers are former catalog editors who supervise staff maintaining online records; all are certainly concerned with the quality and integrity of the database. Others began their professional lives as supervisors of retrospective conversion projects; now they are likely to be involved in conversion of files of machine-readable records from one format to another.

As ways of adding records to databases have multiplied and the need to report data to other entities such as utilities and union lists has grown, database managers have had to become experts in record-transfer processes. More than any other staff in

technical services, they have needed to understand the detailed structure of the records that form the database. This has meant developing a thorough understanding of the MAchine-Readable Cataloging (MARC) format in which records are communicated, as well as the internal formats used in the database. The scope of the databases managed is also unclear and changing. Typically, database managers have been responsible for bibliographic, holdings, and authority records; indeed, management of those records is the focus of this chapter. Increasingly, however, database managers are being asked to deal with other types of files including abstracts, indexes, and full-text databases.

Chapter Content and Organization

If it is difficult to define the position of database manager, it is equally difficult to decide what topics in the literature are relevant. Since the work of the database manager and of everyone else in technical services is so interdependent, there is a sense in which everything written for technical services staff is relevant to the database manager and vice versa. Indeed, a great deal of what is written for public services staff is equally relevant, since records are created for use, not for their own sake. The major topics chosen for this chapter are MARC formats, record conversion, quality control and database management, and record import and export. Though the choice is arbitrary to some extent, record structure, conversion, transfer, and quality are certainly within the purview of the typical database manager.

Determining what type of literature is relevant is also difficult. The database manager is expected to be both technical expert and manager, able to deal with a multitude of small details while preserving the broadest possible perspective on providing patron service through bibliographic access. The database manager must be able to decipher a hex dump to determine why a particular record is not being processed correctly on the same day she or he writes a position paper on the application of a new standard. Certainly no one has written a textbook on how to be a library database manager. While guidebooks, handbooks, and manuals exist for some tasks, they do not exist for the task as a whole. The neophyte database manager inevitably longs for some "how-to" information. Unfortunately, much of the how-to literature is of poor quality or so context-specific as to be of little general use. And realistically, it is easier to learn the how to's than to develop a broad perspective on one's own.

It is my hope that the resources listed in this chapter will provide some sense of the range of tasks involved in database management, how these tasks can be accomplished, and why they are done. Brief introductions define the scope of each section. Sections begin with a list of relevant organizations and other forums for discussion, since personal contact is so important when the literature is deficient. Next, relevant standards and format documents are listed, as they are critical reference tools for the database manager. Comments on groups of articles and books indicate the ways in which they may be useful, while the summaries provided in the annotations should help the reader decide if the content of a specific item is relevant.

KA
General Works

As noted in the introduction to this chapter, there are no textbooks, guides, or manuals that address, either from an introductory or an overview perspective, the responsibilities typically handled by database managers in libraries. Likewise, no journals focus solely on this position or responsibilities. Practitioners turn to many resources to find answers, follow developments, and gain information.

KAA
Periodicals

Following are periodicals that most commonly have articles of interest to individuals responsible for database management and quality control, record conversion, record import and export, and associated tasks. Important articles are published in other periodicals as well.

KAA1. *Advances in Library Automation and Networking: A Research Annual.* Edited by Joe A. Hewitt. Greenwich, Conn.: JAI Press. v. 1– , 1987– . Annual. ISSN 1048-4752.

For annotation, *see* AF3.

KAA2. *Bulletin of the American Society for Information Science.* Silver Spring, Md.: American Society for Information Science. v. 1– , June/July 1974– . Bimonthly. ISSN 0095-4403.

For annotation, *see* AF6.

KAA3. *Cataloging & Classification Quarterly.* New York: Haworth Press. v. 1– , Fall 1980– . Quarterly. ISSN 0163-9374.

For annotation, *see* CAE3.

KAA4. *Computer Communication Review.* New York: Association for Computer Machinery Special Interest Group on Data Communication. v. 1– , 1971– . ISSN 0146-4833.

Covers many aspects of computing with emphasis on communication hardware and software.

KAA5. *Computers in Libraries.* Westport, Conn.: Meckler. v. 9– , 1989– . ISSN 1041-7915. Continues *Small Computers in Libraries.*

Addresses a wide range of software applications for personal computers and for small and large computers.

KAA6. *Information Technology and Libraries.* Chicago: Library and Information Technology Association. v. 1– , Mar. 1982– . Quarterly. ISSN 0730-9295. Continues *Journal of Library Automation.*

For annotation, *see* AF10.

KAA7. *Journal of the American Society for Information Science.* New York: John Wiley & Sons for the Society. v. 21– , Jan./Feb. 1970– . Ten times a year. ISSN 0002-8231. Continues *American Documentation.*

For annotation, *see* AF11.

KAA8. *Library Hi Tech.* Ann Arbor, Mich.: Pierian Press. v. 1– , Summer 1983– . Monthly, plus special issues. ISSN 0737-8831.

For annotation, *see* AF12.

KAA9. *Library Resources & Technical Services.* Chicago: Association for Library Collections and Technical Services, ALA. v. 1– , Winter 1957– . Quarterly. ISSN 0024-2527.

For annotation, *see* AF13.

KAA10. *Library Software Review: SR.* Westport, Conn.: Meckler. v. 3– , Mar. 1984– . Bimonthly. ISSN 0742-5759. Continues *Software Review: SR.*

For annotation, *see* AF14.

KAA11. *Library Technology Reports.* Chicago: American Library Association. v. 12– , 1976– . Bimonthly. ISSN 0024-2586.

For annotation, *see* AF16.

KAA12. *LITA Newsletter.* Chicago: Library and Information Technology Association, ALA. no. 1– , Winter 1980– . Frequency varies; occasional supplements. ISSN 0196-1799.

For annotation, *see* AF17.

KAB
Sources of Expertise

In addition to the following sources of expertise, many of the automated library systems (NOTIS, INOVAC, etc.) have user groups and electronic discussion groups devoted to system-specific topics.

KAB1. American Society for Information Science (ASIS). Headquarters: 8729 Georgia Avenue, Suite 501, Silver Spring, MD 20910-3602. Executive Director: Richard B. Hill.

For annotation, *see* AGA1.

KAB2. ALA Association for Library Collections and Technical Services (ALCTS). Executive Director: Karen Muller.

For annotation, *see* AGA3.

KAB3. ALA ALCTS/CCS Catalog Management Discussion Group.

Serves as a forum for discussion of problems, techniques, and developments in catalog management, i.e., the preservation of the integrity of the catalog through maintenance of records following initial cataloging. It is of particular interest to those charged with quality control. Open to anyone interested in participation.

KAB4. ALA ALCTS/LITA/RASD Committee on Machine-Readable Bibliographic Information (MARBI).

Reviews proposals for changes in the MARC formats and the development of new formats and participates in the development of needed related standards. It also serves as part of the USMARC Advisory Group to the Library of Congress. Members are appointed by the participating ALA divisions, but meetings are open to all interested parties.

KAB5. ALA Library and Information Technology Association (LITA). Executive Director: Linda J. Knutson.

For annotation, *see* AGA5.

KAB6. ALA LITA/ALCTS Retrospective Conversion Interest Group.

Provides information for those planning or involved in retrospective conversion projects, emphasizing technological approaches to conversion. Open to anyone interested in participation.

KAB7. ALA LITA MARC Format for Holdings Interest Group.

Provides a forum for discussion of the development and implementation of the MARC format for holdings and for encouragement of its use. Anyone who is interested may participate in the work of the group.

KAB8. USMARC-L [electronic discussion group].

For annotation, *see* EAF3.

KB
MARC Formats

Walt Crawford (*see* KBC2) has called USMARC "the most expensive content designation standard in the library community . . . and . . . also the most beneficial." Indeed, it is hard to fathom the extent to which the standardization it provides has fostered the exchange of bibliographic and authority data.

The cataloger (one hopes) is most concerned about the content of a record and views MARC format simply as a means of structuring that content so that it can be manipulated by machine; the database manager, however, is most concerned about the structure itself, particularly with its accuracy. (*See* chapters C, Descriptive Cataloging, and E, Authority Control, for discussion of MARC format from the cataloging perspective.) Though most automated systems do not use strict MARC format internally (and their internal formats, which vary considerably, are outside the scope of this chapter), it is widely recognized that any North American library system ought to be MARC-compatible—that is, it ought to be able to import MARC records as well as export them *without loss of content or content designation.*

Of course there are a multitude of ways in which to develop an understanding of the MARC formats. Experienced database managers inevitably will remember poring over record dumps and trying to decipher programmers' notes in an effort to determine why records could not be processed. The literature provides very little help with these kinds of practical problems. It does, however, provide a broad perspective on the development and use of the formats.

Inevitably, one begins with the format documents themselves, and learns that a MARC record has three elements: (1) an overall structure based on the requirements of American National Standards Institute (ANSI) Z39.2, a standard for exchange of bibliographic records; (2) content designation, including tags, indicators, subfield codes, and coded data that are defined in the format documents; and (3) content that is defined by other documents, such as the *Anglo-American Cataloguing Rules*, second edition, revised 1988 (CBA1), and Library of Congress *Subject Headings* (DD15).

This general understanding can be supplemented by reading such excellent general works on the subject of the MARC format as those of Crawford (KBC3) and Gredley and Hopkinson (KBC4); by comparing the features of USMARC or CAN/MARC with those of other MARC formats, particularly UNIMARC, which was designed to be the intermediary format between national formats; and by reviewing the history of MARC formats.

Work on the first MARC format began in the mid-sixties at the Library of Congress with the MARC pilot project and the MARC I format, later revised to the MARC II format that is still with us. The original format was used for monographic materials, but through the seventies formats were published for several other materials, including serials, films, music, and manuscripts. (The last-named never gained widespread acceptance.)

This rapid growth and concern about the complexity and growing divergence of the formats led the Association of Research Libraries (ARL) to commission a study by Kaye Gapen (KBE3) to consider the question of whether the formats should be simplified. She concluded that the most useful form of simplification would be the development of greater consistency across formats. ALA's RTSD/LITA/RASD Committee on the Representation in Machine-Readable Form of Bibliographic Information (MARBI) responded by commissioning John Attig to write a paper (KBE1) defining the concept of a MARC format and by adopting a set of underlying principles upon which future work on the formats would be based.

The remaining years of the eighties were notable for the expansion of the formats to cover additional types of bibliographic material, including computer files and archival collections and manuscripts, and additional types of records, including authority records, holdings records, and classification records. Another key accomplishment was work on the integration of the bibliographic formats, a process that was expected to be completed in 1993. In addition to providing a consistent set of definitions across types of materials, format integration extends to all materials the concepts of seriality and processing control, derived from the AMC (Archival and Manuscripts Control) format.

As one considers the future of the MARC formats, the question of whether they can be extended to cover still more types of records, such as those for abstracting and indexing and full-text data, seems to be a key factor in their continued viability. Other vexing details, such as means of linking records, have not been solved to everyone's satisfaction, hence the divergence among USMARC, UKMARC, and UNIMARC, for instance. As use of the formats for records in many non-Roman scripts has grown, the need to accommodate a single global character-set standard has become more apparent. Finally, discussion between those who want theoretically pure formats and those whose primary consideration is practical usefulness will continue. In all discussions of the future, one salient fact should be kept in mind: The MARC formats are *communication* formats. Records may be stored internally in systems in many formats to take advantage of a wide variety of developing system features. To send those records to multitudes of other systems, however, export in a standard format will be required.

KBA
Standards

A basic understanding of the overarching standards upon which the MARC formats are based will aid the database manager in understanding the general structure of MARC format records.

KBA1. American National Standards Institute. *American National Standard Code for Information Interchange.* New York: ANSI, 1977.

ANSI X3.4 defines the ASCII character set, which is the basic character set used in MARC records.

KBA2. National Information Standards Organization (U.S.). *American National Standard: Extended Latin Alphabet Coded Character Set for Bibliographic Use.* New Brunswick, N.J.: Transaction Publishers, 1992.

ANSI/NISO Z39.47 defines the ANSEL character set, which is used as an extension of the ASCII character set in MARC records.

KBA3. _____. *Information Interchange Format: American National Standard for Information Interchange Format.* New Brunswick, N.J.: Transaction Publishers, 1992.

ANSI/NISO Z39.2 specifies the requirements for a generalized interchange format for bibliographic and other records. The standard allows a wide range of options; the format of MARC records is a specific implementation that employs choices among those options.

KBB
Format Documents

Database managers will refer to the MARC format documents frequently as they answer questions and resolve problems. Developing a general understanding of formats other than USMARC should improve one's understanding of the format most frequently used.

CAN/MARC

The CAN/MARC format documents (KBB1–KBB4), like their USMARC counterparts, provide definitions of content designation of the data carried in the formats. In general, CAN/MARC is highly similar to USMARC but includes additional fields, subfields, and indicators. Perhaps the most notable additions to the bibliographic and authorities formats are the definition of numerous 9XX fields to carry parallel data in another language and the definition of a leader value to indicate the degree of completeness of bilingual data.

KBB1. *Canadian MARC Communication Format: Authorities.* 3rd ed. Ottawa, Ont.: Canadian MARC Office, National Library of Canada, 1988.

For annotation, *see* DD6.

KBB2. *Canadian MARC Communication Format: Bibliographic Data.* Ottawa, Ont.: Canadian MARC Office, National Library of Canada, 1988.

KBB3. *Canadian MARC Communication Format: Holdings Data.* Ottawa, Ont.: Canadian MARC Office, National Library of Canada, 1990.

KBB4. *Canadian MARC Communication Format: Minimal Level.* 2nd ed. Ottawa, Ont.: Canadian MARC Office, National Library of Canada, 1991.

UNIMARC

KBB5. *UNIMARC/Authorities: Universal Format for Authorities.* Munich and New York: K. G. Saur, 1991.

See also annotation under EAB5. Guidelines for use and examples should prove helpful to those designing conversion programs between UNIMARC and other MARC formats.

KBB6. *UNIMARC Manual.* London: IFLA Universal Bibliographic Control and International MARC Programme, British Library Bibliographic Services, 1987.

This document serves as both the definitive description of the format and a handbook on its use. Its intended audiences are those converting records from a national format to UNIMARC for exchange purposes and those developing national formats that may be based upon UNIMARC. However, many readers will find it interesting to compare various aspects of UNIMARC with other MARC formats. Notable for its wealth of examples, which are explained at a level of detail that should expedite the creation of conversion programs.

USMARC

KBB7. *Format Integration and Its Effect on the USMARC Bibliographic Format.* Washington, D.C.: Cataloging Distribution Service, Library of Congress, 1992.

This document begins with a brief history of work on format integration, including a description of its basic elements. A summary version of the integrated format follows, with all changes highlighted for easy reference. Appendixes list all content designators that have been made obsolete, deleted, or added or whose names have been changed.

The following supplementary documents are lists of codes to be used in portions of MARC records specified in the format documents.

KBB8. *USMARC Code List for Countries.* Washington, D.C.: Cataloging Distribution Service, Library of Congress, 1988.

KBB9. *USMARC Code List for Geographic Areas.* Washington, D.C.: Cataloging Distribution Service, Library of Congress, 1988.

KBB10. *USMARC Code List for Languages.* Washington, D.C.: Cataloging Distribution Service, Library of Congress, 1989.

KBB11. *USMARC Code List for Relators, Sources, Description Conventions.* Washington, D.C.: Cataloging Distribution Service, Library of Congress, 1990.

The USMARC format documents define the conventions used to explicitly identify, characterize, and support manipulation of the data carried in each format. Each definition includes (1) a content designation listing; (2) a definition and scope statement; (3) guidelines for applying content designation, including examples; (4) input conventions; (5) information on related USMARC documents or fields; (6) a history of content designation; and (7) anticipated changes in content designation. Notable appendixes include lists of required data elements for minimal-level records in the bibliographic format, a summary of data-coding interdependencies in the authorities format, and a statement of the relationship between the ANSI standards for holdings display and the MARC format in the holdings format.

KBB12. *USMARC Concise Formats for Bibliographic, Authority, and Holdings Data.* Washington, D.C: Cataloging Distribution Service, Library of Congress, 1988– . Loose-leaf.

See also annotation under CBB1. Format for classification data added with Update no. 2 (1992). New edition cumulates updates in base text.

KBB13. *USMARC Diskette Label Specifications.* Washington, D.C.: Network Development and MARC Standards Office, Library of Congress, 1991.

These supplementary documents provide technical information on record structure, character sets, and magnetic tape and diskette formats for those involved in the design and maintenance of systems used for processing MARC records.

KBB14. *USMARC Format for Authority Data: Including Guidelines for Content Designation.* Washington, D.C.: Cataloging Distribution Service, Library of Congress, 1987– . Loose-leaf.

See also annotation under DD7. The 1991 edition consists of base text plus updates numbers 1–4 cumulated into the base text.

KBB15. *USMARC Format for Bibliographic Data: Including Guidelines for Content Designation.* Washington, D.C.: Cataloging Distribution Service, Library of Congress, 1988– . Loose-leaf.

See also annotation under CBB2. The 1992 edition consists of base text plus updates numbers 1–4 cumulated into the base text.

KBB16. *USMARC Format for Classification Data: Including Guidelines for Content Designation.* Washington, D.C.: Cataloging Distribution Service, Library of Congress, 1990– . Loose-leaf.

For annotation, *see* DC5.

KBB17. *USMARC Format for Holdings Data: Including Guidelines for Content Designation.* Washington, D.C.: Cataloging Distribution Service, Library of Congress, 1989– . Loose-leaf.

Defines the codes and conventions that identify elements in USMARC holdings reports for serial and nonserial items. Includes examples illustrating proper usage and guidelines for using the format.

KBB18. *USMARC Format: Proposed Changes.* Washington, D.C.: Network Development and MARC Standards Office, Library of Congress, 1987– . Irregular.

These proposals are the basis of MARBI and USMARC Advisory Group discussions. They are also available from USMARC-L (KAB8).

KBB19. *USMARC Specifications for Record Structure, Character Sets, Tapes.* Washington, D.C.: Cataloging Distribution Service, Library of Congress, 1990.

Provides technical information about USMARC record structure, character sets, and tape format. Essential for those who exchange USMARC records on magnetic tape.

KBC
MARC Formats: General

Resources in this group should provide the reader with an overall understanding of the MARC formats and of the specific issue of MARC compatibility.

KBC1. Byrne, Deborah J. *MARC Manual: Understanding and Using MARC Records.* Englewood, Colo.: Libraries Unlimited, 1991.

See also annotation under CBD2. A useful, though uneven, outline for anyone new to the task of database management. In the section dealing with the MARC formats, her concentration on patterns in the formats and reminders about the usefulness of particular data elements are helpful. In the section dealing with the use of MARC records, her description of tape characteristics is particularly clear; the chapter on database processing serves as an excellent outline for preprocessing tasks; and her focus on library and vendor responsibilities provides an excellent framework for decision making. The book lacks detail at points, quotes overextensively from source materials, and emphasizes OCLC.

KBC2. Crawford, Walt. "Library Standards for Data Structures and Element Identification: U.S. MARC in Theory and Practice." *Library Trends* 30 (Fall 1982): 265–81.

Crawford evaluates the USMARC formats as standards for data structure and element identification on the basis of data entry and maintenance requirements, content restrictions, storage and processing requirements, and data retrieval and manipulation capabilities. Also discusses degrees of MARC compatibility.

KBC3. _____. *MARC for Library Use: Understanding Integrated USMARC.* 2nd ed. Boston: G. K. Hall, 1989.

See also CBD3. Discussion of the structure of USMARC and each of the MARC formats. The tables of field frequencies in the Research Libraries Information Network (RLIN) database for each type of material are of particular interest. Extensions of USMARC used by the bibliographic utilities and the importance of MARC compatibility in bibliographic systems are also covered. The novice will find the book eminently readable and comprehensible, but the experienced user of the formats will also find interesting information and opinions. Useful extensive glossary.

KBC4. Gredley, Ellen, and Alan Hopkinson. *Exchanging Bibliographic Data: MARC and Other International Formats.* Chicago: American Library Association, 1990.

Gredley and Hopkinson begin with a brief discussion of the nature of bibliographic data and devote the majority of their book to a discussion of widely used communication formats for bibliographic data—notably USMARC, UKMARC, CAN/MARC, and UNIMARC, as well as the Common Communication Format (CCF) and the *Reference Manual for Machine-Readable Bibliographic Descriptions*, compiled and edited by H. Dierickx and A. Hopkinson (2nd rev. ed. Paris: General Information Programme and UNISIST, UNESCO, 1981). The book ends with a brief discussion of the use of records in these formats in national and local systems. Though the work has a definite British slant, North American readers will find it includes much useful information. Extensive footnotes, a glossary, and illustrations add value.

KBC5. McPherson, Dorothy S. "MARC Compatibility: A TESLA Survey of Vendors." *Information Technology and Libraries* 4 (Sept. 1985): 241–46.

Results of a TESLA survey of forty-eight library automation vendors. Generally, vendors were asked if their systems could accept, store, and output MARC format bibliographic records. Though the answers demonstrated a relatively high degree of MARC compatibility, McPherson suggests asking potential vendors a detailed list of questions to ensure that libraries will be able to move from one system to another and share records with others.

KBC6. Renaud, Robert. "Resolving Conflicts in MARC Exchange: The Structure and Impact of Local Options." *Information Technology and Libraries* 3 (Sept. 1984): 255–61.

Renaud discusses four options for resolving conflicts when records created using a nationally accepted version of the MARC format are loaded into a system that has a conflicting internal format. He suggests further research on the extent to which national and internal MARC formats vary and the extent to which those variations impede the exchange of records.

KBD
UNIMARC

KBD1. Bossmeyer, Christine. "Linking Techniques in UNIMARC." In *UNIMARC in Theory and Practice: Papers from the UNIMARC Workshop, Sydney, Australia, August 1988*, edited by Sally H. McCallum and Winston D. Roberts, 19–30. London: International Federation of Library Associations and Institutions, 1989.

Bossmeyer describes record linkage, field linkage, and file linkage techniques in UNIMARC. Record linking in UNIMARC involves the use of embedded fields to describe vertical, horizontal, and chronological relationships. Field linkages are used between data in different

scripts, and file linkages are used between bibliographic and authority records.

KBD2. McCallum, Sally H. "Basic Structure of UNIMARC." In *UNIMARC in Theory and Practice: Papers from the UNIMARC Workshop, Sydney, Australia, August 1988*, edited by Sally H. McCallum and Winston D. Roberts, 5–18. London: International Federation of Library Associations and Institutions, 1989.

In this excellent tutorial, McCallum describes the principles used in the development of the UNIMARC format, the basic structure of UNIMARC records, and the definition of each block within the record.

KBD3. _____. "Using UNIMARC: Prospects and Problems." *International Cataloguing* 14 (Apr./June 1985): 16–17.

Description of the Library of Congress efforts to develop a conversion program from USMARC to UNIMARC that would allow it to provide records to subscribers in other countries in the UNIMARC format and to receive UNIMARC records for conversion to USMARC. She argues that resolution of problems encountered is necessary because use of UNIMARC provides the most efficient means of international record exchange.

KBD4. Truitt, Marc. "USMARC to UNIMARC/Authorities: A Qualitative Evaluation of USMARC Data Elements." *Library Resources & Technical Services* 36, no. 1 (Jan. 1992): 37–58.

See also annotation under EAD21. Following a basic comparison of data elements in the USMARC and UNIMARC authorities formats, Truitt presents examples of conversion of data from USMARC to UNIMARC. He argues that UNIMARC more effectively expresses linkages and relationships among headings and records in ways that can be machine recognized and processed, and that USMARC should be enhanced to provide the means to express these relationships.

KBE
USMARC

HISTORICAL DEVELOPMENT

KBE1. Attig, John C. "The Concept of a MARC Format." *Information Technology and Libraries* 2 (Mar. 1983): 7–17.

This pivotal paper, requested by MARBI, initiated discussion of format integration. Following a thorough discussion of the concept of a "format," Attig proposes that the MARC Formats for Bibliographic Data be consolidated in a single format; inconsistencies in definition of content across existing formats be resolved in the new format; and distinct formats be retained for functionally different types of records, e.g., bibliographic and authority records.

KBE2. Avram, Henriette D. "Machine-Readable Cataloging (MARC) Program." Vol. 16, *Encyclopedia of Library and*

Information Science, 380–413. New York: Marcel Dekker, 1975.

A succinct description of the early development of the MARC format, discussing the MARC pilot project, the beginning of the MARC distribution service, the RECON pilot project, the development of ANSI and International Organization for Standardization (ISO) standards for bibliographic information interchange, and the development of the ALA character set. Though the paper is mostly of historical interest, the trends Avram recognizes are still being played out.

KBE3. Gapen, D. Kaye. *Simplification of the MARC Format: Feasibility, Benefits, Disadvantages, Consequences.* Washington, D.C.: Association of Research Libraries, 1981.

Gapen's position paper was commissioned by the ARL Task Force on Bibliographic Control and written from the perspective of an administrator concerned with the costs and benefits of using the MARC format. Gapen concludes that the degree of specificity that characterizes the formats is needed for machine manipulation of data both in online retrieval systems and for batch products, and that the only kind of "simplification" needed is greater consistency across types of materials.

KBE4. McCallum, Sally H. "MARC Record-Linking Technique." *Information Technology and Libraries* 1 (Sept. 1982): 281–91.

McCallum describes the technique for linking related records adopted for the USMARC formats in 1982 following discussion of a variety of linking methods. Linking entry fields are used to identify the related title. This technique differs substantially from that used in other MARC formats, notably UKMARC, that use embedded record techniques.

KBE5. *MARC XX Project.* [oral history] 1988–1990.

These interviews with Henriette Avram, Larry Buckland, Paul Fasana, Kay Guile, Fred Kilgour, Barbara Markus, Lucia Rather, and William Welsh, underwritten by ALA and conducted on the twentieth anniversary of the MARC format, describe early work on the use of computers in library work and the development of the MARC format. Tapes and transcripts (329 leaves) are held at the Library of Congress; transcripts are held by the Columbia University Oral History Research Office.

KBE6. *The USMARC Formats: Background and Principles.* Washington, D.C.: Network Development and MARC Standards Office, Library of Congress, 1989.

This statement, adopted by MARBI in 1982 and revised in 1989, provides a basic description of the MARC formats. Fundamentally, USMARC records have three elements: (1) structure, which is based on ANSI standard Z39.2; (2) content designation, which identifies and characterizes the data elements in the record and is defined in the USMARC Format documents; and (3) content, which is based on standards outside the format such as cataloging codes. The document describes each of these elements in some detail and notes historical variations from the principles that underlie their construction.

DEVELOPMENT OF SPECIFIC FORMATS

Resources in this section describe the development and basic features of some of the more recent MARC formats. They provide the database manager with a general understanding of the features and uses of each format. Titles dealing with the specific application of a format are more useful to other technical services staff and, thus, are outside the scope of this chapter. *See* Chapter G (Serials Management) for additional resources on MARC holdings format.

KBE7. Gertz, Janet, and Leon J. Stout. "The MARC Archival and Manuscripts Control (AMC) Format: A New Direction in Cataloging." *Cataloging & Classification Quarterly* 9, no. 4 (1989): 5–25.

Gertz and Stout trace the development of the MARC AMC format, the character of archives and manuscripts, and the use of the AMC format for cataloging. The article serves as an excellent introduction both to archival practice and to the AMC format.

KBE8. Guenther, Rebecca S. "The Development and Implementation of the USMARC Format for Classification Data." *Information Technology and Libraries* 11 (June 1992): 120–31.

Describes the development of the USMARC format for classification data, its general features, and its possible uses for online classification and building online shelflists, maintenance of classification schedules, and provision of an alternative form of subject access in online databases. Database managers will need to be aware of implementation requirements if the format is to realize its potential usefulness.

KBE9. Hirshon, Arnold. "Considerations in the Creation of a Holdings Record Structure for an Online Catalog." *Library Resources & Technical Services* 28 (Jan./Mar. 1984): 25–40.

While Hirshon endorses the need for a MARC format for holdings, he points out further needs for the holdings formats used in local systems. In particular, he emphasizes the need for "transactional" data elements that describe the status of material in a maintenance format in addition to the "archival," or permanent, information carried in a communications format.

KBE10. Sapp, Linda H. "The USMARC Format for Holdings and Locations." *Drexel Library Quarterly* 21 (Winter 1985): 87–100.

Outlines the issues confronted in the early stages of development of the USMARC format for holdings, including the scope of data to be included in the format, its relationship to bibliographic data, use of the data within automated systems, and the complexity of the format. Some issues have been resolved; others are still being discussed.

KBE11. *USMARC Format for Holdings and Locations: Development, Implementation, and Use.* Edited by Barry

B. Baker. Technical Services Quarterly, Monograph Supplement, no. 2. New York: Haworth Press, 1988.

See also annotation under GG1. The papers in this book describe the development of the holdings format and early implementation efforts by local system developers and vendors. They serve as an excellent introduction both to the format and to some of the problems associated with implementation. Issues confronted include the need for more detailed guidelines and examples for recording holdings, the display of holdings and the relationship of the format to the standards for display, compression and expansion of data, and the use of the format as a basis for serials control systems. The solutions described vary, and, while some of the problems mentioned have since been resolved within the format itself, the process of further refinement continues.

KBE12. Weber, Lisa. "Record Formatting: MARC AMC." *Cataloging & Classification Quarterly* 11, nos. 3/4 (1990): 117–43.

Summarizes the major differences between MARC AMC and the MARC format as designed for other materials: it is not media-specific, it accommodates control over processes, and it emphasizes intrarecord links. Weber points out that with format integration, processing control will be available for all formats. Meanwhile, she believes that the format is significantly changing the practice of describing archival materials by encouraging standardization of what had been highly idiosyncratic work.

RECENT DEVELOPMENTS

The following resources can provide the reader with a basic understanding of the ongoing process of format integration, which was expected to be completed in 1994 and will affect processing of all bibliographic MARC records, and an understanding of proposals to build a national pattern database, so that serials publication pattern data could be shared in much the same way that bibliographic data is currently shared. At the 1992 ALA Midwinter Meeting, Faxon announced plans to create such a database, which should accelerate implementation of the holdings format.

KBE13. Bales, Kathleen. "Format Integration: Coordinating the Implementation." *Information Technology and Libraries* 9 (June 1990): 167–73.

Bales stresses the need for a coordinated implementation of format integration among the bibliographic utilities and LC because so many records are exchanged between systems. Items for consideration are how and when to remap data and file structure and indexing implications.

KBE14. Clack, Mary Elizabeth, and others. "The Balance Point: The National Shared Pattern Database." *Serials Review* 17, no. 3 (Fall 1991): 67–76.

See also annotation under GG4. Contributors to this column discuss various aspects of a shared pattern database, including the role of CONSER in its creation, its economics, conceptual and administrative issues, and the value of extending such a database to include shared holdings.

KBE15. Davis, Stephen P. "Format Integration: Handling Serials and Mixed Media." *Information Technology and Libraries* 9 (June 1990): 162–67.

Presents two aspects of format integration in detail: the use of a repeatable, self-defining 006 field to describe serially issued nontextual items and mixed media items and the extension of the use of the 007 field to all possible cases.

KBE16. Evans, Katherine G. "MARC Format Integration and Seriality: Implications for Serials Cataloging." *The Serials Librarian* 18, nos. 1/2 (1990): 37–45.

Evans describes the effect of format integration on serials cataloging, pointing out both the general notion of seriality for items in all formats and the specific changes in fields in serials records. She notes that specifics of using linking entry fields in records for nonserial titles and using fields previously defined for formats other than serials in serials records have not yet been worked out.

KBE17. Gibbs, George E. "Applying Format Integration: An Operational Test." *Information Technology and Libraries* 9 (June 1990): 173–78.

Gibbs reports the results of an informal test of the application of the integrated MARC format at UCLA. He concludes that the vast majority of cataloging will not be affected except superficially. He also categorizes the types of changes that are possible and suggests that standards-making bodies issue guidelines on the use of the integrated format.

KBE18. McCallum, Sally H. "Format Integration: Handling the Additions and Subtractions." *Information Technology and Libraries* 9 (June 1990): 155–61.

McCallum details the data elements that were extended, made obsolete, deleted, and added to the US-MARC format and the principles upon which decisions were made during the format integration process. One important goal is to allow all types of materials to be controlled serially and archivally.

KBE19. Postlethwaite, Bonnie S. "Publication Patterns, the USMARC Holdings Format, and the Opportunity for Sharing." *Information Technology and Libraries* 9 (Mar. 1990): 80–88.

See also annotation under GG11. To avoid redundant data creation by many institutions, Postlethwaite suggests the creation of a national publication pattern database that includes timely, accurate data distributed at frequent intervals. Possible sponsors include CONSER, SISAC, the bibliographic utilities, subscription agents, and publishers. Postlethwaite recommends the adoption of the CONSER model.

FUTURE DEVELOPMENTS

KBE20. Aliprand, Joan M. "Nonroman Scripts in the Bibliographic Environment." *Information Technology and Libraries* 11 (June 1992): 105–19.

Discusses the ways in which romanization distorts information, the current accommodation of non-Roman scripts in USMARC, and the development of a universal character set through the efforts of the Unicode Consortium and the group working on the development of ISO 10646. Though ensuring correct import and export of existing character sets is often a difficult enough aspect of the database manager's work, thinking about future capabilities is also necessary.

KBE21. Brownrigg, Edwin, and Brett Butler. "An Electronic Library Communications Format: A Definition and Development Proposal for MARC III." *Library Hi Tech 8,* no. 3 (1990): 21–26.

Brownrigg and Butler outline a proposal to develop an extended version of MARC format that would include standards for "access formats" for abstracting and indexing data and "document formats" for storage, transmission, and display of machine-readable text or images. The format would be built upon a variety of existing standards for descriptive and access information, communication protocols, and document representation.

KBE22. Hinnebusch, Mark. "METAMARC: An Extension of MARC Format." *Information Technology and Libraries* 8 (Mar. 1989): 20–33.

Hinnebusch proposes a multilevel MARC record structure in which a single METAMARC record could contain single or multiple MARC or non-MARC records in horizontal, vertical, or chronological relationship. The examples he gives of useful applications of the new format include records for titles in a monographic series, records for articles in a periodical issue, and records for a serial that has undergone title changes.

KBE23. Leazer, Gregory H. "An Examination of Data Elements for Bibliographic Description: Toward a Conceptual Schema for the USMARC Formats." *Library Resources & Technical Services* 36 (Apr. 1992): 189–208.

Leazer uses the theory of the conceptual schema, a tool developed for database management in the computing world, to analyze the USMARC formats. The conceptual schema defines the types of data and data elements to be included in the database, the function of each data element, and the rules of form that govern each data element. Leazer concludes that the USMARC formats do not adhere to a rigorous conceptual plan. He fails, however, to develop a convincing argument that theoretical purity enhances practical usefulness.

KC
Conversion

Some database managers were retrospective conversion managers first; others became retrospective conversion managers because they were already responsible for the database. Though machine-readable records for current cataloging sometimes comprise the initial database, most libraries undertake some retrospective conversion of manual records. Realization that catalog users prefer to use a single catalog led many small to medium libraries to convert all of their records some time ago. That trend has accelerated to the point where many very large libraries have completed or are engaged in full retrospective conversion.

Some of the issues that were debated at length in the early years of conversion projects have been resolved. It has become obvious that complete cataloging records in MARC format are needed to take full advantage of the capabilities of automated systems, allow libraries to convert to second and third generation systems, and allow them to share their records with other libraries. Recataloging rather than conversion has proved impractical except in very limited cases, but significant automated upgrading of records, particularly provision of *AACR2* (CBA4) and *AACR2R* (CBA1) forms of headings, has become commonplace.

On the other hand, some early hopes have yet to be realized. Most disappointing, perhaps, is the fact that a single national database of converted records does not exist, either physically or virtually. The ARL plan for coordinated national retrospective conversion has borne little fruit. Thus, planners must still consider multiple record sources and techniques for conversion.

Retrospective conversion, or recon, however, is the sole topic covered in this chapter for which there is plenty of "how-to" information, ranging from books that cover the process generally to articles covering many specific aspects. Unfortunately, much of this information dates from the mid-eighties, when interest in recon was high. Thus, information on vendor capabilities in particular is rather dated. Important topics still not fully covered in the literature include segmenting large projects for maximum efficiency; developing productive vendor relationships after the contract is signed; and systematic cleanup and enhancement of records following retrospective conversion, either through automated or manual techniques.

As recon projects have been completed, database managers have turned their attention to conversion of existing files of machine-readable records. Typical tasks include creating a single database of records from multiple sources, either for a single institution or multiple institutions; conversion of records from one local system to another; and conversion of records not previously in MARC format (e.g., holdings records) to MARC format. Surprisingly little has been written on this important topic, though the articles included in this chapter do provide some useful information. In particular, very little has been written about working with vendors, especially multiple vendors, to accomplish these tasks.

STANDARDS

KC1. "Proposed Guidelines for a Program for Coordinated Retrospective Conversion of Bibliographic Records of Monographs in United States and Canadian Libraries." Washington, D.C.: Association of Research Libraries, 1985. Also printed in *LC Information Bulletin*, (March 25, 1985).

The proposed guidelines define record fullness, procedures for recording name and subject headings, and encoding requirements for records to be converted under the aegis of ARL's coordinated retrospective conversion plan. Though the plan was never truly implemented, the guidelines may provide recon project planners with a useful basis for defining these requirements.

RETROSPECTIVE CONVERSION: PLANNING

The articles by Beaumont and Cox (KC3) and by Carter and Bruntjen (KC5) attempt to provide overall planning guidance for retrospective conversion projects. Other works in this section cover specific aspects of planning, including management issues, productivity, and costs. Since so many articles deal with choice of recon alternatives, these are in separate sections.

KC2. Adler, Anne G., and Elizabeth A. Baber. *Retrospective Conversion: From Cards to Computer.* Ann Arbor, Mich.: Pierian Press, 1984.

This collection of papers describing early, relatively large-scale conversion projects provides very useful examples of the detailed specifications for treatment of source documents (typically shelflist cards) that must be prepared either for outside vendors or in-house project staff. Otherwise, it is outdated because of changes in technology.

KC3. Beaumont, Jane, and Joseph P. Cox. *Retrospective Conversion: A Practical Guide for Libraries.* Westport, Conn.: Meckler, 1989.

Beaumont and Cox provide an excellent outline of most aspects of the retrospective conversion process, emphasizing planning and decision making based on library needs and careful option analysis. It will be up to the library to expand the outline to include more details. The long section on MARC records, aimed at small to medium libraries, is far less useful. An appendix lists retrospective conversion vendors and their services.

KC4. Broadway, Rita, and Jane Qualls. "Retrospective Conversion of Periodicals: A Shoestring Experience." *The Serials Librarian* 15, nos. 1/2 (1988): 99–119.

This article provides a useful warning to planners through its frank description of the sorts of problems that plague many recon projects. These include lack of sufficient space and equipment, deficiencies in training, high staff turnover, lack of communication between the departments involved in the project, lack of objectives and deadlines, and a general sense that conversion work is not particularly important.

KC5. Carter, Ruth C., and Scott Bruntjen. *Data Conversion.* White Plains, N.Y.: Knowledge Industry Publications, 1983.

A basic outline for planning conversion projects, discussing purposes, project analysis and design, and comparison of conversion alternatives. Though the work serves to establish a basic mindset, it lacks significant details at all points. References at the ends of chapters, as well as lists of libraries doing conversion projects, consultants on data conversion, and conversion vendors, are outdated.

KC6. Epstein, Susan Baerg. "Retrospective Conversion Revisited, Parts 1, 2, and 3." *Library Journal* 115 (15 May 1990): 56–58; (1 June 1990): 94–96; (1 July 1990): 66–69.

Epstein covers basic planning tasks, record sources, and database cleanup, providing many useful reminders about the need for care in the construction of a database.

KC7. Johnson, Carolyn A. "Retrospective Conversion of Three Library Collections." *Information Technology and Libraries* 1 (June 1982): 133–39.

Johnson argues that use of the number of records updated per hour using a bibliographic utility as the basic measure of productivity is misleading since much of the conversion process is done offline. She suggests that if statistics are to be compared, the quality of existing cataloging, the quality of the source database, the hit rate in the source database, special requirements for special collections, and staff skills must be comparable.

KC8. Lambrecht, Jay H. "Reviving a Conversion Project: Strategies to Complete the Task." *College & Research Libraries* 51 (Jan. 1990): 27–32.

Lambrecht discusses the process of adjusting qualitative standards and production norms for recon projects with low or declining productivity.

KC9. Peters, Stephen H., and Douglas J. Butler. "A Cost Model for Retrospective Conversion Alternatives." *Library Resources & Technical Services* 28 (Apr./June 1984): 149–62.

A model for comparing costs per record converted using various retrospective conversion alternatives. For each step in the process, labor, equipment/supply, and vendor/bibliographic utility costs are determined. While use of the model will rationalize cost comparisons to some extent, significant costs such as those for supervision and training must also be considered in a full cost analysis.

KC10. Purnell, Kathleen M. "Productivity in a Large-Scale Retrospective Conversion Project." *Proceedings of the ASIS Annual Meeting* 20 (1983): 177–79.

Purnell describes management issues and problems encountered in a REMARC conversion project at Johns Hopkins. Difficulties encountered included high staff turnover, balancing online and offline work, and off-hours supervision.

KC11. Ra, Marsha. "The Need for Costing in a Cooperative Retrospective Conversion Project." *Technical Services Quarterly* 4, no. 4: (Summer 1987): 39–48.

Ra suggests controlling retrospective conversion costs by defining project goals, setting standards, and developing a work plan. Thus, there will be less temptation to do more than originally intended, thereby raising costs. Though she uses a cooperative project as the basis of her remarks, her comments are equally applicable to a single institution.

KC12. "Retrospective Conversion: Issues and Perspectives." Edited by Jon Drabenstott. *Library Hi Tech* 4, no. 2 (1986): 105–20.

In this forum, the contributors collectively note the need for automation planners to understand the technical aspects of retrospective conversion and appropriate standards to employ in order to effectively integrate recon into a total automation plan and devote sufficient resources to the process.

KC13. Valentine, Phyllis A., and David R. McDonald. "Retrospective Conversion: A Question of Time, Standards, and Purpose." *Information Technology and Libraries* 5 (June 1986): 112–20.

Valentine and McDonald note the basic factors affecting conversion costs: definition—i.e., reproduction versus upgrading of an existing record, standards of acceptance for a matching record, method of conversion, hit rate in a source database, and standards for conversion of nonhits. The bulk of their article is a detailed study of the cost of converting records in house using RLIN.

RETROSPECTIVE CONVERSION: GENERAL ALTERNATIVES

Authors of articles in this group describe general alternatives for conducting recon projects and the ba-

ses for choosing among alternatives. These should provide the reader with a general framework for evaluation of specific alternatives.

KC14. Boss, Richard W., and Hal Espo. "Standards, Database Design, and Retrospective Conversion." *Library Journal* 112 (1 Oct. 1987): 54–57.

Boss and Espo describe various means of retrospective conversion, including offline matching of search keys against vendor files, online matching against optical disks or bibliographic utilities, and direct keying of records. They emphasize the need for conversion of full cataloging records and adherence to standards for content and format.

KC15. Epstein, Susan Baerg. "Converting Bibliographic Records for Automation: Some Options." *Library Journal* 108 (1 Mar. 1983): 474–76.

Outlines three basic conversion methods: (1) online matching against a full database, (2) creation of search keys to be matched against a full database, and (3) direct keying of full records. Several recon services are described briefly.

KC16. Kallenbach, Susan F. "Retrospective Conversion." In *Crossroads: Proceedings of the First National LITA Conference*, edited by Michael Gorman, 64–70. Chicago: American Library Association, 1984.

Reviews the basic factors influencing decisions about choices of recon methods: project parameters; the nature of source data; time, staff, and equipment needs; standards for converted records; and the nature of a source database. Briefly describes the advantages and disadvantages of in-house and vendor conversion.

KC17. Lisowski, Andrew, and Judith Sessions. "Selecting a Retrospective Conversion Vendor." *Library Hi Tech* 1, no. 4 (Spring 1984): 65–68.

Lisowski and Sessions focus on choosing a conversion vendor, as opposed to choosing a conversion method. Factors to be considered are editing capabilities, error rate, ability to meet a schedule, compatibility of records with a local system, and extent of library staff involvement needed. The authors emphasize the need to review converted records on an ongoing basis to ensure adherence to the contract.

KC18. Racine, Drew. "Retrospective Conversion: A Challenge (Still) Facing Academic Libraries." *Show-Me Libraries* 36 (Oct./Nov. 1984): 39–43.

Racine suggests choosing between two basic alternatives for recon, an in-house project versus a project done under contract by a vendor based on resource inventory and on desire for control rating. The greater the resources (space, staff, time, money) and the greater the desire for control, the higher the indication that an in-house project is preferable.

RETROSPECTIVE CONVERSION:
SPECIFIC ALTERNATIVES

This group of resources describes use of specific methods of retrospective conversion. Methods include use of microcomputers either to record search keys to be matched against a full database or to access optical disk files and select and edit records, and conversion of records by vendors based on either the vendor database or the library's own records. Though the information is usually institution or project specific, the details provided should enable the reader to evaluate the usefulness of the method in another context. Some authors also mention method-specific problems.

KC19. Banach, Patricia, and Cynthia Spell. "Serials Conversion at the University of Massachusetts at Amherst." *Information Technology and Libraries* 7 (June 1988): 124–30.

Description of a conversion project done by OCLC that was based on brief paper records generated from a non-MARC serials database. The contract with OCLC specified matching criteria, choice of record when OCLC had multiple matches, splitting of latest-entry records into successive-entry records, and addition of any access points not already on the OCLC record.

KC20. Beaumont, Jane. "Retrospective Conversion on a Micro: Options for Libraries." *Library Software Review* 5 (July/Aug. 1986): 213–18.

Beaumont outlines hardware needed, databases available, types of access, software features, output products, and costs for microcomputer-based retrospective conversion. The two basic procedures in use of micros are to create search keys to be matched against vendor databases and to search optical disk databases to identify, edit, and download records.

KC21. Bocher, Robert. "MITINET/retro in Wisconsin Libraries." *Information Technology and Libraries* 3 (Sept. 1984): 267–74.

Bocher describes use of MITINET/retro, one of several micro-based systems for creating search keys to match against a full database. Users first search one of two COM catalogs (the Wisconsin statewide database or English language LC titles) and note matching record numbers on shelflist cards and then key these numbers plus local data. The use of check digits on record numbers does prevent keying errors, and a menu approach does speed entry of local data. However, the two-step process is inherently inefficient.

KC22. Callahan, Patrick F. "Retrospective Conversion of Serials Using OCLC." In *Projects and Procedures for Serials Administration*, compiled and edited by Diane Stine, 115–44. Ann Arbor, Mich.: Pierian Press, 1985.

Report of an in-house conversion using the OCLC database at the Center for Research Libraries. In this highly organized project, flow charts, decision charts, and detailed written procedures were used to train clerical staff to do online work, professional catalogers to edit a printout of each title, and supervisors to review the work of both. The high level of control it is possible to assert under these conditions should mean that converted records are of high quality. However, costs will obviously be very high.

KC23. Desmarais, Norman. "BiblioFile for Retrospective Conversion." *Small Computers in Libraries* 5 (Dec. 1985): 24–28.

Desmarais describes a test of Library Corporation's BiblioFile for retrospective conversion at Providence College. Users search a CD-ROM file of records, edit retrieved records, and either save them to disk or pass them to a local system if an interface is available. The advantages of this type of system are a known, fixed cost for unlimited access and lower cost per record as more records are used.

KC24. Douglas, Nancy E. "REMARC Retrospective Conversion: What, Why, and How." *Technical Services Quarterly* 2, nos. 3-4 (Spring/Summer 1985): 11–16.

See annotation for KC25.

KC25. Drake, Virginia, and Mary Paige Smith. "Retrospective Conversion with REMARC at Johns Hopkins University." *Information Technology and Libraries* 3 (Sept. 1984): 282–86.

The articles by Douglas (KC24) and by Drake and Smith report typical conversion projects using Carrolton Press's REMARC database at the University of California Riverside and Johns Hopkins. Search keys consisting of either an LC control number plus initial letters of the first two words of the title or title/place/date plus local data are keyed to floppy disk, then matched against a full database. Since REMARC records are missing some data elements, many libraries choose to append selected bibliographic fields to the records. The REMARC database is now available on optical disk, which eliminates problems with multiple matches and reduces the number of probable mismatches.

KC26. Ferrell, Mary Sue, and Carol A. Parkhurst. "Using LaserQuest for Retrospective Conversion of MARC Records." *Optical Information Systems* 7 (Nov./Dec. 1987): 396–400.

Description of the use of GRC's LaserQuest to convert serials records at the University of Nevada and Nevada State. LaserQuest software allows the user to search a CD-ROM database, edit retrieved records, key original records, and save records to diskette. This type of product allows the verification and editing possible on a bibliographic utility without the associated telecommunications costs. However, the database is smaller, and the quality of non-LC records is uncertain.

KC27. Hanson, Heidi, and Gregory Pronevitz. "Planning for Retrospective Conversion: A Simulation of the

OCLC TAPECON Service." *Information Technology and Libraries* 8 (Sept. 1989): 284–94.

Hanson and Pronevitz conducted a very thorough simulation of conversion using OCLC's TAPECON service, in which Ohio State's brief circulation records would be matched against the OCLC database and replaced with full records. Two major concerns were the extent of incorrect matches and the quality of the matched records. Thorough analysis of available brief records is needed to gauge the probable extent of problems.

KC28. Hubbard, William J., and Jeanette Remer. "Retrospective Conversion Blitzkrieg—Is Microcon the Answer?" *Technical Services Quarterly* 8, no. 2 (1990): 17–23.

Hubbard and Remer describe the use of OCLC's Microcon service at Jacksonville State University. Standard OCLC search keys and local data are keyed to floppy disk, then matched against the OCLC database. Single hits are returned, printouts of multiple hits must be reviewed by the library and the correct record number resubmitted. One advantage of this process is that the user's holding library symbol is set on OCLC whenever a matched record is returned.

KC29. Lisowski, Andrew. "Vendor-Based Retrospective Conversion at George Washington University." *Library Hi Tech* 1, no. 3 (Winter 1983): 23–26.

Reports a project in which records were keyed directly from shelflist cards by a vendor. The major anticipated disadvantage of this approach was that no upgrading of records, e.g., use of *AACR2* (CBA4) access points or addition of access points, was possible. Unanticipated problems included a higher-than-expected error rate and difficulties loading records in a local system.

RETROSPECTIVE CONVERSION: SPECIAL CASES

Authors in this section deal with conversion of specific types of records, including those for government documents, holdings, music, and serials. Their practical advice should aid readers dealing with the same kinds of records.

KC30. Bratcher, Perry. "Music OCLC Recon: The Practical Approach." *Cataloging & Classification Quarterly* 8, no. 2 (1987/88): 41–48.

Bratcher describes a small-scores conversion project done at the University of Northern Kentucky and gives some practical advice on use of OCLC for this purpose.

KC31. Christ, Ruth, and Selina Lin. "Serials Retrospective Conversion: Project Design and In-House Implementation." *Cataloging & Classification Quarterly* 14, nos. 3/4 (1992): 51–73.

In addition to providing an excellent checklist of questions concerning project design for serials conversion, Christ and Lin list the advantages and disadvantages of

deriving serial records from national databases versus keying them directly into a local system.

KC32. Epstein, Susan Baerg. "Converting Records for Automation at the Copy Level." *Library Journal* 108 (1 Apr. 1983): 642–43.

Epstein describes the two typical methods for creating item records and labeling items, use of random labels, and generation of item-specific labels. She also mentions one less commonly used technique: "borrowing" another library's database of both bibliographic and item information and editing it to match one's own collection.

KC33. Heitshu, Sara C., and Joan M. Quinn. "Serials Conversion at the University of Michigan." *Drexel Library Quarterly* 21 (Winter 1985): 62–76.

Heitshu and Quinn give a detailed description of the planning and execution of a large-scale (81,000-title) RLIN serials conversion project at the University of Michigan.

KC34. Koth, Michelle, and Laura Gayle Green. "Workflow Considerations in Retrospective Conversion Projects for Scores." *Cataloging & Classification Quarterly* 14, nos. 3/4 (1992): 75–102.

Presents work flow for seven music-scores–conversion projects at various types of institutions. Their analysis of the advantages and disadvantages of each approach should be very helpful to those planning scores conversions.

KC35. Stachacz, John C. "Small College Experiences in Retrospective Conversion of Periodicals." *Information Technology and Libraries* 8 (Dec. 1989): 422–30.

Report of the conversion of serials titles at Dickinson College. Useful features of the project were a complete inventory of serials conducted before the project began so that holdings information could be included in records and customization of "indexed in" information in converted records to cover index titles held by the college. Overall procedures for the project would probably be workable only for small-scale projects.

KC36. Tucker, Ruth W. "Music Retrospective Conversion at the University of California at Berkeley." *Technical Services Quarterly* 7, no. 2 (1989): 13–28.

Tucker describes University of California, Berkeley, music-scores–conversion projects done (following the guidelines adopted by the Associated Music Libraries Group) on RLIN by local staff and under contract by OCLC staff. She notes that attempting to create a definitive national record is costly because of the oddities of music publishing patterns, the need for extensive authority work, the relative lack of machine-readable bibliographic and authority records for music, difficulties in identifying matching records, and complex holdings information.

KC37. Tull, Laura. "Retrospective Conversion of Government Documents: The MARCIVE GPO Tape Clean-up Project." *Technicalities* 9 (Aug. 1989): 4–7.

Reports a cooperative project between MARCIVE, Inc., and Louisiana State, Rice, and Texas A & M libraries to correct and enhance the database of GPO (Government Printing Office) records so that it could be used by other libraries for retrospective conversion. Major tasks included elimination of duplicate records; creation of complete serial and monographic series records; considerable authority work, particularly on subject headings and corporate names; correct tagging of various document numbers; and addition of missing OCLC numbers.

FILE CONVERSION

Though the task of converting existing machine-readable records falls to the database manager just as often as that of converting paper records to machine-readable format, and frequently requires more intellectual effort, far less has been written about the topic. Resources following provide a bare outline of the scope and types of problems and required tasks. They may provide some general background for the reader faced with similar conversion projects.

KC38. Babel, Deborah B. "Archival Tape Processing: Considerations for a Network." *Technical Services Quarterly* 4, no. 1 (Fall 1986): 11–18.

Analyzes the anticipated process for creating online catalogs for the three institutions that form the Western North Carolina Library Network. Steps would include de-duping transaction files on the basis of OCLC number, consolidation of holdings information on a single record, and an *AACR2* (CBA4) upgrade as done by OCLC on its database.

KC39. Bills, Linda G., and Linda W. Helgerson. "CD-ROM Public Access Catalogs: Database Creation and Maintenance." *Library Hi Tech* 6, no. 1 (1988): 67–86.

Bills and Helgerson summarize the results of a survey of tape processing services offered by eight major vendors. Sources of records that can be processed, de-duping and record merging, handling of location and holdings information, ongoing maintenance of the resulting database, authority control and other types of corrections, extraction of database subsets, reports and statistics provided, and transportability to other systems are covered. The information from the surveys provides an excellent summary of general vendor capabilities; current capabilities of any specific vendor should be ascertained.

KC40. Caplan, Priscilla. "Retrospective Duplicate Resolution for the Harvard Distributable Union Catalog." *Information Technology and Libraries* 1 (June 1982): 142–43.

Suggests criteria for selecting a master record among transactions records for multiple libraries and consolidation of data for all locations on that record. A newly defined local data field was used to record location and holdings information. Most records were consolidated by machine, but a significant percentage required human review.

KC41. Chickering, Susan, Teresa Strozik, and Gail Gulbenkian. "A Conversion of Serials Records: OCLC LDR to VTLS USMARC Format." *Information Technology and Libraries* 9 (Sept. 1990): 263–71.

The authors describe mapping of OCLC LDR data to the VTLS USMARC holdings format at Hamilton College. Despite minor problems, mapping to paired 853/863 data fields proved possible.

KC42. Copeland, Nora S. "Testing Data Migration." In *Information Technology, IT's for Everyone: Proceedings of the LITA Third National Conference*, edited by Thomas W. Leonhardt, 166–68. Chicago: American Library Association, 1992.

Drawing on general software design literature, Copeland describes the purposes and qualities of good specifications for data conversion as well as the process of testing conversion programs. An understanding of these basic ideas is critical for anyone attempting to convert files of records.

KC43. Coyle, Karen. "Record Matching: A Discussion." *Information Technology and Libraries* 4 (Mar. 1985): 57–59.

Coyle summarizes an ALA conference discussion of similarities and differences among record-matching algorithms used by OCLC, RLIN, WLN, and the University of California Division of Library Automation. She concludes that the algorithms are strikingly similar considering that they were independently developed and that the differences often depend on whether the system retains or discards matching records.

KC44. Coyle, Karen, and Linda Gallaher-Brown. "Record Matching: An Expert Algorithm." *Proceedings of the ASIS Annual Meeting* 22 (1985): 77–80.

The authors describe the record-matching algorithm developed for California's MELVYL system in order to provide the user with a single record for each unique item. The process employed has two stages: first a character-by-character match on a few data elements, followed by a more detailed match on additional data elements. All data elements are compared in normalized form, and varying weights are given for perfect, embedded, and keyword matches.

KC45. Dalehite, Michele I. "MARC Format on Tape: A Tutorial." In *From Tape to Product: Some Practical Considerations on the Use of OCLC-MARC Tapes*, edited by Barry B. Baker and Lynne D. Lysiak, 15–38. Ann Arbor, Mich.: Pierian Press, 1985.

While the general information on MARC format in Dalehite's presentation is available elsewhere, she provides a very clear explanation of OCLC-specific MARC data and its uses in processing records for database creation. Her list of problems common to many OCLC records should be helpful to anyone who must process a file of OCLC transactions.

KC46. Hartmann, Anne-Marie. "Converting from the OCLC Serials Control Subsystem to MicroLinx." *Serials Review* 14, no. 4 (1988): 7–19.

Hartmann describes conversion from the OCLC SCS to Faxon's MicroLinx system at Queens College. Problems encountered included fields not included on the OCLC tape, note fields that exceeded length limitation in MicroLinx, nonstandard use of the SCS call number field, and pattern and holdings information for serials with complicated patterns.

KC47. Lowrey, James R., and Paul V. Hardiman. "Using a Text-Processing Language for Serial Record Conversion." *Information Technology and Libraries* 4 (Dec. 1985): 356–58.

Lowrey and Hardiman describe the use of a program written in SPITBOL, a text-processing language, to convert serial records from a local batch system to PERLINE (Blackwell's serials check-in system).

KC48. McPherson, Dorothy S., Karen E. Coyle, and Teresa L. Montgomery. "Building a Merged Bibliographic Database: The University of California Experience." *Information Technology and Libraries* 1 (Dec. 1982): 371–80.

The authors describe the tasks involved in creating the MELVYL database. These include translating input from a variety of sources into a standard format, replacing existing records with new versions based on a maintenance key and a version identifier, and merging records for the same bibliographic entity. A composite record is created in which each unique version of a field is stored with appropriate "ownership" bits set.

KC49. McQueen, Judy. "Record Matching: Computers Cannot See That Which Is Obvious to 'Any Idiot' . . . and Vice Versa." *Information Today* 9 (Dec. 1992): 41–44.

Reports the use of LC and OCLC control numbers in record matching, noting that these unique standard numbers are very useful match criteria, provided their integrity has not been violated by sloppy cataloging. She also provides some useful reminders about the need to adequately specify input data and review output data during matching.

KC50. Pope, Nolan. "Processing OCLC Archive Tapes for the FOCUS System: University of Florida." In *From Tape to Product: Some Practical Considerations on the Use of OCLC-MARC Tapes*, edited by Barry B. Baker and Lynne D. Lysiak, 87–97. Ann Arbor, Mich.: Pierian Press, 1985.

Rather than focusing on the mechanics of processing records for database creation, Pope emphasizes the kinds of general and institution-specific data anomalies that must be dealt with programmatically because of changes in library practice and automated systems over time, inconsistencies in data entry, and errors. Though he points out the need for documentation of local practices, he admits relying on cataloger memory. Others may find that sampling records provides a more accurate view of actual practice.

KC51. Reynolds, Dennis. "Entry of Local Data on OCLC: The Options and Their Impact on Processing of Archival Tapes." *Information Technology and Libraries* 1 (Mar. 1982): 5–14.

Using data from a survey conducted by the Bibliographic Center for Research, Reynolds cites several examples of practices that cause problems when multi-institution products are created from OCLC tapes: use of combinations of means of indicating location for the same collection, use of the 590 field for multiple types of data, failure to record multiple copies or withdraw copies on OCLC, and failure to code fixed-field data elements. He suggests developing and documenting consistent practices with tape processing needs in mind.

KC52. Sawyer, Jeanne C. "An Archive Tape Processing System for the Triangle Research Libraries Network." *Library Resources & Technical Services* 26 (Oct./Dec. 1982): 362–69.

The designers of the Triangle Research Libraries Network system wanted to accommodate two features that are not typical of OCLC tapeloaded catalogs: retention, in some instances, of multiple records with the same OCLC control number and replacement of *either* bibliographic or holdings data. Though the solutions devised are relatively creative within this specific context, online record entry and editing capabilities would obviously allow far greater flexibility.

KC53. Winter, Frank. "Conversion of a Non-MARC Database to MARC." *Information Technology and Libraries* 8 (Dec. 1989): 442–51.

Winter describes the conversion of records in a local format developed by the University of Saskatchewan to MARC format records that could be loaded in a Geac system. Techniques used in the conversion process were format recognition using ISBD punctuation (to identify subfield boundaries and assign subfield codes) and searching text strings. Though the conversion program was sophisticated, the resulting database was not completely standard.

KD
Quality Control and Database Maintenance

Quality control is often thought of as "getting it right the first time" and maintenance as "getting it right the second time." These definitions overlook maintenance as an ongoing activity that not only corrects but enhances records. Database managers are more than "database janitors," continually cleaning things up; they are also "database architects," continually constructing.

These tasks are apparently considered rather mundane, and the literature on the topic is not extensive. There are, however, some articles on specific techniques for maintaining quality and doing maintenance. Some focus on machine validation and error reporting, others on training techniques and cooperative efforts. Maintenance often is thought of as responding to reports of individual errors. Rarely is consideration given to the method of systematic maintenance, which seeks types and patterns of errors and designs and effectively uses machine-generated exception reports.

An even more important element often missing from the literature is a strong sense of the purpose of quality control and maintenance work. Though they may bemoan an emphasis on strict mechanical accuracy, writers have little to offer in its place. Happy exceptions are Horny (KD3), who focuses on the importance of considering user needs in defining quality; Graham (KD2), who emphasizes the distinction between the essential and the useful in cataloging records; and Mandel (KD4), who develops a model for quantifying costs and benefits of various methods for achieving quality. Their ideas deserve further development.

PHILOSOPHY AND MANAGEMENT ISSUES

Those who are developing maintenance procedures may seek insights into the purpose of their efforts and some of the management issues involved. These sources will help.

KD1. Davis, Betty Bartlett. "Managing the Online Bibliographic Database for an Integrated Library System." *Technical Services Quarterly* 5, no. 1 (1987): 49–56.

Davis points out the need for organizational change and reconsideration of work flow with the implementation of an integrated system allowing all technical services staff to share the same bibliographic record. She also notes the fact that traditional organizational demarcations tend to blur under these circumstances.

KD2. Graham, Peter S. "Quality in Cataloging: Making Distinctions." *The Journal of Academic Librarianship* 16 (Sept. 1990): 213–18.

Graham argues forcefully that concern for quality should not lead to diminished cataloging productivity, which will make fewer materials available to patrons. Philosophically, he emphasizes consideration of what is essential and what is merely useful in the cataloging record. Practically, he suggests more careful consideration of costs.

KD3. Horny, Karen L. "Quality Work, Quality Control in Technical Services." *The Journal of Academic Librarianship* 11 (Sept. 1985): 206–10.

See also annotation under AH18. Horny emphasizes the key role that a definition of user needs plays within any

definition of quality and the important contribution managerial skills make to quality control. She believes the effective manager will strike a dynamic balance between quality and productivity.

KD4. Mandel, Carol A. "Trade-offs: Quantifying Quality in Library Technical Services." *The Journal of Academic Librarianship* 14 (Sept. 1988): 214–20.

See also annotation under AHB9. Mandel stresses the need for quantitative analysis of various alternatives for achieving higher quality and productivity in technical services operations. Further development of the model she presents could provide more accurate assessments of both costs and benefits to users and to other libraries.

SPECIFIC TECHNIQUES

The following sources focus on specific techniques for improving record quality or doing record maintenance, including procedural changes, automated error detection, and shared maintenance. Together with those in the next section, they provide practical ideas for possible implementation.

KD5. Ballard, Terry, and Arthur Lifshin. "Prediction of OPAC Spelling Errors through a Keyword Inventory." *Information Technology and Libraries* 11 (June 1992): 139–45.

Ballard and Lifshin describe the results of their analysis of spelling errors in a database of 310,000 records. They recommend the use of keyword indexes to systematically identify and correct spelling errors, as well as the use of spell checkers on files of new records.

KD6. Clark, Sharon E., and Winnie Chan. "Maintenance of an Online Catalogue." *Information Technology and Libraries* 4 (Dec. 1985): 324–38.

Description of some of the problems faced by the University of Illinois at Urbana-Champaign in maintaining dual online catalog and circulation systems. Machine assistance from the WLN software for the maintenance of headings in authority and bibliographic records and the use of locally developed microcomputer programs for maintenance of the circulation system do improve efficiency in what is an inherently inefficient setup.

KD7. Edgerton, Janet Gebbie, and Raymond G. Taylor. "Detection and Analysis of Editing Activity in an Online Bibliographic System." *Information Technology and Libraries* 10 (Mar. 1991): 55–57.

The authors (*see also* KD14) offer the results of a study of the use of the North Carolina State system intended to determine why some attempts to edit records in an online system fail and what can be done to reduce the number of failures. One useful finding was that procedural idiosyncracies often led to failure. More careful design of procedures should thus lead to the correction of more errors.

KD8. Hanscom, Martha J., Carol J. White, and Carol C. Davis. "The OCLC Enhance Program: Some Practical

Considerations.'' *Technical Services Quarterly* 4, no. 2 (Winter 1986): 21–28.

The authors describe the benefits of the University of Wyoming's participation in the OCLC Enhance program, especially the improved staff morale that resulted from the opportunity to engage in shared maintenance, thereby improving the quality of a national database.

KD9. Hays, Kathleen M. ''Changing Standards of Quality Control in an Automated System.'' *Technical Services Quarterly* 6, nos. 3–4 (1989): 49–55.

Hays notes that the assistance in error detection provided by an automated system at the Sioux City, Iowa, public library has led to a decreased emphasis on strict mechanical accuracy and greater economy of effort.

KD10. O'Neill, Edward T., and Diane Vizine-Goetz. ''The Impact of Spelling Errors on Databases and Indexes.'' In *National Online Meeting: Proceedings*, edited by Carol Nixon and Lauree Padgett, 313–20. Medford, N.J.: Learned Information, 1989.

Examines the types of spelling errors commonly found in databases and their impact on usability and performance. The feasibility of using spelling checkers and other correction techniques to reduce errors is investigated.

KD11. _____. ''Quality Control in Online Databases.'' *Annual Review of Information Science and Technology* 23 (1988): 125–56.

O'Neill and Vizine-Goetz provide an excellent discussion of the concept of quality control and describe work on manual approaches to authority control, self-checking data, automated data validation, authority control, duplicate detection, and automated checking of spelling. The bibliography is eclectic and extensive, though now somewhat dated.

KD12. Sawyer, Jeanne C., and Jinnie Y. Davis. ''Automated Error Detection in Library Systems.'' In *Crossroads, Proceedings of the First National LITA Conference*, edited by Michael Gorman, 213–17. Chicago: American Library Association, 1984.

Sawyer and Davis describe the kind of errors that can be detected by an automated system in the content designation and content of bibliographic, authority, and holdings records. Ideally, some errors will be corrected automatically rather than merely being reported. In determining which errors to report, system designers need to consider both how difficult the error is to detect and what impact it has on retrieval.

KD13. Striedieck, Suzanne. ''Online Catalog Maintenance: The OOPS Command in LIAS.'' *Cataloging & Classification Quarterly* 6, no. 1 (Fall 1985): 21–32.

Reports the use of the ''OOPS'' command in Penn State's LIAS system, which allows patrons and staff to send error messages to database maintenance staff using a simple online command. Ease of reporting means that more errors are identified and corrected, increasing confidence in the accuracy of the database.

KD14. Taylor, Raymond G., and Janet Gebbie Edgerton. ''Utilization of Commands in an Online Bibliographic Editing System.'' *Information Technology and Libraries* 9 (Dec. 1990): 337–40.

See annotation for KD7.

SPECIFIC CONTEXTS

Articles in this group also discuss particular means of doing maintenance or particular techniques for achieving higher quality of records. However, the suggestions are context specific and thus may be of particular interest to those who are working in similar contexts.

KD15. Bland, Robert N. ''Quality Control in a Shared Online Catalog Database: The Lambda Experience.'' *Technical Services Quarterly* 4, no. 2 (Winter 1986): 43–58.

Bland contends that the tension between the pragmatic view—that a high-quality catalog is one providing effective access to users—and the normative view—that high quality means a catalog in which records adhere to standards—makes quality control issues in a shared database difficult to resolve. In their implementation of guidelines for database maintenance, the users of SOLINET's Lambda system attempted to incorporate both viewpoints.

KD16. Calk, Jo. ''Quality Control in Developing an Interinstitutional Database.'' *Library Hi Tech* 4, no. 1 (1986): 85–90.

Calk describes the quality-control mechanisms used by WLN, including extensive machine review of new records, human review of selected member-input records by a central database-maintenance unit, and general database maintenance performed by both central maintenance and member-library staff.

KD17. DiCarlo, Michael A. ''Sequential Analysis as a Sampling Test for Accuracy of Retrospective Conversion.'' In *Conference on Integrated Online Library Systems: September 23 and 24, 1986, St. Louis, Missouri: Proceedings*, compiled and edited by David C. Genaway, 248–57. Canfield, Ohio: Genaway & Associates, 1987.

DiCarlo suggests the use of sequential analysis as a means of enforcing contractual quality-control standards for retrospective conversion projects.

KD18. Hart, Amy. ''Operation Cleanup: The Problem Resolution Phase of a Retrospective Conversion Project.'' *Library Resources & Technical Services* 32 (Oct. 1988): 378–86.

Emphasizes that guidelines developed for editing the problem records identified during retrospective conversion should be consistent with the guidelines used for all records. Also points to the need to document solutions so they will be standardized.

KD19. Juneja, Derry C. ''Quality Control in Data Conversion.'' *Library Resources & Technical Services* 31 (Apr./June 1987): 148–58.

Juneja emphasizes the importance of adherence to standards and guidelines in retrospective conversion projects—creating full MARC records, following standards for required data elements such as those adopted by ARL, and communicating local practices and requirements to vendors clearly and in detail.

KD20. Kruger, Kathleen Joyce. "MARC Tags and Retrospective Conversion: The Editing Process." *Information Technology and Libraries* 4 (Mar. 1985): 53–57.

Argues that the quality of recon records is highly dependent upon the application of consistent rules for editing records. In addition to providing some details concerning the editing rules adopted for a small conversion project at Colorado State University, Kruger derives some general principles for editing records.

KD21. Mifflin, Ingrid, and Jean Williams. "Online Catalog Maintenance: The Role of Networks, Computers, and Local Institutions." *Information Technology and Libraries* 10 (Dec. 1991): 263–74.

Mifflin and Williams discuss the concepts of shared and automated database maintenance in the context of the relationship between the Washington State University Library (WSU) and WLN. All WLN libraries share the benefits of maintenance done by other consortium participants. The concept of shared maintenance and automated distribution of corrections deserves further serious exploration in other contexts.

KD22. Saylor, Louise V. "Cooperative Cataloging Quality Control in the OCLC Pacific Network." *Information Technology and Libraries* 25 (Sept. 1986): 235–39.

Reports the efforts of PACNET to improve the quality of member records input in OCLC through the establishment of a peer council and workshops conducted by network staff.

KD23. Stankowski, Rebecca House. "Bibliographic Record Maintenance and Control in a Consortium Database." *Cataloging & Classification Quarterly* 12, no. 2 (1990): 47–62.

An account of the quality-control issues faced by a consortium of Indiana public and academic libraries using a Geac system. They addressed these problems by creating a bibliographic control policy manual to which all members agreed to adhere and by mounting a series of projects to correct records online.

KE
Record Import and Export

Tapeloading was the first method used to create local systems databases. Records typically were created on a bibliographic utility, copied to tape, and then loaded into the local system. Tapeloading is still the only means by which records enter some systems and is used on occasion for almost all systems, especially for large files of records. It is currently the usual means by which local systems send records back to the utilities or send files of data to union lists or other cooperatively created databases.

Most local systems, however, have developed online input capabilities, and most also have developed additional methods of transferring records from other sources. Typically, these are of the computer-to-terminal variety. The user searches a bibliographic utility via a standard connection and transfers the record to a terminal (or PC) attached to the local system. The local system then processes and loads the record.

Early transfer formats were essentially screen dumps, so that local system software had to be changed each time the utility changed the screen format. More recently, the utilities have implemented MARC export capabilities, and local system vendors have developed software to convert those records as they are transferred. While this method works reasonably well in day-to-day technical services operations, it has two major drawbacks. First, it is a one-way transfer, and libraries need to report data back to the utilities for the purposes of resource sharing just as much as they need to draw data from them. Second, while it works well for individual records, it does not work well for transfer of large files of records.

Despite their prevalence, very little has been written about either tapeloading or computer-to-terminal transfer. Since computer-to-computer transfer overcomes the limitations of these two methods, it has captured the attention of most writers.

In North America, protocols for computer-to-computer transfer of bibliographic data have developed under the umbrella of the Open Systems Interconnection (OSI) Reference Model promulgated by the International Organization for Standardization. The first project to commit to this model was the Linked Systems Project between the Library of Congress, the Research Libraries Group (RLG), WLN, and later OCLC. The most tangible result of that project is the process for contribution of records to and distribution of the LC authority file, which has been operational for some time now. The National Coordinated Cataloging Program (NCCP) hopes to develop a similar process for records exchange.

A less tangible, but eventually more important, result of the Linked Systems Project has been the development of Z39.50 (KE2), the protocol for intersystem search and retrieval. Though the standard has broader applicability, implementation efforts to date have focused on bibliographic retrieval systems. In the absence of fully developed OSI networks, most applications have actually been developed in a Transmission Control Protocol/Internet Protocol (TCP/IP) environment.

What Z39.50 does, in essence, is allow the user of one library's database to search the databases of other libraries that have adopted the protocol as if the user were searching the local catalog. Commands are entered and results displayed in the native mode of the home system. Since retrieved bibliographic records are transported in MARC format, they can, if desired, be incorporated into the local system. If the protocol were broadly implemented, a single search could be routed to multiple systems in an order based on the likelihood of obtaining useful results. For any user, the "catalog" becomes all catalogs linked by the protocol and interconnected networks. Recent development efforts have focused on expansion of the protocol to deal with other types of data, including abstracting and indexing data, full text, and images.

The papers from the OCLC/RLG seminar on data exchange (KE11) will provide the reader with a general overview of the current state of record transfer and future possibilities. However, both vendor and utility capabilities are changing rapidly. Use of the Internet File Transfer Protocol (FTP) is growing: both RLIN and OCLC plan to receive records from local systems via FTP in the near future, RLIN expects to implement a generalized FTP export capability, CARL is pulling records for its customers from OCLC using FTP, and the Linked System Project participants will probably begin using FTP to exchange records. Use of Z39.50 is quickly moving beyond the developmental stage: Geac has operational Z39.50 capabilities; Z39.50 products from several other vendors are in the final development stages; and several library systems, notably California's MELVYL system and Penn State's LIAS, have installed Z39.50 servers.

To evaluate options for record transfer effectively over the coming years, the database manager will need to develop a basic understanding of the standards for computer-to-computer transfer as well as a general perspective on what their application might accomplish. The remainder of the items in the chapter should aid in that task. One might well begin with those with a less-technical focus, but some degree of technical understanding is eventually necessary.

STANDARDS

KE1. International Organization for Standardization. *Information Processing Systems: Open Systems Interconnection: Basic Reference Model.* Geneva, Switz.: ISO, 1984.

ISO 7498 provides a model within which standards for communication between disparate computers can be de-

veloped. It describes seven layers through which communication occurs: (1) the physical layer, (2) the link layer, (3) the network layer, (4) the transport layer, (5) the session layer, (6) the presentation layer, and (7) the application layer. Numerous protocols have been developed and standardized for each layer. In the United States, the Linked Systems Project was the first networking project to use the model.

KE2. National Information Standards Organization (U.S.). *ANSI Z39.50, Information Retrieval Service and Protocol: American National Standard Information Retrieval Application Service Definition and Protocol Specification for Open Systems Interconnection.* New Brunswick, N.J.: Transaction Publishers, 1992.

ANSI/NISO Z39.50 provides the framework for development of intersystem searching protocols. The objective is to make intersystem searching transparent to the user; search commands are entered and results are displayed in the native mode of the home system. Though the protocol was initially developed for bibliographic data, its implementors also have begun to turn their attention to retrieval of other data, such as full text and images.

OPEN SYSTEMS INTERCONNECTION REFERENCE MODEL (OSI)

Most of the articles in this group are highly technical. Denenberg's 1985 article (KE6) provides the best general introduction to the model.

KE3. Arbez, Gilbert, and Leigh Swain. "OSI Conformance Testing for Bibliographic Applications." *Library Hi Tech* 8, no. 4 (1990): 119–36.

Arbez and Swain provide an overview of Open Systems Interconnection (OSI) conformance testing for bibliographic applications based on their experience in testing the ISO Interlibrary Loan protocol at the National Library of Canada. They discuss standards for conformance testing in general as well as the specific features of this particular set of tests and note the additional need for interoperability testing.

KE4. Davison, Wayne E. "OSI Upper Layers: Support for Applications." *Library Hi Tech* 8, no. 4 (1990): 33–42.

Davison clearly describes the functions of the upper three layers of the Open Systems Interconnection model (*see* KE1), describes the role of protocols associated with each layer, and summarizes the purposes of related application service elements.

KE5. Denenberg, Ray. "Data Communications and OSI." *Library Hi Tech* 8, no. 4 (1990): 15–32.

A brief overview of the seven OSI layers, a discussion of the data communications standards associated with each layer, and a detailed description of the lower four layers and the architectural concepts for those layers. Concludes with a comparison of the OSI protocols and the TCP/IP protocols.

KE6. _____. "Open Systems Interconnection." *Library Hi Tech* 3, no. 1 (1985): 15–26.

In this exceptionally clear explanation of OSI, Denenberg describes the functions and purposes of each of the seven layers in the model. Layers one through four are needed to achieve reliable data transmission; layers six and seven are needed for exchange of information by end users; and level five serves as a bridge between the two. A summary, an explanation of X.25, and a glossary add to the usefulness of the article.

LINKED SYSTEMS PROJECT

Articles by Avram (KE7), Davison (KE8), and Mc-Callum (KE13 and KE14), as well as some of the chapters in *The Linked Systems Project* (KE11), are of general interest; the remainder will be of interest to those with a relatively strong technical background.

KE7. Avram, Henriette D. "The Linked Systems Project: Its Implications for Resource Sharing." *Library Resources & Technical Services* 30 (Jan./Mar. 1986): 36–46.

Avram gives a short history of the Linked Systems Project (LSP), which she describes as an attempt to achieve single network efficiency in the face of the reality of multiple networks. The first of the applications programs, which allows transmission of authority records to and from the bibliographic utilities and LC, has been operational for some time.

KE8. Davison, Wayne E. "The WLN/RLG/LC Linked Systems Project." *Information Technology and Libraries* 2 (Mar. 1983): 34–46.

Davison describes the criteria specified for a telecommunications link for Linked Systems Project, the development of that link, and the implementation of the authorities application. The article is notable for its perception of the broad importance of LSP as "the foundation for a national bibliographic network."

KE9. Denenberg, Ray. "Linked Systems Project, Part 2: Standard Network Interconnection." *Library Hi Tech* 3, no. 2 (1985): 71–79.

Denenberg reminds readers that "LSP was perhaps the first major networking project in the world to commit to OSI" and describes the choices made for OSI layers four through seven for the Standard Network Interconnection (SNI) component of LSP.

KE10. _____. "The LSP/SNI Test Facility." *Library Hi Tech* 4, no. 1 (1986): 41–49.

Traces the development at the Library of Congress of a test system for validation of Standard Network Interconnection (SNI) protocols by vendors. The test system was developed to limit the cost of testing and to overcome the technical difficulties encountered in initial testing by LC, WLN, and RLG.

KE11. Fenly, Judith G., and Beacher Wiggins, eds. *The Linked Systems Project: A Networking Tool for Libraries.* Dublin, Ohio: OCLC, Inc., 1988.

This comprehensive set of papers on LSP covers its history, the standard network interconnection protocols, record transfer, information retrieval, NACO use of LSP, and projected NCCP use, as well as the first bibliographic utility to support local system implementation of LSP. Most of the information in the book is available elsewhere, but it serves as a historical compendium.

KE12. "Implementation of the Linked Systems Project: A Technical Report." *Library Hi Tech* 3, no. 3 (1985): 87–107.

Reports the development of the Standard Network Interconnection (SNI) at LC, WLN, RLG, and OCLC, focusing on hardware and software used and on the development and testing of software.

KE13. McCallum, Sally H. "Linked Systems Project in the United States." *IFLA Journal* 11 (1985): 313–24.

McCallum describes LSP as an example of data exchange between dissimilar computer systems based on protocols compatible with OSI (*see* KE1). LSP tasks were divided into two parts: developing a telecommunications facility that conforms to the OSI model and developing interfaces to existing applications. The first such application was development of cooperative authority file maintenance by LC, WLN, RLIN, and OCLC.

KE14. _____. "Linked Systems Project, Part 1: Authorities Implementation." *Library Hi Tech* 3, no. 2 (1985): 61–68.

McCallum explores three aspects of the authorities implementation portion of the Linked Systems Project—record contribution, record distribution, and intersystem searching—and discusses some of the procedural and technical problems solved as work progressed.

ANSI/NISO Z39.50

Despite the technical nature of the topic, all of the articles in this group are very readable, and each of the authors provides a broad perspective on the importance of Z39.50 (KE2) in addition to details about it.

KE15. Buckland, Michael K., and Clifford A. Lynch. "The Linked Systems Protocol and the Future of Bibliographic Networks and Systems." *Information Technology and Libraries* 6 (June 1987): 83–88.

Buckland and Lynch discuss Z39.50 (KE2) as an application level protocol within the OSI model. They believe that in the short term, developers are likely to focus on interoperability between OSI protocols and other protocols such as Systems Network Architecture (SNA) and TCP/IP. They also argue that Z39.50 should evolve to support transmission of other types of bibliographic information, such as abstracting and indexing data and textual databases, which would require the development of standard communications formats for these types of data.

KE16. _____. "National and International Implications of the Linked Systems Protocol for Online Bibliographic Systems." *Cataloging & Classification Quarterly* 8, nos. 3/4 (1988): 15–33.

Buckland and Lynch contend that application of Z39.50 (KE2) will lead to a redefinition of the national and indeed international database. The catalog available to the user will no longer be the local catalog, but all catalogs connected to a network.

KE17. Hinnebusch, Mark. "Z39.50: A Path for Implementation." *Computers in Libraries* 11 (Sept. 1991): 30–31.

Presents some of the issues concerning the use of Z39.50 (KE2) that still need resolution and the process through which the Z39.50 Implementor's Group is working on those issues.

KE18. Lynch, Clifford. "Access Technology for Network Information Resources." *Cause/Effect* 13 (Summer 1990): 15–20.

Lynch clearly outlines the types of information retrieval problems facing scholars and how use of Z39.50 (KE2) will alleviate some of them. The article serves as an excellent general introduction to the standard and its applicability.

KE19. _____. "The Client-Server Model in Information Retrieval." In *Interfaces for Information Retrieval*, edited by Martin Dillon, 301–18. Westport, Conn.: Greenwood Press, 1991.

Lynch's key point is that the capabilities of Z39.50 (KE2) must be comparable to those of the best existing user interfaces in which database and interface are tightly coupled. He then outlines some of the additional work that must be done on the standard to improve its usefulness.

KE20. _____. "Information Retrieval as a Network Application." *Library Hi Tech* 8, no. 4 (1990): 57–72.

Lynch describes the OSI (KE1) model as "a new paradigm for developing information systems" and emphasizes the fact that work on OSI has been an effort to understand distributed computing rather than simply codify existing practices. He discusses the ways in which Z39.50 (KE2) is superior to other standards for information retrieval. Sidebars in the article describe the work of the Z39.50 implementors group, LC's work as the Z39.50 maintenance agency, and the differences between Z39.50 and related international standards.

KE21. _____. "The Z39.50 Information Retrieval Protocol: An Overview and Status Report." *Computer Communication Review* 21 (Jan. 1991): 58–70.

Because the intended audience for this article is the broader computer networking community, Lynch emphasizes the wide applicability of Z39.50 (KE2) in his description of its development and operation and implementation projects. Along the way, he clears up several misconceptions.

KE22. McGill, Michael J., Larry L. Learn, and Thomas K. G. Lydon. "A Technical Evaluation of the Linked Systems Project Protocols in the Name Authority Distribution Application." *Information Technology and Libraries* 6 (Dec. 1987): 253–65.

After providing background information on the development of LSP, the authors evaluate its operation at OCLC in functional, operational, and performance terms. Problems that need to be addressed are failure to fully conform to the OSI model (KE1), slow data transmission, and frequent failure to establish connections.

THE CURRENT STATE
OF RECORD TRANSPORT

KE23. Bales, Kathleen. "Local System and Bibliographic Utility Data Exchange: Future Methodologies." *Information Technology and Libraries* 10 (June 1991): 108–11.

Bales discusses near-term options for transferring records between bibliographic utilities and local systems, including tapeloading, terminal transfer of MARC formatted records, and computer-to-computer transfer based on either OSI (KE1) or TCP/IP file transfer mechanisms. She stresses the need for a more interactive relationship between the utilities and local systems and raises a long series of questions about types of data to be transferred.

KE24. Bishoff, Liz. "Local System and Bibliographic Utility Data Exchange: Current Approaches." *Information Technology and Libraries* 10 (June 1991): 105–8.

Bishoff outlines the history of the record-transfer process, including tapeloading, transfer via screen dumps, and MARC export facilities. She notes the need for eventual implementation of Z39.50 protocols (KE2) but focuses on nearer term solutions such as utilization of electronic file transfer capabilities and using local system terminals to access bibliographic utilities.

KE25. Lowell, Gerald R. "Local Systems and Bibliographic Utilities: Data Exchange Options: Keynote Address." *Information Technology and Libraries* 10 (June 1991): 99–104.

Lowell describes the context in which record exchange between local systems and bibliographic utilities currently occurs. The barriers to effective exchange he identifies include variations in local system implementation, in the design and use of bibliographic utilities, and in local work-flow procedures, as well as technological problems. In his view, an effective system would be flexible, cost-effective, and work-flow efficient. He suggests two major steps in this direction: creation of a single national utility and use of a single national information network.

KE26. _____. "Local Systems and Bibliographic Utilities in 1992: A Large Research Library Perspective." *The Journal of Academic Librarianship* 16 (July 1990): 140–44.

Lowell reports the results of a survey of technical services directors of twenty-five large research libraries. Respondents generally expected that their local systems would be the database of record, that they would be using more than one utility, and that transfer of records from the utility would be via a downloading capability while transfer of records to the utility would be via tapeloading.

KE27. Nevins, Kate, and Larry L. Learn. "Linked Systems: Issues and Opportunities (or Confronting a Brave New World)." *Information Technology and Libraries* 10 (June 1991): 115–20.

Nevins and Learn remind readers that even when the technical problems of linking systems have been solved, the organizational problems remain, as cooperating enti-ties try to work out policies and procedures, set fair pricing structures, and provide adequate user support.

KE28. Stovel, Lennie. "Evaluating Your Options." *Information Technology and Libraries* 10 (June 1991): 111–15.

Stovel discusses the factors affecting transfer of records between the utilities and local systems, including local-system capabilities, utilities capabilities, local-computing environments, and local priorities and commitments.

L

Access Services

Farideh Tehrani

Overview

The creation of a department of access services in American libraries during the last decade points to a significant conceptual and organizational change. The use of the term "access services" in place of "circulation" can be attributed to the expanding role and added responsibilities of this department. While the term "circulation" prevails in many libraries, the broader term "access services" seems more descriptive to a number of librarians. In this context, the term "access" applies to *how desired information resources are retrieved and presented physically to the inquirer, once locations of resources are known.*

Factors strengthening the concept of "access" over "ownership" include the tremendous increase in print and nonprint resources, the broadening of library missions, service to a more demanding clientele, limited library budgets, and advances in technology. No library can own everything necessary to serve the ever-changing needs of its users. Cooperation and sharing, facilitated by information technology, are the bywords, as libraries can no longer function efficiently in isolation. Library walls are "removed," and distance is no obstacle. The measure of a library's success extends beyond its hold-

ings to how well it provides access to needed materials, wherever located. The term "access services" fits the times.

Traditional circulation activities encompass such functions as charging out, checking in, or discharging items, returning materials to library shelves, collecting fines and fees, providing information on lost books, and maintaining the collection in good condition. Today, whether the department is called "circulation" or "access services," it is charged in many libraries with additional responsibilities such as interlibrary loan and document delivery services.

In 1991, half the respondents to a survey of academic and research libraries (LA2) reported having a department known as "access services." The specific functions of these departments vary from library to library, but they all conduct activities related to physical access to library collections. These usually include circulation of library-owned materials and course-related reserve collections and may include interlibrary-loan operations, document-delivery services, current periodical and newspaper handling, stack maintenance, audiovisual collections, microforms, storage facilities, patron behavior, library security, and library-wide support for automation.

In most cases, the department reports to the head of public service or directly to the director. The increasing interrelationship of access services and technical services, however, justifies the editor's decision to include this area and its resources in a comprehensive technical services guide.

Chapter Content and Organization

Information sources included in this chapter are presented under seven section headings: general works, including periodicals; collection maintenance; circulation; interlibrary loan; document delivery; patron behavior; and security, theft, and mutilation. Special effort has been made to include major information resources that have appeared since 1987. Occasionally, older publications of special significance also are included. Except in a few cases, journal articles of less than five pages have been excluded.

LA
General Works

LA1. McCombs, Gillian M., ed. *Access Services: The Convergence of Reference and Technical Services.* New York: Haworth Press, 1991. Also published as *The Reference Librarian* 34 (1991).

See also annotation under AH31. Explores the growing need for libraries to emphasize access instead of ownership and, hence, combine technical and public services functions toward the common goal of improving access. Articles include discussion on how this change will affect the role of librarians, the structure of academic-library staff, and methods of increasing access.

LA2. Steel, Virginia, comp. *Access Services: Organization and Management.* SPEC Kit, no. 179. Washington, D.C.: Office of Management Services, Association of Research Libraries, 1991.

Reports the result of a 1991 survey on current trends in the organization of access services and circulation services of seventy-six North American academic and research libraries.

LA3. Whitlatch, Jo Bell. "Access Services." In *Academic Libraries, Research Perspectives,* edited by Mary Jo Lynch and Arthur Young, 67–105. Chicago: American Library Association, 1990.

Deals with the role of accessibility in determining use of information source; user interaction with library staff

and bibliographic systems; physical access to library buildings; and access to documents both within libraries and from remote locations.

LAA
Textbooks, Guides, and Manuals

LAA1. ALA ACRL Access Policy Guidelines Task Force. "ACRL Guidelines for the Preparation of Policies on Library Access": A Draft. *College & Research Libraries News* 53, no. 11 (Dec. 1992): 709–10.

This document, now in draft form, will replace the 1975 *Access Policy Guidelines.* It is designed to assist individual libraries in addressing practical questions relating to access and to serve as a guideline or checklist for the development of individual policies. It is divided into the following sections: Introduction, Access to Facilities, Bibliographic Access, Collection Management, Preservation, Access to Services.

LAA2. Baker, Sharon L., and F. Wilfred Lancaster. *The Measurement and Evaluation of Library Services.* 2nd ed. Arlington, Va.: Information Resources Press, 1991.

Chapters 2–6 deal with accessibility and convenience in library use, materials-centered and use-centered approaches in collection evaluation, and evaluation of materials delivery and in-house use. This second edition combines the main features of 1977 and 1978 works by Lancaster. Includes a large number of evaluative studies that have been conducted since the publication of the first edition. Synthesizes major findings of past evaluation efforts for the benefit of practicing librarians. Reviews a substantial body of literature on evaluation for each library service area.

LAA3. Battaile, Connie. *Circulation Services in a Small Academic Library.* Westport, Conn: Greenwood Press, 1992.

For new circulation librarians, a general guide to the underlying concerns of circulation activity. Provides specific examples. Chapters on the circulation department head, circulation process, other circulation department functions, "things" (books, stacks), and "people." Bibliography.

LAA4. Evans, G. Edward, Anthony J. Amodeo, and Thomas L. Carter. *Introduction to Library Public Services.* 5th ed. Englewood, Colo.: Libraries Unlimited, 1992.

The present edition of this comprehensive textbook represents a complete revision. It includes several chapters dealing with access services: interlibrary loan, circulation services, reserve services, and security issues. New lists of suggested readings have been added at the end of each chapter for the benefit of students.

LAA5. Kohl, David F. *Circulation, Interlibrary Loan, Patron Use, and Collection Maintenance: A Handbook for Library Management.* Santa Barbara, Calif.: ABC Clio Information Services, 1986.

Designed for library managers and decision makers, this handbook presents summaries of individual research findings grouped by subjects. A list of 807 journal articles surveyed in the preparation of the handbook is included. Comprehensive, but now more than seven years old.

LAA6. McCabe, Gerard B., ed. *Academic Libraries in Urban and Metropolitan Areas: A Management Handbook.* Westport, Conn.: Greenwood Press, 1992.

Describes services to internal and external populations; security, safety, and preservation; and management perspectives. In its twenty-two chapters on various aspects of urban academic libraries, includes discussion of external-use access, circulation policies, services to faculty, networking among libraries, joint-use library services at distant campuses, and legal aspects of collection security.

LAA7. Paietta, Ann Catherine. *Access Services: A Handbook.* London: Library Association; Jefferson, N.C.: McFarland Publishers, 1991.

This comprehensive handbook offers discussions on circulation control, traditional interlibrary loan and photocopying operations, impact of telefacsimile transmission on information delivery, stack management, staffing, training, labor relations, confidentiality of information, security, patron and social issues, and facilities management.

LAB
Periodicals

LAB1. *Interlending & Document Supply.* Boston Spa, West Yorkshire, Eng.: Document Supply Centre, Publishing Section, British Library. v. 1– , 1971– . Quarterly. ISSN 0264-1615.

Covers a wide range of activities relating to document provision and supply, from traditional approaches to the use of advanced technologies both within and between countries. Former titles: *NLL Review* (1971/1972), *BLL Review* (1973–1977), *Interlending Review* (1978–1982). Includes bibliography, index, and cumulative index.

LAB2. *Journal of Interlibrary Loan & Information Supply.* Binghamton, N.Y.: Haworth Press. v. 1– , 1990– . Quarterly. ISSN 1042-4458.

Devoted to interlibrary loan problems and the expanding roles of interlibrary loan librarians in North America; includes some articles of international scope. Intended as "a broad-based, practical yet professional periodical." Includes both practical and research-based articles. Reviews.

LAB3. *Library & Archival Security.* Binghamton, N.Y.: Haworth Press. v. 2– , 1978– . Quarterly. ISSN 0196-0075. Continues *Library Security Newsletter.*

See also annotation under IAG15. Publishes papers on any aspect of crime and disruption affecting libraries, the impact of crime, crime-prevention and security programs, and some aspects of preservation. Includes advertisements, book reviews, abstracts, bibliography, index.

LAC
Sources of Expertise

PROFESSIONAL ASSOCIATIONS

LAC1. ALA. Association of College & Research Libraries (ACRL). Executive Director: Althea H. Jenkins.

See also annotation under GAE5. Of particular interest here is the Access Policy Guideline Task Force.

LAC2. ALA. Coordinating Committee on Access to Information.

This special committee was established by ALA Council in 1989 to facilitate the development and maintenance of a comprehensive set of information-access policies for ALA in cooperation with all Association units. ALA staff liaison: Mary Jo Lynch, and others.

LAC3. ALA. Library Administration and Management Association (LAMA). Executive Director: Karen Muller.

The Systems and Services Section (SASS) of LAMA studies and evaluates the application of new technology in services, and the management thereof, for the improvement of library services and systems. Of particular interest within SASS is the Circulation Services Committee.

LAC4. ALA. Reference and Adult Services Division (RASD). Executive Director: Andrew M. Hansen.

See also annotation under HAE3. Access services are addressed by several groups within RASD, including its Management and Operation of Public Services Section (MOPSS). The Interlibrary Loan Committee of MOPSS has subcommittees on Continuing Education and Training, National Interlibrary Loan, and an Interlibrary Loan Discussion Group.

LAC5. International Federation of Library Associations and Institutions (IFLA). Headquarters: c/o The Royal Library, POB 95312, 2509CH The Hague, The Netherlands. Secretary General: Paul Nauta.

See also annotation under AGA4. The IFLA Section on Interlending and Document Delivery deals specifically with these topics of interest to access services librarians.

ELECTRONIC DISCUSSION GROUPS

LAC6. CIRCPLUS. [electronic discussion group]

CIRCPLUS is a discussion forum for issues relating to circulation, reserve room, stack maintenance, and similar activities in libraries. Daniel Lester is the list owner. To subscribe, send a message to **LISTSERV@VIDBSU** (BITNET) or **LISTSERV@IDBSU.IDBSU.EDU** (IN-

TERNET) with the command: **SUBSCRIBE CIRCPLUS [your name]**.

LAC7. ILL-L. [electronic discussion group]

This group discusses policies, procedures, and problems having to do with interlibrary loan. To subscribe, send a message to **LISTSERV@UVMVM** (BITNET) with the command: **SUBSCRIBE ILL-L [your name]**.

LB
Collection Maintenance

The main objective of collection maintenance, sometimes called stack maintenance or stack management, is to ensure that all library materials are maintained in good condition and are readily accessible to library patrons. At any given time, the location of each item should be known to those responsible for the maintenance of the collection. "Not-on-shelf" and similar dead-end answers frustrate even the most patient library patrons.

Physical arrangement of the collection varies according to the type of materials, frequency of use, the collection size, and the nature of the library services. All types of physical arrangements must consider the needs of the library patrons and the ease of access. Special types of material requiring special consideration include fiction, nonfiction, rare books, picture books, bound periodicals, newspapers, atlases, globes, phono-records, compact discs, videos, microforms, filmstrips, transparencies, slides, pamphlets, games, models, and art prints.

To ensure that all returning materials are back in their proper places, managers must integrate shelving, reshelving, shelf-reading, shifting, and inventory-taking into the process of orderly maintenance of the stacks. Identification of damaged books for repair and lost or stolen items for replacement is also considered central to proper stacks maintenance. Rapidly growing collections may necessitate moving a part of or the entire collection from one building to another. This complicated task definitely requires systematic planning.

To provide effective lending services to patrons and at the same time to ensure the return of each item, virtually all types of libraries have developed circulation policies. These policies take into consideration all types of library materials and various categories of users. For instance, in academic libraries faculty-borrowing privileges are often different from those of students. Also treated differently are secondary client groups or nonaffiliated borrowers such as alumni, faculty spouses, special-privilege borrowers, and students and faculty members of institutions that participate in a cooperative program. In public libraries, primary users are adult residents. Children and young adults are also served freely. Nonresidents and people who do not pay taxes or work in the library's service area may be asked to pay a small fee. In general, public libraries are willing to encourage secondary and outside borrowers to use the library.

Patrons are informed of the library's lending rules and regulations; unfortunately, not all patrons manage to respect them. Thus, a system of fines for overdue or lost items is enforced. The actual collection of fines and fees and the billing responsibility are also assigned to the access services staff.

Sheila Intner in her *Circulation Policy in Academic, Public, and School Libraries* (LB7) identifies four trends that have, in recent years, motivated librarians to examine and reformulate existing circulation policies. These are the accountability of library administrations for service and expenditures, budget problems, broadening service goals, and cooperative ventures.

LB1. Bede, Mitchell W. "On the Use of Positive Reinforcement to Minimize the Problem of Overdue Library Materials." *The Journal of Library Administration* 9, no. 3 (1988): 87–101.

Proposes the use of positive reinforcement to minimize overdues and prevent the resentment frequently created by fines and other sanctions. Outlines general concerns about the use and misuse of operant conditioning techniques and discusses the benefits to be derived from this approach.

LB2. Burgin, Robert, and Patsy Hansel. "Library Overdues: An Update." *Library & Archival Security* 10, no. 2 (1990): 51–75.

Results of a 1986 survey of seventy public library systems in North Carolina to determine the relationships between overdues and activities designed to tackle the problem. This study, replacing two studies the authors conducted on the same subject in 1981 and 1983, measures the effectiveness of various overdues strategies.

LB3. Cooper, Michael D. "A Cost Comparison of Alternative Book Storage Strategies." *Library Quarterly* 59 (July 1989): 239–60.

Develops a cost methodology to use in deciding the location, type of shelving, and type of access for academic-library book-storage programs. Includes the cost of selecting materials for storage, processing, transporting, and circulating from the storage facility. Based on data from the University of California, San Diego.

LB4. Haka, Clifford H., and Nancy Stevens. *A Guidebook for Shelf Inventory Procedures in Academic Libraries.* Occasional Paper, no. 10. Washington, D.C.: Office of Management Studies, Association of Research Libraries, 1985.

Identifies the benefits derived from conducting a shelf inventory. Describes how to determine the costs and provides a set of procedures with flow charts. Examples from an inventory conducted at the University of Kansas illustrate the procedures. Results of a survey of ARL institutions are cited. A selected bibliography is included.

LB5. Henshaw, Rod, and Cordelia Swinton. "The Penn State Annex: A Model for Implementing a Successful Collection Storage Program." *Technical Services Quarterly* 7, no. 4 (1990): 11–19.

Describes the Pennsylvania State University Libraries storage program. Emphasis is on careful planning, implementation, and follow-up assessment through the integrated local online public access catalog, automated circulation systems, delivery service, and telefacsimile.

LB6. Hubbard, William J. *Stack Management: A Practical Guide to Shelving and Maintaining Library Collections.* Chicago: Amercian Library Association, 1981.

Revises William Jesse's 1952 publication, *Shelf Work in Libraries,* that dealt with problems of collection management in the postwar era. Discusses the management of collections: shelving, reshelving, shelf reading, inventory, and shifting and moving. Hubbard also considers storing and care of books. Includes discussion of various shelving units for libraries, such as revolving and sliding shelf systems, parallel sliding case systems, and perpendicular sliding case systems.

LB7. Intner, Sheila S. *Circulation Policy in Academic, Public, and School Libraries.* New Directions in Information Management, no. 13. New York: Greenwood Press, 1987.

Summarizes policies and procedures based on a survey of approximately sixty academic, public, and school libraries. Intended for those concerned with the use of library materials, i.e., library staff members, both professional and paraprofessional, educators, library and information students, and end users of the services.

LB8. Mackey, Kitty J. "Automating Overdues in a Non-Automated Library: The HyperCard Solution." *College & Research Library News* 50 (Jan. 1989): 23–27.

Provides an overview of the problem of manually generating weekly overdue notices at the Mickel Library, Converse College, Spartanburg, South Carolina. Discusses the development of Overdue Writer, a program using Apple Computer's HyperCard software.

LB9. Nelms, Willie, and Diane Taylor. "The Art of Overdues." *Public Library Quarterly* 9, no. 1 (1989): 13–18.

Looks at one method, adopted by the Sheppard Memorial Library, Greenville, North Carolina, to deal with the problem of overdue books.

LB10. Spicer, Claudia A. "An Inventory for the '80s." *Collection Building* 8, no. 3 (1987): 16–18.

Discusses the inventory of the main collection of Tutt Library at Colorado College, a private liberal arts college in Colorado Springs. The chief aim was to obtain precise information to assist in the selection of a security system, online catalog, and circulation system.

LB11. Treadwell, Jane. "Determining a Fair Price for Lost Books: A Case Study." *Library & Archival Security* 9, no. 1 (1989): 19–29.

Examines how one library considers the issues of book loss and replacement costs. Circulation records from a six-month period were analyzed for pattern of book loss and to determine what the replacement charges should be for in-print and out-of-print books.

LB12. Tucker, Dennis C. *From Here to There: Moving a Library.* Bristol, Ind.: Wyndham Hall Press, 1987.

Considers all aspects of planning for a move, including preliminary activities such as weeding, cleaning, fumigating, and deacidifying. It points to many administrative considerations, such as selection of a director to manage the move, hiring of professionals and other helpers, scheduling of work, and communicating with the staff and the public.

BIBLIOGRAPHIES

LB13. Christensen, John O. *Management of Circulation in Libraries in the 1980's: A Selective Bibliography.* Public Administration Series—Bibliography P-2711. Monticello, Ill.: Vance Bibliographies, 1989.

Includes approximately 200 publications up to September 1988. Foreign-language entries were not included.

LC
Circulation

Circulation is a central function of libraries that lend their materials for use outside the library premises. In these libraries, such activities as collection development, organization of library materials, creation of the libraries' bibliographical databases, and stack maintenance are in large part conducted to bring success to the library's circulation function.

As soon as technological advances permitted the automation of library operations, automating circulation became the first priority for most libraries. In early 1940, card-based batch processing found its place in a number of libraries. But according to *Library Technology Reports* of July 1986 (LC9) "the first commercial online library system developed for installation in a local library was a circulation system. CLSI's LIBS 100 system was the first such system and was delivered to the first customer in 1973.''

During the last two decades, circulation operations of hundreds of libraries have been automated. Some small and medium-sized libraries that could not individually afford automation have joined together and cooperatively maintain an online system to benefit from the numerous advantages of automation. Yet, many libraries still conduct this activity manually. There are indeed a number of economical and reliable manual methods that small libraries still employ to serve their patrons.

Few libraries enter into automation just to reduce the cost of lending services. Quality of service to patrons is the primary motivation. Circulation automation can provide crucial management statistics and can help to improve quality of the collections and better use of space. It facilitates collection-use studies, and helps identify little- or never-used materials for more economical storage. Libraries maintaining a common database can inform users not only of what they possess individually but of what exists anywhere among the participating libraries. Without automation, interlibrary loan could not have had the success it enjoys today both nationally and internationally. The enormous number of publications on circulation automation, of which a selection is included below, reflects the spread of online systems.

LC1. Baker, Peter. "Implementing CLSI in Warwickshire County Library." *Program* 21 (Oct. 1987): 350–59.

Shows the stages in selecting the CLSI system and problems faced in converting diverse existing computer-based systems to an integrated system at Warwickshire County Library, Birmingham, U.K.

LC2. Bluh, Pamela. "Barcoding a Library Collection." *Law Library Journal* 82 (Fall 1990): 727–36.

Discusses the factors to be considered before embarking on bar coding, which links materials and patron records to bibliographical records. Based on experience at University of Maryland Law Library.

LC3. Brophy, Peter, and others. *DOBIS/LIBIS: A Guide for Librarians and System Managers.* Aldershot, Eng., and Brookfield, Vt.: Gower, 1990.

This guide attempts to give a general nonparochial perspective on the functionality and operation of the library automation system DOBIS/LIBIS. Chapter 8 deals with circulation. Includes a list of worldwide users and a bibliography.

LC4. Burrell, Quentin L. "A Third Note on Ageing in a Library Circulation Model: Applications to Future Use and Relegation." *Journal of Documentation* 43 (Mar. 1987): 24–45.

Explains a circulation model for academic research libraries that uses the mixed model, incorporating aging of library materials to predict future use of monographs and to suggest weeding procedures based on frequency of circulation. Longitudinal studies are examined and statistical details are appended.

LC5. Camp, John A., and others. "Survey of Online Systems in U.S. Academic Libraries." *College & Research Libraries* 48 (July 1987): 339–50.

Includes circulation and interlibrary loan along with other library technical operations. Considers methods of financing, use of systems personnel, backup systems, types of computers, sources for systems, and functions within systems.

LC6. Cerveny, William. "Implementing a Computerized Film Rental System." *Community & Junior College Libraries* 5, no. 2 (1988): 35–46.

Examines aspects of the audiovisual rental process appropriate for automation at Oakton Community College, Des Plaines, Illinois. Focuses on dBASE III and suggests plans for future actions.

LC7. Dasgupta, Krishna. "Computer Library Services: Automated Circulation Control in the USA (CLSI, OCLC, and C/W MARS)." *International Forum on Information and Documentation* 14 (Oct. 1989): 24–30.

The contributions of three major systems (CLSI, OCLC, and C/W MARS) are presented in detail. Also discusses the technology in automated circulation in the United States during the mid- to late 1980s.

LC8. Dewey, Patrick. "Public Libraries That Circulate Software." *Technical Services Quarterly* 7, no. 3 (1990): 57–65.

Describes software circulation policies in five libraries, all of which indicate that the operation is viable. Lists rules and ways of circulating software that have been distilled from these projects, bearing in mind copyright considerations. Also discusses hardware lending.

LC9. Fayen, Emily Gallup. "Automated Circulation Systems for Large Libraries." *Library Technology Reports* 22 (July/Aug. 1986): 385–469.

Reviews automated circulation systems for large libraries. Discusses the background and development of automated circulation systems and the reasons for automating. Looks at the requirements for circulation systems. Lists eighteen automated circulation systems available in the United States. Glossary.

LC10. Frederick, Janet. "Database and Collection Preparation for Automated Circulation." *Technical Services Quarterly* 5, no. 2 (1987): 35–46.

Illustrates archival tape processing that includes item-record creation. Discusses using preassigned bar-code or optical character reader (OCR) labels generated by vendors versus using nonassigned labels. Shows the magnitude of and problems associated with labeling a collection and offers alternatives when possible. Gives examples of various methods of labeling, including factors to be considered for ongoing labeling of new acquisitions and material being retrospectively converted. Useful for those who are beginning the transition from manual to automated circulation.

LC11. Freese, Melanie. "Missing Links: Smart Barcodes and Inventory Analysis at Hofstra University's Axinn Library." *Library & Archival Security* 9, no. 1 (1989): 3–17.

Gives an account of the massive bar coding of the circulating collection at Hofstra University, Hempstead, New York, in 1987. A combination of smart and dumb bar codes, prepared by the bibliographic utility ATLAS, was used. A partial inventory of the collection was achieved.

LC12. Garcia, C. Rebecca, and Frank R. Bridge. *Small Libraries Online: Automating Circulation and Public Access Catalogs: Participant Workbook.* Austin, Tex.: Texas State Library, 1989.

Includes step-by-step implementation plans for automating library circulation. Provides appendixes: Glossary, Sample Long-Range Automation Plan, Using MARC Records, Minicomputer and Microcomputer System Comparison, Automation Vendor List, Data Conversion Vendor List, and Functional Specifications. Includes a bibliography.

LC13. Hughes, James R., and Carol K. Moskun. "Building for Performance: Discovery Place." *Aslib Proceedings* 42 (Mar. 1990): 97–109.

Explains "Discovery Place," an integrated system developed by Systemhouse for the Columbus Metropolitan Library in Ohio. In addition to circulation, includes catalog maintenance, catalog searching, and online public access catalog modules. The system was built on Tandem hardware and became operational in 1988.

LC14. Logan, Susan J. "The Ohio State University's Library Control System: From Circulation to Subject Access and Authority Control." *Library Trends* 35 (Spring 1987): 539–54.

Reports the evolution of the library control system at the Ohio State University Library from a circulation control system to a full online catalog with subject access and authority control. Focuses on users' needs.

LC15. Saffady, William. "Automated Circulation Control Systems." In his *Introduction to Automation for Libraries*, 189–214. 2nd ed. Chicago: American Library Association, 1989.

Intended for librarians, information specialists, and library school students. Surveys those aspects of information technology most significant for library operations.

LC16. Stoll, Karen S. "Installation of the Geac System at Los Alamos National Laboratory Library." *Science & Technology Libraries* 9 (Fall 1988): 11–19.

Demonstrates the process of selecting and implementing a turnkey Geac computer system for automated circulation—as well as acquisitions and cataloging—operations.

LC17. Tague, Jean, and Isola Ajiferuke. "The Markov and the Mixed-Poisson Models of Library Circulation Compared." *Journal of Documentation* 43 (Sept. 1987): 212–35.

Two dynamic models of library circulation, the Markov model originally proposed by Morse and the mixed-Poisson model proposed by Burrell and Cane, are applied to a large eleven-year university circulation data set from the University of Saskatchewan. Discusses the outcome and indicates that neither model fits the data.

LC18. Thomason, Nevada Wallis. *Circulation Systems for School Library Media Centers: Manual to Microcomputer.* Littleton, Colo.: Libraries Unlimited, 1985.

Designed to help school library media specialists become familiar with the components of an efficient circulation system. Emphasizes evaluation of systems, hardware, and software. Divided into two parts: (1) manual and semiautomatic systems and (2) computer-based systems. Though any publication dealing with automation dates quickly, much of this book remains extremely useful. Appendixes on sample circulation policies, circulation software, helpful publications, and addresses for manufacturers and suppliers. Bibliography.

LC19. Westlake, Duncan R. "The Circulation Package—Geac Patron Query." In his *Geac, A Guide for Librarians and Systems Managers*, 79–146. 2nd ed. With contributions by Alison M. Hunter and Margaret Sheridan. Aldershot, Hants, Eng.: Ashgate Publishing Co., 1992.

Discusses Geac's comprehensive circulation package software for libraries. Describes Geac's library system, which began with the circulation system and then expanded to other areas.

BIBLIOGRAPHIES

LC20. *Library Circulation Systems and Automation: An Annotated Bibliography, 12-Year Cumulation, 1977–1988.* Chicago: Library Administration and Management Association, American Library Association, 1989.

This bibliography is the work of two LAMA committees: the Publications and Bibliographic Committee of the System and Services Section and its predecessor, the Circulation System Evaluation Committee of the Circulation Services Section. It was cumulated from yearly bibliographies in *LAMA Newsletter* and *Library Administration and Management.* Annotations were written by various individuals over the years, but all entries were reviewed by the Publications and Bibliographic Committee.

LD
Interlibrary Loan

Libraries have been forced to give up the notion of self-sufficiency as a result of ever-growing fields of specialization, drastic increases in numbers of publications, greater patron demands, and limited library budgets. To satisfy the needs of users, most libraries have come to depend on cooperative plans and resource sharing, aided by advances in information technology. Interlibrary loan (ILL) can be defined as the lending of materials by one library to another for use by a patron. In fact, most libraries physically transfer monographs and other substantive works through interlibrary loan but respond to ILL requests for journal articles by providing photocopies, which then become the property of the requestor. Thus, document delivery (the provision of copies of original resources) through various technologies is a topic closely related to interlibrary loan. The subsection following this one deals specifically with document delivery, including telefacsimile transmission.

As online databases in many fields have tipped off users to resources available far and wide, the number of ILL requests has grown rapidly. Beginning in the early 1970s, an increasing number of libraries began to use online interlibrary loan. Online ILL enables libraries to electronically initiate, verify, and respond with high speed to ILL requests. Locating needed items and their delivery has become easier and faster. The success rate in responding to requests has made the public want even more.

The online system also enables librarians to maintain all records and statistics files electronically. Many libraries have completely abandoned their manual record keeping. In 1984, the ALA began to include a section on ILL electronic format in its *Interlibrary Loan Practices Handbook* (LD32).

Success in user satisfaction brought with it two major problems, cost and overload, as many libraries were inundated by requests for books held in collections elsewhere. The question of user fees became a major concern. New methods of charging for services are now continually under study. Some libraries charge the same fee for all ILL transactions, and some may have a different fee structure for out-of-state requests. Cooperative borrowing agreements in which participants charge each other nothing is a current trend.

GENERAL WORKS

LD1. American Library Association, Interlibrary Loan Subcommittee on Continuing Education and Training, Interlibrary Loan Committee, Reference and Adult Services Division. "Interlibrary Loan Training and Continuing Education, Model Statement of Objectives." *RQ* 31 (Winter 1991): 177–84.

Based on a national survey conducted in 1989, this study codifies a core list of knowledge, skills, and accompanying objectives for training and continuing education programs in interlibrary loan.

LD2. Arthur Young Management Consultants. *The Interlibrary Transport Schemes.* British Research Paper, 22. Boston Spa, West Yorkshire, Eng.: British Library Document Supply Centre, 1987.

The final report of a study, undertaken throughout the United Kingdom and Ireland, on delivery methods in support of interlending and new technology for the electronic transmission of documents.

LD3. Bevan, Simon J. "Integrated Interlibrary Loans: LIBERTAS at Cranfield." *Program* 24 (July 1990): 221–32.

Describes the workings of this Information Systems module in general terms and discusses some of the implications for libraries. It describes the main problems, both in the installation and in the system itself, and the main advantages, which are the addition of increased numbers of access points, the loan analyses available, and the overall saving of staff time. Based on experience at the Cranfield Institute of Technology in England.

LD4. Bonk, Sharon. "Interlibrary Loan and Document Delivery in the United Kingdom." *RQ* 30 (Winter 1990): 230–40.

Summarizes the structure of interlibrary loans in the United Kingdom and discusses the changing technology, economics, and political dimensions of interlibrary loans. Parallels to and implications for American libraries are presented.

LD5. Boucher, Virginia, and Susan Fayad. *Library Resource Sharing in Colorado.* Denver, Colo.: Colorado State Library, 1988.

Based on a resource-sharing study conducted from September 1987 to June 1988 for the Colorado State Library to assess the status of interlibrary loan, reference referral, and document delivery among libraries in Colorado. Evaluates services and recommends improvements.

LD6. British Library Document Supply Centre. *Modeling the Economics of Interlibrary Lending.* Report. Nov. 1989. Boston Spa, West Yorkshire, Eng.: The Centre, 1990.

Report of a seminar organized in 1988 by the British Library Document Supply Centre (BLDSC) in conjunction with the London and South Eastern Library Region (LASER) to discuss the future of interlibrary lending in the United Kingdom.

LD7. Chang, Amy. "A Database Management System for Interlibrary Loan." *Information Technology and Libraries* 9 (June 1990): 135–43.

Demonstrates the increasing complexity of dealing with interlibrary loan requests and describes a database management system for interlibrary loans used at Texas Tech University. System functions are described, including file control, record maintenance, and report generation.

LD8. Comeaux, Elizabeth Anne, and Susan Willcox. "Automating Interlibrary Loan Statistics." *Technical Services Quarterly* 8, no. 3 (1991): 35–57.

Discusses the new interlibrary loan statistical system at the Brisco Library, Texas Health Science Center, San Antonio. Describes technical aspects of the system, various files, downloading programs, reporting programs, the copyright-compliance programs, invoicing programs, and benefits and limitations of the system.

LD9. Cornish, Graham P., and Alison Gallico, eds. *Interlending and Document Supply.* Proceedings of the First International Conference held in London, Nov. 1988. Boston Spa, West Yorkshire, Eng.: Office for International Lending, International Federation of Library Associations and Institutions, 1989.

This conference was organized jointly by the editorial office of the *Journal of Interlending and Document Supply* and IFLA Office for International Lending, both based at the British Library Document Supply Centre. Approximately 230 delegates attended from twenty-eight countries. Papers dealing exclusively with the United States and Canada were "Current Patterns of Library Telefacsimile Applications in the United States," "Library Applications of Facsimile in Pennsylvania: The Experience of One U.S. State," and "The Role of OCLC in Interlending."

LD10. Dalrymple, Prudence Ward, and others. "Measuring Statewide Interlibrary Loan among Multitype Libraries: A Testing of Data Collection Approaches." *RQ* 30 (Summer 1991): 534–44.

A study that designed and tested an interlibrary loan measurement tool to be used by all types and sizes of libraries in Illinois. Topics discussed include data collection processes, use of information for resource sharing, and a continuing education program to help librarians use the ILL forms. Sample forms are appended.

LD11. Day, Janice, and Arden Matheson. "ACUILLA: A Microcomputer-Based Interlibrary Loans Management Package." *Microcomputers for Information Management* 5 (June 1988): 93–111.

Highlights the development of a microcomputer-based package for data management in interlibrary loan services at the University of Calgary libraries. The ACUILLA system was developed to enhance productivity by reducing the number of paper files and the amount of manual record keeping. It manages both lending and borrowing activities and reports.

LD12. Dutcher, Gale A. "DOCLINE: A National Automated Interlibrary Loan Request Routing and Referral System." *Information Technology and Libraries* 8 (Dec. 1989): 359–70.

Explains the DOCLINE Interlibrary loan request routing and referral system made available to the United States biomedical libraries by the National Library of Medicine. The system permits users to create, receive, and update requests; monitor status; and receive messages and statistic reports.

LD13. Fiels, Keith, and Ronald P. Naylor, eds. *Delivery of Information and Materials between Libraries: The State of the Art.* Proceedings of the June 1990 ASCLA Multi-LINCS Pre-Conference. Chicago: Association of Specialized and Cooperative Library Agencies, American Library Association, 1991.

Includes nine of the twelve papers presented at the ASCLA Multi-LINCS preconference. Conference addressed the use of telefacsimile, van delivery, commercial delivery services, and evolving communications technology for full-text transmission.

LD14. Gadsden, S. R., and R. J. Adams. *The Administration of Interlibrary Lending by Microcomputer.* Library and Information Research Report, no. 30. Boston Spa, West Yorkshire, Eng.: British Library, 1984.

Authors describe the design and development of an interlibrary loan administration system using a standard data management software package that runs on microcomputers. The package was developed in response to a systems analysis of interlending departments and a questionnaire survey. A brief report, interesting for its analysis of functions, tasks, information needs, and flow charts of processes.

LD15. Hert, Carol Anne. "Predictors of Interlibrary Loan Turnaround Times." *Library & Information Science Research* 9 (July/Sept. 1987): 213–34.

To identify which variables have a significant effect on predicting turnaround times, the following factors were included in a model: document characteristics (publication age, language, document type, and subject), request characteristics (patron type, staffing levels, number of daily requests, and number of concurrent requests from a patron), and fulfillment group (the library or group of libraries from which the material was requested).

LD16. *Interlibrary Loan Trends: Making Access a Reality.* SPEC Kit, no. 184. Washington, D.C.: Office of Managment Services, Association of Research Libraries, 1992.

Sample documents collected from ARL libraries as a result of a survey on ILL policies and procedures. Includes brief bibliography.

LD17. Jackson, Mary E., ed. *Research Access through New Technology.* New York: AMS Press, 1989.

Comprehensive discussions on interlibrary loan and document delivery services. Series of essays intended for interlibrary loan librarians, public service administrators, and library school faculty with interest in resource sharing.

LD18. Klein, Penny, and Nancy S. Hewison. "QuickDOC: An Interlibrary Loan Department in a Microcomputer." *Medical Reference Services Quarterly* 10 (Summer 1991): 11–32.

QuickDOC, a software program, has been designed to expedite and organize the process of requesting loans, keeping records, and preparing reports on ILL activity. The software communicates with DOCLINE, the automated ILL and referral system of the National Library of Medicine, and simplifies the management of all borrowing and lending regardless of how requests are transmitted.

LD19. Lewis, Malcolm, ed. *Sets of Vocal Music: A Librarian's Guide to Interlending Practice.* Lincoln, Eng.: Archives and Documentation Centres, International Association of Music Libraries, 1989.

Prepared by a team of music librarians for library staff to obtain and supply sets of vocal music to their users in the United Kingdom.

LD20. Lingle, Virginia A., and Dorothy L. Malcom. "Interlibrary Loan Management with Microcomputers: A Descriptive Comparison of Software." *Medical Reference Services Quarterly* 8 (Summer 1989): 41–64.

Examines the use of microcomputers in managing interlibrary loan processing and record keeping. Discusses various software options ranging from using dedicated interlibrary loan management software to the development of database management programs. Descriptive profiles and sample input screens of a number of software packages are presented.

LD21. Miller, Connie, and Patricia Tegler. "An Analysis of Interlibrary Loan and Commercial Document Supply Performance." *Library Quarterly* 58 (Oct. 1988): 352–66.

Reports on a study at the University of Illinois at Chicago comparing the performance of commercial document suppliers with traditional interlibrary loans. Deals with document supply changes, locally based commercial suppliers, foreign-language materials published before 1970, technical reports, proceedings, cost, speed of supply, and success rate.

LD22. New Jersey Library Network, Committee on Policies, Procedures, and Protocols. *Final Report to the State Librarian.* Trenton, N.J.: New Jersey State Library, 1988.

The committee's work was to articulate goals and establish performance targets for three required New Jersey library network services: supplemental reference, ILL, and citation/location. Emphases were placed on output measures. The report is presented in three parts: Definitions and Performance Targets, Cost Requirement Issues, and Recommendations.

LD23. Puvogel, Cole. "Characteristics of Interlibrary Loan Usage in a Small College Library." *Journal of Interlibrary Loan & Information Supply* 1, no. 2 (1990): 46–59.

Discusses the characteristics of users of interlibrary loan at one small college library. Some of the factors examined include the number of students and faculty who use ILL, the general subject areas they request, and their willingness to pay for those materials. Student requests, in particular, were reviewed using a variety of factors. Those included were class standing, type of material requested, number of items received, and trends in usage throughout the year.

LD24. Robinson, Barbara. *Costing Question Handling and ILL/Photocopying, A Study of Two State Contract Libraries in New Jersey.* 3 vols. Trenton, N. J.: The New Jersey State Library, 1989.

This study was conducted to determine the cost to the New Jersey State Library and Newark Public Library if they were to deliver reference and interlibrary loan services to all libraries in the state. The study also considered the strategies to be used by the state in compensating the two libraries for these services. The study focused on cost alone; it did not attempt to consider the quality or efficiency of the services. Reports are presented in three volumes: 1, The Study Process, Findings, and Recommendations; 2, Annexes; and 3, The Executive Summary.

LD25. Smith, Christine H., ed. *Open Systems Interconnection: The Communications Technology of the 1990's.* Papers from the preconference seminar held at London, Aug. 12–14, 1987. IFLA Publications, no. 44. New York: K. G. Saur, 1988.

The Open Systems Interconnection (OSI) is seen as an opportunity to overcome the incompatibilities between different bibliographic utilities. OSI facilitates resource sharing among libraries and between libraries and related information sectors. Papers presented in this conference, representing many countries, deal with data interchange, document creation for interchange, implementation of library application layer protocols, and plans for OSI implementations in libraries. (*See also* KE3–KE6.)

LD26. Sweetland, James H., and Darlene E. Weingand. "Interlibrary Loan Transaction Fees in a Major Research Library: They Don't Stop the Borrowers." *Library & Information Science Research* 12 (Jan. 1990): 87–101.

An eighteen-month study of large specialized research libraries suggested that negative effects of charging for ILL are less than expected. Possible reasons for this finding are explored.

LD27. Turner, Fay. "The Interlibrary Loan Protocol: An OSI Solution to ILL Messaging." *Library Hi Tech* 8, no. 4 (1990): 73–82.

Examines the protocol that permits exchange of ILL messages between bibliographic institutions using different computer systems and communication services. Approved as a draft International Standard by the ISO.

LD28. Weaver-Meyers, Pat, Shelly Clement, and Carolyn Mahin. *Interlibrary Loan in Academic and Research Libraries: Workload and Staffing.* OMS Occasional Paper, no. 15. Washington, D.C.: Office of Management Services, Association of Research Libraries, 1988.

An overview of interlibrary loan staffing patterns based on a survey of 116 members of the Association of

Research Libraries (ARL) conducted in 1988. Reflects current technologies and services in academic and research libraries.

LD29. Weetman, Jacqui, and Barry West, eds. *Interlend '88.* Proceedings of a One-Day Seminar for Inter-Library Loans Librarians in Academic Libraries, in Association with Council of Polytechnic Librarians. June 29, 1988. Coventry Polytechnic, Eng.: Council of Polytechnic Librarians, 1988.

Addresses the questions of how the interlibrary loan service of large libraries will be able to cope with the potential of vastly increased interlibrary loan demand and compensation.

TEXTBOOKS, GUIDES, AND MANUALS

LD30. Alabama Public Library Service. *The ALIN Manual: The Alabama Public Library Service Interlibrary Loan Manual.* 2nd ed. Montgomery, Ala.: The Service, 1990.

This loose-leaf procedures manual of interlibrary loan policies is designed to assist libraries throughout Alabama requesting materials and information through Alabama Library Information Network (ALIN). Interlibrary loan between a library in Alabama and one in another state is governed by the policies set forth in the national *Interlibrary Loan Code, 1980* (*see* LD42), adopted by the American Library Association.

LD31. Alaska State Department of Education, Division of State Libraries and Archives. *Interlibrary Loan, the Key to Resource Sharing: A Manual of Procedures and Protocols.* A State-Federal Program under the Library Services and Construction Act, P.L. 91-600 as Amended. Juneau, Alaska: Division of State Libraries and Archives, Alaska State Department of Education, 1989.

Provides general guidelines for maximum utilization of library resources through interlibrary loan service in Alaska. Includes appendixes and a glossary.

LD32. Boucher, Virginia. *Interlibrary Loan Practices Handbook.* Chicago: American Library Association, 1984.

A manual describing the procedures for implementing the policies outlined in national and international interlibrary loan codes. Also addresses adherence to local interlibrary loan codes and electronic mail. Chapters cover instructions for borrowing libraries; instructions for lending libraries; interlibrary loan, reproduction, and the copyright law; dissertations and theses; interlibrary cooperation; international interlibrary loan; and management of interlibrary loan. Brief bibliographies with each chapter. Extensive appendixes include sample forms, policies, codes, and guidelines. Concludes with "Bibliography of Verification Sources."

LD33. Canadian Library Association, Interlibrary Loan Committee. *CLA/ASTED Interlibrary Loan Procedures Manual.* Ottawa, Ont.: CLA, 1989.

Revision prepared with the assistance of Association pour l'avancement des sciences et des techniques de la documentation (ASTED) and adopted officially by the Canadian Library Association (CLA), this manual is for the use of libraries conducting interlibrary loan service under the terms of CLA/ASTED ILL Code. Each library should develop its own internal procedures to carry out the procedures outlined in this document.

LD34. Cornish, Graham P. *Model Handbook for Interlending and Copying.* Boston Spa, West Yorkshire, Eng.: Office for International Lending, International Federation of Library Associations and Institutions, 1988.

Serves as a useful model in the preparation of a handbook for a particular situation but is not a set of detailed instructions on how to operate interlibrary loan functions in a given situation. Recommends steps to be taken by the requesting library and the source library. It also considers international interlibrary loan requests. Appendixes include a selected bibliography, a model code, and a guideline for procedures.

LD35. Research Libraries Group. *RLG Shared Resources Manual.* 4th ed. Mountain View, Calif.: RLG, 1992.

This manual represents contributions from the RLG Public Service Committee, Central Staff, and all RLG member institutions. Produced in loose-leaf form to facilitate updating. Chapters 5–7 are dedicated to ILL networks, borrowing and lending, and photocopying. The first edition (1982) was based on an earlier RLG publication, *Shared Resources: Interlibrary Loan and On-Site Access,* volume 2 of the *Public Service Manual,* May 1980.

LD36. Talley, Marica D., and Virginia A. McNitt. *Automating the Library with askSam: A Practical Handbook.* Westport, Conn.: Meckler, 1991.

Conceived in 1983, askSam is a text-oriented database management system for personal computers from askSam Systems. Chapter 6 of this handbook deals with borrowing file, directory file, and lending file of interlibrary loan.

DIRECTORIES

LD37. Barwick, Margaret M., comp. and ed. *A Guide to Centres of International Lending and Copying.* 4th ed. Boston Spa, West Yorkshire, Eng.: IFLA Office of International Lending, and The British Library Document Supply Centre, 1990.

A handy reference work for those actively involved in international lending. The first edition appeared in 1975 under the title *A Brief Guide to Centres of International Lending and Photocopying.* Information contained in this guide was gathered by means of a questionnaire. This edition includes 140 countries. Entries are arranged alphabetically according to the English name of the country.

LD38. British Library Document Supply Centre. *Inter-Regional Transport Scheme: Directory and Operating Instruc-*

tions. Boston Spa, West Yorkshire, Eng.: The Centre, 1989.

Based on the British Library Document Supply Centre's own record, this directory of British libraries with their full addresses and telephone numbers is compiled to aid users of the interregional scheme of document delivery. A transport scheme mnemonic code is provided and an alphabetical index by user name is included.

LD39. Jones, C. Lee, ed. *The Library Fax Directory: Directory of Telefacsimile Sites in North American Libraries.* 7th ed. Bethlehem, Pa.: C. B. R. Consulting Services, Inc. 1992.

This seventh edition lists 4,898 sites in Canada, Mexico, and the United States. Entries arranged alphabetically by state or province and, within each, by the name of the library. Gives addresses, fax numbers, contacts, and phone numbers.

LD40. Morris, Leslie R., and Sandra Chass Morris. *Interlibrary Loan Policies Directory.* 4th ed. New York: Neal-Schuman Publishers, 1991.

A comprehensive tool for finding, reviewing, and comparing the ILL policies of libraries throughout the United States, Puerto Rico, and Canada. Useful to libraries that participate in computerized interlibrary loan services as well as to smaller libraries with no electronic access to this information. Provides information on lending books, periodicals, newspapers, dissertations and theses, government documents, microforms, audiovisual materials, and computer software.

LD41. National Library of Canada, comp. *Interlibrary Loan Directory.* 5th ed., 1989– . Ottawa, Ont.: The Canadian Library Association.

Includes most of the libraries currently listed in the National Library of Canada's annual publication *Interlibrary Loan Services Manual: Symbols of Canadian Libraries* and in PEB/ILL, the National Library's automated interlibrary loan system. This edition consists of a main records section and two indexes: library name index and Utlas WHO code lists. It is updated semiannually through cumulating supplements.

STANDARDS AND GUIDELINES

LD42. American Library Association, Interlibrary Loan Committee, and International Federation of Library Associations and Institutions, Section on Interlending. *Interlibrary Loan Codes, 1980, and International Lending Principles and Guidelines, 1978.* Chicago: ALA, 1981.

Includes "Model Interlibrary Loan Code for Regional, State, Local, or Other Special Groups of Libraries," "The National Interlibrary Loan Code, 1980," and "International Lending: Principles and Guidelines for Procedure (1978)." Endorsed by the board of directors of the ALA Reference and Adult Services Division in June 1980, this "model code" is intended to provide guidelines for any group of libraries interested in developing an interlibrary loan code to meet special needs. The National Interlibrary

Loan Code adopted by the ALA Reference and Adult Services Division in 1980 is designed primarily to regulate lending relations between research libraries and between libraries operating outside network or consortia. The International Lending Principles and Guidelines prepared by the IFLA Office for International Lending was reproduced in this document for dissemination and feedback.

LD43. *Guidelines and Procedures for Telefacsimile Transmission of Interlibrary Loan Requests.* Chicago: Reference and Adult Services Division, American Library Association, 1990.

A two-page leaflet covering telefacsimile transmission of ILL requests. Reprinted from *RQ*, Winter 1990.

LD44. *Guidelines for Borrowing Special Collections Materials for Exhibition.* Chicago: Association of College and Research Libraries, American Library Association, May 1990.

Includes guidelines for requesting and handling the loan and suggestions for lending institutions. Provides a model for a loan agreement form. Guidelines were approved by the ALA Standards Committee at the 1990 ALA Annual Conference and were first publshed in *College & Research Libraries News*, May 1990.

LD45. *Guidelines for Packing and Shipping Microforms.* Chicago: Association for Library Collections & Technical Services, American Library Association, 1989.

A single-page leaflet providing packing and shipping guidelines.

LD46. National Information Standards Organization (U.S.). *Interlibrary Loan Data Elements: American National Standard for Interlibrary Loan Data Elements.* New Brunswick, N.J.: Transaction Publishers, 1990. ANSI/NISO Z39.63-1989.

The objective of this standard is to guide library practitioners and system designers in identifying and presenting data elements used in ILL transactions. It identifies the data elements that must be communicated to ensure efficient and accurate transactions between borrowers and lenders and is applicable to all types of libraries.

BIBLIOGRAPHIES

LD47. "Bibliography of Interlending and Document Supply." *Interlending & Document Supply* 7– , Apr. and Oct. 1979– .

Appearing semiannually in *Interlending & Document Supply*, the bibliography is based on a review of recent literature. Selections are made by scanning relevant secondary services, as well as professional journals.

LD48. Cornish, Graham P., comp. *Cumulative Bibliography on Interlending & Document Supply.* Boston Spa, West Yorkshire, Eng.: Office for International Lending, International Federation of Library Associations and Institutions, 1989.

First appeared in 1979 in *Interlibrary & Document Supply* and continues to appear in this journal twice a year. Not an exhaustive bibliography; includes major papers (in several languages), monographs, and report literature. In 1986 the IFLA Office for International Lending provided a computerized subject and geographical approach to this file through The British Library Document Supply Centre microcomputers. Inquiries for subject search are welcomed, but charges may be made for extensive searches.

LD49. "Interlending and Document Delivery: A Review of Recent Literature." *Interlending & Document Supply* 10– , Jan. and July 1982–   .

Literature reviews by various authors of various aspects of interlibrary loan and document delivery services. It has appeared semiannually since 1982.

LD50. Line, Maurice Bernard. *Line on Interlending: Selected Papers on Interlending and Document Supply*, edited by Graham P. Cornish. Boston Spa, West Yorkshire, Eng.: British Library Document Supply Centre, 1988.

Includes papers of Maurice Line on interlending, a list of his works from 1972 through 1988, and his biography.

LD51. Ozaki, Hiroko. *Interlibrary Loan: A Bibliography, 1982-1987.* Ottawa, Ont.: Library Documentation Center, National Library of Canada, 1987.

Includes general works, automation, policies, procedures, handbooks, and directories. Part II is devoted to Canadian publications and part III to publications of other countries.

LE
Document Delivery

A major element of interlibrary loan services, document delivery deals with the movement, both in hard copy and in electronic format, of materials from suppliers to requesters. Document lending and borrowing takes place directly between libraries involved in the ILL transaction or via commercial or noncommercial document services.

One of the major suppliers of materials to American libraries is the British Library Lending Division, which operates a document supply service. Unlike in the United States, where document delivery is operated on a decentralized basis, in the United Kingdom this service is highly centralized and relies heavily on a single source.

Major U.S. suppliers include both libraries and commercial delivery firms. Among them: Center for Research Libraries; CARL UnCover2; Chemical Ab-

stracts Service; Data Courier; Federal Document Retrieval; Free Library of Philadelphia; Infoquest; Information on Demand; Institute for Scientific Information; Linda Hall Library; Los Angeles Public Library; National Library of Medicine; OCLC ContentsFirst and ArticleFirst; Research Library Group Ariel and CitaDel; Warner-Eddison Associates; Wisconsin Interlibrary Loan Service; and Universities of Arizona, Minnesota, and Washington.

Libraries rely primarily on the U.S. Postal Service for the physical delivery of a document. Other options are library-sponsored delivery services and commercial courier services, such as Federal Express and United Parcel Service. Notable among statewide library-operated services are those of Connecticut and Pennsylvania.

The electronic delivery technologies include telefacsimile, electronic distribution of machine-readable full text, and document images to remote locations from centralized databanks. A prediction in a comprehensive study sponsored by the Council on Library Resources (*Document Delivery in the United States*, LE4) suggested that electronic delivery would not be likely to replace U.S. mail, couriers, and truck delivery systems within the foreseeable future. Electronic delivery has not yet been used extensively by libraries in the United States as a regular method for document delivery, though several test projects are under way. However, perhaps due to the reduction of its cost, the use of telefacsimile has increased.

LE1. Adams, Roy J. *Communication and Delivery Systems for Librarians.* Aldershot, Hants, Eng., and Brookfield, Vt.: Gower Publishing, 1990.

An extensive look at the possibilities that new information and communication technologies hold for libraries. While coverage is much broader than document delivery technologies, this work is an excellent overview and introduction to the whole area of communications technology. Addresses wide-area and local-area networks, social implications of communications technologies, library applications, possible future scenarios, and related topics. Useful glossary.

LE2. Bennett, Valerie M., Sandra M. Wood, and Dorothy L. Malcom. "Criteria-Based Evaluation of Group 3 Level Memory Telefacsimile Equipment for Interlibrary Loan." *Bulletin of the Medical Library Association* 78 (Apr. 1990): 131–39.

This equipment evaluation groups ninety-six hardware features of group 3 telefacsimile equipment into nine broad criteria. Group 3 is the present generation of telefacsimile equipment now in use in libraries. These features formed the basis of a weighted analysis that identified three final candidates, with one model recommended to the Health Science Libraries Consortium (HSLC) of nineteen libraries in Pennsylvania. This article details each of the criteria and discusses features in terms of library applications. The evaluation grid developed in the weighted analysis process should aid librarians charged with the selection of group 3 telefacsimile equipment.

LE3. Boss, Richard W., and Hal Espo. "The Use of Telefacsimile in Libraries." *Library Hi Tech* 5 (Spring 1987): 33–42.

Three issues on adoption of telefacsimile to improve document delivery are discussed: need, copyright, and cost. Covers the use of telefacsimile in libraries through 1986.

LE4. Boss, Richard W., and Judy McQueen. *Document Delivery in the United States: A Report to the Council on Library Resources.* Washington, D.C.: The Council, 1983.

Provides an overview of interlibrary loan, information about major suppliers, analysis of performance of the ILL system, and suggested potential for electronic document delivery. Authors identified trends they expected to develop over the 1980s. Clearly, this publication is a snapshot of the period in which it was written. This report is included here because it is often cited and because many of the authors' assumptions remain valid.

LE5. Braid, Andrew. "Developments in Facsimile and Document Delivery." In *Telecommunications for Information Management and Transfer*, Proceedings of the First International Conference held at Leicester Polytechnic, Apr. 1987, edited by Mel Collier, 174–86. Aldershot, Hants, Eng., and Brookfield, Vt.: Gower Publishing, 1988.

Includes discussions of principles of facsimile transmission; history of facsimile transmission; requirements of a document delivery system; and the British Library Document Supply Centre (BLDSC) plans for electronic document delivery, document scanning, and future developments.

LE6. Brown, Steven Allan. "Telefacsimile in Libraries: New Deal in the 1980s." *Library Trends* 37 (Winter 1989): 343–56.

Discusses telefacsimile technology and its applications for interlibrary loan, document retrieval, and reference services. Speed and cost of service are examined.

LE7. Campbell, Robert M., and Barrie T. Stern. "ADONIS—A New Approach to Document Delivery." *Microcomputers for Information Management* 4 (June 1987): 87–107.

Describes technical and practical aspects of a document delivery system in which materials are stored on optical disks and printed on demand. Copyright problems are reviewed.

LE8. Cawkell, A. E. *A Survey of Imaging Processing and Document Delivery Technology.* British Library Research Paper, 28. Boston Spa, West Yorkshire, Eng.: The British Library Document Supply Centre, 1987.

Includes a detailed examination of cathode ray tube displays and printers and discusses scanning systems, pattern recognition systems, and storage arrangements. The last section of the survey is a description of several major exper-

imental delivery systems, including those of the Library of Congress and the National Library of Medicine.

LE9. Cleveland, Gary. *Electronic Document Delivery: Converging Standards and Technologies.* UDT Series on Data Communication Technologies and Standards, Report no. 2. Ottawa, Ont.: Universal Dataflow and Telecommunications, International Federation of Library Associations and Institutions, 1991.

A study that describes clearly the elements involved in computerized document delivery. Considers technologies, standards, copyright, and bibliographic control. Describes several active electronic document delivery projects.

LE10. Cornish, Graham P. "The British Library Document Supply Centre: A Unique Institution." *Journal of Interlibrary Loan & Information Supply* 1, no. 2 (1990): 27–39.

Discusses functions, collections, structures, and services of the British Library Document Delivery Centre in Boston Spa, West Yorkshire, England.

LE11. Ensign, David. "Copyright Considerations for Telefacsimile Transmission of Documents in Interlibrary Loan Transactions." *Law Library Journal* 81 (Fall 1989): 805–12.

Suggests that making two reproductions in the process of interlibrary loan transactions is not an infringement on the rights of reproduction and distribution reserved to copyright holders when analyzed in terms of fair use, library reproduction, interlibrary loan guidelines, and technological considerations.

LE12. Kent, A. L., K. Merry, and D. Russon. *The Use of Serials in Document Delivery Systems in Europe and the U.S.A.* Paris: International Council for Scientific and Technical Information, 1987.

The study compares usage patterns among several document delivery centers and discusses ways of using the data it incorporates. The participating international document supply centers include British Library Document Supply Centre (BLDSC)–U.K.; Chemical Abstracts Services (CAS)–U.S.A.; Centre de Documentation Scientifique et Technique (CDST)–France; National Library of Medicine (NLM)–U.S.A.; and OCLC–U.S.A.

LE13. Leach, Ronald G., and Judith E. Tribble. "Electronic Document Delivery: New Options for Libraries." *The Journal of Academic Librarianship* 18, no. 6 (1993): 359–64.

Authors examine several remote and on-site access sytems: Carl UnCover 2, Faxon Finder and Faxon Xpress, OCLC's ContentsFirst and ArticleFirst, RLG's CitaDel, UMI's ProQuest MultiAccess Systems, and Adonis. They suggest five evaluative criteria for selecting a system.

LE14. *Measuring the Performance of Document Supply Systems.* Prepared by the IFLA International Office for UAP. Paris: General Information Programme and UNISIST, UNESCO, 1987.

Prepared by Maurice B. Line, under a contract with IFLA. This manual can be applied in a wide range of countries. It describes the factors affecting demand for document supply and the nature of performance measures. Principal measures discussed include the proportion of document requests that are met; speed of requesting, processing, and supplying; and user satisfaction.

LF
Patron Behavior

The public has traditionally viewed the library as a quiet, comfortable, and safe place conducive to study and reading. But today the reality seems to be somewhat different, especially in public libraries. Anyone is free to enter a public library, no identification is required, and no questions are asked about the purpose of the visit. Public libraries tend to be in population centers, open a long day, and climate-controlled; they have comfortable seating. These factors attract both "serious" users and people who may disturb the study environment and even threaten the safety of library users and staff. In 1984, Bruce Shuman (*River Bend Revisited: The Problem Patron in the Library*, LF4) categorized "problem patrons" in five classes: (1) eccentric behavior: patrons who talk to themselves, gesture nonthreateningly at other library patrons or staff, hum, wear bizarre clothing, etc.; (2) mental illness; (3) noncompliance with library rules; (4) harassment of library staff or other patrons; (5) intentional misbehavior, which includes physical violence, destruction and mutilation of materials, and assaults on the physical building. See LG, following, for resources dealing with security, theft, and mutilation.

There are also those who come to the library to sleep, whose body odors offend nearby patrons and staff, and who rant or complain loudly. In dealing with each incident, librarians must somehow balance the comfort and safety of their well-behaved patrons with their mission of access for all. The literature on patron behavior is filled with suggestions about appropriate library staff responses and protection measures, such as closed-circuit television, plainclothes guards, alarms, and communication links with police. In the final analysis, each library can provide only the protection it can afford. Although school, college, and university libraries generally serve homogeneous patron groups and function within a controlled environment, they are not free from most of these behavioral problems.

LF1. Greater Victoria Public Library. *Problem Patron Manual.* Victoria, B.C.: The Library, 1990.

Deals with disruptive behavior of children and adults, harassment, assault, drinking, drugs, the emotionally/mentally disturbed, panhandlers, sexual deviants, the mutilation of library materials, vandalism, and theft.

LF2. Salter, Charles A., and Jeffrey L. Salter. *On the Frontlines: Coping with the Library's Problem Patrons.* Englewood, Colo.: Libraries Unlimited, 1988.

Begins with the description of twenty-four actual cases and then discusses causes and types of mental illness, how to prepare for and confront a problem patron, and the training for successful problem coping. Includes sources of help for librarians and appendixes, a bibliography, and an index.

LF3. Shuman, Bruce A. "Problem Patrons in Libraries, A Review Article." *Library & Archival Security* 9, no. 2 (1989): 3–18.

A discussion of various factors related to patron behavior, followed by a review of selected recent literature on the subject. The emphasis is on public libraries.

LF4. ———. *River Bend Revisited: The Problem Patron in the Library.* Phoenix: Oryx Press, 1984.

Presents forty case studies of problem situations that might arise in public libraries and provides questions for discussion but no definitive answers. Intended for use in workshops, training programs, and graduate programs. An excellent starting point for developing an emergency policy and procedures manual in all types of libraries.

BIBLIOGRAPHIES

LF5. Dole, Wanda W. *The Literature of Library Violence, 1959–1989: An Annotated Bibliography.* Vance Bibliographies, Public Administration Series: Bibliography, P-2892. Monticello, Ill.: Vance Bibliographies, 1990.

A literature review concerning problem patrons and disruptive behavior in libraries. Includes causes of such behavior and suggested solutions. Fully annotated and arranged by subject.

LG
Security, Theft, and Mutilation

The theft and mutilation of materials are devastating problems for libraries. Untold thousands of pages of mutilated journals and books have to be replaced annually. The cost is high, and limited library budgets cannot withstand these additional expenses. Library crime represents much more than financial loss: If irreplaceable books and unique manuscripts are stolen, the library community is deprived of these resources forever.

Library security goes far beyond concern with the loss of precious items. It embraces a host of other problems, ranging from petty vandalism to bomb threats, from minor verbal abuse to physical attack and violence. A 1989 ARL survey (LG2) divided library security into three major areas: (1) general building security—access to the building, distribution of keys, patrols or monitors, intrusion prevention, lighting, work environment after dark; (2) problem behavior—noise, disorderly conduct, abusive and/or criminal behavior; and (3) emergencies—power outage, bomb threat, fire, natural disaster. See section LF for resources on patron behavior.

Administrators place the human-safety factor high in their security program priorities. Librarians in charge of public services, as skillful as they may be, should not be expected to cope with the full range of library security problems.

In a large, busy library, human-guard systems cannot be entirely effective; electronic security systems may provide a better result. The literature is filled with information on the evaluation of various systems. Since the needs of libraries are different, no one system is recommended as suitable for all libraries.

(*See also* the section on Disaster Control, Recovery, and Insurance in Chapter I, Preservation.)

LG1. Beisler, Lynn, and others. "Emerson College Library Security Guidelines." *Library & Archival Security* 10, no. 1 (1990): 43–54.

Includes security of library building; security at the circulation desk; and security for patrons, staff, and equipment. Discusses measures used in Emerson College in Massachusetts related to opening and closing the building, locking the front door, general security and alarm systems, problem patrons and theft-detection systems, and media and computer equipment.

LG2. Bingham, Karen Havill, comp. *Building Security and Personnel Safety.* SPEC Kit, no. 150. Washington, D.C.: Office of Management Services, Association of Research Libraries, 1989.

A compilation of internal documents dealing with general security at various U.S. universities. Covers responsibility of security personnel, building security policies and procedures, problem behavior policies, and emergency procedures. Includes a selected reading list.

LG3. Harrison Bahr, Alice. "Electronic Collection Security Systems Today: Changes and Choices." *Library & Archival Security* 11, no. 1 (1991): 3–22.

Looks at the growing number of operational possibilities for electronic security systems, how gradual system development brought them about, and the new questions they pose about how to select systems.

LG4. _____. "Library Security Information and National Institute of Justice Clearinghouses." *Library & Archival Security* 10 (1990): 59–66.

Discusses the services and resources offered by the National Criminal Justice Reference Service (NCJRS) that are of use to librarians seeking information about library thefts, security programs, and electronic security systems.

LG5. *Insuring Library Collections and Buildings.* SPEC Kit, no. 178. Washington, D.C.: Office of Management Services, Association of Research Libraries, 1991.

For annotation, *see* IF12.

LG6. Jackanicz, Donald W. "Theft at the National Archives: The Murphy Case, 1962–1975." *Library & Archival Security* 10, no. 2 (1990): 23–50.

Studies the Murphy case as an example of archival thievery on a grand scale. This large theft of documents from the National Archives in Washington forced that institution to reconsider its methods of monitoring researcher access to facilities and documents.

LG7. Lilly, Roy S., Barbara F. Schloman, and Wendy Lin Hu. "Ripoffs Revisited: Periodical Mutilation in a University Research Library." *Library & Archival Security* 11, no. 1 (1991): 43–70.

Reports on a survey at Kent State University in Kent, Ohio, to determine the extent of students' experiences regarding mutilated periodicals and their attitudes toward mutilation and other aspects of the library. Discusses implications of the results for library action and future research.

LG8. Lincoln, Alan Jay. "Computer Security." *Library & Archival Security* 11, no. 1 (1991): 157–71.

Looks at security problems of computers in libraries. Suggests that microcomputers are highly vulnerable to theft and damage and that security planning should include policies to cover personnel, physical security, and response to security violations.

LG9. _____. "Library Legislation Related to Crime and Security." *Library & Archival Security* 10, no. 2 (1990): 77–101.

Presents examples of legislation focused on protecting the library from theft and other security-related offenses.

LG10. _____. "Library Legislation Related to Crime and Security, Part Two." *Library & Archival Security* 11, no. 1 (1991): 71–101.

Presents legislation from individual U.S. states relating to the theft or mutilation of library materials.

LG11. _____, **ed.** "Protecting the Library." *Library Trends* 33, no. 1 (Summer 1984): 1–94.

Examines a full range of issues related to protecting the library—from the causes and impact of crime to physical and legislative measures for preventing and controlling it. Eight authors contributed articles to this special issue.

LG12. _____. "Vandalism: Causes, Consequences and Prevention." *Library & Archival Security*. 9, nos. 3/4 (1990): 37–61.

A discussion of the meaning of vandalism is followed by an examination of why vandalism may be tolerated in some situations. The author describes several vandalism types and motives and stresses the importance of group support. Patterns of vandalism are presented for both the nation as a whole and for public libraries. The author examines several options for reducing and preventing vandalism.

LG13. Saulmon, Sharon A. "Book Security System Use and Costs in Southwest Public Libraries." *Library & Archival Security* 88 (Fall/Winter 1988): 25–35.

Reports on a survey to assess the use of book-security systems in large public libraries in the Southwest. The survey showed that the majority did have a security system and only a few breakdowns were reported. False alarms caused some public relation problems. Formalized cost-benefit analyses typically had not been conducted.

LG14. Scherdin, Mary Jane. "Security Systems Protect Audiovisual Materials." *Library & Archival Security* 11, no. 1 (1991): 23–34.

Suggests that audiovisual materials can be protected with security systems traditionally used for books; smaller targets can be placed directly on media. Indicates that low-level magnetic fields can be used to deactivate and reactivate targets without damaging the contents of magnetic media.

LG15. Treadwell, Jane. "Determining a Fair Price for Lost Books: A Case Study." *Library & Archival Security* 9, no. 1 (1989): 19–26.

For annotation, *see* LB11.

LG16. Tryon, Jonathan S. "Premises Liability for Librarians." *Library & Archival Security*. 10, no. 2 (1990): 3–21.

Informs the library administrator of the law of negligence as it applies to premises liability. Covers what care is owed to whom, the concept of negligence, the obligation to protect patrons from crimes or other harms of third parties, the risks involved in protecting library property, and some of the defenses to the tort of negligence.

Author/Title Index

The index is arranged according to the *ALA Filing Rules* except that numbers are filed as if spelled out, and & is filed as if spelled *and*. Initial articles have been omitted from titles.

Some persons and organizations listed in the index have served as authors, compilers, and editors. The titles by these entities are subarranged alphabetically without regard to the "comp." and "ed." designations. However, titles for which where are joint authors are filed after those of single authorship (or compilership or editorship), and the authors are arranged alphabetically by the surname of the second author (or compiler or editor). Titles by the same group of joint authors (or compilers or editors) are subarranged alphabetically.

For specific Divisions, Committees, or Round Tables within the American Library Association, *see* that specific name.

G

Gadsden, S. R., and R. J. Adams. *Administration of Interlibrary Lending by Microcomputer*, LD14

Gale Directory of Databases, FAF2

Gale Directory of Publications and Broadcast Media, GAB2

Galejs, J. E. "Economics of Serials Exchanges," BE8

Ganzmann, J. "Criteria for the Evaluation of Thesaurus Software," FE4

Gapen, D. K. *Simplification of the MARC Format*, KBE3

"Gaping Black Hole in the Bibliographic Universe," P. Frantz, FB14

Garcia, C. R., and F. R. Bridge. *Small Libraries Online*, LC12

Garfield, E. *Citation Indexing: Its Theory and Application in Science, Technology, and Humanities*, FAD12

Garlick, K., and M. A. Smith. *Materials at Risk*, IK6

Garnett, A. "Worm's Eye View of the Out-of-print Market," BD5

Garnett, T. "Development of an Authority Control System for the Smithsonian Institution Libraries," EE8

Garrison, W. A. "Practical Considerations in Using the Machine-Readable LCSH," EC9

Gatenby, J. "Analysis of the Justification for New Filing Rules," FAB6

Gaunt, M. I. "Machine-Readable Literary Texts," HD27

Gay and Lesbian Library Service, C. Gough and E. Greenblatt, eds., HD11

"Geac Acquisitions System as a Source of Management Information," C. P. Hawks, BC10

Geiser, E. A., and A. Dolin. *Business of Book Publishing*, BH4

Gellatly, P., ed. *Good Serials Department*, GB6

Geller, S. B. *Care and Handling of Computer Magnetic Storage Media*, IID3

Genaway, D. C. "Administering the Allocated Acquisitions Budget," HG3

Genzel, P., ed. *Studies in the International Exchange of Publications*, BE9

"Geographic Indexing for Bibliographic Databases," L. L. Hill, FC4

Gertz, J., and L. J. Stout. "MARC Archival and Manuscripts Control (AMC) Format," KBE7

Gesellschaft für Information und Dokumentation. *Thesaurus Guide*, DD34, FAE3

"Getting Started in Computerized Indexing," K. P. Jones, FF9

Getty Art History Information Program, DD39

Getty Conservation Institute Newsletter, IAG11

Getz, M. "Electronic Library," HAG3

———. "Electronic Publishing," GC8

——— and D. Phelps. "Labor Costs in the Technical Operation of Three Research Libraries," AHB5

Gibb, I. P., ed. *Newspaper Preservation and Access*, IIG2

Gibbs, G. E. "Applying Format Integration," KBE17

——— and D. Bisom. "Creating an Interactive Authority File for Names in the UCLA ORION System," EE9

"Gifts and Block Purchases," W. W. Dole, BE7

Gifts and Exchange Function in ARL Libraries, J. V. Nilson, comp., BE13

Gifts and Exchange Manual, A. H. Lane, BE11

"Gifts and Exchange Operations," M. T. Reid, B14

"Gifts and Exchanges," J. W. Barker, BE3

"Gifts and Exchanges," M. Clark, BE5

"Gifts and Exchanges," R. M. Magrill and J. Corbin, BE12

"Gifts and Exchanges in U.S. Academic Libraries," M. Kovacic, BE10

"Gifts—The Answer to a Problem," T. C. White, J. M. Morgan, and G. A. Gordon, BE18

Gilchrist, A., and D. Strachan, eds. *UDC: Essays for the New Decade*, DC27

Gill, S. L. *File Management and Information Retrieval Systems*, FAD13

Gilman, L. B. "Scholarly Publishing Imbroglio," GF7

Gilroy, J. "Expert System for Classification," DD50

Ginneken, J. van. *770 Articles and Books on Serials*, GAC1

Glaister, G. A. *Glaister's Glossary of the Book*, BAC2

Glaister's Glossary of the Book, G. A. Glaister, BAC2

Glazier, E. "Bibliographic Utilities and the Automation of Authority Files," EF6

Gleason, M. L. "Training Collection Development Librarians," HB17

——— and R. C. Miller. "Technical Services: Direction or Coordination?" AH14

"Global Change Capabilities to Improve Authority Control in an Online Catalog," J. A. Fox and K. Kanafani, EE7

Glogoff, S., and J. P. Flynn. "Developing a Systematic In-House Training Program for Integrated Library Systems," AHD7

Glossary of Imaging Technology, Association for Information and Image Management, JAB1

Glossary of Indexing Terms, B. Buchanan, FAE1

Glossary of Micrographics, JAB1

Glossary of Reprography and Non-impact Printing Terms for the Paper and Printing Industries, Technical Association of the Pulp and Paper Industry, Printing and Imaging Committee, JAB3

Godden, I. P., ed. *Library Technical Services: Operations and Management*, AA4

———, K. W. Fachan, and P. Smith, comps. *Collection Development and Acquisitions 1970–1980*, HAB3

Goehner, D. M. "Vendor-Library Relations," BI4

Goldman, H., and C. Havens. "Authority Control Efficiency Increase," EE10

——— and D. M. Smith. "Name Authority in a NOTIS Environment—Auburn University Libraries," EE11

Good Serials Department, P. Gellatly, ed., GB6

Goode's World Atlas E. B. Espenshade, ed., CCB10

Gordon, P. L., ed. *Book of Film Care*, IIF3

Gorman, G. E., and B. R. Howes. *Collection Development for Libraries*, HAA3

——— and J. J. Mills. "Evaluating Third World National Bibliographies as Selection Resources," HD38

Gorman, M. "Authority Control in the Prospective Catalog," EE12

———. *Concise AACR2*, CBC1

———. "Fear of Filing," FAB7

——— and Associates. *Technical Services Today and Tomorrow*, AA5

——— and P. Winkler, eds. *Anglo-American Cataloging Rules*, North American Text, CBA3

——— ——— eds. *Anglo-American Cataloguing Rules*, 2nd ed., CBA4

Letters for the International Exchange of Publications, A. Allardyce, BE1

Leung, C. H. C. "Architecture of an Image Database System," FC6

_____ and others. "Retrieval by Content in an Image Database," FC7

Lewis, M., ed. *Sets of Vocal Music*, LD19

Libbey, M. C., ed. "Education for Technical Services," AA9

Librarian's CD-ROM Handbook, N. Desmarais, JAE3

Librarians Collection Letter, HAD6

Libraries and Archives, S. G. Swartzburg and H. Bussey, IG16

Libraries and Expert Systems, C. McDonald and J. Weckert, eds., AHC12

Libraries, Erotica, Pornography, M. Cornog, ed., HD9

"Library Acquisitions and the Antiquarian/OP Book Trade," J. Fouts, BD4

Library Acquisitions: Practice and Theory, BAD6, HAD7

Library Adminstration and Management Association (ALA), LAC3

Library and Archival Disaster, IF6

Library & Archival Security, IAG15, LAB3

Library and Archives Conservation, G. M. Cunha and D. G. Cunha, IAD4

Library and Information Services Today, FAI4

Library and Information Technology Association (ALA), AGA5, JAH4, KAB5

_____ /ALCTS CCS Authority Control in the Online Environment Interest Group, EAF1

_____ /ALCTS MARC Format for Holdings Interest Group, KAB6

_____ /ALCTS Retrospective Conversion Interest Group, KAB7

_____ National Conference, AGB5

"Library Applications of Knowledge-Based Systems," J. M. A. Cavanagh, AHC5

"Library Approval Plans," G. J. Rossi, BB16

Library Binding, IB4

Library Binding Institute Standard for Library Binding, P. A. Parisi and J. Merrill-Oldham, eds., IB9

Library Bookseller, BAD7

Library Cataloging and Authorities Discussion Group *see* AUTOCAT

Library Circulation Systems and Automation, LC20

Library Conservation, J. P. Baker and M. C. Soroka, eds., IAI2

Library Conservation News, IAG16

Library Cooperation and Networks, A. Woodsworth, CAD4

"Library Development," D. Burlingame, ed., HG20

Library Disaster Preparedness Handbook, J. Morris, IF8

Library Fax Directory, C. L. Jones, ed., LD39

Library Forms Illustrated Handbook, E. Futas, AE2

Library Hi Tech, AF12, CAE7, KAA8

Library Hi Tech News, CAE8

"Library Legislation Related to Crime and Security," A. J. Lincoln, LG9

"Library Legislation Related to Crime and Security, Part Two," A. J. Lincoln, LG10

"Library Management and Emerging Technology," S. K. Martin, AH30

"Library Management and Technical Services," J. S. Cargill, ed., AH7

Library Manager's Guide to Automation, R. W. Boss, AH4

Library, Media, and Archival Preservation Glossary, J. N. DePew with C. L. Jones, IAB1

Library, Media, and Archival Preservation Handbook, J. N. DePew, IAE1

"Library of Congress: A More-Than-Equal Partner," W. J. Welsh, ID13

Library of Congress Catalog, Motion Pictures and Filmstrips, CCA6

Library of Congress, Catalog Publication Division. *CD MARC Names*, CCB1, EAC1

_____ _____ *Name Authorities.* Cumulative Microform Edition, CCB2, EAC3

_____ _____ *Name Authorities.* [database on magnetic tape], EAC2

_____ *Cataloging Service Bulletin*, CAE4, CBC10, DAC2, EAE3

_____ *Cataloging Service Bulletin Index 1–56*, N. B. Olson, comp., CBC13

_____ *Index to the Library of Congress Service Bulletin, 1–120*, N. B. Olson, comp., CB12

Library of Congress Classification, Library of Congress, Subject Cataloging Division, DC22

Library of Congress Classification—Additions and Changes, Library of Congress, Subject Cataloging Division, DC23

"Library of Congress Classification and the Computer," N. J. Williamson, FB36

"Library of Congress Classification Numbers as Subject Access Points in Computer-based Retrieval," W. H. High, FB17

Library of Congress Classification Schedules Combined with Additions and Changes through 1991, Library of Congress, DC20

"Library of Congress Classification System in an Online Environment," L. M. Chan, FB7

" 'Library of Congress Classification System in an Online Environment': A Reaction," J. D. Saye, FB28

Library of Congress Filing Rules, Library of Congress, Processing Services, FAB9

Library of Congress Information Bulletin, EAE8

Library of Congress. *Library of Congress Classification Schedules Combined with Additions and Changes through 1991*, DC20

_____ Network Development and MARC Standards Office. *Content-Enriched and Enhanced Subject Access in USMARC Records*, FB20

_____ _____ *Enhancing USMARC Records with Table of Contents*, FB21

_____ Office for Subject Cataloging Policy. *Free-Floating Subdivisions*, DD19

_____ _____ *LC Classification Outline*, DC21

_____ _____ *LC Period Subdivisions under Names of Places*, DD9

_____ _____ *LC Subject Headings: Weekly Lists*, DD10, EAC4

_____ _____ *Subject Cataloging Manual: Subject Headings*, DD20

Library of Congress Optical Disk Pilot Program, Optical Disk Print Pilot Project, A. Fischer and T. Swora, JH12

Library of Congress, Photoduplication Service. *Specifications for Microfilming Manuscripts*, JI23

_____ _____ *Specifications for Microfilming of Books and Pamphlets in the Library of Congress*, JI24

_____ Processing Services. *Library of Congress Filing Rules*, FAB9

Library of Congress Romanization Tables, CBC8

Library of Congress Rule Interpretations, CBC11, EAE5

Library of Congress Subject Authority Control, Association for Library Collections and Technical Services, Cataloging and Classification Section, Subject Analysis Committee, Ad Hoc Subcommittee on Library of Congress Authority Control: Scope, Format, and Distribution, EC1

Manual of AACR2 Examples for Liturgical Works and Sacred Scriptures, J. D. Kellen, CBD45

Manual of AACR2 Examples for Technical Reports, E. Swanson, CBD46

Manual of European Languages for Librarians, C. G. Allen, CCB5

Map Cataloging Manual, CBD11

Map Librarianship, M. L. Larsgaard, IIC3

MARBI *see* Association for Library Collections and Technical Services/LITA/RASD Committee on Machine-Readable Bibliographic Information

MARC *see also* Machine Readable Cataloging

"MARC Archival and Manuscript Control (AMC) Format," J. Gertz and L. J. Stout, KBE7

"MARC Compatibility," D. S. McPherson, KBC5

MARC for Library Use, W. Crawford, CBD3, KBC3

"MARC Format Integration and Seriality," K. G. Evans, KBE16

"MARC Format on Tape," M. I. Dalehite, KC45

MARC Manual, D. J. Byrne, CBD2

"MARC Record-Linking Technique," S. H. McCallum, KBE4

"MARC Tags and Retrospective Conversion," K. J. Kruger, KD20

MARC XX Project, [oral history] 1988– 1990, KBE5

Marchant, M. P., and M. M. England. "Changing Management Techniques as Libraries Automate," AH29

Mareck, R. "Practicum on Preservation," HF12

"Marketing Theory Applied to Price Discrimination in Journals," J. A. Talaga and J. W. Haley, GF21

Markey, K., and K. S. Calhoun. "Unique Words Contributed by MARC Records with Summary and/or Contents Notes," FB23

—— and D. Vizine-Goetz. *Characteristics of Subject Authority Records in the Machine-Readable Library of Congress Subject Headings,* EC13

"Markov and the Mixed-Poisson Models of Library Circulation Compared," J. Tague and I. A. Ajiferuke, LC17

Marks, K. E., and S. P. Nielsen. "Longitudinal Study of Journal Prices in a Research Library," GF12

Martin, D., and P. Wenzel. "Retrieval Effectiveness of Enhanced Bibliographic Records," FB24

Martin, M. S. "Automation in Technical Services," AHB10

Martin, S. K. "Library Management and Emerging Technology," AH30

"Mass Buying Programs," C. Bucknall, HD8

Mass Deacidification, Committee on Institutional Cooperation, Task Force on Mass Deacidification, IE2

"Mass Deacidification for Libraries," G. M. Cunha, IE3

"Mass Deacidification for Libraries: 1989 Update," G. M. Cunha, IE4

Mass Deacidification Systems, K. Turko, IE10

Massonneau, S. "Reclassification and Barcoding," DB4

Materials at Risk, K. Garlick and M. A. Smith, IK6

Materials Budgets in ARL Libraries, P. Johnson, HG12

"Matrix Management," P. Johnson, AH24

Matters, M. "Authority Files in an Archival Setting," EAD15

—— "Authority Work for Transitional Catalogs," EAD16

Matthews, F. W. "Sorting a Mountain of Books," IF7

Matting and Hinging of Works of Art on Paper, M. A. Smith, comp., ICB11

Maxwell, M. F. *Handbook for AACR2 1988 Revision,* CBC2

McCabe, G. B., ed. *Academic Libraries in Urban and Metropolitan Areas,* LAA6

McCallum, S. H. "Basic Structure of UNIMARC," KBD2

—— "Format Integration: Handling the Additions and Subtractions," KBE18

—— "Linked Systems Project in the United States," KE13

—— "Linked Systems Project, Part 1: Authorities Implementation," KE14

—— "MARC Record-Linking Technique," KBE4

—— "Using UNIMARC," KBD3

McClung, P. A. "Costs Associated with Preservation Microfilming," JH10

—— ed. *Selection of Library Materials in the Humanities, Social Sciences, and Sciences,* HE17

McClure, C. R., and others. *Planning and Role Setting for Public Libraries,* AHA5, HAC14

McCombs, G. M., ed. *Access Services: The Convergence of Reference and Technical Services,* AH31, LA1

—— "Technical Services in the 1990s," AH32

McCullough, K., E. D. Posey, and D. C. Pickett. *Approval Plans in Academic Libraries,* BB12

McDonald, C., and J. Weckert, eds. *Libraries and Expert Systems,* AHC12

McDonald, D. R. "Data Dictionaries, Authority Control, and Online Catalogs," EE22

McGill, M. J., L. L. Learn, and T. K. G. Lydon. "Technical Evaluation of the Linked Systems Project Protocols in the Name Authority Distribution Application," KE22

McIlwaine, I. C. *Guide to the Use of the UDC,* DC29

McKay, S. C., and B. Landesman. "SISAC Bar Code Symbol," GG9

McKern, D., and S. Byrne. *ALA Target Packet for Use in Preservation Microfilming,* JI25

McKinley, M. "Serials Departments," GB7

—— "Vendor Selection," GD11

McMillan, G. "Embracing the Electronic Journal," GC15

McPheron, W., ed. *English and American Literature,* HE18

McPherson, D. S. "MARC Compatibility," KBC5

—— K. E. Coyle, and T. L. Montgomery. "Building a Merged Bibliographic Database," KC48

McQueen, J. "Record Matching," KC48

McTeigue, B. "Indexing Journal Articles Directly into the Classified Catalogue," FB22

McWilliams, J. *Preservation and Restoration of Sound Recordings,* III4, JAA3

Measurement and Evaluation of Library Services, S. L. Baker and F. W. Lancaster, LAA2

Measuring Academic Library Performance, N. A. Van House, B. T. Weil, and C. R. McClure, AHA8, HAC16

"Measuring Statewide Interlibrary Loan among Multitype Libraries," P. W. Dalrymple and others, LD10

Measuring the Performance of Document Supply Systems, M. B. Line, LE14

Meckler, A. M. *Micropublishing,* JF10

Media Access and Organization, C. O. Frost, CBD32

Media Programs, American Association of School Librarians and

Paper Conservation: Current Issues and Recent Developments, P. Luner, ed., IE5

Paper Conservation News, IAG20

Paper Conservator, IAG21

Paquette, J. "What Goes to the Storage Facility," HF6

Paris, J. *Choosing and Working with a Conservator*, ICB8

"Paris Principles," International Conference on Cataloguing Principles, CBA5

Parisi, P. A., and J. Merrill-Oldham, eds. *Library Binding Institute Standard for Library Binding*, IB9

Parker, J. M. "Scholarly Book Reviews in Literature Journals as Collection Development Sources for Librarians," HD39

Parker, L. M. P., and R. E. Johnson. "Does Order of Presentation Affect Users' Judgment of Documents?" FB27

Parker, T. A. "Integrated Pest Management for Libraries," IG11

Parkhurst, T. S. "Serial Pricing and Copyrights," GC26

"Parlez-Vous X12?" J. Mutter, BC14

Pascarelli, A. M. "Coping Strategies for Libraries Facing the Serials Pricing Crisis," GF18

Pasterczyk, C. E. "Quantitative Methodology for Evaluating Approval Plan Performance," BB14

Paton, C. A. "Whispers in the Stacks," III5

"Patron-use Software in Academic Library Collections," D. M. Beaubien and others, IID1

Paul, H. "Serials Processing," GD2

Pederson, T. L. "Theft and Mutilation of Library Materials," IK10

Pence, C. "Audiovisual Resources on Preservation Topics," IK11

Peniston, S. *Thesaurus of Information Technology Terms*, FAE4

"Penn State Annex," R. Henshaw and C. Swinton, LB5

Performance Appraisal of Collection Development Librarians, J. Siggins, HB12

"Periodical Prices," A. Okerson, GF17

Periodicals in College Libraries, J. Hastreiter, L. Hardesty, and D. Henderson, HD36

Permanence/Durability of the Book, IE6

Permuted Medical Subject Headings, DD23

Perryman, W. R., and L. Wilkas, eds. *International Subscription Agents*, BAB6, GAB8

"Personal Name Variations," T. S. Weintraub, EB23

"Perspective on Library Book Gathering Plans," E. J. Lockman, E. Laughrey, and K. Coyle, BB11

Peters, P. E. "Making the Market for Networked Information," GC27

Peters, S. H., and D. J. Butler. "Cost Model for Retrospective Conversion Alternatives," KC9

Petersen, H. C. "Economics of Economics Journals," GF19

——— "Variations in Journal Prices," GF20

Peterson, E., and B. Johnson. "Is Authority Updating Worth the Price?" EF11

"Phased Preservation," P. Waters, ICB12

Phelps, D. "Cost Impact on Acquisitions in Implementing an Integrated Online System," BC16

Phillips, F. "Developing Collecting Policies for Manuscript Collections," HC10

Phillips, L. L., and W. Lyons. "Analyzing Library Survey Data Using Factor Analysis," AHA6

Photo-Copying, C. Clark, JB2

Photocopy Services in ARL Libraries, Association of Research Libraries, Office of Management Studies, JG2

Photograph Preservation and the Research Library, J. Porro, ed., IIH6

Pickett, A. G., and M. M. Lemcoe. *Preservation and Storage of Sound Recordings*, III6

Picturescope, IIH7

Pierce, S. J., ed. *Weeding and Maintenance of Reference Collections*, HF7

Pietris, M. K. D. "Characteristics of LC Subject Headings That Should Be Taken into Account When Designing On-Line Catalogues," EC16

——— "Library of Congress Subject Headings: Past Imperfect, Future Indicative," EC17

Piggott, M. *Cataloguer's Way Through AACR2*, CBC4

——— *Topography of Cataloguing*, FAC22

Pilette, R., and C. Harris. "It Takes Two to Tango: A Conservator's View of Curator/Conservator Relations," ICB9

Pionessa, G. F. "Serials Replacement Orders," GD21

Piternick, A. B. "Serials and New Technology," GC17

Pitkin, G. M., ed. *Cost-Effective Technical Services*, AHB12

Pitschmann, L. A. "Organization and Staffing," HB6

PLA *see* Public Library Association

Planning Academic and Research Libraries, K. D. Metcalf, IG8

Planning and Role Setting for Public Libraries, C. R. McClure and others, AHA5, HAC14

Planning for Preservation, M. V. Cloonan, IH3

"Planning for Retrospective Conversion," H. Hanson and G. Pronevitz, KC27

Planning Guide for Information Power, American Association of School Librarians, HAC1

Planning in OCLC Member Libraries, M. E. L. Jacob, ed., AH22

PLMS *see* Association for Library Collections and Technical Services, Preservation of Library Materials Section

"Policy and Planning," D. Farrell, HC3

Policy and Practice in Bibliographic Control of Nonbook Media, S. S. Intner and R. Smiraglia, CBD32

Policymaking for School Library Media Programs, M. Karpisek, AB4

Polyester Film Encapsulation, ICA5

Polysulfide Treatment of Microfilm Using IPI SilverLock™, J. M. Reilly, JE5

Pope, N. "Processing OCLC Archive Tapes for the FOCUS System," KC50

Porro, J. *Photograph Preservation and the Research Library*, IIH6

Postlethwaite, B. S. "Publication Patterns, the USMARC Holdings Format, and the Opportunity for Sharing," GG11, KBE19

"Postmodern Culture: Publishing in the Electronic Medium," E. Amiran and J. Unsworth, GC4

Potter, W. G. "Form or Function?: An Analysis of the Serials Department in the Modern Academic Library," BG9

Powell, N., and M. Bushing. *Collection Assessment Manual*, HH34

Practical Approval Plan Management, J. S. Cargill and B. Alley, BB6

"Practical Considerations in Dealing with LCSH-mr," J. Rood, EE27

"Practical Considerations in Using the Machine-Readable LCSH," W. A. Garrison, EC9

Practical Guide to Preservation in Schools and Public Libraries, M. K. Sitts, IAD6

Practice for Operational Procedures/ Inspection and Quality Control of First-Generation Silver-Gelatin Microfilm of Documents,

for Information and Image
Management, JI18
Spreitzer, F., ed. *Microforms in
Libraries,* JD1
Spyers-Duran, P., ed. *Approval and
Gathering Plans in Academic
Libraries,* BB19
―――― "Cost of Library
Technologies," AHB15
St. Clair, G., and J. Treadwell.
"Science and Technology
Approval Plans Compared," BB18
―――― ―――― and V. Baker. "Notable
Literature of the 1980s for
Technical Services," AD7
St.-Laurent, G. *Care and Handling of
Recorded Sound Materials,* III7
*Stability, Care and Handling of
Microforms, Magnetic Media and
Optical Disks,* W. Saffady, IIA6,
JE12
"Stability of Black-and-White
Photographic Images, with Special
References to Microfilm,"
J. M. Reilly and others, IIE4
"Stability of Cellulose Ester Base
Photographic Film,"
P. Z. Adelstein and others, JE1
Stachacz, J. C. "Small College
Experiences in Retrospective
Conversion of Periodicals," KC35
Stack Management, W. J. Hubbard, LB6
*Staff Personality Problems in the Library
Automation Process,* J. E. Daily,
AHD5
*Staff Training and User Awareness in
Preservation Management,*
W. L. Boomgaarden, IK1
"Stalking the Elusive Grey
Literature," P. Allison, HD15
*Standard Cataloging for School and Public
Libraries,* S. S. Intner and
J. Weihs, eds., CAA6
*Standard Citation Forms for Published
Bibliographies and Catalogs Used in
Rare Books Cataloging,*
P. VanWingen and S. P. Davis,
CBD9
*Standard for Information and Image
Management: Micrographics―ISO
Resolution Test Chart No. 2:
Description and Use,* American
National Standards Institute, JI12
*Standard for Information and Image
Management: Reader-Printers for
Transparent Microforms―
Performance Characteristics,*
Association for Information and
Image Management, JI33
*Standard for Information and Image
Management: Readers for Transparent
Microforms―Methods for Measuring
Performance,* Association for

Information and Image
Management, JI31
*Standard for Information and Image
Management: Readers for Transparent
Microforms―Performance
Characteristics,* Association for
Information and Image
Management, JI32
*Standard for Information and Image
Management: Recommended Practice
for Inspection of Stored Silver-Gelatin
Microforms for Evidence of
Deterioration,* Association for
Information and Image
Management, JI19
*Standard for Information and Image
Management: Recommended Practice
for Microphotography of Cartographic
Materials,* Association for
Information and Image
Management, JI20
Standard Periodical Directory, GAB11
"Standards and Specifications,"
M. Chase, JI22
"Standards, Database Design, and
Retrospective Conversion,"
R. W. Boss and H. Espo, KC14
"Standards for Automated
Acquisitions Systems,"
S. R. Bullard, BC6
"Standards for College Libraries,
1986," Association of College and
Research Libraries, HAC10
"Standards for Community, Junior
and Technical College Learning
Resources Programs," Association
of College and Research Libraries
and Association for Educational
Communications and Technology,
HAC12
Standards for Electronic Imaging Systems,
M. Mier and M. Courtot, eds.,
JI28
"Standards for Two-Year College
Learning Resources Programs,"
Association for Educational
Communications and Technology/
Association of College and
Research Libraries Joint
Committee, HAC3
"Standards for University Libraries,"
Association of College and
Research Libraries, HAC11
"Standing Orders and Approval
Plans," D. Alessi and K. Goforth,
BB1
Stankowski, R. H. "Automated
Acquisitions and OCLC," BC20
―――― "Bibliographic Record
Maintenanace and Control in a
Consortium Database," KD23
Starbird, R. W., and G. C. Vilhauer.
*Manager's Guide to Electronic
Imaging,* JD2

"State of Authority," N. Baer and
K. E. Johnson, EAD4
Statement of Principles, International
Conference on Cataloguing
Principles, Paris, France, 1961,
CBA5
*Statistical Applications in Library
Technical Services,*
S. A. Burkholder, ed., AHA1
Statistics for Library Decision Making,
P. Hernon, AHA2
*Statistics for Managing Library
Acquisitions,* E. D. Hardy, ed.,
BG3
"Status of Imaging," W. Thom, FC10
Steel, V., comp. *Access Services:
Organization and Management,* LA2
Steele, V., and S. D. Elder. *Becoming a
Fundraiser,* HG21
Stenstrom, P. F. "Current
Management Literature for
Technical Services," AD8
Stephens, D. "Stitch in Time: The
Alaska Cooperative Collection
Development Project," HI7
Stern, B. "The New ADONIS," GC20
―――― and R. M. Campbell.
"ADONIS," GC21
Stevenson, C. G. *Working Together:
Case Studies in Cooperative
Preservation,* ID12
Stevenson, G., and S. Stevenson.
"Reference Services and Technical
Services," AH36
Stielow, F. J., and H. R. Tibbo.
"Collection Analysis in Modern
Librarianship," HH10
Stippe, H. L. P., ed. *Cartographic
Materials,* CBD10
"Stitch in Time: The Alaska
Cooperative Collection
Development Project,"
D. Stephens, HI7
STM Book News, GAD12
STM Newsletter, GAD12
Stoll, K. S. "Installation of the Geac
System at Los Alamos National
Laboratory Library," LC16
Stolow, N. *Conservation and Exhibitions,*
IG14
Storage and Preservation of Microfilms,
IIE6
"Storage of Maps on Paper,
Microforms, Optical Disks, Digital
Disks and Magnetic Memories,"
L. Cruse, IIC1
"Storing Color Materials,"
H. Wilhelm, IIH3
*Storing, Handling, and Preserving
Polaroid Photographs,* IIH11
Story, K. O. *Approaches to Pest
Management in Museums,* IG15
"Story of Permanent/Durable Book
Paper," V. W. Clapp, IE1

297

D. C. Lee and L. A. Lockway,
HH19

"Using LaserQuest for Retrospective
Conversion of MARC Records,"
M. S. Ferrell and C. A. Parkhurst,
KC26

"Using UNIMARC," S. H. McCallum,
KBD3

USMARC Code List for Countries, CBB3,
KBB8

USMARC Code List for Geographic Areas,
CBB4, KBB9

USMARC Code List for Languages,
CBB5, KBB10

*USMARC Code List for Relators, Sources,
Description Conventions,* CBB6,
KBB11

*USMARC Concise Formats for
Bibliographic, Authority, and
Holdings Data,* CBB1, KBB12

USMARC Diskette Label Specifications,
KBB13

USMARC Format for Authority Data,
DD7, EAB6, KBB14

USMARC Format for Bibliographic Data,
CBB2, KBB15

"USMARC Format for Classification
Data: Development and
Implementation," R. S. Guenther,
DC4

*USMARC Format for Classification Data:
Including Guidelines for Content
Designation,* DC5, KBB16

"USMARC Format for Holdings and
Locations," L. H. Sapp, KBE10

*USMARC Format for Holdings and
Locations: Development,
Implementation, and Use,*
B. B. Baker, ed., GG1, KBE11

USMARC Format for Holdings Data,
KBB17

USMARC Format: Proposed Changes,
KBB18

*USMARC Formats: Background and
Principles,* KBE6

USMARC-L, EAF3, KAB8

*USMARC Specifications for Record
Structure, Character Sets, Tapes,*
KBB19

"USMARC to UNIMARC/
Authorities," M. Truitt, EAD21,
KBD4

"Utility of a Recommended Core
List," J. M. Budd, HH24

"Utilization of Commands in an
Online Bibliographic Editing
System," R. G. Taylor and
J. G. Edgerton, KD14

*Utlas MARC Coding Manual for
Authorities,* E. Black, ed., DD8,
EAA6

V

Valentine, P. A., and D. R. McDonald.
"Retrospective Conversion: A
Question of Time, Standards, and
Purpose," KC13

"Value and Evaluation," D. Henige,
HH4

Van House, N. A., B. T. Weil, and
C. R. McClure. *Measuring
Academic Library Performance,*
AHA8, HAC16

——— and others. *Output Measures for
Public Libraries,* AHA7, HAC17

Van Order, P. J. *Collection Program in
Schools,* HE26

——— "School Libraries," HE27

Van Order, R. "Content-Enriched
Access to Electronic Information,"
FB32

"Vandalism," A. J. Lincoln, LG12

VanWingen, P., and S. P. Davis.
*Standard Citation Forms for
Published Bibliographies and Catalogs
Used in Rare Books Cataloging,*
CBD9

"Variation in Personal Names in
Works Represented in the
Catalog," E. E. Fuller, EB6

"Variations in Journal Prices,"
H. C. Petersen, GF20

"Variations in Personal Name Access
Points in OCLC Bibliographic
Records," A. G. Taylor, EB17

Vasiljev, A. "Enhancement of the
Subject Access Vocabulary in an
Online Catalogue," FB33

Vassie, R. "Reflection of Reality—
Authority Control of Muslim
Personal Names," EB20

"Vendor-Based Retrospective
Conversion at George Washington
University," A. Lisowski, KC29

"Vendor-Controlled Order Plans,"
R. M. Magrill and J. Corbin, BB13

"Vendor Evaluation," Vendor Study
Group, BF20

"Vendor-Library Relations,"
D. M. Goehner, BI4

"Vendor Performance Evaluation as a
Model for Evaluating
Acquisitions," D. Alsbury, BF1

"Vendor Selection," M. McKinley,
GD11

"Vendor Studies Redux,"
J. W. Barker, BB2

Vendor Study Group. "Vendor
Evaluation," BF20

Ventress, A. "Use Surveys and
Collection Analysis," HF20

Vickery, A., and H. Brooks. "Expert
Systems and Their Applications in
LIS," AHC13

Vickery, B. C. *Faceted Classification,*
DC6

——— and A. Vickery. *Information
Science in Theory and Practice,*
FAD26

Video Round Table (ALA), JAH5

Vilhauer, J. *Introduction to
Micrographics,* JC4

"Visual Access to Visual Images,"
H. Besser, FC1

Vizine-Goetz, D., and K. Markey.
"Characteristics of Subject
Heading Records in the Machine-
Readable Library of Congress
Subject Headings," EC20

Vleduts-Stokolov, N. "Concept
Recognition in an Automatic Text-
Processing System for the Life
Sciences," FF15

*Vocabulary Control for Information
Retrieval,* F. W. Lancaster, DD43,
EC10, FE5

*Volume and File Structure of CD-ROM
for Information Exchange,* National
Information Standards
Organization (U.S.), JI29

VPIEJ-L, GAE4

W

Waegermann, C. P. *Handbook of Optical
Memory Systems,* JC10

Wajenberg, A. S. "Authority Work,
Authority Records, and Authority
Files," EE32

Walch, V. I. "Checklist of Standards
Applicable to the Preservation of
Archives and Manuscripts," IAF4

Walfish, B. "Hebrew and Yiddish
Personal Name Authorities under
AACR2," EB21

Walker, G. "Preservation Decision-
Making and Archival
Photocopying," JG7

——— "Preserving the Intellectual
Content of Deteriorated Library
Materials," JH3

——— and J. P. Hudson. "Research
Methodology in Technical
Services," AD9

——— and others. "Yale Survey,"
IH17

Walker, T. C., and R. K. Miller.
*Electronic Imaging and Image
Processing,* JC11

Walton, R. "Shared Automated
Library Systems," AHB16

"Wanted: Fully Automated Indexing,"
R. Purcell, FF13

Warzala, M. "Approval Plan versus
Standing Order," BB20

Waters, D. J. "Electronic Technologies
and Preservation," JD3

——— *From Microfilm to Digital
Imagery,* JH16

Subject Index

The numbers following citations are page numbers, not citation numbers.